THE ZONDERVAN
ENCYCLOPEDIA
OF THE BIBLE

THE ZONDERVAN
ENCYCLOPEDIA
OF THE BIBLE

Volume
4
M – P

Merrill C. Tenney, General Editor / Moisés Silva, Revision Editor

Revised, Full-Color Edition

ZONDERVAN.com/
AUTHORTRACKER
follow your favorite authors

ZONDERVAN

The Zondervan Encyclopedia of the Bible
Copyright © 2009 by Zondervan
First edition copyright © 1975, 1976 by Zondervan

Requests for information should be addressed to:
Zondervan, *Grand Rapids, Michigan* 49530

Library of Congress Cataloging-in-Publication Data

The Zondervan encyclopedia of the Bible / Moisés Silva, revision editor ; Merrill C. Tenney, general editor. — Rev. full-color ed.
    p. cm.
Rev. ed. of: The Zondervan pictorial encyclopedia of the Bible.
Includes bibliographical references.
ISBN 978-0-310-24134-8 (hardcover, printed)
ISBN 978-0-310-24136-2 (set)
1. Bible — Encyclopedias. I. Silva, Moisés. II. Tenney, Merrill Chapin, 1904-1985. III. Zondervan pictorial encyclopedia of the Bible. IV. Title: Encyclopedia of the Bible.
BS440.Z63 2009
220.3 — dc22   2009004956

All Scripture quotations, unless otherwise indicated, are taken from the *Holy Bible, New International Version*®. NIV®. Copyright © 1973, 1978, 1984 by International Bible Society. Used by permission of Zondervan. All rights reserved.

Any Internet addresses (websites, blogs, etc.) and telephone numbers printed in this book are offered as a resource. They are not intended in any way to be or imply an endorsement by Zondervan, nor does Zondervan vouch for the content of these sites and numbers for the life of this book.

All rights reserved. No part of this publication may be reproduced, stored in a retrieval system, or transmitted in any form or by any means — electronic, mechanical, photocopy, recording, or any other — except for brief quotations in printed reviews, without the prior permission of the publisher.

Interior design by Tracey Walker

Printed in China

09 10 11 12 13 14 15 • 23 22 21 20 19 18 17 16 15 14 13 12 11 10 9 8 7 6 5 4 3 2 1

IMAGE SOURCES

The Amman Archaeological Museum. Amman, Jordan.
Todd Bolen/www.BiblePlaces.com
The British Museum. London, England.
The Cairo Museum. Cairo, Egypt.
The Church of Annunciation Museum. Nazareth, Israel.
Direct Design. Amarillo, Texas.
The Egyptian Ministry of Antiquities.
The Ephesus Archaeological Museum. Selchok, Turkey.
The Eretz Israel Museum. Tel Aviv, Israel.
The House of Anchors. Kibbutz Ein Gev. Sea of Galilee, Israel.
International Mapping.
The Isma-iliya Museum. Isma-iliya, Egypt.
The Israel Museum, Jerusalem, courtesy of the Israel Antiquities Authority.
The Istanbul Archaeological Museum. Istanbul, Turkey.
Dr. James C. Martin.
The Jordanian Ministry of Antiquities. Amman, Jordan.
Ministero per I Beni e le Attivita Culturali—Soprintendenza Archaeologica di Roma. Rome, Italy.
Mosaic Graphics.
Musée du Louvre. Paris, France.
Phoenix Data Systems
Z. Radovan/www.BibleLandPictures.com
Reproduction of the City of Jerusalem at the time of the Second Temple—located on the grounds of the Holy Land Hotel, Jerusalem.
Sola Scriptura. The Van Kampen Collection on display at the Holy Land Experience. Orlando, Florida.
The Turkish Ministry of Antiquities. Ankara, Turkey.
The Yigal Allon Center. Kibbutz Ginosar, on the western shore of the Sea of Galilee, Israel.

ABBREVIATIONS

I. General

א	(Aleph) Codex Sinaiticus
A	Codex Alexandrinus
AASOR	Annual of the American Schools of Oriental Research
AB	Anchor Bible
ABD	*Anchor Bible Dictionary*
ABR	*Australian Biblical Review*
ad loc.	*ad locum*, at the place
AHR	*American Historical Review*
AJA	*American Journal of Archaeology*
AJP	*American Journal of Philology*
AJSL	*American Journal of Semitic Languages and Literature*
AJT	*American Journal of Theology*
Akk.	Akkadian
ANE	Ancient Near East(ern)
ANEP	*The Ancient Near East in Pictures Relating to the Old Testament*, ed. J. B. Pritchard (1954)
ANET	*Ancient Near East Texts Relating to the Old Testament*, ed. J. B. Pritchard, 3rd ed. (1969)
ANF	Ante-Nicene Fathers
ANRW	*Aufstieg und Niedergang der römischen Welt* (1972–)
aor.	aorist
APOT	*Apocrypha and Pseudepigrapha of the Old Testament*, ed. R. H. Charles, 2 vols. (1913)
Apoc.	Apocrypha
approx.	approximate(ly)
Aq.	Aquila
ARAB	*Ancient Records of Assyria and Babylonia*, ed. D. D. Luckenbill, 2 vols. (1926–27)
Arab.	Arabic
Aram.	Aramaic
Arch	Archaeology
ARM	*Archives royales de Mari*
Assyr.	Assyrian
ASV	American Standard Version
AThR	*Anglican Theological Review*
AUSS	*Andrews University Seminary Studies*
B	Codex Vaticanus
b.	born
BA	*Biblical Archaeologist*
BAR	*Biblical Archaeology Review*
BASOR	*Bulletin of the American Schools of Oriental Research*
BASORSup	*Bulletin of the American Schools of Oriental Research Supplemental Studies*
BBR	*Bulletin for Biblical Research*
BC	F. J. Foakes-Jackson and K. Lake, eds., *The Beginnings of Christianity*, 5 vols. (1920–33)
BDAG	W. Bauer, *A Greek-English Lexicon of the New Testament and Other Early Christian Literature*, 3rd ed., rev. F. W. Danker (2000)
BDB	F. Brown, S. R. Driver, and C. A. Briggs, *A Hebrew and English Lexicon of the Old Testament* (1907)
BDF	F. Blass, A. Debrunner, and R. W. Funk, *A Greek Grammar of the New Testament and Other Early Christian Literature* (1961)
BDT	*Baker's Dictionary of Theology*, ed. E. F. Harrison (1960)
BECNT	Baker Exegetical Commentary on the New Testament
BETS	*Bulletin of the Evangelical Theological Society*
BHK	*Biblia Hebraica*, ed. R. Kittel, 3rd ed. (1937)
BHS	*Biblia Hebraica Stuttgartensia*, ed. K. Elliger and W. Rudolph (1983)
Bib.	*Biblica*
BJRL	*Bulletin of the John Rylands Library*
BKAT	Biblischer Kommentar, Altes Testament
BNTC	Black's New Testament Commentaries
BRev	*Bible Review*
BSac	*Bibliotheca Sacra*
BWL	*Babylonian Wisdom Literature*, ed. W. G. Lambert (1960)
BZ	*Biblische Zeitschrift*
C	Codex Ephraemi Syri
c.	*circa*, about

CAH	*Cambridge Ancient History*	*DOTT*	*Documents from Old Testament Times*, ed. D. W. Thomas (1958)
CANE	*Civilizations of the Ancient Near East*, ed. J. M. Sasson, 4 vols. (1995)	*DPL*	*Dictionary of Paul and his Letters*, ed. G. F. Hawthorne et al. (1993)
CBQ	*Catholic Biblical Quarterly*	DSS	Dead Sea Scrolls
CBSC	Cambridge Bible for Schools and Colleges	E	east
CD	Cairo: Damascus (i.e., *Damascus Document*)	EA	El-Amarna Tablets. See *Die el-Amarna-Tafeln, mit Einleitung und Erläuterung*, ed. J. A. Knudtzon, 2 vols. (1908–15; suppl. by A. F. Rainey, 2nd ed., 1978)
cent.	century		
CEV	Contemporary English Version		
cf.	*confer*, compare	*EBC*	*The Expositor's Bible Commentary*, ed. F. E. Gaebelein et al., 12 vols. (1979–92)
CGTC	Cambridge Greek Testament Commentary	*EBr*	*Encyclopedia Britannica*
ch(s).	chapter(s)	ed(s).	editor(s), edited, edition
CT	*Christianity Today*	e.g.	*exempli gratia*, for example
CIG	*Corpus inscriptionum graecarum*	*EGT*	*Expositor's Greek Testament*, ed. W. R. Nicoll, 5 vols. (1897–1910)
CIL	*Corpus inscriptionum latinarum*		
CIS	*Corpus inscriptionum semiticarum*	Egyp.	Egyptian
col(s).	column(s)	EKKNT	Evangelisch-katholischer Kommentar zum Neuen Testament
COS	*The Context of Scripture*, ed. W. W. Hallo, 3 vols. (1997–2002)	*EncBib*	*Encyclopaedia Biblica*, ed. T. K. Cheyne and J. S. Black, 4 vols. (1899–1903)
CRINT	Compendia rerum iudaicarum ad Novum Testamentum	*EncJud*	*Encyclopedia Judaica*, 16 vols. (1972)
D	Codex Bezae	Eng.	English
d.	died, date of death	*ERE*	*Encyclopedia of Religion and Ethics*, ed. J. Hastings, 13 vols. (1908–27)
DAC	*Dictionary of the Apostolic Church*, ed. J. Hastings, 2 vols. (1915–18)	ERV	English Revised Version
DBI	*Dictionary of Biblical Interpretation*, ed. J. H. Hayes, 2 vols. (1999)	esp.	especially
		ESV	English Standard Version
DBSup	*Dictionnaire de la Bible: Supplément*, ed. L. Pirot and A. Robert (1928–)	et al.	*et alii*, and others
		ETR	*Etudes théologiques et religieuses*
DCG	*Dictionary of Christ and the Gospels*, ed. J. Hastings, 2 vols. (1906–08)	*ETSB*	*Evangelical Theological Society Bulletin*
		Euseb.	Eusebius
DDD	*Dictionary of Deities and Demons in the Bible*, ed. K. van der Toorn et al., 2nd ed. (1999)	*EvQ*	*Evangelical Quarterly*
		EvT	*Evangelische Theologie*
		Exp	*The Expositor*
DJD	Discoveries in the Judaean Desert	*ExpTim*	*Expository Times*
DJG	*Dictionary of Jesus and the Gospels*, ed. J. B. Green et al. (1992)	ff.	following (verses, pages, etc.)
		FCI	*Foundations of Contemporary Interpretation*, ed. M. Silva, 6 vols. in 1 (1996)
DLNT	*Dictionary of the Later New Testament and Its Developments*, ed. R. P. Martin and P. H. Davids (1997)		
		fem.	feminine
DNTB	*Dictionary of New Testament Background*, ed. C. A. Evans and S. E. Porter (2000)	*FFB*	*Fauna and Flora of the Bible*, UBS Handbook Series, 2nd ed. (1980)
		fig.	figure, figurative(ly)
DOTHB	*Dictionary of the Old Testament: Historical Books*, ed. B. T. Arnold and H. G. M. Williamson (2005)	fl.	*floruit*, flourished
		FOTL	Forms of the Old Testament Literature
		ft.	foot, feet
DOTP	*Dictionary of the Old Testament: Pentateuch*, ed. T. D. Alexander and D. W. Baker (2003)	GCS	Die griechische christliche Schriftsteller

ABBREVIATIONS

Ger.	German
GKC	Gesenius-Kautzsch-Cowley, *Gesenius' Hebrew Grammar*, 2nd ed. (1910)
Gk.	Greek
GNB	Good News Bible
HAL	*Hebräisches und aramäisches Lexikon zum Alten Testament*, by L. Koehler et al., 5 fascicles (1967–95)
HALOT	*Hebrew and Aramaic Lexicon of the Old Testament*, by L. Koehler et al., 5 vols. (1994–2000)
HAT	Handbuch zum Alten Testament
HDB	Hastings' *Dictionary of the Bible*, 5 vols. (1898–1904); rev. ed. in 1 vol. by F. C. Grant and H. H. Rowley (1963)
Heb.	Hebrew
HGHL	*Historical Geography of the Holy Land*, by G. A. Smith, 25th ed. (1931)
Hitt.	Hittite
HibJ	*Hibbert Journal*
HJP	*A History of the Jewish People in the Time of Jesus Christ*, by E. Schürer, 5 vols., 2nd ed. (1885–90); rev. ed., *The History of the Jewish People in the Age of Jesus Christ (175 B.C.–A.D. 135)*, by G. Vermès and F. Millar, 4 vols. (1973–87)
HNT	Handbuch zum Neuen Testament
HNTC	Harper's New Testament Commentaries
HTKAT	Herders theologischer Kommentar zum Alten Testament
HTKNT	Herders theologischer Kommentar zum Neuen Testament
HTR	*Harvard Theological Review*
HUCA	*Hebrew Union College Annual*
IB	*Interpreter's Bible*, ed. G. A. Buttrick et al., 12 vols. (1951–57)
ibid.	*ibidem*, in the same place
ICC	International Critical Commentary
id.	*idem*, the same (as previously mentioned)
IDB	*Interpreter's Dictionary of the Bible*, ed. G. A. Buttrick, 4 vols. (1962); supplementary vol., ed K. Crim (1976)
i.e.	*id est*, that is
IEJ	*Israel Exploration Journal*
Ign.	Ignatius
illus.	illustration
impf.	imperfect
impv.	imperative
inscr.	inscription
Int	*Interpretation*
IPN	*Die israelitischen Personennamen*, by M. Noth (1928)
Iren.	Irenaeus
ISBE	*International Standard Bible Encyclopedia*, ed. M. G. Kyle, 4 vols. (1929); rev. ed., G. W. Bromiley, 4 vols. (1979–88)
JANESCU	*Journal of the Ancient Near Eastern Society of Columbia University*
JAOS	*Journal of American Oriental Society*
JASA	*Journal of the American Scientific Affiliation*
JB	Jerusalem Bible
JBL	*Journal of Biblical Literature*
JBR	*Journal of Bible and Religion*
JCS	*Journal of Cuneiform Studies*
JE	*The Jewish Encyclopedia*, ed. I. Singer, 12 vols. (1925)
JEA	*Journal of Egyptian Archaeology*
JETS	*Journal of the Evangelical Theological Society*
JJS	*Journal of Jewish Studies*
JNES	*Journal of Near Eastern Studies*
JNSL	*Journal of North Semitic Languages*
Jos.	Josephus
JPOS	*Journal of the Palestine Oriental Society*
JPS	Jewish Publication Society, *The Holy Scriptures according to the Masoretic Text: A New Translation …* (1945)
JQR	*Jewish Quarterly Review*
JR	*Journal of Religion*
JRS	*Journal of Roman Studies*
JSJ	*Journal for the Study of Judaism in the Persian, Hellenistic, and Roman Periods*
JSNT	*Journal for the Study of the New Testament*
JSOT	*Journal for the Study of the Old Testament*
JSP	*Journal for the Study of the Pseudepigrapha*
JSS	*Journal of Semitic Studies*
JTS	*Journal of Theological Studies*
KAI	*Kanaanäishce und aramäische Inschriften*, by H. Donner and W. Röllig, 2nd ed., 3 vols. (1966–69)
KAT	Kommentar zum Alten Testament
KB	L. Koehler and W. Baumgartner, *Lexicon in Veteris Testamenti libros*, 2nd ed. (1958; for 3rd ed., see *HAL*)

KD	C. F. Keil and F. Delitzsch, *Biblical Commentary on the Old Testament*, 25 vols. (1857–78)
KEK	Kritisch-exegetischer Kommentar über das Neue Testament (= Meyer-Kommentar)
KJV	King James Version
Lat.	Latin
LCL	Loeb Classical Library
lit.	literal(ly), literature
LN	J. P. Louw and E. A. Nida, *Greek-English Lexicon of the New Testament Based on Semantic Domains*, 2 vols., 2nd ed. (1989)
LSJ	H. G. Liddell, R. Scott, and H. S. Jones, *A Greek-English Lexicon*, 9th ed., with rev. supplement (1996)
LXX	The Seventy = Septuagint
Maj. Text	Majority Text
masc.	masculine
mg.	margin
mi.	mile(s)
MM	J. H. Mouton and G. Milligan, *The Vocabulary of the Greek Testament* (1930)
MNTC	Moffatt New Testament Commentary
MS(S)	manuscript(s)
McClintock and Strong	J. McClintock and J. Strong, *Cyclopedia of Biblical, Theological, and Ecclesiastical Literature*, 12 vols. (1867–87)
MT	Masoretic text
N	north
n.	note
NA	Nestle-Aland, *Novum Testamentum Graecum*
NAB	New American Bible
NAC	New American Commentary
NASB	New American Standard Bible
NBD	*New Bible Dictionary*, ed. J. D. Douglas et al.; unless otherwise noted, references are to the 3rd ed. (1996)
NCB	New Century Bible
NCBC	New Century Bible Commentary
NCE	*New Catholic Encyclopedia*, ed. W. J. McDonald et al., 15 vols. (1967)
NCV	New Century Version
n.d.	no date
NE	northeast
NEAEHL	*The New Encyclopedia of Archaeological Excavations in the Holy Land*, ed. E. Stern et al., 4 vols. (1993)
NEB	New English Bible
neut.	neuter
NewDocs	*New Documents Illustrating Early Christianity*, ed. G. H. R. Horsley and S. Llewelyn (1981–)
NHC	Nag Hammadi Codex
NHL	*Nag Hammadi Library in English*, ed. J. M. Robinson, 4th ed. (1996)
NIBCNT	New International Bible Commentary on the New Testament
NIBCOT	New International Bible Commentary on the Old Testament
NICNT	New International Commentary on the New Testament
NICOT	New International Commentary on the Old Testament
NIDNTT	*New International Dictionary of New Testament Theology*
NIDOTTE	*New International Dictionary of Old Testament Theology and Exegesis*
NIGTC	New International Greek Testament Commentary
NIV	New International Version
NIVAC	New International Version Application Commentary
NJB	New Jerusalem Bible
NJPS	*Tanakh: The Holy Scriptures. The New JPS translation according to the Traditional Hebrew Text*
NKJV	New King James Version
NLT	New Living Translation
NovT	*Novum Testamentum*
NPNF	Nicene and Post-Nicene Fathers
NRSV	New Revised Standard Version
NT	New Testament
NTAp	*New Testament Apocrypha*, ed. E. Hennecke, 2 vols., trans. R. McL. Wilson (1963–65); unless otherwise indicated, references are to the rev. ed. by W. Schneemelcher, trans. R. McL. Wilson (1991–92)
NTD	Das Neue Testament Deutsch
NTS	*New Testament Studies*
NW	northwest
OCD	*Oxford Classical Dictionary* (1949)
ODCC	*Oxford Dictionary of the Christian Church*, ed. F. L. Cross and E. A. Livingstone, 3rd ed. (1997)
Onom.	Eusebius's *Onomasticon*, according to E. Klostermann, ed., *Das Onomastikon der biblischen Ortsnamen* (1904)

op. cit.	*opere citato*, in the work previously cited	SHERK	*The New Schaff-Herzog Encyclopedia of Religious Knowledge*, 13 vols. (1908–14)
orig.	original(ly)		
OT	Old Testament	SIG	*Sylloge inscriptionum graecarum*, ed. W. Dittenberger, 4 vols., 3rd ed. (1915–24)
OTL	Old Testament Library		
OTP	*Old Testament Pseudepigrapha*, ed. J. H. Charlesworth, 2 vols. (1983–85)		
		sing.	singular
		SJT	*Scottish Journal of Theology*
p., pp.	page, pages	SP	Sacra Pagina
pass.	passive	*ST*	*Studia theologica*
PEQ	*Palestine Exploration Quarterly*	Str-B	H. L. Strack and P. Billerbeck, *Kommentar zum Neuen Testament aus Talmud und Midrash*, 6 vols. (1922–61)
Pers.	Persian		
pf.	perfect		
PG	*Patrologia graeca*, ed. J.-P. Migne, 162 vols. (1857–96)		
		Sumer.	Sumerian
		s.v.	*sub verbo*, under the word
PJ	*Palästina-Jahrbuch*	SW	southwest
pl.	plural	Syr.	Syriac
PL	*Patrologia latina*, ed. J.-P. Migne, 217 vols. (1844–64)	Symm.	Symmachus
		Tac.	Tacitus
POxy	Oxyrhynchus Papyri	TDNT	*Theological Dictionary of the New Testament*, ed. G. Kittel and G. Friedrich, 10 vols. (1964–76)
prob.	probably		
Pseudep.	Pseudepigrapha		
ptc.	participle	TDOT	*Theological Dictionary of the Old Testament*, ed. G. J. Botterweck and H. Ringgren (1974–)
PTR	*Princeton Theological Review*		
RA	*Revue d'assyriologie et d'archéologie orientale*		
		TEV	Today's English Version
Rahlfs	A. Rahlfs, *Septuaginta, id est, Vetus Testamentum graece iuxta LXX interpretes*, 3rd ed. (1949)	Tg.	Targum
		Theod.	Theodotion
		THKNT	Theologischer Handkommentar zum Neuen Testament
RB	*Revue biblique*		
RE	*Realencyclopädie für protestantische Theologie und Kirche*, ed. J. J. Herzog and A. Hauck, 24 vols. (1896–1913)	*ThTo*	*Theology Today*
		TNIV	Today's New International Version
		TNTC	Tyndale New Testament Commentaries
REB	Revised English Bible	TOTC	Tyndale Old Testament Commentaries
repr.	reprint(ed)	TR	Textus Receptus
rev.	revised	trans.	translation, translator, translated
RevExp	*Review and Expositor*	TWNT	*Theologisches Wörterbuch zum Neuen Testament*, ed. ed. G. Kittel and G. Friedrich, 10 vols. (1932–79)
RevQ	*Revue de Qumran*		
RGG	*Die Religion in Geschichte und Gegenwart*, ed. K. Galling, 7 vols., 3rd ed. (1857–65)		
		TynBul	*Tyndale Bulletin*
		TZ	*Theologische Zeitschrift*
Rom.	Roman	UBS	United Bible Society, *The Greek New Testament*
RSPT	*Révue des sciences philosophiques et théologiques*		
		UF	Ugarit-Forschungen
RSV	Revised Standard Version	Ugar.	Ugaritic
RV	Revised Version	UM	*Ugaritic Manual*, by C. H. Gordon, 3 parts (1955)
S	south		
SacBr	A. F. Rainey and R. S. Notley, *The Sacred Bridge: Carta's Atlas of the Biblical World* (2005)	UT	*Ugaritic Textbook*, by C. H. Gordon, 3 parts (1965)
		v., vv.	verse, verses
Sansk.	Sanskrit	*VT*	*Vetus Testamentum*
SE	southeast	viz.	*videlicet*, namely
sec.	section	v.l.	*varia lectio*, variant reading

vol(s).	volume(s)	Hos.	Hosea
vs.	versus	Joel	Joel
Vulg.	Vulgate	Amos	Amos
W	west	Obad.	Obadiah
WBC	Word Biblical Commentary	Jon.	Jonah
WEB	World English Bible	Mic.	Micah
WH	B. F. Westcott and F. J. A. Hort, *The New Testament in the Original Greek*, 2 vols. (1881)	Nah.	Nahum
		Hab.	Habakkuk
		Zeph.	Zephaniah
WTJ	*Westminster Theological Journal*	Hag.	Haggai
ZAW	*Zeitschrift für die alttestamentliche Wissenschaft*	Zech.	Zechariah
		Mal.	Malachi
ZDMG	*Zeitschrift der deutschen morgenländischen Gesellschaft*		
ZDPV	*Zeitschrift der deutschen Palästina-Vereins*		
ZNW	*Zeitschrift für die neutestamentliche Wissenschaft*		
ZRGG	*Zeitschrift für Religions und Geistesgeschichte*		

New Testament

Matt.	Matthew
Mk.	Mark
Lk.	Luke
Jn.	John
Acts	Acts
Rom.	Romans
1 Cor.	1 Corinthians
2 Cor.	2 Corinthians
Gal.	Galatians
Eph.	Ephesians
Phil.	Philippians
Col.	Colossians
1 Thess.	1 Thessalonians
2 Thess.	2 Thessalonians
1 Tim.	1 Timothy
2 Tim.	2 Timothy
Tit.	Titus
Phlm.	Philemon
Heb.	Hebrews
Jas.	James
1 Pet.	1 Peter
2 Pet.	2 Peter
1 Jn.	1 John
2 Jn.	2 John
3 Jn.	3 John
Jude	Jude
Rev.	Revelation

II. Books of the Bible
Old Testament

Gen.	Genesis
Exod.	Exodus
Lev.	Leviticus
Num.	Numbers
Deut.	Deuteronomy
Josh.	Joshua
Jdg.	Judges
Ruth	Ruth
1 Sam.	1 Samuel
2 Sam.	2 Samuel
1 Ki.	1 Kings
2 Ki.	2 Kings
1 Chr.	1 Chronicles
2 Chr.	2 Chronicles
Ezra	Ezra
Neh.	Nehemiah
Esth.	Esther
Job	Job
Ps.	Psalm(s)
Prov.	Proverbs
Eccl.	Ecclesiastes
Cant.	Canticles (Song of Songs)
Isa.	Isaiah
Jer.	Jeremiah
Lam.	Lamentations
Ezek.	Ezekiel
Dan.	Daniel

Apocrypha

1 Esd.	1 Esdras
2 Esd.	2 Esdras (= *4 Ezra*)
Tob.	Tobit
Jdt.	Judith
Add. Esth.	Additions to Esther
Wisd.	Wisdom of Solomon

Sir.	Ecclesiasticus (Wisdom of Jesus the Son of Sirach)	2 En.	2 Enoch
Bar.	Baruch	4 Ezra	4 Ezra (= 2 Esdras)
Ep. Jer.	Epistle of Jeremy	Jub.	Book of Jubilees
Pr. Azar.	Prayer of Azariah	Let. Aris.	Letter of Aristeas
Sg. Three	Song of the Three Children (or Young Men)	Life Adam	Life of Adam and Eve
		3 Macc.	3 Maccabees
Sus.	Susanna	4 Macc.	4 Maccabees
Bel	Bel and the Dragon	Mart. Isa.	Martyrdom of Isaiah
Pr. Man.	Prayer of Manasseh	Pss. Sol.	Psalms of Solomon
1 Macc.	1 Maccabees	Sib. Or.	Sibylline Oracles
2 Macc.	2 Maccabees	T. Benj.	Testament of Benjamin (etc.)
		T. 12 Patr.	Testaments of the Twelve Patriarchs
		Zad. Frag.	Zadokite Fragments

III. Pseudepigrapha

As. Moses	*Assumption of Moses*
2 Bar.	*2 Baruch*
3 Bar.	*3 Baruch*
1 En.	*1 Enoch*

Other Christian, Jewish, and Greco-Roman texts are referred to by their standard abbreviations. See, e.g., *The SBL Handbook of Style* (1999), ch. 8, appendix F, and appendix H.

THE ZONDERVAN ENCYCLOPEDIA OF THE BIBLE

Northern portion of the Masada plateau, with a view of Herod's palaces.

M

M. The symbol used to designate material peculiar to Matthew; for some scholars, the symbol represents an independent literary source used by this evangelist. B. H. Streeter proposed that M originated c. A.D. 60, probably in JERUSALEM, and that Matthew used it — along with the Gospel of Mark and some additional tradition from ANTIOCH OF SYRIA — to produce his gospel (*The Four Gospels: A Study of Origins* [1924], ch. 9). See GOSPELS; MATTHEW, GOSPEL OF.

Maacah (person) may′uh-kuh (מַעֲכָה *H5082*, perhaps "dull" or "oppression"). KJV also Maachah; TNIV Maakah. At least nine OT figures, both male and female, have this name. **(1)** Son of NAHOR by his concubine Reumah; nephew of ABRAHAM (Gen. 22:24). He may have been the ancestor of the people who inhabited a region by the same name. See MAACAH (PLACE). Some have thought that this Maacah was a daughter, not a son, of Nahor.

(2) Sister or wife of MAKIR son of MANASSEH (1 Chr. 7:15–16). The passage appears to speak of two different women named Maacah, one of whom was Makir's sister (v. 15) and another one his wife (v. 16). The Hebrew text of v. 15 is difficult, however, and the KJV takes it to mean that Makir "took to wife *the sister* of Huppim and Shuppim, whose sister's name was Maachah" (not a likely interpretation of the Hebrew). Many scholars emend the verse to say, "Makir took a wife, and her name was Maacah" (or the like). In either case, the passage would then refer to only one woman named Maacah, Makir's wife, who bore him two sons, Peresh and Sheresh. (For other emendations and further discussion, see G. N. Knoppers, *I Chronicles 1–9*, AB 12 [2004], 454–55.)

(3) Second concubine of CALEB son of Hezron (1 Chr. 2:48). His first concubine was EPHAH (v. 46).

(4) Wife of JEIEL, who was a descendant of BENJAMIN and the "father" (i.e., founder or a civic leader) of GIBEON (1 Chr. 9:35; the name Jeiel is missing from the MT of the parallel passage, 8:29, but most versions insert it).

(5) Daughter of TALMAI king of GESHUR; she became a wife of DAVID and bore ABSALOM during David's reign at HEBRON (2 Sam. 3:3; 1 Chr. 3:2). Absalom fled for safety to his mother's homeland after he killed his half-brother AMMON (2 Sam. 13:37–38).

(6) Father of Hanan; the latter was one of David's mighty warriors (1 Chr. 11:43).

(7) Father of Shephatiah; the latter was an officer over the tribe of SIMEON during the reign of David (1 Chr. 27:16).

(8) Father of the PHILISTINE king ACHISH (1 Ki. 2:39). Many believe this Maacah is the same as MAOCH (1 Sam. 27:2; the two forms may be variant spellings of the same name); others question this identification, since it would mean that the reign of Achish lasted at least forty years.

(9) Daughter of Abishalom (ABSALOM), favorite wife of REHOBOAM, and mother of Abijam (ABIJAH; 1 Ki. 15:2; 2 Chr. 11:20–22). Elsewhere she is called "Micaiah daughter of Uriel of Gibeah" (2 Chr. 13:2 NRSV), but the name MICAIAH may be a scribal error or an alternate form of Maacah (cf. NIV), while the word "daughter" here may mean "granddaughter" (cf. NIV mg.). Some argue, however, that this Maacah was in fact the granddaughter of Absalom; this view assumes that Absalom's daughter TAMAR was the wife of Uriel.

Another difficulty is raised by 1 Ki. 15:10, which says with respect to ASA, Abijah's son, that "his mother's name was Maacah daughter of Abishalom" (NRSV). Three solutions are possible. (a) Asa

3

was Abijah's brother rather than his son, a view that requires emending v. 8. (b) Two different women, both named Maacah, are involved: one (v. 2) was the actual daughter of Absalom and the mother of Abijah, while the other (v. 10) was the granddaughter of Absalom and the mother of Asa. (c) More likely, only one person, Abijam's mother (i.e., Asa's grandmother), is involved, and "mother" in vv. 10 and 13 means "grandmother" (cf. NIV). In any case, the biblical writer tells us that Asa deposed his grandmother (or mother!) Maacah from her royal position (*gĕbîrâ* H1485, "queen mother") because of her idolatry (v. 13).

Maacah (place) may´uh-kuh (מַעֲכָה H5081 [מַעֲכָת in Josh. 13:13b], perhaps "dull" or "oppression"; gentilic מַעֲכָתִי H5084, "Maacathite" [KJV, "Maachathi" and "Maachathite"]). KJV Maachah; TNIV Maakah; NRSV also Maacath (only Josh 13:13b). A small Aramean state SE of Mount HERMON. See ARAM (COUNTRY). It bordered GESHUR on the S and may have crossed the JORDAN to ABEL BETH MAACAH on the W. JAIR son of Manasseh made conquest of the land (Deut. 3:14; Josh. 12:5), and it was assigned to the half tribe of MANASSEH (Josh. 13:29–30). Both the Maacathites and the neighboring Geshurites remained in occupancy of their lands after Jair's conquest (Josh. 13:13; NRSV, "Maacath"). During the reign of DAVID, the king of Maacah contributed 1,000 men as mercenaries to aid AMMON in war with Israel (2 Sam. 10:6–8; 1 Chr. 19:6–7). (See B. Mazur in *JBL* 80 [1961]: 16–28.) L. J. WOOD

Maacath, Maacathite may´uh-kath, may-ak´uh-thit. See MAACAH (PLACE).

Maachah, Maachathi, Maachathite may´uh-kuh, may-ak´uh-thi, may-ak´uh-thit. KJV forms of MAACAH and Maacathite.

Maadai may´uh-di (מַעֲדַי H5049, short form of מַעֲדְיָה H5050, "ornament of Yahweh" [see MOADIAH]). One of the sons of Bani who gave up their foreign wives in the time of EZRA (Ezra 10:34; called "Momdius" in 1 Esd. 9:34).

Maadiah may´uh-di´uh. See MOADIAH.

Maai may´i (מְעַי H5076, derivation uncertain). A priestly musician who participated in the dedication of the rebuilt wall of Jerusalem under EZRA (Neh. 12:36; his name is one of several omitted in the LXX).

Maakah may´uh-kuh. TNIV form of MAACAH.

Maaleh-acrabbim may´uh-leh-uh-krab´im. See AKRABBIM.

Maani may´uh-ni (Μααντ). (1) Ancestor of a family of temple servants (NETHINIM) who returned from the EXILE (1 Esd. 5:31; KJV, "Meani"; RSV, "Meunites"). See MEUNIM.

(2) KJV Apoc. variant form of BANI (1 Esd. 9:34).

Maarath may´uh-rath (מְעָרָת H5125, possibly "barren [field]"). A town in the hill country of the tribe of JUDAH (Josh. 15:59). Maarath is listed between GEDOR and BETH ANOTH, so it was probably a few miles N of HEBRON, but its precise location is unknown. Some have thought it is the same as MAROTH (Mic. 1:12), but the context seems to place this town too far W.

Maareh-geba may´uh-ri-gee´buh. Transliteration used by some versions (e.g., NJPS) to render the difficult Hebrew phrase *maʿărēh-gābāʿ*, referring to a place where the men of Israel lay in ambush and from which they rushed forth to attack the Benjamites (Jdg. 20:33; KJV, "the meadows of Gibeah"). On the basis of the SEPTUAGINT and the VULGATE, the NIV and other versions read *maʿărab-gābāʿ*, "west of Gibeah."

Maasai may´uh-si (מַעְשַׂי H5127, short form of מַעֲשִׂיָהוּ H5129, "work of Yahweh" [see MAASEIAH]). KJV Maasiai. Son of Adiel, listed among the first priests that returned from the EXILE and resettled in Jerusalem (1 Chr. 9:12). Because Maasai seems to correspond to AMASHSAI in a parallel passage (Neh. 11:13), some have argued that they are the same person and that the latter form is the result of scribal error.

Maaseiah may´uh-see´yah (מַעֲשִׂיָהוּ H5129 [in 1–2 Chr.], מַעֲשִׂיָה H5128 [in Ezra, Neh., and Jer., except Jer. 35:4], "work of Yahweh" [cf. MAASAI; see also BAASEIAH and HOSHAIAH #2]). **(1)** One of the Levites who played the lyre when the ARK OF THE COVENANT was brought to Jerusalem (1 Chr. 15:18, 20).

(2) Son of Adaiah; he was one of the commanders under JEHOIADA who took part in the revolt against ATHALIAH (2 Chr. 23:1).

(3) An officer under King UZZIAH who took part in mustering the army (2 Chr. 26:11).

(4) Son of King AHAZ; all that is known about him is that he and two royal officials were assassinated by an Ephraimite warrior named Zicri (2 Chr. 28:7).

(5) The ruler of Jerusalem at the time of King JOSIAH; he was among those sent to repair the temple (2 Chr. 34:8).

(6) Father of the priest ZEPHANIAH; the latter figures in the ministry of Jeremiah (Jer. 21:1; 29:25; 37:3). This Maaseiah is perhaps the same as the son of Shallum, a doorkeeper who had a room in the temple (35:4).

(7) Father of the false prophet ZEDEKIAH (Jer. 29:21).

(8–11) Four different men by the name of Maaseiah are listed among those who agreed to put away their foreign wives. Three of them—descendants of Jeshua, Harim, and Passhur respectively—were priests (Ezra 10:18–22; 1 Esd. 9:19–21 [KJV, "Matthelas," "Eanes," "Massias"]); the fourth was a descendant of Pahath-Moab (Ezra 10:30; cf. 1 Esd. 9:30, which has "Moossias" [KJV, "Mossias"], listed as a descendant of Addi).

(12) Father of a certain Azariah who made repairs to the wall of Jerusalem in Nehemiah's time (Neh. 3:23).

(13) One of the prominent men who stood near EZRA when the law was read at the great assembly (Neh. 8:4; called "Baalsamus" [KJV, "Balasamus"] in 1 Esd. 9:43); he is possibly the same as #11 above.

(14) A Levite who helped Ezra instruct the people in the law (Neh. 8:7; called "Maiannas" [KJV, "Maianeas"] in 1 Esd. 9:48).

(15) One of the leaders of the people who signed the covenant of NEHEMIAH (Neh. 10:25); he is possibly the same as #11 or #13 above.

(16) Son of Baruch and descendant of JUDAH through SHELAH; he was an inhabitant of Judah resident in Jerusalem in postexilic times (Neh. 11:5 [KJV has "Shiloni" instead of "Shelah"; NRSV, "the Shilonite"]; apparently the same as ASAIAH in 1 Chr. 9:5). See SHILONITE.

(17) Son of Ithiel and an ancestor of Sallu; the latter was a Benjamite who lived in postexilic Jerusalem (Neh. 11:7).

(18–19) Two priests who participated in the choirs at the dedication of the walls of Jerusalem (Neh. 12:41–42); the first of these played the trumpet. Either or both of these men are possibly to be identified with one or more of the priests mentioned above (##8–10).

(20) KJV form of MAHSEIAH (Jer. 32:12; 51:59).

Maasias may-as′ee-uhs. KJV Apoc. form of MAHSEIAH (Bar. 1:1).

Maasmas may-as′muhs (Μαασμαν, possibly to be understood as accusative of the unattested form Μαασμας). One of a group of leaders sent by EZRA to Iddo to get attendants for the house of God (1 Esd. 8:43; KJV, "Masman"). The parallel list has SHEMAIAH (Ezra 8:16).

Maath may′ath (Μααθ *G3399*, possibly from Heb. מַחַת *H4744* [cf. LXX 2 Chr. 29:12; 31:13; see MAHATH]). Son of Mattathias, included in the GENEALOGY OF JESUS CHRIST (Lk. 3:26).

Maaz may′az (מַעַץ *H5106*, perhaps "angry"; possibly short form of אֲחִימַעַץ *H318* [see AHIMAAZ]). Son of RAM, grandson of JERAHMEEL, and descendant of JUDAH (1 Chr. 2:27).

Maaziah may′uh-zi′uh (מַעַזְיָהוּ *H5069* [1 Chr. 24:18] and מַעַזְיָה *H5068* [Neh. 10:8], "Yahweh is [my] refuge"). **(1)** A priest during the time of DAVID who was the leader of the twenty-third division (1 Chr. 24:18). Some scholars believe that Maaziah here is the family name of a later priestly group. See #2 below.

(2) One of the priests (or priestly families) who signed the covenant of NEHEMIAH (Neh. 10:8).

Mabdai mab′di. KJV Apoc. form of MAMDAI (1 Esd. 9:34).

Macalon muh-kal´uhn (Μακαλοων). A Judean town listed in a postexilic census list (1 Esd. 5:21); the parallel passages have MICMASH (Ezra 2:27; Neh. 7:31).

Macbannai mak´buh-ni (מַכְבַּנַּי H4801, perhaps from a root meaning "wrap around"). KJV Machbanai, NRSV Machbannai; TNIV Makbannai. A Gadite who joined DAVID's forces at ZIKLAG (1 Chr. 12:13). The Gadites are described as "brave warriors, ready for battle and able to handle the shield and spear. Their faces were the faces of lions, and they were as swift as gazelles in the mountains" (v. 8).

Macbenah mak-bee´nuh (מַכְבֵּנָה H4800, perhaps from a root meaning "wrap around"). Also Machbenah; TNIV Makbenah. Son of Sheva and grandson of CALEB, included in the genealogical list of JUDAH (1 Chr. 2:49). However, it may be the name of a town, and the expression "Sheva the father of Macbenah and Gibea" probably indicates that Sheva was the founder of those two cities. Some identify Macbenah with CABBON (Josh. 15:40); others think it was a Calebite settlement in an unknown location S of HEBRON.

Maccabaean, Maccabaeus mak´uh-bee´uhn, -uhs. See MACCABEE.

Maccabee mak´uh-bee. The term *Makkabaios* was a surname given to Judas son of Mattathias (1 Macc. 2:4 et al.; Jos. *Ant.* 12.6.1 §266); it was later applied to his brothers and, more generally, to the anti-Hellenistic party of the 2nd cent. B.C. and to the HASMONEAN dynasty. The derivation of the name Maccabee is quite obscure. If from the verb *kābâ* H3882 (piel "to extinguish"), it may mean "extinguisher [of Hellenism]." More probably it is related to Aramaic *maqqābāʾ* and means either "hammer," referring to his crushing military exploits, or "hammer-head," referring to a physical characteristic (cf. *m. Bek.* 7:1). The latter meaning is preferable because it was common in the Hellenistic world to designate people by their physical characteristics and seems to be the case in the designation of Judas's brothers (1 Macc. 2:2–4).

    I. Historical background
        A. Alexander the Great
        B. Israel under the Ptolemies
        C. Israel under the Seleucids
    II. Maccabean revolt
        A. Antiochus's vengeance
        B. Mattathias
        C. Judas Maccabee
        D. Jonathan

I. Historical background. Only a brief historical summary will be given in order to provide a proper setting for the Maccabean revolt. All dates are B.C.

A. Alexander the Great (356–323). ALEXANDER THE GREAT was born in 356 and from thirteen years of age was taught by Aristotle. He was convinced of the Greek way of life and consequently his dream was to hellenize the world (see HELLENISM). With the death of his father Philip of Macedon in 336, he made immediate plans to invade the Persian empire. He invaded ASIA MINOR in the spring of 334, defeating PERSIA at the Granicus River and continued to push them out of Asia Minor. In October 333 he defeated Darius III at Issus and marched southward conquering TYRE and GAZA. Finally EGYPT was in his control by the winter of 332/1.

Sometime while he was in Palestine (it is difficult to know the exact sequence), according to JOSEPHUS (*Ant.* 11.8.5 §§329–39; cf. also *b. Yoma* 69a), he visited JERUSALEM and offered sacrifices to God in the TEMPLE under the direction of the high priest Jaddua. The priests showed him from the book of Daniel that he was the one predicted to destroy the Persian empire (cf. Dan. 8:5–7, 20–21; see DANIEL, BOOK OF). He accepted this interpretation and, being favorably disposed, granted the request that Jews in Palestine, Babylonia, and Media be allowed to live according to their ancestral laws and be exempt from tribute every SABBATICAL YEAR. Hence there was a friendly relationship between Alexander and the Jews. In the spring of 331 he marched eastward and defeated Persia and declared himself king over Persia by July 330. He died in 323.

B. Israel under the Ptolemies (323–198). Following Alexander's death there was much strife among his generals in their attempt to gain and hold their portions of his kingdom. By 311 SELEUCUS was acknowledged as the ruler of Babylonia, this year marking the commencement of the Seleucid dynasty/era. Palestine was the battlefield for much of the strife. Palestine was under Ptolemaic control (see PTOLEMY) from 323 to 315, when Antigonus (ruler over Asia Minor and N Syria) took possession of it; Ptolemy regained it briefly in 312, but he had to withdraw, leaving Antigonus in control.

In 301 Antigonus was killed in a decisive battle at Ipsus in PHRYGIA. Two years earlier an agreement had been made that on Antigonus's defeat, COELE-SYRIA should be given to Ptolemy. The latter had not taken part in the battle so it was now decided to give it to Seleucus, but Ptolemy forestalled Seleucus and took possession of Palestine. This action was the bone of contention between the two houses for decades to come. Palestine remained under Ptolemaic control until it was lost to the Seleucids in the person of ANTIOCHUS III (the Great) at the Battle of Panias (CAESAREA PHILIPPI of the NT) in 198 (Jos. *Ant*. 12.3.3 §§132–37; cf. Dan. 11:13–16). The Seleucids had now acquired the land which they considered rightly theirs.

C. Israel under the Seleucids (198–63). Israel remained under the Seleucids until POMPEY made it a province of Rome in 63 B.C. The scope of this article deals only with the first sixty-five years of the Seleucids' reign, in conjunction with the Jewish reaction toward them (for the later development, see HASMONEAN). After the victory over the Ptolemies at Panias, Antiochus III granted the Jews freedom of worship according to their laws; allowed them to complete and maintain the temple; exempted the council of elders, priests, and the scribes of the temple from taxes, which exemption the citizens of Jerusalem also enjoyed for the first three years (after that period they were exempted a third part of their taxes); and released the prisoners (Jos. *Ant*. 12.3.3–4 §§138–53). Hence the Jews enjoyed a brief period of tranquillity under the Seleucid rule.

One reason for these developments was that the Seleucids were concentrating their efforts in the western part of their empire. ROME had defeated Hannibal at Zama (near Carthage) in 202 and then the Macedonian monarchy in 197. After making a peace treaty with Ptolemy V Epiphanes (cf. Polybius, *Hist*. 28.20; Appian, *The Syrian Wars* 5; Jos. *Ant*. 12.4.1 §154; Dan. 11:17), Antiochus invaded Thrace in 196, and with the influence of Hannibal he invaded Greece (which the Romans had evacuated) in 194; but the Romans retaliated, defeating him at Thermopylae in 191 and at Magnesia in Asia Minor in 190. A peace treaty was signed at Apamea in 189, where Antiochus agreed to give up Asia Minor N and W of the Taurus Mountains, relinquish much of his military force, and pay a heavy indemnity over a twelve-year period. He had to deliver twenty hostages to Rome until the indemnity was paid, one of the hostages being his son Antiochus IV Epiphanes (Appian, *The Syrian Wars*, 36–39; Polybius, *Hist*. 20–21; Livy, *Hist*. 36–37; Dan. 11:18–19; 1 Macc. 1:10; 8:6–8; Jos. *Ant*. 12.10.6 §414).

Antiochus was succeeded by his second son, Seleucus IV Philopator, in 187. Because of the

Palestine at the time of the Maccabees.

heavy indemnity to be paid to the Romans he had to abstain from expensive adventures. The Jews remember him in his unsuccessful attempt to rob the temple of Jerusalem via his chief minister HELIODORUS (2 Macc. 3:7; cf. also Dan. 11:20). In 175 Heliodorus assassinated Seleucus and attempted to seize the throne, but Antiochus III's third son, Antiochus IV Epiphanes, having just been released from Rome as a hostage, went to Syria and ousted Heliodorus and made himself king. Since his newly acquired kingdom lacked political and financial stability, he attempted to unify it by a vigorous hellenization program (Tac. *Hist.* 5.8).

Religion was one of the unifying factors by which he encouraged the people (c. 169) to worship his own person in the form of the Olympian ZEUS. His title *Theos Epiphanes*, meaning "the manifest god," was changed by his enemies to *Epimanes* (which requires only one letter change in the Greek spelling), meaning "mad man" or "insane" (Polybius, *Hist.* 26.10). Soon after Antiochus's accession he was called upon to settle a dispute between the Jewish high priest ONIAS III, who was pro-Ptolemaic, and Onias's brother JASON (a Gk. name which he preferred over the Heb. name JOSHUA), who was pro-Seleucid. In 174 Jason secured the high priesthood by offering a larger payment of money to Antiochus and by pledging his wholehearted support in the hellenization of the Jerusalemites (1 Macc. 1:10–15; 2 Macc. 4:7–17; Jos. *Ant.* 12.5.1 §237–41). In 171 Jason's friend MENELAUS offered Antiochus 300 more talents than Jason for the position of high priest. Antiochus gladly accepted this, for it would help him financially; and since Menelaus was outside the Aaronic line (according to 2 Macc. 4:23 and 3:4 he was a Benjamite) it would break a great unifying force among the Jews. Jason went into hiding in the Ammonite country.

Next year in 170 the amateur regents Eulaeus and Lenaeus advised their minor king Ptolemy VI Philometor to avenge Panias and recover Coelesyria. Antiochus got wind of their plans and with a large army invaded Egypt in 170/169, defeating Ptolemy VI. He proclaimed himself as king of Egypt and allowed a rivalry to exist in Egypt by making Ptolemy VI Philometor king of MEMPHIS and his brother Ptolemy VIII Euergetes king in ALEXANDRIA (Dan. 11:25–27). On his return from Egypt, Antiochus heard that the Jerusalemites with the help of Jason (who came out of hiding) had forced Menelaus to take refuge in the Acra (a fortress the Seleucids had built in Jerusalem). The Jews had revolted against Menelaus because he plundered the temple, and Antiochus, feeling this was rebellion against himself, decided to subdue Jerusalem (2 Macc. 5:11–17). With Menelaus, Antiochus desecrated and plundered the temple of its treasures, leaving the city under one of his military commanders, Philip, a Phrygian (1 Macc. 1:20–29; 2 Macc. 5:18–22; Jos. *Ant.* 12.5.3 §§246–47).

II. Maccabean revolt

A. Antiochus's vengeance (168–166). The next contact Jerusalem had with Antiochus IV was after his second campaign in Egypt. The rival brothers had agreed to unite against their uncle Antiochus IV. The latter went to Egypt in the spring of 168 and subdued Memphis; but when he was at Eleusis, a suburb of Alexandria, the Roman representative Popillius Laenas (whom Antiochus knew at Rome) handed him an ultimatum from the senate to evacuate Egypt at once (cf. Polybius, *Hist.* 29.2.1–4; 29.27.1–8; Livy, *Hist.* 45.12.1–6; Diodorus Siculus, *Bibl. Hist.* 31.2; Velleius Paterculus, *Hist. Rom.* 1.10.1–2; Appian, *The Syrian Wars* 66; Justinus, *Epitome* 34.3; Dan. 11:28–30). Having learned of Rome's might when he served as a hostage for fourteen years, he quickly retreated.

With bitterness he retreated to Palestine (Polybius, *Hist.* 29.27.9; Dan. 11:30) and determined to make Palestine loyal to himself in order to act as a buffer state between himself and the Romans. Considering himself Zeus Epiphanes, he ordered a cultic hellenization policy in Palestine. In 167 Antiochus determined to exterminate the Jewish religion by forbidding them to live in accordance with their ancestral laws. He forbade the observance of the SABBATH, customary FEASTS, traditional SACRIFICES, and CIRCUMCISION of children, and ordered the destruction of copies of the TORAH. Idolatrous altars were set up, and the Jews were commanded to offer unclean sacrifices and to eat swine's flesh (2 Macc. 6:18). The climactic deed was on Kislev 25 (16 December 167), when the temple of Jerusalem became the place of the worship of the Olympian

The high desert butte of Masada was once fortified by Jonathan Maccabee. (In this aerial view, looking N, the excavations reveal structures from the time of Herod.)

Zeus; swine's flesh was offered upon the altar of the Greek god, which was erected on the altar of burnt offering (Dan. 11:31–32; 1 Macc. 1:41–64; 2 Macc. 6:1–11). These were to be offered on the twenty-fifth day of each month, since that date celebrated the birthday of Antiochus Epiphanes; hence the sacrifices were in effect offered to him.

B. Mattathias (166). Every village in Palestine was required to set up its heathen altar, and imperial legates were present to see that citizens offered the pagan sacrifices. In the village of MODEIN (c. 20 mi. NW of Jerusalem) there lived an aged priest named MATTATHIAS who lived with his five sons—John, Simon, Judas, Eleazar, and Jonathan. Antiochus's agent came to Modein compelling the people to renounce the God of the Hebrews and to offer unclean sacrifices. Mattathias, as an acknowledged leader of the village, was asked to be an example by being the first to make an offering, but he refused. When another Jew stepped out to offer the sacrifice, Mattathias slew both him and the king's legate. He then tore down the altar and proclaimed, "Let every one who is zealous for the law and supports the covenant come out with me" (1 Macc. 2:15–27; Jos. *Ant.* 12.6.1–2 §§265–72; Dan. 11:32–35). Mattathias, his sons, and many followers fled to the mountains. This marked the beginning of the Maccabean revolt.

While hiding, the rebels heard the news that a thousand men, women, and children had been slain because they refused to fight on the Sabbath. To avoid extermination, Mattathias and his friends decided that they could defend themselves even on the Sabbath (1 Macc. 2:19–41). It was about this time that the Hasidim (see HASIDEANS), who were a religious group within JUDAISM with a great passion for the law of God, joined Mattathias in a struggle against hellenization. Mattathias's forces waged war against the Jews who complied with Antiochus, tore down heathen altars, circumcised children who had been left uncircumcised, and exhorted Jews everywhere to follow in their struggle. During this struggle Mattathias died (166), leaving the battle in the hands of his third son Judas, with whom a new era in the fighting commenced (1 Macc. 2:42–70; Jos. *Ant.* 12.6.2–4 §§273–86).

C. Judas Maccabee (166–160)

1. Rededication of the temple (166–164). Mattathias's selection of Judas was the right choice, for he was the terror of his enemies and the pride of his nation. Under him the Maccabean struggle

Judas had regained the entire country, and his next move was to restore the worship in the temple. He marched on Jerusalem and occupied all of it except the Acra. This left him free to restore the temple. He selected priests who had remained faithful, destroyed the altar of the Olympian Zeus and built a new one, and rebuilt and refurbished the temple. And so on Kislev 25 (14 December 164), exactly three years after its desecration, the temple with its altar was rededicated and the daily sacrifices commenced (1 Macc. 4:36–59; 2 Macc. 10:1–8; Jos. *Ant.* 12.7.6–7 §§316–26). This marked the commencement of the Jewish Feast of DEDICATION or Lights (Heb. Hanukkah). Immediately after this, Judas fortified the Jerusalem walls and the city of Beth Zur on the border of IDUMEA. This completes the first stage of the Maccabean war. Up to this point they never experienced defeat.

Marble statue of Zeus, Greek god of the sky (2nd cent. A.D.). The Maccabean revolt was fueled by an altar to Zeus placed in the Jerusalem temple.

went from guerrilla warfare to well-planned battles. In his first year of leadership he became popular and won more volunteers to fight for freedom when he defeated the Syrian governors APOLLONIUS and SERON (1 Macc. 3:10–26; Jos. *Ant.* 12.7.1 §§287–92). Since Antiochus was having troubles in the E, he ordered LYSIAS, regent of the western part of the empire, to make an end of the rebellion and to destroy the Jewish race (1 Macc. 3:32–36; Jos. *Ant.* 12.7.2 §§295–96). Lysias dispatched a large army under the command of Ptolemy, Nicanor, and Gorgias, followed by merchants who expected to purchase Jewish slaves (1 Macc. 3:38–41). But Judas decisively defeated GORGIAS at EMMAUS, causing the Syrian soldiers to flee (1 Macc. 4:1–22; Jos. *Ant.* 12.7.4 §§305–12). In 164 Lysias personally led a larger army to attack Jerusalem from the S, but was completely defeated at BETH ZUR and withdrew to ANTIOCH OF SYRIA (1 Macc. 4:28–35; Jos. *Ant.* 12.7.5 §§313–15).

2. Religious freedom gained (163). The victories of Judas had resulted in making Judea reasonably secure. There were two things Judas still needed to accomplish. First, he and his brothers Jonathan and Simon determined to gain independence for all of Palestine. All the Jews in all of Palestine must be brought under their rule. Therefore Judas carried out several campaigns against IDUMEA in the S, BAEAN in TRANSJORDAN, and AMMON NE of the Dead Sea (1 Macc. 5:1–8). Because other Jewish communities asked for their help, he sent his brother Simon with an army into GALILEE while he and his other brother Jonathan went to GILEAD. Subsequently Judas went against Idumea, capturing HEBRON, and then against the PHILISTINES, capturing ASHDOD (1 Macc. 5:9–68; Jos. *Ant.* 12.8.1–6 §§327–53).

Having accomplished his first goal, Judas now started on his second one, namely, to get rid of the Syrian control of the Acra in Jerusalem. Their domination was a constant reminder that Antiochus's decree forbidding the practice of the Jewish religion had not been withdrawn. In the spring or summer of 163 Judas laid siege to it. There were some Syrian soldiers and Hellenistic Jews who escaped and went to Antioch for help (1 Macc. 6:18–27). Antiochus IV was already dead and was succeeded by his nine-year-old son Antiochus V Eupator. On his deathbed Antiochus

IV appointed one of his friends, Philip, as regent and guardian over Antiochus V, but Lysias, who had been given these privileges at an earlier date, asserted his responsibility by crowning Antiochus V as king (1 Macc. 6:5–17; both were in Antioch when Antiochus IV died). Immediately Lysias and the boy-king went S where he defeated Judas at Beth Zechariah (SW of Jerusalem) and laid siege to Jerusalem (1 Macc. 6:28–54). Judas being in desperate straits because of the food shortage (it was a sabbatical year) was saved when Lysias heard that Philip was marching from Persia to Syria to claim the kingdom for himself. Hence Lysias was anxious to make a peace treaty with Judas and guaranteed him religious freedom, but he did tear down the walls of Jerusalem (1 Macc. 6:55–63). The Jews were still under the Syrian rule, but had obtained religious freedom.

3. Political freedom desired (162–160). Having achieved the goal of the Maccabean revolt, Judas now wanted political independence for the nation. The Syrian government did not want this, so they had to strengthen the Hellenistic element among the Jews. Although the reports are conflicting, it seems that Lysias appointed ALCIMUS (Heb. Jakim, Jehoiakim) as high priest. He was of Aaronic descent, but ideologically a Hellenist (cf. 1 Macc. 7:14; 2 Macc. 14:3–7; Jos. *Ant.* 12.9.7 §§384–88; 20.10.3 §235). This was unacceptable to Judas (prob. because Alcimus was a hellenizer and possibly also Judas may have wanted the position of high priest for himself), so he prevented Alcimus from taking up his position in Jerusalem.

Meanwhile there were political upheavals in Syria. DEMETRIUS, nephew of Antiochus IV and cousin of Antiochus V, escaped from Rome, seized and put to death both Lysias and Antiochus V, and assumed the throne of Syria as Demetrius I Soter. The Hellenistic Jews and Alcimus complained against Judas, and consequently Demetrius confirmed Alcimus as the high priest in 162 and sent him to Jerusalem with an army under general BACCHIDES. Certain scribes and the Hasidim sought to establish peace with Alcimus and Bacchides, which would be a marked split from Judas's ranks. The reason for this move is not mentioned, but probably it was that the Hasidim were satisfied that Alcimus was of the Aaronic line and that the Syrians had guaranteed them freedom of worship.

Alcimus, however, who had promised that he would cause no evil to them, slew sixty of the Hasidim; hence they turned against him and returned to Judas (1 Macc. 7:15–20; Jos. *Ant.* 12.10.2 §§393–97). Alcimus asked Demetrius for more military help against Judas and his followers, who were causing trouble (2 Macc. 14:6). Demetrius sent an army with general NICANOR in order to capture Judas and to confirm Alcimus in the high priesthood. Nicanor on Adar 13 (9 March 161) was defeated and killed at ADASA (the Jews celebrated the victory annually as Nicanor's day) and his army fled to Gazara (GEZER) and was wiped out. Alcimus fled to Syria (1 Macc. 7:26–50; Jos. *Ant.* 12.103–5 §§398–412).

At this stage Judas sent ambassadors to Rome to ask for protection against Syria. This move by Judas reveals his political aspirations. A treaty was concluded, and Rome warned Demetrius that any interference with Judas would mean war with Rome. However, before Rome could have done anything, Demetrius had already taken steps to avenge Nicanor's defeat. Only weeks after the defeat Demetrius sent an army under Bacchides who was accompanied by Alcimus. Because of the might of the Syrian army, many men deserted Judas and in a battle at ELASA (c. 10–12 mi. N of Jerusalem) Judas was slain. His brothers Jonathan and Simon took his body to be buried at Modein (1 Macc. 8:1—9:22; Jos. *Ant.* 12.10.6—12.11. 2 §§413–34).

Tombs of the Maccabees at Modein.

D. Jonathan (160–143). Judas's death was a great blow to morale. His youngest brother Jonathan was selected to succeed him. The Hellenists were in control temporarily while Jonathan and his followers were in the wilderness of TEKOA, only able to carry on guerrilla warfare. Bacchides fortified Jerusalem and other Judean cities against a possible Maccabean attack. In May of 159 Alcimus died and soon after that Bacchides left his command in Judah and returned to Antioch. After two years of peace the hellenizers requested Bacchides to return to Judah, where he suffered defeat at BETHBASI (6 mi. S of Jerusalem). Bacchides made a peace treaty with Jonathan.

This peace treaty greatly weakened the hellenizers, for they no longer enjoyed the undivided support of the Syrian government. Moreover, since Demetrius I did not appoint a high priest after Alcimus's death, they had no real leadership, and certainly with this new peace treaty Jonathan would oppose an appointment of a high priest since he would have authority over Jonathan. After the treaty was signed, Bacchides returned to Antioch and Jonathan made his headquarters at MICMASH (9 mi. N of Jerusalem), where he judged the people, punishing the hellenizers (1 Macc. 9:23–73; Jos. *Ant.* 13.1.1–6 §§1–34). For the next five years Judah enjoyed peace and since a high priest was never selected, Jonathan's power increased.

In 152 Judah was further helped by internal struggles for power in Syria. A pretender, Alexander Balas, who claimed to be the son of Antiochus Epiphanes, challenged Demetrius I. Both vied with each other for Jonathan's support. Demetrius first offered to hand over to Jonathan the Jewish hostages held in the Acra and permitted Jonathan to raise an army. Also Demetrius abandoned all the fortresses except Beth Zur, Acra, and Gazara (cf. 1 Macc. 10:14; 11:41; 13:43). Jonathan exploited the situation and moved his headquarters from Micmash to Jerusalem (1 Macc. 10:1–14; Jos. *Ant.* 13.2.1 §§35–42). Alexander Balas in turn appointed Jonathan high priest (there had been no high priest since Alcimus's death in May of 159) and gave him the title "Friend of the King" (1 Macc. 10:15–21; Jos. *Ant.* 13.2.2 §§43–45).

Not to be outdone, Demetrius offered more promises: exemption from many taxes, surrender of

The burning of the Hanukkah candles even today is used to remember the liberation of Jerusalem by Judas Maccabee.

the Acra, attachment of three toparchies of Samaria to Jerusalem, subsidy of the Jewish army and temple, and money for rebuilding the city walls. Fortunately Jonathan sided with Alexander Balas, for in 150 Demetrius was slain in a battle against Alexander. Alexander made Jonathan general and governor of Judah and was considered one of his chief friends (1 Macc. 10:22–66; Jos. *Ant.* 13.2.3–4 §§46–61; 13.4.1–2 §§80–85). This was certainly a strange alliance—Alexander Balas, professed son of Antiochus Epiphanes, in league with a Maccabean!

In 147 Alexander Balas was challenged by Demetrius's son, Demetrius II Nicator, and was finally defeated and assassinated two years later. Demetrius II was only sixteen years of age when he ascended the throne in 145. Jonathan took advantage of the new king's inexperience and his insecure position on the throne by attacking the Acra, where the hellenizing Jews were still in control. Demetrius demanded that he withdraw the siege and report to him at Ptolemais. Jonathan boldly ordered his men to continue the siege while he went to Ptolemais with many gifts for Demetrius. Impressed by his audacity, Demetrius made him "Friend of the King," confirmed his high priesthood, and granted Jonathan's request of annexation of three districts of Samaria to Judah and exemption from tribute. Demetrius being weakened by the concessions and having trouble with his own army, Diodotus TRYPHO (a general of Alexander Balas) claimed the Syrian throne for Alexander Balas's son, Antiochus VI. Jonathan took advantage of the situation and sided with Trypho, who in turn made Jonathan head of the civil and religious aspects and his brother Simon head of the military.

Jonathan turned to the diplomatic field by sending an embassy to Rome to reconfirm their alliance with Rome. Jonathan's successful campaigns from Gaza to Damascus and his fortification of cities throughout Judah made Trypho apprehensive. By deceit Trypho was able to convince Jonathan to come with him to Ptolemais with only a few men. After Jonathan arrived Trypho arrested him. At Adida (near Modein) Trypho bargained with Jonathan's brother Simon to release Jonathan for 100 talents and two of Jonathan's sons as hostages. Simon complied but Trypho did not

THE MACCABEAN-HASMONEAN PERIOD		
Seleucid Kings	**Jewish Leaders**	**Ptolemaic Kings**
Seleucus I (Nicator) 321–281		Ptolemy I (Soter) 323–285
Antiochus I (Soter) 281–261		
Antiochus II (Theos) 261–246		Ptolemy II (Philadelphus) 285–246
Seleucus II (Callinicus) 246–225		Ptolemy III (Euergetes) 246–222
Seleucus III (Soter) 225–223		Ptolemy IV (Philopator) 221–205
Antiochus III (The Great) 223–187		Ptolemy V (Epiphanes) 204–180
Seleucus IV (Philopator) 187–175		Ptolemy VI (Philometor) 180–145
Antiochus IV (Epiphanes) 175–163	Mattathias 166; Judas 166–160	
Antiochus V (Eupator) 163–162		
Demetrius I (Soter) 162–150	Jonathan 160–143	
Alexander Balas 150–145		Ptolemy VII (Neos Philopator) 145
Demetrius II (Nicator) 145–139	Simon 143–135	Ptolemy VII (Neos Philopator) 145
(Antiochus VI [Epiphanes Dionysus] 145–142)		Ptolemy VIII (Euergetes II *or* Physcon) 145–116
Antiochus VII (Sidetes) 139–129	John Hyrcanus I 135–104	
Demetrius II (Nicator) 129–125		
Antiochus VIII (Grypus) 125/4–113		Ptolemy IX (Soter II *or* Lathyrus) 116–110
Antiochus IX (Philopator Cyzicenus) 113–111		
Antiochus VIII (Grypus) 111–95	Aristobulus 104–103	Ptolemy X (Alexander) 110–109, 108–88
Seleucus VI 95–54	Alexander Jannaeus 103–76	
Antiochus X (Eusebes) 94–83		Ptolemy IX (Soter II *or* Lathyrus) 88–80
Tigranes, King of Armenia 83–69	Salome Alexandra 76–67	Ptolemy XI (Alexander II) 80 (20 days)
		Ptolemy XII (Philopator Philadelphus Neos Dionysus *or* Auletes) 80–51
Antiochus XIII (Asiaticus) 69–65	Hyrcanus II 67 (3 months); Aristobulus 67–63	Cleopatra VII 51–30

free Jonathan. Trypho killed Jonathan at BASKAMA (NE shore of the Sea of Galilee) in 143; he was buried at Modein (1 Macc. 10:67-13:30; Jos. *Ant.* 13.4.3–6 §§86–212). The only remaining son of Mattathias, SIMON MACCABEE, became Jonathan's successor. For his reign and the subsequent period, see HASMONEAN.

(Important works on the Maccabean period include E. R. Bevan, *The House of Seleucus*, 2 vols. [1902]; id., *Jerusalem under the High-Priests* [1904], 69–108; E. J. Bickerman, *From Ezra to the Last of the Maccabees* [1947], 93–145; V. Tcherikover, *Hellenistic Civilization and the Jews* [1959], 117–239; S. K. Eddy, *The King Is Dead* [1961], 183–238; S. Zeitlin, *The Rise and Fall of the Judaean State* [1962], 1:37–140; B. Reicke, *New Testament Era* [1968], 42–62; *HJP*, rev. ed. [1973–87], 1:125–88; E. J. Bickerman, *The God of the Maccabees: Studies on the Meaning and Origin of the Maccabean Revolt* [1979; German orig. 1937]; B. Bar-Kochva, *Judas Maccabaeus: The Jewish Struggle against the Seleucids* [1988]; D. J. Harrington, *The Maccabean Revolt: Anatomy of a Biblical Revolution* [1988]; W. D. Davies and L. Finkelstein, eds., *The Cambridge History of Judaism, Vol. 2: The Hellenistic Age* [1989]; L. L. Grabbe, *Judaism from Cyrus to Hadrian*, 2 vols. [1992], ch. 5; A. I. Baumgarten, *The Flourishing of Jewish Sects in the Maccabean Era: An Interpretation* [1997]; J. Sievers, *Synopsis of the Greek Sources for the Hasmonean period: 1–2 Maccabees and Josephus, War 1 and Antiquities 12–14* [2001]; Y. Aharoni et al., *The Carta Bible Atlas*, 4th ed. [2002], 142–53; L. L. Grabbe, *History of the Jews and Judaism in the Second Temple Period*, 4 vols. [2004–].) H. W. HOEHNER

Maccabees, Books of. A series of books relating events that focus on Judas MACCABEE and other heroes in the Jewish struggle for religious and political freedom; 1 and 2 Maccabees are included in the APOCRYPHA, whereas 3 and 4 Maccabees are usually ranked among the PSEUDEPIGRAPHA. These four books vary greatly in historical reliability, content, and style.

    I. First Maccabees
    II. Second Maccabees
    III. Third Maccabees
    IV. Fourth Maccabees
    V. Canonicity

I. First Maccabees

A. Title. By the late 2nd cent. A.D. the title *ta Makkabaika* ("The Things Maccabean"; EUSEBIUS, *Eccl. Hist.* 6.25.2, quoting ORIGEN) was used to refer apparently to either 1 or 2 Maccabees or both. Possibly only 2 Maccabees was intended, because the surname Maccabeus (meaning "hammerer" or "mallet-headed" or "extinguisher") applies in its strictest sense only to Judas, who dominates all of 2 Maccabees but shares the spotlight with his brothers in the longer history of 1 Maccabees.

JOSEPHUS (*Ant.* 12.6.1 §265) asserts that MATTATHIAS, father of Judas and his four brothers, was descended from Asamonaios. Since the TALMUD refers to this famous family as HASMONEAN, whereas the nickname Maccabee does not occur in Semitic literature before the Common Era (A.D.), it is possible that the original title of 1 Maccabees was "Book of the House of the Hasmoneans." This designation occurs in JOSIPPON (a Hebrew adaptation of Josephus's writings) to indicate a source for the wars of Judas.

Origen knew the book(s) also as *Sarbēthsabanaiel* (Euseb. *Eccl. Hist.* 6.25.2), an obvious Semitic term of uncertain meaning. If it represents Hebrew *śr byt šbnh ʾl*, it would mean "the prince of the house that God built." If it is a badly corrupted title, it might be equivalent to an Aramaic phrase meaning "the book of the house of the princes of God." CLEMENT OF ALEXANDRIA (c. A.D. 195) refers to 1 Maccabees as *to tōn Makkabaikōn* (*Stromata* 1.21 §123), and Eusebius specifically mentions *hē prōtē kaloumenē tōn Makkabaiōn biblos* (*Demonstration* 8.2.72). Greek MSS of the SEPTUAGINT commonly designate 1 and 2 Maccabees as *Makkabaiōn A* and *B*.

B. Unity. In spite of the chronological order and sustained style of the book, scholars have occasionally questioned the authenticity of 1 Macc. 13:43 to 16:24. The material in these chapters was used sparingly if at all by Josephus in his *Antiquities*, so some have concluded that his copy ended prior to this point and that the final chapters were a later addition. A few small contradictions in ch. 14 do lend themselves to this view, but there are discrepancies earlier in the book also. Josephus apparently stopped using 1 Maccabees as a source for the period following Simon's induction as high priest owing to his earlier work, *The Jewish War*, in which he had utilized the material of Nicholas of Damascus. Josephus felt free to modify and amplify his sources, so his switch back to a previous work does not prove that the chapters in question are spurious.

C. Sources. From several standpoints it is clear that written sources were used by the author of 1 Maccabees. Of particular importance are several letters, perhaps accessible to the author from the high priest's archives in the temple (cf. 1 Macc. 14:23; 16:23–24). Chapter 8 contains a letter from Rome confirming an alliance with the Jews, and in spite of earlier skepticism, scholars today accept its genuineness. Another letter from the Roman consul Lucius to Ptolemy Euergetes (15:16–21) explaining the Jewish alliance appears largely authentic. Several letters from Syrian rulers to the Maccabees are likewise included. Most are directed to Jonathan (10:18–20; 11:30–57) and Simon (13:36–40; 15:2–9) and exhibit authenticity except in various details. Correspondence between the Spartans and Jews (ch. 12) is open to question, particularly the letter from the Spartans to Onias (vv. 20–21). A Spartan message to Simon (14:20–23) does at least reflect an official document.

The existence of a "biography" of Judas Maccabeus is postulated on the large proportion of material relating to him. Half of the book covers only seven years (166–160/59 B.C.), in contrast to the twenty-five year span for the rest of the book. In 1 Macc. 9:22 one discovers that the rest of the acts of Judas are not written since they were so numerous. This contrasts with the usual summary of a king's reign found in Scripture (2 Ki. 8:23; 10:34; et al.). It may indicate that the author concentrated only on those events concerning Judas that were recorded.

Judas's biography may not have differed much from the annals that Jonathan and Simon would have kept as high priests. The book ends with a reference to the rest of John Hyrcanus's activities that were recorded in the chronicles of his high priesthood (1 Macc. 16:24). Since John's accession is noted in 1 Maccabees, but little else, the author wishes to indicate an additional source for information regarding him. Chronicles about the rule of Jonathan and Simon were undoubtedly available in the archives also and were utilized in this historical sketch.

D. Authorship. In a period when party divisions were not clearly defined in Judaism, it is difficult to label the author either a Pharisee or a Sadducee. He was a Palestinian who knew the terrain well judging from his precise descriptions of battle locations. Regions outside Palestine are little known to the author. He obviously revered the law and the temple and vigorously opposed paganism. He is careful to avoid the name of God, referring to deity as "heaven" primarily. Such caution reflects the Pharisees' practice of substituting for "Yahweh" lest they profane the divine name.

Perhaps the token summary of John Hyrcanus's reign indicates that the author disapproved of certain tendencies of the Hasmonean rulers. Toward the end of his rule, John openly rebuffed the Pharisees and espoused the Sadducean cause. Dissatisfaction with this policy or the growing worldliness of the king may be reflected in the failure to discuss John's rule. The final verses imply that he had been ruler for some years.

Other factors, however, seem to point toward the Sadducees as the party of the author. He does not refer to the resurrection of the dead, not even when great leaders have fallen (1 Macc. 9:9–10). There is likewise no mention of angels or spirits, and strict Pharisaic Sabbath rules appear to be disregarded at times (2:40–41). Certainly there is no attempt to antagonize the Sadducees.

It would be possible to identify the writer with the Hasideans or Hasidim, the "pious ones," embracing both Pharisees and Essenes. Yet, even the Hasidim are seen in a bad light for accepting Alcimus as chief priest in spite of Judas's objections. Contrary to the suggestion of some, the author probably was not directly related to the Hasmonean family, if one considers his criticism of their policies. It is more likely that he respected them highly while not actually belonging to their clan.

E. Date. Since the author does not side decisively with either the Pharisees or the Sadducees, some scholars point to a date of about 110 B.C. for the book, before John Hyrcanus's split with the Pharisees. The reference to the rest of John's acts in the chronicles of the high priesthood (1 Macc. 16:24) suggests that the author was living toward the end of John's reign (134–104 B.C.) or shortly after his death. Those who do not accept the trustworthiness of the last few verses tend to place the book in the early part of John's rule.

F. Purpose and style. The author aimed at providing a chronological history of the key events surrounding the lives and accomplishments of the Maccabees. He extolled these valiant warriors and the little nation which they led to independence under God. This work may have been an unofficial history geared to rebuke the growing secularization of the Hasmoneans who succeeded the Maccabees.

The structure and purpose of the book parallel EZRA and NEHEMIAH in certain respects. Just as those canonical books record God's providence over Israel under Persian rule, so 1 Maccabees describes God's care during the Greek period. Some assert that this book was written as a sequel to Ezra and Nehemiah. The inclusion of decrees and letters in those two books does resemble the many items of official correspondence cited in 1 Maccabees. Occasionally the flow of the narrative is interrupted by one of these letters, but they are usually well integrated with the writer's own knowledge and other eyewitness accounts, so that the result is a credible history.

Unlike the other books of Maccabees, the style is simple, straightforward, and factual, with little effort to embellish the narrative or to interpret events. References to the OT abound, as the Maccabees draw courage from the heroes of old (1 Macc. 2:26; 4:30; 7:1–20). Scriptural terms and phrases are sprinkled throughout the text (3:45; 9:21–22) and predicted events find some fulfillment. Compare the "great tribulation" (9:27) after Judas's death and the prosperity of the "vine and fig tree" during Simon's reign (14:4, 12; cf. Mic. 4:4).

Several poetic sections, usually dependent on biblical passages, appear in the book. Laments occur most often, mourning Antiochus's destruction of Jerusalem (1 Macc. 1:24–28), the desecration of the temple (1:36–40), the murder of many Hasidim (7:17), and the tragic death of Judas (9:21). The lament in ch. 7 is an adaptation of Ps. 79:2–3. An imprecatory prayer directed against Nicanor occurs in 7:37–38, and eulogies of Judas and Simon are recorded in 3:3–9 and 14:4–15.

G. Contents. The narrative may be outlined as follows:
1. Introduction (1 Macc. 1:1–9)
2. The persecution of Antiochus Epiphanes (1:10–64)
3. The launching of the revolt (ch. 2)
4. The career of Judas (3:1—9:22)
5. The career of Jonathan (9:23—12:53)
6. The career of Simon (13:1—16:16)
7. The accession of John Hyrcanus (16:17–24)

First Maccabees describes the Jewish struggle for independence from the tyranny of ANTIOCHUS Epiphanes in 175 B.C. through the reign of SIMON MACCABEE in 134. After a nine-verse introduction referring to the exploits of ALEXANDER THE GREAT, the division of his empire, and the rise of the SELEUCIDS, the author outlines Antiochus's outrages against the Jews, culminating in the "abomination of desolation" (1 Macc. 1:10–64). Chapter 2 describes the fervent zeal of Mattathias, a priest who, along with his five sons, launched a bitter revolt in MODEIN against Antiochus's soldiers and any Jews who collaborated with the Syrians out of expediency.

The major section of the book records the heroics of Judas, the most illustrious of the five sons. Several victories won after the death of Mattathias enabled Judas to recapture Jerusalem and rededicate the temple (1 Macc. 4:36–61). The Jews purified the temple on the twenty-fifth of Kislev 164, a date commemorated in the Jewish feast of Hanukkah (see DEDICATION, FEAST OF). Judas and his brothers next won victories in GILEAD and GALILEE (5:17–68). After the death of Antiochus (6:1–17), Judas battled various generals and kings, including Antiochus Eupator, Lysias, and Nicanor. A treaty with Lysias (6:55–63) afforded a brief respite during this time. To pressure the Syrians, Judas concluded a treaty with Rome just prior to his death at Elasa against Bacchides (8:1—9:22).

Judas's brother and successor Jonathan achieved further victories against the Seleucids, who were plagued internally with political intrigue. Using this turmoil to advantage, Jonathan received from them the title of high priest. He also maintained peaceful relations with Rome and the Spartans, only to be murdered by his supposed ally, Trypho (1 Macc. 9:23—12:53).

Simon, the surviving brother, ruled from 142 to 134 and gained full political independence by capturing the citadel (Acra), the hated center of Hellenism in Jerusalem, which was manned by a garrison. A special decree set up in the temple guaranteed to Simon and his successors the offices of ruler and high priest until a faithful prophet would arise in Judea (1 Macc. 14:41–44). Antiochus VII even permitted Simon to coin his own money (15:1–9), although he later denied him this valuable concession (15:10–31). Simon and his sons were victorious over Antiochus, but an army officer named Ptolemy assassinated Simon along with two of his sons, Mattathias and Judas (16:3–16). John Hyrcanus, a third son, escaped and assumed control of the government (16:17–24). With the accession of this king, the book ends rather abruptly.

H. Teaching. The providence of God over Israel is paramount in the book, for the Jewish nation was a righteous center in the midst of an ungodly world. Israel was vitally important for other nations (1 Macc. 10:4–5; 11:3–8; 14:10–18), but their attempts to overwhelm her were repulsed by a God who controls history at every turn. Antiochus Epiphanes died because of his wicked acts against Jerusalem (6:1–17).

Numerical superiority means little in battle if the faithful seek God in prayer. Repeatedly, Judas prayed before conflict and encouraged his men to cry to heaven like the faithful of old (1 Macc. 4:10, 30; 7:1–20, 36–38, 41–42). Such trust in God should, however, be coupled with sound military strategy. The Maccabees were instruments of God for the preservation of the faith, and they frequently are compared with OT heroes. Mattathias's death-dealing zeal for the law paralleled Phinehas's slaughter of Zimri (2:26, alluding to Num. 25:10–15). Judas was a savior of Israel (1 Macc. 9:21) like former judges and kings, and his death is lamented in terms used for Saul and Jonathan, "How is the mighty fallen!" (9:21; cf. 2 Sam. 1:19, 25, 27). Victory, however, was due ultimately to God (1 Macc. 5:62), and the Maccabees are not exalted unduly. The success of the ruling family was secondary to the destiny of the nation as a whole (1 Macc. 4:59; 5:16; 7:48–49), and disillusionment with their later policies is implied.

The messianic hope appears in connection with a faithful prophet who would come to deal with the profaned altar (1 Macc. 4:42, 47), and to replace the dynasty of Simon as ruler and high priest (14:41). This "prophet" relates undoubtedly to the prophet like Moses mentioned in Deut. 18:15, 18. Some features of the messianic age are anticipated during Maccabean rule. Simon is praised for bringing peace, so that every man sat under his vine and fig tree (1 Macc. 14:12), a probable allusion to the prophecy of Mic. 4:4. A newly independent Israel must have rekindled hopes for Messiah's coming.

Strict observance of the law was mandatory for the righteous man. Those who apostatized and connived to ruin the faithful were harshly condemned (1 Macc. 3:15; 6:21–22; 7:10). God is a holy God who demands obedience to the principles of the Torah.

I. Original language. Although it is extant only in Greek translation, there is little doubt that the book was first composed in Hebrew. Origen's Semitic designation already has been discussed (see above, section A), and Jerome in his *Prologus Galeatus* states quite clearly that Hebrew was the original language of 1 Maccabees. This Hebrew text apparently lasted in some form until the period of Origen and Jerome, but Josephus utilized only the Greek version in the 1st cent. A.D.

It is possible that Jerome intended "Hebrew" to be understood as Palestinian Aramaic, but the nature of the Greek translation indicates otherwise. Frequently, this literalistic version betrays obvious OT idioms, and on occasion, translation errors are evident due to a faulty understanding of the original. Since the translation shows an awareness of the Greek OT (LXX), he may have been an Alexandrian Jew, preparing his rendition near the start of the 1st Christian cent. Two translations based on the Greek were made into Latin and two into Syriac.

It seems strange that the rabbis failed to preserve the Hebrew original to such a valuable Jewish work. This may reflect the disapproving attitude of influential Pharisees toward the worldliness so evident in the reign of the Hasmonean successors.

J. Chronology. The dates in 1 Maccabees are crucial for the history of this period, for they are given with a precision that indicates the author had access to an official Seleucid chronicle. According to Josephus, the chronology is calculated from the year that Seleucus Nicator controlled Syria, a period beginning with the Battle of Gaza in the summer of 312 B.C. (Jos. *Ant.* 13.6.7). In 1 Macc. 1:10 we read that Antiochus Epiphanes became king in the 137th year of the Greek kingdom, or 175 B.C.

The chronology is complicated, however, by different CALENDARS employed by the Seleucids and the Jews. New Year's Day occurred in the autumn in the Seleucid calendar, which paralleled the preexilic Judean custom for computing kings' reigns from the first day of the seventh month, the present Rosh Hashana. The postexilic Jews observed a spring New Year, following the Babylonian pattern and the ancient Hebrew religious calendar. Dates in 2 Maccabees often are one less than the corresponding date in 1 Maccabees. Antiochus Epiphanes died in 163 B.C. according to 1 Macc. 6:16, but 2 Macc. 9:1 and 11:23 place the same event in 148. Scholars do not agree concerning how this problem can be unraveled. Apparently 1 Maccabees began the second year of the Seleucid era in the autumn of 312, counting the remaining weeks of the summer after the Battle of Gaza as the first year. In 2 Maccabees, the Seleucid era may be calculated from the autumn of 311.

K. Relation to the NT. The Jewish expectation of a messianic age and a prophet who should come (1 Macc. 4:46; 14:41) parallels the attitudes found in the NT. When JOHN THE BAPTIST proclaimed Messiah's coming, Jewish leaders asked him if he was "the prophet" (Jn. 1:21, 25). Probably both groups had in mind Moses' prediction of a great prophet (Deut. 18:15, 18).

Instead of using a name of God, the author consistently refers to deity as "Heaven." The people prayed "to Heaven, to see whether he will favor us" (1 Macc. 4:10). This substitution of the place for the name is compared by some scholars with the term "kingdom of heaven" (Matt. 3:2). This may be virtually equivalent to the closely related "kingdom of God" concept.

While concluding his description of Judas's life, the author declares that the remaining deeds of this hero were not written because they were so numerous. In similar fashion, John summarizes Jesus' life by referring to "many other miraculous signs ... which are not recorded in this book" (Jn. 20:30). If these "many other signs" were to be recorded, even "the whole world would not have room for the books that would be written" (21:25).

II. Second Maccabees

A. Title. As mentioned above (I.A.), the 2nd cent. A.D. title *ta Makkabaika* may have referred exclusively to 2 Maccabees inasmuch as Judas, the focal point of this work, was properly "the Maccabee." The book presents a summary or epitome of a five-volume history by one Jason of Cyrene (2 Macc. 2:23–32). Clement of Alexandria (*Stromata* 4.14 §97) correctly refers to this book as *hē tōn Makkabaikōn epitomē*, "The epitome of the things Maccabean." A more accurate title is given at the end of Codex Venetus: "An epitome of the deeds of Judas Maccabeus."

B. Unity. Since 2 Maccabees is based on the fivefold history of Jason, it is difficult to decide which material was original with the author himself. Within 2 Macc. 3:1—15:36, which constitutes the "epitome" proper, scholars have questioned the inclusion of official documents in ch. 11. Some doubt that either Jason's history or the original 2 Maccabees contained them, but other authorities attribute the documents to Jason. Inasmuch as the work of Jason is no longer extant, most of the arguments of this nature are subjective and anything but conclusive.

Several contradictions and historical problems have cast doubt on the integrity of 2 Maccabees. Chronological errors abound, such as the placing of Antiochus Epiphanes's death prior to the cleansing of the temple by Judas (2 Macc. 1:11–18; 9:1—10:9) or the description of episodes concerning Lysias following Antiochus's decease (11:1–15). In the latter case, the two defeats of Lysias are merged into one badly confused account. Similarly, 8:30–33 relates battles with Timothy and Bacchides that interrupt the account of the victory over Nicanor (8:23–29, 34–36).

With regard to the death of the despicable Antiochus IV, variant accounts are given in 2 Macc. 1 and 9. The author must have noticed the discrepancy but preferred to follow his sources; any tradition of that tyrant's death was worth preserving! Apparently he was bothered little by historical difficulties, avoiding the painstaking care of a thorough historian (2:28). Attempts at rearranging the book to eliminate errors break up whatever continuity remains, for most of the mistakes form an integral part of their present context.

Prefaced to the main body of the text are two introductory letters addressed to the Jews in Egypt (2 Macc. 1:1—2:18). While there is some doubt as to their authenticity, these letters may well have been incorporated by the epitomist himself. The prologue (2:19–32) and epilogue (15:37–39) obviously were written by him.

C. Sources. The bulk of 2 Maccabees comprises an abridgement of a comprehensive history by Jason of Cyrene. This five-volume work has not survived, but many authorities outline the book on the basis of five divisions, which are each concluded with a summary statement (2 Macc. 3:40; 7:42; 10:9; 13:26; 15:37). These sections may correspond to the volumes of Jason's original production. Other scholars contend that the epitomist did not abridge Jason's entire work, since Jason is said to have written about Judas Maccabeus and his brothers (2:19). Simon, the last of the brothers, died in 134 B.C., whereas the events described in 2 Maccabees stop at about 160. A five-volume history might be expected to cover more than the fifteen-year period dealt with in the epitome.

Parts of 2 Maccabees clearly reflect the process of condensation owing to their marked brevity (e.g. 2 Macc. 13:22–26). Chapter 14 strangely omits any reference to Bacchides's efforts to appoint Alcimus the high priest, an event which nevertheless seems presupposed (14:3–4). Yet, other passages, such as those describing the martyrdoms (6:18—7:42), contain abundant detail and may have been amplifications of Jason's narrative.

It is not likely that the epitomist or Jason made use of 1 Maccabees, even though there are many similarities of detail between the two. Some of the sources utilized by Jason and the author of 1 Maccabees may have been identical, however. The biography of Judas (cf. above, I.C) could have been at Jason's disposal, expanded at points by oral tradition about the Maccabean hero. Since several of the dates involving Syrian rulers match those in 1 Maccabees, the epitomist probably had access to a Seleucid chronicle. Numerical notations, such as the number of soldiers involved in battles, do not agree in 1 and 2 Maccabees, so different chronicles may have been followed. The temple archives probably comprised another common source for the two historians. In at least two places (2 Macc. 9:19–27; 11:16–38) documents are quoted which demanded access to those key Jerusalem records if they are indeed reliable quotations. Facts about Onias, Jason, and Menelaus may have been derived from priestly annals chronicling events prior to Judas's triumphs. On the other hand, oral tradition could have been responsible for the circulation of much of this information.

The letters that introduce 2 Maccabees ostensibly were written from Palestine to Egyptian Jews mainly to encourage the remembrance of the purification of the temple by observing Hanukkah (or Feast of Dedication). Two letters appear to be cited (2 Macc. 1:1–9; 1:10—2:18), the first stemming from 124 B.C. and referring to a letter written in 143 (1:7–8). The second letter is more suspect, for it includes some legendary material about the altar (1:18b—2:15) and a story of the death of Antiochus that differs substantially from other accounts. If genuine, this second letter was written about.

D. Authorship. The identification of either Jason or the epitomist who summarized the larger history is difficult. There was a nephew of Judas Maccabeus named Jason (1 Macc. 8:17), and another Jason served as an envoy to Rome, but neither of these men can be connected positively with Jason of Cyrene. The epitomist himself was evidently an Alexandrian Jew, since the letters opening the book

Greek edition (1715) of 2 Maccabees.

were written to the Jews in Egypt, and the rhetorical Greek suits the style of ALEXANDRIA. Perhaps the emphasis upon the Jerusalem temple was a pointed rebuke against the Jewish temple at HELIOPOLIS. Others suggest that 2 Maccabees was composed in ANTIOCH OF SYRIA, for several of the martyrdoms might have happened there (7:3; cf. 6:8).

The author has been variously designated as a PHARISEE or one of the HASIDEANS (Hasidim). Contrasted with the writer of 1 Maccabees, the epitomist stresses such characteristic Pharisaic teachings as predestination, the active intervention of angels on behalf of God's people, and the resurrection of the body. If the epitomist is identified less specifically with the Hasidim, as is the author of 1 Maccabees, it is hard to account for the vast differences between the two books. The Hasidim disapproved of Simon's rule (2 Macc. 10:18–22; 14:17–19), but the Pharisees doubtless shared this sentiment. Unlike 1 Macc. 7:12–16, there is no reference in the epitome to the dispute between the Hasidim and Judas.

A case could also be made for an ESSENE background, for some have noticed several parallels between 2 Maccabees and the Qumran *War of the Sons of Light and the Sons of Darkness* (see DEAD SEA SCROLLS). Both works frown on fighting during the sabbatical year, and slogans written on the banners of the "sons of Light" resemble those used by Judas (2 Macc. 8:23; 12:11; 13:13, 15, 17; 15:7–8). Angels play a large role in the battles, although the *War* scroll emphasizes evil angels also. The importance of restoring true temple worship is another similarity within the two works. On the whole, however, these parallels seem more apparent than real; the Pharisaic identification remains the strongest view.

E. Date. Before examining the date of the extant book, one must investigate Jason's earlier work. The date of that production depends partially on the identification of Jason and the scope of the epitome. If only a portion of Jason's five volumes was abridged, a date far later than Judas must be sought (cf. above, II.C). Even the traditions regarding Judas could have taken a number of years to develop, however, so the date for his history is placed tentatively during John Hyrcanus's reign (134–104), probably after 130. Most authorities assume that Jason wrote before 1 Maccabees was composed.

The date of the epitome itself must be later than 124 B.C., since the first letter cited was written then (2 Macc. 1:9). In the epilogue (15:37), Jerusalem is said to be controlled by the Jews, a power they relinquished to the Romans in 63 B.C. This date may provide a *terminus ad quem* for the writing of 2 Maccabees, although Zeitlin argued for a date during the time of Agrippa I (A.D. 41–44). One may safely assert that the book was in circulation by A.D. 50.

F. Purpose and style. In his zeal to magnify the temple in Jerusalem, the author aimed his book at those Egyptian Jews who may have been supporting the Jewish temple at Heliopolis. These brothers were exhorted by the introductory letters to observe the Feast of Dedication and thus maintain close unity with the Palestinian Jews. As he carefully depicted the events surrounding the desecration and purification of the temple, the epitomist sought to foster proper devotion to the Jerusalem sanctuary. He was also intent on proving God's providential care for his people.

A theological treatise such as 2 Maccabees differed widely from the unadorned, factual approach found in 1 Maccabees. Indeed, so distinct are these two works that one must not label the epitome "the second book of Maccabees," as if it were a continuation of 1 Maccabees. Rather, it is a distinct book about the Maccabean era. In contrast to the straightforward account of 1 Maccabees, the author of 2 Maccabees embellishes and amplifies his material, mixing historical details with a colorful style in order to delight the taste of the reader (2 Macc. 15:39). Thorough historical research was snubbed, while incidents of great interest and emotional appeal were stressed and exaggerated (2:23–32). In general, Jason's history was abridged, but where facts needed to be dressed up the epitomist waxed eloquent. Second Maccabees was unabashedly written for popular consumption in the florid and fluent Greek common in Alexandria during this period. The author displays a large vocabulary in his descriptive zeal.

Because of the writer's religious objective, he emphasizes the supernatural, particularly the effective work of angelic horsemen. Frequently he attaches moral teaching to the outcome of battles. Individual heroism also is highly commended, notably that of Judas himself or of the martyrs.

G. Contents. The material may be outlined as follows:

1. Preface: Letters to the Egyptian diaspora (2 Macc. 1:1—2:18)
2. Prologue (2:19–32)
3. Heliodorus barred from the temple (3:1–40)
4. Desecration of the temple and the faithful martyrs (4:1—7:42)
5. Death of Antiochus and dedication of the temple (8:1—10:9)
6. Judas's victories over Timothy and Lysias (10:10—13:26)
7. Judas's victory over Nicanor (14:1—15:36)

The book covers a fifteen-year period extending from a time just preceding the accession of Antiochus IV in 175 B.C. down to 160. Although it is divided into 15 chapters compared with 16 for 1 Maccabees, it is considerably shorter. Two letters (2 Macc. 1:1–9; 1:10—2:18) from Jews in Palestine to those in Egypt are prefaced to the work (see above, II.C). They contain information about the purification of the temple and the Feast of Dedication, which they are urging their brothers to keep. Then follows the prologue (2:19–32) acknowledging the author's dependence on the history of Jason, which he hopes to abridge with sweat and long hours.

In the first chapter of the epitome proper, the author relates the abortive attempt of Heliodorus, an officer of Seleucus IV, to plunder the temple. A horse with an awesome angelic rider struck Heliodorus dumb and preserved the sanctity of "the place." Chapter 4 outlines the struggles of the Tobiads to gain the high priesthood. Jason and then Menelaus, aided by the Tobiad temple officer Simon, wrested this position from Onias III, mainly through bribes given to Antiochus Epiphanes. As a result, Jerusalem was turned into a Greek city. After miraculous signs in the sky, Jason attacked Jerusalem hoping to regain the high priesthood lost to Menelaus (2 Macc. 5:1–10). Assuming that a major revolt was in progress, Antiochus unleashed a murderous attack on Jerusalem, desecrating and plundering the temple, and forcing Judas to flee to the mountains (5:11–27).

Antiochus dedicated the temple to Zeus and forced the Jews to honor the god Dionysus (2 Macc. 6:1–9). Two women were killed because they circumcised their children, and other Jews were burned to death while keeping the Sabbath (6:10–11). Included among the many martyrs was one Eleazar, a venerable scribe who refused to eat swine's flesh to save his life (6:18–31). More famous are the seven brothers who were tortured to death one by one rather than give up their faith. After exhorting her sons not to recant and then observing the merciless atrocities inflicted on them, the godly mother also died a martyr's death.

The events in 2 Macc. 8–15 parallel 1 Macc. 3–7 in large measure, depicting the accomplishments of Judas. First, victories over Nicanor, Timothy, and Bacchides are recounted. Then 2 Macc. 9 presents an account of the death of Antiochus that differs radically from that of 1 Macc. 6:1–16. Horrible pains plagued the tyrant, and his chariot somehow ran over him (2 Macc. 9:5–8). As worms were eating away his rotting body, Antiochus changed his attitude toward the Jews, sending them a friendly letter and resolving to become a Jew himself (9:11–27).

The cleansing of the temple and the institution of the Feast of Dedication are related in 2 Macc. 10:1–9. This is followed by another invasion of Timothy, whose large army was smashed near Jerusalem by Judas with the aid of five angelic horsemen visible to the enemy (10:24–38). Another horseman dressed in white led the Jewish forces on to victory against Lysias (ch. 11).

A brief peace evaporated as conflicts erupted at Joppa and other cities, and Lysias was again defeated in 163 B.C. (2 Macc. 12–13). This time three years of peace ensued until Demetrius I sent Nicanor to be the Syrian governor of Judea. Intermittent fighting between the rival armies was climaxed by a final battle in which 35,000 Syrians were killed, including Nicanor. A vision in which the priest Onias and Jeremiah appeared to Judas provided important motivation for the army (14:1—15:36). This triumph was thereafter commemorated a day before the Feast of PURIM. In a short epilogue, the author states that he did his best to combine historical details with a style which was hopefully interesting enough to please his readers (15:37–39).

H. Teaching. The temple in Jerusalem is regarded as the best and holiest in the world (2 Macc. 2:19, 22; 5:15; 14:31), and events concerning this sanctuary are extremely important. Heliodorus's unsuccessful attempt to enter and plunder the temple is related, as well as the high priest's fear that "the place" would be dishonored (3:18–21). Antiochus's desecration of the temple is viewed by the author as a heinous deed (5:11—6:9), while Judas gains heroic stature for purifying the sanctuary. At the end of the book, Nicanor's death is attributed to his threat against the temple.

God's providential justice is strongly emphasized, particularly by the exact retribution he meted out to the wicked. Hence, Andronicus was killed at the very place where he had put Onias to death (2 Macc. 4:38), and the agonies endured by Antiochus IV are compared with the tortures he had devised for others (9:5–6). Each punishment corresponded precisely to the crime (13:4–8; 15:32–35).

Even the persecution of the Jews was deserved, for the nation had sinned in supporting pagan practices. Their punishment was a loving discipline for God's people (2 Macc. 1:26; 6:12; 14:15) that would bring the ungodly among them to repentance. On the other hand, the sin of heathen nations was allowed to increase to the point where God had to destroy them (6:12–17). When Israel did keep the law, victory over the enemy was forthcoming (8:34–36).

The power and sovereignty of God are evident in his deeds and names. He is the God who sees all things (2 Macc. 12:22) and has created heaven and earth out of things that did not exist (7:28 NRSV mg.). With a word God can strike dead an invading army of any size (8:18; 15:22). Unlike the usage in 1 Maccabees, names for God occur freely. He is the "Almighty Lord" (3:22; 8:18), "the great Sovereign of the world" (12:15, 28), and "the righteous Judge" (12:6, 41).

In almost every battle angelic horsemen appear to terrify the enemy and bring victory to the Maccabean forces. These dazzling warriors physically repelled Heliodorus (2 Macc. 3:25) or protected Judas (10:29), and with a heavenly rider to lead them the Jews demolished Lysias (11:6–14). Occasionally angels rendered assistance without their steeds (3:26, 33). Horsemen were seen fighting high over Jerusalem for almost forty days. This served as a warning of the impending persecution (5:1–4).

Judas Maccabeus stands out as a champion (2 Macc. 8:36) who, like David, restored the military fortunes of Israel and revitalized the nation's worship (cf. 2 Sam. 6). His purification of the sanctuary is the focal point of the book, but he also receives praise for his fervent prayers (2 Macc. 8:1–5) and his concern for widows and orphans (8:28, 30). To the author, Judas was a blameless man raised up by God at a crucial time.

In a vision seen by Judas before a key battle, the martyred Onias and Jeremiah appeared to encourage the people. Onias prayed for the nation and Jeremiah gave Judas a golden sword to slay the foe (2 Macc. 15:11–14). The concern and intercession of the dead for the living has been developed into a doctrine by the Roman Catholic Church. Conversely, Rome has adopted the practice of praying and offering sacrifices for the dead found in 12:43–46. Neither teaching is found in the OT.

The well-known martyr section (2 Macc. 6:10—7:42) extols the dedicated faithfulness of the victims and makes their actions worthy of emulation. Patristic writers compared the early martyrs favorably with Abraham's sacrifice of Isaac. Their suffering was even regarded as having an atoning value (7:37; 8:3). The aforementioned sacrifice for the dead was also a sin offering to make atonement for some whose pagan involvements had placed their resurrection and eternal destiny in jeopardy. In several places this bodily resurrection of the righteous is strongly emphasized. God will raise up the faithful to everlasting life (7:11, 36; 14:26) and a reunion with one's loved ones (7:6, 14, 19, 29). For the wicked, the future held nothing but punishment and suffering.

I. Original language. There is little doubt that the smooth Greek of the book, though strained at times, does not represent a translation from Hebrew or Aramaic. Unlike 1 Maccabees, there are few Hebraisms pointing to such an original, and an Alexandrian provenience is well-established. Only with regard to the introductory letters have serious attempts been made to posit a Semitic original. Since they stem from Palestine and have some evidences of a Hebraic style, it is possible that they are translations in their present form.

J. Chronology. Second Maccabees is consistent in following the Seleucid calendar, with the New Year falling in autumn (cf. above, I.J). Where 1 Macc. 7:1 mentions a Syrian date, 2 Macc. 14:4 has the same year. When an event concerns the Jews directly, 1 Maccabees employs the Jewish calendar with its spring New Year, but 2 Maccabees retains the Seleucid system (cf. 1 Macc. 6:20 and 2 Macc. 13:1). Hence, a one-year discrepancy occurs in these instances.

K. Relation to the NT. The impact of the martyr section (2 Macc. 6:10—7:42) upon the early church was evident during the Roman persecutions and may be alluded to in Heb. 11:35–38. Some of the faithful heroes were tortured and killed, or "wandered in deserts and mountains, and in caves and holes in the ground" (Heb. 11:38). The terminology closely parallels 2 Macc. 5:27; 6:11; and 10:6; it may reflect upon the afflictions of the Maccabean era (since Heb. 11:4—12:2 is often related to the "honor roll" found in Sir. 44–49, it could be argued that the author of Hebrews had another intertestamental book in mind also). Some scholars see similar allusions in the Pauline literature (e.g., S. A. Cummins, *Paul and the Crucified Christ in Antioch: Maccabean Martyrdom and Galatians 1 and 2* [2001]; see also below, IV.I).

The sequence and meaning of the words *deilandrountes* and *apistountes* (2 Macc. 8:13) resemble *deilois* and *apistois* (Rev. 21:8). The joining of the epithets "cowardly" and "unbelieving" in these two passages could be more than coincidence, and the context in 2 Maccabees would indicate that *apistos G603* does not mean only "faithless" (RSV) or "untrustworthy." An important NT term, *epiphaneia G2211*, occurs frequently in 2 Maccabees, mainly referring to the "appearances" of angels at strategic times (2 Macc. 2:21; 3:24, 33; 12:22). In the NT the "epiphany" of Christ relates to his first coming (2 Tim. 1:10) and especially to his climactic glorious return (2 Thess. 2:8; 1 Tim. 6:14; Tit. 2:13).

III. Third Maccabees

A. Title. The earliest MSS and versions give this book the title 3 Maccabees although it is, strictly speaking, inaccurate. The events described precede the Maccabean era by about fifty years, and none of the Maccabees figures in any of the narratives. In the Greek uncials A (Alexandrinus) and V (Venetus), 3 Maccabees appears next to 1 and 2 Maccabees and may have received its name from this arrangement.

Some scholars consider the book to be a kind of introduction to the books of Maccabees, and Henry Cotton for one placed it first in his *Five Books of Maccabees* (1832). Since 3 Maccabees also deals with a foreign power's attempt to hellenize the Jews, there is some merit to this suggestion. It is true that "Maccabee" was applied to all of Judas's brothers (see above, I.A) and may have been extended to include other heroes of the faith as well.

B. Sources. In spite of the legendary character of much of the book, there is evidence that the author did have certain historical facts at his command. Several accounts resemble the 2nd cent. B.C. history of Polybius, particularly the description of the Battle of Raphia (*Histories* 5.80–86). The material in 3 Macc. 1 regarding Ptolemy IV apparently represents the facts to a large degree. If it were not for certain discrepancies with the *Histories* of Polybius, one would label this as a source for 3 Maccabees, though the author may have depended on his faulty memory for information from that work.

A source that may have been used by both Polybius and the author of 3 Maccabees was the biography of Ptolemy IV written by one Ptolemy of Megalopolis, governor of Cyprus during Philopator's reign. This rather derogatory biography may have furnished the raw material for the embellishments of 3 Maccabees, and it is also known that Polybius lived in Megalopolis. Only a few fragments of this biography are extant, however.

1. Jewish traditions. The fusing of divergent traditions among Egyptian Jewry is particularly evident in the elephant episode (3 Macc. 4–6). Josephus (*Ag. Ap.* 2.5) describes a similar event during the reign of Ptolemy VII Physcon (146–117 B.C.). When the Jews supported the cause of Queen Cleopatra against his own, Physcon planned to release a herd of elephants upon them. As in 3 Maccabees, the drunk beasts attacked and killed many of the king's men. This story must go back to a historical kernel that became associated with more than one Ptolemy in the course of transmission. Similarly, the dichotomy between the Jews of Alexandria and those from the Egyptian interior indicates two traditions. The existence of a festival at Alexandria as well as one at Ptolemais strengthens this hypothesis (6:36; 7:19).

2. Esther. Several motifs seem to be borrowed from the canonical book of ESTHER, which relates the oppression of the Jews by an earlier power. The plot against the king and subsequent rescue through Dositheus (3 Macc. 1:2–3) reminds one of Mordecai's life-saving contribution (Esth. 2:21–23). Like the Jews in Persia, those in Egypt were accused of disloyalty (Esth. 3:8; 3 Macc. 3:19). In both works the attempt to wipe out the Jews backfired as the persecuted gained revenge against the Gentiles (Esth. 9) or their apostate brethren (3 Macc. 7:10–15). To celebrate the deliverances, both books record the establishment of festivals.

3. Second Maccabees. Even more striking are the parallels between 2 and 3 Maccabees. Both books revolve around the forced hellenization of the Jews at the expense of their religious beliefs (2 Macc. 4:9; 6:1–9; 3 Macc. 2:27–30). The attempt of Philopator to enter the Jerusalem temple (3 Macc. 1:9—2:24) closely resembles the thwarted efforts of Heliodorus (2 Macc. 3:7). And the angelic horseman who blocked the path of that Syrian official (2 Macc. 3:25) reminds one of the two angels who panicked the elephants and the Egyptians in 3 Macc. 6:18–21. To preserve the sanctity of the temple, the Jews prayed fervently in both books (2 Macc. 3:15–23; 14:34–36; 3 Macc. 2:1–20). In addition, each work solemnizes God's deliverance with a festival.

C. Authorship. The nature of the Greek used, the emphasis upon Alexandrian Judaism, and the author's knowledge of Egyptian affairs lead scholars to conclude that the author was a Jew living in Alexandria; and his zeal to adhere to the Jewish faith until death links him with the Hasidim. Judging from the parallels of the book with 2 Maccabees, one could identify the author with the Pharisees also. His belief in angels (3 Macc. 6:18) points in this direction, but there is no mention of the resurrection of the body or a future life. Perhaps this omission parallels the arrangement in Daniel, where God's saving providence is emphasized (Dan. 1–6), but the resurrection is outlined only at the end of that book (12:2).

D. Date. Although the occasion for the book need not have been deep distress (see below, III.E), several scholars have favored CALIGULA's persecution of the Jews in A.D. 38–39 as the historical backdrop. That Roman monarch, an advocate of EMPEROR WORSHIP, tried to defile the temple and also set up images in synagogues. If this were the actual situation behind the book, one would expect that these heathen practices would have been vigorously condemned and ascribed to Ptolemy.

Several lines of evidence support a 1st cent. B.C. origin. The author was influenced by 2 Maccabees and was aware of the Greek Additions to the Book of Daniel, particularly the language of the Song of the Three Children (Pr. Azar. 26–27; cf. 3 Macc. 6:6). Linguistic affinities with the Epistle of ARISTEAS strengthens a dating in the last pre-Christian century also. Moreover, the use of a personal name like "Philopator" in formal correspondence (3 Macc. 3:12; 7:1) did not become the practice of the Ptolemies until about 100 B.C. While a 1st cent. B.C. date is more probable, others argue that the composition took place in the Christian era. If so, a time prior to the destruction of the temple in A.D. 70 is demanded, since the temple services are viewed as continuing (1:8).

E. Purpose and style. The author's aim is to comfort and strengthen Jews who were undergoing persecution by providing examples of those who remained true to the faith and were delivered. By providing background stories of this kind, he also made available instructional and religious material for use in the special festivals of the Egyptian Jews. These stories would be of value even in times of relative peace and security. The slaughter of the several hundred apostate Jews would also serve as a warning to any about to abandon the religion of their fathers. An equally potent warning is directed against those individuals or nations that may have been embarking on policies of persecution toward the Jews.

With this apologetic approach, the author uses the style of a historical novel or romance. Various traditions and motifs are combined and embellished to achieve the desired effects. Many of the details are fantastic and incredible, reminiscent of the method of the epitomist. Occasionally scriptural allusions are made to God's intervention in regard to the flood, Pharaoh and the exodus, Sennacherib's army, Daniel and his three friends, and Jonah (3 Macc. 2:1–10; 6:3–8).

The book was composed in good idiomatic Greek, so there is no likelihood of a Semitic original. At times the style becomes bombastic and similar to parts of the SEPTUAGINT.

F. Contents. The narrative may be outlined as follows:
1. Ptolemy Philopator visits the Jerusalem temple (3 Macc. 1:1—2:24)
2. Alexandrian Jews forced to worship Bacchus (2:25–30)
3. Rebellious Jews registered for destruction in hippodrome (2:31—4:21)
4. Alexandrian Jews delivered from elephants in hippodrome (4:22—6:21)
5. Reinstated Jews celebrate (6:22—7:23)

The book is a historical romance setting forth the growing conflict between Ptolemy IV Philopator and the Jews. In the first story (3 Macc. 1:1—2:24) Ptolemy's great victory over Antiochus III at the Battle of Raphia (217 B.C.) is followed by the Egyptian's visit to the Jerusalem temple. His threat to enter the holy place produced bitter grief among the people, who preferred death to the desecration of the temple (1:29). When the high priest Simon prayed eloquently, God answered by paralyzing Ptolemy.

Returning to Alexandria with his desire unfulfilled, the king retaliated by compelling the Jews of that city to sacrifice to Bacchus (DIONYSUS) at the royal temples (3 Macc. 2:25–33). Those who refused would forfeit their rights as citizens and would be branded with the ivy leaf, the symbol of Bacchus. Most of the Jews resisted this order and used bribery to avoid being enrolled as serfs.

In this mosaic from the Roman House at Sepphoris, three satyrs (constant companions of the god Dyonisus or Bacchus) are treading on grapes. According to 3 Maccabees, the Jews in Alexandria were forced to sacrifice to Bacchus or face execution.

Ptolemy then issued an edict to execute all the Jews of Egypt, who were brought in chains to the hippodrome near Alexandria (4:21). Before this slaughter a census of all the Jews was to be taken, but a shortage of pens and papyrus precluded the forty-day effort to complete this registration.

Angered, Ptolemy decreed that 500 intoxicated elephants were to be turned loose against the Jews, but the king overslept one day and completely forgot about the decree the next day. Finally, the elephants were readied and the Jews, led by an old priest named Eleazar, prayed earnestly for deliverance. Two angels appeared to terrify the elephants and soldiers, and the beasts turned to trample many of Philopator's own men (3 Macc. 4:22—6:21).

This remarkable event brought the king to repentance; he released the Jews and reinstated them as loyal citizens. After a week's feast, he also gave them permission to attack those of their own number who had apostatized. They later killed 300 fellow Jews. While journeying homeward, they also celebrated for another week at Ptolemais and decided to commemorate their deliverance with an annual festival (3 Macc. 6:22—7:23).

G. Teaching. As in the first two books of Maccabees, the importance and value of prayer is stressed. During great crises, miracles follow directly upon the prayers of Simon and Eleazar, which are recorded in detail. A corollary to prayer is the saving work of God on behalf of those who trust in him.

The "unconquerable providence" of God who was "aiding the Jews from heaven" (3 Macc. 4:21) is another concept. The Lord does not turn his face away from his people (6:15), for he is the "holy Savior" of Israel (7:16). Even if they sin, God will forgive and deliver them (2:13).

The uniqueness of the Jews and their religion is strongly emphasized. They retain their faith in spite of fierce persecution, and any who would desecrate their temple will face dire consequences (3 Macc. 1:8—2:24). Contrary to the charges of their enemies, they are loyal citizens who have always been an asset to Egypt from the time they first defended her borders (3:21; 6:25; 7:7).

H. Relation to the NT. As in 2 Maccabees (see above, II.K), the noun *epiphaneia* and related words occur several times (3 Macc. 2:9; 5:8, 51). In 6:18 God manifests his face by sending two glorious angels to strike terror into the hearts of the Jews' enemies. The relating of "epiphany" to the appearance or manifestation of angels was characteristic of 2 Maccabees. God manifests his mercy (2:19) and is called the "manifest God" (5:35). Each of these examples helps the interpreter to evaluate the meaning of this term in the NT.

IV. Fourth Maccabees

A. Title. The oldest title of this book, 4 Maccabees (*Makkabaiōn D*), is found in several texts of the LXX (Sinaiticus, Alexandrinus, Venetus) and in later lists. The only justification for the title is that illustrations are largely drawn from 2 Macc. 6–7. A number of church fathers erroneously attributed the work to Josephus and called it "On the Supremacy of Reason" (*peri autokratoros logismou*; cf. Euseb. *Eccl. Hist.* 3.10.6. and Jerome, *On Illustrious Men* 13). Some Greek editions of Josephus's works make "On the Supremacy of Reason" the last chapter. The title is superior to "4 Maccabees" but the latter remains the more common designation.

B. Unity. A few sections are viewed by some as additions to the book, primarily 4 Macc. 17:23–24 and 18:6–19. Their content seems to be at odds with the language and teaching of the rest of the book and with the immediate context. In 18:6–19 the mother of the martyrs makes a speech reviewing the splendid teaching of her deceased husband, instruction that contributed greatly to the valor of their sons. Included in this speech are passages from Deut. 32:39 and Ezek. 37:3, which allude to a physical resurrection, a doctrine largely neglected by the author. It should be noted, however, that these scriptural verses themselves do not refer specifically to a physical resurrection. While this passage may be a digression, its content is consonant with the rest of the book.

C. Sources. There is little question that the author utilized 2 Maccabees as a source for his book. The historical setting given in 4 Macc. 3:19—4:26 is dependent on 2 Macc. 2:1—6:11, although the Seleucid persecution therein described does contain

Greco-Roman pig rattle from Cyprus. Antiochus Epiphanes ordered the Jews in Israel to eat pork or face death.

some variations. For example, in 2 Macc. 3, Heliodorus was the official who tried to enter the temple, while 4 Macc. 4 attributes this deed to Apollonius, governor of Syria. The martyrdom accounts in 4 Macc. 5–18 expand the much briefer description found in 2 Macc. 6–7, and the version of the death of Antiochus Epiphanes given in gruesome detail in 2 Macc. 9 is reflected in 4 Macc. 18:5.

Discrepancies between the two works and the elaborations of 4 Maccabees have cast some doubt on the identification of the source. It is possible that the writer depended on the history of Jason of Cyrene, which stands behind 2 Maccabees, rather than on the epitome itself. Conceivably, both might have been consulted. Yet, the characteristically loose handling of the author's source material need not lead away from 2 Maccabees. His penchant for deviations is evident even in his biblical references, particularly in his discussion of David's thirst (4 Macc. 3:6–16; cf. 2 Sam. 23:13–17).

D. Authorship. As already mentioned, some of the early church fathers named Josephus as the author of 4 Maccabees (see above, IV.A). Internal evidence strongly militates against this view, since the style and content differ radically from the known writings of Josephus. Like Josephus, however, the author was a Jew sympathetic with Pharisaic views. His fervent devotion to the law and belief in angels (4 Macc. 4:10; 7:11) support this identification. By eulogizing the Maccabean martyrs and neglecting the more important military leaders, the author also manifests a pacifistic attitude. Not war but the martyrs who restored the observance of the law are credited with expelling the enemy from the land (18:4).

The author's Hellenistic background stands out in bold relief. Stoic thought forms are used frequently, and a philosophical tone permeates the book. He assumes that his readers are capable of deep thinking and have a philosophical framework themselves. It is evident that the author wishes to retain Greek ideas wherever they do not contradict his Jewish beliefs.

Most scholars hold that the author wrote from Alexandria, since the integration of Greek philosophy with Judaism was felt most keenly there. The Greek style and overall content compare favorably with other Alexandrian literature of this period. Moreover, the important influence of 2 Maccabees upon the book supports this location, for in all probability 2 Maccabees was composed in Alexandria also.

Generally, proof that he was not a Palestinian Jew is based on the reference to a gymnasium "upon" (*epi*) the citadel of Jerusalem rather than "under" it (4 Macc. 4:20). This "error" is mitigated by the less precise meaning of *epi* as "at" or "by" instead of "upon." Usually, however, those who doubt the Alexandrian provenience prefer to locate the author in Antioch of Syria. This argument is posited upon the allegation that the Greek of 4 Maccabees is more Asiatic than Egyptian.

E. Date. The book must have been written after 2 Maccabees and before the destruction of the temple in A.D. 70. Although the date of 2 Maccabees is uncertain, most likely a work dependent on it, such as 4 Maccabees is, could not have been composed before 50 B.C. The *terminus ad quem* is fixed by the assumption that the temple worship had been resumed after Antiochus demolished the cultic functions (4 Macc. 4:20).

A more accurate dating can perhaps be derived from the historical notation that Apollonius was governor of Syria, Phoenicia, and Cilicia (4 Macc. 4:4). The same Apollonius governed Coelesyria and Phoenicia (2 Macc. 4:4). Only from A.D. 18 to 55 was Cilicia joined with Syria and Phoenicia, and this may explain the changed reference.

This span is further narrowed by the failure to allude to Caligula's persecution of 38–39, for the readers can hardly comprehend the atrocities of Antiochus (14:9). If 4 Maccabees had been written after 38, such behavior would have been more easily understood.

F. Purpose and style. The book was written to show the viability of Judaism within a Hellenic world. As he exalted the law and eulogized the Maccabean martyrs, who were loyal to its principles, the author wished also to commemorate those godly heroes who far surpassed Greek stalwarts. By their inspiring example, he exhorted and encouraged others to emulate their faithfulness and live under the control of religious reason.

Apparently the book was presented orally at a special "time" or "season" when the deaths of the martyrs were remembered (4 Macc. 1:10; 3:19). Several suggestions have been made concerning the identity of this occasion. One theory relates the recitation to the custom of Greek and Syriac Christians commemorating the martyrdoms on August 1, a custom partially based on the belief that the martyrs were buried in Antioch. Such a theory demands an Antiochene origin for 4 Maccabees, a supposition with scant support.

Because of the frequent mention of the atonement accomplished by the martyrs, some have associated the book with the Day of Atonement (see ATONEMENT, DAY OF). Evidence for this is meager, but according to a rabbinic legend, synagogue worship for that occasion did include reference to another martyrdom of ten godly men slain by HADRIAN. Another possibility is the Feast of DEDICATION, for the book stresses the purified land and the renewal of keeping the law accomplished by the martyrs (4 Macc. 1:11; 17:21; 18:4). The themes of purification and renewal are closely related to the Feast of Dedication, though with reference to the temple. Since there is no mention of this festival or of any of the Maccabean leaders in the book, even this identification is not convincing.

The form of the book is difficult to evaluate. Evidently it was intended for oral presentation, and some have called it a sermon. Frequently, the author appeals to his audience in sermonic fashion (4 Macc. 18:1, 4), and a religious quality is apparent in the splendid rhetoric. Yet the philosophic framework implies that the form is a literary device rather than an actual Jewish sermon. Scriptural references are confined mostly to the first three chapters.

This work also has been rightly designated a *panegyric*, for the eulogy of the Maccabean martyrs is central to the book. At times the style is impressive and eloquent; vivid description and figures of speech occur often, and occasionally scriptural terminology is used effectively (4 Macc. 6:2). The martyrdom chapters spare no gory detail as they evoke revulsion and respect.

The philosophic vocabulary sometimes demands close reasoning from a well-educated audience. A semiclassical style of Greek is used, replete with numerous optative forms.

G. Contents. The material may be outlined as follows:

1. Introduction (4 Macc. 1:1–30a)
2. OT illustrations of triumph of reason (1:30b—3:17)
3. The Seleucid oppression (ch. 4)
4. The martyrdom of Eleazar (5:1—7:23)
5. The martyrdom of the seven brothers (8:1—14:10)
6. The martyrdom of their mother (14:11—18:24)

The book is a philosophical discourse on the superiority of pious or religious reason in the life of a godly man. It is radically different from the other books of Maccabees, and in spite of a greater number of chapters, it is slightly shorter than 2 Maccabees and only half as long as 1 Maccabees in actual text.

According to his opening statement, the author seeks to demonstrate that religious reason can be the master of one's passions. Stating his theme and method of approach (4 Macc. 1:1–12), he proceeds to define clearly the philosophical terms used (1:13–30a). Then in 1:30b—3:17 OT figures such as Joseph and David are cited to illustrate the triumph of reason. Chapter 4 provides the historical background to the rest of the book by describing the Seleucid persecution against the Jews.

The main proof of his thesis is found in the lives of the Maccabean martyrs, to whom most of the book is dedicated. In 4 Macc. 5:1—6:30 the trial and torture of the faithful priest Eleazar are narrated, followed by a commentary upon that death (6:30—7:23). Then the martyrdom of the seven brothers is presented in great detail, as each one, beginning with the eldest, endures horrible atrocities (8:1—12:20). After some observations upon their bravery (13:1—14:10) the author shifts his attention to the fortitude of the mother in her death (14:11—18:24).

H. Teaching. Fourth Maccabees attempts to synthesize Jewish and Greek thought by showing that the Mosaic law provides the best means of gaining wisdom (4 Macc. 1:16–17). Reason operates most efficiently when the life of wisdom selected by the intellect is in accord with the Jewish law. The oft-repeated "devout [*or* religious] reason" is derived from the phrase *ho eusebēs logismos* (or a variation of it, 1:1 et al.). While such reason can be the master of the passions, it cannot control defects like forgetfulness or ignorance, which are inherent in the mind itself (1:5–6). In the heroic deaths of the martyrs, reason was victorious over passion.

The author divides the passions into pleasure (*hēdonē G2454*) and pain (*ponos G4506*) in Aristotelian fashion, and Stoic influence can be seen in his discussion of desire, joy, fear, and grief (4 Macc. 1:20–23). These emotions are affected by *hē kakoēthēs diathesis*, "the tendency toward evil" (1:25), which is similar to the rabbinic concept of *yēṣer hāṭôb* and *yēṣer hāraʿ* ("the good tendency" and "the evil tendency") struggling within human beings (cf. Gen. 6:5). Unlike the Stoics, the writer denies that reason can eradicate the passions; reason's function is to control the passions, thus avoiding enslavement to them (4 Macc. 3:1–3).

In his delineation of the four cardinal virtues—intelligence (*phronēsis G5860*), justice (*dikaiosynē G1466*), courage (*andreia*; cf. *andrizomai G437* in 1 Cor. 16:13), and self-control (*sōphrosynē G5408*)—the author clearly uses Stoic terminology (4 Macc. 1:6, 18; 3:1). The Hebrew martyrs more than others demonstrated these virtues by enduring a cruel death (9:18). By their heroism, Eleazar and the seven brothers show themselves to be philosophers of distinction, despising the self-gratifying hedonism of their tormentor Antiochus (5:4–12; 8:1–10). Thus, the Jews deserve recognition as philosophers who are actually superior to the Greeks. Further evidence of Stoic background can be seen in the names used for God, particularly *pronoia G4630*, "providence" (9:24; 13:19; 17:22), a term meaning "the world soul" in Stoic thought. "Justice" (*dikē G1472*, 4:21; 8:14, 22) and "power" (*dynamis G1539*, 5:13) are other titles that appear sporadically.

Emphasis is placed also upon the doctrine of immortality, which would bring eternal life for the godly (4 Macc. 9:8; 14:5–6; 17:12) and eternal torment for the wicked (9:9, 31; 12:12, 18; 13:15). In contrast to 2 Maccabees, no clear reference to a bodily resurrection occurs in the book, an omission that reflects the Greek viewpoint of the writer.

Probably the most remarkable passages on vicarious atonement outside of the NT occur in 4 Maccabees, where the blood of the martyrs atones for the sin of the people. The most explicit statement, found in 4 Macc. 17:22, describes their blood as a propitiatory death through which divine Providence saved Israel. By their endurance these martyrs conquered tyranny and cleansed the fatherland (1:11; 18:4). Quite clearly this atonement is expressed as a substitution for the people (6:28–29). An analogous teaching is found in the *Manual of Discipline* from Qumran, which asserts that certain righteous ones within the community atone for iniquity through righteous living and suffering (1QS VIII, 3–4). This same group also makes atonement for the land (VIII, 6–7), a concept similar to "cleansing the fatherland" (4 Macc. 1:11; 18:4).

I. Relation to the NT. There are several points of correspondence between 4 Maccabees and the writings of Paul, leading some scholars to suggest that Paul could have been the author if he had not been saved. Both men had Pharisaic backgrounds and were familiar with the philosophies of the day, particularly Stoicism. The recognition that reason—or the law—cannot fully control the mind (4 Macc. 1:5–6) is similar to Paul's admission in Rom. 7 that sin led him against his will.

When Paul declared in 1 Cor. 13:3 that he would gain nothing if he gave his body to be burned without love, he may have been counteracting the glorification of martyrdom so characteristic of 4 Maccabees. That same chapter on love ends with the mention of faith, hope, and love—the greatest of which is love (v. 13). These three may have been intentionally contrasted with the four Stoic virtues of intelligence, justice, courage, and self-control—the greatest of which was intelligence (4 Macc. 1:18–19).

Paul's teaching about the vicarious suffering of Christ parallels to some extent the substitution of the martyrs for the people (4 Macc. 6:28–29). The propitiatory blood of Christ stressed in Rom. 3:25 resembles the propitiatory death of the martyrs through which Israel was saved (17:22). Similarly, the book of Hebrews refers to the sanctifying effect of the blood of Christ (Heb. 1:3; 2:11; 10:10, 14, 29; 13:2), while 4 Maccabees describes the purifying of the Jews and Israel through the martyrs' blood (4 Macc. 1:11; 6:29; 17:21–22). Christ's death, however, has a worldwide application.

Hebrews 11:34–35 already has been discussed with regard to 2 Maccabees, but a possible relationship with 4 Maccabees also exists. The faith that motivated the great heroes of Heb. 11 is likewise stressed in the suffering of the Maccabean martyrs (4 Macc. 16:22; 17:2). The opening verses of Heb. 12 can be instructively compared with 4 Macc. 17:11–16. In the latter passage, the world and "the life of men" are the ones observing the martyrs enduring torture. In v. 10 they are described as *eis theon aphorōntes* "looking to God"; in Heb. 12:2 persevering believers surrounded by a cloud of witnesses are *aphorōntes eis ... Iēsoun*, "looking to (Jesus)." This verb is rare in both the LXX and the NT, and the contextual similarities to 4 Maccabees as well as the connection with Heb. 11 may indicate a relationship between the two books.

In the Johannine writings, an interesting comparison can be made with the word *nikaō* G3771, "to conquer," in 4 Maccabees. Frequently it means to endure suffering faithfully (4 Macc. 6:10; 7:4, 10–11; 9:6) and to overcome tyranny (1:11; 9:30; 16:14). It is used in John of overcoming the world (Jn. 16:33; 1 Jn. 5:4–5) and the evil one (1 Jn. 2:13–14), or of patient endurance (Rev. 2:7, 11, 17, 26; 3:5, 12, 21). In Rev. 7:15 and 4 Macc. 17:18 the slain martyrs appear before God's throne.

V. Canonicity. First and Second Maccabees were declared to be canonical by the Council of Trent in 1546, although some leading Roman Catholic scholars contemporary with Luther denied their right to this status. Protestants have relegated these two books to the APOCRYPHA, while acknowledging the high quality of 1 Maccabees. Early church fathers made frequent use of both books, but Origen, and particularly Jerome, who had broad acquaintance with Hebrew and the views of the Jews, excluded them from their lists of canonical writings. The latter scholar omitted them from his famous Vulgate. Only AUGUSTINE gave 2 Maccabees canonical ranking, and he equivocated at that.

Third Maccabees was regarded as canonical only by the Eastern churches (Greek, Syriac, and Armenian), which also received 1 and 2 Maccabees. Although it does appear in the Codex Alexandrinus of the LXX and the Syriac Peshitta, 3 Maccabees was not even included among the Apocrypha proper by Protestants.

In spite of the influence of 4 Maccabees among martyrologies and its presence in key MSS of the LXX (including Sinaiticus and Alexandrinus), it was rarely considered canonical. A few church fathers may have ascribed authority to it owing to its wide circulation and gripping message. See also CANON (OT).

(Significant editions and commentaries include *APOT*, 1:59–173 and 2:653–85; S. Tedesche and S. Zeitlin, *The First Book of Maccabees* [1950], and *The Second Book of Maccabees* [1954]; M. Hadas, *The Third and Fourth Books of Maccabees* [1953]; J. C. Dancy, *A Commentary on 1 Maccabees* [1954]; F.-M. Abel and J. Starcky, *Les Livres des Maccabées*, 3rd ed. [1961]; J. A. Goldstein, *I Maccabees*, AB 41 [1976]; J. J. Collins, *Daniel, First Maccabees, Second Maccabees* [1981]; J. A. Goldstein, *II Maccabees*, AB 41A [1983]; *OTP*, 2:509–64. Introductory works and monographs include W. O. E. Oesterley, *An Introduction to the Books of the Apocrypha* [1935], 300–327; R. H. Pfeiffer, *History of New Testament Times, with an Introduction to the Apocrypha* [1949], 461–522; K. D. Schunck, *Die Quellen des I und II Makkabäerbuches* [1954]; R. Doran, *Temple Propaganda: The Purpose and Chracter of 2 Maccabees* [1981]; D. J. Harrington, *Invitation to the Apocrypha* [1999], chs. 10–11, 15, 17; D. S. Williams, *The Structure of 1 Maccabees* [1999]; D. A. deSilva, *Introducing the Apocrypha: Message, Context, and Significance* [2002], chs. 11–12, 16, 18; S. R. Johnson, *Historical Fictions and Hellenistic Jewish Identity: Third Maccabees in its Cultural Context* [2004]; N. C. Croy, *3 Maccabees*

[2006]; D. A. DeSilva, *4 Maccabees* [2006]. See also the titles listed under MACCABEE.)   H. WOLF

Maccabeus mak´uh-bee´uhs. See MACCABEE.

Macedonia mas´uh-doh´nee-uh (Μακεδονία *G3423*; gentilic Μακεδών *G3424*, "Macedonian"). Also Macedon. In NT times a Roman senatorial province encompassing much of what is now northern GREECE.

I. Geography. A land of high mountains, broad rivers, and fertile valleys in the center of the Balkan peninsula, Macedonia was bounded in antiquity by Illyria (see ILLYRICUM) on the W, Moesia to the N, and Thrace (see THRACIA) to the E. It was separated from Thessaly to the S by the Pindus mountains. Four important river basins mark the terrain: the Haliacmon, Axius, Strymon, and Nestus. The three-pronged Chalcidice peninsula, which projects into the northern AEGEAN SEA, is one of the significant geographic features. The region boasted of rich farm land and timber, extensive deposits of silver and gold, a long seacoast of good harbors, and a hardy population of mixed non-Indo-European, Thracian, Illyrian, and Macedonian origin.

II. History. The kingdom of Macedonia was established in the 7th cent. B.C., but the first 200 years of its history are almost unknown. It was founded by Perdikkas I. His successors, known only by name, include Philip I, Alexander I, Perdikkas II, and Archelaus (c. 413–399 B.C.). Thucydides (*Hist.* 2.100) remarks that Archelaus did more than his predecessors to build up the military might of the nation.

Under Philip II (359–336 B.C.) the power of Macedonia began to influence both Greece and the E. At this time the Persian threat to the Greek city-states was great. Philip by bribery, persuasion, and force managed to rally Greece against the Persians. After the battle of Chaeronea, he was named *stratēgos autokratōr* at the synod of CORINTH. However, he was assassinated by a Macedonian noble in 336 before he could embark upon his long-planned campaign against PERSIA. Philip's successor was his son, Alexander III (see ALEXANDER THE GREAT). Though only a young man of eighteen, he embarked upon a campaign of conquest such as the world has seldom seen. In twelve years he conquered Egypt, Persia, Babylonia, and parts of India, only to die of a fever at the age of thirty-three.

The success of the small kingdom of Macedonia can be accounted for in the military skills of Philip and Alexander. Philip, while a hostage at Thebes, had opportunity to study the tactics of the Greek military genius Epaminondas. The latter had begun to use a flexible mode of attack rather than the rigid phalanx of four to eight men deep. He employed an oblique order of attack that used the central phalanx to stabilize the line. Because each man was individually less protected on the right side, Greek armies tended to bear to the right when they attacked. This tendency left them open to attack on the exposed flank. Epaminondas grasped this weakness and successfully used cavalry on one flank to concentrate the attack. Philip also learned at Thebes the importance of patriotism, which too often was lacking in the mercenary soldiers customarily employed by the Greek city-states.

Philip continued scientific analysis in military maneuvers. He developed a sophisticated attack force that consisted of the phalanx at the center, now equipped with much longer poles and cavalry on both flanks. The light cavalry on the left was merely defensive. The heavy cavalry was on the

Macedonia.

right, protected on its left by heavily armed but mobile infantry, and on the right by light cavalry. When the enemy was confronted, the phalanx held the center while the cavalry on the right attacked in echelon. This basic style of attack was successful in encircling and routing the enemy on every occasion it was employed by Philip and Alexander.

Alexander's premature death in 323 B.C. introduced a tremendous struggle for power throughout the empire. In Greece proper his regent, Antipater, ruled for a short time and selected Polyperchon as his successor. However, Antipater's son Cassander soon gained control. He and his son Alexander were then recognized as kings of Macedonia until 294. Thereafter the Antigonids, descendants of one of Alexander's generals, assumed control of the Greek mainland until the Roman intervention. The period from 294 to 197 was marked by internal disorders and an invasion of migrating Gauls. In other parts of the empire two dynasties were established by Alexander's generals, the Seleucid empire in Syria and the Ptolemaic in Egypt (see SELEUCUS; PTOLEMY). A fourth kingdom, Thrace, disappeared when Lysimachus, one of Alexander's generals, died childless.

All of the Greek mainland came under Roman rule in the middle of the 2nd cent. B.C. After the Romans under L. Aemilius Paulus defeated its forces in 168 at Pydna, Macedonia was organized as a semi-independent republican federation modeled on the Achaean and Aetolian Leagues. It was divided into four districts: (1) the region between the Strymon and Nestus Rivers; (2) the region between the Strymon and Axius Rivers including the Chalcidice; (3) the region from the Axius River to the Peneius River in Thessaly; (4) the mountainous lands to the NW. The capitals of these regions were respectively AMPHIPOLIS, THESSALONICA, Pella, and Pelagonia. However, the independent status was short lived. Andriscus, who claimed to be the son of Perseus, tried to reconstitute the Macedonian monarchy in 149 B.C. A Roman army under Q. Caecilius Metellus put down the revolt, and in 146 Macedonia was reorganized as a Roman province. The new province included portions of Illyria and Thessaly. Thessalonica became the seat of the Roman government, although the four capital districts were still recognized.

The senatorial province was administered by a propraetor (a PRAETOR sent to govern a province) with the title of PROCONSUL. The province of ACHAIA, which comprised central Greece and the Peloponnesus, was associated with it. It was usually administered by a legate from Macedonia. Several times the two are mentioned together in the NT, but Macedonia always is given priority (Acts 19:21; Rom. 15:26; 2 Cor. 9:2; 1 Thess. 1:7). From A.D. 15 to 44 Macedonia was combined with Achaia and Moesia into a large, imperial province. Macedonia was then ruled by a legate from Moesia. In A.D. 44 it reverted back to its original status as a senatorial province.

The province was strategically and commercially important because of the famous VIA EGNATIA, which extended across its territory from the Adriatic to Thrace. The highway started at the seaports of Dyrracium and Apollonia, which were opposite S Italy; extended across the mountains to the port of Thessalonica; and from there to a second Apollonia on the N Aegean, AMPHIPOLIS, PHILIPPI, and NEAPOLIS. According to the geographer Strabo, it terminated beyond the Hebrus River at Kypsela in Thrace. In all it was 535 Roman miles long. The apostle Paul no doubt traveled on it from Neapolis to Philippi and Thessalonica (Acts 16:11–12; 17:1).

III. Biblical and extrabiblical references. Macedonia is mentioned in 1 and 2 MACCABEES and alluded to in the book of DANIEL. First Maccabees begins with a description of the exploits of Alexander and the division of the empire upon his death (1 Macc. 1:1–9). In 1:1 he is said to have come from the land of KITTIM. In 8:2 an account is given of the way in which the Romans overcame Philip V and Perseus, who was called the king of Kittim. In 2 Macc. 8:20 the name Macedonians is applied to mercenary soldiers in the service of the Seleucid kings.

Daniel described the kingdom of Macedonia as a kingdom of bronze (Dan. 2:39) and as a rough he-goat (8:5). The goat had one horn between his eyes that was broken and from which came four horns. From one of the four horns came a king who became very powerful and troubled the people of God. This is interpreted as referring to

Alexander, who was succeeded by his four generals. A descendant of one of them was the notorious ANTIOCHUS Epiphanes (175–163), who laid waste the sanctuary of the Jews at Jerusalem. In Dan. 11 a description is given of the conflicts between the Ptolemies and Seleucids. Prediction was made of the marriage of Berenice, daughter of Ptolemy Philadelphus, to Antiochus Theos, which brought a temporary respite in their struggle for power. Further prophecies were made regarding conflicts between the two houses that lasted until the Roman intervention.

Numerous references are made to the cities of Macedonia in Acts and the Pauline epistles. Flourishing churches were established by PAUL in the important cities of PHILIPPI, THESSALONICA, and BEREA (Acts 16:8—17:15). When Paul departed from the region, SILAS and TIMOTHY continued the work (17:14–15; 18:5). GAIUS and ARISTARCHUS, who were Macedonians, were Paul's traveling companions in the E. Because of their association with him, they faced danger during the riot at EPHESUS (19:29). SECUNDUS, also a Macedonian, waited for Paul at TROAS when the latter left Philippi for the last time on his way to Jerusalem (20:4). Paul's converts in Macedonia made a collection for the poor at Jerusalem (Rom. 15:26). They also ministered to the needs of Paul himself (2 Cor. 8:1–5; Phil. 4:15). In epistles addressed to the PHILIPPIANS and the THESSALONIANS, Paul warmly commended them for their faith and love.

(See further S. Casson, *Macedonia, Thrace and Illyria* [1926]; U. Wilcken, *Alexander the Great* [1932]; W. A. Heurtley, *Prehistoric Macedonia* [1939]; N. G. L. Hammond et al., *A History of Macedonia*, 3 vols. [1972–88]; M. Sakellariou, ed., *Macedonia: 4,000 years of Greek History and Civilization* [1983]; N. G. L. Hammond, *The Miracle that was Macedonia* [1991]; R. Billows, *Kings and Colonists: Aspects of Macedonian Imperialism* [1995]; M. Girtzy, *Historical Topography of Ancient Macedonia: Cities and Other Settlement-Sites in the Late Classical and Hellenistic Period* [2001]; J.-N. Corvisier, *Philippe II de Macédoine* [2002].)

A. RUPPRECHT

Machaerus muh-kihr´uhs (Μαχαιροῦς; cf. Jos. *War* 7.6.1 §168). The name Machaerus does not occur in the NT, although JOSEPHUS (*Ant.* 13.5.2 §119) reports that JOHN THE BAPTIST was imprisoned and beheaded at this fortress. According to the account in the Gospels (Matt. 14:3–12; Mk. 6:17–29; Lk. 3:19–20), it was during the celebration of his birthday that HEROD Antipas ordered the death of John the Baptist.

Herod the Great built a prison and fortress at Machaerus (view to the W). It was probably here that his son Herod Antipas executed John the Baptist.

Machaerus (modern Mukawir) is located E of the DEAD SEA on a high mountain overlooking the sea. In the 1st cent. B.C. it was fortified by Alexander Jannaeus (see HASMONEANS), and later Herod the Great constructed an impressive palace on a hill opposite the fortification (Jos. *War* 7.6.2 §§171–77). Herod Antipas possessed it when he received the territory of PEREA.

Scattered remains of the fortress, palace with the roadway joining them, and aqueducts and cisterns, are visible today. In the early summer of 1968, Jerry Vardaman excavated in various areas of the site. The termination of the pottery sequence near the end of the 1st cent. indicates abandonment of the site after the Herodian period. The attractive view of the Dead Sea, the commanding position with Herodium and Alexandrium visible on the W bank, and the presence of hot springs nearby no doubt made this a delightful residence for the healthy and ailing Herods. (See *ABD*, 4:457–58.)

B. VAN ELDEREN

Machbannai mak´banai. KJV form of MACBANNAI.

Machbenah mak-bee′nuh. See MACBENAH.

Machi may′ki. See MAKI.

Machir, Machirite may′kihr, may′kuh-rit. See MAKIR.

Machmas mak′muhs. KJV Apoc. form of MICMASH (1 Macc. 9:73).

Machnadebai mak-nad′uh-bi. See MACNADEBAI.

Machpelah mak-pee′luh (מַכְפֵּלָה *H4834*, always with the definite article, meaning "the double [cave]"). The burial place that ABRAHAM purchased of EPHRON, the HITTITE of HEBRON, now located under the Ḥaram el-Khalil in Hebron. The name does not occur outside Genesis and always designates the sepulchres of the patriarchs.

The occasion of the mention of Machpelah was the death of SARAH and the necessity to find a secure sepulchre for her, himself and their posterity. Analysis of Gen. 23 and Hittite law codes have shown that Hittites of Anatolia maintained an outpost at Hebron at this time (cf. M. R. Lehmann in *BASOR* 129 [Feb. 1953]: 15–18; however, see HITTITE IV.A.1). The process of negotiation was perfect etiquette and custom that still prevail in many Arab communities, but in Abraham's case the price finally paid was deliberately exorbitant, and the offer first of the land for nothing is not to be considered a true offer. The high price was prompted by the aversion of the native Hittites to have a non-Hittite acquire proprietary, hence citizenship, rights in their midst. They could hardly deny the privilege to Abraham since he was a prince of God (Gen. 23:5–6), but sought to dissuade him by the excessive price asked. Abraham was not so easily put off, and going on the strength of God's promises that he should inherit the land (12:7; 13:15; et al.), he took the first step to this end as a token of his belief in God's promises and unhesitatingly paid the price demanded.

The record simply locates the cave "in Machpelah" (Gen. 23:17), "near Mamre" (23:19; 25:9 [NRSV, "east of Mamre"]), "in the field" (25:9; 49:30; 50:13). Abraham was buried there by ISAAC and ISHMAEL; Isaac and REBEKAH were likewise buried in Machpelah, and JACOB required that his sons bury him in the same field, where he had buried LEAH (49:30). By this Jacob expressed the same confidence in the promises of God that was exhibited by Abraham his grandfather. However, though the record locates the cave opposite Mamre, yet it is only a general term and no other landmarks are given by which to locate it, indicating that the site was obviously known, and that the name was sufficient to localize it. Ḥaram el-Khalil lies NE from the tell of Hebron across the vale on the lower slope of the N ridge on its S side.

According to Acts 7:16, Jacob and his sons "were brought back to Shechem and placed in the tomb that Abraham had bought from the sons of Hamor at Shechem" (cf. Josh. 24:32). The apparent discrepancy with Genesis is attributed by some to Samaritan influence; others think that the two transactions (Abraham's and Jacob's) have been telescoped into one event (see F. F. Bruce, *The Acts of the Apostles: The Greek Text with Introduction and Commentary*, 3rd ed. [1990] 196; C. K. Barrett, *A Critical and Exegetical Commentary on the Acts of the Apostles*, ICC, 2 vols. [1994–98], 1:351). JOSEPHUS (*War* 4.9.7) was the next earliest writer to mention Machpelah; he comments that the "monuments" of Abraham were being "shown to this very time" in the "small" city of Hebron. He records that Isaac was buried by his sons beside his wife in the same cave. From that time to this a connected witness places Abraham's tomb in the present city of Hebron under the present Ḥaram.

This Ḥaram is today a Muslim sanctuary, but in 1967 the cenotaphs marking the burials were removed from their inner rooms to an outer court. The sanctuary itself sets NE to SW, measuring 197 ft. long by 110 ft. wide with masonry walls 8–9 ft. thick. The stonework up to the cornice atop the pilasters is homogeneous and Herodian, while that above is Muslim. Around the exterior at about the line of the floor within occur a series of pilasters about 3 ft. 9 in. wide, spaced approximately 7 ft. apart, providing for 16 on the sides and 8 on the ends. Entrance to the Ḥaram is along the SW side from the N to the S between adjacent buildings. The visitor is required to wait in a vestibule before proceeding into an arched aisle at the westerly side; from there a court opens off with the cenotaphs of

Jacob and Leah, formerly each in its own chapel on the N side, while those of Abraham and Sarah are to the S.

A former church, now a mosque, occurs to the S of these memorial rooms; here were located the cenotaphs of Isaac and Rebekah. All the men were placed on the easterly side of the sanctuary. The location of each of the cenotaphs of Isaac and Rebekah supposedly mark the location of their bodies in the cave below, which is reported to extend under the entire church. In the mosque is found a low curb with a brass plate viewing hole, located over a small room of the cave below (about 12 ft. square). A small mosque outside the Ḥaram commemorates Joseph's reburial from Shechem on account of the antipathy between Jews and Samaritans.

The history of Machpelah since Genesis is obscure down to the Christian era. Perhaps Isa. 51:1b–2a ("Look to the rock from which you were cut / and to the quarry from which you were hewn; / look to Abraham, your father, / and to Sarah, who gave you birth") is a veiled reference to the cave. The later veneration of the site by Jews and Muslims alike supports the view that knowledge of the cave was not lost. The book of JUBILEES frequently mentions Abraham's "house" in Hebron (*Jub.* 29.17–20; 31.5; et al.). In Latin tradition it was called *baris Abraham* (palace of Abraham; see R. H. Charles, *Testament of the Twelve Patriarchs* [1908], 247). Comparison with Herodian stonework of the temple in Jerusalem makes it certain that the Ḥaram enclosure in Hebron was built by HEROD the Great to memorialize for all later time the location of the cave. This included apparently an entrance and vestibule before the double cave, and on an upper level erected the memorial to which Josephus referred.

In the time of Eudoria of Justinian (c. early 6th cent. A.D.) the church, now a mosque, was built, a detail recorded c. 570 by an anonymous visitor who also recorded seeing the tombs of the patriarchs. In 670 Arculf recorded the presence of the cenotaphs. In 980 Muqaddasi recorded the cenotaphs located as of recent times (G. Le Strange, *Palestine under the Moslems* [1890]); the monuments of Isaac and Rebekah were built by the Mamelukes but those of Abraham and Sarah came from the Abbasid or Omayyad periods. The Calif Mahdi is reported by Nasir-i-Kosru in 1047 that he constructed the present access in 918, possibly due to the obstruction of Joseph's tomb to the E.

In 1119 the bones of the patriarchs were reportedly found when access through the church floor at the peephole was made to a vestibule below to the two chambers to the W. These same chambers are reported to have been visited by an English officer in 1917 through an opening hidden since the Crusades. (See further L. H. Vincent et al., *Hebron, le Haram el Khalil, sepulture des Patriarchs* [1923]; R. de Vaux in *DBSup*, 5:618–627; D. M. Jacobson in *PEQ* 113 [1981]: 73–80; N. Miller in *BAR* 11/3 [May-June 1985]: 26–43.) H. G. STIGERS

Macnadebai mak-nad′uh-b*i* (מַכְנַדְבַי *H4827*). Also Machnadebai; TNIV Maknadebai. One of the descendants of Binnui who agreed to put away their foreign wives (Ezra 10:40; possibly called *Mamnitanaimos* in the parallel passage, 1 Esd. 9:34a, but this name may correspond to MATTANIAH in Ezra 10:37). Some believe that the MT is corrupt here and (on the basis of 1 Esd. 9:34b, *ek tōn huiōn Ezōra*) emend *maknadbay* to *mibběnê ʿazzûr*, "from the descendants of Azzur," thus beginning a new set of names.

Macron may′kron (Μάκρων). Ptolemy Macron, son of Dorymenes, was governor of COELESYRIA and PHOENICIA under ANTIOCHUS IV Epiphanes (2 Macc. 8:8). PTOLEMY VI Philometor had committed CYPRUS to him earlier, but Macron had deserted to Antiochus (10:13). He had influence with Antiochus, for he was able to win favor for a certain Menelaus who already had been convicted of wrongdoing (4:45–47). LYSIAS, left in charge of the country while Antiochus was away in Persia, chose Macron, along with two others, to lead in battle against the Jews under Judas MACCABEE. Their army totaled 47,000, besides help from two other sources, but still they were defeated by the aroused Jews (1 Macc. 3:38–60; 4:1–25). Some time later, Macron came to show favor toward the Jews, and for this, Antiochus V Eupator (son and successor of Antiochus Epiphanes) deposed him; in disgrace, Macron poisoned himself (2 Macc. 10:10–13). L. J. WOOD

Madaba. See MADEBA MAP; MEDEBA.

Madai may′di (מָדַי H4512, meaning unknown). Son (or descendant) of JAPHETH and grandson (or more distant descendant) of NOAH (Gen. 10:2; 1 Chr. 1:5). The Hebrew term is elsewhere rendered "Medes" (e.g., 2 Ki. 17:6) or "Media" (e.g., Esth. 1:3). See MEDIA.

Madeba map mad′uh-buh. An early Christian mosaic, set into the floor of a 6th-cent. Greek Orthodox church in the town of Madeba, Jordan (see MEDEBA). Almost 40 ft. long, it is the earliest known map of the Holy Land. See CARTOGRAPHY, BIBLICAL.

Madiabun muh-di′uh-buhn. KJV Apoc. form of EMADABUN (1 Esd. 5:58).

Madian may′dee-uhn. KJV Apoc. form of MIDIAN (Jdt. 2:26).

Madmannah mad-man′uh (מַדְמַנָּה H4526, "dung place" [possibly referring to the surrounding manured land; cf. MADMEN and MADMENAH]). One of the "southernmost towns of the tribe of Judah in the Negev toward the boundary of Edom" (Josh. 15:31; cf. v. 21). Elsewhere a man named SHAAPH, one of the sons of CALEB, is described as "the father of Madmannah" (1 Chr. 2:49), which probably means that he was the founder or civic leader of the town. Many scholars believe that Madmannah is the same as BETH MARCABOTH, a city taken from JUDAH's allotment and transferred to the tribe of SIMEON (Josh. 19:5, cf. v. 9; 1 Chr. 4:31; however, J. Simons, *The Geographical and Topographical Texts of the Old Testament* [1959], §317.29–30, argued that it was the same as MECONAH). The town is identified by some with modern Khirbet Umm ed-Deimneh, and by others with nearby Khirbet Tatrit, both about 9 mi. NE of BEERSHEBA.   L. J. WOOD

Madmen mad′muhn (מַדְמֵן H4522, "dung place" [cf. MADMANNAH and MADMENAH]). A town in MOAB against which JEREMIAH prophesied (Jer. 48:2). It is often identified with modern Khirbet Dimneh, some 10 mi. E of the DEAD SEA and 7.5 mi. N of KIR HARESETH. It is possible that either as a result of scribal error or for literary reasons (altering the spelling to mock the Moabites), an original *dimôn* was changed to *madmēn*. See DIMON.

Madmenah mad-mee′nuh (מַדְמֵנָה H4524, "dung place" [cf. MADMANNAH and MADMEN]). An unidentified place, apparently near ANATHOTH, mentioned in Isaiah's description of the Assyrian advance upon Jerusalem (Isa. 10:31).

madness. Ancient people were universally in awe of mental illness and attributed it to some activity of a DEMON. In the OT insanity was regarded as the punishment of God upon those who disobeyed his laws (Deut. 28:28). SAUL was perhaps the most notable figure in the OT to reveal such affliction, and the statement was made, "Now the Spirit of the LORD had departed from Saul, and an evil spirit from the LORD tormented him" (1 Sam. 16:14). When DAVID fled from Saul, he found it expedient to act the part of a madman in the presence of ACHISH because he feared him (21:12–15).

The NT also reflected the conviction of the ancient world that demons and devils were active agents behind all mental and emotional abnormality. When a man was deranged, he was described as being possessed; and there were many exorcists who practiced among the Jews, representing themselves as having power over the demons. Jesus' experience in the country of the GERASENES was typical (Mk. 5:1–20). The madman lived among the tombs, being described as having an unclean spirit. This violent creature could not be restrained. After Jesus' ministry to him, he was described as "dressed and in his right mind" (v. 16).

The belief that the human MIND was subject to the control of spirits is evidenced in many ancient cemeteries where skulls have been found that were trepanned. A hole had been bored in the skull in many instances, and from subsequent bone growth and the smallness of the hole (too small to be of any surgical value), it is evident that the operation had been performed to let the evil spirit out. It is known that the disk of bone removed by such a surgical procedure often was worn as an amulet around the patient's neck to ward off the return of the spirit. In one cemetery, out of 120 skulls six had been trepanned, which would show the intensity of the belief of the ancient world in the control of spirits over human minds. It was thought that there were seven and one half million such demons, one or more for every human malady. See DISEASE; LUNATIC. H. L. DRUMWRIGHT, JR.

Madon may′don (מָדוֹן *H4507*, "[place of] contention"). A royal city of the Canaanites in GALILEE whose king, JOBAB, joined JABIN king of HAZOR in his unsuccessful alliance against Israel (Josh. 11:1 [LXX *Marrōn*]; 12:19). The proposal that Madon should be identified with modern Khirbet Madin (c. 10 mi. ENE of NAZARETH and a short distance from Qarn Ḥaṭṭin) has little in its favor other than name similarity. Because the SEPTUAGINT uses *Marrōn* also where the MT has *mērôm* (11:5, 7), many scholars suspect textual corruption and identify Madon with MEROM (prob. some 20 mi. farther N), near which the battle took place. (Cf. Y. Aharoni, *The Land of the Bible: A Historical Geography*, rev. ed. [1979], 117–18.) See also SHIMRON (PLACE).

Maelus may′uh-luhs. KJV Apoc. variant of MIJAMIN (1 Esd. 9:26).

Maerus may′uh-ruhs. See AMRAM #2.

Magadan mag′uh-dan (Μαγαδάν *G3400*). A locality on the W shore of the Sea of Galilee to which Jesus came after feeding the 4,000. The name appears only in Matt. 15:39 (KJV, "Magdala," following the Majority text), while the parallel passage reads DALMANUTHA (Mk. 8:10). Magadan and Dalmanutha may have been contiguous; and possibly Magadan was identical with, or at least included in, MAGDALA, the home of MARY Magdalene. L. J. WOOD

Magbish mag′bish (מַגְבִּישׁ *H4455*, possibly from a root meaning "to pile up" or "to be massive"). Either the ancestor of some Israelites who returned from EXILE or, more likely, a town in JUDAH resettled by them (Ezra 2:30; the name is omitted in the parallel list, Neh. 7:33, whereas 1 Esd. 5:21 has "Niphish" [KJV, "Nephis"]). If it is a town, its location is unknown; proposals include Khirbet el-Makhbiyeh (c. 3 mi. SW of ADULLAM) and Khirbet Qanan Mugheimis (a bit farther S).

Magdala, Magdalene mag′duh-luh, -leen (Μαγδαλά *G3401* [not in NIV], prob. from Heb. מִגְדָּל *H4463*, "tower"; gentilic Μαγδαληνή *G3402*). Apparently the home of MARY Magdalene, who is mentioned a number of times in the Gospels (Matt. 27:56 et al.). The name Magdala itself does not

Small stone structures from ancient Magdala. (View to the NE.)

occur in any textually secure passage, although it is found in a few MSS at Mk. 8:10 (where the original reading is no doubt DALMANUTHA); it also occurs in many MSS, followed by the KJV, at Matt. 15:39 (where the earliest texts, as well as most modern versions, read MAGADAN). Magdala is sometimes linked with *migdāl nûnayyāʾ*, "Fish Tower," a place mentioned in the TALMUD as being one *mil*, or less than a mile, from TIBERIAS (*b. Pesaḥim* 46a). It is also thought to be the same as *Taricheas* (Tarichea or Tarich[a]eae), "Fish-Salting," an important town mentioned several times by JOSEPHUS (*War* 1.8.8 §180 et al.) and usually identified with modern Majdal, 3 mi. NW of Tiberias (for a discussion of the conflicting evidence, see G. A. Smith, *Historical Geography of the Holy Land*, 25th ed. [1931], 292–93). Majdal (also Mejdel) stands at a strategic road junction, and so perhaps justifies the name—a tower or fortification, some strong point, perhaps, on a vital crossroad. (See further *ABD*, 4:463–64.)

E. M. BLAIKLOCK

Magdiel mag′dee-uhl (מַגְדִּיאֵל *H4462*, "gift of God"). Descendant of ESAU, listed among the clan chiefs of EDOM (Gen. 36:43; 1 Chr. 1:54). His name may have been preserved in an ancient locality (see Euseb. *Onom.* 124.22–23).

Maged may′gid. KJV Apoc. alternate form of MAKED (1 Macc. 5:36).

Magi may′jī (pl. form of Latin *magus*, from Gk. μάγος *G3407*, in turn a borrowing of Old Pers. *maguš*; cf. Heb. רַב *H4454*, "official"). The Magi first appear in history by being identified as a tribe of the emerging Median nation in the 7th cent. B.C. (see MEDIA). Within this tribe there was a strong tradition that favored the exercise of sacerdotal and occult powers within the frame of their religious system, on the part of those who were capable of such activity. Thus the Magi became a hereditary priesthood, often possessing great political power, in the Median, Babylonian, Persian, and Parthian empires. In Hellenistic and Roman times the word was corrupted into a common noun meaning "magician" or "sorcerer" (cf. Acts 13:6, 8). The term *Magi* is used by the NIV and some other modern versions in the Matthean nativity story, where the KJV and NRSV render the Greek word as "wise men" (Matt. 2:1, 7, 16).

I. Religion. The original religious system of the Magi, possibly of SCYTHIAN origin, seems to have been based on philosophical concepts they shared with some segments of the Hellenic world, in particular an emphasis on the primacy of the elements: fire, water, earth, and air. Fire seems to have become the principal element of their worship, which was centered about an altar on which burned a perpetual flame believed to have been kindled from heaven. Blood sacrifices of domestic animals, including horses, were offered on a separate altar lit from the fire altar. Little of the victim was burned, and the remainder was consumed by the worshiper and the priests. The meaningful element of the sacrifice was considered to be the life of the victim rather than its flesh.

The Magian priesthood dressed in white robes and wore tall, somewhat conical hats made of felt that had long side flaps covering their cheeks as far as the chin. They carried small bundles of divining rods known as *barsoms* with which they officiated at sacrifices; these rods also were utilized in divining and soothsaying by arranging them in various patterns on the ground while chanting their incantations.

They admitted of no personal gods and permitted no images. Temples, as far as is known, were of no monumental distinction and were apparently little more than shelters for the sacred fire. The priests believed in the destruction of certain unclean forms of life—reptiles and insects—and were equally concerned with maintaining the sanctity of the previously mentioned physical elements. In this latter activity the disposition of the bodies of the dead became a major problem that was solved in either of two different ways: the bodies could be exposed to birds of prey, or they could be interred, if first completely sealed in a covering of wax.

The absence of any compelling theology was remedied by the introduction of ZOROASTRIANISM in the 6th cent. B.C., and its establishment as the state religion of PERSIA by DARIUS I (the Great). The Magi, anxious to maintain their religious and political favor, acceded to the royal decree, but did so without negating their original elemental philosophy or greatly altering their rituals.

At its best, the syncretistic Magian religion of Achaemenid days (i.e., during the height of the Persian empire) had much in common with the religion of the Jews. Each had its monotheistic concept of one beneficent creator, author of all good, who in turn was opposed by a malevolent evil spirit. Each had its hereditary priesthood, which became the essential mediator between God and man by virtue of a blood sacrifice. Each depended on the wisdom of the priesthood in DIVINATION (the URIM AND THUMMIM of the Levite was used in a way similar to that of the barsoms of the Magi), and to each was attributed considerable prophetic insight and authority. Their mutually held concepts of CLEAN and unclean forms of life and vegetation, and their positive attitude toward the four elements in material life as well as in religious symbolism are worthy of note.

II. History. The early Magian system was decreed to be the state religion of Media by Cyaxares, king of the Medes, late in the 6th cent. B.C., after some Magi who were considered to be expert in the interpretation of DREAMS had been attached to the Median court. It was in this dual capacity, whereby civil and political counsel was invested with religious authority, that the Magi became powerful figures in the empire.

NERGAL-SHAREZER, called the *rab-māg* in the service of NEBUCHADNEZZAR of BABYLON, is mentioned by name as one of the principal officials of the court (Jer. 39:3, 13). Such prominence is not surprising when it is remembered that this was a coalition government of Babylonians and Medes. Median, and consequently Magian, ambition was to be reckoned with again in the early Persian empire.

CYRUS the Persian had wrested the government from the old Median line of Cyaxares and Astyages and had established the supremacy of Persia over Media. At the same time he acknowledged the role of the Magi as the supreme priestly caste of the empire. While they waited their time, the Magian opportunity to reassert Median supremacy came during the reign of CAMBYSES and Bardiya (Smerdis), sons of Cyrus. During the palace intrigue that culminated in the murder of Bardiya (and the suicide of Cambyses), the Magi were in sufficiently high position to implement a conspiracy of their own. One of their own number, Gaumata (Pseudo-Smerdis) by name, actually usurped the throne. Such usurpation was severely punished by Darius the Great, who destroyed the immediate conspirators as well as the ambitious Gaumata himself. However severely these political aspirations were rebuked, the Magi were not deprived of their priestly status, nor were they removed from their office of being diviners and advisers to the King. XERXES, the son of Darius, is mentioned as having consulted the Magi when formulating his plans for the invasion of Greece.

With the PARTHIAN revolt against the SELEUCIDS in the mid-3rd cent. B.C., the Magi again appeared, being incorporated into the constitutional government of the empire. As the Medes (and the Magi) had been accorded considerable deference when absorbed into the Babylonian and Persian empires, so the Persians (and the Magi) were conferred much privilege by their less sophisticated Parthian overlords. Magian Zoroastrianism was reinstated as the state religion.

A constitutional council, known as the Megistanes, was instituted whose duty was to assist in the election (and, if need be, the deposition) of the monarch, and to serve as his advisers in governing the nation. The Magian hierarchy was accorded the senior position in this council. The upper house was composed of the hereditary priesthood of the Magi, while the lower house was composed of appointees who were collectively known as the *Sophi* (wise men).

Artist's conception of the Magi who came to visit Jesus. Their presence fueled the fear of King Herod.

Apparently the Parthians, though showing considerable respect for the Persians and the Magi, were never enthusiastic converts to Zoroastrianism. By the 3rd cent. A.D. they had largely reverted to their original idolatry and ancestor worship, coupled with much of the popular religious syncretism of the day. The Magi, in turn, lost much of their influence except in Persia proper, where they still were accorded their traditional veneration. Some of their vassal kings may have themselves been Magi.

In their traditional way the Persians and the Magi waited and plotted. They overthrew the Parthian rule and reimposed the rule of native (Sassanian) Persian monarchs. The Magi again were granted the highest religious and governmental powers. Zoroastrianism was reinstated as the state religion, and this situation prevailed until the empire fell to Islam in the 7th cent. A.D. In ensuing years, Zoroastrian refugees, doubtless with Magi among them, migrated to India, where their descendants are still to be found among the Parsees. (See further E. M. Yamauchi, *Persia and the Bible* [1990], ch. 13.)

III. OT references.
As noted previously, the untranslated title of Nergal-Sharezer, the chief of the Magi at the court of Nebuchadnezzar, is mentioned in Jer. 39:3, 13. Magi of lesser rank serving at the same court as advisers and interpreters of dreams are, in all probability, mentioned in the accounts given in Dan. 2:10, 27; 4:7, 9; 5:11. In these references the term *māg* is not used. Instead we find an Aramaic term, *ḥarṭōm H10282*, usually translated "magician." As noted previously in the definitions, the concept of magician in the form of a common noun was developed as a corruption of the older proper noun of Magus or Magian. In spite of older usage of the Hebrew term, it is not unlikely that in this context the officials referred to are Magians rather than magicians. It must be remembered that the Babylonian court of that day was of combined Babylonian and Median influence, and in naming the soothsayers for each group the Babylonians are simply referred to as such. However, the author, who was obviously pro-Median in his sympathies, would scarcely have omitted mention of their senior Median counterparts.

It is to be noted that JEREMIAH, writing objectively from outside the court milieu, uses the appropriately untranslated term *Rabmag* when referring to the chief Magian. DANIEL, on the other hand, writing from within, chose to make a distinction by translating the Median proper noun into an Aramaic common noun. The king, as a reward for services rendered, apparently appointed Daniel to the office of Master of the Magians (i.e., the Rabmag). As pro-Median as Daniel may have been, he was nevertheless fiercely proud of his Jewish identity and chose to describe the Magian office to which he had been appointed by official decree (rather than by hereditary right) with an appropriate Jewish term. Had he done otherwise, he would tacitly have identified himself as a Mede of Magian ancestry. This could also have had serious repercussions in the ranks of the Magi themselves, who doubtless would have resented the appropriation of their hereditary name by an appointee from outside their ranks. In his account Daniel evidently attempted to make it quite clear that he recognized the distinction. It is noteworthy that when Daniel did become the intended victim of a plot fomented by jealousy (Dan. 6), it was at the hands of regional governors (satraps) rather than the Magian dominated hierarchy of the court.

IV. NT references.
In identifying the Magi in Matthew's account of the birth of Christ (Matt. 2:1, 7, 16), it is necessary to call attention to some significant historical background. Since the days of the prophet Daniel in the 6th cent. B.C., the fortunes of Persia and the Jewish nation had been closely intertwined. There is a strong probability that a Jewish-Median conspiracy had accomplished the fall of Babylon and gained for Cyrus the Persian undisputed supremacy of the ancient world. Persian gratitude was magnanimous. With the exception of the interlude during the reign of Cambyses, the consistent Persian policy toward the reemerging Jewish nation was overwhelmingly supportive.

Both nations had in their turn fallen under Seleucid domination in the wake of Alexander's conquests. Subsequently both had regained their independence—the Jews under Maccabean leadership, and Persians as the dominantly ruling group within the Parthian empire. It was at this time that the Magi, in their dual priestly and governmental office, composed the upper house of the council of the Megistanes whose duties included the absolute choice and election of the king of the realm. It was, therefore, a group of Persian-Parthian king makers who entered Jerusalem in the latter days of the reign of HEROD.

Herod's reaction was understandably one of fear when one considers the background of Roman-Parthian rivalry that prevailed during his lifetime. POMPEY, first Roman conqueror of Jerusalem in 63 B.C., had attacked the Armenian outpost of Parthia. In 55 B.C. Crassus led Roman legions in sacking Jerusalem and in a subsequent attack on Parthia proper. The Romans were decisively defeated at the battle of Carrhae with the loss of 30,000 troops, including their commander. In retribution, moreover, the Parthians counterattacked with a token invasion of Armenia, Syria, and Palestine. Nominal Roman rule was reestablished under Antipater, the father of Herod, who in his turn retreated before another Parthian invasion in 40 B.C. Mark Antony reestablished Roman sovereignty three years later, and like Crassus before him also embarked on a similarly ill-fated Parthian expedition. His disastrous retreat was followed by another wave of invading Parthians that swept all Roman opposition completely out of Palestine (including Herod himself, who fled to Alexandria and then to Rome). With Parthian collaboration, Jewish sovereignty was restored and Jerusalem was fortified with a Jewish garrison.

Herod had by this time secured from AUGUSTUS Caesar the title of king of the Jews. However, it was not for three years, including a five months' siege by Roman troops, that the king was able to occupy his own capital city. Herod had thus gained the throne of a rebellious buffer state that was situated between two mighty contending empires. At any time his own subjects might again be instrumental as a fifth column in bringing the Parthians to their aid.

At the time of the birth of Christ (prob. c. 4 B.C.), Herod was certainly close to his last illness. Augustus was also aged; and Rome, since the retirement of TIBERIUS, was without any experienced military commander. Pro-Parthian Armenia was fomenting revolt against Rome (a revolt that was successfully accomplished within two years). The time was ripe for another Parthian invasion of the buffer provinces, except for the fact that Parthia itself was racked by internal dissension. Phraates IV, the unpopular and aging king, had once been deposed, and it was not improbable that the Persian Magi were already involved in the political maneuvering requisite to choosing his successor.

It is possible that the Magi might have taken advantage of the king's lack of popularity to further their own interests with the establishment of a new dynasty, which could have been implemented only if a sufficiently strong contender could be found. At this point in time it was entirely possible that the messianic prophecies of the OT, culminating in the writings of Daniel, one of their own chief Magians, was of profound motivating significance. The promise of divinely imposed world dominion at the hands of a Jewish monarch was more than acceptable to them. Their own Persian and Medo-Persian history was studded with Jewish nobles, ministers, and counselors; and in the great Achaemenid days some of the kings themselves were apparently partly of Jewish blood.

In Jerusalem the sudden appearance of the Magi, probably traveling in force with all imaginable oriental pomp, and accompanied by adequate cavalry escort to insure their safe penetration of Roman territory, certainly alarmed Herod and the populace of Jerusalem, as is recorded by Matthew. It would seem as if these Magi were attempting to perpetrate a border incident that could bring swift reprisal from Parthian armies. Their request of Herod regarding him who "has been born king of the Jews" (Matt. 2:2) was a calculated insult to him who had contrived and bribed his way into that office. (Because of the three gifts mentioned in the biblical narrative, early Christians deduced that the visitors were three kings [cf. Ps. 68:29]; subsequent legends attributed to them the names of Gaspar, Melchior, and Balthasar.)

In the providence of God, the messianic prophecy of the kingdom was not then fulfilled; the Magi, being "warned in a dream" (a type of communication most acceptable to them), "returned to their own country" (Matt. 2:12) with empty hands. Within two years Phraataces, the parricide son of Phraates IV, was duly installed by the Magi as the new ruler of Parthia. (It should be noted, however, that most scholars view these Magi more generally as Mesopotamian astrologers or "wise men" with some knowledge of Hebrew traditions, and not necessarily as officials involved in Parthian politics. See ASTROLOGY.)

In the book of Acts, reference is made to a certain Simon who "had practiced sorcery" (Acts 8:8; the verb is *mageuō* G3405) and who used to amaze people with his MAGIC (v. 11, *mageia* G3404). See SIMON MAGUS. In addition, a man in CYPRUS named BAR-JESUS or ELYMAS is specifically called a *magos* (13:6, 8). In the western Hellenistic and Roman world, this term was used in general description of any juggler, magician, or astrologer; such implication may have been intended here. Some of these magi, however, may have been of Median or Persian descent and may have laid claim to some degree of mystical authority. It also is possible that some of them were Jews descended from appointed Magi of Daniel's day. Elymas could have been such a person. It is doubtful that the PROCONSUL, described as "an intelligent man" (v. 7), would have employed a total impostor. D. W. JAYNE

magic and sorcery. In its widest sense, magic is "the science of the occult," that is, the attempt to influence persons and events by recourse to superhuman powers. The word derives from the MAGI, a priestly caste in MEDIA whose functions have largely been associated with "magic" ever since. They claimed to mediate between gods and human beings, conducted sacrifices, supervised the disposal of the dead, interpreted dreams, omens, and celestial phenomena, and foretold the future. The term *magic* came into the Greek world (*mageia* G3404) from Persia and thence into the Roman (Lat. *magus*); gradually it acquired a pejorative sense, which the word *sorcery* has possessed to an even greater degree. (The large number of Hebrew terms for the various magical practices are noticed below.)

Traditionally, a distinction has been made between "black" and "white" magic. The former is a means of invoking evil upon one's enemies, with the aid of evil spirits, curses, and spells: it presupposes malevolent powers who are willing to be manipulated. "White" magic postulates benevolent powers through whom good ends can be achieved and evil spells undone. In a well-known definition,

J. G. Frazer wrote, "Magic is a kind of savage logic, an elementary species of reasoning, based on similarity, contiguity and contrast" (*The Golden Bough: A Study in Magic and Religion*, 3rd ed. [1917–20], 1:61). This often is compared with the systematic procedures of science.

I. Magic in the ANE. The Hebrews are portrayed in the OT within a world in which magic had been practiced for many centuries. The Persian Magi were, in fact, relative late-comers.

In Sumero-Akkadian folklore, gods as well as people needed the services of magic (see SUMER; ASSYRIA AND BABYLONIA). Thus, in the Babylonian "Creation Epic," Ea-Enki was the "Lord of Incantation," and his son MARDUK defeated the female deity TIAMAT because his spells were more potent than hers. Handbooks have survived which list a wide range of errors that bring evil on humans, with appropriate rites of purification (See E. Reiner, *Surpu: A Collection of Sumerian and Akkadian Incantations* [1958]). A manual "Maglu" similarly prescribes ritual for warding off the effects of black magic. The cult of DIVINATION was highly developed: tablets survive describing many omens observable in the heavens, in human events, in the flight of birds, and in the organs of animals. Hence the reference in Nahum to Assyria as "the mistress of sorceries" (Nah. 3:4).

In EGYPT, magic had been equally prominent. It was under the patronage of the leading gods Thoth and Isis (see OSIRIS), and papyri provide abundant detail. Magic was learned in temple schools ("the House of Life"), and priesthoods devoted especially to the art. The lore was extended to the dead, who needed their own magical equipment to preserve them in the next life. The manual "Instructions for King Merikare" (c. 2200 B.C.) shows how closely magic was linked with medicine in Egypt. The interpretation of dreams was a highly sophisticated art, and Egyptian magicians were also renowned as wonder-workers, the evidence of their extraordinary feats (going back to the 3rd millennium) being recorded in the "Tales of the Early Magicians" (see A. H. Gardiner in *ERE*, 8:262–69, for six categories of Egyptian magic).

As in Assyria and Babylonia, so in early Canaanite epics both divine and human magic

Babylonian astrological tablet in cuneiform script, giving omens regarding lunar eclipses.

were practiced. In the "Epic of Baal," for example, the victory of Mot over BAAL is reversed by the goddess ANATH through magical means: and in the "Legend of Keret," king of UGARIT, the god EL carries out elaborate rituals to restore the king to health. Other epics mention the practice of augury and astrology by women. Evidence of Canaanite magic is relatively plentiful in the OT, and will be summarized below.

II. The OT and magic. In the light of this universal phenomenon, its impact on the life of Israel was inevitable. The OT is clear-cut in its message: as in other areas of their spiritual development, the uniqueness and power of the revelation of Yahweh were here apparent.

The reality of occult powers is acknowledged, but magic and sorcery are consistently forbidden. A notable passage is Deut. 18:10–14: "Let no one be found among you who … practices divination or sorcery, interprets omens, engages in witchcraft, or casts spells, or who is a medium or spiritist or who consults the dead. Anyone who does these things is detestable to the LORD. … The nations you will dispossess listen to those who practice sorcery or divination. But as for you, the LORD your God has not permitted you to do so." This passage incorporates practically all the OT types of magic, except those practiced by Egyptians and Babylonians (cf. Lev. 19:26; note also the general terms used in Exod. 22:18; 2 Ki. 9:22; et al.).

Faithful Hebrews were trained from childhood to regard as dangerous superstition much of the religious practice around them; it could not coexist with the pure WORSHIP of Yahweh. Those who became mediums or wizards were to be put to death (Lev. 20:27). The same uncompromising attitude is found in the prophets (e.g., against necromancy, Isa. 8:19; against DIVINATION, Jer. 27:9–10; against witches, Ezek. 13:18). A long list of the finery of women includes several articles used as charms (Isa. 3:18–23).

Genesis contains some instructive examples: the power of the spoken word and the irrevocability of blessings and cursings (Gen. 27:18–40); the use of mandrakes as a love-philter (30:14–18); Jacob's peeled rods in connection with animal breeding (30:37–41). Of special note are the TERAPHIM, figurines that were virtually household gods and used for divination (Laban, 31:30–35; cf. Micah, Jdg. 17:1–6; and Michal, 1 Sam. 19:13–16, where a larger image is suggested). Teraphim are condemned everywhere as a piece of Canaanite IDOLATRY. In the narrative of JOSEPH (Gen. 41) the special gift of dream interpretation given to him is to be noted, surpassing that of Pharaoh's magicians.

In Exodus, the encounter between Moses and Aaron and Pharaoh's magicians and sorcerers (Exod. 7–8) accords with evidence of wonder-working magic in Egypt. The signs of the serpent rod and the plagues, however, were given not merely to outdo Egyptian wizardry; they demonstrated the OMNIPOTENCE of the God of Israel—"I will bring judgment on all the gods of Egypt. I am the LORD" (12:12). In Numbers the story of BALAAM is instructive (Num. 22–24). The Moabite BALAK hires Balaam, who was a diviner (22:7) accustomed to "look for omens" (24:1 NRSV; NIV, "resort to sorcery"). He was to injure the Israelites by his curses; however, he was granted prophetic powers and blessed them instead, under the guidance of God (23:20, "he has blessed, and I cannot change it").

Many other OT practices come under the general heading of divination. Casting lots to discover the divine will was very frequent: Lev. 16:8; Num. 26:55; Josh. 7:14; Jdg. 20:9; 1 Sam. 10:20 are illustrations of a wide variety of circumstances. Particular methods are sometimes mentioned (e.g., belomancy, the shaking of arrows in a quiver, Ezek. 21:21), but most significant are the URIM AND THUMMIM, kept on the breastplate of the high priest in the EPHOD. They were probably a pair of sacred objects for casting lots, and fell into disuse by the prophetic period (Num. 27:21; Deut. 33:8, 10; 1 Sam. 28:6). Dreams and visions often are recorded as means of divine communication; they could either be sent unsolicited or sought after (cf. Deut. 13:1–15, "one who foretells by dreams"). Necromancy, or the consultation of the dead, is strongly condemned. Best-known is the medium of ENDOR consulted by SAUL (1 Sam. 28:7–19) in spite of his show of obedience in the banishing of mediums and wizards. Linked with necromancers are the FAMILIAR SPIRITS said to possess them.

In 2 Kings are found the best examples of royal attitudes to magic. JEZEBEL is condemned as a sorceress (2 Ki. 9:22), and MANASSEH's apostasy included BAAL worship, human sacrifice, soothsaying and augury, and dealing with mediums and wizards (21:3–6). By contrast, JOSIAH his grandson "got rid of the mediums and spiritists, the household gods, the idols and all the other detestable things seen in Judah and Jerusalem" (23:24).

Finally, the book of Daniel reflects the opposition of Jewish faith and Babylonian magic. The young captives surpassed in skill all Nebuchadnezzar's magicians, particularly in the interpretation of dreams and visions (Dan. 1:17–20; at 2:2 sorcerers and Chaldeans [NIV, "astrologers"] are added). Daniel as chief of the whole class is given the name BELTESHAZZAR (4:8; the name itself may be an invocation, "[may] Bel protect his life") but declares the superiority of the "God in heaven" as revealer of mysteries (2:28). It is notable that astrology was not practiced in early Jewish history, and is indeed belittled by Isaiah as part of Babylonian error: "Let your astrologers come forward, those stargazers who make predictions month by month, let them save you from what is coming upon you" (Isa. 47:13; cf. Jer. 10:2).

III. The NT and magic. The OT repugnance for magic was inherited by the Christian church in a world that was as thoroughly imbued with such practices as ever. The Epistles therefore echo OT denunciations: PAUL lists witchcraft among the "acts of the sinful nature" that bar people from God's kingdom (Gal. 5:20), and in the somber description of 2 Tim. 3:1–9, the godless are compared to the magicians JANNES AND JAMBRES who withstood MOSES (in v. 13, "impostors" may also describe sorcerers). In Revelation sorcery appears among those practices that merit judgment (Rev. 9:21; 18:23; 21:8; 22:15).

The Gospels mention certain Pharisaical customs that appear to have bordered on the superstitious—the wearing of PHYLACTERIES (Matt. 23:5) and repetitious prayers (6:7), but the former practice did have a higher significance for the pious (cf. Exod. 13:9, 16; Deut. 6:8). What is emphasized is the supremacy of Christ over the spirit world (Mk. 3:22, 23; Lk. 10:17–20). Sorcerers appearing in Acts are SIMON MAGUS and ELYMAS (cf. also Acts 16:16–18 and 19:14–17).

(See further T. W. Davies, *Magic, Divination and Demonology among the Hebrews and Their Neighbours* [1898]; G. Coutenau, *La magie chez les Assyriens et les Babyloniens* [1947]; M. F. Unger, *Biblical Demonology* [1952], 107–64; A. L. Oppenheim, *The Interpretation of Dreams in the Ancient Near East* [1956]; G. Luck, *Arcana Mundi: Magic and the Occult in the Greek and Roman Worlds: A Collection of Ancient Texts* [1985]; A. Jeffers, *Magic and Divination in Ancient Palestine and Syria* [1996]; F. Graf, *Magic in the Ancient World* [1997]; H.-J. Klauck, *Magic and Paganism in Early Christianity: The World of the Acts of the Apostles* [2000]; A. Mastrocinque, *From Jewish Magic to Gnosticism* [2005]; M. Labahn and L. J. Lietaert Peerbolte, eds., *A Kind of Magic: Understanding Magic in the New Testament and Its Religious Environment* [2007]; *ABD*, 4:464–71.)

B. F. HARRIS

magistrate. This English term, referring to an official entrusted with the administration of laws, is used to render the Aramaic terms *šĕpaṭ H10735*, "judge" (Ezra 7:25), and *tiptāy H10767*, "[police] officer" (Dan. 3:2–3). It also renders Greek *archōn G807*, "ruler," in one passage (Lk. 12:58) and especially *stratēgos G5130* (Acts 16:20–38). The latter was a common term in classical Greek literature for a high military officer and is usually translated "general" or "captain" (e.g., Acts 4:1; see CAPTAIN OF THE TEMPLE). In Hellenistic times, however, it was used as the equivalent for a large number of technical terms denoting Roman provincial officials.

In the context in Acts 16, *stratēgos* is used as the title of the Roman official of the colony of PHILIPPI and probably stands for the Latin *duumviri* (also *duoviri*), referring to the magistrates of the colony. This Greek term, however, was used also of the much higher Roman official, the PRAETOR. In the provincial colonial seats of the Roman empire there often were several of these officials whose power included paramilitary and police affairs as well as administrative and political functions. There were usually three to five such officials who levied taxes, commanded the Roman garrison, tried criminal cases, and kept civil order. Frequently the names of the magistrates appear on the local coinage of the Asiatic provinces. The precise differentiation between the Greek *archōn* and *stratēgos*, as they appear together in Acts 16:19b–20a, is that most likely the second word is a subclass of the first and refers to the Roman judges of the court, a usage that would accord with extrabiblical sources.

(See further D. Magie, *Roman Rule in Asia Minor* [1950]; M. Rostovtzeff, *The Social and Economic History of the Hellenistic World*, vol. 1 [1953]; A. H. M. Jones; *The Later Roman Empire: A Social, Economic and Administrative Survey*, 2 vols. [1964]; C. K. Barrett, *A Critical and Exegetical Commentary on the Acts of the Apostles*, ICC, 2 vols. [1994–98], 2:789.) See also CITY AUTHORITIES.

W. WHITE, JR.

Magnificat mag-nif'uh-kat. The title given to Mary's psalm of praise (Lk. 1:46–55), drawn from the first line of the Latin VULGATE, "Magnificat anima mea Dominum" ("My soul magnifies the Lord"). The passage is similar to the prayer or song of HANNAH (1 Sam. 2:1–10) and contains allusions to it. It is one of the three psalms in Hebrew poetic style in this narrative of the birth of our Lord. The text makes a most fitting ending to the expectations of the OT covenant which looked forward to the consummation of the promised blessing to ABRAHAM through the MESSIAH. The utter humility of the means by which God is pleased to bring this grace to his people is glorified as a singular instance of his sovereign power. The psalm also initiates the age of the messianic fulfillment. (Cf. S. Farris, *The Hymns of Luke's Infancy Narratives: Their Origin, Meaning and Significance* [1985], 108–26.)

The text in its medieval guise as "The Canticle of the Blessed Virgin" has had wide acceptance in all branches of Christendom. Since the codification of the worship service by Pope Gregory the Great (590–604) and the official acceptance of the rule of St. Benedict (480–543), the Magnificat has been sung in the Roman Catholic Church at Vespers (evening prayers). In the Reformation and evangelical churches it has often been paraphrased and sung as a congregational hymn. Some of the greatest works of Christian art have been produced around the Magnificat themes. Artists, poets, and musicians have celebrated its theme of joy at the salvation now graciously offered mankind through the gift of his Messiah. See also BENEDICTUS.

W. WHITE, JR.

Magog may'gog (מָגוֹג *H4470*, possibly from Akk. *māt gugi*, "land of Gyges" [cf. *NIDOTTE*, 4:686]; Μαγώγ *G3408*). In Ezek. 38:2 and 39:6, Magog is described as a land in which (or people over which) GOG acts as chief ruler. The name appears first in the Table of NATIONS for one of the sons (or descendants) of JAPHETH (Gen. 10:2; 1 Chr. 1:5), who are eponymous ancestors of national groups. JOSEPHUS (*Ant.* 1.6.1) identifies Magog with the SCYTHIANS of the far N. Resemblance of names has caused some to identify Gog with Gyges (Gugu) of LYDIA, and so Magog with Lydia. Ezekiel's association of Gog and Magog with peoples at the extremities of the then known world (Ezek. 38:2) suggests that they might be interpreted in a representative and eschatological sense rather than identified particularly (Rev. 20:8 uses the terms this way). Ezekiel sees them as representing northern nations (Ezek. 38:16), who in the "latter days" come against Israel in battle and experience God's wrath in defeat. (For bibliography, see Gog.) L. J. Wood

Magor-Missabib may´gor-mis´uh-bib (מָגוֹר מִסָּבִיב *H4474*, "terror all around"). The name that Jeremiah gave to Pashhur, the priest who beat him and put him in stocks (Jer. 20:3–4). In describing the coming of the Babylonian army, Jeremiah used the same phrase (meaning "terror on every side") on a number of occasions to press home the terrible truth. In one of his sermons, for example, he says, "Do not go out to the fields or walk on the roads, for the enemy has a sword, and there is terror on every side" (6:25). This expression is in fact the theme of Jeremiah's preaching (cf. 20:10; 46:5; 49:29; cf. Lam. 2:22). The phrase appears also in Ps. 31:13. E. B. Smick

Magpiash mag´pee-ash (מַגְפִּיעָשׁ *H4488*, derivation uncertain). An Israelite leader who sealed the covenant of Nehemiah (Neh. 10:20). Some think that the personal name Magpiash may have been derived from Magbish (Ezra 2:30) if the latter was the village settled by the family (cf. H. G. M. Williamson, *Ezra-Nehemiah*, WBC 16 [1985], 324).

Magus may´guhs. See Magi; Simon Magus.

Mahalab may´huh-lab (from a conjectured place name, מְחֶלֶב). A border town within the tribal territory of Asher, near Aczib and the Mediterranean Sea (Josh. 19:29 NRSV). The MT, however, reads *meḥebel*, "from the territory" (cf. KJV, "from the coast to Achzib"; NIV, "in the region of Aczib"). The conjecture *meḥalleb* is based on Codex Vaticanus of the Septuagint (*kai apo Leb*, "and from Leb," which suggests that the MT reading may have resulted when a scribe transposed the consonants *l* and *b*) and on the fact that a town named Maḥalliba is mentioned in an inscription by Sennacherib (*ANET*, 287). If this proposal is correct, Mahalab probably should be identified with Ahlab (Jdg. 1:31), which in turn may be the same as modern Khirbet el-Maḥalib, some 4 mi. NE of Tyre (see Y. Aharoni, *The Land of the Bible: A Historical Geography*, rev. ed. [1979], 235; *ABD*, 4:471–72).

Mahalah may´huh-lah. KJV alternate form of Mahlah (only 1 Chr. 7:18).

Mahalaleel muh-hay´luh-lee´uhl. KJV form of Mahalalel.

Mahalalel may-hal´uh-luhl (מַהֲלַלְאֵל *H4546*, "praise of God" or "God shines"; see Noth, *IPN*, 205, and J. D. Fowler, *Theophoric Personal Names in Ancient Hebrew* [1988], 126–27; Μαλελεήλ *G3435*). KJV Mahalaleel; KJV NT, Maleleel. **(1)** Son of Kenan and grandson of Enosh in the line of Seth (Gen. 5:12–17; 1 Chr. 1:2); included in the genealogy of Jesus Christ (Lk. 3:37; NRSV, "Mahalaleel"). Some relate this name with Mehujael, grandson of Enoch in the line of Cain (Gen. 4:18).

(2) Descendant of Perez and ancestor of Athaiah, a postexilic Judahite who settled in Jerusalem (Neh. 11:4).

mahalath, mahalath leannoth may´huh-lath, may´huh-lath-lee-an´oth (מָחֲלַת *H4714* and לְעַנּוֹת *H4361*). Musical terms of uncertain meaning found, respectively, in the titles of Pss. 53 and 88. The first term is often interpreted as referring to a musical instrument, such as the flute; and if the word *leʿannôt* is analyzed as the piel infinitive of the verb ʿ*ānâ H6702*, the phrase could mean "[upon] a flute for singing." According to a different analysis, the phrase indicates a tune perhaps entitled "The Suffering of Affliction" (so NIV mg.). See also music VI.

Mahalath (person) may´huh-lath (מָחֲלַת *H4715*). **(1)** Daughter of Ishmael (Gen. 28:9). Esau married her because his previous marriages to Canaanite women had displeased Isaac (v. 8). Mahalath may be the same as the Basemath mentioned in 36:3, but some scholars argue that the two passages preserve conflicting traditions.

(2) Daughter of Jerimoth and Abihail, granddaughter of David, and wife of Rehoboam (2 Chr. 11:18). She gave birth to three sons (v. 19).

Mahali may´huh-li. KJV alternate form of Mahli (only Exod. 6:19).

Mahanaim may´huh-nay´im (מַחֲנַיִם *H4724*, "double camp"; variously transliterated and translated in the LXX). A city in N TRANSJORDAN, important especially in the time of the monarchy. Mahanaim, according to Gen. 32:2, was named by JACOB after he left LABAN, his father-in-law, and met God's angels on the way back to Canaan. The Hebrew word *maḥănayim* H4724 looks like a dual noun, although it may not have originally been so (cf. v. 10, where the expression "two groups" or "two camps" renders Heb. *šĕnê maḥănôt*, plural of *maḥăneh* H4722).

Mahanaim was on the border between the tribes of GAD (Josh. 13:26) and MANASSEH (v. 30). It also was one of the Transjordanian CITIES OF REFUGE (21:38) and one of the LEVITICAL CITIES (1 Chr. 6:80). Later the town became the seat of AHINADAB, one of SOLOMON's district governors (1 Ki. 4:14). There may be a mention of Mahanaim in Cant. 6:13 (NIV, "the dance of Mahanaim"; NRSV, "a dance before two armies").

It is in connection with DAVID, however, that Mahanaim is most frequently mentioned. After SAUL died, a civil war was beginning in Israel. ABNER, Saul's general, wanted ISH-BOSHETH, a son of Saul, to be king (2 Sam. 2:8). From their base of operations at Mahanaim, Abner and Ish-Bosheth went to GIBEON, where a war by representation was fought around the great pool. After an indecisive outcome and some foul play by Abner, JOAB (David's general) chased Abner back to Mahanaim (2:29). Presumably it was there that RECAB and BAANAH murdered Ish-Bosheth (4:5–7).

In the war between David and ABSALOM, David made his headquarters temporarily at Mahanaim (2 Sam. 17:24–27 and 19:32). At this time the battle of the forest of Ephraim occurred, where Absalom was caught by his hair in a tree and subsequently slain by Joab. Apparently David was at Mahanaim when news of Absalom's death came and he wept, crying out, "O my son Absalom! My son, my son Absalom! If only I had died instead of you—O Absalom, my son, my son!" (18:33).

The Bible gives little information to identify the site, apart from the deduction in Gen. 32:22 that it was N of the JABBOK River. Various proposals have been made, including modern Khirbet Maḥneh and Tell er-Reheil, but the most likely site is western Telul edh-Dhahab, that is, Tell edh-Dhahab el-Gharbi, on the N bank of the Jabbok and some 7 mi. E of the Jordan (just NW of T. edh-Dhahab esh-Sherqiyeh, which is identified with PENUEL). (See E. Kraeling, *Bible Atlas* [1956], 204–6; Y. Aharoni, *The Land of the Bible: A Historical Geography*, rev. ed. [1979], 34, 314; *ABD*, 4:472–73.)

R. L. ALDEN

Mahanaim.

Mahaneh Dan may′hun-uh-dan′ (מַחֲנֵה־דָן H4723, "camp of Dan"). Also Mahaneh-dan. A place between ZORAH and ESHTAOL (i.e., 14–15 mi. W of Jerusalem) where "the Spirit of the LORD began to stir" SAMSON (Jdg. 13:25; KJV, "the camp of Dan"). The area received its name because 600 Danites camped there before attacking the Ephraimites (18:12). The latter passage describes the place as being "west" (lit., "behind") KIRIATH JEARIM, which seems inconsistent with 13:25. Some scholars suspect textual corruption in 13:25; others speculate that two different places had the same name; still others interpret "west of Kiriath Jearim" loosely. In any case, the precise location of Mahaneh Dan is unknown. (See the discussion in *ABD*, 4:473–74.)

Maharai may′huh-ri (מַהְרַי H4560, possibly "impetuous [*i.e.*, for Yahweh]"). A warrior from the town of NETOPHAH who became one of DAVID's Thirty (2 Sam. 23:28; 1 Chr. 11:30). Elsewhere he is identified as a descendant of ZERAH and as an army commander in charge of the division for the tenth month (1 Chr. 27:13).

Mahath may′hath (מַחַת H4744, perhaps "harsh" [cf. *HALOT*, 2:572, "terror" or "hard"]). **(1)** Son of AMASAI, descendant of KOHATH, and ancestor of the musician HEMAN (1 Chr. 6:35).

(2) Son of Amasai (prob. different from #1 above); this Mahath was a Kohathite Levite who assisted in the reforms of King HEZEKIAH (2 Chr. 29:12) and is probably also to be identified with the Mahath who was one of the supervisors of the temple offerings (31:13).

Mahavite may′huh-vit (מַחֲוִים H4687, derivation unknown). Epithet applied to ELIEL, one of DAVID's mighty warriors (1 Chr. 11:46); it serves to distinguish him from the Eliel in the following verse. The term, which occurs only here, appears to be a gentilic, but its reference is unknown. Many scholars emend the text to *hammaḥnî*, "the Mahanite" (alternatively *hammaḥănaymî* [*BHS*]; see MAHANAIM), or to *hammeʿônî*, "the Maonite" (see BAAL MEON and MAON), but these forms too are unattested.

Mahazioth muh-hay′zee-oth (מַחֲזִיאוֹת H4692, prob. from a root meaning "vision"). Son of HEMAN, the king's seer (1 Chr. 25:4). The fourteen sons of Heman, along with the sons of ASAPH and JEDUTHUN, were set apart "for the ministry of prophesying, accompanied by harps, lyres and cymbals" (v. 1). The assignment of duty was done by lot, and the twenty-third lot fell to Mahazioth, his sons, and his relatives (25:30).

Maher-Shalal-Hash-Baz may′huhr-shal′al-hash′baz (מַהֵר שָׁלָל חָשׁ בַּז H4561, prob. "hurry [to seize] plunder, hasten [to seize] spoil"). A symbolic name given to one of the sons of Isaiah to signify the speedy destruction of REZIN and PEKAH by the king of ASSYRIA (Isa. 8:1, 3). In this phrase, the roughly synonymous verbs *māhar* H4554 and *ḥûš* H2590 ("to hurry, hasten, be quick") are usually understood as imperatives, but it is possible to take them as participles ("the one who hurries … who hastens"; for these and other interpretations see H. Wildberger, *Isaiah 1–12: A Commentary* [1991], 332). On the significance of the passage as a whole, see ISAIAH, BOOK OF, VI.A.

Mahlah mah′luh (מַחְלָה H4702, possibly "weak"). **(1)** The eldest of the five daughters of ZELOPHEHAD of the tribe of MANASSEH (Num. 26:33). Since Zelophehad had no sons, his daughters requested ELEAZAR the priest that they be allowed to inherit their father's property, and the request was granted on condition that they marry into their father's tribe (27:1–11; 36:11; Josh. 17:3–4). This decision was very important and became a precedent.

(2) Son (or daughter) of HAMMOLEKETH, who was apparently the sister of GILEAD; included in the genealogy of MANASSEH (1 Chr. 7:18). It is unclear why the name of Mahlah's father is not given. See ABIEZER #1.

Mahli mah′li (מַחְלִי H4706, derivation uncertain; gentilic מַחְלִי H4707, "Mahlite"). **(1)** Son of MERARI and grandson of LEVI (Exod. 6:19; Num. 3:19; 1 Chr. 6:19, 29; 23:21; 24:26, 28; Ezra 8:18). His offspring, the Mahlites (Num. 3:33; 26:58), along with their brothers, the Mushites (see MUSHI), were responsible for carrying the frames of the TABERNACLE with its bars, pillars, bases, and all the accessories attached to these things (Num. 4:31–33). (For the significance of the inclusion of the name Mahli in the various lists, see *ABD*, 4:476.)

(2) Son of Mushi, grandson of Merari, and thus nephew of #1 above (1 Chr. 6:47; 23:23; 24:30). He is listed as an ancestor of ETHAN, one of the Levites that DAVID put in charge of the temple music (cf. 6:31, 44).   E. B. SMICK

Mahlon mah′lon (מַחְלוֹן H4705, possibly "sickly"). Son of ELIMELECH and NAOMI; first husband of RUTH (Ruth 1:2, 5; 4:10). He and his brother KILION, as well as their father, died in MOAB. (On the possible significance of his name, see *ABD*, 4:476–77.)

Mahol may′hol (מָחוֹל H4689, "[round or circle] dance"). A term used to designate the father of four sages who are compared with SOLOMON for wisdom (1 Ki. 4:31). Elsewhere, however, their father is said to be ZERAH (1 Chr. 2:6). Since *māḥôl* means "dance," and two of these sages, HEMAN and ETHAN, are ascribed authorship of one psalm each (Heman, Ps. 88; Ethan, Ps. 89), it is likely that "sons of Mahol" is an appellative expression indicating membership in a musical guild. These men apparently were dancers whose activity played an important role in religious exercises (cf. Ps. 149:3; 150:4).   L. J. WOOD

Mahseiah mah-see'yah (מַחְסֵיָה H4729, "Yahweh is [my] refuge"). KJV Maaseiah. Father of NERIAH and grandfather of BARUCH and SERAIAH; the latter two men assisted the prophet JEREMIAH (Jer. 32:12; 51:59; Bar 1:1 [KJV, "Maasias"]).

Maianeas may-an'ee-uhs. KJV Apoc. form of MAIANNAS (1 Esd. 9:48).

Maiannas may-an'uhs (Μαιννας). A Levite who helped EZRA instruct the people in the law (1 Esd. 9:48 NRSV; KJV, "Maianeas"). The RSV calls him "Maaseiah" on the basis of the parallel (Neh. 8:7).

maid, maiden. The English term *maid* (already found in Middle English) is a short form of *maiden*, both of which mean "unmarried young woman," usually applied to virgins. The shorter form, however, often has the more specific meaning of "female servant," its most common modern use. The KJV uses *maid* (in both the general and the specific meaning) over forty times to render several Hebrew and Greek words. Modern versions as a rule apply this term only to servants and thus employ it less frequently (similar terms used include *maidservant* and *slave-girl*; cf. also *handmaid* and *handmaiden* in the KJV).

The fuller term, *maiden*, occurs twenty-six times in the KJV as the translation of such words as Hebrew *naʿărâ* H5855, "girl," and *bĕtûlâ* H1435, "virgin" (cf. both terms in Gen. 24:16). The NRSV, by contrast, uses it only seven times in Song of Solomon to render several Hebrew words (Cant. 1:3 et al.) and once elsewhere to render *bĕtûlâ* (Amos 5:2). In the NIV, *maiden* occurs sixteen times, usually as the translation of *bĕtûlâ* (e.g., Ps. 78:63), but

Young Palestinian maiden.

a few times it renders *ʿalmâ* H6625 (Gen. 24:43; Ps. 68:25; Prov. 30:19; Cant. 1:3).

The latter Hebrew term, *ʿalmâ*, has proven controversial because of its use in Isa. 7:14. Following the SEPTUAGINT (which uses *parthenos* G4221 here [also in Gen. 24:43]), the KJV translates "virgin," as does the NIV. Many scholars, however, argue that it should be rendered "young woman" (cf. NRSV). It is true that Hebrew *ʿalmâ* does not fully correspond to English *virgin*, but it may well indicate a marriageable young woman, who in that culture would have been presumed to be a virgin. In this respect, English *maiden* may be a close equivalent of this Hebrew word. See discussion under VIRGIN.

mail. See ARMOR, ARMS IV.B.

Makaz may'kaz (מָקַץ H5242, derivation uncertain). One of four towns within the second of the twelve districts that supplied provisions for SOLOMON and the royal household (1 Ki. 4:9); governed by BEN-DEKER, this district was apparently in the N SHEPHELAH, but the precise location of Makaz is unknown.

Makbannai mak'banai. TNIV form of MACBANNAI.

Makbenah mak-bee'nuh. TNIV form of MACBENAH.

Maked may'kid (Μακεδ). A strong city in GILEAD from which Judas MACCABEE rescued Jews who were being threatened by their pagan neighbors (1 Macc. 5:26, 36; KJV, "Maged"). Maked must have been E of the Sea of Galilee, apparently between BOSOR and CHASPHO (CASPIN), and some have identified it with modern Tell el-Jemid.

Makheloth mak-hee′loth (מַקְהֵלֹת *H5221*, "places of assembly"). A stopping place of the Israelites, between Haradah and Tahath, during their forty years of wilderness wanderings (Num. 33:25–26). The location is unknown.

Maki may′ki (מָכִי *H4809*, possibly short form of MAKIR). Also Machi. Father of Geuel, who was one of the twelve spies sent out to reconnoiter the Promised Land; he represented the Gadites (Num. 13:15). See GAD, TRIBE OF.

Makir may′kihr (מָכִיר *H4810*, prob. "bought"; gentilic מָכִירִי *H4811*, "Makirite"). **(1)** Son of MANASSEH (through an Aramean concubine, 1 Chr. 7:14) and grandson of JOSEPH. Makir may have married a woman "from among the Huppites and Shuppites" (so NIV, v. 15, but NRSV has, "Machir took a wife for Huppim and for Shuppim" [similarly NJPS]). In any case, his wife MAACAH bore him two sons (Pesher and Sheresh, v. 16); his son GILEAD may have been borne by another wife. We read that the children of Makir "were placed at birth on Joseph's knees," apparently an adoption ritual (Gen. 50:23). A daughter of Makir married the Judahite HEZRON and bore him SEGUB, who became the father of JAIR (1 Chr. 2:21–23).

Makir's descendants, the Makirites, are at the head of the list of Israelites who came out of Egypt (Num. 26:29). Makir's son Gilead gave his name (or was named for?) the area in TRANSJORDAN that his family inhabited (Num. 27:1; 32:39–40). In addition, BASHAN was allotted to the Makirites because they were "great soldiers" (Josh. 17:1; NRSV, "because he [Makir] was a warrior"). Makir's great-grandson, ZELOPHEHAD, had no sons and thus his daughters claimed the inheritance (Num. 27 and 31). Further light is thrown on the exact situation regarding the Makirites and their inheritance in Josh. 13:29–31, which records the method by which the tribe of Manasseh was divided: half the family of Makir moved into Transjordan, while the other half went with that portion of the tribe of Manasseh that settled in Palestine proper.

(2) Son of Ammiel and probably a descendant of #1 above. This Makir is identified as a citizen of LO-DEBAR in whose house MEPHIBOSHETH the son of JONATHAN stayed (2 Sam. 9:4–5). He subsequently helped DAVID when the latter went into exile (17:27–29). (For other scholarly reconstructions of the family of Makir, see *ABD*, 4:458–60, s.v. "Machir.")   E. B. SMICK

Makkedah muh-kee′duh (מַקֵּדָה *H5218*, possibly related to a root that in Aram. means "to be clean"). A Canaanite royal city taken by JOSHUA in his battle with the southern confederacy of five kings (Josh. 10:10–29). These kings, having been defeated at GIBEON, fled first eastward toward BETH HORON and then southward toward AZEKAH and Makkedah. The kings sought refuge, under pressure of Joshua's attack and God's rain of "stones," in a cave near Makkedah. There Joshua killed them in the presence of his men. Then Joshua took the city of Makkedah nearby, killing the king (10:28).

The town was in the SHEPHELAH and was later incorporated into the tribe of JUDAH, in the same district as LACHISH (Josh. 15:41). Its precise location is uncertain, however. Though mentioned with Azekah in the story, it need not have been near it, for the two cities are recorded in different lists in Josh. 15 (Azekah in vv. 33–36; Makkedah in vv. 37–41). Proposed sites include Khirbet el-Kheishum (between Azekah and BETH SHEMESH), Khirbet el-Kum (el-Qom, c. 6 mi. ESE of Lachish; cf. A. F. Rainey in *BASOR* 251 [Summer 1983]: 1–22; *NEAEHL*, 4:1233–35), and Tell Bornaṭ (c. 5 mi. NE of Lachish; favored by Z. Kallai, *Historical Geography of the Bible* [1986], 381, but see LIBNAH). Joshua's route in the conquest of the individual cities (Makkedah, Libnah, Lachish, Eglon, Hebron, Debir; see Josh. 10:28–39) may favor the first site mentioned. (See E. G. Kraeling, *Bible Atlas* [1956], 138; D. Baly, *Geographical Companion to the Bible* [1963], 175.)   L. J. WOOD

Maknadebai mak-nad′uh-bi. TNIV form of MACNADEBAI.

Maktesh mak′tesh. KJV transliteration of *maktēš H4847* in Zeph. 1:11, "Howl, ye inhabitants of Maktesh, for all the merchant people are cut down;

all they that bear silver are cut off." This Hebrew term occurs in only two other places: (1) Jdg. 15:19, where it is usually translated "hollow" in an attempt to fit the context (a place God opened so that water might come out of it); and (2) Prov. 27:22, where it evidently refers to an object used for grinding, thus "mortar." In Zeph. 1:11, it is unclear whether the term is used as a proper name (thus KJV and NJPS ["Machtesh"]; cf. also NRSV, "the Mortar") or as a common noun (cf. NIV, "the market district," since its inhabitants are merchants). In favor of taking it as a name is the mention of the FISH GATE and the Mishneh (see SECOND DISTRICT) in the previous verse. In either case, it must have been a well-known place in JERUSALEM, and it may have been so named because it was a hollow place in shape like a mortar (or perhaps it was a section where grinders of grain worked).

Malachi, Book of mal´uh-k*i* (מַלְאָכִי H4858, "my messenger"). The last book among the twelve Minor Prophets.

    I. Background
   II. Unity
  III. Authorship
  IV. Date
   V. Place of origin
  VI. Destination and occasion
 VII. Purpose
VIII. Canonicity
  IX. Text
   X. Content
  XI. Theology

I. Background. With the prophecies of HAGGAI and ZECHARIAH, the book of Malachi is of great importance in supplying information about the period between the return from the EXILE and the work of EZRA and NEHEMIAH because of the scarcity of sources, both secular and religious, that relate to this period of Hebrew history. While the prophecy is not dated in the opening verses in the manner of some others, it is possible from an examination of the internal evidence to locate the activities of the author within the period of Persian suzerainty over Palestine (see PERSIA). This latter is evident from the mention in Mal. 1:8 of the *peḥâ* H7068, referring to the office of civil governor in the Persian empire, to which further references are found in Neh. 5:14 and Hag. 1:1.

Obviously then, the historical background of the prophecy is that of the postexilic period in Judea. Yet the book portrays religious and social conditions that point to a time subsequent to that of Haggai and Zechariah. The fact that sacrifices were spoken of as being offered in the TEMPLE (Mal. 1:7–10; 3:8) implies not merely that the structure had at last been completed, but also that it had been standing for a considerable time. In addition, the rituals of the cultus had become well established once more (1:10; 3:1, 10), and this would point to a date later than 515 B.C. That the prophet may actually have uttered his complaints against the priests and people in the following century seems highly probable from the fact that a certain degree of laxity had crept into cultic worship. The priests were not observing the prescriptions relating to the nature and quality of the animals offered for sacrifice (1:8), and had gone one step further in their attitude of indifference to the sacrificial requirements of the Lord by offering polluted bread before him. Indeed, the prophet rebuked them sharply because their general attitude showed that they had become tired of the ritual procedures connected with worship (1:13).

Clearly the initial enthusiasm that must have attended the opening of the second temple had diminished, and with a lessening of zeal came a more casual attitude toward the prescriptions of cultic worship. This degree of neglect also extended to the payment of requisite TITHES (Mal. 3:8–10), which were important for the support of both the

Because Israel was using blemished and diseased animals in worship, Malachi called for the people's repentance.

moral and religious leadership which would have enabled the returned community to avoid much of the current distress. Far from honoring their God in sacrifice and cultic worship, the priests had been indifferent and even contemptuous in discharging their duties. They condoned the offering to God of animals that would have been pronounced unworthy of the service of the civil Persian governor (1:7–8), and their behavior contrasted unfavorably with that of pagan Gentile cults, where the sacrificial tariffs were much more stringent. Whereas the primitive Levitical priesthood had displayed spiritual integrity, its postexilic successors were in danger of falling into the evil ways of their preexilic forebears. The true priest must be essentially an evangelist, and a "messenger of the Lord Almighty" (2:6–7).

In the third oracle (Mal. 2:10–16), the prophet concerned himself with the problem of mixed marriages and divorces among the laity. The whole issue had arisen because the Israelites had disregarded the implications of the covenant for community life. As a result, they had felt free to leave the fellowship of the THEOCRACY in their search for suitable marital partners, and had imported alien women with strange beliefs which by nature were contrary to those of the law. Such actions could hardly go unpunished (2:12), nor could the people make legitimate protest when they received the due reward of their sins, since they had only themselves to blame (2:13). See DIVORCE; MARRIAGE.

The coming of God in an act of judgment was the subject of the fourth prophetic oracle (Mal. 2:17–3:5). God had grown tired of the common complaint that, by not interfering, he was actually condoning the prosperity of the wicked (2:17), and leading his people to think that there was no justice in human life. Because he was morally and ethically consistent, he would come suddenly upon the nation in judgment, being heralded in this intent by means of his messenger. His purpose would be to separate the faithful from the impious, and the temple priesthood would be the first to feel the weight of his judgments. Once the cultus had been purified and the worship of the temple had been made more acceptable (3:3–4), the lay members of the theocracy would themselves be judged. All who had been guilty of religious or moral crimes would be condemned (3:5), and the covenantal ideals of purity and holiness would be reestablished. In consequence of these procedures, the offerings of Judah and Jerusalem would once again be pleasing to God.

The fifth oracle (Mal. 3:6–12) laid the responsibility for the current displeasure of God squarely upon the shoulders of the people. Because God was ethically consistent, his attitude toward them could not change without a good reason. A change had in fact occurred because the people had disobeyed his laws, and his former feelings of graciousness could be restored only when the repatriates submitted in obedience to his demands. The offense about which Malachi complained in particular was their failure to pay the tithe laid down by the law (Num. 18:21). Only when this deficiency had been remedied would their land again bear fruit, and freed from the devastation of locust plagues, it would be the envy of their neighbors for productivity (Mal. 3:8–12).

The final oracle of the prophecy (Mal. 3:13—4:3) dealt again with the problem of evil in human life (cf. 2:17). The devout members of the theocracy, perplexed by the fact that arrogant and willful unbelievers in the nation seemed to be more prosperous than their fellowmen and under no apparent reproach from God, had begun to question the value of a life lived in obedience to the commands of God (3:13–15). In reply the prophet indicated that a "scroll of remembrance" was kept before the Lord, in which the deeds of the righteous were recorded (3:16). When the day of judgment upon sinners came into being, the Lord would remember the virtuous life of the faithful and would make it clear that his service brings its own rich blessings. The promised judgment would see sinners destroyed for their iniquity, while the pious believers would enjoy felicity and blessedness (4:1–3).

The concluding verses of the prophecy (Mal. 4:4–6) have been regarded by some scholars as an editorial addition to the entire book, on the ground that they either summarized the message of Malachi or that they indicated that the people should henceforth look to the traditional Mosaic law now that the voice of prophecy had ceased.

XI. Theology. The spirituality of Malachi is akin to that of the 8th and 7th cent. B.C. prophets. He recognized the absolute lordship of the God of Israel and the implications of the COVENANT relationship for the growth and well-being of the postexilic theocratic community. Personal commitment to the claims of God could alone insure blessing and peace, either for the individual or the nation. Although Malachi, with EZEKIEL, laid considerable stress on the importance of proper ritual procedures in worship as a means of preserving a pure and holy nation, he never condoned ritual as a substitute for an obedient heart. The true service of God included moral rectitude, justice and mercy, as well as correct ritual forms.

Important also in the theology of Malachi was his insistence that the first step toward a proper spiritual relationship with God was true REPENTANCE. Because of the many objections that had been raised against the traditional approach to the problem of evil, Malachi found it necessary to emphasize that iniquity would not go unpunished for ever, but that a just and holy God would exact proper recompense in due time. His ESCHATOLOGY drew heavily upon prophets such as AMOS and ZEPHANIAH in outlining the conditions that would obtain in the DAY OF THE LORD. It would be a time of calamity rather than blessing, in which deluded sinners would be punished for their violations of covenant love.

Malachi, however, also introduced an original theme, namely the concept of a book of remembrance in which the deeds of the righteous were recorded. This development was important in subsequent thought relating to the idea of a life beyond death. Another significant emphasis was upon the personage of a forerunner who would herald the coming of the Lord at the time of judgment. Since this individual was identified with a revived ELIJAH (cf. 2 Ki. 2:11), it would seem probable that the forerunner was thought of as a prophetic figure who would offer a disobedient people one last chance of repentance before the onset of divine judgment. Christ regarded the prophecy as foreshadowing the work of JOHN THE BAPTIST (Mk. 9:11–13), and the early church saw in the relationship between the work of the Baptist and that of Jesus the fulfillment of this prophecy (Mk. 1:2; Lk. 1:17).

(Significant commentaries include H. G. Mitchell et al., *A Critical and Exegetical Commentary on Haggai, Zechariah, Malachi and Jonah*, ICC [1912]; W. C. Kaiser, Jr., *Malachi: God's Unchaging Love* [1984]; R. L. Smith, *Micah-Malachi*, WBC 32 [1984]; P. A. Verhoef, *The Books of Haggai and Malachi*, NICOT [1987]; E. H. Merrill, *Haggai, Zechariah, Malachi: An Exegetical Commentary* [1994]; D. L. Petersen, *Zechariah 9–14 and Malachi: A Commentary*, OTL [1995]; D. Stuart in *The Minor Prophets: An Exegetical and Expository Commentary*, ed. T. McComiskey [1992–98], 3:1245–1396; A. E. Hill, *Malachi*, AB 25D [1998]; R. A. Taylor and R. Clendenen, *Haggai, Malachi*, NAC 21A [2004].

(See also W. O. E. Oesterley and T. H. Robinson, *An Introduction to the Books of the Old Testament* [1934], 427–33; R. K. Harrison, *Introduction to the Old Testament* [1968], 958–62; B. Glazier-McDonald, *Malachi: The Divine Messenger* [1987]; J. M. O'Brien, *Priest and Levite in Malachi* [1990]; G. P. Hugenberger, *Marriage as a Covenant: A Study of Biblical Law and Ethics Governing Marriage, Developed from the Perspective of Malachi* [1994]; and the bibliography compiled by W. E. Mills, *Zechariah and Malachi* [2002].)   R. K. HARRISON

malachite. This English term, referring to a bright green-colored valuable ore of COPPER (hydrated basic carbonate of copper), is used by the NEB to translate a Hebrew word of uncertain meaning that occurs only once (Esth. 1:6; the NIV and other versions render it PORPHYRY). Malachite often shows different shades of color following a concentrically banded arrangement and is sometimes used for ornamental purposes. It is found together with other ores of copper in the zone of weathering or oxidation of copper deposits, with large amounts of ornamental quality in the Ural Mountains near Nizhni-Taglish. Malachite was an important ore in the copper deposits worked in ARABAH (cf. Deut. 8:9), and some may have been of ornamental quality.   D. R. BOWES

Malachy mal′uh-kee. KJV Apoc. form of MALACHI (2 Esd. 1:40).

Malcam mal′kam (מַלְכָּם *H4903*, from a root meaning "king"). KJV Malcham; TNIV Malkam. **(1)** Son of SHAHARAIM and descendant of BENJAMIN;

a family head (1 Chr. 8:9). Malcam was one of seven children that were born to Shaharaim in MOAB by his wife HODESH after he had divorced Hushim and Baara (v. 8).

(2) The same Hebrew form occurs in the last phrase of Zeph. 1:5, which speaks of idolaters who swear both by Yahweh and by *malkām*. The SEPTUAGINT (Old Greek) translators, reading the same vowels as does the MT, analyzed the form as the noun *melek H4889* plus the third masculine plural pronominal suffix, and rendered it *tou basileōs autōn*, "their king." These and other early translators, however, were working with an unvocalized Hebrew text (thus simply *mlkm*). The Lucianic recension of the Greek version, reading *milkōm* (*H4904*), transliterates the word as *Melchom* (similarly the Syriac Peshitta and the Latin Vulgate). Most modern versions take this second approach (as they do also in Jer. 49:1, 3; and cf. 2 Sam. 12:30 = 1 Chr. 20:2; Amos 1:15). Many believe that MILCOM is an alternate name for MOLEK. It is less clear whether *malkām* in these passages should be regarded as an alternate form of *milkōm* or, more likely, as an incorrect analysis preserved by the Masoretes.

Malcham mal'kam. KJV form of MALCAM.

Malchiah mal-ki'uh. See MALKIJAH.

Malchiel, Malchielite mal'kee-uhl, mal'kee-uh-lit. See MALKIEL.

Malchijah mal-ki'juh. See MALKIJAH.

Malchiram mal-ki'ruhm. See MALKIRAM.

Malchishua mal'ki-shoo'uh. See MALKI-SHUA.

Malchus mal'kuhs (Μάλχος *G3438*, prob. from an Arabic name meaning "king"). A servant of the high priest (CAIAPHAS); according to John, Simon PETER struck him with a sword and cut off his right ear when Jesus was arrested (Jn. 18:10). Although this incident is also recorded in the Synoptic Gospels (Matt. 26:51; Mk. 14:47; Lk. 22:50–51 [Luke adds the information that Jesus healed his ear]), John alone reports that his name was Malchus and that it was Peter who struck him. Because the name occurs in NABATEAN and Palmyrene inscriptions (cf. also Jos. *Ant.* 14.14.1 §370 et al.), some have thought that Malchus was an Arabian slave. John also reports that another servant of the high priest who was a relative of Malchus was also present during the arrest of Jesus and thus was able to identify Peter (Jn. 18:26). The Gospels do not state why Peter would have chosen to strike Malchus in particular, but it is likely that the latter, representing the high priest, played a significant role in the arrest.

Maleleel muh-lee'lee-uhl. KJV NT form of MAHALALEL.

Malkam mal'kam. TNIV form of MALCAM.

Malkiel mal'kee-uhl מַלְכִּיאֵל *H4896*, "God is [my] king" [cf. MALKIJAH]; gentilic מַלְכִּיאֵלִי *H4897*, "Malkielite"). Also Malchiel. Son of BERIAH, grandson of ASHER, and eponymous ancestor of the Malkielite clan (Gen. 46:17; Num. 26:45; 1 Chr. 7:31).

Malkijah mal-ki'juh (מַלְכִּיָּה *H4898* and מַלְכִּיָּהוּ *H4899* [only Jer. 38:6], "Yahweh is [my] king"; cf. MALKIEL and MELECH). Also Malchiah (nine times in KJV and three times in NRSV), Malchijah (six times in KJV, twelve times in NRSV, and twice in NRSV Apoc.), Melchiah (KJV only Jer. 21:1), Melchias (three times in KJV Apoc. and once in NRSV Apoc.). A rather common Hebrew theophoric name borne by men of exilic and postexilic times who seem to be mostly priests (or Levites) and royalty. The inconsistency in the English spelling between "Malchiah" and "Malchijah" has no textual basis (the NRSV has "Malchiah" only in Jeremiah); the NIV uses "Malkijah" throughout.

(1) Son of Ethni, descendant of LEVI, and ancestor of the musician ASAPH (1 Chr. 6:40).

(2) A priest who received the fifth lot of the twenty-four divisions in DAVID's time (1 Chr. 24:9).

(3) A man identified as "the king's son" (which prob. indicates that he was a royal official with police duties; see R. de Vaux, *Ancient Israel* [1961], 119–20); he was owner of the cistern into which JEREMIAH's enemies cast him while King ZEDEKIAH pretended to be powerless to stop them (Jer. 38:6). Some believe that this Malkijah is the same man identified elsewhere in Jeremiah as the father of Pashhur (21:1; 38:1). It is also possible that he is the same Malkijah listed as an ancestor of Adaiah, the head of a priestly family who resettled in Jerusalem after the exile (1 Chr. 9:12; a fuller genealogy is given in Neh. 11:12).

(4–6) In a list of Israelites who pledged themselves to put away their foreign wives, three are named Malkijah, two of whom were descendants of Parosh (Ezra 10:25, but NRSV emends the second to Hashabiah on the basis of Septuagint here and at 1 Esd. 9:26), and the third a descendant of Harim (Ezra 10:31; called a descendant of Annan in 1 Esd. 9:32). This third Malkijah may be the same as the son of Harim who helped repair the wall of Jerusalem (Neh. 3:11).

(7) Son of Recab and ruler of Beth Hakkerem; he was in charge of repairing the Dung Gate (Neh. 3:14).

(8) A goldsmith who "made repairs as far as the house of the temple servants and the merchants, opposite the Inspection Gate, and as far as the room above the corner" (Neh. 3:31).

(9) One of the prominent men (not identified as priests) who stood near Ezra when the law was read at the great assembly (Neh. 8:4; 1 Esd. 9:44). If this Malkijah was a priest, he may be the same as #10 or #11 below.

(10) A priest who sealed the covenant of Nehemiah (Neh. 10:3). He may be the same as #11 below.

(11) A priest or Levite listed among those who assisted Nehemiah in the dedication of the rebuilt walls of Jerusalem (Neh. 12:42).   E. B. Smick

Malkiram mal-ki′ruhm (מַלְכִּירָם H4901, "[my] king is exalted"). Son (or descendant) of King Jeconiah, that is, Jehoiachin (1 Chr. 3:18).

Malki-Shua mal′ki-shoo′uh (מַלְכִּי־שׁוּעַ H4902, "[my] king is salvation"). KJV Melchi-shua (in 1 Sam.) and Malchi-shua (in 1 Chr.); NRSV, Malchishua. The third son of King Saul (1 Sam. 14:49; 1 Chr. 8:33; 9:39). The Philistines killed him at the battle of Gilboa (1 Sam. 31:2; 1 Chr. 10:2).

Mallos mal′uhs. KJV Apoc. form of Mallus (2 Macc. 4:20).

Mallothi mal′uh-thi (מַלּוֹתִי H4871, from מָלַל H4910, "to speak"). Son of Heman, the king's seer (1 Chr. 25:4). The fourteen sons of Heman, along with the sons of Asaph and Jeduthun, were set apart "for the ministry of prophesying, accompanied by harps, lyres and cymbals" (v. 1). The assignment of duty was done by lot, and the nineteenth lot fell to Mallothi, his sons, and his relatives (25:30).

mallow. This term (which strictly speaking refers to various herb plants of the *Malvaceae* family) is used in the KJV and NRSV to render Hebrew *mallûaḥ* H4865, found only once (Job 30:4; in addition, the NRSV uses it in 6:6 and 24:24 as an emendation on the basis of the lxx). The Hebrew word is evidently related to *melaḥ* H4875, "salt" (cf. NIV, "salt herbs"; NJPS, "saltwort") and is usually thought to refer to the *Atriplex halimus*, which grows in salty regions, such as the shores of the Dead Sea. It is a loose-spreading, half-evergreen shrub, growing to a height of 8–9 ft., with light greenish-gray leaves. It belongs to the *Chenopodiaceae* family and rarely produces flowers. The leaves are edible, and were eaten by the poorer Israelites as a kind of salad. The plant is sometimes referred to as the sea orache or as the (Spanish) sea purslane. (See *FFB*, 136–37.)

W. E. Shewell-Cooper

Malluch mal′uhk (מַלּוּךְ H4866, variant מַלּוּכִי H4868 [Neh. 12:14, *Qere* מְלִיכוּ], from a root meaning "king"). TNIV Malluk. **(1)** Son of Hashabiah, descendant of Levi through Merari, and ancestor of the musician Ethan (1 Chr. 6:44).

(2) One of the descendants of Bani who agreed to put away their foreign wives (Ezra 10:29; called "Mamuchus" in 1 Esd. 9:30).

(3) One of the descendants of Harim who agreed to put away their foreign wives (Ezra 10:32).

(4) One of the priests who signed the covenant of Nehemiah (Neh. 10:4).

(5) One of the leaders of the people who signed the covenant of Nehemiah (Neh. 10:27). Possibly the same as #2 or #3 above.

(6) One of the priests (or priestly families) who returned from the exile with Zerubbabel (Neh. 12:2). He is probably the same person mentioned later, when a certain Jonathan is listed as the head of the family of Malluch (v. 14; KJV, "Melicu"; NRSV, "Malluchi"). (See *ABD*, 4:488.)

S. Barabas

Malluchi mal′uh-k*i*. See Malluch #6.

Malluk mal′uhk. TNIV form of Malluch.

Mallus mal′uhs (Μαλλός). KJV Mallos. An important coastal city in Cilicia whose inhabitants (*Mallōtai*), along with those of Tarsus, rebelled when Antiochus Epiphanes gave their cities to his concubine as a present (2 Macc. 4:20). According to Strabo (*Geogr.* 14.5.16), Mallus was on a height near the Pyramus River.

Malta mawl′tuh (Μελίτη G3514). A Mediterranean island lying between Sicily and Africa. The name occurs once in the NT as the place where Paul was shipwrecked on his journey to Rome (Acts 28:1; KJV, "Melita"). Some early writers, apparently confused by the reference to Adria earlier in the text (27:27), identified the island with Mljet (Meleda), which is much farther N, well into the Adriatic Sea, off the coast of Dalmatia. Also unpersuasive is the recent view that it should be identified with Kefallinia (Cephalonia, ancient Cephallenia), the largest of the Ionian Islands off the W coast of Greece (see discussion in F. F. Bruce *The Acts of the Apostles: The Greek Text with Introduction and Commentary*, 3rd ed. [1990], 530).

Paul and the other travelers stayed in Malta three months (Acts 28:11). Its inhabitants treated the survivors with "unusual kindness" (v. 1; cf. v. 10). Soon after reaching the island, Paul was bitten by a snake, but nothing happened to him, so the islanders thought he was a god (vv. 3 – 6). The chief official, Publius, welcomed Paul and the others in his home. Publius's father was sick and Paul healed him; as a result, "the rest of the sick on the island" came to the apostle, and they too were healed (vv. 7 – 9).

Located 90 mi. from Syracuse, the great commercial center of the W Mediterranean, Malta occupied a strategic position in the ancient world. Endowed with good harbors safe from the stormy waters of the sea, it offered a convenient haven for commercial traffic moving both E – W and N – S.

The island of Malta.

Some 18 mi. long and 8 mi. wide, it was barren and arid, with few natural resources other than building stone. The eastern half, however, was somewhat productive; olive oil, wool, and lapdogs are mentioned as commodities that were profitable.

Malta shows evidences of early habitation. There are remains of Neolithic culture antedating 2000 B.C., and also traces of a Bronze Age culture from about the 14th cent. Then follows a blank period lasting until about 1000 B.C., when the Phoenicians colonized the island, drawn by its favorable location for trade (see Phoenicia). The result was an outburst of commercial activity that made the island prosperous. A colony was even established in N Africa.

Next to control Malta were the Carthaginians, who ruled the Mediterranean from the 6th to the 3rd centuries. Their presence is attested by coins and inscriptions, although these are meager when compared to the Greek material found there. This suggests that ties to Carthage were not very strong, nor relations cordial. The Carthaginians were very harsh in their treatment of the people and levied oppressive taxes upon the island. During the 3rd cent. B.C., Carthage and Rome engaged in a series of wars for mastery of the W Mediterranean, and in the course of the struggle Malta passed into Roman hands (218 B.C.), though Carthaginian and Greek elements remained strong for a long time afterward.

The Romans granted Malta the status of a municipium, which allowed them to control their own domestic affairs. It seems, too, that the island acquired Roman CITIZENSHIP, although it is not clear just when this took place. Cicero and others speak of the beauty and elegance of the houses on Malta, and of the prosperity of the island, indicating a high degree of civilization and wealth. Under AUGUSTUS, the island was seemingly administered by an official who was known by the people of Malta as "chief" or "first man" of the island (Gk. *ho prōtos*, Acts 28:7). Tradition has it that Publius, who held this position when Paul was shipwrecked there, was the first Christian convert in Malta, and that from this time there developed a Christian community. Catacombs from the 4th and 5th centuries A.D. give evidence of Christian influence on the island. When Rome fell, approximately at the end of the 4th cent., the island became Byzantine in culture, and finally in the 9th cent. passed into the hands of the Arabs. (See further Pauly-Wissowa, *Real-Encyclopädie der classischen Altertumswissenschaft*, 15/1 [1931], 543–47; W. G. Berg, *Historical Dictionary of Malta* [1995]; C. Cassar, *A Concise History of Malta* [2000]; *ABD*, 4:489–90.)

R. C. STONE

Mamaias muh-may′uhs. KJV Apoc. variant of SHEMAIAH (1 Esd. 8:44).

Mamdai mam′di (Μαμδαι). One of the descendants of BANI who agreed to put away their foreign wives in the time of EZRA (1 Esd. 9:34; KJV, "Mabdai").

Mamitanemus (Μαμνιταναιμος, var. Μαμταναιμος). One of the descendants of BANI who agreed to put away their foreign wives (1 Esd. 9:34 NRSV [KJV, "Mamnitanaimus"; RSV emends to "Machnadebai"; see MACNADEBAI]; possibly corresponding to MATTANIAH in Ezra 10:37).

mammon mam′uhn. This term, derived from Greek *mamōnas* G3440 (via the Latin VULGATE) comes ultimately from Aramaic *māmôn*, "wealth" (emphatic state *māmônāʾ*), the etymology of which is disputed (see E. Nestle in *EncBib*, 3:2914–15). The equivalent Hebrew term appears in various postbiblical writings (e.g., 1QS VI, 2; *m. ʾAbot* 2:12). In Matt. 6:24 and Lk. 16:13, the term is personified, and the NIV translates, "You cannot serve both God and Money." In Lk. 16:9, Jesus speaks of "the mammon of unrighteousness" (equivalent to "the unrighteous mammon," v. 11), which the NIV renders as "worldly wealth" (more negative is the NRSV rendering, "dishonest wealth"). There has been much discussion of the implications of unrighteousness in connection with WEALTH, but the simplest explanation seems to be that material riches (whether money or gems or landed property) is a resource open to misuse and characteristically employed by wicked, unscrupulous men for wicked purposes. Yet it is possible for a true servant of God to use wealth for good and salutary purposes, and thus procure for himself treasure in heaven such as money cannot buy.

G. L. ARCHER

Mamnitanaimus. See MAMITANEMUS.

Mamre (person) mam′ree (מַמְרֵא *H4935*, derivation uncertain). An AMORITE, brother of ESHCOL and ANER, who apparently resided near HEBRON (Gen. 14:13, 24). All three were allies of ABRAHAM when LOT was rescued from KEDORLAOMER. The expression "the great trees of Mamre the Amorite" (v. 13; cf. 13:18) suggests that he owned the place that came to be known by his name. See MAMRE (PLACE). However, some scholars believe that there is confusion in the text and that the names of all three brothers refer to localities.

Mamre (place) mam′ree (מַמְרֵא *H4934*, derivation uncertain). After LOT separated from Abram (ABRAHAM), the latter "moved his tents and went to live near the great trees of Mamre at Hebron, where he built an altar to the LORD" (Gen. 13:18). Abraham was still living there when he entertained the three heavenly visitors (ch. 18). It was in Mamre that he prayed for the deliverance of SODOM and GOMORRAH. After SARAH died, he bought a burial plot from EPHRON the HITTITE. Thus Abraham came into possession of the field of MACHPELAH, which is E of Mamre, and there he buried his wife (23:17–20). The four other times Machpelah is mentioned are always in relation to Mamre (23:19; 25:9; 49:30; 50:13). (See the recent monograph by D. Jericke, *Abraham in Mamre* [2003].)

Through the centuries there have been several places vying for the site of Mamre and Abraham's oaks. The first problem in establishing its identity is the great antiquity of the place—nearly 4,000 years (and oaks do not live that long). Moreover,

Traditional tomb of Isaac in the Machpelah (Hebron).

the building and destruction of shrines by Jews, pagans, and Christians have focused undeserved attention on some places and perhaps obscured the true site. Khirbet Nimreh and ʿAin Nimreh (Ruin and Spring of Nimreh) have a name similar to Mamre. They are about 1.5 mi. NNW of Hebron. However, the most widely accepted site today is Ramat el-Khalil, "The high place of the friend (of God)," which is c. 2.5 mi. N of Hebron. An enclosure of huge proportions built by HEROD is there. It may have marked where the site was thought to be in NT times. Chalcolithic and Early Bronze remains found in the vicinity show at least that it is an ancient site.

If Machpelah is indeed under the mosque at Hebron, then Ramat el-Khalil does not lie *before* it (in the usual sense of the word in Hebrew, i.e., E of Hebron). On the other hand, if Hebron were generally approached from the N, then this Hebrew preposition would not be out of order in describing the relationship between the two places. (See A. E. Mader, *Mambrie: Die Ergebnisse der Ausgrabungen im heiligen Bezir Râmet et-Ḫalêl in Sudpalästina,*

2 vols. [1957]; *NEAEHL*, 3:939–42. For the view that Mamre corresponds to Hittite *miu-mar*, "friendship," which is semantically equivalent to Hebron, and that therefore Gen. 14:13 originally said, "Abram was dwelling at the Amorite sanctuary of Alliance," see Y. L. Arbeitman in *ABD*, 4:492–93.) See also MAMRE (PERSON).

R. L. ALDEN

Mamuchus muh-myoo´kuhs. KJV Apoc. form of MALLUCH (1 Esd. 9:30).

Mamukan mi-myoo´kuhn. TNIV form of MEMUCAN.

man. See ADAM; HUMAN NATURE; SOCIETY.

man, new. The words *eis hena kainon anthrōpon*, "into one new man," occur in Eph. 2:15 with reference to the unity that Jews and Gentiles enjoy in Christ. This article, however, deals with the phrase as it occurs in two other passages. In Eph. 4:24, *ho kainos anthrōpos* ("the new man") is contrasted with *ho palaios anthrōpos* ("the old man," v. 22). In Col. 3:10, instead of the adjective *kainos* G2785, PAUL uses the synonym *neos* G3742 (with *anthrōpos* G476 understood), also contrasted with *palaios* G4094 (v. 9). The NIV and the NRSV render both constructions as "the new self." The phrase, in general terms, refers to human beings as changed by the HOLY SPIRIT through faith in Jesus Christ. Some believe that *neos* points to the idea in respect to its historical context, while *kainos* in respect to its quality of perennial newness. The distinction is blurred, however, by the fact that in these two passages the one idea is qualified by the other.

"Newness" is a special predicate of the gospel order of things in Scripture (see NEW, NEWNESS), and thus "new man" is associated with the new covenant (Jer. 31:31; Heb. 8:8), in contrast with the first or old covenant, which was "obsolete," "aging," and about to "disappear" (Heb. 8:13). Other associated references are to the new creation (2 Cor. 5:17; Gal. 6:15) and the new birth (Jn. 3:3, 7; 1 Pet. 1:23; 2:2). Paul talks of newness of life and spirit (Rom. 6:4; 7:6) in contrast with "the old way of the written code" (7:6), "the old self" (Eph. 4:22; Col. 3:9), "the old yeast" (1 Cor. 5:7), "your former way of life" (Eph. 4:22; cf. 1 Pet. 1:14; 2 Pet. 1:9). The new self or new nature is part of the future renewal of all things in Christ (future in Matt. 19:28; Acts 3:21; Rev. 21:4; but it operates now, Jn. 3:18–21; 11:24–25; 1 Jn. 2:8).

I. Significance in NT usage. The term has, in the first place, reference to individual believers, for by becoming Christians (normally expressed in BAPTISM, Rom. 6:1–7) they enter on a life "in Christ" so radically new as to be based upon a prior death with him. "New" here is contrasted with the former way of life to which a person is born as a human being. It is spiritual, as opposed to carnal (Rom. 8:4–11); it is also contrasted with what is natural (1 Cor. 2:14–15) and with life under prescribed behavior patterns (Rom. 7:6).

For Paul and his contemporaries, this overlapped a further reference to the claims of Judaism as an old-established religion. So the new covenant replaces the old, decaying one (Heb. 8:13); believers are ransomed from it as "the empty way of life" (1 Pet. 1:18). The Christian stands in the new relationship to God foretold by the prophets (e.g., Ezek. 36:24–27) through the events of Calvary and Pentecost, and the powers of the new age are already at work in him (1 Cor. 10:11; Heb. 6:5).

This relegation of the old religion embodied in Jewish ordinances abolished the greatest single racial distinction, namely, the Jewish possession of divine REVELATION (Rom. 9:4; Eph. 2:11–22). In its place appears a new kind of humanity—what may be called a "third race" in which this distinction and therefore all the old racial and cultural differences are irrelevant. This truth gives the "new man" its corporate significance with a creative, supraracial unity, "in this one body" (Eph. 2:16; "body" here is ambiguous, perhaps deliberately so; cf. Col. 3:15).

The newness of the gospel extends even beyond history to cosmic proportions. The regenerate person is a new creation (*kainē ktisis*, 2 Cor. 5:17; Gal. 6:15); he belongs to a second Adam (1 Cor. 15:45) and is remade in the image of his Creator (Col. 3:10).

II. Theological significance. The phrase in general refers to the subject of REGENERATION. The question arising here is, What, in fact, is "new" in regenerate individuals? Interpretations range from a Socinian conception of a new and perfect moral law, to Tillich's "New Being" in the existential trend set by Kierkegaard (see P. Tillich's sermon, "The Yoke of Religion," in *The Shaking of the Foundations* [1957]). The first is not new, but an intensification of Jewish moralism; but the idea of the "New Being," a partaking of a new order of reality in which all religion is irrelevant, strikes at the continuity expressed by "man" in our phrase, for man is, by definition, *homo religiosus*. It is tempting to take a hint from IGNATIUS (*Eph.* 20.1) and equate the "new man" with Jesus himself. But there is a distinction: the believer is a new person, born anew, but not Jesus Christ reborn. Reformed theology, following John Calvin and based on the two primary texts, has specified righteousness, holiness, and true knowledge as the "new" elements of regenerate persons.

The difficulty arises in understanding this truth in the light of the Christian's only too obvious inconsistencies. Possibly one may understand it more easily as a fact progressing through concentric circles of influence. (1) There is a new relationship with God whereby a person, sins and all, comes under God's favorable consideration and pleasure. Everything is instantaneously new because it is placed in a new light. (2) Consequently, God's Spirit implants new motives of LOVE and FAITH which replace the old domination of self-sufficiency and extend their influence progressively over the old system of motivation. (3) The outward behavior is modified correspondingly, and in particular the attitudes and relationships toward other people are changed. Thus regenerate human beings are still human—even, until the PAROUSIA, sinners—but their environment, and their inner principle of life are new: both are, in fact, Jesus Christ. "Jesus Christ brought nothing that was new; he made all things new in himself." (See T. Boston, *Human Nature in its Fourfold State* [1720, repr. 1964]; J. Stewart, *A Man in Christ* [1935]; B. Kenrick, *The New Humanity* [1958]; J. R. Stott, *Men Made New* [1966]; H. Darling, *Man in Triumph* [1969], esp. ch. 4.) See also HUMAN NATURE. J. PECK

man, old. The expression *ho palaios anthrōpos*, "the old man," occurring three times in the NT, refers to the unregenerate nature and activities that characterized a person prior to his new life "in Christ." It is frequently translated "the old self" or "the old nature." PAUL states in Rom. 6:6 that "our old self" was crucified with Christ, and exhorts Christians to live conscious of this fact. In Eph. 4:22 he urges his converts to "put off your old self, which is being corrupted by its deceitful desires," and in Col. 3:9, similarly, he pleads for honesty on the basis of having "taken off your old self with its practices." In this period in redemptive history between the finished work of Christ in the past and the consummation of God's plan in the future, Christians live as citizens of two worlds who are constantly conscious of (1) the crucified nature of "the old man," and yet (2) the need to deaden the effects of that depravity in their lives which will be eradicated finally when Christ comes again. This tension, experienced by all believers, provides the context for almost all of the exhortations in the NT. See MAN, NEW.

R. N. LONGENECKER

Manaen man′uh-en (Μαναήν *G3441*, from מְנַחֵם *H4968*, "comforter" [see MENAHEM]). One of the five "prophets and teachers" listed as ministering in the church at ANTIOCH OF SYRIA (Acts 13:1). The others were BARNABAS, Simeon NIGER, LUCIUS of Cyrene, and Saul (PAUL). Manaen's position indicates a man of spiritual power and influence. Nothing further is known about Manaen beyond Luke's designation of him as one "who had been brought up with Herod the tetrarch." The relation to HEROD Antipas has been interpreted as "foster-brother" (ASV), "childhood companion" (Berkeley), "intimate friend" (MM, 615), or "member of the court" (cf. NRSV). Whatever the precise meaning, it was a relationship of honor and distinction. But it points to a striking contrast between the lives of the two men. Some think Manaen may have been related to an earlier man named *Manaēmos*, an ESSENE who was a friend of Herod the Great (Jos. *Ant.* 15.10.5 §§373–78).

D. E. HIEBERT

Manahath (person) man′uh-hath (מָנַחַת *H4969*, prob. "resting [place]"). Son of SHOBAL and grandson of SEIR the HORITE (Gen. 36:23; 1 Chr. 1:40); he was a chieftain living in EDOM (Gen. 36:21). See also MANAHATHITE.

Manahath (place) man′uh-hath (מָנַחַת *H4970*, prob. "resting [place]"). A city to which certain sons or descendants of EHUD—described as heads of families among the Benjamites who lived in GEBA—were deported (1 Chr. 8:6). The town is usually identified with modern el-Malḥah, about 4 mi. SW of Jerusalem. It has also been argued, however, that Manahath should be sought in GILEAD and identified with modern Maḥnah, about 8 mi. SE of JABESH GILEAD (see E. A. Knauf in *ABD*, 4:493–94).

E. B. SMICK

Manahathite man′uh-ha′thit (מָנַחְתִּי *H4971*, gentilic of מָנַחַת *H4969*). KJV Manahethite. A clan descended from CALEB through HUR. According to 1 Chr. 2:54, the descendants of SALMA (son of Hur) included "half the Manahathites," while v. 52 says that the descendants of SHOBAL (another son of Hur) included "half of the Menuhoth" (NRSV, following the MT). Many scholars believe that *mĕnuḥôt* must be a variant (or textual corruption) of *mānaḥtî* and therefore read "half the Manahathites" in v. 52 as well (so NIV; cf. KJV). A more difficult problem is raised by the fact that a HORITE (Edomite) named Manahath is identified as son of Shobal. See MANAHATH (PERSON). Since the Calebites lived in the S of Palestine, some scholars argue that the Manahathites were in fact connected with this Manahath, and that their presence in the Calebite genealogy is evidence of Edomite penetration into Judah (cf. *ABD*, 4:494). Others, however, believe that the Manahathites received their name from the town or district in which they lived. See MANAHATH (PLACE).

Manahethite man′uh-heh′thit. KJV form of MANAHATHITE.

Manasseas muh-nas′ee-uhs (Μανασσηας, Gk. form of MANASSEH). One of the descendants of Addi who agreed to put away their foreign wives (1 Esd. 9:31).

Manasseh (person) muh-nas′uh (מְנַשֶּׁה *H4985*, "one who causes to forget"; gentilic מְנַשִּׁי *H4986*, "Manassite"; Μανασσῆς *G3442*). KJV Apoc. and NT Manasses. (1) The older of two sons born to JOSEPH and his Egyptian wife ASENATH (Gen.

41:50–51; 46:20). The name is evidently derived from the verb *nāšâ* H5960, "to forget," and Joseph interprets it by the statement, "God has made me forget all my trouble and all my father's household" (41:51). When Joseph brought his sons EPHRAIM and Manasseh to his father for his blessing, JACOB adopted them as his own, placing them on an equality with his own sons as progenitors of separate tribes (48:1–5). In blessing the two boys, Jacob subordinated Manasseh the elder to Ephraim the younger, who thus inherited the position of privilege, the blessing of the FIRSTBORN (48:13–14).

Notwithstanding his subordination in the INHERITANCE, Manasseh was to be blessed by the Angel who had delivered Jacob from all harm (Gen. 48:16) and was to become a great people (48:19; Jacob's statement in v. 20, "In your name will Israel pronounce this blessing, saying, 'May God make you like Ephraim and Manasseh,'" is the basis of the benediction Jewish parents pronounce upon their sons on the Sabbath and holy days). According to a Jewish tradition (preserved in *Targum Pseudo-Jonathan*), Manasseh was a steward in the house of Joseph and acted as interpreter in Joseph's conversation with his brothers (42:23). The same tradition records that Manasseh was possessed of unusual physical strength, which he demonstrated when he retained SIMEON (42:24). It was Manasseh's Aramean concubine who gave birth to MAKIR, whose descendants became the tribe of Manasseh (1 Chr. 7:14). See MANASSEH (TRIBE).

(2) Son of HEZEKIAH and king of Judah from c. 696 to 641 B.C. (2 Ki. 21:1; 2 Chr. 33:1). Manasseh was only twelve years of age when he succeeded his father as king (according to a different system of CHRONOLOGY, Manasseh was coregent with his father for ten years). His reign of fifty-five years was the longest in Judah's history, and its events are recorded in 2 Ki. 21:1–18 and 2 Chr. 33:1–20. Judah, during practically the entire reign of Manasseh, was a tribute-paying province of the Assyrians. This situation began under TIGLATH-PILESER III when the Assyrian came to the help of AHAZ against PEKAH of the northern kingdom and REZIN of Syria (Aram), and continued so on through the reign of ESARHADDON (c. 681–669) and ASHURBANIPAL (c. 669–630). In the Assyrian inscriptions of these kings, Manasseh is specifically referred to as a vassal king. Each of these Assyrian rulers invaded and plundered Egypt, and Manasseh sent a contingent of troops to aid their armies in these campaigns. See JUDAH, KINGDOM OF II.B.

Second Chronicles describes the arrest of Manasseh and his deportation to Babylon in chains by "the army commanders of the king of Assyria." The Chronicler declares that from the prophetic point of view Manasseh's arrest and deportation was the result of the judgment of God upon the king's wickedness (2 Chr. 33:9–11). Scholars disagree as to why the Assyrians forced Manasseh to go to Babylon. It may not necessarily have been because of Manasseh's rebellion against Assyria, for which there is no clear evidence. It may have been the way by which the Assyrians forced the Judean king to demonstrate his loyalty as a vassal. This procedure apparently was an Assyrian policy toward vassals whose loyalty was in doubt. Assyrian inscriptions give no specific suspicious act of Manasseh as the reason for his arrest. In Ashurbanipal's record of his first campaign against Egypt, he lists twenty-two vassal kings among whom is Manasseh. A rebellion of serious proportions erupted in 652 B.C. against Ashurbanipal, led by his brother Shamash-shumukin of Babylon. The civil war raged for four years and ended with the defeat of Babylon. If Manasseh had been interested in throwing off the yoke of Ashurbanipal, this would have been his time for action. Some scholars find no problem in Manasseh's journey by coercion to Babylon, followed by his restoration to his throne. The Assyrian records report the parallel case of Pharaoh NECO I, who was also one of the royal prisoners of Ashurbanipal and then restored to Egypt.

The Assyrian kings of this period spent much of their time in Babylon. In the course of his imprisonment, Manasseh repented of his sins and was restored to his kingdom (2 Chr. 33:12–13). A penitential psalm attributed to Manasseh is included in the apocryphal Prayer of Manasseh, probably from the Maccabean period. See MANASSEH, PRAYER OF. It is an attempt to give expression to Manasseh's repentance and faith at the time of his arrest by the Assyrians. His religious reforms when he was restored were superficial, for he did not remove the HIGH PLACES of paganism (2 Chr. 33:17). Upon his return from Babylon, Manasseh gave himself to a program of building, measures of defense, and administration besides the religious reforms. Considering his fifty-five-year reign, very little is known of these activities. His reign was a period of great material prosperity due to his cooperation with the Assyrians. Assyrian records list Manasseh along with other subjects who paid tribute (2 Chr. 33:12–19).

The reign of Manasseh is distinguished by his personal responsibility for the religious syncretism of his time, which gained him the reputation of being the typical evil king of Judah. According to the account in 2 Ki. 23:26–27, his was the most immoral reign of all the kings and was the reason for the ultimate collapse of the southern kingdom. He was greatly influenced by Assyria, and inscriptions excavated at GEZER disclose Assyrian presence there and the use of the Assyrian language and methods of dating. Manasseh's active leadership in the promotion of pagan practices was perhaps prompted by interests that were more political than religious. There was a great surge of paganism involving the spread of the various cults, with their mythologies emanating from the great population and culture centers of the Assyrian empire. The resulting religious syncretism as it involved Judah is referred to by Isaiah (Isa. 2:6–8). The popular religion of Judah became a medley of Assyrio-Babylonian cults, the Canaanite FERTILITY CULT of Baalism (see BAAL), and Yahwism. Ezekiel's picture of the situation is quite vivid (Ezek. 8). The most degraded aspects of this pagan cultus was human sacrifice, and like Ahaz before him Manasseh "sacrificed his sons in the fire in the Valley of Ben Hinnom" (2 Chr. 33:6).

The record in 2 Ki. 21:1–18 and 24:3–4 emphasizes three degrading aspects of the regime of Manasseh: upon his accession to the throne he led in a reaction against the reforms instituted by his father Hezekiah; he accelerated the development of heathenism in the country; he instituted a bitter persecution of the prophetic party that opposed the popular syncretism led by the king. He "filled Jerusalem with innocent blood" (2 Ki. 24:4), and the prophets were put to the sword (Jer. 2:30). Rabbinical literature places emphasis upon the idea that Manasseh was even more evil than Ahaz, and that he killed ISAIAH, who had fled and hidden in a tree, by sawing him asunder. When Manasseh's immediate successor, JOSIAH, came to the throne, the supreme need was religious revival (2 Ki. 23:26). Jeremiah said that Manasseh's sin had yet to be expiated (Jer. 15:4; cf. 2 Ki. 23:26). Manasseh is included in the GENEALOGY OF JESUS CHRIST (Matt. 1:10). (See P. S. F. van Keulen, *Manasseh through the Eyes of the Deuteronomists: The Manasseh Account (2 Kings 21:1–18) and the Final Chapters of the Deuteronomistic History* [1996].)

(3) Father of Gershom and grandfather of JONATHAN; the latter was a priest for the Danites (Jdg. 18:30 KJV, following the MT). See DAN (PERSON AND TRIBE). The NIV and other versions, however, read MOSES. It is generally presumed that the reading in the MT is an intentional misspelling, since the Jonathan referred to is said to be a priest of the idolatrous shrine of MICAH. Thus Jonathan's grandfather was probably Moses, but his name was changed to Manasseh to avoid stigmatizing the revered name and sparing Moses the humiliation of having an idolatrous descendant. The change was accomplished by merely inserting a small *nun* (נ) between the first two letters of the name for Moses. This not only removed the stigma but also gave to the man a name familiar to the Hebrews as an idolater. Hubert Grimme's attempt to equate the names Moses and Manasseh on the basis of the Sinai inscriptions has been generally rejected by scholars.

(4) One of the descendants of PAHATH-MOAB who agreed to put away their foreign wives (Ezra 10:30; called "Manasseas" in 1 Esd. 9:31).

(5) One of the descendants of HASHUM who agreed to put away their foreign wives (Ezra 10:33; 1 Esd. 9:33).

(6) According to JOSEPHUS, Manasseh was the name of a man that NEHEMIAH describes as follows: "One of the sons of Joiada son of Eliashib the high priest was son-in-law to Sanballat the Horonite. And I drove him away from me" (Neh. 13:28). Josephus (*Ant.* 11.7.2) reports that he married Nicaso, daughter of SANBALLAT, and was consequently deposed from the priesthood by Nehemiah. Josephus also describes how the high priest JADDUA, Manasseh's brother, expressing the feeling of the people of Jerusalem, presented Manasseh with

the alternative of putting away his wife or leaving the priesthood. Manasseh went to Sanballat and told him that although he loved his wife he could not leave the priesthood. Upon Sanballat's promise that he would build with the approval of the king a temple on Mount GERIZIM where Manasseh should be the high priest, Manasseh stayed with his wife and father-in-law (*Ant.* 11.8.2–4) and thus became the high priest of the schismatic temple.

A. C. SCHULTZ

Manasseh (tribe) muh-nas′uh (מְנַשֶּׁה H4985, "one who causes to forget"; gentilic מְנַשִּׁי H4986, "Manassite"; Μανασσῆς G3442). KJV NT Manasses. One of the twelve tribes of Israel descending from MANASSEH, the grandson of JACOB through JOSEPH; the other Joseph tribe was EPHRAIM. At the time of the exodus, Manasseh numbered 32,200 (Num. 1:35; 2:21) while Ephraim had 40,500 (1:32, 33; 2:19). At the time of Israel's conquest of Canaan forty years later, Manasseh had increased to 52,700 (26:34), while Ephraim had fallen to 32,500 (26:37). At the time of the entrance into Canaan, Manasseh was sixth in the numerical strength of the twelve tribes, being surpassed by Judah, Issachar, Zebulun, Dan, and Asher.

During the journey through the wilderness, the position of Manasseh was on the W side of the TABERNACLE with Ephraim and Benjamin (Num. 2:18–24). The head of the tribe was Gamaliel son of Pedahzur (1:10; 7:54). According to *Targum Pseudo-Jonathan*, the standard of the RACHEL tribes—Manasseh, Ephraim, and Benjamin—carried the figure of a boy with the statement, "The cloud of the Lord rested on them until they went forth out of the camp." The TALMUD says that Manasseh's tribal banner was a black flag carrying the embroidered figure of a unicorn. The tribe of Manasseh was represented by Gaddi, son of Susi, when MOSES sent the twelve spies to survey the land of Canaan (13:11).

Manasseh took an important part in the victories of Israel over her enemies. The biblical account describes how the descendants of MAKIR son of Manasseh took GILEAD and conquered the AMORITES (Num. 32:39). JAIR the Manassite took the whole region of BASHAN and called the villages HAVVOTH JAIR after his own name (32:41; Deut. 3:14; 1 Chr. 5:18–22). Another Manassite, NOBAH, captured KENATH and its villages, then renamed it after himself (Num. 32:42). Troops of the tribe of Manasseh contributed effectively to the victories of the conquest under the leadership of JOSHUA (Josh. 22:1–7). At the conclusion of the fighting, the tribe of Manasseh cooperated with the Reubenites and the Gadites in building an altar by the Jordan; this action nearly led to civil war in Israel because it was misinterpreted by the other tribes (Josh. 22:10–34). Other prominent leaders from Manasseh included the judge GIDEON, who with a small army defeated the Midianites (Jdg. 6:15). Gideon's son ABIMELECH maintained himself at the head of a short-lived kingdom in the territory of Manasseh (ch. 9). Also from Manasseh was the judge JEPHTHAH, who defeated the Ammonites (ch. 11).

The territory occupied by Manasseh lay on both banks of the JORDAN River. On the E bank its territory was farthest N, adjacent to SYRIA and especially

The tribal territories of Manasseh.

View E across the tribal territory of Manasseh at the Jezreel Valley with Jokneam in the foreground.

adapted for the raising of cattle. On the W bank it was on the northern and most fruitful area of the mountain of Ephraim. The boundaries of the two sections of Manasseh cannot be drawn with exactness. Eastern Manasseh seems to have extended from the JABBOK to Mount HERMON in the N, and western Manasseh lay N of Ephraim extending to the slopes of Mount Carmel (cf. Josh. 17:15; see CARMEL, MOUNT). Thirteen cities in the eastern area of Manasseh were assigned to the Levites, and ten in the western section (21:5–6). GOLAN, a city of refuge, was in the eastern area of Manasseh. Although Manasseh was larger numerically than Ephraim about the time of the conquest of Canaan, in later times Ephraim surpassed Manasseh in population, wealth, and power. Western Manasseh apparently was never able to dominate completely the Canaanites in its area (17:12; Jdg. 1:27). See TRIBES, LOCATION OF, I.C and IV.B.

When DAVID was made king at HEBRON, 18,000 men came from the western half-tribe of Manasseh to join the movement (1 Chr. 12:31), while eastern Manasseh was represented in the 120,000 troops who came together with the men of Reuben and Gad. When David organized his administration under the leadership of "capable men" (26:31), he found Joel son of Pedaiah in W Manasseh, and in E Manasseh he appointed Iddo son of Zechariah (27:20–21). In spite of its being a part of the northern kingdom of Israel, Manasseh participated in the revival and reform movements in the southern kingdom. Manassites were involved in the revival under ASA, in the Passover celebration in the reign of HEZEKIAH, and in his attack upon idolatry. They were also involved in the reform of JOSIAH and the restoration of the TEMPLE (2 Chr. 15:9; 30:1, 10–11, 18; 31:1; 34:6, 9). The eastern tribe of Manasseh was more exposed to the attacks of the Arameans and Assyrians than other parts of the country. Manasseh suffered the same fate as the other northern tribes in the deportations by TIGLATH-PILESER III and later by SARGON at the time of the fall of SAMARIA in 722 B.C.

Manasseh eventually lost its identity in becoming assimilated with the people of the new environment after the destruction of the northern kingdom, whose gods the Manassites came to worship. The biblical account emphasizes that the children of Manasseh were among those who proved themselves "unfaithful to the God of their fathers and prostituted themselves to the gods of the peoples of the land, whom God had destroyed before them" (1 Chr. 5:25).

In Pss. 4:7 and 108:8 Manasseh is called a most precious possession of God. Ezekiel has a place for the tribe of Manasseh in his picture of the future

(Ezek. 48:4), and John includes the tribe in his vision described in Rev. 7:6.   A. C. Schultz

Manasseh, Prayer of muh-nas′uh. KJV Prayer of Manasses. A relatively brief (fifteen verses) penitential prayer that constitutes a separate book of the Apocrypha.

I. Background. Of exceptional beauty and poignancy, this prayer embodies the best of Jewish piety and is attributed (but only in the title) to Manasseh, the king whose reign was the longest (696–642 B.C., but prior to 686 prob. as coregent with Hezekiah) and one of the most regrettable in the history of Judah. Manasseh, according to the OT account (2 Ki. 21:1–18; 2 Chr. 33:1–9), turned from the ways of his father Hezekiah to a renewal of idolatry and to various iniquitous practices, including the burning of his sons as offerings to pagan deities, as well as the shedding of "much innocent blood" (2 Ki. 21:16). The Chronicler gives us the additional information that God brought the Assyrians upon Jerusalem in judgment causing Manasseh to be taken captive to Babylon. (The exact date of this event is unknown, but it may have been c. 648 in connection with a widespread rebellion against Ashurbanipal.)

In his dire need Manasseh turned to the Lord in repentance, and the Lord heard his cry and brought Manasseh back to Jerusalem where he tried his best to undo in a few years the tragic deeds of his past. The Chronicler, in closing the narrative concerning Manasseh, twice refers to a prayer by Manasseh that is to be found in "the annals of the kings of Israel" and also in "the records of the seers" (2 Chr. 33:18–19). Unfortunately, neither these early sources nor the original prayer has survived. It is almost certain that what is known by the title "Prayer of Manasseh" is the creation of a much later author designed to fit the prayer mentioned in 2 Chr. 33.

II. Author and date. The author of the prayer is unknown. That he lived much later than the time of Manasseh seems probable from the form, content, and language of the prayer. The form follows a liturgical pattern that was common during the three or four centuries before the coming of Christ. Despite the fact that the author has specifically attempted to relate the content of the prayer to the situation of Manasseh (cf. the reference to the setting up of abominations and the iron fetters in Pr. Man. 10), a number of the concepts of the prayer are more suitable to a later age, and particularly to postexilic Judaism. It seems probable that the author was a Hellenistic Jew, but it cannot be ascertained beyond doubt whether he wrote in Greek or in Hebrew. If he wrote in Greek, his language contains several Hebraisms and possibly also reflects the influence of Septuagint phraseology. All of this uncertainty makes the determination of an approximate date difficult. The majority of scholars date the prayer sometime in the period 2nd cent. B.C. to the 1st cent. of our era, but the probability would seem to lie in favor of the earlier part of this time span, particularly the Maccabean era (see Maccabee).

III. Content. The author follows a well-defined pattern in formulating the prayer. He begins (Pr. Man. 1–7) with an ascription of sovereignty and glory to the Creator who by virtue of his incomparable greatness is unapproachable, yet who has promised mercy and forgiveness having "appointed repentance for sinners, so that they may be saved" (v. 7). The verses that follow contain a moving confession of sin which is made in the first person (vv. 8–10). Thereupon comes the plea for mercy and forgiveness (vv. 11–14), and the prayer concludes with a doxology, the final words of which are reminiscent of the traditional ending of the Lord's Prayer, "and yours is the glory forever. Amen."

IV. Purpose and theology. If the prayer may correctly be placed in the Maccabean age, the purpose in the author's mind is readily apparent. Presumably it was written to fill the void caused by the unavailability of the documents that originally contained the prayer. The author, however, wrote not merely to satisfy this deficiency but also to speak a word to those of his own generation who had made the mistake of lapsing into idolatry. If there had been hope for the wicked Manasseh, the implied argument runs, how much more was there hope for the writer's own contemporaries. A number of the theological ideas of the prayer, although not impossible in an earlier period, fit well what is known of postexilic Judaism. This is particularly true of the emphasis upon God as "the God of those who repent" (Pr. Man. 13), and the "God of the righteous" (v. 8), but also of other emphases, such as the sinlessness of the PATRIARCHS (v. 8), the combination of universalism and particularism (God, as sovereign Creator and as specially related to the patriarchs, vv. 1–2, 8), and the power of the "glorious name" (v. 3). The prayer, however, by its nature centers upon the two main theological ideas of the abundance of God's mercy and the efficacy of sincere repentance.

V. Canonicity and text. Although the prayer appears as part of the Apocrypha, it is not included among the books finally accepted as canonical by the Roman Catholic Church in the deliberations of the Council of Trent. It was not a part of the original VULGATE (JEROME appears not to have known of it) nor was it originally to be found in the SEPTUAGINT. The earliest literary evidence concerning the prayer is its presence in the 3rd-cent. Syriac work, DIDASCALIA APOSTOLORUM (2.21), from which it was also taken up into the 4th-cent. writing, APOSTOLIC CONSTITUTIONS. (The lateness of this evidence has, unnecessarily, caused some scholars to date the prayer in the Christian era.) The prayer is found in CODEX ALEXANDRINUS (5th cent.) among the collection of Odes appended to the Psalms. Only in some later MSS was the prayer ever associated with 2 Chronicles, and after the Council of Trent the work was customarily relegated to an appendix.

The Greek text is available in some editions of the SEPTUAGINT (e.g., Ode 12 in Rahlfs's *Septuaginta*). English translations are available in Protestant editions of the Apocrypha, where it has held a place since its initial appearance in the Bible of Thomas Matthew (1537). (See further H. E. Ryle in *APOT*, 1:612–24; W. O. E. Oesterley, *The Books of the Apocrypha* [1915], 404–10; E. J. Goodspeed, *The Story of the Apocrypha* [1939], 52–56; R. H. Pfeiffer, *History of New Testament Times, with an Introduction to the Apocrypha* [1949], 457–460; B. M. Metzger, *An Introduction to the Apocrypha* [1957], 123–28; D. J. Harrington, *Invitation to the Apocrypha* [1999], ch. 13; D. A. deSilva, *Introducing the Apocrypha: Message, Context, and Significance* [2002], ch. 14.)   D. A. HAGNER

Manasses muh-nas´eez. KJV Apoc. and NT form of MANASSEH.

Mandaic man-day´ik. See MANDEAN.

Mandean man-dee´uhn. Also Mandaean. This term (from an Aram. word meaning "knowledge") refers to a member of Mand(a)eism, a religious community that claims to have originated in Palestine, with JOHN THE BAPTIST regarded as one of its prophets; its earliest extant writings (bowls with magical texts) are from 4th-cent. MESOPOTAMIA. A number of Mandean villages still survive today, mainly in S Iraq. The Mandean religion is a form of GNOSTICISM, with complex MYTHS based on a strong DUALISM between light (life, goodness, spirit) and darkness (death, evil, matter); it is also characterized by intricate rituals. The Mandean language, usually referred to as Mandaic, is a form of E ARAMAIC. (See E. S. Drower, *The Mandaeans of Iraq and Iran: Their Cults, Customs, Magic, Legends, and Folklore*, 2nd ed. [1962]; E. M. Yamauchi, *Gnostic Ethics and Mandaean Origins* [1970]; K. Rudolph, *Mandaeism* [1978]; N. Deutsch, *The Gnostic Imagination: Gnosticism, Mandaeism, and Merkabah Mysticism* [1995]; J. J. Buckley, *The Mandaeans: Ancient Texts and Modern People* [2002].) See also MANICHEAN.

mandrake. The English term *mandrakes* is the usual rendering of the Hebrew word *dûdāʾim* H1859 (a pl. form related to *dôd* H1856, "beloved"), which occurs only in Gen. 30:14–16 and Cant. 7:14. It is thought that it refers to the *Atropa mandragora*, an herb like the deadly nightshade, and therefore a member of the same family. This plant bears yellow fruits, somewhat smaller than the tomato, and has an "acquired," pleasant taste. Because of its reputation as an aphrodisiac, it is sometimes known as the "love apple," and it is called by the Arabs "a devil's apple." The description in Genesis of RACHEL's conversation with LEAH certainly gives the impression that the mandrake was thought to be a love potion. The plant was used in ancient times as a purgative and anesthetic, and is considered poisonous. Its near relation, *Atropa belladonna*, is the source of Atropine, an important medicinal drug.

The Royal Horticultural Society's *Dictionary of Gardening* names the plant *Mandragora officinarum*, and describes the fruit as a globose berry. This plant has a large tap root; it produces leaves like a primrose, and blue or greenish-white flowers similar to those of the potato. The yellow plum-like fruits invariably lie in the middle of the rosette of leaves, rather like the eggs of some bird in a nest. There is little doubt that its amorous properties are pure superstition, but the plant is certainly found in Palestine.

According to Cant. 7:13, "The mandrakes send out their fragrance," and it is this statement that has made some feel that the plant could not have been *Mandragora*, which has no definite scent—no more, for instance, than the tomato. Some have therefore argued that the plant must be *Citrus medica*. In view of where the mandrakes were found by Reuben, the writer feels this idea quite unacceptable. (See *FFB*, 138–39.) See also flora (under *Solanaceae*). W. E. Shewell-Cooper

maneh may'neh. KJV term for mina (only Ezek. 45:12).

Manes may'neez. See Manichean.

manger. A receptacle for feeding livestock. The NIV uses this term as the rendering of Hebrew *ʾēbûs H17*, "feeding trough" (Job 39:9; Prov. 14:4; Isa. 1:3; KJV and NRSV have "crib"), and most versions use it to translate Greek *phatnē G5764* in the nativity story (Lk. 2:7, 12, 16). This Greek term sometimes has the broader meaning of "stall" or "stable" (cf. possibly Lk. 13:15). In the ANE, animals might be kept in outdoor enclosures with lean-to roofing, or in permanent shelters made of stone and mud-wall, or in cave stalls. When Joseph and Mary were unable to find room in the "inn" (prob. a private home or a public shelter), they sought refuge in some kind of stable, perhaps next to the inn, though it is not possible to ascertain what type of animal shelter this was.

In early Christian tradition, the place of our Lord's birth was thought to be a cave, and a number of possible sites were revered in and about Bethlehem. The present Church of the Nativity on a slight rise of hillside in Bethlehem covers one of these ancient grotto stalls. The traditional artistic representation in Western churches is influenced to a great extent by the work of the Renaissance painters, who naturally portrayed the scene of virgin and

A stone feeding trough or manger at Megiddo.

child in the heavy wooden constructions of Europe. In the ANE, however, such stalls and mangers usually were cut from the natural stone of the caves or transported into the shelter. Many examples of such stone fodder troughs have been found. In the scenes from Dura-Europos and other early decorated churches, it is such stone mangers that are shown. The essential character of the narrative of Jesus' birth is clear, irrespective of the exact state of the manger: Jesus Christ was born in the humblest and lowliest of surroundings among the poor of the Jewish people. W. White, Jr.

Mani may'ni (Μανι). **(1)** The ancestor of several Israelites who agreed to put away their foreign wives (1 Esd. 9:30; called Bani in Ezra 10:29).

(2) See Manichean.

Manichean man'uh-kee'uhn. Also Manichaean, Manichee. A follower of the teachings of Mani (also Manes, from Gk. *Manēs*). The term is sometimes applied more broadly to a believer in dualism. Born of Parthian princely blood in 216, probably in Babylonia, Mani was under Mandean influence as a child, and claimed to have received his first revelation at the age of twelve. He first preached in India, but later, during the long and tolerant reign of Shapur (c. 242–273), he made numerous converts in Babylonia, Media, and Parthia. Upon the accession of Bahram I in 273, ZOROASTRIANISM gained the upper hand; the Manicheans were persecuted, and Mani died in prison (prob. 276). Mani taught that Buddha, Zoroaster, and Jesus were great prophets, but that he was the last and greatest. His system was a dualism in which God opposed matter. See GNOSTICISM. The elect among his followers abstained from meat, all killing of animals and plants, and sexual relations. The influence of this teaching lasted over a millennium. (See S. N. C. Lieu, *Manichaeism in the Later Roman Empire and Medieval China: A Historical Survey* [1985]; P. A. Mirecki and J. BeDuhn, eds., *The Light and the Darkness: Studies in Manichaeism and Its World* [2001]; P. A. Mirecki in *ABD*, 4:502–11.)

P. WOOLLEY

Manichee man´uh-kee. See MANICHEAN.

Manius, Titus may´nee-uhs, ti´tuhs (Τίτος Μάνιος). Titus Manius was one of two Roman legates who, in 164 B.C., sent a letter to the Jewish people confirming the concessions that had been made to them by LYSIAS after he had been beaten by them in battle, and offered to act in their behalf in the coming negotiations with ANTIOCHUS Epiphanes at Antioch (2 Macc. 11:34; see MACCABEE). Attempts to identify Titus Manius have not been successful.

S. BARABAS

manna man´uh. This term is a transliteration of Greek *manna* G3445, which is the usual SEPTUAGINT rendering of Hebrew *mān* H4942. (The stricter Gk. transliteration *man* occurs in LXX Exod. 16:31–35; some believe that the choice of *manna* in Num. 11:6–9 et al. may have been influenced by a Gk. word that has the same form and that means "small grain.") When the Israelites saw the "thin flakes like frost" that God had miraculously provided as food (lit., "bread") for them, they asked, *mān hûʾ*, "What is it?" (Exod. 16:15), and so they called the substance *mān* (v. 31). This food is also described as "white like coriander seed," and we read that it "tasted like wafers made with honey" (v. 31). According to Num. 11:7–8, "The manna was like coriander seed and looked like resin. The people went around gathering it, and then ground it in a handmill or crushed it in a mortar. They cooked it in a pot or made it into cakes. And it tasted like something made with olive oil." In Exod. 16:13–14, the manna is associated with the dew, and Ps. 78:24–25 says that God "rained down manna for the people to eat, / he gave them the grain of heaven. / Men ate the bread of angels; / he sent them all the food they could eat."

God provided the manna on a daily basis to the Israelites through all the years of their wanderings (Exod. 16:35; Josh. 5:12). They were told to take only one *omer* (about two liters) per person, but on the sixth day they were to take twice as much so that it would last them through the SABBATH (Exod. 16:16–30). Following the Lord's command, MOSES instructed AARON to put some manna in a jar that was to be kept in the TABERNACLE as a memorial for future generations (vv. 31–34; cf. Heb. 9:4). Near the end of the Israelites' wandering, Moses explained to them that the manna was part of God's testing: "He humbled you, causing you to hunger and then feeding you with manna, which neither you nor your fathers had known, to teach you that man does not live on bread alone but on every word that comes from the mouth of the LORD" (Deut. 8:3; cf. v. 16; Neh. 9:20). (See P. Maiberger, *Das Manna: Eine literarische, etymologische und naturkundliche Untersuchung*, 2 vols. [1983].)

The Lord Jesus quoted this last text to SATAN at the time of his temptation in the wilderness (Matt. 4:4; Lk. 4:4; see TEMPTATION OF CHRIST). Later in his ministry, after miraculously providing bread to the crowds, some people challenged him by pointing out that God had given manna to the Israelites in the desert (Jn. 6:31). In response, Jesus claimed that he himself was the "bread from heaven" (vv. 32–35, 41, 48–51, 58; see P. Borgen, *Bread from Heaven: An Exegetical Study of the Concept of Manna in the Gospel of John and the Writings of Philo* [1965]). And in the book of Revelation, the glorified Lord says to the church in PERGAMUM: "To him who overcomes, I will give some of the hidden manna" (Rev. 2:17), which probably refers to the eschatological fellowship believers will enjoy with Christ at the MESSIANIC BANQUET (cf. 19:9; for a discussion of various views, see G. R. Osborne, *Revelation*, BECNT [2002], 147–48).

Some believe that the manna was a gum-resin, which exuded from trees such as *Alhagi maurorum* (called the prickly alhagi and sometimes the Sinai manna). Two other trees that are found in Palestine and could produce similar globules of gum are *Fraxinus ornus*, a flowering ash, and *Tamarisk gallica* (or *T. nilotica*), variety *manifera*. See also BREAD V.

W. E. SHEWELL-COOPER

Manoah muh-noh´uh (מָנוֹחַ *H4956*, "[place of] rest"; cf. NOAH). The father of SAMSON. Manoah lived in ZORAH, a town in the tribal territory of DAN before the Danites moved N to take the city of LAISH. Manoah's wife, who was sterile, received a message from the angel of the Lord, announcing the birth of a son, who was to be a NAZIRITE (Jdg. 13:2–5). Manoah asked God for instruction on how to bring up the boy (v. 8). On a second appearance of the angel, Manoah did not request a repetition of the promise, but with implicit faith said, "When your words are fulfilled, what is to be the rule for the boy's life and work?" (v. 12). After another reminder of a perpetual Nazirite vow (Num. 6), which was to begin with the child's mother, Manoah sought to reward the messenger with food, but was told instead to prepare a burnt offering. It seems strange that Manoah did not know that the messenger was the angel of the Lord (v. 16), but his wife had said merely, "He looked like an angel of God, very awesome" (v. 6). Manoah realized that he was indeed the angel of the Lord when he ascended in the flame of the offering into heaven (v. 21). Manoah responded with fear, but his wife, who remains nameless, seemed to have a better understanding of the divine will (vv. 22–23).

E. B. SMICK

man of lawlessness, man of sin. See ANTICHRIST.

mansion. This term, which in present English usually refers to an imposing house, is used by the NIV a few times (e.g., for the expression "great houses," Amos 3:15). The KJV uses it only once in the well-known words of Jesus, "In my Father's house are many mansions" (Jn. 14:2), but the meaning here is certainly not "palatial residence." The English term *mansion* used to mean simply "dwelling," and thus in the 17th cent. it was an appropriate rendering of the Greek term here, *monē G3665* (derived from the verb *menō G3531*, "to remain, dwell," which is used frequently in Jn. 14–15). This noun occurs in only one other place in the NT—in this same chapter, where Jesus says, "If anyone loves me, he will obey my teaching. My Father will love him, and we will come to him and make our home [*monē*] with him" (14:23; here the KJV renders it "abode"). On this basis it has been argued that v. 2 does not refer (at least not exclusively) to HEAVEN, but to the presence of Christ in the believer's heart. (See R. H. Gundry in *ZNW* 58 [1967]: 68–72.)

mantelet. This English term, referring to a movable shelter used to protect besiegers, is used by the NRSV to render Hebrew *sōkēk H6116*, a term of uncertain meaning that occurs only once (Nah. 2:5; KJV, "defence"; NIV, "protective shield"). The sense of "protection" is supported by ancient versions (LXX, *prophylakē*; Vulg., *umbraculum*). Assyrian bas-reliefs depict thick shields made of reeds behind which the besieging archers stand (see *ANEP*, nos. 368 and 369). See ARMOR, ARMS.

J. REA

mantle. This English term, referring to a loosely worn upper garment, occurs frequently in the KJV and other versions (rarely in the NIV, which prefers CLOAK). One's daily work was performed while usually wearing only an undergarment such as a waist cloth or TUNIC. In bad weather and for protection by night, an upper garment was added.

In the Bible several words are used for the upper garment. Common in the OT is Hebrew *śimlâ H8529*, which seems to refer to garments in general (e.g., Gen. 9:23; 35:2; 37:34; 41:14; 44:13; Deut. 8:4; 10:18; cf. *śalmâ H8515*, Exod. 22:9 et al.), and also more specifically to an article of clothing that was used as a protective covering to be used with some form of undergarment (Exod. 12:34; Deut. 22:3). Frequently it is difficult to determine precisely what type of garment is meant. In the NT the corresponding Greek word is *himation G2668* (Matt. 5:40; Lk. 8:27).

A type of mantle mentioned several times is the *mĕʿîl* H5077. From its apparent association with men of high social position, or of the priestly order, one may likely infer that it was more ornate and elaborate than the ordinary robe. This was the type of garment that was made annually for young SAMUEL by his mother (1 Sam. 2:19) and which he wore on important occasions (15:27; 28:14). It also is mentioned in reference to SAUL (24:4, 11), JONATHAN (18:4), and DAVID (1 Chr. 15:27). Mention is made of robes and embroidered garments elsewhere (Exod. 28:31; 2 Sam. 13:18; Job 29:14; Ps. 109:29; Isa. 59:17).

A third type of mantle was the *ʾadderet* H168, a garment of distinction worn by kings (Jon. 3:6), and especially by prophets (1 Ki. 19:13, 19; 2 Ki. 2:8, 13–14; Zech. 13:4). Made of animal hair, this type of robe was one of the objects coveted by ACHAN (Josh. 7:21, 24). A comparable NT term is *stolē* G5124, which important people wore (Mk. 12:38; Lk. 20:46). Martyrs are described as being given a white robe (Rev. 6:11). It is also the garment of the redeemed (7:9, 13). (See M. G. Houston, *Ancient Egyptian and Persian Costume and Decoration*, 2nd ed. [1954]; ANEP, figs. 1–66 and passim; *BA* 24 [1961]: 119–28.) See also COAT; DRESS; ROBE.

S. WOUDSTRA

Manual of Discipline. See DEAD SEA SCROLLS IV.

manuscript. A handwritten document (from Latin *manus*, "hand," and *scriptus*, "written"). Prior to the invention of printing, any document, whether a work of literature or a private writing, was written by hand and was thus a "manuscript" (although in present-day English the term is also used of typewritten compositions).

Manuscripts have been made of many materials, including CLAY TABLETS, wax tablets, LEATHER, broken pieces of pottery (see OSTRACA), cloth, and the bark of trees. The Jews commonly used SCROLLS of leather for the MSS of their Scriptures. For 4,000 years, PAPYRUS scrolls were commonly used to write documents. The scroll form began to be replaced by the CODEX or modern book form near the beginning of the Christian era. About the 4th Christian cent., papyrus was replaced largely by PARCHMENT (or vellum). Paper, invented in China and introduced into the Western world through the Arabs, began to replace parchment about the 12th cent. See WRITING.

Manuscripts of the Bible are more numerous than those of any other ancient literature. Most ancient works have either not survived at all or are extant in only one MS or in a few; some exceptional writings (such as the *Iliad* and the *Odyssey*) have survived in several hundred copies. In contrast, the Bible is extant in thousands of MSS, varying from small fragments to complete Bibles, both in the original languages and in numerous ancient translations. See TEXT AND MANUSCRIPTS (OT); TEXT AND MANUSCRIPTS (NT).

J. H. GREENLEE

Maoch may´ok (מָעוֹךְ H5059, derivation uncertain, but possibly a variant of מַעֲכָה H5082, which may mean "dull" or "oppression"). TNIV Maok. Father of ACHISH, who was the PHILISTINE king of GATH with whom DAVID and his men took refuge when they were fleeing SAUL (1 Sam. 27:2; cf. 1 Ki. 2:39). See MAACAH #8.

Maok may´ok. TNIV form of MAOCH.

Maon (person) may´on (מָעוֹן H5062, "dwelling"). Son of Shammai, descendant of CALEB, and "father" of BETH ZUR (1 Chr. 2:45). The latter description means either that he was the ancestor of the people of Beth Zur or the founder of that city. It is also possible that the name in this passage is a collective for the people of the town of Maon,

Medieval Hebrew scroll (14th cent.) opened to Gen. 4.

and that they were the ones who founded the city of Beth Zur. See Maon (place); Maonites.

S. Woudstra

Maon (place) may´on (מָעוֹן *H5063*, "dwelling"). A town in the hill-country of Judah, in the same district as Carmel and Ziph (Josh. 15:55). It is identified with modern Khirbet Ma‛in, situated on a hilltop about 8 mi. SSE of Hebron. Hiding from Saul, David and his men took refuge in the Desert of Maon (1 Sam. 23:24–25), which was a wilderness area E and SE of the town. Maon was the residence of Nabal, whose widow Abigail became the wife of David (25:1–2). (See *NEAEHL*, 3:942–44.)

S. Woudstra

Maonites may´uh-n*i*ts (מָעוֹן *H5062*, "dwelling"). Name given to a group of people who were hostile to Israel (Jdg. 10:12; lit., "Maon"). They are probably not to be connected with the town of Maon; see Maon (place). Perhaps these people are the same as the Meunites (1 Chr. 4:41; 2 Chr. 20:1; 26:7), but this identification is by no means established.

S. Woudstra

maps. See cartography, biblical.

Mara mair´uh (מָרָא *H5259*, "bitter" [possibly an Aram. formation corresponding to Heb. מָרָה *H5288*; see Marah]). The name that Naomi chose for herself when she returned from Moab to her native country, bereaved of her husband and sons. Earlier, Naomi had said to her two daughters-in-law, "It is more bitter [*mar H5253*] for me than for you" (Ruth 1:13). When she arrived in Bethlehem, she asked the women of the town not to call her Naomi: "Call me Mara, because the Almighty has made my life very bitter [*mārar H5352*]" (v. 20).

Marah mair´uh (מָרָה *H5288*, "bitter"). The name that the Israelites gave to a place (between Etham and Elim) where they found water that was brackish and undrinkable (Exod. 15:23; Num. 33:8–9). They had traveled in the Desert of Shur without finding water (Exod. 15:22). When the people came to the spring and were unable to drink from it, they murmured against Moses. Then the Lord showed Moses a piece of wood, which he threw into the

This oasis may be the site of biblical Marah.

water, thereby miraculously sweetening the spring (vv. 24–25). The location of Marah is uncertain, but proposals include modern ‛Ain Hawarah (some 47 mi. SE of Suez) and Bir Mara (much farther N, only 10 mi. E of Suez).

S. Woudstra

Maralah mahr´uh-luh (מַרְעֲלָה *H5339*, possibly "mountain ledge"). A town on the W border of the tribal territory of Zebulun between Sarid and Dabbesheth (Josh. 19:11; RSV, "Mareal"). Maralah was in the Valley of Jezreel, but its precise location is uncertain. Possible identifications are modern Tell el-Ghaltah (about 7 mi. NNW of Megiddo) and, more likely, Tell Thorah (2 mi. closer to Megiddo).

maranatha mair´uh-nath´uh (μαράνα θά *G3448*, from Aram. מָרָנָא תָא, "our Lord, come!" or מָרַן אֲתָא, "our Lord has come"). This term, which is a transliteration of two Aramaic words, occurs once in the NT (1 Cor. 16:22, after an anathema against anyone who does not love the Lord) and once in the Apostolic Fathers (*Didache* 10.6). The first part of the phrase is the Aramaic word for "lord, master" (vocalized either *mar* or *mār*) with the suffix of the first person plural pronoun (resulting in the form *māran* or, if the older form of the suffix is used, *māranaʾ*; see G. Dalman, *Grammatik des jüdisch-palästinischen Aramäisch*, 2nd ed. [1905], 152 n. 3). The second part is a form of the Aramaic word for "to come": either the third person perfect *ʾătāʾ*, "has come," or the second person imperative *tāʾ*, "come!"

The rendering "Our Lord has come" makes good sense, especially if a eucharistic background is assumed (the context in *Didache* 10.6 definitely centers on the Lord's table). If so, the reference is either to the INCARNATION or to his presence at the EUCHARIST. Most scholars, however, prefer the meaning "Our Lord, come!" in view of the parallel expression, "Come, Lord Jesus" (Rev. 22:20). This rendering too is fitting to the LORD'S SUPPER, at which time Jesus' death is proclaimed "until he comes" (1 Cor. 11:26).

A eucharistic context is made further plausible by the following consideration. An Aramaic expression in a letter addressed to a Greek-speaking group appears very strange indeed, unless it be a form consecrated in the worship of the earliest Christian community in Jerusalem, and with which all Christians, whatever their native language, would become familiar (something like AMEN or HALLELUJAH). The Lord's Supper would easily fit that picture. In spite of these arguments, the identification of the context of "maranatha" with the Eucharist remains speculative, and some able scholars offer alternative views, notably C. F. D. Moule (in *NTS* 8 [1960]: 307–10), who envisions this expression as a part of a curse or of a solemn asseveration.

If the imperative is preferred, the term *maranatha* would be a very early evidence of a prayer addressed to Jesus as Lord. It bears witness in any case to the fact of a Palestinian recognition of Christ as LORD. (J. A. Fitzmyer, *A Wandering Aramean: Collected Aramaic Essays* [1979], ch. 5, esp. p. 124, provides evidence that the Aram. word could mean "the Lord" in an absolute sense with reference to Yahweh. See also R. G. Kuhn in *TDNT* 4:466–72, which has a lucid discussion with extensive bibliography up to 1937.) R. NICOLE

marble. Limestone (calcium carbonate) or dolomite (calcium-magnesium carbonate) that has been recrystallized under metamorphic conditions, either by heat adjacent to a large igneous intrusion or by heat and pressure in the earth's crust, particularly in mountain belts. However, the term *marble* often is also applied to some special types of nonmetamorphic limestone. The stone is capable of high polish (Lat. *marmor*, "shining stone") and was much used in ARCHITECTURE, as in the building of Solomon's TEMPLE (1 Chr. 29:2, where the Hebrew term is *šayiš* H8880), with pillars of marble being used as a representation of strength (Cant. 5:15, Heb. *šēš* H9253). In addition, the use of marble as a paving stone was widespread, although other polished material also was used for this purpose (Esth. 1:6; see MALACHITE).

Marble was used for making jars and other ornamental vessels (Rev. 18:12; Gk. *marmaros* G3454), particularly those varieties showing variegated patterns resulting from their formation with concentric color-zones in stalagmitic deposits. Such marble commonly was referred to as ALABASTER and used for making ointment jars (Matt. 26:7; Mk. 14:3; Lk. 7:37; Gk. *alabastros* G223). It also was referred to as onyx-marble, with Algerian ONYX being used in buildings of Carthage and Rome.

Much of the marble for sculpture came from Greece, especially the Pentelic marble from Mount Pentelicus in Attica and the Parian marble from the isle of Paros. Carrara marble, which is found in the Apuan Alps, Italy, and is used by many sculptors of the present day, was employed in Rome for architectural purposes in the time of AUGUSTUS. (See H. H. Read, *Rutley's Elements of Mineralogy*, 26th ed. [1970], 270–77.) D. R. BOWES

Marcheshvan (מַרְחֶשְׁוָן, not found in the OT; prob. of Persian origin). The postbiblical name for the eighth month (October-November), corresponding to Canaanite BUL and Babylonian *Arahsamna* ("eighth month"). The name is already attested in the Aramaic papyri from ELEPHANTINE. It is also known as Heshvan. S. BARABAS

Marcion mahrʹshuhn (Μαρκίων). A native of Sinope in PONTUS, Marcion moved to ROME c. A.D. 140 and joined the church there but in 144 was excommunicated for his heretical opinions (however, an earlier date for Marcion's work is argued by R. J. Hoffmann, *Marcion: On the Resti-*

tution of Christianity* [1984], 44–47). The sect he founded spread widely and was for a time a serious menace to the church. Strongly anti-Jewish, he distinguished the merely just God of the OT from the loving God and Father of Jesus revealed in the NT, and accordingly rejected the OT altogether (see A. von Harnack, *Marcion: The Gospel of the Alien God* [1990; German orig. 1924]). He believed that only PAUL had truly grasped the contrast of law and gospel, so the Pauline letters (purged of what he considered Jewish accretions) formed the basis of his canon. See CANON (NT).

Marcion's *Gospel* was not an independent work, but an expurgated version of Luke, adapted to Marcion's own doctrinal theories. It does not appear that Marcion added much if anything of his own. According to IRENAEUS (*Haer.* 1.25.1, trans. W. W. Harvey), he excised "all that is written about the birth of the Lord and many things from the teaching in his discourses, in which he clearly confessed the Creator of this universe as his Father." Other deletions include the baptism and temptation narratives, which were inconsistent with Marcion's docetic CHRISTOLOGY. Altogether he omitted between a quarter and a third of Luke's gospel.

A second view, which would make Luke dependent on Marcion's *Gospel* and not the reverse, seems in H.-C. Puech's words "paradoxical and impossible to maintain" (*NTAp* [1963–65], 1:348), but a third theory has been advanced by J. Knox, namely, that what Marcion used was an *Urlukas*, an earlier and shorter version that was later expanded by the church "in the interest of anti-Marcionite polemic" (*Marcion and the New Testament* [1942], ch. 4). The difficulty is that there is no evidence for such an *Urlukas* (Streeter's conjectured Proto-Luke is another matter), and Irenaeus within half a century of Marcion is quite unambiguous. (See now J. B. Tyson, *Marcion and Luke–Acts: A Defining Struggle* [2006].)

The reasons for Marcion's choice of Luke have been debated. Was it the only gospel he knew, or the gospel of his native Pontus? Or did he make a deliberate choice? Matthew, of course, would be out of the question because of its strong Jewish flavor, but what of Mark or John? Probably use of John would have been difficult to reconcile with Marcion's view of the relations of Paul and the Twelve, and this gospel has a mystical background out of keeping with Marcion's spirituality (H. E. W. Turner, *The Pattern of Christian Truth: A Study in the Relations between Orthodoxy and Heresy in the Early Church* [1954], 172). Mark was never widely popular in the early church, and is mostly incorporated into Luke. That Marcion's *Gospel* was an adaptation of one of the church's Gospels shows the prestige they were already beginning to enjoy even at this early period. (See R. M. Grant, "Marcion, Gospel of," in *ABD*, 4:516–20.)

Because Marcion's edition of Luke and Paul is quoted extensively by other writers, these citations are an important source for the work of NT textual criticism. See TEXT AND MANUSCRIPTS (NT). The textual variants that have survived in these quotations shed significant light on the transmission of the NT text, and at least some of them have a claim to originality. (See J. J. Clabeaux, *A Lost Edition of the Letters of Paul* [1989]. More generally, G. May and K. Greschat, eds., *Marcion und seine kirchengeschichtliche Wirkung* [2002], which includes several articles in English and an important bibliography.) See also ANTI-MARCIONITE PROLOGUES; MARCIONITE PROLOGUES TO PAUL. R. McL. WILSON

Marcionite Prologues to Paul mahr´shuh-nit. The earliest MSS of the VULGATE, as well as some Old Latin MSS, include brief introductions (no longer than three sentences) to the letters of PAUL. These prologues are already attested in the 4th-cent. commentaries of Marius Victorinus. The origin of this material is shrouded in controversy, but many believe that it was produced by a Marcionite community because some of the comments imply an order for the Pauline letters that corresponds to the edition of the NT prepared by MARCION. Moreover, the material includes an emphasis on Paul as the true apostle that is consonant with Marcionite concerns. The evidence is ambiguous, however, and apparently the orthodox church was not aware that the prologues had a heretical origin. (See *ABD*, 4:520–21.)

Marcus mahr´kuhs. KJV alternate form of *Mark*. See MARK, JOHN.

Marcus Aurelius mahr´kuhs aw-reel´yuhs. Roman emperor from A.D. 161 until his death in 180.

Born in 121 (and originally named Marcus Annius Verus), he was adopted in 138 by Antoninus Pius (emperor 138–161). Marcus Aurelius was made consul at the age of nineteen, and sometime during his twenties he became a committed STOIC. Upon the death of Pius, he was named emperor and took the name Antoninus. (His adoptive brother, Lucius Verus, shared the throne until the latter's death in 169.) The empire enjoyed a period of internal peace and prosperity during the rule of Marcus Aurelius, but much of his time was spent fending off the PARTHIANS and various Germanic tribes. Although he viewed Christians as a danger to the state and persecuted them, his administration was generally marked by leniency and benevolence. Marcus Aurelius is best known for his *Meditations*, an assortment of philosophical and religious reflections published after his death. This work, second only to the *Discourses* of EPICTETUS in importance, has proven to be a strikingly popular expression of Stoic thought. (See A. R. Birley, *Marcus Aurelius: A Biography*, rev. ed. [1988]; P. Hadot, *The Inner Citadel: The Meditations of Marcus Aurelius* [1998]; M. Morford, *The Roman Philosophers: From the Time of Cato the Censor to the Death of Marcus Aurelius* [2002].)

Mardocheus mahr′duh-kee′uhs. KJV Apoc. form of MORDECAI (Add. Esth. 11:2 et al.).

Marduk mahr′dyook (מַרְדֻּךְ H5281, from Akk. *Mar(u)duk*). A Babylonian deity (Jer. 50:2; KJV and other versions, MERODACH; cf. also the personal names EVIL-MERODACH, MERODACH-BALADAN, MORDECAI). Already known in SUMER in the 3rd millennium B.C., Marduk became chief god of the Babylonian pantheon at the time of HAMMURABI. To him were transferred the functions and exploits of the storm-god and creator ENLIL. His principal temple was the Esagila ("the house that lifts up its head") in BABYLON. In the myth and ritual of the Babylonian New Year Festival each spring, his victory as champion of the gods was celebrated. Marduk was given the title BEL ("Lord") and eventually became known primarily by that name (cf. Isa. 46:1; Jer. 50:2; 51:44). (See E. Dhorme, *Les religions de Babylonie et d'Assyrie* [1945], 139–50; W. Sommerfield, *Der Aufstieg Marduks* [1982]; *ABD*, 4:522–23; *DDD*, 543–49.) L. WALKER

Marduk-Baladan mahr′dyook-bal′uh-duhn. TNIV form of MERODACH-BALADAN.

Mareal may′ree-uhl. See MARALAH.

Mareshah (person) muh-ree′shuh (מָרֵשָׁה H5359, possibly "head place"). **(1)** Son of Mesha (or of Ziph), grandson (or great-grandson) of CALEB, and father of Hebron (1 Chr. 2:42 NIV). The MT appears to have suffered scribal corruption, and it is possible that "Mesha" in the first part of the verse should be "Mareshah" also (so LXX), in which case Mareshah would be the firstborn of Caleb and the father of Ziph (cf. NRSV mg.). See HEBRON (PERSON) #2.

(2) Son of LAADAH and descendant of JUDAH (1 Chr. 4:21). However, in the phrase "Laadah the father of Mareshah," *father* could mean "founder" or "civic head," in which case the reference would be to MARESHAH (PLACE).

Mareshah (place) muh-ree′shuh (מָרֵשָׁה H5358 [מראשה in Josh. 15:44], "head place, summit"). A town in the SHEPHELAH of JUDAH, in the same district as LIBNAH (Josh. 15:44). Mareshah is identified with modern Tell Sandaḥannah, about 3 mi. NE of LACHISCH. The town was strengthened by REHOBOAM in the early 9th cent. B.C. (2 Chr. 11:8). ASA met a threateningly large Ethiopian army under ZERAH nearby in the Valley of ZEPHATHAH. Victorious by divine aid, Asa drove the enemy back to GERAR, 30 mi. SW of Mareshah (2 Chr. 14:9–15).

The Royal Inscription of Esarhaddon (680–669 B.C.), which describes his rebuilding of the temple of Marduk in Babylon.

General overview of the ruins at Mareshah.

A prophet from Mareshah, Eliezer son of Dodavahu, foretold the failure of Jehoshaphat's naval expedition bound for Tarshish, because of the unholy alliance with Ahaziah of Israel (2 Chr. 20:35–37). In a play on words, Micah speaks of a conqueror (*yōrēš*) who will be brought against Mareshah (Mic. 1:15). During the exile, the Edomites infiltrated S Judah, and Mareshah — thereafter commonly known as Marisa — became a capital city. Beginning early in the 3rd cent. B.C., the place was successively occupied by the Seleucids (Syrians), the Ptolemies (Egyptians), and again by the Seleucids. About 250 B.C. a Sidonian colony under Apollophanes settled in Marisa, which archaeological discoveries confirm.

Even under Egyptian rule, the Sidonians began to use Greek names instead of Phoenician. Excavations reveal a Grecian style city, with right angle streets and a number of houses in regular blocks. The place was the center of Idumean slave trade in the 3rd cent. B.C. (see Idumea). In Maccabean times, Marisa retained its importance. It is mentioned in connection with Judas Maccabee (1 Macc. 5:66; KJV, "Samaria"). Gorgias, governor of Idumea, took refuge there in 164 B.C. (2 Macc. 12:35). About the year 110, John Hyrcanus apparently subdued the city, circumcising such Idumeans as chose to remain (Jos. *Ant.* 13.9.1; see Hasmonean II.A). In 63 B.C., Pompey recovered Marisa for the Idumeans; and c. 57 B.C., Gabinius, Roman governor of Syria, rebuilt its fortifications. Caesar's rule brought the city into Judah's bounds, and in 47 B.C. he appointed Hyrcanus as high priest, and Antipater as procurator (*Ant.* 14.5.4; 14.8.5; 14.10.3–6). Later, Antipater's son, Herod, fled to Marisa escaping from Antigonus and allies (*Ant.* 14.13.9). In 40 B.C. the place was destroyed and never rebuilt. Eleutheropolis, about two Roman miles away, became the important regional city. (See *ABD*, 4:523–25; *NEAEHL*, 3:948–57.)

R. F. Gribble

Mari mah′ree. An important ancient city of western Mesopotamia; excavations at Mari have yielded many significant discoveries.

I. Location. The city of Mari was situated c. 7 mi. NW of modern Abu-Kemal at Tell Hariri. Its importance and its prosperity were due to its strategic location at the intersection of two caravan roads: one beginning on the Mediterranean coast and passing across the Syrian desert to the Euphrates, and the other beginning in N Mesopotamia and passing southward through the valleys of the Khabur and Euphrates Rivers. This strategic location is reflected not only in the fabulous wealth of the city but also in the truly international character of its population, including cultured Babylonians, Assyrians, W Semites from the kingdom of Yamkhad-Aleppo, Hurrians, and seminomadic Khaneans, Suteans, and Benjaminites. It was the center of an important AMORITE kingdom c. 1800–1700 B.C. and preserves in the personal names of many of its citizens at that time an important part of the documentation for the little known Amorite language. See ASSYRIA AND BABYLONIA.

II. Excavations. Between 1933 and 1939 six seasons of excavations took place at Tell Hariri under the auspices of the Louvre Museum and directed by André Parrot. The Second World War interrupted the excavations until 1951, when work was resumed. Four further campaigns were undertaken until 1956, when work was discontinued again as a consequence of the Suez incident. The chief buildings were: (1) a temple dedicated to the goddess ISHTAR, (2) a ZIGGURAT or stage-tower, and (3) a 300-room palace at the center of the mound and dating to the period of the 1st dynasty of Babylon (c. 1850–1750 B.C.). New campaigns were directed by J. Margueron from 1979 to 1985, focusing on the city itself and its integration with the region as a whole (see the latter's reports in the journal *Mari: Annales de recherches interdisciplinaires*, beginning with vol. 1, 1982).

In the palace area the excavators found c. 20,000 cuneiform tablets, most of which date from the reigns of Yasmakh-Adad (c. 1796–1780), under whose reign the palace was begun, and Zimri-Lim (c. 1779–1761), under whom it was finished. Both of these kings were contemporaries of HAMMURABI of Babylon (c. 1792–1750). With the exception of a few religious texts composed in HURRIAN, the documents were written in Akkadian (see LANGUAGES OF THE ANE II.A).

Several rooms contained chiefly texts of an economic, administrative, or judicial nature, while others contained the royal correspondence. King Yasmakh-Adad corresponded with his father, King Shamshi-Adad I of Assyria (c. 1814–1782), with his brother, King Ishme-Dagan I (1781–1742), and with several of his officials (Tarīm-shakin, Hasidān, Ishar-Līm, Il-asu, and Yawi-Ila). He also corresponded with other kings, including Hammurabi of Babylon and Ishkhi-Aadad of Qatna. King Zimri-Lim's correspondence was with King Hammurabi of Babylon, King Yarīm-Līm of Aleppo, and other royal personages. Among his officials he corresponded with Kibri-Dagan, governor of Terqa; Bakhdi-Lim, prefect of the palace of Mari; Mukannishum; Yasīm-Sumu; and Shunukh-rakhalu.

Several letters addressed to King Zimri-Lim concern prophetic utterances pronounced in the name of Adad or Dagan. These are instructive in their similarities and differences with biblical prophecy.

III. History. The earliest known example of a king claiming to have conquered Mari is Eannatum of LAGASH (c. 2500 B.C.). Around 2350 Sargon the Great of AKKAD made the same claim. During the 3rd dynasty of UR (c. 2113–2006) Mari was ruled by governors (*šakkanakkū*) of the kings of Ur. But c. 2017 Ishbi-Erra, who hailed from Mari and was an official of Ibbi-Sin, king of Ur (c. 2029–2006), seized control of the city of Isin, when it was cut off from Ur by rampaging Amorites. When Ur fell in 2006, Ishbi-Erra of Isin and Naplanum of Larsa became the leading powers in Babylonia.

Some time later Yakhdun-Lim, king of Khana (c. 1830–1800), conquered the city of Mari and incorporated it in his realm. But not long thereafter he was defeated by King Shamshi-Adad I of Assyria (c. 1814–1782). In c. 1800 Yakhdun-Lim lost his life in a palace revolution perhaps instigated by Shamshi-Adad, and his son Zimri-Lim fled

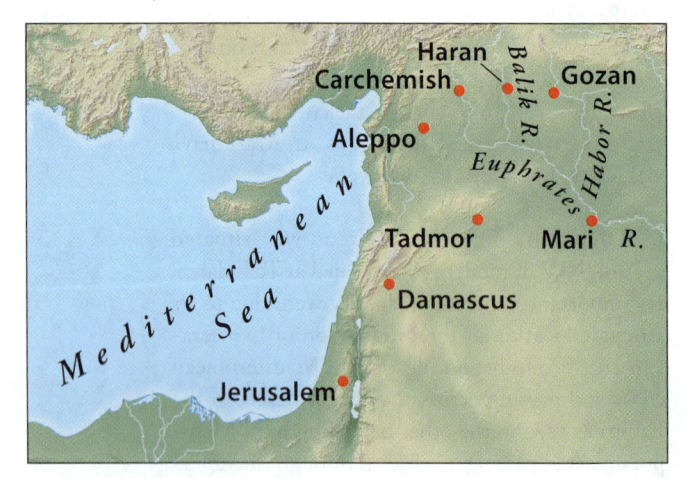

Mari on the Euphrates River.

to Syria. Four years later Shamshi-Adad installed his son Yasmakh-Adad as vice-king of Mari (c. 1796–1780). When Shamshi-Adad died (1782), Zimri-Lim secured the assistance of Ibal-pi-El II of Eshnunna (c. 1790–1761) and the king of Aleppo to drive Yasmakh-Adad from the throne of Mari. After an independent rule of nineteen years (c. 1779–1761), Zimri-Lim was reduced to the status of a vassal king or governor of the city, when Hammurabi of Babylon conquered Mari in 1761. As a vassal of Hammurabi, Zimri-Lim continued to rule Mari until the Kassites destroyed the city in 1742.

IV. Mari's contribution to OT studies. From a linguistic point of view the Mari texts have aided OT study in the wealth of Amorite personal names, many of which resemble those in the Hebrew Bible. Also of interest to OT students are the so-called "Yahweh names" of Mari. These names (Yawi-Addu and Yawi-El) are not only reminiscent of OT personal names like Joel (= Yawi-El), but have raised the question of whether Yawi was a divine name at Mari. Opinions differ, but it seems unlikely in view of the fact that the word Yawi never occurs with the determinative for deity (i.e., ᴰYawi). More likely *yawi* is a verb telling what the gods Addu and El had done or were expected to do. The OT name of Israel's God, Yahweh, may indeed contain that same verb as a description of the unnamed God (cf. Exod. 3:14; see GOD, NAMES OF).

A second contribution to OT study afforded by the Mari texts lies in the description of the customs of the nomadic peoples surrounding Mari (Khaneans, Suteans, and Benjaminites). The latter in particular have been suspected as relatives of the OT tribe of BENJAMIN, although it is not even clear that the Mari name DUMU.MEŠ *Ya-mi-na* is to be read as *banū Yamina*, which would seem to be a necessary first postulate in any such theory. But whether or not the DUMU.MEŠ *Yamina* are "Benjaminites," the customs held by all these nomadic groups provide interesting insights into certain OT practices of the Israelites.

(The texts have been published in the series *Archives royales de Mari: Transcription et traduction des textes cunéiformes* [1950ff.]. See further A. Parrot, ed., *Studia Mariana* [1950]; M. Noth, *Mari und Israel* [1953]; Georges Roux, *Ancient Iraq* [1964], 164–77, 189–201; G. E. Mendenhall in *The Biblical Archaeologist Reader*, 2 [1964], 3–20; A. Parrot, *Mari, capital fabuleuse* [1974]; J. Margueron, *Recherches sur les palais mésopotamiens de l'Age du Bronze*, 2 vols. [1982]; A. Malamat, *Mari and the Early Israelite Experience* [1989]; M. Anbar, *Les tribus amurrites de Mari* [1991]; G. D. Young, ed., *Mari in Retrospect: Fifty Years of Mari and Mari Studies* [1992]; A. Malamat, *Mari and the Bible* [1998]; D. E. Fleming, *Democracy's Ancient Ancestors: Mari and Early Collective Governance* [2004]; J.-C. Margueron, *Mari, métropole de l'Euphrate au IIIe et au début du IIe millénaire av. J.-C.* [2004]; *ABD*, 4:525–38.) H. A. HOFFNER, JR.

Mariamme (Μαριάμμη, from מִרְיָם *H5319*; see MIRIAM). Traditionally spelled Mariamne. A HASMONEAN princess, famous for her beauty (Jos. *Ant.* 15.2.5 §23), who became the second wife of HEROD the Great. This marriage strengthened the position of Herod (a foreigner from IDUMEA) as ruler of the Jews. Mariamme bore him four children, but she was accused of unfaithfulness, and Herod, who was exceedingly jealous, had her executed (*Ant.* 15.2.9 §§81–87; 15.7.5 §§232–36). The name Mariamme was borne by another wife of Herod the Great, by Herod's son Archelaus, and by others in the Herodian family.

Marimoth mair´i-moth. KJV Apoc. form of MERAIOTH (2 Esd. 1:2).

mariner. See SAILOR.

Marisa mahr´uh-suh. Greek form of MARESHAH (1 Macc. 5:66 [KJV follows the variant "Samaria"]; 2 Macc. 12:35).

mark. This English noun is used variously to translate a number of Hebrew and Greek words in the Bible. For example, Hebrew *ʾôt H253* (more frequently translated SIGN) occurs with reference to the mark that God placed "on Cain so that no one who found him would kill him" (Gen. 4:15; the nature of the sign is not known). Similarly the noun *tāw H9338* (also the name of the last letter of the Heb. ALPHABET, which in the earlier script looked like an X) can refer to a mark placed on the forehead (Ezek.

9:4 [used with the cognate verb *tāwâ H9344*], 6). In the NT, the KJV uses "mark" to render Greek *skopos G5024* ("that which one looks or aims at," thus "end, goal") in the well-known passage where Paul compares the Christian life to a race and says that he presses toward the goal (Phil. 3:14). Paul uses a different term, *stigma G5116*, when he refers to the scars he bears in his body as a result of his suffering for the sake of Jesus (Gal. 6:17). When the book of Revelation speaks of the "mark of the beast" (Rev. 16:2 et al.), which the Antichrist will require of all people during his reign of terror in the tribulation period, the term used is *charagma G5916* (from *charassō*, "to cut, engrave, inscribe").

Mark, Gospel of. The second account of the gospel of Jesus Christ, according to the present common order of listing in the NT canon. See also Mark, John.

    I. Background
        A. Geographical
        B. Historical
        C. Religious
    II. Unity
    III. Authorship
        A. External evidence
        B. Internal evidence
        C. The author
    IV. Date
        A. Traditional view
        B. Today's view
    V. Place of origin
    VI. Destination
    VII. Occasion
    VIII. Purpose
    IX. Canonicity
        A. Second century
        B. Third century
        C. Fourth century
    X. Text
    XI. Special problems
    XII. Content
        A. The period of preparation
        B. The Galilean ministry
        C. The Perean ministry
        D. The Judean ministry
        E. The passion narrative
        F. The resurrection
    XIII. Theology
        A. Christology
        B. Soteriology

I. Background

A. Geographical. The geographical setting of Mark's gospel is mainly the Palestine of Jesus' day. Palestine proper, between the Mediterranean Sea (Great Sea) and the Jordan Valley, consisted of Galilee in the N, Samaria in the center, Judea in the S, and Idumea below this. On the other side of the Jordan, E of Judea, was Perea; N and E of Perea was the Decapolis ("Ten Cities"); W and N of Galilee was Phoenicia (modern Lebanon), with its two main cities of Tyre and Sidon.

B. Historical. Practically all of Mark's gospel relates to the public ministry of Jesus. During this period Galilee and Perea were ruled by Herod Antipas, son of Herod the Great (see Herod V). Judea, Samaria, and Idumea were governed by the Roman procurator (or prefect) Pontius Pilate, who had been directly commissioned by the Emperor Tiberius.

Roman domination of Palestine had begun in 63 B.C., when Pompey took Jerusalem, by which time the Jews were accustomed to paying taxes to their foreign rulers. These taxes were somewhat oppressive. Everything, it seemed, was taxed — animals, fruit trees, homes, whatever a man owned. This is one reason the tax collectors (called "publicans" in the KJV) were hated by their fellow Jews. They symbolized foreign oppression, and their business contacts with Gentiles rendered them ceremonially unclean. They were despised and ostracized by the pious "people of God."

C. Religious

1. The synagogue. Solomon's temple was destroyed in 586 B.C. The Jewish captives in Babylonia would naturally wish to assemble for worship and the reading of their sacred Scriptures. Probably the earliest beginnings of the synagogue are to be found at this time, but the wide spread of this new institution seems to have taken place in the Persian period, as a result of Ezra's work.

By the time of Christ the number of synagogues had multiplied greatly. According to rabbinic tradition there were 480 of them in Jerusalem when the temple was destroyed in A.D. 70. Many of them were built for the convenience of Jewish pilgrims coming from various foreign countries. On the hill OPHEL (the SE ridge of Jerusalem), an inscription was found that describes such a place. It reads thus: "Theodotus, son of Vetenus, priest and synagogue ruler, grandson of a synagogue ruler, built the synagogue for the reading of the Law and for the teaching of the commandments, and the guest house and the rooms and supplies of water as an inn for those who are in need when coming from abroad, which synagogue his fathers and the elders and Simonides founded."

Wherever there were ten adult male Jews in a town or village, a synagogue was to be established. Since the Jews were widely scattered over the Mediterranean world and the Mesopotamian region after the Babylonian conquest of Jerusalem, synagogues were found almost everywhere. (In the book of Acts are mentioned two cities apparently without synagogues—LYSTRA and PHILIPPI.) The synagogues were centers of education as well as places of worship. The public reading and expounding of the law was the leading function that took place.

2. The Sabbath. The main feature that outwardly distinguished Jews from all others was their observance of the SABBATH day. This lasted from sunset Friday night until sunset Saturday. During this time no work was to be done. No devout Jew was permitted to walk more than the "Sabbath day's walk" (Acts 1:12), which was about half a mile. Sabbath observance was one of the crucial issues that the Pharisees raised with Jesus.

3. The sects. There were three main religious sects in the JUDAISM of Jesus' day. The dominant one was the PHARISEES, mentioned a hundred times in the NT. The SADDUCEES were second in importance, named fourteen times. The third sect, that of the ESSENES, is not mentioned at all. In general it may be said that the Sadducees held control of the temple worship and the Pharisees oversaw the teaching in the synagogues, while the Essenes preferred to live in secluded groups.

The Pharisees were the men who came into most frequent conflict with Jesus. Many of them gave undue emphasis to minute rules and regulations governing the everyday life of the people. They stressed the importance of almsgiving, fasting, and public prayers. They also emphasized strict separation from all UNCLEANNESS, including unclean people. The latter would embrace not only Gentiles but also Jews who failed to observe the law meticulously. Jesus called them hypocrites because much of this was done for outward show, whereas he emphasized the inner attitude. Of course, not all the Pharisees were hypocrites. Many were sincerely pious. But Jesus charged many of them with inconsistency and insincerity.

The Pharisees accepted the whole of the OT as their sacred Scriptures. In addition, they gave great authority to "the tradition of the elders." These were rabbinical interpretations and applications of the Mosaic law. They covered every aspect of the daily life of the people. Jesus accused the Pharisees of making the TRADITION of the elders more binding than the law that God gave to Moses (Mk. 7:9–13).

The Sadducees came into direct conflict with Jesus only near the close of his ministry. When he cleansed the temple he threatened their prestige as well as their pocketbooks. Actually it was a clash of authority. So in the last hours before Christ was condemned and crucified the Sadducees, particularly the chief priests, led the opposition. They were the ones who agitated the people to demand his death.

This 1st-cent. synagogue at the Herodium functioned like others throughout Israel that served as centers for worship and education.

It is thought that the name Sadducee was derived from ZADOK, a priest in the time of DAVID and SOLOMON. He was thought of as the father of the Jerusalem priesthood. The Sadducees probably arose as a party in Judaism during the Maccabean period (see MACCABEE). They are first mentioned by JOSEPHUS in the days of John Hyrcanus (135–104 B.C.; see HASMONEAN II.A).

Josephus also states that the Sadducees denied the RESURRECTION of the body (cf. Matt. 22:23; Mk. 12:18; Lk. 20:27) as well as all future punishments and rewards. They held that the soul perishes with the body. Acts 23:8 states that they denied the existence of angels and spirits. They also rejected the oral law, or "the tradition of the elders" (Mk. 7:3), giving almost exclusive attention to the TORAH (the Pentateuch). After the destruction of the temple in A.D. 70, the Sadducees largely disappeared.

The Essenes are described by PHILO JUDAEUS, the famous Alexandrian Jew (c. 10 B.C. to c. A.D. 45). Most of the early information about them comes from Josephus (c. A.D. 37–100). In his autobiography (*Life*) he tells how at the age of sixteen he decided to investigate the three main sects of Judaism. After three years in the Judean wilderness, where he may well have visited the Essenes, he returned to Jerusalem and joined the Pharisees. The Essenes, like the Pharisees, were probably successors of the Hasidim (see HASIDEANS). But the Essenes were more ascetic and rigid than the Pharisees.

With the discovery of the DEAD SEA SCROLLS in 1947, the knowledge of the Essenes was greatly broadened. They practiced a communal ownership of property. Celibacy was common, although marriage was evidently permitted. The members of the community were governed by strict rules of conduct. They avoided the temple at Jerusalem as being unclean. The Scriptures were studied daily and especially on the Sabbath. The Essenes had a strong messianic hope.

II. Unity. It is popular today to talk about the sources of the second gospel. But most scholars agree that it comes from the hand of one author. The last twelve verses, as will be noted, were perhaps not a part of the original Gospel of Mark. Aside from those, no serious question is raised as to the unity of the book.

III. Authorship. All four Gospels are anonymous; so the matter of authorship can be established only by careful investigation.

A. External evidence. By external evidence is meant the testimony of early church writings as to who wrote this gospel.

1. Second century. The only certain noncanonical Christian writing from the 1st cent. is Clement of Rome's *First Epistle to the Corinthians* (A.D. 95; see CLEMENT, EPISTLES OF). One of Clement's quotations (*1 Clem.* 46:8) bears a resemblance to Mk. 9:42, but direct quotation cannot be proved. The earliest certain witness to the authorship of Mark's gospel comes from the 2nd cent.

The early church historian EUSEBIUS (A.D. 326) quotes PAPIAS (c. A.D. 140) as saying: "And John the presbyter also said this, Mark being the interpreter of Peter, whatsoever he recorded he wrote with great accuracy, but not, however, in the order in which it was spoken or done by our Lord, but as before said, he was in company with Peter, who gave him such instruction as was necessary, but not to give a history of our Lord's discourse: wherefore Mark has not erred in any thing, by writing some things as he has recorded them; for he was carefully attentive to one thing, not to pass by any thing he had heard, or to state any thing falsely in these accounts" (Euseb. *Eccl. Hist.* 3.39). Six statements are made here by Papias: (1) Mark was the "interpreter" (perhaps, translator) of PETER; (2) he wrote accurately, but not necessarily in chronologi-

Roman coin of the 1st/2nd cent. depicting the running boar, mascot of the Tenth Legion. Mark appears to have written his gospel with a Roman audience in view.

cal order; (3) he was not himself a follower of Jesus; (4) he was a companion of Peter; (5) he has not recorded the discourses of Christ; (6) his account is reliable.

Justin Martyr (c. A.D. 150) quotes Mk. 3:17 as from "Peter's Memoirs." The Anti-Marcionite Prologue to Mark (A.D. 150–180), which comments that Mark was called "stump-fingered" because he had small fingers, says that "he was the interpreter of Peter. After the death of Peter he wrote down this same Gospel in the regions of Italy." Irenaeus (c. A.D. 185), as quoted by Eusebius, says that after the "departure" (death?) of Peter and Paul, "Mark, the disciple and interpreter of Peter, also transmitted to us in writing what had been preached by Peter" (Euseb. *Eccl. Hist.* 5.8).

Clement of Alexandria (c. A.D. 195) has this to say about the origin of the Gospel of Mark: "When Peter had proclaimed the word publicly at Rome, and declared the gospel under the influence of the spirit; as there was a great number present, they requested Mark, who had followed him from afar [for a long time], and remembered well what he had said, to reduce these things to writing, and that after composing the gospel he gave it to those who requested it of him. Which, when Peter understood, he directly neither hindered nor encouraged it" (Euseb. *Eccl. Hist.* 6.14; there are two other similar statements by Clement). Finally, Tertullian (c. A.D. 200), in his book *Against Marcion* (4.5), says that the gospel "which Mark published may be affirmed to be Peter's, whose interpreter Mark was."

2. Third century. It is generally agreed that the greatest Bible scholar in the early church was Origen (d. c. A.D. 254). In his *Commentary on Matthew* he declares that the four Gospels "are the only undisputed ones in the whole church of God throughout the world." After discussing Matthew, he writes: "The second is according to Mark, who composed it as Peter explained to him, whom he also acknowledges as his son in his general Epistle, saying, 'The elect church in Babylon salutes you, as also Mark my son'" (Euseb. *Eccl. Hist.* 6.25).

3. Fourth century. The year after the famous Council of Nicaea (A.D. 325), Eusebius wrote his *Ecclesiastical History*, the most important single sourcebook for the history of the early church. It has an entire chapter on the Gospel according to Mark. Eusebius writes: "So greatly, however, did the splendour of piety enlighten the minds of Peter's hearers, that it was not sufficient to hear but once, nor to receive the unwritten doctrine of the gospel of God, but they persevered in every variety of entreaties, to solicit Mark as the companion of Peter, and whose gospel we have, that he should leave them a monument of the doctrine thus orally communicated in writing. Nor did they cease their solicitations until they had prevailed with the man, and thus became the means of that history which is called the gospel according to Mark. They say also that the apostle (Peter), having ascertained what was done by the revelation of the spirit, was delighted with the zealous ardour expressed by these men, and that the history obtained his authority for the purpose of being read in the churches" (2.15). Eusebius says he learned this from Clement of Alexandria's writings.

Jerome, in his *Commentary on Matthew* (c. A.D. 380), writes: "Second, Mark, the interpreter of the apostle Peter and the first bishop of the church of Alexandria, who himself did not see the Lord the Saviour, but narrated those things which he heard his master preaching, with fidelity to the deeds rather than to their order." It is generally agreed that Jerome is mistaken in saying that Mark was the first bishop of Alexandria. But the rest of his statement agrees with the previous ones we have noted.

In all of these quotations, there is a general agreement on two matters: (1) the second gospel was written by Mark; (2) this gospel gives us the preaching of Peter. The point on which there is some difference of opinion is as to whether Mark wrote his gospel before or after the death of Peter. This affects the date, as will be noted later, but the matter of authorship is unaffected. Vincent Taylor declares: "There can be no doubt that the author of the Gospel was Mark, the attendant of Peter" (*The Gospel according to St. Mark*, 2nd ed. [1966], 26). Other scholars, however, are skeptical of this tradition and emphasize the period of oral transmission that must have preceded the writing of the gospel.

B. Internal evidence. This section deals with what we find in the Gospel of Mark itself. Does it point to Mark as the writer?

1. Petrine characteristics. There is general agreement among the early church fathers that Mark's gospel reproduces the preaching of PETER. When we turn to the gospel, we can find Peter's personality on almost every page. Peter was impulsive, aggressive, active. That is the character of the gospel.

Undoubtedly the main characteristic of Mark's gospel is action. If one examines carefully a harmony of the Synoptic Gospels, it soon becomes clear that Mark has most of the miracles but few of the parables. Long sections of the harmony have parallel columns of material from Matthew and Luke, with nothing from Mark. In such cases the material almost always consists of the sayings of Jesus. Matthew and Luke devote much of their space to Jesus' teachings; Mark majors on action. This is what one would expect if Mark is reproducing the preaching of Peter.

This rapidity of action is highlighted by the frequent use of the Greek word *euthys* G2317, "straightway, immediately, at once" (although it can have the weakened sense of "then," as in Mk. 1:21 et al.). It occurs forty-two times in this short gospel, as against seven times in the much longer Matthew, three times in John, and only once in Luke. In two passages in the Gospel of Mark the word is repeated three times in three consecutive verses. A glance at the first chapter of Mark shows that almost every verse begins with "and." As someone has said, "The narrative almost runs." It might well be suggested that while John in his gospel gives us a studied portrait of Jesus, and Matthew and Luke offer a series of colored slides, Mark gives a moving picture of his public ministry.

Another characteristic is vividness of detail. While Mark's gospel is the shortest, its individual narratives are usually longer than the corresponding accounts in Matthew and Luke, sometimes two or three times as long. This difference is due to the addition of details that add vividness to the narrative. (Some of these will be noted under "Content.") Such style is what one would expect from Peter. He was a man of the out-of-doors and thus more observant than a bookish person.

A third characteristic is picturesqueness of description. Peter might be expected to use colorful words in his preaching, and this is what one finds in Mark's gospel. In connection with the feeding of the 5,000, Mark alone observes that the people reclined on the green grass. The word he uses for "groups" (Mk. 6:40 KJV) literally means "flower beds." Thousands of people in bright-colored oriental garments of red, yellow, and blue seated in groups on the green grass of the hillside—it was a picture photographed on Peter's memory. He probably used this expression in his preaching and Mark has retained it for us in his gospel.

2. Roman characteristics. Perhaps one reason Mark majors on Jesus' activity rather than his teachings is that, according to early church tradition, he was writing at ROME. The Romans glorified action. The Greeks gave primary emphasis to intellectual pursuits, but the Romans sought military conquest.

Mark presents Jesus to the Romans as a man of action. They were not so much concerned about a person's ancestry as with his ability. Mark has no genealogies of Jesus as in Matthew and Luke. Similarly, he omits all reference to Jesus' birth and childhood. With only a brief introduction—John the Baptist's ministry, followed by Jesus' baptism and temptation—he plunges immediately into the public ministry of the Master. In Mark's gospel there are only thirteen verses of introduction, compared with 76 in Matthew and 183 in Luke. The Romans did not ask "Where did he come from?" or "What did he say?" but "What has he done?" That is the question that Mark answers for them regarding Jesus. He presents Christ as the mighty Conqueror over demons, disease, and death. Even the winds and the waves were subject to his "Peace, be still."

In keeping with the tradition that this gospel was written in Rome is the fact that it contains more Latinisms than any other book in the NT. Three of the ten terms of Latin origin that he uses are in his gospel only. He also has some distinct Latin idioms and translates Jewish terms into Roman equivalents (e.g., Mk. 12:42). He explains Jewish customs for his Roman readers. An outstanding example is that of the ceremonial washing before eating (7:3–4).

Artist's rendering of a trammel boat on the Sea of Galilee. Jesus called James and John to ministry from their occupation as fishermen.

Other examples are the beliefs of the Sadducees (12:18) and the custom of fasting (2:18). All these Markan items fit in well with the tradition that he wrote his gospel in Rome.

C. The author. The first mention of Mark (the person) is in Acts 12:12. When Peter was released from prison, he went "to the house of Mary the mother of John, also called Mark, where many had gathered and were praying." This was in Jerusalem, fourteen years after Jesus' death. It is thought by some that this home may have been the place of the LAST SUPPER and of the events on the day of PENTECOST.

When BARNABAS and Saul (PAUL) returned to ANTIOCH OF SYRIA from their "famine visit" to Jerusalem (Acts 11:27–30), they took John along with them (12:25). Here again it is added, "also called Mark." He accompanied the two leaders on their first missionary journey. He is described in KJV as their "minister" (13:5), but the Greek word means "subordinate, attendant, helper." John acted as their assistant, not as their preacher.

But at PERGA in PAMPHYLIA, John Mark turned back to Jerusalem (Acts 13:13). His action was due probably to a combination of homesickness, fear of the dangers in the mountains ahead, and resentment that Paul had become the leader of the party instead of John's relative Barnabas. When they started out it was "Barnabas and Saul" (13:2). When they left CYPRUS it was "Paul and his companions" (13:13). This change of leadership was hard for the young man to take, and he failed. (It is also possible that Paul's leadership marked a change in tactics—going directly to the Gentiles—that disturbed John Mark's Jewish sensibilities.) When Paul suggested a second missionary journey, Barnabas wanted to give John another chance, but Paul refused. The result was that Barnabas took John and returned to Cyprus, where he disappears from the biblical narrative. Paul chose a new associate, SILAS, and went overland to GALATIA (15:36–41).

Fortunately, the story of Mark does not end there. Paul speaks of Mark as his companion in Rome (Col. 4:10; Phlm. 24). And finally in 2 Tim. 4:11 the apostle pays high tribute to Mark's service. He also is mentioned by Peter as "my son Mark" (1 Pet. 5:13). John was his Jewish name, Mark his Roman name. See further MARK, JOHN.

IV. Date. There is wide agreement today that Mark is the earliest of the four Gospels. When was it written?

A. Traditional view. Adolph Harnack, in *The Date of the Acts and the Synoptic Gospels* (1911), presents the classical argument for dating Mark in the 50s. It starts with the date of Acts, which closes with Paul's two years' imprisonment in Rome (A.D. 59–61 or 60–62). Since the story stops at this point, the natural deduction is that the book of Acts was completed at this time (c. A.D. 62; see ACTS OF THE APOSTLES). Unquestionably Luke's gospel is "the former treatise" (Acts 1:1), and so it must have been written about A.D. 60 (see LUKE, GOSPEL OF). Presumably Matthew appeared in the same general period of time (see MATTHEW, GOSPEL OF). According to the commonly held two-document theory, both Matthew and Luke made

At times, the Romans would crucify their victims by hanging them on a tree.

use of Mark as a historical source. If so, then this shortest of the Gospels must have been written in the 50s. (For the view that Matthew's gospel was written first, see W. R. Farmer, *The Synoptic Problem* [1964]). See also GOSPELS.

B. Today's view. It already has been noted that there is a discrepancy at one point in the witness of the early church fathers to Mark's gospel. Some say it was written before Peter's death, others after his death. Today a majority of NT scholars agree in dating the Gospel of Mark c. A.D. 65–70. Matthew and Luke are placed ten or twenty years later. For Mark's gospel, D. A. Hayes says: "Some time between A.D. 60 and 70 it is possible that the work was begun and revised and completed" (*The Synoptic Gospels and the Book of Acts* [1919], 123). Donald Guthrie writes: "It is not in fact impossible to regard both Clement and Irenaeus as correct, if Mark began his Gospel before and completed it after Peter's death; a suggestion which merits more consideration than it generally receives." He goes on to say: "Another possibility is that Irenaeus was not referring to Peter's death at all, but to his departure from the place where Mark was.... In this case it would also be possible to accept the statements of both Irenaeus and Clement, and this solution seems the more preferable" (*New Testament Introduction: Gospels and Acts* [1961], 69; differently in the revised one-vol. ed. [1990], 85). That is, Mark wrote his gospel after Peter's departure from the city but before Peter's death. This would be in the 50s or early 60s. (For an even earlier date, see J. G. Crossley, *The Date of Mark's Gospel: Insights from the Law in Earliest Christianity* [2004].)

The dating of the Gospels is not a matter of primary importance. The earlier the dates, of course, the nearer the Gospels come to the actual time of Jesus' earthly ministry. It should be remembered, however, that most conservative scholars agree in dating John's gospel about A.D. 85–95. The essential factor is the recognition of the divine INSPIRATION of these accounts of Jesus' life and ministry. Since they were written by men, it is our responsibility to investigate as carefully as possible the details of their human origin. It is obvious that the early church was interested in this matter, and so should we be. (For the view that Mark is a redaction of a "secret" gospel, see MARK, SECRET GOSPEL OF.)

V. Place of origin. The majority voice of the early church says that Mark wrote his gospel in Rome. The character of the book fits well with this tradition. CHRYSOSTOM does say that Mark's gospel was written in Egypt, but few modern scholars have accepted this suggestion. J. V. Bartlet (*St. Mark*, NCB [1922], 35–38) even suggested Antioch, but his arguments do not seem convincing. Rome still holds the field.

VI. Destination. Mark's gospel clearly was intended for Gentile readers. Not only does the author explain Jewish customs and use a high number of Latinisms, but he also translates the numerous ARAMAIC terms he uses (cf. Mk. 3:17; 5:41; 7:11, 34; 10:46; 14:36; 15:22, 34). These Aramaic words give a primitive touch to this gospel and lend some weight to the idea of an early date. One cannot be certain of a definite locality for the destination of Mark's gospel, but it can be safely assumed that it was written for Gentiles, not Jews.

VII. Occasion. It is obvious that the matter of the occasion for the writing of Mark's gospel cannot be settled dogmatically as long as there is uncertainty as to whether Mark wrote before or after Peter's death. In either case the occasion was probably the desire of the Christians to have the substance of Peter's preaching in written form.

VIII. Purpose. The first verse of this gospel indicates its purpose: to give the good news about Jesus Christ, the Son of God. It has been increasingly recognized in recent scholarship that Mark has a theological purpose. This does not in any way call in question the historicity of the narrative. It simply means that the author had in mind a definite doctrinal aim. He is writing history. At the same time he is writing more than history; his gospel has a strong theological thrust. It was written to proclaim the fact that Jesus Christ is Son of God and Savior. So Mark's main purpose was evangelistic, as is true of the other Gospels.

IX. Canonicity. By canonicity is meant acceptance by the church at large. This judgment was finally expressed officially in its councils.

A. Second century. In 1740 L. A. Muratori discovered and published a descriptive list of books of the NT recognized in Rome near the end of the 2nd cent. (A.D. 170–190). The list was in a badly mutilated MS from the 7th or 8th cent., kept in the Ambrosian Library at Milan. Unfortunately, the first part is broken off, so that it often is referred to as the Muratorian Fragment (see MURATORIAN CANON). The opening incomplete sentence reads: "… at which, however, he was present, and so set them down." Since the document goes on to say: "The third of the Gospel (according to Luke) …" and then next discusses John's gospel, there seems to be no reasonable doubt that the first two books discussed were the Gospels of Matthew and Mark. This constitutes evidence that these four Gospels were all accepted in Rome at the end of the 2nd cent. This is corroborated by quotations from Justin Martyr and Irenaeus.

B. Third century. By the end of the 2nd cent. and beginning of the 3rd it is obvious that Mark's gospel was accepted throughout Christendom. We have testimonies, given above, from North Africa, Egypt, and Italy to this effect. It was given apostolic authority as representing the preaching of Peter.

C. Fourth century. When Athanasius sent out his Easter Letter in 367, he listed exactly the twenty-seven books of the NT as sacred Scripture to be read in the churches of his diocese. In 397 the Council of Carthage made this official. From that time until the Reformation the canon of the NT was settled and stable. Mark was included. See further CANON (NT).

X. Text. The main textual problem relating to Mark's gospel concerns the last twelve verses (Mk. 16:9–20). These—called the Long Ending—are not found in the two oldest Greek uncial MSS, CODEX VATICANUS and CODEX SINAITICUS, from the 4th cent. They also are omitted in one of the oldest versions, the Sinaitic Syriac, as well as most of the Armenian MSS. Clement of Alexandria and Origen evidently had no knowledge of these verses. See TEXT AND MANUSCRIPTS (NT).

Several uncial MSS of the 7th, 8th, and 9th centuries have an alternative, shorter ending. It is found also in a few minuscules and several ancient versions. It reads: "But they reported briefly to Peter and those with him all that they had been told. And after this Jesus himself sent out by means of them, from east to west, the sacred and imperishable proclamation of eternal salvation." Anyone familiar with the early church will easily recognize that this reading is not genuine. Its last sentence is simply not in the language of the 1st cent. Several MSS have both the Long and the Short Ending. This fact militates somewhat against the genuineness of either one.

The prize MS in the United States (Washingtonensis or W, 5th cent.) has a long insertion after Mk. 16:14 in the Long Ending. It reads: "And they excused themselves, saying, 'This age of lawlessness and unbelief is under Satan, who does not allow the truth and power of God to prevail over the unclean things of the spirit. Therefore reveal thy righteousness now'—thus they spoke to Christ. And Christ replied to them, 'The term of years for Satan's power has been fulfilled, but other terrible things draw near. And for those who have sinned I was delivered over to death, that they may return to the truth and sin no more, that they may inherit the spiritual and imperishable glory of righteousness that is in heaven'" (see B. M. Metzger and B. D. Ehrman, *The Text of the New Testament: Its Transmission, Corruption, and Restoration*, 4th ed. [2005], 81). It hardly needs to be said that this is spurious. Its language clearly condemns it.

Regarding the last twelve verses found in the KJV, H. B. Swete writes: "As to the origin of this ending there can be little doubt. It has been written by some one whose copy of the Gospel ended at *ephobounto gar* ["for they were afraid"], and who desired to soften the harshness of so abrupt a conclusion, and at the same time to remove the impression which it leaves of a failure on the part of Mary of Magdala and her friends to deliver the message with which they had been charged" (*The Gospel according to St. Mark*, 2nd ed. [1902], cviii).

Two other factors argue against the genuineness of this Long Ending. One is that the language of the original does not fit Mark very well. The other is a somewhat awkward connection between Mk. 16:8 and 9. Guthrie (*New Testament Introduction*, 73) notes that vv. 9–20 "seem to be composed from material drawn from the other three Gospels," and so "this ending wears the appearance of compilation distinct from the rest of the Gospel." His conclusion is: "It would seem that the only course open is to admit that we do not know the original ending" (ibid., 74).

Another textual issue that has raised considerable interest is the claim by the Spanish Jesuit scholar and papyrologist, José O'Callaghan, that several NT fragments, including one that contains part (seventeen letters) of Mk. 6:52–53, were discovered among the DEAD SEA SCROLLS of Qumran Cave 7 (for the first account of his findings, see *Bib* 53 [1972]: 91–100). Although this claim has been strongly supported by a few (notably C. P. Thiede, *The Earliest Gospel Manuscript? The Qumran Papyrus 7Q5 and Its Significance for New Testament Studies* [1992]), scholarly reaction has been largely negative (cf. B. M. Metzger, *The Text of the New Testament*, 3rd ed. [1992], 264–65; for a strong rejection based on microscopic analysis, see R. H. Gundry in *JBL* 118 [1999]: 698–707). About half of the letters cannot be read with certainty, and the identification rests on two or three assumptions that, while possible, are debatable. (On textual issues more generally, see now H. Greeven and E. Güting, *Textkritik des Markusevangeliums* [2005].)

XI. Special problems. Aside from the matter of the ending of Mark, there are not many crucial problems connected with this book. One point that has been raised is this: If Mark is giving us Peter's preaching, why does he omit three striking incidents about this disciple that are narrated in Matthew's gospel? These are Peter's walking on the water (Matt. 14:28–33), the paying of the temple tax (17:24–27), and the statement about the keys to the kingdom of heaven (16:19). These omissions may reasonably be explained as due to modesty on Peter's part. In his preaching he was concerned to exalt Christ, not himself. It is worth noting that in Mark's gospel Peter is never mentioned alone except in connection with his being rebuked by Jesus. This is the kind of humility that one would expect to find in Peter after Pentecost.

The incident of the young man in GETHSEMANE has caused considerable comment. Mark records: "A young man, wearing nothing but a linen garment, was following Jesus. When they seized him, he fled naked, leaving his garment behind" (Mk. 14:51–52). This little item seems like a senseless intrusion into the account of Jesus' agony and arrest in the garden. The only logical deduction would seem to be that the young man was John Mark himself. This is his modest way of saying, "I was there." A. E. J. Rawlinson (*St. Mark* [1925], 215) says: "The story certainly reads like a personal reminiscence."

It is not difficult to make a possible reconstruction of what happened that night. If the Last Supper took place in the home of John Mark's mother, one may assume that JUDAS ISCARIOT, who had left the table early, would lead the mob back there to arrest Jesus. When he arrived he discovered that the Master and his disciples had already left, so he went on to the MOUNT OF OLIVES to find him. Wakened by the noise and seeing the torches and weapons, young John Mark could easily sense the situation. He hastily threw a linen cloth around himself and hastened out into the night to warn Jesus. By the time he arrived at the garden the soldiers were already there, and he himself was almost arrested.

XII. Content. The Gospel of Mark may be divided into six main sections:

    A. The period of preparation (Mk. 1:1–13)
    B. The Galilean ministry (1:14—9:50)
    C. The Perean ministry (10:1–52)
    D. The Judean ministry (11:1—13:37)
    E. The passion narrative (14:1—15:47)
    F. The resurrection (16:1–20)

A. The period of preparation (Mk. 1:1–13). The first verse of this book seems to be a sort of title: "The beginning of the gospel of Jesus Christ, the Son of God" (1:1 KJV). Many of the early church fathers took this to be a heading for the ministry of JOHN THE BAPTIST, which in turn was viewed as the beginning point in the gospel story. Modern scholars, however, usually think of it as a title to the entire gospel. The "beginning of the gospel" is the ministry of Jesus, including his death and resurrection.

The word GOSPEL means "good news." It was not used for a book of the NT until the time of JUSTIN MARTYR, in the middle of the 2nd cent. In the 1st cent. it meant the oral message of SALVATION through Jesus Christ. The earliest Greek MSS label this book simply *Kata Markon*, "According to Mark." The early church spoke of *one* gospel, narrated "according to" Matthew, Mark, Luke, and John. The phrase, "the gospel of Jesus Christ," probably means "the good news about Jesus Christ" (objective genitive; cf. NIV) rather than the good news preached by Jesus (subjective genitive). This understanding fits the character of this gospel, which gives a minimum of the teachings of Christ, but rather portrays his redemptive ministry. The last phrase, "the Son of God," is omitted in some MSS, but most modern scholars accept it as genuine. It fits in with Mark's consistent emphasis on the DEITY OF CHRIST as demonstrated in his ministry. The good news is not about a mere man—his human birth is not mentioned in this gospel—but about the Son of God who became the Savior.

Mark's account of the ministry of John the Baptist (Mk. 1:2–8) is briefer than Matthew's or Luke's. He does not tell of John's discussion with various groups. Peter's forceful personality is probably reflected in the stronger terms that Mark uses, as compared with Matthew and Luke. A case in point is his description of the heavens being "torn open" at the time of Jesus' baptism (1:10). The term here is *schizō G5387*; Matthew and Luke use the weaker verb *anoigō G487*, "open." The temptation of Jesus is recorded in two short verses by Mark (1:12–13), whereas Matthew and Luke spell out the three specific attacks of "the devil" (Mark prefers "Satan"). Even in this brief account Mark adds the graphic detail: "He was with the wild animals." And again he uses a stronger term than Matthew and Luke: "And immediately the Spirit driveth him into the wilderness" (KJV). The Greek verb here (*ekballei*, pres. of *ekballō G1675*) also illustrates Mark's fondness for the historic present to add vividness to the narrative—probably reflecting Peter's frequent use of it in his preaching. There are 151 historic presents in Mark's gospel; Matthew retains only 21 of these.

B. The Galilean ministry (Mk. 1:14—9:50). Matthew and Mark agree that Jesus began his great Galilean ministry after the arrest and imprisonment of John the Baptist (Matt. 4:12; Mk. 1:14). They also indicate that Christ's opening message was, "Repent, for the kingdom of heaven [God] is near" (Matt. 4:17; cf. Mk. 1:15)—an echo of John the Baptist's preaching.

The call of the first four disciples is recorded similarly in Matthew and Mark. Typically the latter adds a slight touch. He says that JAMES and John (see JOHN THE APOSTLE) left their father ZEBEDEE in the boat "with the hired men" (Mk. 1:20). This assures us that the father was not left helpless, to carry on alone. It also suggests that he was fairly well off financially. It was successful businessmen that the Master called to work with him. The account of Jesus casting a demon out of a man in the synagogue on the Sabbath day (1:21–28) is closely paralleled in Luke. The healing of Peter's mother-in-law (1:29–31) is recorded in all three synoptics. Twice in this brief memo Mark uses his favorite word "immediately" (*euthys*).

The account of the sunset healing service (Mk. 1:32–34) probably preserves Peter's reaction to the vast crowd outside: "The whole town gathered at the door." This, of course, is hyperbole, but that is the way it looked to Peter as he stood in the doorway of his house, which Jesus made his home when in CAPERNAUM. Typical of Mark's (Peter's) graphic language is the wording of 1:35. Mark uses three adverbs to emphasize how early it was when Jesus rose and went out to a quiet place to pray. This may well reflect Peter's consternation when he wakened in the morning and found the Master gone. He alone says that they "hunted him down" (NRSV; Gk. *katadiōkō* G2870)—another of those forceful expressions. The SERMON ON THE MOUNT (Matt. 5–7) is omitted by Mark, although a few of its sayings are paralleled in his gospel. Mark has only one of the long discourses of Jesus, the so-called Olivet Discourse (Mk. 13).

Mark's narrative of the healing of the leper (Mk. 1:40–45) includes the verb *splanchnizomai* G5072, "to feel compassion," indicating Jesus' reaction to human need. The healing of the paralytic (2:1–12) has two added touches in Mark, as compared with Matthew and Luke. So large a crowd had gathered "that there was no room left, not even outside the door" (v. 2). This was doubtless Peter's house, where Jesus was "at home" (v. 1 NRSV), and the apostle had clear recollections of the crowded conditions. Also Mark says that they "made an opening in the roof" (v. 4), digging a hole through which to lower the paralytic in front of Jesus. Peter would not forget the damage to his house! (Luke mentions "tiles" [Lk. 5:19], which suggests that it was an expensive roof.) Another added detail in Mark is the fact that the paralytic was carried by four people (Mk. 2:3). This information gives the clear picture of four men each taking hold of a corner of the pallet on which the paralytic lay, and using it as a stretcher to carry him to Jesus. There is a Roman touch here. Mark alone uses for "mat" the term *krabaton* G3187 (v. 4), a word borrowed from Latin that originally meant the bed roll of a Roman soldier. It was nothing more than a padded quilt.

The call of Levi (Mk. 2:13–17) is recorded in all three synoptics, as is also the question about fasting (2:18–22). Typically Mark says that John's disciples and the Pharisees "were fasting" (v. 18). This pinpoints the incident as occurring on a fast day and thus indicates the occasion for the question. Those who were fasting saw Jesus' disciples eating. They wanted to know why.

In Mk. 2:1—3:6 are included five incidents in which Jesus ran into conflict with the Pharisees. In connection with his healing the paralytic (2:1–12), he was criticized for declaring the man's sins forgiven; only God had this authority. Then he was castigated for eating with tax collectors and sinners (2:15–17). The Pharisees probably thought Jesus was less religious because his disciples were not fasting (2:18–22). The fourth conflict concerned the disciples working on the SABBATH day, because they picked some heads of wheat, rubbed off the husks in their hands, and blew away the chaff (2:23–28). They were harvesting, threshing, and winnowing! The fifth was a criticism of Jesus for healing on the Sabbath (3:1–6). The Pharisees allowed such healing only in case of an emergency, if the afflicted person might die before the next day.

Mark 3:7–12 has a summary statement about Jesus healing many people on the shores of the Lake of Galilee. Mark adds the picture of Jesus sitting in a boat a little offshore so as not to be crushed

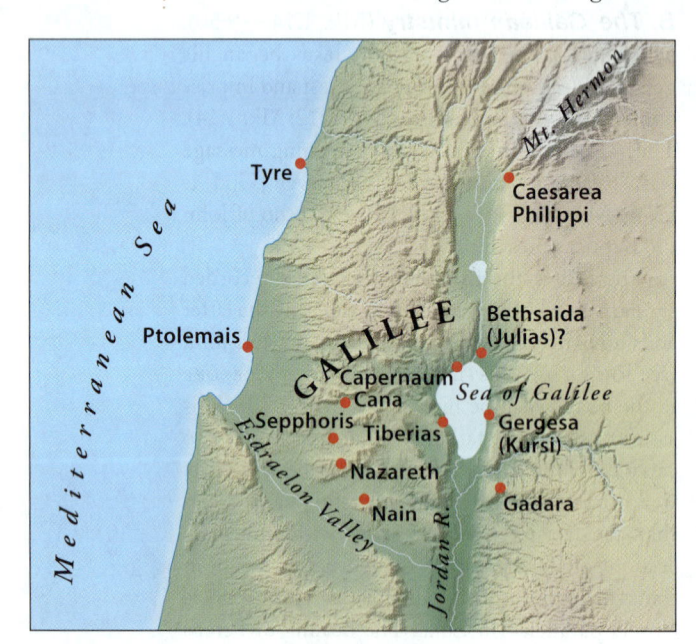

Jesus in Galilee.

by the large crowd (v. 9). This passage is followed by the call of the twelve apostles (3:13–19). Mark adds the twofold purpose of their appointment: "that they might be with him and that he might send them out to preach" (v. 14). Preparation must precede preaching.

It often has been pointed out that Mark portrays the strenuous life of Jesus more forcibly than the other Gospels. An example of this is the unique item in Mk. 3:20–21: "Then Jesus entered a house, and again a crowd gathered, so that he and his disciples were not even able to eat. When his family heard about this, they went to take charge of him, for they said, 'He is out of his mind.'" At the same time Mark gives more emphasis than the other Gospels to the rest Jesus sought to take. Five times he is described as withdrawing from the crowds and seeking a quiet place outside Galilee.

Another characteristic of Mark's gospel is its emphasis on the looks and gestures of Jesus. A good example is Mk. 3:5, "He looked around at them in anger ... deeply distressed at their stubborn hearts." Another example is Mark's added phrase: "Then he looked at those seated in a circle around him" (3:34). Observant Peter caught these items and wove them vividly into his preaching. We are indebted to Mark for communicating them.

Matthew gives seven of Jesus' PARABLES of the kingdom (Matt. 13). Mark has two of them: the sower (Mk. 4:1–20) and the mustard seed (4:30–32). In addition it includes the parable of the seed growing secretly (4:26–29), the only one found in this gospel alone. Altogether Mark has only four parables, as against fifteen in Matthew and nineteen in Luke (this enumeration is based on R. C. Trench's list of thirty in his *Notes on the Parables of Our Lord* [1882]). In contrast there are eighteen miracles in Mark, compared with twenty-one in Matthew and twenty in Luke—both much longer books. Mark majors on action.

In the miracle of the stilling of the storm (Mk. 4:35–41) Mark adds that Jesus was "in the stern" (v. 38) of the boat, asleep "on a cushion"—the steersman's leather-covered pad. The story of the GERASENE demoniac (5:1–20) offers a good example of how Mark often gives a much fuller record of an incident. Mark's account has 325 words, as against 136 in Matthew. The description of the demoniac (vv. 3–5) is far more vivid than that found in the other two Gospels.

Much the same holds true for the twin miracles (told together) of the healing of the woman with a hemorrhage and the raising of JAIRUS's daughter (Mk. 5:21–43). Once more, Mark has 374 words, whereas Matthew uses 135. A significant Markan addition is found in vv. 29b–30: "and she felt in her body that she was freed from her suffering. At once Jesus realized that power had gone out from him." Christ paid a price to heal people; he was conscious that power went out of him. Mark also adds here the Aramaic expression, TALITHA KOUM, and then translates it for his Roman readers: "Little girl, I say to you, get up" (5:41).

In connection with the rejection of Jesus by his neighbors at NAZARETH, Mark alone records that "he was amazed at their lack of faith" (Mk. 6:6). In only one other instance is it stated that Christ marveled, and that was at the faith of a foreigner, a Roman centurion (Matt. 8:10; Lk. 7:9). The mission of the Twelve (Mk. 6:7–13) is found in all three synoptics. Mark adds the interesting detail that Jesus sent them out "two by two" (v. 7). There are obvious advantages in companionship and encouragement, as well as protection.

In the account of John the Baptist's death (Mk. 6:14–29) Mark refers to the ruler of Galilee as "King Herod" (v. 14). Matthew and Luke more precisely call him TETRARCH (Matt. 14:1; Lk. 9:7). At Rome, where Mark was probably writing, it was common to refer to rulers in the E generally as kings. Mark's account, again, is much longer than the only parallel (Matt. 14:1–12). The vividness of his narrative shows up especially in his addition, "So Herodias nursed a grudge against John and wanted to kill him. But she was not able to, because Herod feared John and protected him, knowing him to be a righteous and holy man. When Herod heard John, he was greatly puzzled; yet he liked to listen to him" (Mk. 6:19–20).

In the feeding of the 5,000 (Mk. 6:30–44), the only miracle of Jesus recorded in all four Gospels, Mark has some typical additions. He tells how Jesus said to the Twelve: "Come with me by yourselves to a quiet place and get some rest" (6:31). The reason was that "so many people were coming and going that they did not even have a chance to eat" (v. 31).

Mark alone records the question of the disciples: "Are we to go and spend that much on bread and give it to them to eat?" (v. 37).

In connection with Jesus walking on the water (Mk. 6:45–52) Mark adds the observation, "for they had not understood about the loaves; their hearts were hardened" (v. 52). The account of the healings at GENNESARET (6:53–56) is much more vivid and full than the parallel in Matt. 14:34–36. In the discussion of what defiles a person (Mk. 7:1–23) Mark explains for his Roman readers the Jewish ceremony of hand-washing (vv. 3–4). He also uses, typically, the Aramaic term CORBAN and then interprets its meaning. Significantly he adds the momentous statement that by his teaching here Jesus "declared all foods 'clean'" (v. 19). Mark closes this incident with a list of sins (vv. 21–22) that parallels passages in Paul's epistles. Whereas Matthew has seven sins in his parallel account (Matt. 15:19), Mark has thirteen.

Matthew and Mark both record the miracle of Jesus casting the demon out of the SYROPHOENICIAN woman's daughter (Matt. 15:21–28; Mk. 7:24–30). Mark alone notes: "He entered a house and did not want anyone to know it; yet he could not keep his presence secret" (v. 24). This fits Mark's emphasis on the Master's attempts to get away from the crowds in order to teach his disciples privately.

Two miracles of Jesus are recorded only by Mark. The first is the healing of the deaf mute (Mk. 7:31–37). The other is the healing of the blind man of BETHSAIDA (8:22–26). They have some common elements. In both cases Christ took the victim aside from the crowd, possibly in order to avoid the confusion that often comes to deaf and blind people when surrounded by noise and people. The Master Healer wanted their undivided attention. In both instances, also, he used spittle and touched the afflicted part of the body. The first miracle has another Aramaic word, EPHPHATHA, translated "be opened." The second miracle has a feature not found elsewhere in the miracles of Jesus: the healing took place in two stages. Why? Alexander Maclaren suggests that Jesus was "accommodating the pace of his power to the slowness of the man's faith" (*Expositions of Holy Scripture: St. Mark Chaps. I to VIII* [1893], 326).

Matthew and Mark alone tell about the feeding of the 4,000 (Matt 15:32–38; Mk. 8:1–10). They also refer back to both feedings (Matt. 16:5–12; Mk. 8:14–21). A significant detail is that in all six references to the feeding of the 5,000 (Matt. 14:20; 16:9; Mk. 6:43; 8:19; Lk. 9:17; Jn. 6:13) the same Greek word for "basket" is used (*kophinos* G3186) and in all four references to the feeding of the 4,000 (Matt. 15:37; 16:10; Mk. 8:8, 20) another Greek word (*sphyris* G5083) is employed. This is a strong argument in favor of two separate feedings (rather than a duplicate of one historical feeding): there is no confusion in the careful use of these terms.

One of the great turning points in Jesus' life and ministry came at CAESAREA PHILIPPI far to the N (Mk. 8:27–30). Jesus had gone there to be alone with his disciples. He asked them a pertinent question: "Who do people say that I am?" They gave various answers, then he asked them: "Who do you say I am?" As the spokesman for the apostles, Peter replied, "You are the Christ" (i.e., the MESSIAH). This confession of his messiahship was followed by Jesus' first prediction of his PASSION (8:31–33). Until the apostles recognized him as Messiah, he could not tell them about his coming death and resurrection. Mark says that he "began to teach them" about this (cf. Matt. 16:21). It is clear that the confession at Caesarea Philippi marks a shift in the Master's ministry. Up to this point he had spent most of his time with large crowds—teaching, preaching, healing. From that time he gave major attention to instructing his disciples and preparing them for the day when they would take over in his place. Peter rebuked Jesus for talking about his death. The Master, in turn, rebuked the disciple who was acting the part of "Satan" (adversary) in tempting him to turn aside. Then follows Jesus' important teaching on the meaning of DISCIPLESHIP (8:34—9:1). All three Synoptic Gospels have the key saying of Christ: "If anyone would come after me, he must deny himself and take up his cross and follow me" (8:34). This is the cost of discipleship.

The TRANSFIGURATION (Mk. 9:2–8) was one of the high points of Jesus' ministry. Its purpose for the disciples was probably to confirm Peter's confession of his deity. For him it was a bright moment of glory before the humiliation and suffering of the cross. Only Peter, James, and John were present. They were also the only disciples with Jesus at the raising of Jairus's daughter, and when he prayed in Gethsemane. Seeing Elijah on the mount caused the three apostles to ask Jesus about the prophecy that Elijah would come back to earth (9:9–13). Jesus indicated that the prediction had been fulfilled in the coming of John the Baptist (cf. Matt. 17:13).

At the foot of the mountain Jesus healed an epileptic boy (Mk. 9:14–29). Once again, Mark gives by far the most graphic of the three accounts, describing the helplessness of the lad and the agony of the father (vv. 20–26). He also notes the amazement of the crowd when Christ approached (v. 15), perhaps due to the afterglow on his face. Jesus then gave a second prediction of his passion (9:30–32). As usual, the disciples did not understand. Their Master was trying to tell them that he was not going to Jerusalem to display his power and glory by setting up an earthly kingdom; he was going there to die! A most pathetic incident follows. The disciples were disputing about which of them was the greatest (9:33–37). Jesus pointed out to them that true greatness is shown by humility and service—"If anyone wants to be first, he must be the very last, and the servant of all" (v. 35).

Both Mark and Luke tell how John reported that he had forbidden a certain man to cast out demons in Jesus' name because he was not following them (Mk. 9:38–41; Lk. 9:49–50). The Master reproved the sectarian spirit of his disciple. Christ emphasized the seriousness of tempting others to sin (Mk. 9:42–48) by saying it would be better for the tempter to be drowned in the ocean with a heavy millstone around his neck than to lead any one astray. He also said that it would be better for a man to lose a hand, foot, or eye than to be cast into hell. The short saying about SALT (9:49–50) is paralleled in the SERMON ON THE MOUNT (Matt. 5:13). Salt is a type of the saving grace of God.

C. The Perean ministry (Mk. 10:1–52). The beginning of ch. 10 narrates Jesus' leaving Galilee for the last time and going SE to Perea (across the Jordan). Here the Pharisees questioned him on the matter of DIVORCE (10:1–12). This was a perennial problem in Judaism. Christ emphatically asserted that God's will was MARRIAGE for life. He said: "Anyone who divorces his wife and marries another woman commits adultery against her" (v. 11). Then Mark adds a Roman touch: "And if she divorces her husband and marries another man, she commits adultery" (v. 12). Matthew omits this last comment, because Jewish women could not divorce their husbands but Roman women could.

Jesus' reproof of the disciples for rebuking mothers who brought their children to him (Mk. 10:13–16) is included in all synoptics, though Mark adds a characteristic detail: "he took the children in his arms ... and blessed them." The story of the rich young ruler (10:17–31) evidently made a profound impression, for it is recorded at length in all three Synoptic Gospels. Typically, Mark says: "a man ran up to him and fell to his knees before him" (10:17; Matthew simply says that he "came up to him"). Mark's pictures are so graphic that an artist could draw them. The three accounts portray the sadness of the ardent young seeker as he refused to pay the price of discipleship—leaving all to follow Jesus. Perhaps significantly, by way of contrast, this incident is followed by Christ's third prediction of his passion (10:32–34), somewhat more detailed than the previous two. Graphically Mark describes how, as they were on the road to Jerusalem, Jesus was "leading the way, and the disciples were astonished, while those who followed were afraid" (v. 32). Possibly the set look of determination on his face frightened them.

The tragic story that follows (Mk. 10:35–45) is almost unbelievable in the light of these three passion predictions. James and John, who had seen Jesus' glory on the mount, had become obsessed with the idea that the King was about to take his throne at Jerusalem. They wanted the highest places of honor on either side of him. The Master had to rebuke this self-seeking spirit of his two disciples. He warned them that suffering, not glory, lay just ahead. He also had to rebuke the self-righteous indignation of the other ten disciples. Again he declared, "whoever wants to become great among you must be your servant, and whoever wants to be first must be slave of all" (vv. 43–44). Perhaps no other virtue was emphasized by Jesus more frequently than HUMILITY. This and service are the two signs of real greatness.

As he left Jericho for Jerusalem, Christ healed blind BARTIMAEUS (10:46–52). Typically, Mark gives and explains this Aramaic name (*bar* means "son"). And as usual, he adds a vivid touch: "Throwing his cloak aside, he jumped to his feet and came to Jesus" (v. 50). The reader can easily visualize the scene.

D. The Judean ministry (Mk. 11:1—13:37). The so-called TRIUMPHAL ENTRY of Jesus into Jerusalem (11:1–10) is recorded in all three Synoptic Gospels. It was a messianic act, the King offering himself to his nation in fulfillment of the prophecy in Zech. 9:9.

Mark spells out more carefully than the others the sequence of events at the beginning of passion week. The triumphal entry on Sunday ended with Jesus surveying the temple and then going out to BETHANY for the night. On Monday morning, on the way back into the city, he cursed the barren fig tree (Mk. 11:12–14). Entering Jerusalem, he cleansed the temple (11:15–19), driving the dirty, noisy, smelly market out of the Court of the Gentiles. Tuesday morning the disciples noticed that the fig tree had withered, and Jesus taught them an important lesson of faith and forgiving prayer (11:20–25). When he reached the temple, the members of the SANHEDRIN demanded that he tell them where he got his authority to cleanse the temple (11:27–33). After disposing of them, Jesus told the parable of the wicked husbandmen (12:1–12), which the religious leaders realized was aimed at them (v. 12).

Probably on Wednesday, Christ was asked three questions, noted in each of the synoptics. First came the Pharisees and Herodians, asking whether they should pay taxes to the emperor (Mk. 12:13–17). Whichever way Jesus answered, he would be trapped. His well-known handling of this problem is a classic. Next came the Sadducees, with a catch-question about the resurrection (12:18–27), in which they did not believe. After Jesus had pointed out the absurdity of their reasoning, a scribe asked him which was the chief commandment (12:28–34). For good measure the Master defined both the "first" and "second" commandments. Mark alone portrays this scribe as being friendly to Jesus (vv. 32–34). When he had been questioned three times, Christ proceeded to ask his opponents a question: How could the Messiah be David's son and lord at the same time? (12:35–37). The answer is clear to us now, but it was not to the religious experts of that day. Jesus warned the people against the hypocrisy of the Pharisees (12:38–40). Then he sat down opposite the treasury in the Women's Court of the temple and watched a poor widow put in two tiny copper coins (12:41–44), all that she had. The lesson is clear. One's giving is measured not by the amount given but by how much is left over.

Mark 13 often is called the "Little Apocalypse." Jesus predicted the destruction of the temple, which took place in A.D. 70, and discussed the signs of his SECOND COMING. This so-called Olivet Discourse is the only long discourse of Jesus found in all three Synoptic Gospels.

E. The Passion narrative (Mk. 14:1—15:47). The anointing at Bethany (14:3–9) is described at this point by Mark and Matthew, but this event probably took place on the previous Friday or Saturday, as indicated in Jn. 12:1–8. Then comes Judas's plot to betray Jesus (Mk. 14:10–11) and the preparation for the PASSOVER (vv. 12–16). The Last Supper (vv. 17–21) was followed by the institution of the LORD's SUPPER (vv. 22–25). On the way out to the garden, Christ predicted Peter's denials (vv. 26–31). The prayer in Gethsemane (vv. 32–42) is given rather fully in all three synoptics, as is also Jesus' arrest (vv. 43–52) and his trial before the Sanhedrin (vv. 53–72). This is followed by the trial before PILATE (15:1–15), the mocking by the soldiers (vv. 16–20), the crucifixion (vv. 21–41), and the burial (vv. 42–47).

F. The resurrection (Mk. 16:1–20). As already noted (see above, section X), the last twelve verses of Mark are probably not a part of the original work. That would leave only the first eight verses of this chapter. These tell of MARY Magdalene and three other women coming to the tomb on Sunday morning. A "young man" (an angel) was sitting in the tomb and told them that Jesus had risen. The women were to tell his disciples "and Peter" that he would meet them in Galilee. The Markan addition of Peter's name fits this gospel well. Peter would never forget how Jesus had sent this comforting word specifically to him. Because no postresurrection appearances of Jesus are mentioned in these first eight verses, the various endings of the gospel (16:9–20 and others) were evidently added to fill up the gap.

XIII. Theology. It used to be said that Mark was the historical gospel and John the theological one. Since the middle of the 20th cent., however, much attention has been given to the fact that there is a strong theological thrust in Mark's gospel. This is found especially in two fields.

A. Christology. The first verse, which is probably the title of the gospel, reads: "The beginning of the gospel of Jesus Christ, the Son of God." This implies that one of Mark's main purposes was to demonstrate the DEITY OF CHRIST. This he does by showing that Jesus exercised authority over demons, disease, and death, as well as the physical elements.

Of the expression SON OF GOD Vincent Taylor writes: "Beyond question this title represents the most fundamental element in Mark's Christology" (*St. Mark*, 120). It occurs five times (Mk. 1:1; 3:11; 5:7; 14:61; 15:39). Taylor also makes the startling statement: "Mark's christology is a high christology, as high as any in the New Testament, not excluding that of John" (ibid., 121). Along with the other two synoptics, Mark records the Father's voice at the baptism and the transfiguration identifying Jesus as "my beloved Son." There is no doubt here about a clear affirmation of the full deity of the One who was both SON OF MAN and Son of God. See CHRISTOLOGY.

B. Soteriology. The main passage on this subject is Mk. 10:45, the greatest theological statement in this book. It reads: "For even the Son of Man did not come to be served, but to serve, and to give his life as a ransom for many." Jesus did not come to sit on an earthly throne, surrounded by a host of servants to wait on him. He came to be the Servant of humanity, but more than that, its Savior.

The word for ransom here, *lytron G3389*, was used in the 1st cent. for the ransom price paid to free a slave. Similarly, Jesus paid the ransom price to free men and women from the slavery of sin. Moreover, in the phrase "for many," the word translated "for" is *anti G505*, which frequently carries the meaning "instead of, in place of." Jesus' ATONEMENT "for" us was vicarious or substitutionary. He died in our place, taking our guilt upon himself. This truth is briefly but beautifully expressed by Mark in this great soteriological passage.

(Since the first edition of this encyclopedia, the Gospel of Mark has been the object of intensive scholarly study. For a helpful survey of the history of recent research, see the introductory chapter in W. R. Telford, ed., *The Interpretation of Mark*, 2nd ed. [1995], which also reprints some of the more influential essays. Significant commentaries include H. B. Swete, *The Gospel according to St. Mark*, 2nd ed. [1902]; C. E. B. Cranfield, *The Gospel according to St. Mark*, CGTC [1959]; V. Taylor, *The Gospel according to St. Mark*, 2nd ed. [1966]; R. A. Cole, *The Gospel according to Mark*, TNTC, 2nd ed. [1989]; R. A. Guelich, *Mark 1—8:26*, WBC 34A [1989]; M. D. Hooker, *The Gospel according to Saint Mark*, BNTC [1991]; R. H. Gundry, *Mark: A Commentary on His Apology for the Cross* [1993]; P. Lamarche, *Evangile de Marc: Commentaire* [1996]; E. Trocmé, *L'Evangile selon saint Marc* [2000]; J. Marcus, *Mark*, AB 27–27A, 2 vols. [2000–]; C. A. Evans, *Mark 8:27—16:20*, WBC 34B [2001]; B. Witherington III, *The Gospel of Mark: A Socio-Rhetorical Commentary* [2001]; J. R. Edwards, *The Gospel according to Mark* [2002]; J. R. Donahue and D. J. Harrington, *The Gospel of Mark*, SP 2 [2002]; R. T. France, *The Gospel of Mark: A Commentary on the Greek Text*, NIGTC [2002]; M. E. Boring, *Mark: A Commentary* [2006]; A. Yarbro Collins, *Mark: A Commentary*, Hermeneia [2007].

(Among numerous monographs, note the following: W. Marxsen, *Mark the Evangelist* [1969]; T. J. Weeden, *Traditions in Conflict* [1971]; J. D. Kingsbury, *The Christology of Mark* [1984]; C. C. Black, *The Disciples according to Mark: Markan Redaction in Current Debate* [1989]; H. Räisänen, *The "Messianic Secret" in Mark* [1990]; C. Bryan, *A Preface to Mark: Notes on the Gospel in Its Literary and Cultural Settings* [1993]; W. R. Telford, *The Theology of the Gospel of Mark* [1999]; D. N. Peterson, *The Origins of Mark: The Markan Community in Current Debate* [2000]; R. Watts, *Isaiah's New Exodus in Mark*, rev. ed. [2000]; T. R. Hatina, *In Search of a Context: The Function of Scripture in Mark's Narrative* [2002]; B. J. Incigneri, *The Gospel to the Romans: The Setting and Rhetoric of Mark's Gospel* [2003]; P. Bolt, *The Cross from a Distance: Atonement in Mark's Gospel* [2004]; J. G. Crossley, *The Date of Mark's Gospel: Insights from the Law in Earliest Christianity* [2004]; F. J. Moloney, *Mark: Storyteller, Interpreter, Evangelist* [2004]; H. N. Roskam, *The Purpose of the Gospel of Mark in Its Historical and Social Context* [2004]; S. W. Henderson, *Christology and Discipleship in the Gospel of Mark* [2006]; and the bibliography compiled by W. E. Mills, *The Gospel of Mark* [2002].)   R. EARLE

Mark, John mahrk, jon (Μᾶρκος *G3453*, Ἰωάννης *G2722* [see JOHN]). Son of a Christian woman named Mary (see MARY #2), cousin of BARNABAS, assistant to PAUL and Barnabas, and traditionally the author of the second gospel. See MARK, GOSPEL OF.

The name *Iōannēs* is derived from the Hebrew *yôḥānān H3419*, meaning "Yahweh is gracious," and points to his Jewish heritage. *Markos*, on the other hand, is the common Greek form of the Latin *Marcus* ("large hammer") and served as John's surname (Acts 12:12). Other examples of Jews bearing Latin or Greek names in addition to their Hebrew names are common in the NT (e.g., Acts 1:23; 10:18) and in some cases may indicate Roman CITIZENSHIP, in others perhaps a previous life of slavery to a Roman family. The nickname *kolobodaktylos*, or "stump-fingered," was applied to John by some early Christian writers. While various explanations have been advanced for this nickname, it is most natural to take it as referring to an actual physical impairment, due to either congenital or accidental reasons.

Concerning the family of John Mark, his mother was named Mary (Acts 12:12) and he was the cousin of Barnabas (Col. 4:10). Barnabas was a Levite, a native of CYPRUS, and a land owner (Acts 4:36–37). The household of Mary is pictured also as being of considerable means, boasting at least one servant girl and having sufficient space to accommodate a sizable prayer meeting (Acts 12:12–13). Of the father of Mark, nothing is known with certainty, but since the house is called Mary's, one may assume that he had died prior to this time. The fact that PETER, upon his miraculous release from prison, knew where to find the praying church, implies that the household held a position of some prominence among the early Jewish Christians in Jerusalem.

Concerning the early life of Mark, there is no direct information. However, judging from the fact that Peter was welcomed at the house of Mary and from information in the first epistle that bears that apostle's name (1 Pet. 5:13), one may say that Mark had a particularly close relationship with Peter, probably dating from the early days of the church in Jerusalem. Later traditions likewise bear out a close association between Peter and Mark. The young man who fled naked from the betrayal scene in GETHSEMANE (Mk. 14:51–52) often is thought to have been John Mark. None of the known facts are against this suggestion, and it was certainly not rare for an author to omit mention of his own name in his writings (cf. Jn. 21:24).

As far as the more explicit record of the NT is concerned, the first significant event in the life of John was the fact that, when Paul and Barnabas returned to ANTIOCH OF SYRIA from their famine relief mission to Jerusalem in c. A.D. 46, they brought him with them. Shortly after, Paul and Barnabas set out on the first missionary journey with Mark as their *hypēretēs G5677* or "helper" (Acts 13:5). The young man's ministry with the two great missionaries often has been taken as being roughly equivalent to that of a modern-day business manager serving a traveling team. The term generally indicates an official assistant quite distinct from what is implied by *doulos G1528* ("slave"), for example. Interestingly, Luke uses the phrase *hypēretai tou logou*, "servants of the word" (Lk. 1:2), seemingly to indicate those who were committed to writing the events of the gospel or otherwise paid careful attention to them. It is precisely this type of function, the note-taking from the preaching of Peter, which PAPIAS assigns to Mark (see Euseb. *Eccl. Hist.* 3.39). Indeed, A. Wright argued that Mark's ministry was that of an official catechist (see *ExpTim* 21 [1910–11]: 211–16 and 22 [1910–11]: 358–62).

Whatever the specific nature of Mark's assistance may have been, the record does indicate that Mark left the two senior men at PERGA, the capital of the religion of ARTEMIS in PAMPHYLIA, and returned to Jerusalem (Acts 13:13). No one can know the reason for Mark's return. In any case, Paul was later to regard Mark's action as desertion, for when the time came for the second journey, Barnabas desired that his younger cousin should accompany them again, but Paul steadfastly refused (Acts 15:37–38). So sharp was the contention between the two elder missionaries that, in the end, Paul departed with Silas while Barnabas took Mark and set sail for his native Cyprus. (Paul's firmness on this matter has led some scholars to believe that Mark, because of Jewish scruples, may have earlier objected to the apostle's distinctive mission to the Gentiles, that is, his gospel of freedom without the intermediary role of Judaism. See PAUL III.A.)

Mark now drops out of the account of Acts, which is wholly concerned with the further activities of Paul. The Pauline correspondence indicates that within a decade or so of the rift, the relationship between Paul and Mark had improved greatly. In Col. 4:10 Paul includes Mark among the few of the circumcision who labored with him and provided him with some comfort. Indeed, Mark appears to have been chosen by the great apostle to make some representation to Colosse. Paul makes further mention of Mark as his fellow worker in Phlm. 24. By the time of the writing of 2 Timothy, Mark and TIMOTHY are together, probably in Asia Minor, and Paul expresses his final, gratifying tribute for the young man: "he is helpful to me in my ministry" (2 Tim. 4:11).

Beginning with PAPIAS in the first half of the 2nd cent., the early church consistently ascribed to Mark the task of having interpreted for Peter in Rome and of having written the second gospel (see the various traditions in Euseb. *Eccl. Hist.* 2.15–16; 3.39; 5.8; 6.14). Mark also is said to have established churches in ALEXANDRIA in Egypt (ibid. 2.16). A later and somewhat legendary tradition states that early in the 9th cent., Mark's remains were taken from Alexandria and placed under the church of St. Mark in Venice. (See E. M. Blaiklock, *The Young Man Mark* [1965], 9–21, and bibliography under MARK, GOSPEL OF.)   H. G. ANDERSEN

Mark, Qumran fragments of. See MARK, GOSPEL OF, X.

Mark, Secret Gospel of. In 1958, the well-known scholar Morton Smith (1915–1991), while cataloguing manuscripts at the Greek Orthodox monastery in Mar (SE of Jerusalem), discovered a letter that purports to have been written by CLEMENT OF ALEXANDRIA. This document refers to a "secret" and "more spiritual" gospel written by Mark (in addition to the canonical gospel), which was intended only for "those who are being initiated into the great mysteries." The document includes excerpts from this otherwise unknown gospel. (See M. Smith, *Clement of Alexandria and a Secret Gospel of Mark* [1973].) Although some have dismissed this letter as a forgery (no scholar other than Smith has seen it), many believe it is genuine. However, controversy has raged about the authenticity and significance of the gospel to which it refers. A few writers have accepted and developed Smith's view that the Secret Gospel predates the canonical Gospel of Mark, but after a detailed discussion, R. H. Gundry concludes that the material should be regarded "as apocryphal non-Marcan additions to canonical Mark" (*Mark: A Commentary on His Apology for the Cross* [1993], 603–23, esp. 621). Similarly, J. Marcus believes that if this work really existed, it must have been "a late edition of Mark that reveals the concern for esotericism typical of second-century Alexandrian Christianity" (*Mark 1–8*, AB 27 [1999], 51). (See now the monographs by J. Dart, *Decoding Mark* [2003], and S. G. Brown, *Mark's Other Gospel: Rethinking Morton Smith's Controversial Discovery* [2005], as well as the summary of research and reviews by P. Foster in *ExpTim* 117 [2005]: 46–52, 64–68.)

market, marketplace. There is little mention of marketplaces in the OT (cf. 1 Ki. 20:34 NIV; Ps. 55:11 NRSV). In the NT, however, the Greek

In the 1st cent., goods were sold and bartered in the marketplace much as they are in parts of Jerusalem today.

term *agora G59* occurs eleven times, mainly in the Gospels, where the reference is to typically Eastern (rather than Greek) marketplaces, much like the bazaars of present-day oriental towns. Not only were they used for buying and selling of goods, but a variety of other activities centered there: it was an open place where children engaged in their sports (Matt. 11:16; Lk. 7:32), laborers were hired (Matt. 20:3), greetings were exchanged (Matt. 23:7; Lk. 11:43), and the sick were brought for healing (Mk. 6:56). On the other hand, the two market places mentioned in Acts were in Greek cities and were typically Hellenic: surrounded by colonnades, temples, and public buildings, and adorned with statues, they were centers of public life, lending themselves to such uses as the holding of trials (Acts 16:19) and as centers for public disputation (17:17). (See B.-Z. Rosenfeld and J. Menirav, *Markets and Marketing in Roman Palestine* [2005].)   R. C. STONE

Marmoth mahr´moth. KJV Apoc. form of MEREMOTH (1 Esd. 8:62).

Maroth mair´oth (מָרוֹת *H5300*, prob. "bitter [things]"). An otherwise unknown town mentioned in a difficult passage that contains a number of wordplays (Mic. 1:12). MICAH's prophecy reads literally, "For she who inhabits Maroth is in labor pains [*ḥîl H2655*] for good." Some emend the verb to a form of *yāḥal H3498*, "to wait" (cf. NRSV, "For the inhabitants of Maroth wait anxiously for good"). The NIV apparently retains the MT reading but supplies "waiting" to complete the sense ("Those who live in Maroth writhe in pain, / waiting for relief"). D. R. Hillers (*Micah*, Hermeneia [1984], 26) suggests that the word for "good" (*ṭôb H3202*), which can be used to describe wine and perfume (Cant. 1:2–3), here has the sense "sweet," thus contrasting with the name Maroth, "bitter." The imprecations in this passage (Mic. 1:10–16) are against the enemies of Judah and refer to places mostly in the SHEPHELAH, but the location of Maroth cannot be determined. Some have suggested it is the same as MAARATH, an unlikely identification.

marriage. The legal union of a man and woman as husband and wife.

I. Marriage in historical perspective
  A. Early Palestinian family life
  B. Marriage in biblical times
  C. Marriage in postbiblical Judaism
II. Various cultural traits
  A. Bars to marriage
  B. Choosing the bride
  C. Mohar—the price of the wife
  D. Marriage formalities and ceremonies
III. Dissolution of marriage
  A. Historic developments
  B. Deterrents to divorce
  C. Kinds of divorce
  D. Divorce and the support of the children
  E. Divorce procedures
  F. The levirate marriage
IV. Succession and inheritance
V. The status of women
  A. Virgins
  B. Married women
  C. Widows
  D. Adultery
VI. The Status of children
  A. Childbirth
  B. Naming the child
  C. Child rearing
VII. Mixed marriages and the future of the Jewish family

I. Marriage in historical perspective. Modern sociologists recognize the distinction between marriage as an act, event, or even a process, and the FAMILY as a social institution. Marriage is the legal union of a man and a woman and the ceremony initiating and celebrating them as husband and wife. The family is the social institution developed around the child-mother relationship and creating the social climate in which human nature may be conditioned and realized. Marriage and family, therefore, constitute two distinct systems even though they are found within a single nexus. This is particularly true in contemporary Western society, where marriages often do not produce children for several years. The family is a more complicated and binding system than the marriage. It binds parents to children. It places the children under the obligation of the parent. It makes it incumbent upon the couple to care for relatives and sometimes even for the servants.

There are many categories of social facts that are difficult to classify properly and clearly as belonging to the study of marriage or to that of the family. Such social facts are therefore treated by various authorities in either one or in both of these areas designated as marriage and family. Looking to the evolution of marriage in historic perspective, of primary concern in this presentation are the characteristics and the features identified with marriage in the Bible lands through the various stages and periods of history.

A. Early Palestinian family life. Various elements were incorporated by the Hebrew people into their culture as they were influenced by Arameans (see ARAM), AMORITES, and a large mixture of the blood of that central Asiatic race from which the HITTITES and HURRIANS descended. The evidence for a prehistoric stage of polyandrous marriage among the ancestors of the Hebrew people is of no great weight. However, the evidence for the presence of so-called matriarchate or "mother-right" is of far greater significance. The value of this evidence must be appraised with moderation, for some of the arguments are far-fetched and rather weak.

ARABIA was the cradle land of the Semitic society. Authoritative sources offer evidence that a number of deviations from normal monogamous marriage were well known in early Arabia, and therefore among the primitive Semites. Worthy of mentioning particularly are three types of deviations: (1) *Polyandry*, a family system that includes a plurality of husbands; (2) *Beena-marriage*, in which the husband goes to live in the wife's village and the children are regarded as members of her tribe (cf. JACOB's marriage to LEAH and RACHEL, Gen. 29:28); (3) *Mot-a marriage*, which differs from Beena-marriage only because of its temporary nature.

The question whether the clan has preceded the family as the first social unit in the early stages of development was proposed by W. Robertson Smith, who, at the beginning of his discussion on relations of gods and men in the oldest Semitic communities, considered the clan as the earliest social unit (*Religion of the Semites* [1894], 35). This theory is not supported by the present sociological research. By his investigations Robert H. Lowie makes it probable that the earliest social unit is the family, and that larger social groups such as clans and "sibs" came later as natural developments (*Primitive Society* [1920], 4–8).

In harmony with the views sustained by later sociological inquiry, what was the nature of the marriage ties in the earlier stages? Some scholars claim that in the primitive society monogamous marriage was practically unknown. They claim that promiscuity characterized the relation of the sexes. E. Westermarck argued for permanent mating (*History of Human Marriage* [1922], passim). The progress of knowledge appears to have vindicated the correctness of his position. He argued that polyandry did not represent the earliest stages of the evolution of human marriage, but rather degenerations from the primitive types.

B. Marriage in biblical times. The Bible contains evidence of a certain evolution of marital relations without presenting exclusive clear patterns.

1. Marriage in the OT. The most fruitful sources for the understanding of the nature of the family ties are to be found in the OT. The story of the CREATION of the first two human beings reveals monogamous marriage as the expression of the will of God. Polygamy first appeared in the reprobate line of CAIN when LAMECH took two wives. In the period of the PATRIARCHS evidence is offered that ABRAHAM married his own half-sister. Later the laws of MOSES prohibited such marriages. In patriarchal times cases were recorded, like that of JACOB, when the same man married two sisters. Again, later, the law of Moses prohibited such marriages. Many of the institutions developed in the patriarchal period later disappeared.

The creation of new marital relations in the early OT period must be understood against the background of the relationships and roles ascribed to various members of the family. The relationships between brothers were of fundamental significance. A brother in that era meant all the members of a family, or even a tribe. Each brother was obligated to offer protection and help to all the other brothers, when conditions made his services necessary. The GOEL (meaning "protector" or "redeemer") was a close relative bound to redeem his brother from slavery (see REDEMPTION), to buy the family patrimony sold under necessity, to bury his deceased brother or sister, to observe the LEVIRATE LAW, and to take upon himself the obligation of blood vengeance for a murdered brother (see AVENGER OF BLOOD). Clear distinctions of relationship degrees were not easily made because of the wider, larger, and more inclusive consanguinal family structure of their society.

Under the judges and the monarchy, Israel shifted toward a wider practice of polygamy. Bigamy was recognized as a legal fact (Deut. 21:15–17), but it is clear that the most common form of marriage in Israel was monogamy. No cases of bigamy among the commoners are found in the books of Samuel and Kings. The OT WISDOM Literature, which provides a picture of the society for this period, never mentions polygamy. The image of a monogamous marriage was in the minds of those prophets who represented Israel as the one wife chosen by the one and only God, Yahweh. Ezekiel developed the same metaphor into an allegory (Ezek. 16).

2. Marriage in postexilic times. In the postexilic period the family underwent changes but remained essentially oriental and patriarchal in character. Monogamy was the general practice. The father had the responsibility of educating his sons and training them in some practical and useful trade. The Hebrew traditions helped to preserve some high standards of OT and postexilic sexual morality by comparison with other ANE peoples.

There is no direct information about the period of the second temple. From the APOCRYPHA it appears that they continued to be monogamous (cf. TOBIT, a family tale that never refers to any other kind but monogamous families), although not without exception. Selection of mates, the nature and the size of the dowry, and other decisions were made normally by the parents.

The papyri of ELEPHANTINE show that the *mohar* or "dowry" was considered the property of the woman, even though usually it was given to her father. In the period of the second temple, the *mohar* was replaced by the sum registered in the *ketubah* ("marriage contract"). For a virgin bride the amount suggested was fifty silver shekels; if the bride was widowed or divorced, the amount was reduced to half.

According to the law, *kiddushin* meant that the bride could have been bought (betrothed), whether by money, by writ (a brief contract), or by cohabitation. Betrothal by contract was suspended before the Middle Ages. In the case of betrothal by cohabitation the man and the woman entered a private chamber, having first declared to witnesses their intention to become betrothed. At the end, and following the period of the second temple, it was customary for the wedding of a virgin to be held on a Wednesday. This arrangement offered the husband, if he found the absence of the tokens of virginity, the necessary time to bring the case to court on Thursday. The widows and the divorcees were married on Thursdays so that they could enjoy with their husbands uninterrupted two days before the Sabbath.

The prevailing Jewish concept was that marriage was the proper state for a man.

3. Marriage in the NT and in the early church. Marriage received the sanction of JESUS CHRIST himself. Jesus preached mercy along with justice. An uncompromising view of adultery and other sexual offenses is evidenced throughout the NT (e.g., Matt. 5:27–30). PAUL recognized the value of both marriage and celibacy (1 Cor. 7:1–9; Eph. 5:22–33). The special insistence on purity for Christians is in all probability a good indication of the laxity of the age (Acts 15:29; 1 Cor. 5:11; Gal. 5:16–21).

Early in the history of the church the idea of virginity as a state of purity, especially pleasing to Christ, took roots among Christians and later received the sanction and the encouragement of the church fathers. Marriage has never been explicitly condemned or forbidden by Christian teachers, but it was placed third and lowest in the scale of Christian purity. The highest is absolute virginity. The next lowest is celibacy adopted after marriage or after the death of the husband. Marriage was regarded only as the third best choice, a substitute for a worse state, that of illicit sexual intercourse.

CLEMENT OF ALEXANDRIA, who died c. A.D. 215, declared that marriage as a sacred image must be kept pure from those things which defile it. In like manner IGNATIUS (*Epistle to Polycarp*) and Athenagoras pled for Christians to maintain the purity of the marriage state. JEROME, who at the close of the 4th cent. preached the beauties of the monastic life, showed his growing antipathy to the married state. He based his strong opinion on the oft-quoted statement of Paul, "It is better to marry than to burn." He used to say: "It is good to marry simply because it is bad to burn." In like manner Ambrose and AUGUSTINE manifested high appreciation for celibacy. Under such influences the praise of celibacy became more insistent, and the deeply felt depreciation of marriage more simply and seriously accepted.

C. Marriage in postbiblical Judaism. The regenerative forces of the Jewish people were greatly enhanced by the institution of Jewish marriage. The Jew's whole life, including his sexual instincts, was scrupulously subjected to the supervision of religion. Social factors, such as the increasing concentration of the masses within the lower middle class, contributed to a greater exercise of sexual self-control. In this realm of human behavior the rabbis chose the path of moderation. They fought with relative effectiveness all forms of licentiousness. They did not consider the sexual appetite as evil in itself (as some church fathers interpreted Paul).

The legislators of the TALMUD neither elevated marriage to the position of a sacrament nor did they regard it as a mere contract in civil law. The act establishing the communion between husband and wife was termed *kiddushin*, or "sanctification," without implying the indelible character of a sacrament. In general, married life was regarded as sacred and under the direct ordering and control of Providence. The ascetic trends that ran through Talmudic Judaism had no bearing whatsoever upon marriage.

The Talmudic writers were determined to promote marriage. It was especially vital for Judaism to build the strength of the family structure as a good foundation of their ethnic life. They were willing to relax some ancient customs, such as to reduce the acquisition of a wife to "mere mutual consent," in order to facilitate marriage. The rabbis in the 3rd cent., however, outlawed this informal type of marriage, penalizing the transgressors by public flogging.

Rabbinic law treated illegitimate children almost on a par with the legitimate offspring. They enjoyed the full rights of inheritance of the estates of their fathers. JOSEPHUS correctly summarized the point of view held by the rabbis saying that the law recognizes no sexual connections except the natural union of husband and wife, and that only for the procreation of children. To avoid temptation, the sages recommended early marriages. The traditional *mohar* constituted serious limitations for many Jews interested in marriage, particularly after the ravages of the BAR KOKHBA revolt and after they became a little more urbanized.

Charitable provision for needy brides eventually became the major responsibility of the community. Others had to choose between married life and scholarly pursuits. The rabbis felt the need of a compromise in such cases and to relax somehow the legal requirements. "If one's soul is longing for learning he could postpone the assumption of marital relations beyond the stated age of eighteen." This was in a period of heavy taxes when students could scarcely marry and study at the same time. Some remained single to the age of thirty and even forty. To encourage both learning and marriage, some men of wealth selected promising young students for their daughters and helped them through their early difficult years. The rabbis were quick to recognize and advocate such preferential treatment as a matter of good general policy.

The Jewish institutional traits of marriage were the subject of continuous development through the centuries. The priestly benediction of the union is mentioned neither in the Bible nor in the Talmud. The Talmud recommended that a "congregation"

Medieval (11th cent.) *ketubah* or marriage contract from Palestine.

should be instituted for the purpose of celebrating a wedding. The presence of ten adult males was regarded as desirable. In the Middle Ages many Jewish communities formalized this desire into a binding statute. In the 10th cent. marriages were performed before a congregation in the bridegroom's abode or in the synagogue.

By the 14th cent. the *huppah* (actual cohabitation) had become a mere religious emblem. Instead of a real room, it became a symbolical room, a canopy, or even a veil or garment (*tallit*) thrown over the heads of the bridal pair. In the 10th cent., the introduction of liturgical marriage hymns had become noticeable. On the whole at this time the Jews had become more tolerant in regard to mixed marriages. The Jews were reluctant, however, to consider marriage with the families of the newcomers in the community. This was due partly to fear, caused by the newcomers, partly to the long history of persecution suffered by Jews from the hands of the foreigners among whom they lived, and partly to the spirit of exclusiveness and pride of the Jewish people.

Time has refined some of the grosser elements connected with weddings. The bridal procession leading the party from the home of the bride to the home of the bridegroom was changed in the Middle Ages, with the party going to the synagogue and not to the bridal chamber. Wedding odes were characteristic of medieval Jewish weddings; so were songs and jests in which wit and merriment scintillated to the end. The seven-day wedding feast was marked by incessant performances, which were not interrupted by the Sabbath. Wit of another kind was displayed at the wedding table. The wedding discourse by the rabbi was a conspicuous function.

II. Various cultural traits

A. Bars to marriage. In early Israel it was a general practice for a man to marry within his own clan (Gen. 24:4; 28:2; 29:19; Jdg. 14:3). Long after the tribal framework of Israel's life had been broken up, marriage within the same family was still considered ideal. An early prohibition was related to seniority, as when LABAN said, "It is not our custom here to give the younger daughter in marriage before the older one" (Gen. 29:26); such custom was found in China, and among Semitic and Aryan peoples.

Cousin marriages were common in Israel during biblical times and continue to be preferred even today among the Middle East Arabs. Cases of consanguineous marriages are reported in the Bible. ABRAHAM married his half-sister, SARAH (Gen. 20:12). AMNON apparently could have married TAMAR, his half-sister (2 Sam. 13:13), but in the priestly code such marriages were forbidden (Lev. 18:6–18; 20:17–21; cf. Deut. 27:22). The law of Moses also prohibited marriages between a man and his aunt (Exod. 6:20; Lev. 18:12–13; 20:19; Num. 26:59) and between a father and his daughter, or mother and son (Lev. 18:7).

People related by marriage could not marry each other (Lev. 18:8, 14–17; 20:12, 14, 20–21; Deut. 27:23). Marriage simultaneously to two sisters was also forbidden (Lev. 18:18). The rabbis added some other twenty to the forbidden degrees. They were mostly extensions of the existing Torah prohibitions; for instance, a man was forbidden to marry the wife of his father's half-brother.

Marriage with Canaanites was prohibited (Deut. 7:3). Priests were forbidden to marry a harlot or a divorcee (Lev. 21:7). A high priest was prohibited to marry a widow and was restricted to one wife (Lev. 21:13–14). According to the later Jewish law, the consent of parents was no legal requirement when the parties to the marriage were of age. M. Mielziner (*The Jewish Law of Marriage and Divorce in Ancient and Modern Times*, 2nd ed. [1901]) states that because of the high respect and veneration in which father and mother have ever been held among Israelites, "the cases of contracting marriage without the parents' consent belonged to the rarest exceptions." One very important reason for the connection between filial submissiveness and religious beliefs was no doubt the extreme importance attached to the curses and blessings of parents. The Israelites believed that parents, and especially a father, could by their blessings or curses determine the destiny of their children.

Marriages with foreign women did take place, as in the case of ESAU, JOSEPH, MOSES, DAVID, SOLOMON, AHAB, and others. Many of these were marriages of kings that were partly inspired by political considerations. The kings, however, encouraged a fashion that spread to their subjects. After the settlement in Canaan, an embargo on racially and ethnically mixed marriages was considered necessary (Exod. 34:15–16; Deut. 7:3–4). Mixed marriages nevertheless continued, as in the case of BATHSHEBA (2 Sam. 11:27) and HIRAM (Huram, 1 Ki. 7:13–14). Deuteronomic law takes for granted that non-Israelite women captured in war will be married by their captors. This custom was not considered an infringement of Israel's law. The actual prohibitions probably date from the days of monarchy when national and religious solidarity were considered to be of the greatest importance. The attitude of the ESSENES and the sectaries of QUMRAM toward marriage, as revealed in the DEAD SEA SCROLLS, suggests that a definite laxity had developed in regard to the prohibited degrees.

B. Choosing the bride. It appears that both boys and girls were married very young. Later the rabbis fixed the minimum age for marriage at twelve for the girls and thirteen for the boys. The parents usually made the decisions for the young people. However, there were love marriages in Israel. The young man could make his preferences known or he could make his own decision without consulting his parents. He could make his own decisions even against the wishes of his parents.

C. Mohar—the price of the wife. The word *mōhar* H4558 ("bridal price, dowry") occurs only three times in the Bible (Gen. 34:12; Exod. 22:16; 1 Sam. 18:25). The *mohar* is usually a present to the bride's father, either in the form of a sum of money or its equivalent in kind, such as an unusual deed. The *mohar* is not a fixed sum; it depends upon the social standing and the wealth of the parties concerned. For a compulsory marriage after a virgin had been raped, the law prescribed the payment of fifty shekels of silver (Deut. 22:29). The ordinary *mohar* must have been less. A fiancé could compound for the payment of the *mohar* by providing a service, such as Jacob did for Leah and Rachel, David did for Michal, and Othniel for Caleb's daughter.

In the thinking of the Israelites, the *mohar* seems to have been not so much a price paid for the woman as a compensation given to the family. It is also probable that the father enjoyed only the usufruct of the *mohar*, which actually reverted to the daughter at the time of succession, or if her husband's death reduced her to penury. Thus the *mohar* is a compensation to the father for the loss of his daughter as well as the means of providing her with certain necessities. Its fundamental purpose seems to be to insure the woman against being left unsupported if widowed.

Gifts presented by the bridegroom on the occasion of the wedding were quite different from the *mohar* (Gen. 34:12). The presents were rewards for the acceptance of the proposal of marriage. In general the custom of providing a dowry never took root in Jewish territory. Fathers gave with their daughters no gifts other than maidservants. There were special cases when fathers gave portions of land with their daughters. (The Babylonian law required the bride's parents to make their daughter a wedding gift or settlement which remained her property, the husband receiving the interest as income on it.)

In order to protect the wife in the event of her becoming widowed or divorced, it was established by the Jewish law that before the nuptials the husband was to make out an obligation in writing, which entitled her to receive a certain sum from his estate in case of her divorcement. This obligation was termed *ketubah*, the marriage deed. For the security of the wife's claim to the amount fixed in the *ketubah* all the property of the husband, both real and personal, was mortgaged. The *ketubah* is still retained in most Jewish marriages, though it has little legal significance in many countries.

In the Talmudic law the mutual consent of the parties to marry each other has to be legally manifested by a special formality, which gives validity to the marriage contract. The usual formality is called *kaseph*, "money." The man gave to his chosen bride a piece of money, even a *peruta* (the smallest copper coin in use in Palestine), or any object of equal value, in the presence of two witnesses, with the words, "Be consecrated to me." In the Middle Ages the piece of money was replaced with a plain ring.

At the time of the Talmud, the gifts the bride brought with her from her parents began to be known as a *neduniah*, "dowry." The sum involved was registered in the *ketubah*. If it was money that the husband would invest in his business, he promised to repay his wife, under specific conditions, the full amount plus one-third interest. If it consisted of clothing and household goods, their value was registered but the husband was committed only to repayment of the value less one-fifth, to allow for depreciation.

D. Marriage formalities and ceremonies. In the ANE marriage was a civil matter. The marriage deed was a legal contract defining the rights of the parties concerned. For the Israelites it was a COVENANT (*běrit* H1382).

Since early times, there have been two stages to a Jewish marriage: betrothal and marriage proper. The betrothal is a legally binding promise of marriage (Deut. 20:7). A man betrothed was exempt from military service. The betrothed woman was regarded as though she were already married. Any other man who violated her was stoned to death as an adulterer. The rabbis continued the distinction between the two stages of marriage, calling them *kiddushin* (betrothal) and *huppah* (the word means "canopy," representing the actual ceremony of bringing home the bride).

1. Kiddushin. According to the law the bride might be bought (betrothed) by money, by writ (a brief contract), or by cohabitation. (Betrothal by contract was suspended before the Middle Ages and is now almost unknown.) In the case of betrothal by cohabitation, the man and woman entered a private chamber, having first declared to witnesses that their actions would count as a betrothal. At the time of the RESTORATION and thereafter, the betrothed girl was expected to remain virgin. During and after the persecutions of ANTIOCHUS Epiphanes, however, the requirement of chastity was relaxed, and the betrothed girl was permitted sexual relations with her future husband. During the NT times this manner of betrothal was disapproved because of its licentious nature. This left the betrothal by money as the last alternative. In the early Middle Ages betrothal by ring was introduced into Palestine, and this practice has remained the custom ever since.

2. Huppah. The actual wedding ceremony of bringing home the bride was a time for rejoicing. The chief element was the entry of the bride into the bridegroom's house. The bridegroom was the king for a week. During the whole week he wore his festal clothes, did not work, and merely looked on at the games—except that now and then the queen joined in a dance. Accompanied by his friends with tambourines and a band, they went to the bride's house where the wedding ceremonies were to start. The bride, richly dressed and adorned with jewels (Ps. 45:14–15), usually wore a veil, which she took off only in the bridal chamber. Escorted by her companions, she was led to the home of the bridegroom.

Love songs were sung in praise of the bridal pair. Speeches were made in their honor, exalting the graces of the newly wedded. Big feasts were prepared in the house of the bride and sometimes in the bridegroom's parents' house. At the close of the feast the bride was conducted by her parents to the nuptial chamber (Jdg. 15:1). The bride remained veiled throughout all these ceremonies (Gen. 29:23). After the wedding night, it was customary for the bride's parents to preserve the blood-stained sheet as proof of the girl's virginity (Deut. 22:13–21). The duty of preserving evidence of the bride's antenuptial chastity was intended as a safeguard against the slanders of a malicious or inconstant husband. There were no marriage festivities for concubines.

III. Dissolution of marriage

A. Historic developments. The fundamental principle of the government of the patriarchal family was the absolute authority of the oldest male ascendant, who was the lawgiver and the judge, and whose rule over his wives, children, and slaves was supreme. This power remained his right throughout the subsequent history of the Jewish people, although in the course of time it was greatly modified and curtailed.

As far back as the history of domestic relations can be traced, the husband's right to divorce was absolutely untrammeled. It was only with the gradual breakup of the patriarchal system, and the substitution of an individualistic system for a socialistic state, that the woman acquired, at first merely negative rights, such as protection against her husband's rights, and finally, positive rights.

This ancient right of the husband, to divorce his wife at his pleasure, is the central thought in the entire system of Jewish divorce law. It was not until the 11th cent. of the common era that, by the decree of Rabbi Gershom of Mayence, the absolute right of the husband to divorce his wife at will was formally abolished, although it had already been for all practical purposes nonexistent in Talmudic times.

The OT, written at a time when the domestic law of the patriarchal family was in full vigor, accepted divorce as a matter of fact. Divorce is the legal dissolution of the marriage relation while both parties are still alive. The ethical principle of marriage is certainly against such a dissolution, but many believe that the ethical principle is not always sufficient for life's actual circumstances. For further discussion, see DIVORCE.

B. Deterrents to divorce. In the following cases the wife could not be divorced: (1) if the husband accused his newly married wife of antenuptial unchastity, and the charge proved to be slanderous; (2) if the husband ravished his wife before marriage; (3) if the wife had become insane or an alcoholic; (4) if the wife was in captivity, in which case it was the duty of the husband to ransom her; (5) if she was the minor wife; (6) if the wife became a deaf-mute after the marriage.

Another deterrent to divorce was the legal necessity for the husband to seek help of one learned in the law, who usually tried to bring reconciliation. The husband also was compelled to pay the wife her dowry and a certain amount of money from what was brought to him by the bride or her parents at the time of the marriage. Gradually men became accustomed to going to the rabbi when they wished to divorce; and, forgetting their ancient rights, they accepted new guiding principles regulating marital relations.

C. Kinds of divorce. Four kinds of divorce were possible on the basis of the rabbinical law: (1) Divorce by mutual agreement of the parties; in this case the wife was entitled to receive the dowry fixed in the *ketubah*. (2) Divorce enforced upon the wife on the petition of the husband; in this case the wife as the guilty party forfeited her dowry. (3) Divorce enforced upon the husband on the petition of the wife; the husband was compelled to give her the bill of divorcement and to pay her dowry. (4) Divorce enforced by court, without petition of either of the parties.

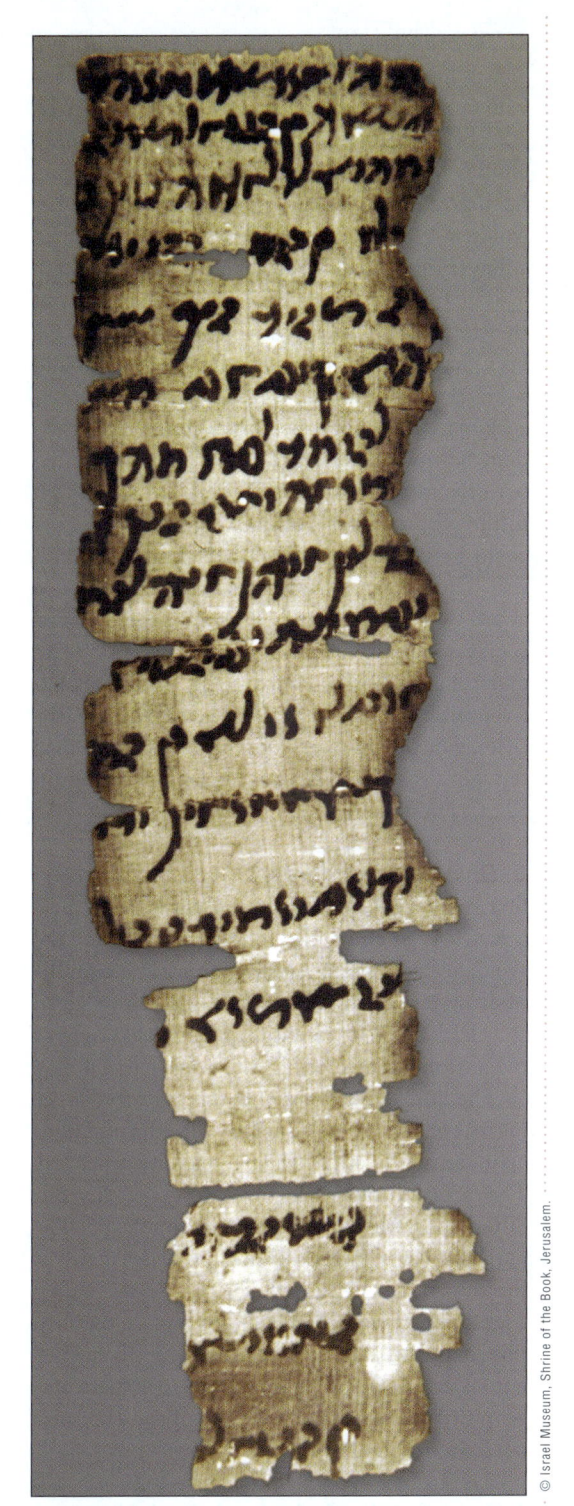

This papyrus, written in Aramaic, contains a marriage contract (from Wadi Murabbaʿat, A.D. 117).

D. Divorce and the support of the children. The influences that modified the legal status of the wife (according to the decree issued around A.D. 1025 by Rabbi Gershom ben Yehudah of Mayence), entitling her to demand and receive a divorce from her husband, affected her rights with respect to her children. In Talmudic times she seems to have had stronger rights than her husband to their custody.

The first regulations concerning the custody of the children of a divorced woman appear to have been made during the early Mishnaic period and were related exclusively to the charge and care of sucklings. Rabbinical decisions concerning children beyond nursing age provide evidence that both the male and the female children were given to the mother. However, the custody of the boys could be claimed by the father after their sixth year. The Roman law gave the court the power to award the custody of the children of the divorced couple according to its discretion. The Jewish law, under the decision of Rabban Ulla, held the father responsible for the support of his son while in the custody of the divorced wife until he had reached the age of six. The father was required by the law in all cases to support his daughter.

E. Divorce procedures. Divorce procedures, at first simple, became complex. By using technical forms, lawyers and judges sought precision and the avoidance of dispute and litigation. The complicated system of procedure among the Jews acted as a check on the theoretically unrestricted right of the husband to divorce his wife at his pleasure.

The husband had not only the right to divorce his wife but also to link the divorce with conditions upon the fulfillment of which its validity depended. The husband could make his own death the condition upon which the divorce became valid. The purpose of this, in all likelihood, was the desire of the husband to give his wife the chance of avoiding a levirate marriage. With a bill of divorce that had this condition, at the moment of his death she was not his widow, but a divorced woman: not any longer restricted to marry any of the husband's brothers but free to marry any man of her own choice.

1. Causes favoring the husband. The husband was entitled to divorce in the following cases: (1) the wife's adultery, and even on strong suspicion of adultery; (2) the wife's public violation of moral decency; (3) the wife's change of religion or evidence of disregard for the ritual law in the management of the household; (4) the wife's obstinate refusal of connubial rights for a full year; (5) the wife's refusal to follow him to another domicile; (6) when the wife insulted her father-in-law, in the presence of her husband, or when she insulted her own husband; (7) when the wife suffered certain incurable diseases, rendering cohabitation impractical or dangerous.

2. Causes favoring the wife. Jewish women could obtain divorce on their own rights, in the following cases: (1) *False accusation of antenuptial incontinence.* PHILO JUDAEUS has recorded the fact that the woman was entitled, if she wanted, to be released from the marriage with the man who by his false accusation had become odious to her.

(2) *Refusal of conjugal rights.* The Torah says, "her food, her raiment, her duty of marriage shall he not diminish" (Exod. 21:10 KJV). This was obligatory on the husband, so its refusal constituted good ground for divorce.

(3) *Impotence.* If the marriage was childless after ten years of cohabitation and the wife charged the husband with physical impotence, she was entitled to divorce.

(4) *Vow of abstinence.* Under the Mosaic law, the husband had the right to annul the vows of his wife. If after the annulment of her vow, she persisted in her resolution, she was released from the payment of the *ketubah*, if he chose to divorce her, since the wife provided the cause for divorce. For the same reason the wife could choose to divorce her husband.

(5) *Physical blemishes.* If the husband was afflicted with any serious disease such as leprosy, or if he was engaged in some malodorous business such as gathering dog's dung, the wife was entitled to a divorce.

(6) *Nonsupport.* When the husband could no longer give her the absolute necessities of life, he was obligated, on her application, to give her a divorce; and her *ketubah* remained a lien on all his subsequently acquired goods, until he had paid it in full.

(7) *Restricting the wife's lawful freedom.* Where the wife by a vow deprived herself of any right or

privilege, and the husband did not absolve her, as he might have done, she was entitled to a divorce. When the husband treated his wife tyrannically and sought to deprive her of her lawful freedom, she was entitled to a divorce.

(8) *Wife beating and desertion* will cause the court to compel the husband before desertion to give his wife a bill of divorce.

(9) *Licentiousness.* As long as polygamy and concubinage were legally sanctioned, there was a marked distinction made between the sexual immorality of the husband and that of the wife. Technically, adultery at that time could be committed only by the wife. After a change in the sex mores, with a more rigid acceptance of monogamy, the licentious conduct of the husband was deemed more serious, and his wife was entitled to divorce him on grounds of adultery.

(10) *Crime.* The husband's committing of a crime that compelled him to flee from the country gave the wife the right to petition for divorce.

Betrothal among the Jews in the old days took place twelve months before marriage. The bride being in all respects bound as a wife, she could be freed only by death or divorce, under the same divorce laws as the married woman.

F. The levirate marriage. The Mosaic law (Deut. 25:5–10) provided for the possibility and necessity, at the death of one brother, to have his childless wife marry one of the surviving brothers. The first son of this union was to be regarded as the son of the dead brother.

The purpose of the levirate marriage or LEVIRATE LAW was: (1) to prevent the name of the dead brother from being put out of Israel (Deut. 25:6; Ruth 4:15); (2) to restore the name of the dead to his inheritance (Ruth 4:5); (3) to keep the family property intact. The child born of levirate marriage would be the heir of the dead husband; he would also be the heir of his real father. This fits the purpose of preserving and consolidating a family property.

The custom went through a process of development before being written in Deuteronomy. At first the levirate law was binding on the entire family of the dead husband (Gen. 38). In the code of Deuteronomy the obligation was limited to the brothers only, and moreover, to brothers living together.

The woman's brother-in-law could refuse levirate, but his reputation would suffer as he was subjected to the ceremony of *halitzah* (Deut. 25:7–10). The obligation was not superseded if the deceased left daughters.

Elsewhere (Lev. 18:16) the law forbids, without any qualification, marriage with a deceased brother's wife. Some believe that this represents a clear collision of codes. Others suppose that an exception was made in the case of a childless widow. The famous disputation with the SADDUCEES clearly implies that the levirate law was regarded as binding in the time of Jesus (Matt. 22:25–32).

IV. Succession and inheritance. The rule of primogeniture or BIRTHRIGHT was generally accepted in Israel. The rule held good throughout Israel's history, was confirmed by the MISHNAH and TALMUD, and is valid to this day in Jewish religious law. Every FIRSTBORN was considered sacred to God in Israel. The firstborn humans were redeemed and were not sacrificed as were the animals (Exod. 13:15); the consecration of all Levites to the service of God was regarded as a suitable substitute for the rest of the people (Num. 3:12–13; 8:16–18).

The firstborn received the prime choice of the inheritance. He was expected, however, to share it equally and by lot with the others. Upon the death of his father, he inherited twice the share of his brothers in the family property (Deut. 21:17). At the same time he became the head of the family. While his father was living, the eldest son was second in rank and authority and had special religious, social, and economic responsibilities. The Jewish father, according to Israelite custom, was expected to make a will before his death (2 Sam. 17:23; 2 Ki. 20:1; Isa. 38:1). In so doing, however, the father was legally restrained from trying to deprive his oldest son of his right to a double share in the inheritance.

Only legitimate sons were entitled to inherit. Children of CONCUBINES were not included in the inheritance. A Hebrew father could declare the sons of his concubines legitimate during his lifetime. In the case of Abraham, he could have made Ishmael his legal heir. According to the Bible record, however, he received a command from God to comply with the wishes of his wife, Sarah (Gen. 21:10–12). The sons of Bilhah and Zilpah born "upon the knees" of their mistresses (30:3 Heb.), ranked with the sons of Rachel and Leah (49:1–28).

As a general rule the daughters were not included in the inheritance of their fathers. There were exceptions, as when a man had no sons. In such a case, in order to keep the estate within the tribe, the girls were expected to marry men of their father's tribe and were entitled to their father's inheritance. Cases in point were the daughters of ZELOPHEHAD (Num. 27:1–11; 36:1–12), and the daughters of ELEAZAR who were married to their own cousins (1 Chr. 23:22). JOB's three daughters apparently inherited equally with their brothers (Job 42:15)—but Job was not necessarily a Hebrew.

When a man died leaving neither sons nor daughters, his relatives were the heirs and not his wife. A childless widow would be remarried under the levirate law, or else return to her father's house (Gen. 38:11; Lev. 22:13; Ruth 1:8). A widow with adult sons would expect them to support her, but if she had small children it was her job to administer her husband's estate until they grew up and entered into their inheritance.

V. The status of women. A Hebrew WOMAN's status was inferior to that of women in Egypt, who were found to serve as heads of their families, or in Babylon, where a woman could acquire property, be a party to a contract, and share in her husband's inheritance. In Israel a woman could own only her marriage portion of the dowry, and even this was administered by her husband. She was excluded from her husband's inheritance but had the right to administer her husband's estate until her sons became of age after their father's death. Nevertheless, the status of Israelite women was far higher than that of the Assyrian women, who were treated as beasts of burden.

The birth of children, especially of boys, usually heightened the status of women. The law commanded that children honor their mother on an equal basis with their father. A wife, if divorced, regained her freedom and enjoyed the right to remarry. A wife could never be sold by her husband. Israelite women did play a part in various religious gatherings and rituals, bringing sacrifices in their own name (Lev. 12:6, 8; 1 Sam. 1:23–24), partaking of the sacred meal (Deut. 12:12, 18; 14:22, 29), and offering prayers at the shrines (1 Sam. 1:9–12). They even played their part in public affairs. Only a general atmosphere of social respect for them could have produced women of the caliber of MIRIAM, DEBORAH, JAEL, HULDAH, and ATHALIAH.

A. Virgins. A girl was expected to be chaste until marriage. The bride's parents had the responsibility to preserve the evidence of their daughter's virginity, the blood-stained garment or sheet from the nuptial bed. Such proofs were preserved in case the husband accused his wife of unchastity. In the case that he was found to be a liar he was first whipped, then fined twice the amount of a normal dowry (Deut. 22:13–19). However, if the accusations were true the wife was stoned (22:20–21). See VIRGIN.

B. Married women. The Israelite law has developed detailed and strict regulations governing a woman's sexual role and life. Her rights were few, her obligations many. With a few exceptions she was deprived of the right to divorce her husband. Legally she was regarded as a piece of his property. The generally accepted sexual double standards placed upon her the burden of the code of sexual morality.

C. Widows. The only certain provision for WIDOWS in the law and tradition was the dowry and the marriage settlement she had received under the *ketubah*. She could choose to remarry one of her brothers-

A young boy learning to read. Giving birth elevated the status of women within biblical culture.

in-law under the levirate law. She was also free to remain with her husband's family or to return to the house of her father (Gen. 38:11; Ruth 1:8–9). If she was the daughter of a priest she was free to partake of priestly portions as before her marriage (Lev. 22:13). The widows with children were in the most pitiable condition, and the Bible makes reiterated appeals for charity toward them (Exod. 22:21–23; Deut. 10:18; Isa. 1:17). The Code of HAMMURABI and the Ugaritic Aghat Epic (see UGARIT) show that widows did not have legal status and were in great need of protection all over the ANE, in Israel as much as in Assyria and Babylon.

D. Adultery. According to the Jewish law, ADULTERY was the most serious violation of a marriage or betrothal contract by the woman. A husband's infidelity did not constitute adultery among the Jews, just as among the Greeks and the Romans. The misconduct by the wife was considered to be the "great sin" in the OT and various Egyptian and Ugaritic texts. Adultery by either a married woman or a betrothed girl was considered to be not only a crime against the husband, but also a deep moral offense. Both the lover and the unfaithful wife were liable to suffer the death penalty (Lev. 20:10; Deut. 22:22–27). The wife accused of infidelity had to undergo the ordeal of the BITTER WATER (Num. 5:12–31) in order to prove her innocence or guilt.

VI. The status of children

A. Childbirth. The role of professional midwives helping at the time of childbirth is clearly indicated (Gen. 35:17; Exod. 1:16). Two customary ways are mentioned as means by which CHILDBEARING was helped among the people of the ANE, and particularly among the Jews. One text dealing with childbirth (Exod. 1:16) uses the term ʾobnayim H78 (lit., "two stones"), which may refer to a delivery stool, suggesting a woman in labor sat on two stones placed at a small distance from each other (some argue, however, that the word refers to the baby's genitalia). Children are described also as being born on the knees of another person (Gen. 30:3), probably of a MIDWIFE or a relative helping the mother.

In the case of multiple births, the rights of the firstborn were well guarded and the birth sequence carefully noted (Gen. 25:25; 38:27). The newborn was washed with care, rubbed with salt, and wrapped in swaddling clothes (Job 38:8–9; Ezek. 16:4). The mother or wet nurse, if the family was wealthy, was responsible for nursing the baby. Usually the baby was weaned at the age of three (2 Macc. 7:27). On the day the baby was weaned, a feast apparently was arranged (Gen. 21:8).

B. Naming the child. The child was named as soon as it was born. Sometimes the mother was expected to name the child (Gen. 29:32; 30:24; 35:18; 1 Sam. 1:20), sometimes the father (Gen. 16:15; 17:19; Exod. 2:22). In many cases the names chosen included (at the beginning or end) the divine element *El*, as in AZAREL and ELEAZAR (both meaning "God has helped"), or *Yah(u)*, as in HANANIAH and JEHOHANAN ("Yahweh is/has been gracious"). Sometimes such names appeared shorter, for instance NATHAN for ELNATHAN ("God has given"). Other more popular names were those of living things, such as DEBORAH ("honey-bee"), expressing the wish that the child would have the positive qualities of its namesake. Occasionally the children were given names from the plant world, or an outstanding trait or feature, or an event coinciding with his birth. An example of a biblical name of the latter type is ICHABOD ("inglorious," 1 Sam. 4:21).

After the restoration and especially during the NT period, ARAMAIC names became quite common. At about the same time these were found beside or instead of Hebrew names. The practice of modern times of naming a boy at his CIRCUMCISION is mentioned only in the NT (Lk. 1:59; 2:21) and not in the OT.

C. Child rearing. The relation of Hebrew parents and children is consonant with a family of the patriarchal type. The father was responsible for the training of his children, including the religious education. It was expected from him to "direct his children and his household after him to keep the way of the LORD by doing what is right and just" (Gen. 18:19). Every Hebrew male child was circumcised on the eighth day of his life and thus set apart to Yahweh (17:10). In the earlier years the child was under the close care of his mother. After his fifth birthday the boy came more directly under the care of his father, who instructed him in the Torah. Moreover, every father was expected to teach his son a trade as a means of livelihood.

At about the time of Christ, Rabbi Joshua ben Gamala instituted schools apart from the homes in every town and village of Palestine. The chief subject matters in the new schools continued to be the Mosaic law and the two portions of the Talmud, the MISHNAH and the GEMARA. Because of the intercourse with Greece, it is likely that the GREEK LANGUAGE was also studied.

The education of girls was not neglected. Above all things their education was designed to fit them for their special sphere of responsibility, the management of the household. They were helped to become better wives and better mothers also through their participation in the family worship and the study of the sacred writings. The Hebrew family was, therefore, an institution of significant moral, religious, social, and economic value.

VII. Mixed marriages and the future of the Jewish family. Although not encouraged but rather forbidden, marriages with foreign women did take place among the Israelites both before they had any real appreciation for a sense of national unity and later throughout their history. Esau married two Hittite women (Gen. 26:34); Joseph, an Egyptian (41:45); Moses, a Midianite (Exod. 2:21); David, an Aramean (2 Sam. 3:3); Solomon, a harem with many foreign women (1 Ki. 11:1); Ahab, a Phoenician (16:31).

These were all marriages of kings or prominent men. They began, however, a fashion that spread among their subjects and the commoners. Earlier, in connection with the settlement in Canaan, the need to protect the religion and high national interests had brought about an embargo on mixed marriages (Exod. 34:15–16; Deut. 7:3–4). The mixed marriages nevertheless continued; Bathsheba married a Hittite (2 Sam. 11:3), and Huram's mother married a Phoenician (1 Ki. 7:13–14).

The more rigid prohibitions date from the days of the monarchy, when the national and the religious solidarity were so important for the security of the nation. The matter came to a crisis after the EXILE (Ezra 10). During the Hellenistic period the need to preserve the purity of the Jewish community prompted the reinforcement of restrictions relating to mixed marriages.

Mixed marriages are much more readily accepted in modern Judaism. Many however are really disturbed about the trends and developments. David Kirshenbaum (*Mixed Marriage and the Jewish Future* [1958]) feels that "slowly and unperceptibly, like cancer cells, the disease of mixed marriages penetrates, consumes and destroys the Jewish family and the Jewish hope of survival." He appears to be convinced that the Jewish home has become spiritually empty. Mixed marriages have a dangerously disruptive effect. There will be no longer any historic Jewish continuity if the rate of mixed marriages increases among the Jews. There will be no point of contact among the past, present, and future. Coupled with a general acceptance of mixed marriages is the religious and spiritual laxity of the Jewish parents. In many cases they completely neglect the spiritual upbringing of their children.

At the same time, considering all the threatening forces, one cannot be but deeply impressed by the strength and solidarity of the Jewish family. Through the centuries, the Jewish family, probably more than any other influence, has been responsible for the continuing vitality and for the survival of this nation of wonder, the most peculiar among all the nations of the world.

(See further D. W. Amram, *The Jewish Law of Divorce* [1896]; E. Westermarck, *The Future of Marriage in Western Civilization* [1936]; W. Goodsell, *A History of Marriage and the Family* [1939], 1–53; S. R. Brav, *Marriage and the Jewish Tradition* [1951]; O. L. Yarbrough, *Not Like the Gentiles: Marriage Rules in the Letters of Paul* [1985]; G. P. Hugenberger, *Marriage as a Covenant: A Study of Biblical Law and Ethics Governing Marriage, Developed from the Perspective of Malachi* [1994]; M. L. Satlow, *Jewish Marriage in Antiquity* [2001]; J. Evans Grubbs, *Women and Law in the Roman Empire: A Sourcebook on Marriage, Divorce and Widowhood* [2002]; C. Hayes, *Gentile Impurities and Jewish Identities: Intermarriage and Conversion from the Bible to the Talmud* [2002]; D. Instone-Brewer, *Divorce and Remarriage in the Bible: The Social and Literary Context* [2002]; K. M. Campbell, ed., *Marriage and Family in the Biblical World* [2003]; W. Deming, *Paul on Marriage and Celibacy:*

The Hellenistic Background of 1 Corinthians 7, 2nd ed. [2004]; G. Beattie, *Women and Marriage in Paul and His Early Interpreters* [2005].)   P. TRUTZA

marrow. A connective tissue found in the cavities of the bones. It produces blood platelets to aid in blood clotting, red blood cells for carrying oxygen, and white blood cells for combating infection. There are two kinds of bone marrow, red and yellow. Red marrow preponderates in childhood and represents a more active phase of blood cell formation. Yellow marrow, characterized by more fat tissue, is increased in the healthy adult (cf. Job 21:24; Heb. *mōaḥ H4672*). The marrow in adults reverts to red marrow following serious blood loss or body stress. The marrow cavity of long bones ends at the joints so that it is completely surrounded by bone cortex. This clear demarcation is referred to in a well-known NT passage that emphasizes the discerning power of the word of God (Heb. 4:12; Gk. *myelos G3678*). The English term also has a figurative meaning, "choice food," and is used in that sense once in the KJV (Ps. 63:5) and once in the NRSV (Isa. 25:6).   P. E. ADOLPH

Marsanes. A non-Christian Gnostic text included in the NAG HAMMADI LIBRARY (NHC X, 1). Composed in Greek, probably in the 3rd cent. A.D., this tractate is preserved in a Coptic translation, but the MS is very fragmentary. Regarded as an apocalypse, and influenced by Platonism, it apparently describes the experience of a prophet who had a visionary experience as he ascended into the heavens. The document also discusses the symbolical meaning of the letters of the alphabet. (English trans. in *NHL*, 460–71.)

Marsena mahr-see´nuh (מַרְסְנָא *H5333*). One of "the seven nobles of Persia and Media who had special access to the king and were highest in the kingdom" (Esth. 1:14). Queen VASHTI was banished by Ahasuerus (XERXES) on their advice.

marsh. Because of the dryness of the climate, there are very few marshes (Heb. *biṣṣâ H1289*) in PALESTINE, except along the DEAD SEA. In Ezek. 47:11 the prophet foretells future blessings for Israel, and writes that the marshes around the sea (prob. the Dead Sea) shall not be sweetened, but left as beds for digging salt. The references in Job 8:11 and 40:21 are probably to marshes in Egypt, since there are many in the NILE delta. The term *ʾăgam H106*, usually rendered "pool, pond," is translated "marsh" once in the NIV and other versions (Jer. 51:43).
     S. BARABAS

marshal. See CAPTAIN.

Marshes near Lake Timsah in Egypt.

Mars' Hill. See Areopagus.

Martha mahr´thuh (Μάρθα *G3450*, from Aram. מָרְתָא, "lady, mistress, hostess" [fem. of מַר, "lord, master"]). The sister of Mary and Lazarus, all three being among the special friends of Jesus (Jn. 11:5). Their home is clearly stated by John to be in Bethany in Judea (Jn. 11:1), but Luke does not name the village (Lk. 10:38). The topographical context of Lk. 10 suggests that the village might be in Galilee, but there is no certainty about this. Some explain this apparent discrepancy with John's account by suggesting that Luke has placed the event too early in the ministry of Jesus, but it is more likely that Jesus visited the home in Bethany on a journey to Jerusalem unrecorded by the synoptists (cf. Jn. 10:22–23).

Martha appears three times in the gospel narratives (Lk. 10:38–42; Jn. 11:1–44; 12:2). The historical accuracy of the accounts in Luke and John is supported by the consistent characterization in these two independent records. In both, Martha is busy serving at table and tends to be outspoken, in contrast to Mary's quieter devotion to Jesus. Luke's statement that Martha received Jesus into her house (Lk. 10:38) implies that she was mistress of the house, probably being the elder sister; but there is no evidence that she was married to Simon the leper or was his widow. If one assumes that the event of Jn. 12:1–8 is the same as that of Matt. 26:6–13 and Mk. 14:3–9, Martha is serving in Simon's house, and Lazarus and Mary are also present, but so were other guests. Martha's aptitude for serving was sufficient reason for her assistance on this special occasion.

Jesus' affectionate rebuke (Lk. 10:41–42) was evoked by Martha's failure to recognize the primary importance of his teaching. Her activity was not out of place but out of proportion. Jesus did not condemn Martha's work, but her excessive attention to material provision, which disturbed her peace of mind, prompted criticism of both Mary and Jesus, and robbed her of the benefit of receiving the Lord's instruction. Both Martha and Mary expressed the same faith in Jesus' power to save Lazarus from dying (Jn. 11:21, 32). The Lord would not have spoken to her the profound truth of Jn. 11:25–26 did he not know that she was sufficiently receptive to hear it. Her declaration of belief rose to the highest level (11:27), but her hesitancy of faith (v. 39) shows that she did not yet realize its full implications. (See B. Witherington III, *Women in the Ministry of Jesus* [1984], 100–116; P. F. Esler and R. A. Piper, *Lazarus, Mary and Martha: A Social-Scientific and Theological Reading of John* [2006].)

J. C. Connell

martyr. A person who suffers death for refusing to renounce a religion. The English term derives (through Latin) from the Greek *martys G3459* (genitive *martyros*), meaning "a witness," that is, someone who can assert what he himself has seen and heard. Because in the early church those who witnessed to Christ often gave their lives for their faith (cf. "the blood of your witness [NIV, martyr] Stephen," Acts 22:20 NRSV; "Antipas, my faithful witness, who was put to death in your city," Rev. 2:13), the sense of the term became specialized. See also testimony.

In the OT, the people of Israel were the primary witnesses (Heb. *ʿēd H6332*, Isa. 43:10–12; 44:8), but the prophets in the special sense held that position with a special commission (Isa. 6:9–10; Jer. 1:5). In the NT the church was the witness that was to take the gospel to the whole world (Lk. 24:48; Acts 1:8), but like the prophets, the apostles had a special position, since they witnessed not only to Christ's teaching and works, but also from personal experience to his resurrection (Acts 1:1, 2–22). They received special authority from Christ, who himself was the ultimate witness (Rev. 1:5; 3:14).

Persecution, however, soon arose from both Jew and Gentile, with the result that many of those who bore faithful witness experienced physical attack and even death. Stephen the deacon (Acts 7:57–60) and James the brother of John (12:2) were two of the earliest witnesses who suffered the extreme penalty for witnessing to Christ. Others followed in their train, including the apostles Peter, Paul, and a number of lesser fame (Rev. 20:4). Those who so suffered became in a special sense witnesses to Christ (cf. Heb. 11), which led the church to accord them a special place in its tradition, as those who had given the utmost in witness by being faithful unto death.

In post-NT times the tendency became common to regard those who died for their witness as having a special place in heaven, with special rights of intercession. Under the influence of Neo-Platonism, this led to the development of the idea of "saints" who had the privilege of intercession for Christians upon earth. The NT, however, provides no ground for such beliefs, since it gives no place of special privilege even to those who have as "martyrs" died for the faith.

(See further H. B. Workman, *Persecution in the Early Church: A Chapter in the History of Renunciation* [c. 1906]; W. H. C. Frend, *Martyrdom and Persecution in the Early Church: A Study of Conflict from the Maccabees to Donatus* [1965]; D. Seeley, *The Noble Death: Graeco-Roman Martyrology and Paul's Concept of Salvation* [1990]; A. Droge and J. Tabor, *A Noble Death: Suicide and Martyrdom Among Greeks and Romans, Jews and Christians in the Ancient World* [1992]; M. Cormack, ed., *Sacrificing the Self: Perspectives on Martyrdom and Religion* [2002]; E. A. Castelli, *Martyrdom and Memory: Early Christian Culture Making* [2004].)   W. S. REID

Martyrdom and Ascension of Isaiah. See ASCENSION OF ISAIAH.

marvel, marvelous. These English terms are used frequently in the KJV (where the adjective is spelled "marvellous"), almost always with reference to divinity. OT writers extolled God's "marvelous works," including his CREATION and his SALVATION (1 Chr. 16:24; Job 5:9 [NIV, "miracles"]; Pss. 96:3; 98:1; cf. 1 Pet. 2:9 [NIV, "wonderful"]). Prophets predicted his marvelous work of REDEMPTION through the MESSIAH (Ps. 118:23; Isa. 29:14 [NIV, "wonder"]; Zech. 8:6). Significantly, Jesus himself, his message, and his works were marvelous. "The child's father and mother marveled at what was said about him" by SIMEON (Lk. 2:33). NICODEMUS, the Jews, and all the people marveled at his teaching (Jn. 3:7; 5:20, 28; 7:15, 21). Jesus' works repeatedly made the crowds marvel (Matt. 8:27; Mk. 5:20; Lk. 8:25; 11:14). Jesus, in turn, marveled at the great faith of the centurion (Matt. 8:10), and at the unbelief of the Nazarene citizens (Mk. 6:6). In most of these NT passages the NIV uses various synonyms; see ASTONISHMENT.   G. B. FUNDERBURK

Mary mair′ee (Μαρία *G3451*, occurring frequently in the indeclinable form Μαριάμ, from Heb. מִרְיָם *H5319*; see MIRIAM). The name was made famous by the sister of MOSES. Possibly its prevalence in NT times was due to the popularity of MARIAMME, the last of the HASMONEANS and wife of HEROD the Great. Six (or seven) women of this name are mentioned in the NT.

(1) MARY, MOTHER OF JESUS. See separate article.

(2) Mother of John Mark (see MARK, JOHN). Though mentioned only once by name in the NT (Acts 12:12), this Mary must have been prominent in the Jerusalem church. She was related to BARNABAS (Col. 4:10), and her large home was used

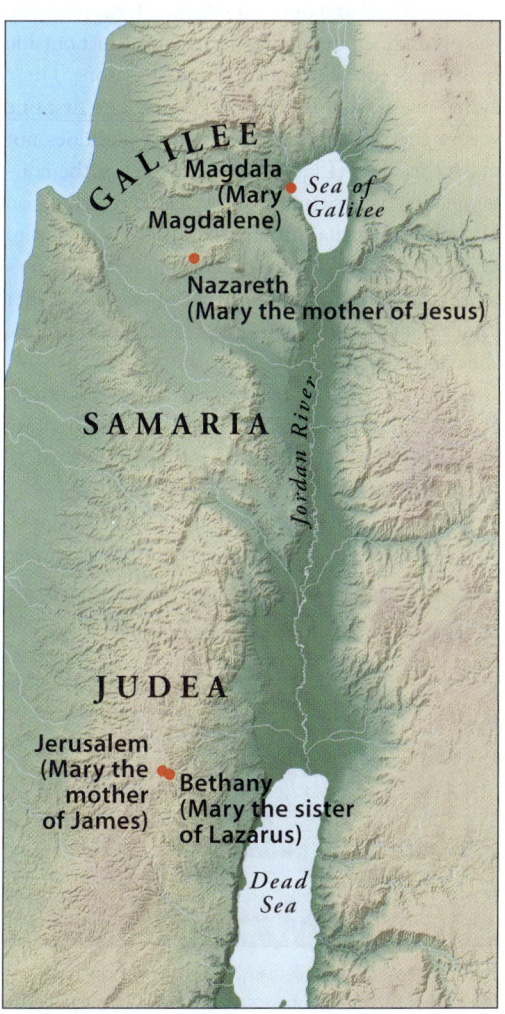

Many different Marys are mentioned in the Gospels.

by the apostolic church for assembly (Acts 12:12; mention is made of servants, v. 13). Peter's knowledge of where to go to find the believers indicates an established practice. It was likely the most adequate home in Jerusalem available for such meetings. Apparently she had not sold her property for communal distribution (Acts 4:34–37). She used it for the common good. It is pure conjecture that the Last Supper was in her "upper room" (Lk. 22:12), but early Christianity found in her home a frequent meeting place. A by-product of her hospitality and faithfulness was the missionary service of her son, John Mark.

(3) Sister of LAZARUS and MARTHA, from BETHANY (Jn. 11:1). Jesus appreciated Mary of Bethany as a special friend and devoted follower. Jesus probably was entertained frequently in this home just outside Jerusalem, especially during the feast seasons. Three events reveal what is known of Mary. The first one was in the Bethany home, though Luke does not make this clear (Lk. 10:38–42). Mary is the contemplative type, sitting at Jesus' feet and feeding on his words. Martha, in her frustration, objected to doing all the work, but Jesus complimented Mary's sense of values. She realized that there were higher values than physical comforts. Having found them, she was allowed to keep them.

The second cluster of reactions relates to the death and restoration to life of Lazarus (Jn. 11:1–46). Mary and Martha first sent word to Jesus in PEREA of the illness of Lazarus (v. 3). When Jesus delayed his coming and Lazarus died, Mary was deeply affected. She sat still in the house among the comforters when Martha went to meet Jesus (v. 20). When Jesus sent for her, she came quickly (vv. 28–29). Faith and sorrow mingled in her words, "Lord, if you had been here, my brother would not have died" (v. 32). Throughout, Martha was still the manager and Mary was the sensitive, contemplative soul.

The third event is a dinner, perhaps in gratitude for Jesus' raising Lazarus (Jn. 12:1–8; cf. Matt. 26:6–10 and Mk. 14:3–9, where Mary is not named, and where the event is said to take place in the home of SIMON the leper). Both Jesus and Lazarus are at the table. The atmosphere is charged with impending crisis. No one can think of an appropriate word or action. Suddenly the quiet, contemplative Mary bursts forth with an impulse that has been growing in her heart. The ALABASTER cruse of precious imported perfume from INDIA, which represented a year's wages and which had been reserved much as a dowry for a great day—would not that express her feelings to her wonderful Lord? Forgetting her reserve in the intensity of her act, she pushed past the reclining forms, broke the expensive jar and poured the oil on the head of Jesus. Recoiling from the gaze of the guests, no doubt, she pulled back from the center of attention, stopping at Jesus' feet with the remainder of the PERFUME, dripping it on his feet and lovingly wiping the feet with her hair. To "practical" men, it was a stupid waste, but Jesus considered it a most beautiful tribute paid to him. Such love is precious. (This anointing is not to be confused with the one in Galilee, Lk. 7:36–50; see D. A. Carson, *The Gospel according to John* [1991], 425–27, which also discusses the differences between John and Matthew/Mark.)

(4) Mother of James the younger and of Joseph/Joses (Matt. 27:56; 28:1 ["the other Mary"]; Mk. 15:40, 47). See JAMES III and JOSEPH #12. A problem arises in relation to the husband of this Mary. Most English versions mention "Mary the wife of Clopas" as present at the cross (Jn. 19:25; the Gk. reads simply, "Mary of Clopas"). But James the younger is regularly designated "son of Alphaeus" (Matt. 10:3; Mk. 3:18; Lk. 6:15). Is the same Mary wife of CLOPAS (to be distinguished from CLEOPAS) and of ALPHAEUS? That would be possible if Clopas and Alphaeus are names of the

The Church of Lazarus in Bethany. It was in this town that Mary, her brother Lazarus, and her sister Martha frequently opened their home to Jesus.

same person or if there was a second marriage. An alternate possibility is suggested by the Arabic version, which renders John's reference as "Mary the daughter of Clopas" (see E. Bishop in *ExpTim* 73 [1961–62]: 339). In any case, it is quite unlikely that this Mary should be identified with the sister of Mary in Jn. 19:25, since two sisters would not normally bear the same name. The church father Hegesippus refers to a Clopas who is said to have been a brother of Jesus' father, Joseph (Euseb. *Eccl. Hist.* 3.11; 4.22). If this is true, and if Clopas and Alphaeus are the same person, then Mary of Clopas and Mary the mother of Jesus were sisters-in-law. According to some scholars, "Mary of Clopas" (a description found only in Jn. 19:5) is not the same as the mother of James and Joseph/Joses, but altogether a different person, about whom nothing else is known.

In any case, Mary the mother of James the younger and of Joseph/Joses was one of the Galilean women who, having been healed of evil spirits and infirmities, followed Jesus and supported him financially (Mk. 15:40; Lk. 8:2–3). It is interesting to note that two mothers with their sons thus joined the group and at least three of the four sons became apostles. According to the records, this Mary accompanied Jesus to Jerusalem (Matt. 27:56; Mk. 15:41), witnessed the crucifixion (Matt. 27:55, 56; Mk. 15:40; Lk. 23:49), observed the entombment (Matt. 27:61; Mk. 15:47; Lk. 23:55), joined in the securing of spices for anointing Jesus' body (Mk. 16:1; Lk. 23:56), saw the empty tomb and heard the angelic announcement of Jesus' resurrection (Matt. 28:1–7; Mk. 16:2–7; Lk. 24:1–7), reported to the apostles what she had seen and heard (Matt. 28:8; Lk. 24:9–11), and even saw the resurrected Jesus (Matt. 28:9–10).

(5) Mary Magdalene, so called after the name of her native city, MAGDALA, on the W bank of the Sea of Galilee, 3 mi. NW of TIBERIAS. On the site are now the squalid hovels of Majdal (Mejdel). A. Edersheim says the ancient city was famous for dye works and fine woolen textures (*The Life and Times of Jesus the Messiah*, 8th ed. [1900], 1:571). Trade, shipbuilding, fishing, fish curing, and agriculture also brought great wealth to the city; its moral corruption was also notorious (ibid., citing *y. Ta'an.* 69a).

Jesus had driven seven demons out of Mary Magdalene (Lk. 8:2; cf. Mk. 16:9). This obviously meant that she was a healed invalid, not a rescued social derelict. There is no evidence that she was promiscuous, much less a harlot for hire. That she was a person of means is evident from her ability to support Jesus from her means. Her obvious leadership among the women hardly reflects a scarlet past. (There is certainly no ground for identifying her with the anonymous sinful woman of Lk. 7:37; otherwise, NT usage would normally have kept her anonymous.) She is mentioned more often than most of the other believing women, and usually first. A dozen references show her as healed of evil spirits or infirmities (Lk. 8:2), following Jesus from Galilee and ministering to him (Matt. 27:56), beholding the crucifixion from afar (Mk. 15:40), standing by the cross (Jn. 19:25), locating the tomb (Matt. 28:1; Mk. 15:47), watching the tomb (Matt. 27:61), coming early to the tomb with spices (Mk. 16:1; Jn. 20:1), being first to see the risen Lord (Mk. 16:9), and reporting the resurrection to the disciples (Lk. 24:10; Jn. 20:18).

(6) An early Christian who "worked very hard" for the church in Rome (Rom. 16:6; KJV, "who bestowed much labour on us [*hymas*]", following the TR). It is not possible to determine whether this Mary was a Jewish Christian or a Gentile (the Latin *Maria*, not as the Hebrew name but as the feminine form of *Marius*, was common in Rome).

(See further S. Andrews, *The Life of our Lord Upon the Earth* [1862], 281–86, 596–612; J. Lange, *The Life of the Lord Jesus Christ* [1872], 1:441; 2:258–59, 489; 3:21–23, 365–67; 4:253–54, 470–71; B. Witherington III, *Women in the Ministry of Jesus* [1984]; C. M. and J. A. Grassi, *Mary Magdalene and the Women in Jesus' Life* [1986]; J. Schaberg, *The Resurrection of Mary Magdalene: Legends, Apocrypha, and the Christian Testament* [2002]; F. Stanley Jones, ed., *Which Mary? The Marys of Early Christian Tradition* [2002]; A. G. Brock, *Mary Magdalene, the First Apostle: The Struggle for Authority* [2003]; H. E. Hearon, *The Mary Magdalene Tradition: Witness and Counter-Witness in Early Christian Communities* [2004].)   W. T. DAYTON

Mary, Birth of. Also *Descent of Mary* or *Genealogy of Mary* (Gk. *Genna Marias*). A Gnostic document known only from its mention by EPIPHANIUS (*Pan.* 26.12.1–4; K. Holl's ed., 1:290–91). It identifies the Zechariah of Matt. 23:35 with the father of JOHN THE BAPTIST, and says he was killed because he told of his vision in the temple (Lk. 1:9–12) of a man having the form of a donkey. This detail conforms with pagan polemic against the God of the Jews, and the work appears to show violent hostility to Judaism. (English trans. in *NTAp* [1991], 1:395–96). See also MARY, GOSPEL OF; MARY, GOSPEL OF THE BIRTH OF.   R. McL. WILSON

Mary, Descent (Genealogy) of. See MARY, BIRTH OF.

Mary, Gospel of. An apocryphal Gnostic document preserved fragmentarily in the Berlin Codex (BG 8502, 1). It reports that the disciples were grieved after the resurrected Jesus departed from them, and that MARY (Magdalene) encouraged them by recounting to them her vision of "the soul" ascending and being questioned by "the powers." Both Andrew and Peter were skeptical that the Savior had said such "strange" things, but Levi persuaded them to listen to her. This tractate is a Coptic translation of a Greek original, and a 3rd-cent. Greek papyrus discovered at Oxyrhynchus in Egypt preserves two small sections (with substantial differences). (English trans. in *NHL*, 523–38; discussion in *ABD*, 4:583–84. For the view that the work is not Gnostic and that it is based on tradition earlier than the NT Gospels, see E. A. de Boer, *The Gospel of Mary: Beyond a Gnostic and a Biblical Mary Magdalene* [2004]).

Mary, Gospel of the Birth of. A Latin account of the birth and childhood of MARY, MOTHER OF JESUS, included among the works attributed to JEROME (*PL* 30:307ff.), but actually a much later (possibly 8th cent.), shorter, and improved edition of the first part of the *Gospel of Pseudo-Matthew*, which in turn is based on the *Protevangelium of James*. See JAMES, PROTEVANGELIUM OF; PSEUDO-MATTHEW, GOSPEL OF. There is a certain irony in the attribution, in view of Jerome's pronounced opposition to such apocryphal literature.

The text begins with Mary's parents, Joachim and Anna, and tells of their blameless life. Because of Joachim's childlessness, his offering is rejected by the high priest Issachar (in the *Protevangelium* and *Pseudo-Matthew* the name is Reuben); Joachim retires to his flocks, but an angel appears to him, and also to Anna. The document then relates the birth of Mary, her presentation in the temple, and her upbringing there. At the age of fourteen, virgins resident in the temple are required to marry, but Mary is reluctant. A council summoned by the high priest resolves to seek divine guidance, which is soon forthcoming. Joseph (here not a widower, as in the *Protevangelium*, though advanced in years) is chosen by a miraculous sign, and they are betrothed. Joseph goes to Bethlehem, while Mary returns to her parents' home in Galilee, where the ANNUNCIATION takes place. Joseph on his return finds her with child, but in his perplexity is reassured by an angel. The document closes with a brief statement about the birth of Jesus.

This outline is enough to reveal the document's affinity with the earlier chapters of the *Protevangelium*. Reference to Joseph's previous marriage has been removed as heretical (according to Jerome, the "brothers" of Jesus were cousins), as have elements felt to be offensive (e.g., the episode of the midwife). The book is later than the 6th-cent. *Decretum Gelasianum*, which does not mention it, but is quoted at the end of the 10th cent. by Fulbert of Chartres. It has been argued that the author was Paschasius Radbertus, abbot of Corbie in the 9th cent. (see *Revue Bénédictine* 46 [1934]: 265ff.). Through its incorporation in the *Golden Legend* of James de Voragine (1298), the work enjoyed a wide circulation. (English trans. in *Ante-Nicene Christian Library* 16 [1870]; see also É. Amann, *Le Protévangile de Jacques et ses remaniements latins* [1910].)

R. McL. WILSON

Mary, mother of Jesus mair'ee (Μαρία *G3451*, occurring frequently in the indeclinable form Μαριάμ, from Heb. מִרְיָם *H5319*; see MIRIAM).

   I. Biblical information
      A. Lineage
      B. The betrothal
      C. The annunciation
      D. The visit to Elizabeth
      E. The birth and infancy narratives

F. Life in Nazareth
G. Incidents during Christ's ministry
H. At the cross and after the resurrection
II. Worship of Mary
A. Mother of God
B. Perpetual virginity
C. Immaculate conception
D. Bodily assumption

I. Biblical information

A. Lineage. In Lk. 1:36 Mary is called a relative of ELIZABETH, who was a descendant of AARON (1:5). This connection may be thought to suggest that Mary too belonged to the tribe of LEVI (cf. *T. Sim.* 7), but other indications argue strongly that she, like JOSEPH, was of royal lineage (some think that the phrase "of the house of David" in Lk. 1:27 [NRSV] may apply either to "virgin" or to "Joseph"). The references to the Davidic lineage by Elizabeth and ZECHARIAH (Lk. 1:32, 69) and the frequent, and unchallenged, public address of Jesus by the title "Son of David" (Matt. 9:27; 15:22; 20:30–31; Mk. 10:47–48) possibly imply that on his mother's side as well as Joseph's, Jesus was of David's line. The Sinaitic Syriac text of Lk. 2:4 reads, "because they were both of the house of David." It is unlikely, however, that Lk. 3:23–38 gives the genealogy of Mary, as some have thought. See GENEALOGY OF JESUS CHRIST.

The *Protevangelium of James* calls Mary's parents Joachim of Nazareth and Anna of Bethlehem (see JAMES, PROTEVANGELIUM OF). The only member of her family mentioned in Scripture is her sister (Jn. 19:25). Comparison with Mk. 15:40 and Matt. 27:56 makes it almost certain that this sister was SALOME, wife of ZEBEDEE, in which case JAMES and JOHN THE APOSTLE were cousins of Jesus. (The alternative suggestion, which identifies "his mother's sister" with "Mary the wife of Clopas," involves the most unlikely requirement that two sisters bore the same name.)

B. The betrothal. Mary was brought up in NAZARETH and probably was still in her teens when she was betrothed. In the 4th-cent. *History of Joseph the Carpenter,* she was said to be twelve when she was betrothed to Joseph, a widower of ninety with a grown-up family (see JOSEPH THE CARPENTER, HISTORY OF). The biblical picture, however, suggests a young man entering marriage for the first time. Betrothal was in Jewish custom almost tantamount to MARRIAGE. A declaration was made to the prospective bride, and a small gift given her as a pledge, in the presence of witnesses; or else the declaration might be in writing. From this time the woman was called "wife"; if her betrothed should die before the marriage was consummated, she became a widow and the custom of LEVIRATE LAW might apply to her. She could not be dismissed from the betrothal relationship except through a writing of divorce, and any sexual relationship during the betrothal period was treated as adultery. In the case of a virgin, the betrothal lasted about a year. See MARRIAGE.

C. The annunciation (Lk. 1:26–38). During this period of betrothal, the angel GABRIEL appeared to Mary and greeted her with the words, "Greetings, you who are highly favored! The Lord is with you" (1:28). The address *kecharitōmenē* (from *charitoō* G5923) means that Mary has received grace, not that she has grace to bestow. The following clause may be interpreted as a wish, "the Lord *be* with you," or as a statement defining the grace Mary had received. The additional words in the KJV, "Blessed art thou among women," have some MS support, but are most likely a gloss from Elizabeth's words (v. 42). Mary was puzzled by the greeting and evidently frightened, for the angel continued,

Illustration of a cave home. While at her home in Nazareth, Mary received word of the special child she would bear.

telling her not to be afraid, and that she would conceive and bear a son whom she would call Jesus. He would be called the Son of the Most High and would, as David's descendant, reign over Israel for ever. Mary made the natural inquiry, "How will this be ... since I am a virgin?" Her reply does not indicate doubt or disbelief of the message, as Zechariah's had done (1:18), but rather perplexity as to the method of fulfillment.

Gabriel replied, "The Holy Spirit will come upon you, and the power of the Most High will overshadow you. So the holy one to be born will be called the Son of God" (Lk. 1:35), thus confirming the virginal conception. Belief in the VIRGIN BIRTH of Christ is dependent almost entirely on the records of Matthew and Luke. There is no reference to it in the remainder of the NT. In Gal. 4:4, PAUL writes that Jesus was born of a "woman" (*gynē G1222*) instead of using the word "virgin" (*parthenos G4221*). But his point is the real humanity of Christ, not the marital state of Christ's mother. The variant reading of Matt. 1:16 given in a few MSS, "Joseph, to whom the virgin Mary was betrothed, begat Jesus who is called Christ," is certainly a scribal error, repeating the formula of earlier verses. It would, in any case, be quite impossible to take the word "begat" in the normal biological sense in the same verse that describes Mary as "virgin." The references to Joseph as Jesus' father (Matt. 13:55; Lk. 2:33, 48) imply the family and social position Joseph occupied, not physical paternity.

The angel then told Mary that Elizabeth, in her old age, had conceived a son six months earlier, "For nothing is impossible with God" (Lk. 1:37). A great deal was implied by Mary's words of meek acceptance, "I am the Lord's servant. ... May it be to me as you have said" (v. 38). It was the devout maiden's humble acceptance of the embarrassment, suspicion, and misunderstanding that would undoubtedly follow. See ANNUNCIATION.

D. The visit to Elizabeth (Lk. 1:39–56). Shortly after the angel's departure, Mary went to visit the home of Zechariah and Elizabeth. Luke states merely that this was in a city of Judah in the hill country (1:39). Tradition identifies the town as ʿAin Karim, a village 5 mi. W of Jerusalem; if so, Mary traveled some 80 mi. from Nazareth (many think that the couple lived even further S, in the area around HEBRON). On entering the house, she was surprised by Elizabeth's greeting, "Blessed are you among women, and blessed is the child you will bear!" (v. 42), and by her reference to Mary, not as a relative, but as "the mother of my Lord" (v. 43). Doubtless the promises she had received through Zechariah would have filled Elizabeth with hopes for the early appearance of the Messiah; now there was the physical sign of the movement of the babe in her womb, as well as the inspiration of the Holy Spirit (v. 41) to grant recognition of the one who was to be born, and to pronounce blessing on the mother who believed God's message.

The song that follows, known as the MAGNIFICAT, is attributed to Elizabeth by three Old Latin MSS and by Niceta of Remesiana; but all Greek and most Latin MSS, and almost all patristic references, speak of it as Mary's. The Magnificat is more calm and majestic than the ecstatic outburst of Elizabeth, and is modeled on the OT Psalms, especially the song of HANNAH (1 Sam. 2:1–10). It is a meditation in four strophes. The first two give Mary's personal praise and the reason for it; the third speaks of God's larger purposes in the shaping of human history; the last returns to the immediate fulfillment of God's mercy promised to Israel. The theme in general is of God's gracious dealing with the humble and poor, while he shows his strong power against the rich and the mighty. Mary stayed with Elizabeth for three months (Lk. 1:56, in all probability up to the birth and circumcision of John, vv. 57–79).

E. The birth and infancy narratives. It was probably some time after Mary returned to Nazareth that "she was found to be with child through the Holy Spirit" (Matt. 1:18). Joseph, being a just but also kindly man, planned to divorce her quietly rather than expose her to public disgrace, but he was reassured by the message of an angel, given in a dream, that Mary's child was conceived by the Holy Spirit. He was instructed, as Mary had already been (Lk. 1:31), to call the baby's name JESUS ("Yahweh is salvation"), "because he will save his people from their sins" (Matt. 1:21). Immediately Joseph took Mary to his home as his wife, but had no sexual intercourse with her until after the birth of Jesus (v. 25).

If we had only Matthew's account, we would have thought Joseph and Mary belonged to BETH-LEHEM, but Luke makes it clear that the birth of Jesus occurred in Bethlehem only because of the CENSUS, which brought his parents to their ancestral home town. Luke's accuracy has been challenged on the grounds that there is no record of a census at the time of Jesus' birth; that no one would be required to journey eighty miles or more to fill out a census paper; and that the census taken when QUIRINIUS was governor of SYRIA was in A.D. 6–7, long after Jesus' birth. The conclusion drawn is that Matthew and Luke brought Bethlehem into the picture only to make the record fulfill the prophecy of Mic. 5:2.

William M. Ramsay discusses the question carefully in his book, *Was Christ Born at Bethlehem?* (1898). He produces evidence from Egyptian papyri that a census was taken in the Roman world every fourteen years, so one would have occurred about 8–7 B.C., and it may have been somewhat delayed in Palestine. In a census in A.D. 104, people in Egypt were required to return to their own town for enrollment. When Quirinius was appointed governor of Syria in A.D. 6, it was his second such appointment; he may well have been an additional legate to Sentius Saturninus at the time of the earlier census. There seems no valid reason, therefore, to reject the historicity of Luke's clear statement about the circumstances of Jesus' birth.

The census would account for the shortage of accommodation in Bethlehem. The INN (*katalyma* G2906, Lk. 2:7), probably a simple lodging place, was full. Somewhere nearby, perhaps in a cave, as some apocryphal gospels say, Jesus was born and laid in a MANGER (*phatnē* G5764, v. 12)—not a stall, but probably a feeding trough for animals.

Out in the fields a group of shepherds stood guard over their flock that night. Such flocks were always needed for the sacrifices of the temple at Jerusalem, a mere six miles away. Informed of the birth by an angel, the shepherds went to Bethlehem, found the babe wrapped in swaddling cloths lying in a manger, and excitedly repeated the message they had received. For many, the shepherds' words were a passing wonder (Lk. 2:18). "But Mary treasured up all these things and pondered them in her heart" (v. 19).

There is no indication in Matthew's account how long after the birth it was when the "wise men" or MAGI (Gk. *magoi*, from *magos* G3407) came, following the lead of the star they had seen in the E, in search of the one born king of the Jews (Matt. 2:1–12). Their inquiry in Jerusalem perturbed HEROD, who verified from the chief priests and scribes the anticipated birthplace of the Messiah, then sent the wise men to Bethlehem. By this stage the holy family was in a house, where the wise men offered their gifts of gold, frankincense, and myrrh. This may have occurred before or after the CIRCUMCISION, which took place on the eighth day, when the baby was given his angel-conferred name of Jesus. They stayed in the environs of Jerusalem until two further requirements of the Jewish law were fulfilled. For every firstborn child, a redemption price of five silver shekels (approximately ten days' wages for a laborer) had to be paid to the temple a month after the birth (Num. 18:16). Then, forty-one days after the birth for a boy, the ceremony of the mother's purification took place (Lev. 12:2–4). For convenience, these two ceremonies were commonly combined in one visit to the temple, as was the case here. The offering for a mother's purification was a lamb and a turtle-dove or a young pigeon. Joseph and Mary offered the alternative permitted to a mother too poor to afford a lamb, namely, two turtle-doves or pigeons (Lk. 2:24).

During the course of the presentation in the temple, two aged Hebrew saints came in and praised God at the recognition of the infant Redeemer. SIMEON held the babe in his arms and blessed God for the gift of salvation (Lk. 2:29–32, a passage referred to as the NUNC DIMITTIS, after the first two words in the VULGATE). He then blessed the parents and prophesied to Mary that the child would cause the downfall of many, and the rising of many others, in Israel. He would be spoken against as he revealed the thoughts of human hearts. And for Mary herself, a sword would pierce through her own soul, as she saw her son so treated. The long-widowed prophetess ANNA, aged eighty-four, likewise gave thanks to God and spoke to others about the child.

Luke's account suggests that the family returned immediately to Nazareth (Lk. 2:39), but Matthew tells how, after the departure of the wise men,

Joseph, being warned by an angel in a dream, fled in haste by night, with Mary and Jesus, to Egypt, staying there in safety until after Herod's death, about the end of March, 4 B.C. No indication is given of the length of stay in Egypt or the exact location. Ancient legends say they spent two years at Matareeh, a few miles NE of modern Cairo, but others have argued for a sojourn as short as a month or two. After this, they returned to Israel, and avoiding JUDEA, where Archelaus now reigned (see HEROD IV), made their home in Nazareth.

F. Life in Nazareth. Jesus' development is described as that of an entirely normal boy in Luke's restrained and dignified account (Lk. 2:40–52). It was a godly Jewish home in which Jesus was taught the Scriptures, reverent obedience to parents, and the love of God. Every year the family journeyed to Jerusalem to celebrate the PASSOVER Feast. It was during one such annual visit, when Jesus at the age of thirteen entered the responsibilities of a "son of the commandment" (*bar mitzvah*), that he stayed behind and was found in the temple after three days, listening to the teachers and asking intelligent and perceptive questions. Mary was astonished and indignant as she rebuked him, "Son, why have you treated us like this? Your father and I have been anxiously searching for you" (v. 48). His reply, "Didn't you know I had to be in my Father's house?" (v. 49), was in turn a gentle rebuke. Mary should have sensed the early call of his divine mission.

The home in Nazareth was one full of boys and girls, for Joseph and Mary had at least six other children (Mk. 6:3; the view that Joseph had children from a previous marriage lacks evidence). Jesus, as the eldest, followed his father's trade as a carpenter. From the total silence of the later gospel story, we conclude that Joseph died before Jesus entered upon his public ministry (legend says in his eighteenth year). If so, for many years Jesus stood by his widowed mother in the responsibility of bringing up the younger members of the family, which may well account for his not entering his public ministry until he was about thirty (Lk. 3:23).

G. Incidents during Christ's ministry. Mary was present at the marriage in CANA to which Jesus and his disciples were invited. She evidently bore some responsibility in the arrangements, perhaps as a close relative. When the supply of wine was exhausted, she informed Jesus of the fact (Jn. 2:1–3). Perhaps she thought to hasten his public manifestation; this consideration would explain the gentle rebuff in Jesus' words (v. 4), which probably mean, "Woman, you have no right to determine my mission. This is not yet my hour for open manifestation." Our Lord thus asserted his independence and sole authority in fulfilling his God-given task. Mary accepted this, retiring from the scene after she instructed the servants to obey his every command (v. 5).

It would seem that after this time Mary and Jesus' brothers made their home in CAPERNAUM with Jesus (Jn. 2:12), while his sisters, probably married, stayed on in Nazareth (Mk. 6:3). They did not normally accompany him on his preaching tours, but on one occasion, perhaps fearful for his safety, they came to the outskirts of the crowd, seeking him (Matt. 12:46–50; Mk. 3:31–35; Lk. 8:19–21). Almost certainly the phrase *hoi par' autou* in Mk. 3:21 means "his family"; their reaction to Jesus at this stage was to say, "He is out of his mind," and they came seeking to restrain him. Jesus' reply when told that his family was calling him (vv. 34–35) indicates that he viewed them as not doing the will of God; those who do are truly mother and brothers to him. The only other allusion to Mary during his ministry is the cry of the unknown woman in the crowd, "Blessed is the mother who gave you birth and nursed you!" (Lk. 11:27). Again on this occasion, Jesus emphasized that physical relationship to him did not confer blessing; only obedience to God's message could do so.

H. At the cross and after the resurrection. Only John states that Mary was present at the CRUCIFIXION with the BELOVED DISCIPLE, and that Jesus said to her, "Dear woman, here is your son," and to the disciple, "Here is your mother" (Jn. 19:26–27). Why did Jesus give Mary into the care of her nephew John rather than one of her own sons? It may have been because they, as yet, did not believe in him (Jn. 7:5), or because they were married men (1 Cor. 9:5) while John single. Or it may be that Jesus merely intended John to take her away from the harrowing scenes of the crucifixion, and he did so from that hour. However, traditions say that she lived the rest of her life with John, either in JERUSALEM or accompanying him to EPHESUS.

The only further mention of Mary is after the ASCENSION OF CHRIST, when Mary and Jesus' brothers, now in Jerusalem, joined the eleven apostles in prayer while they waited for the promised gift of the HOLY SPIRIT (Acts 1:14). It was perhaps the appearance of the resurrected Christ to James (1 Cor. 15:7) that brought to his brothers the faith they notably lacked during his ministry, and brought full assurance to Mary. They were all doubtless in the full company of 120 persons (Acts 1:15) present at the choosing of MATTHIAS to replace JUDAS ISCARIOT and who were filled with the Holy Spirit on the day of PENTECOST (2:1–4). (See R. E. Brown et al., ed., *Mary in the New Testament* [1978]; D. Flusser et al., *Mary: Images of the Mother of Jesus in Jewish and Christian Perspective* [1986].)

II. Worship of Mary. There is no hint anywhere in the NT of veneration offered to Mary. Jesus expressly warned against such (Lk. 11:27–28). Rather, the picture of Mary given in the NT is of a humble village maiden who typifies all that is finest and noblest in Jewish womanhood. Her purity, simplicity, deep spiritual sensitivity, and complete obedience to God stand out; her careful training of her son in his early years, her complete confidence in him as shown in the incident at Cana, her utter loyalty as shown by her presence at the cross, even though it seems there were times when she did not fully understand him—all prepared her for the position she took among the earliest disciples in acknowledging him as Lord and Christ (Acts 2:36).

Nor is there any evidence of prayer made, or worship offered, to Mary during the first four centuries. The later cult of the worship of Mary has developed on the flimsy foundation of three passages in Luke—the greeting of Gabriel (Lk. 1:28); the greeting of Elizabeth (v. 42), and the grateful words of Mary in the *Magnificat*, "From now on all generations will call me blessed" (v. 48). These passages emphasize the unique high privilege bestowed on this specially chosen maiden, but in no way suggest that worship should be offered her, which belongs only to God. Upon the brief biblical details of her life has been woven an intricate web of legend, largely fictitious and quite unreliable, and upon this has been built a complex structure of dogma that has developed and increased through the centuries. There are four main tenets of this dogma.

A. Mother of God. In the 4th and 5th centuries, controversy raged around the propriety of applying the term *theotokos*, "Godbearer" or "mother of God," to Mary. The title was intended to confirm the full DEITY OF CHRIST. Nestorius proposed the less explicit *christotokos*, but this, along with his other teaching, was condemned at the Council of Ephesus in 431, where it was affirmed that in Christ there were not two persons but one ("the perfect existing God made at the same time perfect man, made flesh of the Virgin"). The expression, then, does not mean "mother of the divine nature." On the understanding that the reference is only to Jesus' human nature, both Lutheran and Reformed confessions at the time of the Reformation allowed the term, but it has never been popular among Protestants. It is as mother of God that Mary is termed *mediatrix*, not, in the thought of the Roman communion, to take the place of Christ as sole MEDIATOR between God and man (1 Tim. 2:5), but to mediate between Christ and mankind as she did at Cana (Jn. 2:3).

B. Perpetual virginity. The phrase "born of the Virgin Mary," used in the APOSTLES' CREED, is held to imply not only that Mary was a virgin when she conceived, but also "in birth and after birth." The apocryphal *Protevangelium of James* states that Jesus was born miraculously, leaving Mary's virginity intact. It is held that Mary's words to Gabriel, "I know not a man" (Lk. 1:34 KJV) indicate that she was under a vow of perpetual virginity, in which case it is difficult to explain why she had earlier become betrothed to Joseph. As to the BROTHERS OF JESUS, these are regarded either as children of Joseph by an earlier marriage (the view of the apocryphal gospels, commonly called the *Epiphanian* view, after Epiphanius who argued it c. 382), or as cousins, children of Clopas and the Virgin's sister, also called Mary (the *Hieronymian* view, after Jerome, about the same time).

This doctrine has no explicit support in the NT, and the application of OT texts such as Cant. 4:12 and Ezek. 44:2 to Mary is quite unjustified. While the use of the words "before" (Matt. 1:18), "until" (Matt. 1:25), and "firstborn" (Lk. 2:7) may not constitute absolute proof, they agree with the frequent references in the NT to Jesus' brothers, indicating that after a perfectly normal birth (Lk. 2:5), Mary lived with Joseph as man and wife, and enjoyed the blessing of a large family (the *Helvidian* view, after Helvidius). Had it not been for the pressures of ASCETICISM, which in these early centuries regarded celibacy as an ethically higher state than marriage and all sexual relations as inherently part of sinful flesh, it is certain no other interpretation would ever have been thought of.

C. Immaculate conception. AUGUSTINE is the first notable theologian to declare that Mary was free from actual SIN (*Nature and Grace* 36). Later theologians discussed whether she was free, not only from actual sin, but also from original sin, like Eve in her innocence. Thomas Aquinas (*Summa theologiae* 3.27–30) taught that though Mary contracted original sin, between conception and birth, by God's miraculous power, the "inflammation of sin was rendered harmless," and then completely removed at her conception of Christ. Duns Scotus opposed this view, and taught that she was preserved immaculate from all stain of original sin at the first instant of her conception. This latter view was promulgated as Roman Catholic dogma by Pope Pius IX in 1854.

D. Bodily assumption. The earliest versions of this legend come from the later 4th cent. and show widely varying details, the one common feature being that Mary was miraculously transported, body and soul, to heaven by Jesus. The legend has no historical evidence, is foreign to Scripture, and contrary to all extant writings of the first three centuries. But the "feast of the Assumption" has long been observed as August 15 in the Christian calendar, and the ASSUMPTION OF THE VIRGIN was proclaimed a part of official Roman Catholic dogma by Pope Pius XII in 1950. (See J. B. Carol, ed., *Mariology* [1955]; A. J. Tambasco, *What Are They Saying about Mary?* [1984]; S. J. Boss, ed., *Mary: The Complete Resource* [2007].)

D. G. STEWART

Masada muh-sah′duh (Μάσαδα [Strabo, *Geogr.* 16.2.44, Μοασάδα], from Aram. מְצָדָא [cf. Heb. מְצָד H5171], "stronghold"). First identified by E. Smith and E. Robinson with a rock called by the local inhabitants Qaṣr es-Sebbe, Masada is a natural fortress in the eastern Judean Desert on the western shore of the DEAD SEA, located some 50 mi. S of Khirbet QUMRAN. The upper plateau of the boat-shaped rock covers 20 acres and rises abruptly, almost perpendicularly 440 yards above its surroundings.

According to JOSEPHUS (*War* 7.8.3), the natural advantages of this remote mountain were first recognized by Jonathan MACCABEE, the high priest who fortified it. However, Josephus meant probably Alexander Jannaeus, HASMONEAN ruler of JUDEA (103–76 B.C.), as indicated now by the excavations. During this general period several structures and buildings were constructed, including four small palaces at the center. The prominent role of Masada in the history of Judea, however, coincides with the decline of the Hasmonean dynasty, espe-

King Herod fortified the southern portion of his kingdom with various outposts including Masada.

cially from 42 B.C. in the struggle between the house of Antipater, the father of HEROD, and the legitimate ruling dynasty. The same year Masada fell to Herod's followers but remained besieged by the Hasmoneans for some years, who were conscious of its importance (Jos. *War* 1.7.7–9; *Ant.* 14.14.6).

Herod kept his family at Masada during the years of his struggle for power in Judea. Only in 39–38 B.C. did he succeed in moving his family to the more secure SAMARIA (Jos. *War* 1.13.7–9; 1.15.1–4; *Ant.* 14.13.8–9). After having established his rule in Judea (37 B.C.), Herod began a large-scale building scheme of fortresses in Judea to secure his rule internally as well as against any external threat (*War* 7.13.7–8). Masada probably was rebuilt around 35 B.C. Herod built there, according to Josephus's detailed account (*War* 1.15.1–4), casemate walls strengthened with towers, the palace, cisterns, and storerooms.

Following Herod's death (4 B.C.) and the exile of his son Archelaus (A.D. 6), a small Roman garrison seems to have been established at Masada. At the beginning of the first war against the Romans, sixty years later, Masada was taken by a group of ZEALOTS (Jos. *War* 2.17.2). Herod's armories there were broken into and large quantities of weapons were taken to Jerusalem and distributed to the insurgents (*War* 2.17.8). For the six following years the community on Masada seems to have practiced a normal way of life without being seriously involved in the war with the Romans. See WARS, JEWISH.

This almost impregnable fortress, however, did not escape the fate that fell upon other parts of the country. Two or three years after the fall of Jerusalem (A.D. 70) this last stronghold to survive the war with the Romans had to defend itself against a vast Roman army. The tenth legion (Fretensis) with numerous auxiliary forces led by the governor Flavius Silva had been moved to Masada. Eight camps and a circumvallation wall were put up around the fortress. Access to the fortifications of Masada for heavy siege machines was provided by an extensive rampart erected on the western side of the rock (*War* 7.8.5).

Masada was besieged and attacked for seven months during the autumn of A.D. 72 or 73 and the winter and spring of the following year. It was then that the Romans succeeded in creating a breach in the wall. Several attempts by the defenders to check the breach failed, and hopes to survive the Roman attack consequently faded (*War* 7.8.5). Their leader, Elazar Ben Yaiʾr, persuaded his 960 followers—men, women, and children—to take their own lives, and to die as free people rather than to be enslaved by the Romans. When the Romans entered the fortress the next day they encountered only seven survivors—two women and five children. All the others had taken their own lives after having burned their belongings (*War* 7.9.1–2).

Masada remained deserted until modern times except for a short interval during the 5th and 6th cent., when a small community of monks settled there and erected a small church and some cells. Many explorers and scholars have been attracted to this site ever since it was identified in the 19th cent. Their careful descriptions and observations are of great importance to any further study.

The large-scale excavations that began in 1963 were preceded by two rather small but very important projects. A study of the Roman camps and siege works was carried out in 1932 by Schulten and Lammerer (see A. Schulten, "Masada, die Burg des Herodes und die römischen Lager," *ZDPV* 56 [1933]: 1–185). A survey and a small-scale excavation were carried out by an expedition headed by M. Avi-Yonah, M. Avigad, and Y. Aharoni of the Hebrew University during three weeks in 1955 and 1956 (see their report, "The Archaeological Survey

Northern portion of the Masada plateau, with a view of Herod's palaces.

of Masada, 1955–1956," *IEJ* 7 [1957]: 1–60). Extensive excavations were undertaken for twelve months in 1963–1965. The work was led by Yigael Yadin under the auspices of the Hebrew University, the Israel Exploration Society, and the Department of Antiquities of the State of Israel.

Herod's storehouses at Masada.

Herod's palaces, storerooms, fortifications, and elaborate water supply arrangements known already from Josephus' writings, besides a well-appointed bath house, were brought to light. The architectural and ornamented elements from this period uncovered at Masada are of the greatest importance for the understanding of the transitional period in architecture and art lying between the Hellenistic and the Roman period.

The Zealots and their families settled mainly in the casemate walls. The community's daily life is well attested. Household installations and utensils as well as pieces of furniture and attire were unearthed. A synagogue and some ritual baths also were found. The extremely dry climate helped to preserve organic materials, above all PARCHMENT and PAPYRUS. In addition to this, several hundred OSTRACA inscribed in Hebrew and Aramaic, as well as some in Greek and Latin, were found.

The scrolls identified include fragments of Genesis, Leviticus, Deuteronomy, Ezekiel, and Psalms, as well as apocryphal texts in Hebrew, namely Ecclesiasticus, a fragment of the *Book of Jubilees*, and a sectarian text comprising verses from "The Heavenly Sabbath Sacrifices" of a QUMRAN type. The uniformity of these fragments found among the burned debris (A.D. 73) with the scrolls found at Qumran point to the connections that must have existed between the Masada community and the Judean desert sect. See DEAD SEA SCROLLS.

Conspicuous remains of the Roman siege works are scattered around Masada and serve as a reminder of an outstanding chapter in the history of the Jewish people. Some scholars question, to varying degrees, the view that the Jewish resistance and mass suicide at Masada was an act of great heroism, but the story has had an extraordinary impact on the psyche of modern Israel. (See further Y. Yadin, *Masada: Herod's Fortress and the Zealots' Last Stand* [1966]; *Masada: The Yigael Yadin Excavations 1963–1965, Final Reports*, 6 vols. [1989–99]; N. Ben-Yehuda, *The Masada Myth: Collective Memory and Mythmaking in Israel* [1995]; J. F. Hall and J. W. Welch, *Masada and the World of the New Testament* [1997]; *NEAEHL*, 3:973–85.)

G. FOERSTER

Masaloth mas´uh-loth. KJV Apoc. form of MESALOTH (1 Macc. 9:2).

Maschil mas´kil. See MUSIC VI.A.

Mash mash (מַשׁ *H5390* [not in NIV]). Son of ARAM and grandson of SHEM, listed in the Table of the NATIONS (Gen. 10:23 KJV and most versions). On the basis of the parallel passage (1 Chr. 1:17), as well as the SEPTUAGINT reading (*Mosoch*) in both passages, the NIV reads MESHECH. However, Meshech is the name of one of the sons of JAPHETH (Gen. 10:2), so many scholars believe that Mash is original in Gen. 10:23. The identification of Mash with a people group or a geographical location has eluded scholars. Various proposals have been made, however, including MESHA (v. 30, perhaps in ARABIA) and Mount Masius (Tur ʿAbdin, in N MESOPOTAMIA).

Mashal may´shuhl (מָשָׁל *H5443*; a common word with the same form, מָשָׁל *H5442*, means "saying, proverb"). Variant form of MISHAL (1 Chr. 6:74).

Masiah muh-si´uh (Μασιας). Ancestor of a family of SOLOMON's servants who returned from the EXILE with ZERUBBABEL (1 Esd. 5:34; KJV, "Masias"). The name is not found in the parallel passages (Ezra 2:57; Neh. 7:59).

Masias muh-si′uhs. KJV Apoc form of MASIAH.

Maskil mas′kil. See MUSIC VI.A.

Masman. KJV Apoc. form of MAASMAS (1 Esd. 8:43).

mason. This English term is used to render the participle of the Hebrew verb *gādar H1553* ("to build a wall") in two passages that refer to the skilled workers who repaired the TEMPLE (2 Ki. 12:12; 22:6). The noun *ḥārāš H3093* ("craftsman, artificer") can also be used with the same meaning in similar contexts (with *ʾeben H74*, "stone," 2 Sam. 5:11; 1 Chr. 22:15; with *qîr H7815*, "wall," 1 Chr. 14:1; by itself, 2 Chr. 24:12). Another term, *ḥōṣēb H2935* ("quarryman, stonecutter"), can also be rendered "mason" (Ezra 3:7).

In ancient times the best masons were from PHOENICIA (2 Sam. 5:11; 1 Chr. 14:1). DAVID and SOLOMON used foreign artisans from that country (2 Sam. 5:11; 1 Chr. 22:2). Palestine abounds in limestone of a quality suitable for building material. The greatest examples of the mason's skill were found in JERUSALEM, MEGIDDO, and SAMARIA; but it is possible that they were built by Phoenician workmen. In NT times the most magnificent building made of stone was HEROD's temple. Herod erected many impressive public buildings in various parts of his kingdom, and even in cities outside his dominion.

The OT refers to cutting the STONES in the quarry (1 Ki. 5:17; 6:7), the hewing of wine vats (Isa. 5:2) and of tombs in the solid rock (Isa. 22:16), and the cutting and shaping of stones for various constructions (Exod. 20:25; 1 Ki. 5:17; Amos 5:11). Two kinds of hammers were used, a large one for quarrying (Jer. 23:29) and a smaller one for dressing the stones (1 Ki. 6:7). In the famous SILOAM inscription the workmen say that they used a small pickaxe for cutting out the water tunnel. A bronze relief from the time of SHALMANESER III shows Assyrian stonemasons carving the royal image with their implements. See also ARCHITECTURE.   J. L. KELSO

Masorah muh-sor′uh (postbiblical מְסוֹרָה or מָסוֹרָה, from מָסַר *H5034*, "to select," later "hand over, transmit"; cf. מֹסֶרֶת *H5037*, "binding," later מָסוֹרֶת, "tradition"). Also Masora and Massora(h). A systematic collection of textual notes made by medieval Hebrew scholars, called the *Masoretes*. In their production of biblical MSS, they would place a small circle (later called a *circellus*) above or between the words that required comment. Placed usually to the side on the margin, the comment might give statistical information on the word (e.g., that it appears nowhere else in the Hebrew Bible), or indicate that a different word should be read (often the equivalent of a textual variant; see KETIB). Other types of information were also included. These notes, given in highly abbreviated form, constitute the *Masorah parva* ("small"); in addition, lists providing fuller information make up the *Masorah magna* ("large").

In order to preserve accurately the traditional pronunciation, the Masoretes also developed a very sophisticated system for indicating vowels (the Hebrew ALPHABET originally had only consonants) and cantillation ("accents"). At least two major Masoretic schools, the Eastern or Babylonian and the Western or Palestinian (Tiberian), can be traced back to about A.D. 500. Prior to the discovery of the DEAD SEA SCROLLS, all available copies of the Hebrew Bible were those produced by the Masoretes. (See B. J. Roberts, *The Old Testament Text and Versions* [1951], ch. 3; I. Yeivin, *Introduction to the Tiberian Masorah* [1980]; P. H. Keley et al., *The Masorah of Biblia Hebraica Stuttgartensia: Introduction and Annotated Glossary* [1998].) See also TEXT AND MANUSCRIPTS (OT) VI.

Masoretes, Masoretic Text. See MASORAH; TEXT AND MANUSCRIPTS (OT) VI–VII.

Masrekah mas′ruh-kuh (מַשְׂרֵקָה *H5388*, possibly "red" or "vineyard"). The royal city of SAMLAH king of EDOM (Gen. 36:36; 1 Chr. 1:47). The site is unknown, though some have proposed Jebel el-Musraq, about 20 mi. SW of Maʿan in TRANSJORDAN.

Massa mas′uh (מַשָּׂא *H5364*, "burden"). Son of ISHMAEL and grandson of ABRAHAM (Gen.

25:14; 1 Chr. 1:30). Descendants of Massa lived in NW ARABIA, as evidenced by several pieces of information. For example, TIGLATH-PILESER III makes reference to the inhabitants of Masʾa and of TEMA, among others, as paying tribute and as living towards the West (*ANET*, 283b). Tema, the name of Massa's brother, is identified with present Teima, NE of el-ʿUla in NW Arabia. Another brother was DUMAH, and Isaiah wrote of a locality by that name in the vicinity of SEIR, S of the Dead Sea (Isa. 21:11–12).

ASHURBANIPAL contacted both "Nebaiati" and "Qedareans" after moving S of DAMASCUS (*ANET*, 298–300), these people doubtless being descendants of NEBAIOTH and KEDAR respectively, two other brothers (in Ps. 120:5, some scholars emend "Meshech" to "Massa" because it is in parallel with Kedar). In other words, Ishmael's descendants, including those of Massa, settled in NW Arabia, not far from the homeland of their ancestor. Some scholars further identify or otherwise associate Massa with MESHA, a place "in the east country" (prob. Arabia) that, along with SEPHAR, served to delimit the territory occupied by the sons of JOKTAN, a descendant of SHEM through EBER (Gen. 10:30).

According to the RSV (cf. also NJPS), both AGUR and LEMUEL were from Massa (Prov. 30:1; 31:1; the NIV and other versions understand *maśśāʾ* H5363 here as a common noun, "burden, oracle"). If this rendering is correct, the two men may well have descended from the son of Ishmael; or perhaps they lived in an area associated with the Ishmaelite tribe. (See further P. K. Hitti, *The History of the Arabs* [1953], 43; J. Simons, *The Geographical and Topographical Texts of the Old Testament* [1959], 45–46; F. V. Winnett, "The Arabian Genealogies in Genesis," in *Translating and Understanding the Old Testament*, ed. H. T. Frank and W. L. Reed [1970], 171–96, esp. 193–96; I. Ephʿal, *The Ancient Arabs: Nomads on the Borders of the Fertile Crescent, 9th-5th Centuries B.C.* [1982], 218–19 et passim.)   L. J. WOOD

Massah mas′uh (מַסָּה H5001, "testing, trial"; LXX, πειρασμός G4280, "trial, temptation"). An unidentified place near REPHIDIM in the Desert of SINAI where the Israelites quarreled and tested God because of their thirst. The place was also called

The location of Massah and Meribah may have been in the area of Wadi Feiran pictured here.

MERIBAH ("contention"). The two names occur in combination once (Exod. 17:7) and in parallelism twice (Deut. 33:8; Ps. 95:8). The name Massah is mentioned by itself in two other passages (Deut. 6:16; 9:22), and "the waters of Meribah" more frequently (Num. 20:13, 24; Pss. 81:7; 106:32; Meribah Kadesh in Num. 27:14; Deut. 32:51; Ezek. 47:19; 48:28).

Soon after leaving Egypt, the Israelites moved on from the Desert of Sin and camped at Rephidim (Exod. 17:1). Not finding drinking water there, they murmured against MOSES and were almost ready to stone him. At the command of the Lord, Moses went on before the people to the rock at HOREB, which he struck with his staff so that it brought forth water (vv. 2–6). Moses named the location "Testing and Contention" because of the Israelites' faultfinding and their putting the Lord to the test (v. 7).

The account in Num. 20:1–13 refers to an event in Israel's history some forty years later and in a different geographical location (KADESH BARNEA, in S Palestine). Many scholars regard this text as a different strand of tradition (of the same event)

resulting from conflation of sources and conflicting literary purposes. It is better, however, to distinguish this Meribah from "Massah and Meribah." While the two incidents are indeed very similar, the differences are more significant. In the second episode, for example, the Lord commanded Moses to speak to the rock, but instead he struck the rock twice and as a consequence forfeited the right to enter the Promised Land (Deut. 32:51). (See G. W. Coats, *Rebellion in the Wilderness* [1968]; G. J. Wenham, *Numbers: An Introduction and Commentary* [1980], 149–51; W. H. Propp, *Water in the Wilderness* [1987]; B. Levine, *Numbers 1–20*, AB 4 [1993], 490–91.) S. WOUDSTRA

massebah mas′uh-buh. Sometimes *mazzebah*. A transliteration of Hebrew *maṣṣēbâ H5167*, "[cultic] stone" (Gen. 35:20 et al.), used especially by archaeologists with reference to a sacred PILLAR, that is, a stone monument set up as a memorial or as an object of worship.

Massias muh-si′uhs. KJV Apoc. form of MAASEIAH (1 Esd. 9:22).

Massorah, Massorete, Massoretic. See MASORAH.

master. This English term, meaning "lord, owner," is used very frequently to translate a number of biblical words, especially Hebrew *ʾādôn H123* (Gen. 18:12 et al.) and Greek *kyrios G3261* (Matt. 6:24 et al.). See LORD. Other relevant terms include Greek *despotēs G1305* (1 Tim. 6:1–2 et al.) and *epistatēs G2181* (only in Luke, e.g., Lk. 5:5). The KJV uses *master* also in the sense of TEACHER to render Greek *didaskalos* (Matt. 8:19 et al.).

mastic tree. A small evergreen (*Pistacia lentiscus*) of the cashew family, mentioned only in the APOCRYPHA (Sus. 54, Gk. *schinos*). It is the gum or resin that exudes from the trunk when cut that is called *mastic* or *mastich* by the trade. This gum is usually in the form of tear-like, whitish-yellow drops. A third-grade gum is used as varnish. This evergreen shrub can grow up to 20 ft. The flowers have no petals, and its small fruits are first red, then black.

W. E. SHEWELL-COOPER

Mathanias math′uh-ni′uhs. KJV Apoc. form of MATTANIAH (1 Esd. 9:31; NRSV, "Bescaspasmys").

Mathusala muh-thoo′suh-luh. KJV NT form of METHUSELAH.

Matred may′trid (מַטְרֵד *H4765*, possibly from a root meaning "to pursue, drive away"). Daughter of a certain Edomite named ME-ZAHAB (Gen. 36:39; 1 Chr. 1:50). Matrel's daughter, Mehetabel, married Hadad (Hadar), king of EDOM; see HADAD (PERSON) #3. The SEPTUAGINT in Genesis and the Syriac in both passages read "son" instead of "daughter"; because Matred is thought to be a male name, some scholars accept this reading.

Matri may′tri (מַטְרִי *H4767*, lit., "Matrite," the gentilic form of an unattested name related to the noun *māṭār H4764* ["rain"] and possibly meaning "[born during] the rainy season"). Presumably, the head of a Benjamite family. When SAMUEL proceeded to choose a king for Israel, the lot fell on the tribe of BENJAMIN, then on "the Matrite family" (lit. rendering), and from within that clan, on SAUL (1 Sam. 10:21; KJV, "the family of Matri"; NRSV, "the family of the Matrites"; NIV, "Matri's clan"). Nothing more is known about Matri or his family.

Matrite may′trit. See MATRI.

Mattan mat′uhn (מַתָּן *H5509*, possibly short form of מַתַּנְיָהוּ *H5515*, "gift of Yahweh"; see MATTANIAH). **(1)** A priest (perhaps the chief priest) of BAAL during the rule of ATHALIAH. At the time of the overthrow of her reign, the Israelites under the leadership of JEHOIADA the priest destroyed the temple of Baal with its altars and idols, and they also killed Mattan "in front of the altars" (2 Ki. 11:18; 2 Chr. 23:17).

(2) Father of Shephatiah (Jer. 38:1); the latter was one of the officials who heard JEREMIAH preach and recommended that he be put to death (v. 4).

Mattanah mat′uh-nuh (מַתָּנָה *H5511*; a common word with the same form means "gift"). A camping place of the Israelites in TRANSJORDAN, near the end of their wilderness wanderings (Num. 21:18–19). As they traveled from the river ARNON into the territory of SIHON, king of the AMORITES, they came to BEER and then to Mattanah, which was near NAHALIEL (possibly a tributary of the Arnon). The location of Mattanah is unknown, although some think it may be the same as modern Khirbet el-Medeiyineh, 11 mi. NE of DIBON. S. WOUDSTRA

Mattaniah mat´uh-ni´uh (מַתַּנְיָה H5514 and מַתַּנְיָהוּ H5515 [1 Chr. 25:4, 16; 2 Chr. 29:13], "gift of Yahweh"; cf. MATTENAI, MATTHAN, MATTITHIAH). A very common name, also attested (in full or abbreviated form) in various nonbiblical sources. **(1)** Son of HEMAN, DAVID's seer (1 Chr. 25:4). He and his thirteen brothers were set apart "for the ministry of prophesying, accompanied by harps, lyres and cymbal" (v. 1). When lots were cast to determine the duties of the Levitical singers, he, along with his sons and relatives, received the ninth lot (v. 16).

(2) A Levite, descendant of ASAPH and ancestor of JAHAZIEL son of Zechariah; Jahaziel was apparently a prophet in the court of King JEHOSHAPHAT (2 Chr. 20:14).

(3) A Levite, descendant of Asaph, who served during the reign of HEZEKIAH in the work of consecrating the temple (2 Chr. 29:13).

(4) Son of JOSIAH and last king of Judah (2 Ki. 24:17). See ZEDEKIAH.

(5–8) The name of four postexilic Israelites who agreed to put away their foreign wives. They were respectively descendants of Elam (Ezra 10:26; 1 Esd. 9:27 [KJV, "Matthanias"]), Zattu (Ezra 10:27; called "Othoniah" in 1 Esd. 9:28 [KJV, "Othonias"]), Pahath-Moab (Ezra 10:30; called "Bescaspasmys" in 1 Esd. 9:31 [KJV, "Mathanias"]), and Bani (Ezra 10:37; possibly called "Mamitanemus" in 1 Esd. 9:34 [KJV, "Mamnitanaimus"; see also MACNADEBAI]). The correspondences between Ezra and 1 Esdras are uncertain (J. M. Myers provides the lists in parallel columns in *I and II Esdras*, AB 42 [1974], 101–4).

(9) Son of Mica and descendant of Asaph; he was one of the Levites who resettled in Jerusalem (1 Chr. 9:15). When the temple was restored, Mattaniah became "the director who led in thanksgiving and prayer" (Neh. 11:17; 12:8). He may be the same person listed among the "gatekeepers who guarded the storerooms at the gates" (12:25). One of Mattaniah's descendants, Uzzi son of Bani, became chief officer of the Levites (11:22).

(10) Son of Micaiah, descendant of Asaph, and ancestor of Zechariah; the latter was a Levite who played the trumpet in the procession when the walls of Jerusalem were rededicated (Neh. 12:35).

(11) Grandfather of a certain Hanan who assisted in the distribution of supplies for priests and Levites (Neh. 13:13). R. F. GRIBBLE

Mattatha mat´uh-thuh (Ματταθά G3477, from מַתָּתָה, prob. short form of מַתִּתְיָהוּ H5525, "gift of Yahweh"; see MATTITHIAH). Son of NATHAN and grandson or descendant of DAVID (not mentioned in the OT); included in the GENEALOGY OF JESUS CHRIST (Lk. 3:31).

Mattathah mat´uh-thuh. KJV form of MATTATTAH.

Mattathiah mat´-uh-thi´uh. See MATTATHIAS.

Mattathias mat´uh-thi´uhs (Ματταθίας G3478, from מַתִּתְיָהוּ H5525, "gift of Yahweh"; see MATTATTAH, MATTHIAS, MATTITHIAH). **(1)** One of the prominent men who stood near EZRA when the law was read at the great assembly (1 Esd. 9:43 KJV [NRSV, "Mattathiah"]; called MATTITHIAH in Neh. 8:4).

(2) The priestly father of the famous Maccabean line (see MACCABEE), whose five sons carried on the fight for law and liberty after the father's death (1 Macc. 2:1 et al.). He descended from the clan of JOARIB (prob. the same as JEHOIARIB, 1 Chr. 24:7). It was at MODEIN, W of Jerusalem, that the revolt against ANTIOCHUS Epiphanes began. Determined to eradicate Judaism, Antiochus abolished sacrifices, erected pagan altars, even one to ZEUS in the temple, and executed any who possessed the law. Mattathias defied the king, the climax coming when Greek officers under Apelles set up an altar at Modein, demanding sacrifice to heathen gods. Mattathias, refusing, killed the Jew who volunteered, and also the Greek officer, destroyed the altar, and fled to the hills with his followers. He conducted a guerrilla campaign, reversing his early refusal to fight on the Sabbath. At the end of one year (166 B.C.), he died (1 Macc. 2:14–70). In special Hanukkah prayers this patriot is remembered as the spearhead of the warfare for religious freedom.

(3) Son of Absalom; a commander of Maccabean forces warring against DEMETRIUS (1 Macc. 11:70). In the plain of HAZOR, his loyal support enabled Jonathan Maccabeus to convert threatened defeat into victory.

(4) The third (or youngest) son of Simon Maccabeus; with his father and brothers, he was murdered by his brother-in-law Ptolemy at JERICHO c. 134 B.C. (1 Macc. 16:14–16; cf. v. 2).

(5) One of three envoys from NICANOR, a general of Antiochus, regarding a treaty with Judas Maccabeus in 161 B.C. (2 Macc. 14:19).

(6–7) Two men included in Luke's GENEALOGY OF JESUS CHRIST; one is identified as the son of Amos (Lk. 3:25), and the other one as the son of Semein (v. 26). R. F. GRIBBLE

Mattattah mat'uh-tuh (מַתַּתָּה *H5523*, prob. short form of מַתִּתְיָהוּ *H5525*, "gift of Yahweh"; see MATTITHIAH). One of the descendants of Hashum who agreed to put away their foreign wives (Ezra 10:33 [KJV, "Mattathah"]; 1 Esd. 9:33 [KJV, "Matthias"]).

Mattenai mat'uh-n*i* (מַתְּנַי *H5513*, short form of מַתַּנְיָהוּ *H5515*, "gift of Yahweh"; see MATTANIAH). (1–2) The name of two Israelites who agreed to put away their foreign wives. One was a descendant of Hashum (Ezra 10:33; 1 Esd. 9:33 [KJV "Altaneus"]); the other one a descendant of Bani (Ezra 10:37; this name does not occur in 1 Esd. 9:34, unless it corresponds to *Mamnitanamos*, but see MATTANIAH #8).

(3) Head of the priestly family of JOIARIB in the days of the high priest JOIAKIM (Neh. 12:19).

S. BARABAS

Matthan math'an (Ματθάν *G3474*, from מַתָּן *H5509*, possibly short form of מַתַּנְיָהוּ *H5515*, "gift of Yahweh"; see MATTAN, MATTANIAH). Son of Eleazar, father of Jacob, and grandfather of JOSEPH, included in Matthew's GENEALOGY OF JESUS (Matt. 1:15; cf. MATTHAT in Lk. 3:24).

Matthanias math´uh-n*i*´uhs. KJV Apoc. form of MATTANIAH (1 Esd. 9:27).

Matthat math´at (Ματθάτ *G3415* [some MSS Ματθατ], from מַתַּת *H5522*, "gift," possibly short form of מַתִּתְיָהוּ *H5525*, "gift of Yahweh"; see MATTITHIAH). (1) Son of Levi, father of Heli, and grandfather of JOSEPH, included in Luke's GENEALOGY OF JESUS CHRIST (Lk. 3:24). In Matthew's genealogy, Joseph's grandfather has the very similar name MATTHAN (Matt. 1:15), and many scholars have thought that both names refer to the same person, with various solutions (e.g., LEVIRATE marriage) offered to the problem that Joseph's father in Matthew is called Jacob, not Heli. Others argue that Matthan and Matthat are two different people. (See *ABD*, 4:617–18; D. L. Bock, *Luke*, BECNT, 2 vols. [1994–96], 1:918–23.)

(2) Son of a certain Levi, also mentioned in Luke's genealogy (Lk. 3:29).

Matthelas math´uh-luhs. KJV Apoc. variant form of MAASEIAH (1 Esd. 9:19).

Matthew math´yoo (Ματθαῖος *G3414* [sometimes Ματθαῖος], prob. from מַתַּי, short form of מַתִּתְיָהוּ *H5525*, "gift of Yahweh"; cf. T. Zahn, *Introduction to the New Testament*, 3 vols. [1909], 2:524, and see MATTITHIAH). A Jewish TAX COLLECTOR (publican) or revenue officer of CAPERNAUM, called to be a disciple of Jesus (Matt. 9:9; 10:3; Mk. 3:18; Lk. 6:15; Acts 1:13), identified with LEVI son of Alphaeus (Mk. 2:14; Lk. 5:27–29), and traditionally thought to be the author of the first gospel. See MATTHEW, GOSPEL OF, III.

Assuming Matthew wrote the first gospel, no doubt he gives his name as Matthew rather than Levi in order to point out that he was one of the Lord's apostles and at the same time to identify himself with his familiar name, since he was known as Matthew and not as Levi among the Christians. There is no indication that he wished to hide his identity as a tax collector (Matt. 10:3). There were many "converted sinners" like Matthew in the early church. The two separate names should cause no difficulty for Bible students, since double names were common among the Jews, even among Jesus' disciples (Simon PETER, THOMAS Didymus, and prob. BARTHOLOMEW Nathanael). There can be little doubt that Levi and Matthew are one and the same person. Possibly Levi changed his name to Matthew, which means "gift of Yahweh," when he became a member of Jesus' disciples. It is still a common practice for converts on the mission fields to assume new names at their baptism. Matthew's former occupation as a tax collector certainly aided him in keeping excellent records and writing a detailed orderly gospel.

Since all three of the Synoptic Gospels record the calling of Matthew-Levi, one can conclude that his calling to be one of Jesus' disciples was not only a great event in his life, but also a remarkable event in and for the early Christian church. Tax collectors or publicans were considered the lowest state among the Jews together with thieves and harlots. Revenue officers became servants of the hated occupation government of Rome and also of the provincial government under such men as HEROD the Great. Both were known for high taxes, graft, extortion, and stern methods. Sometimes revenue men like Levi purchased the tax franchise for a district and collected revenue of all kinds at a high commission also. Besides, Matthew Levi was a Jew, and this made matters worse because he was considered a renegade and a turncoat by his people. That he should be called to be a member of the twelve disciples was an outstanding symbol of the Christian church in which all people were called to the kingdom by repentance and faith. Matthew makes a special point of quoting Jesus regarding this point (Matt. 21:28–32).

The first three Gospels also record faithfully the fact that immediately after his calling Matthew held a dinner for his tax collector friends and Jesus and his disciples. This was a high point in the new kingdom and the beginning of the missionary thrust of the early church. Levi knew what it meant to be an outcast from his people, and even though he had attempted to turn back, the way would be blocked. He knew the bitterness of separation from his people and the sordid life of the "underworld" in which he lived and operated. Thus, while all three synoptics record Jesus' statement after the dinner, "It is not the healthy who need a doctor, but the sick," only Matthew adds these significant words of Jesus to the Pharisees: "But go and learn what this means: 'I desire mercy, not sacrifice.' For I have not come to call the righteous, but sinners" (Matt. 9:12–13).

In this connection, it is also interesting that Luke alone records that it was Matthew's house and not Jesus' house in which the dinner was held (Lk. 5:29–32). This has led Bible students to conclude that Matthew, deep down, was a conscientious man with deep spiritual troubles and a spiritual concern for his sinful colleagues. He wanted to share the gospel of the kingdom and his wonderful experience with his fellowmen. The fact that he dropped everything readily and followed Jesus seems to indicate that he may have heard Jesus preach and possibly had witnessed some of his miracles.

The daring initiative Jesus took in calling a tax collector into the kingdom, along with many of his friends and followers, must have increased the sharp opposition of the PHARISEES. It is possible that Matthew, bearing the brunt of the Pharisaical criticism, also became one of their bitterest critics in return. His gospel contains some of the sharpest, most scathing rebukes of the Pharisees (Matt. 23:1–37). His gospel highlights Jesus' difficulties with them, their tempting wicked questions, and the manner in which he would "put them down." He records those parables of Jesus that defend the kingdom against the Pharisees and condemns them for their self-righteousness.

There have been attempts to identify Matthew's father ALPHAEUS with the father of James the less, but Matthew and James are never joined together in the list of the apostles, in contrast, for example, to James and John. Matthew's father was an unknown Alphaeus much as Matthew himself was unknown in the church. At least, after his calling he disappears from the scene and is not mentioned by the gospel writers except in the listing of the apostles.

It is still apparent that Matthew is known most of all in the church for writing the first gospel, which the church attributed to him from the 2nd cent. on. If so, this unlikely candidate becomes the author of one of the greatest books ever written. While later scholarship says there are other possible authors of the first gospel, there is no real reason why Matthew-Levi did not write it. His purpose in writing was to bring the Christ of the OT to his fellow countrymen, and show from OT witness that Jesus of Nazareth who called him from his tax collector's post was indeed the Messiah, the Savior of the world and king of the Jews. Reading of the gospel from this point of view becomes indeed a wonderful experience. The divine Word reaches out to all people, both Jew and Gentile. The early Jewish Christians who were driven from Palestine into surrounding countries certainly would want reliable knowledge of Jesus Christ in a written text. Guided by the Holy Spirit, he furnished the church and the world with one of the most influential Christian documents the world has seen.

L. M. PETERSEN

Matthew, Gospel of. The first book of the NT.
    I. Introduction
   II. Title
  III. Author
  IV. Structure and outline
   V. Theme and theological purpose
  VI. Characteristics and special features
 VII. Matthew's use of the OT
VIII. Relation to Mark and Luke
  IX. Time and place of writing
   X. Readers and destination
  XI. Language and text

I. Introduction. The Gospel according to Matthew has always occupied a position of highest esteem in the faith and life of the Christian church. Matthew heads the four GOSPELS and is the first book of the NT, forming a bridge between the Old and New Covenants, and it may be that the early Christians placed it in first position in the NT canon precisely because of the profound influence of its contents on the church and the world.

William Barclay writes, "When we turn to Matthew, we turn to the book which may well be called the most important single document of the Christian faith, for in it we have the fullest and the most systematic account of the life and the teachings of Jesus" (*The First Three Gospels* [1966], 197). The writings of the early church fathers reveal that it was the most frequently quoted and perhaps the most widely read gospel during the first two centuries of the church's history. After the Lord's death and resurrection, there was much interest in knowing who Jesus really was and what he said and did. In fact, many believe the gospel was written to fulfill this need. For this reason the gospel lessons or pericopes from Matthew to be read in the churches have been favored by the liturgies. More

The Lord's Prayer in Hebrew from the Pater Noster Church in Jerusalem. Matthew's version of the Lord's Prayer is the one most widely used in Christian literature.

lessons were chosen from Matthew's gospel than from any other.

It also has had much influence on literature, music, and the fine arts both in and out of the church. Matthew's formulations of favorite texts, such as the BEATITUDES, the LORD'S PRAYER, and the PASSION narrative have been widely used in Christian literature and in the church's preaching and teaching. J. S. Bach used Matthew's version of the Lord's suffering for his great oratorio known throughout the world as the *St. Matthew Passion*. The theology of Matthew, particularly the ethical content, has dominated the church's teaching perhaps even more than the theology of the Gospel of John. Another reason for its wide acceptance has been the apostolic authority associated with Matthew's name, an eyewitness and apostle of our Lord.

In the years both before and after the writing of the gospel, the church had great need for the authoritative Word of our Lord to instruct the faithful and to refute those who would divide the church. It also became popular because of the full and orderly way in which it describes events and records the pronouncements and teachings of the Lord. The unique combination of the Lord's life and teaching, and the theological theme of Jesus as the Messiah, became the final touchstone for its use and authority in the church. The first gospel became a favorite of the church because of its close relationship to the OT. Converts readily saw that it interprets the OT as a Christian book. Whether or not it was the first gospel committed to writing, its position in the NT testifies to its importance and influence in the eyes of Christians through the years, particularly during the first two centuries. Furthermore, it was an ecumenical gospel, upholding both Jewish and Gentile Christianity. All things considered, the first gospel is perhaps the most powerful document ever written.

Matthew's gospel is still doing for the church what it has always done. Because it bridges the OT and NT, it is still basic to both church and the world for the understanding of the teachings of Jesus Christ and of historical Christianity. The amount of literature produced on this book during recent decades indicates that the gospel still commands the attention of the church and biblical scholars. Everyone welcomes new insights into its treasured message. The message contained in Matthew was certainly proclaimed in great detail by the NT prophets and apostles (Eph. 2:20; 3:5) long before it was written down, and those who would learn what was preached and taught during the apostolic era have generally turned to the first gospel.

To get behind all later formulations and systems of Christianity, Matthew merits the attention of Christians everywhere. In our time, with its social turbulence similar to what the early church experienced, the first gospel could restore broken bodies and spirits as in the days of Jesus and the apostles. When asked by a member of a Bible class which of the four Gospels one should read first for a thorough understanding of Christianity, a well-known preacher and Bible scholar recently said, "Naturally, one should read all four Gospels. Which one first? For many years I always pointed to Luke, but in our time I believe I would suggest that one read Matthew first and then the rest of the Gospels in the order listed in the Canon of the NT."

II. Title. The title of this gospel in most modern Bibles reads, "The Gospel according to St. Matthew." This wording is an exact translation of the title in many Greek MSS (*Euangelion kata Maththaion*), but the oldest Greek copies have the shortened form, "According to Matthew" (*Kata Maththaion*). Most scholars believe the original text had no title at all. When the early Christians wished to distinguish one gospel from another, they called the first gospel not the "Gospel of Matthew," as we often say, but "The Gospel *according* to Matthew," to distinguish it from the versions of Mark, Luke, and John. There is only one GOSPEL, but four versions or accounts of it, as even the earliest church fathers recognized (e.g., Irenaeus, *Against Heresies* 3.11.8). The gospel is "God's Story" of salvation and life, the best news story the world has ever heard. The church fathers identified the four gospel writers with the four living beings or beasts named in Rev. 4:6–7 (cf. Ezek. 1:10)—the lion was Mark, the ox was Luke, the flying eagle was John, and the creature with the face of a man was Matthew. This symbolic identification is made in both Christian literature and art.

III. Author. All four of the canonical Gospels are anonymous. None of them begins with words like these, "Matthew, the apostle, to the Jewish Christians of Palestine," as PAUL introduces his apostolic letters (cf. Rom. 1:1–4), and in modern scholarship there has been a great deal of discussion regarding the author of this gospel.

From the earliest times the ancient church was clear, consistent, and unanimous in attributing the first gospel to the apostle MATTHEW. There is no evidence at all that any other author ever claimed to have written the book, nor was it ever attributed to anyone except Matthew. No doubt the early view of Matthean authorship grew out of the detail provided by this book that Jesus "saw a man named Matthew sitting at the tax collector's booth. 'Follow me,' he told him, and Matthew got up and followed him" (Matt. 9:9). The record of Matthew's call in all three synoptics strengthened the view. Scholars believe that the identification became more positive from the fact that Mark and Luke call him by the name of LEVI son of Alphaeus (Mk. 2:14; Lk. 5:27, 29).

The identification was aided by the fact that Jesus attended a dinner in Levi's home and explained the gospel to the Pharisees with the words, "It is not the healthy who need a doctor, but the sick. I have not come to call the righteous, but sinners" (Mk. 2:17; cf. Lk. 5:31–32). The clincher was found in Matt. 10:3, where "Matthew the tax collector" is named among the twelve apostles (cf. Mk. 3:18; Lk. 6:15; Acts 1:13). It is interesting that after his name appears in the lists of the apostles, Matthew disappears from the history of the church as recorded in the NT. Incidents attributed to him later probably are legendary. He is known mainly for his writing of the first gospel—otherwise he would be almost entirely unknown.

Both of Matthew's names are Hebrew. Could it be that he was the son of a man named Levi (thus Matthew ben Levi) and that he was a Levite? Perhaps, as in Peter's case, Jesus gave him the name Matthew as a Christian-Jewish name, because it means "gift of Yahweh." He certainly was a Jew: the gospel that bears his name is Jewish in character and was written mainly for Jewish Christians. If so, he was a chosen vessel, "made to order" for his audience. Luke calls him Levi (Lk. 5:27), and Mark adds "the son of Alphaeus" (Mk. 2:14). It has been pointed out that Matthew-Levi's call was not only daring on the part of Jesus (there was an inherent hatred of tax collectors among the Jews), but also an event in the life of the new kingdom, since it was a symbol of the power of God's grace and Jesus' love for sinners. Only God could change a tax collector named Levi into a Christian apostle named Matthew.

Tax collectors, or *publicani*, were both numerous and dishonest. Moreover, they were in the employ of the hated foreign government that dominated the land and sent taxes collected from both poor and rich alike to far-away Rome. Tax collectors collaborated with the enemy; in fact, they became the *real* enemy because the people did not actually see the government of Herod and Rome. They saw more often the tax collector. Rome did not collect her own taxes. The system was to farm out the taxes and let the collector collect as much over the rate as he could. Rome was satisfied with her quota—the tax collector could keep the balance as a fat commission. A man without a conscience could easily become rich and exploit beyond measure under such a system. Besides, there were many kinds of taxes, and those collected in the line of custom or duty on foreign goods brought into or through the country were the most lucrative. People were not informed of the customs rates and the

View from the Mount of Beatitudes toward the tree-covered hill of Gennesaret (looking W, with the Plain of Gennesaret, Arbel, and the Horns of Hattin in the background). Jesus called Matthew to ministry from his tax collection station, which may have been located on this hill.

collector could collect as much as he could get from each caravan or individual.

No doubt this is the type of tax collecting in which Matthew-Levi was involved in CAPERNAUM of GALILEE. It is not surprising, therefore, that tax collectors among the Jews—and particularly Jews who collected from their own countrymen—were numbered with harlots, thieves, and murderers, not only in the NT but in secular writers as well (Matt. 21:31, 32; Mk. 2:15, 16; Lk. 5:30; Cicero, *De officiis* 1.42). That such people came into the kingdom demonstrated well the power of the gospel to reconcile people to God and to each other. For such a converted Jewish tax collector to write his book to Jews and Gentiles alike would give the gospel a special appeal and acceptance to "sinners." In fact, it is more truthful to state that *only* such a person could write a gospel like that of Matthew-Levi. And since he was also an apostle of the Lord, it was natural for the early church to attribute it to Matthew the publican; the church would simply "know" that he wrote it.

This is a most plausible explanation of the authorship of the first gospel, since the evidence from the NT itself for Matthean authorship is somewhat less than direct. This is, no doubt, the reason the patristic evidence, especially after the first two centuries of the Christian Era, persists. ORIGEN states that "the first gospel was written by Matthew, who was once a tax collector, but who was afterwards an apostle of Jesus Christ, and it was prepared for the converts from Judaism, and published in the Hebrew tongue" (Euseb. *Eccl. Hist.* 6.14.5). IRENAEUS writes: "Matthew also published a book of the gospel among the Hebrews, in their own dialect, while Peter and Paul were preaching the gospel in Rome and founding the church" (*Against Heresies* 3.1.1). EUSEBIUS reports a similar view: "Matthew, who preached earlier to the Hebrews, committed his gospel to writing in his native tongue, and so compensated by his writing for the loss of his presence" (*Eccl. Hist.* 3.24.5). Later JEROME speaks in the same vein in his *Prologue to the Gospels*: "Matthew, the tax collector with the cognomen Levi, is the first of all to have published a gospel in Judea in the Hebrew tongue. It was produced for the sake of those Jews who had believed in Jesus and who were serving the true Gospel at a time when the shadow of the Law had not disappeared." Jerome also writes: "Matthew, who is also called Levi, and who was changed from a tax collector into an apostle, was the first in Judea to compose a gospel of Christ in Hebrew for those of the circumcised who believed. But who later translated it into Greek is not known" (*Illus. Men* 36).

Most scholars believe, however, that the traditional view of Matthean authorship rests squarely upon a sort of double quotation from Eusebius in his famous *Ecclesiastical History* (3.39.16), who quotes PAPIAS as sayings: "Matthew compiled [or arranged] the *logia* [oracles] in the Hebrew language, and each one interpreted them [or translated them] as best he could." The gospel was entitled "According to Matthew," they say, because it contains the translation of his collection of the sayings of Jesus, the LOGIA. By this term Papias did not mean, it is believed, a life of Christ or even a gospel, but a complete record of the sayings of Jesus. Some scholars have identified that record as Q (from German *Quelle*, "source"), a symbol used to refer to an otherwise unknown document thought to be the source of material common to Matthew and Luke (but not found in Mark).

Many believe now, however, that such an identification is highly improbable, since the word *logion* G3359 (pl. *logia*) had been a technical term in Greek from early times to designate a divine oracle or an inspired utterance, like the oracles at Delphi (the word is to be distinguished from *logoi*, pl. of *logos* G3364, "word"). Other scholars, like E. J. Goodspeed, believe that the term *oracles* as used in some NT passages (Rom. 3:2; Heb. 5:12; 1 Pet. 4:11) refers not to a set of OT passages or quotations about the Messiah compiled by Matthew, or prophecies that Christ fulfilled, but to an early Hebrew gospel containing both the words and deeds of Jesus which Matthew had written down from the fixed oral tradition, either in Jerusalem or Antioch. It was assumed that Matthew, being an apostle and one interested in Jesus' words and deeds, must have been the first evangelist to write.

These assertions were expanded into a theory that Matthew wrote the first gospel but that he wrote it in a short form in Hebrew or Aramaic. For these reasons modern scholarship has for the most part abandoned the traditional Matthean authorship and believe the first gospel was ascribed to Matthew only because he was the author of one of its sources and not the author of the entire gospel itself. These suggestions are thought to explain why the first gospel came to bear Matthew's name.

While the view that Matthew originally wrote a gospel to the Hebrews in the Hebrew language, as scholars have deduced from the words of Papias, may still be acceptable to some, this view also has been repudiated by most modern scholars. Even older conservative scholars had their doubts about this theory. They said it would be better to believe that Matthew wrote a gospel in Hebrew and another in Greek. The "translation by inspiration" theory also has little acceptance today. The gospel tradition must have circulated in the early church in ARAMAIC, but the written Gospels we know are Greek books. Advocates of the Aramaic gospel theory were compelled to develop a complicated hypothesis for which there is no real evidence in or outside the gospels themselves.

If Hebrew gospels or written information about the life and words of Jesus were in existence in the first days of the church, and if Paul's Greek mission churches quickly outnumbered the Aramaic churches, any Hebrew originals may have disappeared early. W. G. Kümmel writes: "The oft-repeated thesis that Matthew was the author of a main source of Mt (the 'Logion source' or an Aramaic Mt) and that accordingly the whole was named for the part ... is a completely groundless assumption. We must concede that the report that Mt was written by Matthew 'in the Hebrew language' is utterly false, however it may have arisen" (*Introduction to the New Testament*, rev. ed. [1973], 120–21). Most NT scholars today believe that the internal evidence of all four Gospels indicates that they were composed in Greek, although some of the sources, written or oral, were Aramaic.

The interpretive method known as FORM CRITICISM also has been employed to ascertain the author and explain the nature of the first gospel. Following G. A. Kilpatrick's view (*Origins of the Gospel according to St. Matthew* [1950]) that the first gospel is a product of the Christian community and that the author is really an editor, Krister Stendahl (*The School of St. Matthew* [1954]) developed a theory that the writer or editor of the first gospel was a Christian rabbi who was interested in creating a manual for catechetical teaching in the church. The rabbi was not working alone; an entire school of scribes and teachers was at work in the church of Matthew, a school that was the counterpart of the elders of Judaism. Not an individual, nor the community, but a group is the author. Is not the gospel characterized by a teacher addressed as "Rabbi" by a group of disciples around him? The purpose of the Matthew school was to write a polemic to convert the unbeliever to the validity of Jesus as the Messiah. The structure of the gospel into ordered sections of discourses and narratives indicates that the school attempted to create a manual or textbook for teaching and administration in the church. The school is said to have influenced not only the shape, but also the actual materials of the gospel itself. While this theory throws much interesting light on the first gospel, it still results in an unknown author, and offers no more valid explanation of the character and purpose of the gospel than other views.

NT studies and criticism during the past two centuries, particularly in synoptic gospel studies, should be much appreciated and should not be denigrated in any manner, for much light has been thrown upon the NT. But a penetrating evaluation of all the theories, hypotheses, and conclusions, sometimes offered without solid evidence, indicates that the traditional view of Matthean authorship of the first gospel should not be entirely excluded. The following considerations might be offered.

(a) The quotations from the church fathers relative to the authorship of Matthew may be used on both sides of the question. It is possible that Matthew may have written a gospel in Hebrew of some type for Jewish Christians and converts, and that later he wrote such a gospel in Greek, the gospel that bears his name in the canon. At least, he could have compiled a group of Aramaic sayings or OT prophecies that were applied to our Lord for instructing Jewish Christians. Scholars believe that if he wrote a Greek gospel (the one we have) then he could have used Mark and through Mark included elements of Peter's gospel, particularly in the Antioch area, which would have drawn the Hebrew and Greek elements of the church closer together. This aspect would coincide with one of the purposes of Matthew's gospel.

(b) It must be admitted, however, that no fragment of an Aramaic Matthew has ever been found and that a Greek composition is more plausible than a Greek translation. Matthew's gospel does not give evidence of being a translation, which is one of the weak evidences for the Aramaic theory. The discussion of Papias's statement (preserved by Eusebius writing in the 4th cent.) should not overshadow the 2nd-cent. comment of Irenaeus: "Matthew also issued a written gospel among the Hebrews in their own language, while Peter and Paul were preaching at Rome and laying the foundation of the church" (*Against Heresies* 3.1.1). It seems from this statement that Matthew was considered the author, at least, of a gospel for the Jewish-speaking Christians, and that the appearance of a Greek Matthew would be readily accepted, although one must admit this is in the area of conjecture. But there is strong historical tradition that Matthew actually wrote gospel material.

(c) It is not incredible that Matthew in writing a Greek gospel would use a gospel like Mark. Embodying the Petrine material from Rome would lend itself well to one of his purposes of drawing the Hebrew and Gentile churches together. One must face openly, however, the extreme doubts of some modern scholars (doubts that have caused them to forsake the Matthean authorship) that an eyewitness of the Lord's words and life would lean heavily upon a nonapostolic person like Mark. See MARK, GOSPEL OF.

(d) One must account for the unanimous early tradition that speaks for the Matthean authorship of the first gospel. Matthew certainly had something to do directly with the gospel that carries his name. While it may be true that in ancient times books and documents sometimes were connected with famous names to gain for them recognition and authority, we must remember that Matthew was not one of the great figures of the early church. Hardly anything is known of him. He occupies little space in NT history. If he did not write the first gospel, it is most difficult to explain his connection with the gospel to which his name is attached.

One might ask why Matthew is the only one of the synoptics who is denied authorship. The title *Kata Maththaion* is very old, perhaps as early as A.D. 125, and should imply authorship. Scholars may come to the general conclusion some day that the early church ascribed the first gospel to Matthew not because he was the source of one of its sources, but because he actually wrote it. It should be remembered that many theories which explain the origin of the gospels were brought forth not to ascertain authorship but to account for their similarities and dissimilarities.

(e) Although it may not be considered the strongest argument for authorship, the suggestion of E. J. Goodspeed, noted NT scholar, is worthy of note. He believed that Matthew's occupation as a tax collector highly qualified him to be the official recorder of the works and words of Jesus and that this is the practical reason Jesus called him to be a disciple. Here was a man used to keeping books and records day after day. The entire contents of the gospel bear the marks of a tax collector. The tax collector, it is said, is one man who wrote everything down. "There was doubtless one special thing that Matthew did bring with him. To the rest of the disciples, to the men who worked on the fishing-boats, a pen and a book would be strange and unfamiliar things; but Matthew's work would make him familiar with the act of writing and recording. He left all, but he brought with him a talent that one day in some way he would use for his new Master" (Barclay, *First Three Gospels*, 208). A man like Matthew could hardly keep from writing things down, completely and accurately. Moreover, the character of his gospel reveals the background and thinking of a tax collector. The story of the unforgiving debtor (Matt. 18:23–35) deals in millions of dollars. Throwing a small debtor into prison for a few hundred dollars is part of the vocabulary of a publican.

(f) If the apostle Matthew, one of the Twelve, is not the author of our canonical Matthew, then the author is unknown to us. Two questions in this regard must be faced. How did it happen that the real author was forgotten so soon? And how did Matthew become known as the author? If the tradition that attributes the gospel to Matthew cannot be fully explained or accepted, the alternate author is just as difficult to determine. While Matt. 13:52 ("Therefore every teacher of the law who has been instructed about the kingdom of heaven is like the owner of a house who brings out of his storeroom new treasures as well as old") might be a veiled hint of a single author who was a learned rabbi or scribe, his identity is still unknown. An unknown author of the first gospel may not disturb faithful Christians as long as such a proposal does not obviate the inspiration and authority of the gospel, but there is no reason why an eyewitness and an apostle could not have written the Gospel according to Matthew.

IV. Structure and outline. An examination of the outline and structure of the Gospel of Matthew reveals that it has been both orderly and artistically arranged. Although he has certain theological and didactic aims, Matthew employs the same general historical and chronological framework as Mark and Luke, especially Mark. Yet he marshals his material in a topical way rather than as an exact day-by-day record. In the first gospel we do not look for an exact chronology of events; rather, the events of the Lord's life are written in such an order as to teach certain lessons. Matthew was an evangelist rather than a historian. He always had the church in mind. A rather deliberate artistic arrangement of the material in groups or units of three, five, and seven, is discernible, however. Some scholars, like Goodspeed, believe the gospel is arranged according to the pattern of many ancient Jewish works, for example, the five "books" or main divisions of the PENTATEUCH, the PSALMS, and the MEGILLOTH.

In Matthew each of the five "books" contains a narrative section (Jesus ministering), followed by a "lesson" section (Jesus teaching). Some have observed that Matthew was attempting to create a "New Testament Pentateuch" by this schematic arrangement. An outline of the fivefold narrative-discourse arrangement (alternate "deeds" and "words" sections) may be constructed as follows:

Introduction: Infancy stories (Matt. 1–2)
A. Early ministry of Jesus (chs. 3–7)
   1. Narrative: Galilean ministry (chs. 3–4)
   2. Discourse: Sermon on the Mount (chs. 5–7)
B. Ministry of healing: Discipleship (chs. 8–10)
   1. Narrative: Healing ministry (8:1—9:34)
   2. Discourse: Mission of the disciples (9:35—10:42)
C. Second ministry in Galilee (11:1—13:52)
   1. Narrative: Traveling and healing (chs. 11–12)
   2. Discourse: Teaching in parables (13:1–52)
D. Mission and miracles (13:53—18:35)
   1. Narrative: Life of the church (13:53—17:27)
   2. Discourse: Church discipline (18:1–35)
E. Ministry in Judea (chs. 19–25)
   1. Narrative: Teaching and healing (chs. 19–22)
   2. Discourse: Woes on Pharisees and eschatology (chs. 23–25)
Conclusion: Passion and resurrection (chs. 26–28)

The idea is that as the five books of the Pentateuch contain the laws for the OT people, so the five discourses lay down the ethics that are to guide the life of the Christian. Each one of the divisions is concluded by a repeated formula: "When Jesus had finished these sayings" (Matt. 7:28; 11:1; 13:53; 19:1; 26:1). Some believe these sections were meant to be read in the Christian meetings of worship. The formula might be understood: "Here ends the first, second, third, fourth, and fifth book of the teachings of Jesus the Messiah."

In attempting such a simplified division of the first gospel, however, it should be remembered that in certain instances the material is only generally divided according to this scheme; sharp, rigid sections are not to be expected. The arrangement is neither superficial nor forced but remains more or less topical. For example, some of Jesus' shorter discourses are woven into the narrative sections. It seems strange also to designate the infancy narrative as mere prologue and the important passion, death, and resurrection section as conclusion or epilogue. It is necessary to point out that the first gospel itself says nothing directly about this arrangement. The Markan sequence and geographical framework seem to be the basis of the gospel.

For facility in study and even memorization, as a church manual for discipleship, Matthew seems to have a penchant for grouping his materials also into threes and sevens. The miracles of Matt. 8–9 are divided into groups of three, while ch. 13 has seven parables. And the genealogy that heads the gospel has the double division of three fourteens. No doubt such divisions were to aid the memory. Since the early Christians did not possess books as we know them, things had to be committed to memory if one was to have a "copy" of them. Other examples are easily seen: There are three main events in Jesus' childhood (ch. 2); three temptations (4:1–11); seven strophes (two more than Luke) in the Lord's Prayer (6:9–15); three prohibitions (6:19—7:6); three commands (7:7–20); three miracles of healing (8:1–15); three prayers in Gethsemane (26:39–44); three denials of Peter (26:69–75); seven woes (ch. 23); three questions by Pilate (27:11–17); seven demons (12:45); seven loaves and baskets (15:34, 37); forgiving seven times and seventy times seven (18:22); seven brothers (22:25). It has been said that the gospel's appeal lay not in its narrative or literary power, but in its practical ability to shape the life of the church. It is a gospel that is easy to remember and to use for reference. The arithmetical arrangement seems too prominent to be overlooked.

The gospel also has been divided into three major parts around which the topical materials may be gathered. In this outline, as has been pointed out above, the infancy narratives and the death and resurrection form the prologue and the epilogue:

Prologue: Infancy narratives (chs. 1–2)
First major part: Jesus in Galilee (4:12—13:58)
Second major part: Jesus the Messiah (chs. 14–20)
Third major part: Jesus in Jerusalem (chs. 21–25)
Epilogue: Death and resurrection (chs. 26–28)

Others see in the design of Matthew a double outline or line of thought that can be detected in the formula "from that time on Jesus began to …" The first part of the double outline is primarily biographical, similar to that found in Mark and Luke, with two main points of departure. Point one: "From that time Jesus began to preach" (Matt. 4:17), which activity led to his great preaching ministry and brought him into prominence. Point two: "From that time on Jesus began to explain to his disciples that he must go to Jerusalem" (16:21), which section shows his decline in public favor and his ultimate death on the cross. It seems that the author wishes to emphasize these two poles of Jesus' life and works, and Jesus' entire life is to be conceived as having one divine purpose.

An acceptable and usable outline that takes into consideration a dominant theme of Matthew, that of messianic fulfillment (see below on theological purpose) is the following:

A. Introduction (1:1—4:16). Genealogy. Seven fulfillments of prophecy.

B. First Group of messianic deeds and words. The annunciation of the kingdom and the call to repentance (4:17—7:29).

C. Second group of messianic deeds and words (8:1—11:1). The contradicted Messiah seeks the lost sheep of the house of Israel.

D. Third group of messianic deeds and words (11:2—13:53). The contradicted Messiah conceals the kingdom from those who have rejected it and further reveals it to those who have accepted it (cf. 13:12).

E. Fourth group of messianic deeds and words (13:54—19:1). Toward the new messianic people of God, the church: the Messiah separates his disciples from the mass of old Israel and deepens his communion with his own.

F. Fifth group of messianic deeds and words (19:2—26:1). The Messiah gives his disciples a sure and sober hope.

G. Conclusion (26:2—28:20). The passion, death, and resurrection of the Messiah. The risen Lord in the perfection of his power: the universal commission to the disciples (M. H. Franzmann, *The Word of the Lord Grows* [1956], 175).

A general outline of the subject matter of Matthew's gospel, without specific reference to any schematic structure, is as follows:

A. The infancy stories (1:2—2:23)
   1. The genealogy (1:1–17)
   2. Birth of Jesus (1:18–25)

    3. Visit of Magi (2:1–12)
    4. Flight to Egypt (2:13–23)
 B. The ministry of John the Baptist (3:1—4:11)
    1. The preaching of John the Baptist (3:1–12)
    2. The baptism of Jesus (3:13–17)
    3. The temptation of Jesus (4:1–11)
 C. The ministry in Galilee (4:12–25)
    1. Early ministry of Jesus (4:12–17)
    2. Jesus calls his first disciples (4:18–22)
    3. Jesus preaches in Galilee (4:23–25)
 D. Teaching: The Sermon on the Mount (5:1—7:29)
    1. The Beatitudes (5:3–12)
    2. Christians are salt and light (5:13–16)
    3. Jesus teaches a new law (5:17–48)
    4. Jesus the teacher of ethics (6:1—7:27)
    5. Jesus and his hearers (7:28–29)
 E. Miracles in Galilee (8:1—9:8)
    1. Miracles of healing: leper, slave (8:1–17)
    2. Jesus teaches his disciples (8:18–22)
    3. Jesus stills the storm (8:23–27)
    4. Healing miracles: demoniac, paralytic (8:28—9:8)
 F. Various incidents (9:9–34)
    1. The calling of Matthew (9:9–13)
    2. Jesus teaches about fasting (9:14–17)
    3. More miracles of healing (9:18–34)
 G. Jesus' great mission discourse (9:35—10:42)
    1. Jesus' love for people (9:35–38)
    2. Instructions to the disciples (10:1–15)
    3. Predictions of the future (10:16–25)
    4. Jesus admonishes the disciples to be fearless (10:26–33)
    5. Difficulties and rewards (10:34–42)
 H. Traveling and teaching in Galilee (11:1—12:50)
    1. Jesus tours Galilee (11:1)
    2. The preaching of John the Baptist (11:2–15)
    3. Jesus denounces the Galilean cities (11:16–24)
    4. Jesus' blessing on the troubled (11:25–30)
    5. Teaching and healing in the synagogue (12:1–21)
    6. Jesus and the Pharisees (12:22–45)
    7. Jesus' spiritual family (12:46–50)
 I. Teaching the kingdom through parables (13:1–52)
    1. The seed and the soils (13:1–9)
    2. The purpose and interpretation of parables (13:10–23)
    3. Parable of the tares (13:24–30)
    4. The mustard seed and the leaven (13:31–35)
    5. Interpretation of the tares (13:36–43)
    6. Parables of the treasure, pearl, and net (13:44–51)
    7. The role of the scribe in the kingdom (13:52)
 J. Confession of Christ as the Messiah (13:53—17:27)
    1. Jesus' difficulties in Nazareth (13:53–58)
    2. The murder of John the Baptist (14:1–12)
    3. Various miracles and healings (14:13–36)
    4. Discussions with the Scribes and Pharisees (15:1–20)
    5. Jesus performs more miracles in Galilee (15:21–39)
    6. The Pharisees ask for a sign (16:1–4)
    7. Parable of the leaven (16:5–12)
    8. Peter's confession of the Christ (16:13–20)
    9. Jesus predicts his suffering and death (16:21–28)
    10. The transfiguration (17:1–13)
    11. Healing of the epileptic (17:14–21)
    12. Discussions of the passion (17:22–27)
 K. Jesus' teaching on various subjects (18:1–35)
    1. Status in the kingdom (18:1–5)
    2. The giving of offense (18:6–10)
    3. Parable of the lost sheep (18:11–14)
    4. Admonition on reconciliation (18:15–22)
    5. Parable of the wicked servant (18:23–35)
 L. Jesus' Judean ministry (19:1—22:46)
    1. Jesus' ministry in Perea (19:1–2)
    2. Discussions of marriage and divorce (19:3–12)
    3. Jesus blesses little children (19:13–15)
    4. Jesus and the rich young man (19:16–22)
    5. Jesus' discussion of riches and rewards (19:23–30)

6. Parable of the workers in the vineyard (20:1–16)
  7. Jesus again foretells the passion (20:17–19)
  8. The petition of Zebedee's wife for her two sons (20:20–28)
  9. Healing of the two blind men (20:29–34)
  10. Jesus enters Jerusalem (21:1–11)
  11. Jesus cleans the Temple (21:12–17)
  12. Jesus curses the fig tree (21:18–22)
  13. Discussions in the Temple court (21:23—22:46)
M. Jesus' teaching on the last things (23:1—25:46)
  1. Woes against the Pharisees (23:1–36)
  2. Jesus mourns over Jerusalem (23:37–39)
  3. Jesus' teaching on the end of the world (24:1—25:46)
N. Suffering, death, and resurrection (26:1—28:20)
  1. The beginnings of the passion (26:1–19)
  2. Prediction of the betrayal by Judas (26:20–25)
  3. The Lord's Supper (26:26–29)
  4. Jesus predicts the denial of Peter (26:30–35)
  5. Jesus prays in Gethsemane (26:36–46)
  6. Jesus' arrest, trial, and crucifixion (26:47—27:56)
  7. The burial of Jesus (27:57–66)
  8. Jesus' resurrection and appearance to the disciples (28:1–17)
  9. The Great Commission (28:18–20)

V. Theme and theological purpose. The theme of the first gospel is stated in the lead sentence of the book, "A record [*lit.*, book] of the genealogy of Jesus Christ the son of David, the son of Abraham" (Matt. 1:1). One is reminded of the book of Genesis, which is divided into sections by the use of a similar phrase, "[the book of] the generations of" (KJV Gen. 2:4; 5:1; 6:9; et al.). In the OT the phrase marks a new stage in the development of the promises of the Messiah, carried on until David, where the line ends. Matthew begins his genealogy at this point and shows in detail how Jesus of Nazareth fulfills the OT prophecies. In this manner Matthew imitates the structure of the OT, and perhaps in more than one way provides a definite bridge between the prophets and the NT fulfillment. (See GENEALOGY and GENEALOGY OF JESUS CHRIST.)

All things considered, this is the dominant theme of the gospel, namely, the fulfillment of OT prophecy, and this forms at the same time Matthew's main theological purpose. The purpose is indicated by the genealogy itself; Matthew begins the line with ABRAHAM to show that Jesus is a true Jew while Luke traces him back to ADAM as the true SON OF MAN (Lk. 3:38). If Jesus' lineage can be traced back to Abraham through David, then he is the Messiah, the divine SON OF GOD (Matt. 22:42). If not, theologically speaking, Jesus could not be the One who died and rose again and be the "Sent One."

The first gospel testifies that God is the Lord of all history and salvation and that Jesus Christ is his Son. The works and words of Yahweh are so closely related in both the OT and the NT that God's great works are described simply as the action of his Word (the LOGOS), his only Son. Nowhere is this theme more clearly illustrated than in the Gospel according to Matthew, the gospel of fulfillment. God's promise in the COVENANT of the Messiah and Savior in the OT is fulfilled in the words and deeds of Jesus Christ in the NT. An outstanding example is Jesus before the high priest: "But Jesus remained silent. The high priest said to him, 'I charge you under oath by the living God: Tell us if you are the Christ, the Son of God.' 'Yes, it is as you say,' Jesus replied. 'But I say to all of you: In the future you will see the Son of Man sitting at the right hand of the Mighty One and coming on the clouds of heaven'" (Matt. 26:63–64).

To illustrate his theme, Matthew literally crowds his gospel with the entire Christological and messianic aspects of the OT until he has quoted almost every book in the OT—over fifty quotations in all not counting many echoes and allusions. His OT polemic is not limited to a few scattered references but is by far the most complete collection of passages bearing on the theme "Christ in the Old Testament" given by any NT writer. He quotes chiefly Isaiah, the messianic and evangelical

This picture of the region near Bethlehem reminds us that Matthew frequently quotes the OT (e.g., Mic. 5:2) to show that Jesus fulfilled the predictions associated with the coming Messiah.

prophet, and the Psalms, but his quotes are representative of the entire OT in the Law, the Prophets, and the Psalms. One-fifth of his quotations are from Isaiah. Perhaps no other OT book influenced Matthew as Isaiah did. A study of the use of the OT in Matthew gives some credence to the belief of those who think that the statement of Papias about the Logia of Matthew refers to a collection of OT quotations on Christ the Messiah.

After his famous genealogy, he launches into the lowly birth of the Suffering Servant, quoting Isaiah in fulfillment: "All this took place to fulfill what the Lord had said through the prophet: 'The virgin will be with child and will give birth to a son, and they will call him Immanuel'" (Matt. 1:22–23). After that, prophet after prophet and book after book is quoted by Matthew to illustrate that Jesus is the Messiah foretold by the OT Word. The glory of the Messiah, the ministry of the Messiah, the crucifixion of the Messiah, the resurrection of the Messiah, and the exaltation of the Messiah all receive due attention in Matthew so that his purpose is unmistakable. The Son of Man has come for both salvation and judgment, and in him the present is the substance of the past and the future. No book in the NT sets forth the person of Jesus, his life, and his teaching so clearly as the fulfillment of the Law and the Prophets in Matthew. Some eleven times in the gospel he introduces prophecy with the impressive formula "to fulfill what was spoken through the prophet," the cumulative effect of which is remarkable.

In all this prophecy and fulfillment, the Word does not once lose its character of history. Christianity is portrayed as a historical religion. Events are recorded as happening in the way they did because God had willed that it should be so. Even isolated events, the seemingly unexplained, happened "according to the Scriptures." Thus the Word has a history, being the culmination of God's previous promises and mighty acts. It is history because a real Man comes into history to deal with real people in time and deals with their predicament of sin; it creates history in that the Word is strong and mighty, still fulfilling God's will on earth.

Matthew's gospel also represents a full expansion of the apostolic KERYGMA (proclamation). In keeping with the view that Matthew used as source material the oral Aramaic tradition, his gospel indicates that he followed the outline of this oral preaching. The first generation of Christians, between Jesus' resurrection and the writing of the Gospels, had no complete written documents about Jesus; the only Scripture they had was the OT. The message that is indicated in the speeches of Peter (Acts 3:11–26; 10:36–43) and in certain sections of Paul's epistles (1 Cor. 15:3–7) followed an outline something like this:

1. God's promises in the OT have been fulfilled.
2. The long-awaited Messiah, born of David's line, is here with the kingdom.
3. He is Jesus of Nazareth.
4. In his ministry on earth, he went about preaching and doing good through mighty works of healing and power.
5. He was crucified according to the promise and will of God the Father.
6. He was raised from the dead and exalted at God's right hand.
7. He will come again in glory to judge the living and the dead.
8. Therefore, all should listen to his message, repent, and be baptized for the forgiveness of their sins.

This *kerygma* or "message" was the earliest gospel. Matthew's gospel gives an expanded version of it in great detail. One notices how much space he gives to the passion narrative. This is why the gospel was so popular in the early church. The earliest gospel was not, therefore, the SERMON ON THE MOUNT. That sermon was one of Matthew's special contributions to the teaching and life of the church—the ethical teaching of Jesus (see ETHICS OF JESUS). We should be reminded that this or the fulfillment of the historical interest was not Matthew's primary objective, but a means to an end.

The gospel is not a biography. It is impossible to write a life of Christ. Too few events are extant and only two to three years of Jesus' life at the most are portrayed by all of the Gospels together. The primary concern was not historical completeness *but revelation and theology*. In this concern, Matthew seems to exclude almost all material that is not theologically essential to the messiahship of Jesus. The purpose was completeness of the divine revelation and the culmination of all earlier OT writings. It is not amazing, therefore, that the early Christians considered the OT a true source of the life and works of Jesus and thus placed the OT canon beside the Greek Scriptures. The NT has definite continuity through Jesus Christ with the Messiah and Israel of the OT.

The fulfillment formula of Matthew follows two principles: (1) every event recorded of Jesus was foretold in the OT; (2) every prediction of the Messiah must find a corresponding event in the life of Jesus. Matthew carries these principles to great lengths in his gospel. He demonstrates that the Messiah, descended from Abraham, was born as King of the Jews (Matt. 2:2), entered the Holy City in triumph as a King (21:4), was born of a virgin as foretold by the prophet Isaiah (1:22), was conceived by the Holy Spirit (1:20), was called the Son of God (14:33). As the Messiah on earth, he fulfilled all the prophecies of the Old Covenant: his ministry, use of parables, betrayal, miracles, healing, suffering, death, coming in glory with angels (24:30), and sitting on his throne of glory (25:31), all were foretold in the OT. Matthew covers the entire gamut of the Messiah in the OT, so much so that the NT is, as it were, an OT rerun.

Perhaps the central point of this thesis was Peter's confession of Jesus as the Messiah at CAESAREA PHILIPPI (Matt. 16:13–20). It was all part of the divine messianic plan of the ages and is perhaps why Matthew's gospel was used and read more by early Christians than any other. At the end of his gospel Matthew looks both backward and forward to Jesus Christ when he quotes these words of the Lord: "and teaching them to obey everything I have commanded you. And surely I am with you always, to the very end of the age" (28:20).

A secondary purpose of Matthew's gospel, as was noted above in the section on structure and outline, was to furnish the young church a manual of instruction in doctrine and church practice. Many believe it was not written for private reading and study so much as for the guidance of teachers as they instructed new converts. It is a teaching gospel, quite easy to remember and memorize. Perhaps it was the first textbook in Christian education to be used by the church. It was designed also to be read aloud in the Christian worship services. Besides the messianic fulfillment emphasis, the instruction from the gospel would present the ethical teachings of Jesus and the teaching of love and forgiveness, but these are included in the works and teachings of Jesus the Messiah.

VI. Characteristics and special features.

Matthew's gospel is, first of all, a *mission-type gospel* or a *preaching gospel*. The over-all purpose is to inform, convince, and evangelize the hearers, both Jew and Gentile, regarding the Messiah. The messianic theme makes for the unity of the book. Some have said this gospel is a defense against all Jewish unbelief. It appeals to deep-rooted Jewish messianic beliefs in order to convince all that Jesus of Nazareth is the promised Messiah. Matthew argues from the OT much as most preachers of the early church did.

The messianic theme of Matthew may be outlined as follows:

1. The prophecies of the Messiah fulfilled—the coming (Matt. 1:1—4:11)
2. The teachings of the Messiah—great discourses (4:12—7:29)
3. the Deity of the Messiah revealed—the miracle (8:1—11:1)
4. The kingdom of the Messiah revealed—the parables (11:2—13:53)
5. The redemption of the Messiah proclaimed—the cross (13:54—19:2)
6. The opposition of the enemy—debates with opponents (19:3—26:2)
7. The passion of the Messiah—suffering, death, and resurrection (26:3—28:10)
8. Conclusion: The Great Commission (28:11-20)

If Matthew wrote at a time when Jewish and Gentile Christianity were separate and in opposition, his gospel shows that there is both unity and ecumenicity in the Lord Jesus Christ. For Matthew, Christianity was not a divisive sect that was inventing a Christ or misusing the OT; rather, he shows that the divine purpose of salvation for all was fulfilled in Jesus Christ the Messiah. The gospel is both universal and particular. The first gospel is, therefore, a gospel that teaches universal grace. It is an *ecumenical* gospel (Matt. 9:12-13). The first gospel also teaches much about *the power of the gospel*. The Messiah's call to the Christian is earnest, drastic, and by grace.

All of the basic theology taught in the first gospel certainly had its personal reference to Matthew himself. The manner in which he records his call (Matt. 9:9-13) shows how he appreciated the Savior's love for all. He certainly must have thought of himself when he wrote down the parable of the laborers in the vineyard (20:1-16). By his countrymen he was considered a renegade Jew who had turned his back upon Israel to make profit from the shady tax-collecting system of the Romans and the provincial government. No doubt he was a self-seeking materialist. For him the Lord's call meant a sharp break with the past. The experience of being totally hated by his people and then fully and completely accepted by grace left an indelible mark on Matthew the tax collector. On the one hand, he knew how sin could separate a man from God and his fellowman, and on the other, he realized how gracious was the call to repentance and service. Although he was a most unlikely candidate to be the author of a gospel, he was uniquely prepared to appeal to both Jew and Gentile for faith and commitment to the Messiah of the OT Scriptures.

The Gospel of Matthew emphasizes the *call to repentance and ministry*. It is always a demanding absolute call. It involves the total person facing God. Matthew's gospel is in unswerving opposition to any compromise with evil on the road back to God. No doubt this is why the discipline of winning the sinful brother, an evangelical duty that the church has followed through the centuries, is found alone in Matthew's powerful gospel (Matt. 18:15-35).

Another prominent aspect of Matthew's gospel is the emphasis on the *obedience of faith*. God initiates all dealings with his people on the basis of grace in Christ. Only God is good. The Christian gives himself wholly to the Savior and in faith and service. The sin of the Pharisee was as much half-heartedness as self-righteousness. Matthew, who from a human point of view should be the last to castigate righteous people in the eyes of men, pours the most scathing rebuke on the scribes and Pharisees in the NT for their hypocrisy. He who once forsook the OT and its teachings now becomes its most ardent supporter and interpreter.

Those who have received the grace of God and entered into discipleship have learned from Matthew the true meaning of the gospel and of the kingdom. See DISCIPLE, DISCIPLESHIP. Such discipleship is taught in the parable of the merciless servant (Matt. 18:23–35). A person is set free to forgive and to free others. Matthew teaches not only that the Lord calls the sinner to repentance, but also that those who have become his disciples must daily repent (18:1–4). Every limitation of love is set aside when the Lord asks his disciples to love their enemies (5:44). Impetuous stubborn Peter, the impatient man of Galilee, is asked to forgive his brother not just seven times but seventy times seven (18:21–22). Finally our Lord asks the disciples to make his cross their way of life in ministry and sacrifice (10:38).

The Messiah brings into being a *new universal church*, the new Israel. Both Jews and Gentiles find refuge in it. Matthew is the only evangelist who uses the word CHURCH at all (Matt. 16:18; 18:17). He speaks of the permanence of the church and of discipline and forgiveness within it. The gospel opens with the promise that the Messiah is the IMMANUEL who will be with his people and closes with the promise that this same Jesus, now the risen Christ, will be with his disciples of all nations until the end of time. Such features as the visit of the MAGI to the infant Jesus early in the gospel and Jesus' long ministry in "Galilee of the Gentiles" (4:15) speak of a universal church. Yet this Christian church, universal in its membership, is no new church. It is the old Israel transformed and expanded (10:5).

The first gospel is known also for the extent and manner in which it presents the *ethical teachings of Jesus*. To the evangelist Matthew, as well as to Paul, there is a "law of Christ," a principle of Christian LOVE that becomes imperative for ethical living. Jesus is the great teacher who proclaims a revised law for the new Israel from the mountain in the Sermon on the Mount, even as Moses has spoken divine law on Mount Sinai. The Messiah calls his church not only to repentance, but also to good works. The righteousness of the disciples must exceed that of the Pharisees. Christian life is free but it is moral and responsible, motivated by love. Even if the existing institution had corrupted and perverted the law, nevertheless it was divine revelation. The Messiah comes not to destroy it but to fulfill it and to supply what it lacked. Thus a large part of the Sermon on the Mount is replete with explanations of the law in which Jesus lays down the moral standards of love by which the conduct of Christians is to be judged.

From a practical or methodological viewpoint, the Gospel according to Matthew is a *teaching gospel*. It is characterized by lengthy discourses. It expands the *action* Gospel of Mark, which is more interested in what Jesus did than in what he said. The following is a list of prominent lengthy discourses in the gospel:

Matt. 3:1–12 Preaching of John
5:1—7:29 Sermon on the Mount
10:1–42 The apostolic commission
13:1–52 The parables
18:1–35 The meaning of forgiveness
23:1—25:46 Denunciation and prophecy
28:18–20 The Great Commission

The Gospel of Matthew features a large number of parables. The greatest single group of parables is in Matt. 13. The illustrations are taken from everyday life and portray the nature and demands of the kingdom. Many of them are prophetic. Matthew says that the parables were intended both to reveal and conceal truth (13:10–13). Ten parables in Matthew are not found in any of the other Gospels: tares, hidden treasure, net, pearl of great price, unmerciful servant, laborers in the vineyard, two sons, marriage of the king's son, the ten virgins, and the talents. (There are two miracles that are found only in Matthew's gospel: the two blind men and the coin in the mouth of the fish.)

Matthew alone uses the phrase "the kingdom of heaven" (thirty-three times). Five times he speaks of the "kingdom of God." Matthew's gospel is also a royal gospel. The Messiah is pictured repeatedly as the great King. His lineage is traced back to King David; the Magi ask for the King of the Jews; he is called the "Son of David"; he enters Jerusalem in triumph; Pontius Pilate asks Jesus if he is the King of the Jews; over his cross the words are written, "This is Jesus the King of the Jews"; and in the climax of the gospel he claims all power over heaven and earth. One must conclude that the author of the gospel deliberately presents Jesus as the King.

Matthew's portrayal of Jesus Christ as the Messiah may be *patterned after the experiences of the people of Israel*. Our Lord's relationship to Egypt

Aerial view of the NE shore of the Sea of Galilee, looking toward Capernaum, with Bethsaida Julias in the foreground. The hill rising on the right side of the photograph is a probable location for the feeding of the 5,000.

is particularly significant. As the children of Israel went down into Egypt in infancy and came out of it in the exodus, so Matthew portrays Jesus in his infancy going down to Egypt and coming out of it in fulfillment of the prophecy spoken in Hos. 11:1, "Out of Egypt I called my son" (Matt. 2:15). Another parallel is Jesus' temptation and fasting in the desert forty days and forty nights with Israel's wandering in the desert for forty years (4:1–2).

Matthew's gospel may be characterized as an *ecclesiastical gospel*. Its interests are centered in the church more than those of any of the other Gospels. The church is portrayed as an actual living body of worshipers and servants of Christ. The Sermon on the Mount and the parables in Matthew portray the ideals and life of the Christian congregation. This church is interested in winning all of its erring members (Matt. 18), and our Lord says the gates of hell shall not prevail against it (16:18). The gospel speaks of prayer, giving, Christian rules for marriage and divorce, the sacraments, the teaching, and preaching ministry. In fact, Matthew has much to say about the entire life and practices of the Christian church.

While Matthew's gospel is known for its lengthy discourses or teaching episodes, a main feature for which it is known is its complete form of the *Sermon on the Mount*. It contains the spiritual and moral principles of the new Israel. The ethic Jesus expounded was based upon the inner spirit, selfless love, and responsible evangelical living. It is also an interpretation of the old Mosaic law but not an abrogation of it (Matt. 5:17). All Christians know the formula and authority of the Lord's ethical teaching: "You have heard that it was said to the people long ago. … But I tell you …" (5:21–22 et al.).

Matthew's gospel also is definitely *a Jewish gospel*. The outlook and flavor is Jewish, written by a Jewish Christian to guide the thought and worship of Jewish Christians in Palestine and Syria. The other gospel writers tend to explain Jewish words and phrases (Mk. 7:1–13), but Matthew assumes his readers understand such details.

Another specific feature unique to Matthew is the manner of teaching the gospel through what has been called the *extreme* or *critical case method*. For example, it illustrates the gospel by selecting those instances in which Jesus went to extreme limits to illustrate by word and deed the gracious word of God. According to the Sermon on the Mount, the poor will inherit the earth, and the blessings of the kingdom are promised to the beggar, to the poor in spirit (Matt. 5:3). What superb teaching to point out that the boundless grace of God is as wide and deep as the need of man! The miracles of Jesus are selected in the same manner. Three illustrate the boundless compassion of Jesus. He heals the leper whom no one can help (8:1–4); he assists

With his listeners sitting on the hillsides above the Sea of Galilee, Jesus probably used natural amphitheaters like this along the lakeshore to amplify his voice. (View to the SE.)

the Gentile who is outside the commonwealth of Israel (8:5–13); he restores to health the woman that the culture of the day placed in second place as a creature of God (9:18–22). Troubled Christians throughout the centuries have considered the gospel credible because Jesus called a hated tax collector, a man whom the Jewish authorities always named the sinner and excluded from Yahweh's grace, to be his disciple and apostle (9:9–13).

Matthew shows that our Lord taught by the extreme method in the ethical area. There are no limits of love because Jesus asks his disciples to love even their enemies, which implies that no one can consider another person his enemy (Matt. 5:44). A classic example is Jesus' instruction to Peter that went far beyond the apostle's own estimate of love when he said he should forgive his brother seventy times seven (18:21–22).

Another interesting facet of Matthew's gospel is the use of *extreme opposites* in teaching the gospel. On the one hand, Jesus the Messiah is the son of Abraham the son of David, the high point in Israel's history (Matt. 1:1–17), but immediately Matthew records that the Messiah is not the product of Israel's history itself, but is conceived by God himself from outside history (1:18). Again, the Messiah is the Lord of heaven and earth (28:18), and yet he is sorrowful even to death in his suffering and dies a disgraceful criminal's death on the cross (27:32–54). He sits on the very throne of God and will come to judge the entire world (25:31–33), but on the cross he is forsaken by his Father (27:46). Of course, the most extreme statement of opposites in Matthew's gospel is that the Messiah is Jesus of Nazareth, born of a lowly maiden, a carpenter's son who reduces himself to the form of a servant and suffers and dies for the world; yet he is the Christ, the Son of God, who will rule all things in all ways (28:18). This contrast is the heart of the gospel. The Messiah is divine and yet human. He is a man of history and yet the Son of God of all eternity. He comes from one nation of people on the earth, yet he died for all peoples and is to be preached to all nations for the salvation of all (28:19–20).

Only Matthew records certain events of Jesus' life: Joseph's vision (Matt. 1:20–24), the visit of the Wise Men (2:1–12), the flight of the Christ Child into Egypt (2:13–15), the killing of the infants in Bethlehem (2:16), the dream of Pilate's wife (27:19), the suicide of Judas (27:3–10), the resurrection of the dead at the crucifixion (27:52), the story of the bribed guard (28:12–15), and the Great Commission (28:19–20). These are not found in any of the other Gospels. The same is true of certain parables. Matthew uses the miracles of Jesus to give proof of Jesus' messianic power more than as a part of the narrative of his life, again illustrating his theological interest. A unique feature of Matthew's gospel, which is not usually mentioned, is the ecclesiastical text of 16:18: "And I tell you that you are Peter, and on this rock I will build my church." The passage has influenced the history of the church on earth as much as any other. It is inscribed on the dome of St. Peter's in Rome (*Tu es petrus et super hanc petram aedificabo ecclesiam meam*). No other gospel has these words, not even in a different format.

A close reading of the first gospel reveals a great emphasis on *Jesus' disciples and discipleship*. Matthew gives much space to the instruction of the disciples and apostles. One of Jesus' first acts after his baptism and temptation was the calling of his disciples into ministry. Immediately the teaching is clear that salvation does not originate in the institutional structure of Judaism, but in the deep communion and faith between the Lord and his disciples, the church. Most of our Lord's discourses, which form the backbone of the gospel, are addressed to his disciples. It is interesting that Matthew records much about their call, their training, their failures, their forgiveness, and their reconciliation. The most remarkable revelations of the Messiah—the transfiguration, the miracles, the resurrection, the passion—are shown to the disciples alone. Even the last words of the Messiah in Matthew's record ask his disciples to make disciples of all men (28:19).

Matthew's gospel also has a strong *eschatological content*. Matthew is interested in the SECOND COMING of Jesus. He generally expands the words of Mark or Luke on the subject (Matt. 16:28; 24:30–31; 26:64). He even uses APOCALYPTIC language of the day such as PAROUSIA (24:3). Matthew includes a group of parables that teach and interpret the second coming of Jesus. The other Gospels do not have the following particular parables: the ten virgins (25:1–13); the sheep and goats in the great judgment (25:31–46); the talents (25:14–30). There is an amazing tendency on the part of the writer of Matthew to include lengthy statements on the second coming and to interpret it in terms of deliverance from the troubles of life, eternal relief from a horrible present.

VII. Matthew's use of the OT. Matthew's gospel is saturated with the OT. Over fifty clear quotations, some including several passages, have been lifted from the OT, particularly from the Prophets. In addition to the verbatim quotations, there are many allusions, echoes, single words, and phrases to be found. Much of the language and thought of the gospel is shaped by the form and figure of the Hebrew Scriptures. The OT casts a long shadow over Matthew's gospel. No other evangelist or NT writer, including Paul or the author of Hebrews, drew upon the OT writings as Matthew did. Most of the quotations come through the SEPTUAGINT (LXX, the ancient Greek translation of the OT), although by no means all. As already mentioned, many believe this collection of OT passages represents the Logia of Matthew mentioned by Papias, but this is not at all certain.

The list of quotations below, although not exhaustive, will offer the interested reader a general picture of Matthew's use of the OT in terms of documentation or "proof texts" for his messianic thesis. The list represents the more familiar whole-verse citations, which, when placed in a single group, form an imposing array of messianic witness. Parts of the verses are quoted to indicate the contents of the quotations.

1:23, "The virgin will be with child" (Isa. 7:14)
2:6, "But you, Bethlehem" (Mic. 5:2)
2:15, "Out of Egypt" (Hos. 11:1)
2:18, "A voice is heard in Ramah" (Jer. 31:15)
2:23, "He will be called a Nazarene" (Isa. 11:1)
3:3, "A voice of one calling" (Isa. 40:3)
4:4, "not … on bread alone" (Deut. 8:3)
4:6, "He will command his angels" (Ps. 91:11)
4:7, "Do not put the Lord … to the test" (Deut. 6:6)
4:10, "Worship the Lord" (Deut. 6:13)
4:15–16, "Land of Zebulun" (Isa. 9:1)
5:21, "Do not murder" (Exod. 20:13)

This papyrus from c. A.D. 300 (known as P[37]) contains Matt. 26:19–52; in v. 31 Jesus quotes Zech. 13:7.

5:27, "Do not commit adultery" (Exod. 20:14)
5:48, "Be perfect" (Lev. 19:2)
8:17, "He took up our infirmities" (Isa. 53:4)
9:13; 12:7, "I desire mercy, not sacrifice" (Hos. 6:6)
11:5, "The blind receive sight" (Isa. 29:18)
11:10, "I will send my messenger" (Mal. 3:1)
12:18–21, "Here is my servant" (Isa. 42:1–4)
13:14–15, "You will be ever hearing" (Isa. 6:9–10)
13:35, "I will open my mouth in parables" (Ps. 78:2)
15:4, "Honor your father and mother" (Exod. 20:12)
15:8–9, "people honor me with their lips" (Isa. 29:13)
18:16, "two or three witnesses" (Deut. 19:15)
19:4, "made them male and female" (Gen. 1:26)
19:5, "a man will leave his father" (Gen. 2:24)
19:18–19, "Do not murder ..." (Exod. 20:12–16)
21:5, "Say to the Daughter of Zion" (Isa. 62:11)
21:9, "Hosanna to the Son of David!" (Ps. 118:26)
21:13, "a house of prayer" (Isa. 56:7)
21:16, "From the lips of children" (Ps. 8:2)
21:42, "The stone the builders rejected" (Ps. 118:22)
22:24, "man dies without having children" (Deut. 25:5)
22:32, "I am the God of Abraham" (Exod. 3:6)
22:37, "Love the Lord your God" (Deut. 6:5)
22:39, "Love your neighbor" (Lev. 19:18)
22:44, "Sit at my right hand" (Ps. 110:1)
23:39, "Blessed is he who comes" (Ps. 118:26)
24:7, "Nation will rise against nation" (Isa. 19:2)
24:15, "abomination that causes desolation" (Dan. 9:27)
24:21, "great distress" (Dan. 12:1)
26:31, "I will strike the shepherd" (Zech. 13:7)
26:38, "My soul is overwhelmed" (Ps. 42:6)
26:64, "you will see the Son of Man" (Dan. 7:13)
27:34, "wine ... mixed with gall" (Ps. 69:21)
27:35, "divided up his clothes" (Ps. 22:18)
27:39, "shaking their heads" (Ps. 22:7)
27:43, "He trusts in God" (Ps. 22:8)
27:46, "My God, my God, why ..." (Ps. 22:1)
27:48, "sponge ... wine vinegar" (Ps. 69:21)

VIII. Relation to Mark and Luke. In view of the nature of NT studies during the last two centuries, any discussion of one of the Synoptic Gospels (Matthew, Mark, and Luke) quickly involves the other two. Many modern scholars are certain that Mark wrote his gospel first and that the writer of Matthew (as well as Luke) used Mark's gospel as the basic format and source for his gospel. As we have seen (above, section III), some scholars further conclude that Matthew the apostle could not have written the first gospel, because it is incredible that an apostle would lean so heavily on the writing of one who was not one of the Twelve. Why should Matthew borrow from Mark what he himself had evidently seen as an eyewitness? But if Matthew did not use Mark, why is his gospel so similar to Mark's? Careful Bible students are aware that most of the material in Mark (606 verses out of 661) are found in Matthew. In fact, practically all of Mark's gospel with the exception of some fifty verses are to be found in both Matthew and Luke.

The question of the relationship of Matthew to Mark (and Luke) confronts one immediately with the celebrated question of modern NT scholarship, the synoptic problem—a problem that scholars must live with because no one has come forth with an absolute answer. How does one explain both the similarities and the dissimilarities of the synoptics? If one finally thinks he has the answer to the similarities, the question of the dissimilarities stares him in the face and vice versa. Matthew and Luke hardly ever agree against Mark in parallels. There are also a number of passages common to Matthew and to Luke that Mark does not have at all—generally sayings or parables of Jesus. What was the source of *this* material? Assuming for a moment that all three synoptics were written independently, how does one explain, for example, the minute verbal resemblances between Matthew and Mark? Is it possible that a gospel like Matthew arose and circulated by itself free of other sources and that Mark copied much of Matthew? What single theory will account for all relationships between the first three Gospels?

All three Gospels give a common outline of the story of Jesus. There is a remarkable parallelism between them; the same incidents about Jesus are told in much the same language. One must infer that all the synoptics must have drawn materials from a source or sources that the others also possessed. To discover these sources is the task set by the synoptic problem. An old solution, but one that is not to be discarded (since all theories rely upon it in one way or another) is the *oral gospel theory*. Because of the agreements among the Gospels, a common source of oral tradition about Jesus, it is said, must lie behind them. They all seem to be cut from a single piece of cloth. The oral tradition, embodying the early preaching and teaching of the new church, was available to all gospel writers. On the other hand, each of the writers used the oral source in his own way and according to his own purpose; this would explain the dissimilarities. According to this theory, one studies Matthew as Matthew and is not concerned with the other Gospels. Each one must be studied in its own right. This view seems very acceptable, but in fact the church throughout its history has never ceased to harmonize the Gospels and study them together just *because they are so much alike*, and also *because they are different*—all three synoptics deal with the same Lord and all his people wish to know the whole story. Besides, students of the Gospels also soon discovered that the oral tradition view could not explain the minute parallels in language.

The relation of Matthew with Mark and Luke (or any combination of the three) is best explained if one attributes the similarities and dissimilarities to common use of one or more *written sources*. As the Jewish Christians spread out from Jerusalem and the Gentile Christians were brought into the church through the missionary efforts of the apostles, many questions about Jesus would arise and there would naturally be a demand for the gospel in written form. Perhaps Matthew himself, as Papias suggests, published one of these early documents. Scholars then began to investigate the possible written sources behind the Gospels. The pattern of thought generally ran something like the following: The old view that Matthew was the earliest gospel and that Mark simply made a summary of it is quite impossible. Also unacceptable is the more recent "Aramaic Gospel" view, namely, that Matthew was first written in Hebrew and then translated into Greek (either by Matthew himself or someone else) after Mark was written. Should Mark be an abridgment of Matthew it would also have to be an abridgment of Luke, since the two are closely related. By far the simplest and most natural view of the problem is that which looks upon Matthew and Luke as independent writings, but both of them being based upon Mark who wrote first (since he is the shortest and most fundamental), as one of two sources. Since Matthew and Luke both contain gospel material that Mark does not have, then Matthew and Luke must have used still another source for the common material they both have. Since the common source of Matthew and Luke centers a great deal on the sayings and preaching of Jesus, scholars have called this common source "Q" (from the German word *Quelle* meaning "spring, source").

In this way came into being the so-called "two-document" or "two-source" hypothesis. This explains, scholars say, the fact that Mark is totally contained in the other two synoptics, that it was written first, and that the other Gospels are an expansion of it. The theory accounts for the common material (Matthew used nearly all of Mark, and Luke about one half of Mark), for the linguistic parallels (it is said Matthew repeats about fifty percent and Luke fifty-five percent of Mark's phraseology), and for the common order of events. The second source, Q, accounts for the material Matthew and Luke have that is not found in Mark. Matthew and Luke have in common nearly 200 verses, often in about the same language, which Mark does not have. Since this common material is mostly in the sayings of Jesus, it could have been (and prob. was) something like the Logia attributed to Matthew.

While the two-source theory is acceptable, and even many conservative Bible scholars have favored it, it must be admitted that it is a theory and not a fact, since no document entitled Q has ever been found. It has to be "constructed" from the common material of Matthew and Luke. Also Matthew inserted some material not found in any of the sources mentioned. The same is true of Luke. When the materials which Matthew and Luke use from Mark and Q are isolated, each of these writers still contains much subject matter peculiar to himself. Matthew has more than 300 verses no one else has. Furthermore, the document Q (if it is identified with Matthew's Logia) can mean different things. Is it a Hebrew gospel? A catalog of OT testimonies or proof texts that Jesus is the Messiah? A collection of "oracular utterances"? Sayings of Jesus? In addition to this uncertainty about Q, the weakness of the two-document theory always has been that it does not answer the questions it sets out to explain; instead it raises still others.

Because of these difficulties, some scholars, notably Burnett H. Streeter, expanded the written source theory into a "four-document" hypothesis including a separate written source "L" that Luke alone used and a special source known as "M" that Matthew used. This expanded theory also posited that the four sources came from different centers of the early church: Mark from ROME, M from JERUSALEM, L from CAESAREA, and Q from ANTIOCH OF SYRIA. It is self-evident that four sources, three of which have never been found, is more speculative than two sources. There is also the question whether or not the relationships between the synoptics are *only* documentary. It is also possible that Matthew did not know Mark as a complete document but relied instead upon the fixed oral tradition of the early church, such as one finds in apostolic preaching (e.g., Peter's address on the day of Pentecost, Acts 2:22–36; Paul's speech in Antioch, 13:23–41).

Dissatisfaction with source theories led to the development of FORM CRITICISM. This is an attempt to get behind all written sources to the oral preaching and teaching of the church, which is thought to have developed according to certain patterns or forms that can be determined by applying to the text of our Gospels certain predetermined criteria of literary criticism. A second purpose of the "form" approach is to push on to the shape of the text in the oral tradition before it became "gospel." From the oral tradition it was only a short step for the form critic to an analysis of the historical or cultural context in which the forms grew. This is commonly called the *Sitz im Leben* ("situation in life"), and from it one could reason back to the community that produced the form. It was concluded from this rather complex and subjective process that the Gospels, or the written sources used in them, were really a collection of isolated pieces (parables, miracles, addresses, etc.) which had circulated in the early Christian community before being written down.

A special characteristic of form criticism, as practiced by many of its early proponents, was the belief that these pieces or literary forms were the creation of the worshiping and teaching church and that the forms were "put together" by editors or redactors rather than authors who wrote under the influence of the Holy Spirit. Others, like Kilpatrick and Stendahl, came to the conclusion that not the Christian community but certain schools or groups of teachers and scholars were responsible for creating and shaping the forms. The method also led to great doubts about the historicity of some of the forms and stories that make up the Gospels. The redactors were more interested in certain theological purposes than in the historical context of the form. In the hands of radical scholars, the form-critical method often took on such negative and destructive elements that it fell into disrepute in some quarters, "done in" by its friends more than its enemies.

Form criticism quickly lost ground as an adequate method of explaining the origin of Matthew and the other Gospels. It leaves behind some answers to the familiar questions of the synoptic problem (the similarities and differences of the Gospels are due to use of the forms according to theological interests) but raises other still more significant problems, for example, what role did an apostolic eyewitness like Matthew, or Jesus himself, play in creation of the forms? If the answer is "None," or "Very little," then the inevitable question is, "Why was the gospel material created in the first place?" and one is back where he started. Some scholars believe that the question of the relation of Matthew to Mark and Luke is a problem of authors rather than of documents. If one could discover in some way the possible living contact and interchange between the writers of the first three Gospels, perhaps the right answer could be found. How much did they rewrite and rearrange written sources? Is it at all possible that the three authors could have had contact with each other and fashioned their writings to include the new material they heard from each other?

It must be admitted that none of the theories really explains the synoptic problem completely. Helpful for the explanation of the relationship between Matthew and Mark, however, is the theological purpose of these two evangelists. Although they use the same gospel material, they put it to different uses, organize it into different frameworks, and under the direction of the Holy Spirit, write a gospel for a specific theological and historical purpose. Mark's gospel of action and movement certainly had a different aim than the didactic gospel of fulfillment of Matthew. The intended readers or audience of each gospel also determined the nature of the gospel. This is why four versions of the one gospel is a gift of God to a diverse people of God today just as in ancient times. Each gospel should be accepted as it is and studied as the Word of God in its own right, relevant "now" as "then." See further BIBLICAL CRITICISM IV.A, V.E; GOSPELS.

IX. Time and place of writing. The date of the composition of Matthew's gospel is unknown, and scholars have set the time anywhere between A.D. 50 and 115. Some scholars believe that any date before A.D. 70 is untenable because the statement in the parable of the marriage banquet (Matt. 22:7) about an angry king destroying a city refers to the fall of Jerusalem: "The king was enraged. He sent his army and destroyed those murderers and burned their city." Such a conclusion seems to be too strong for the weak evidence from an incidental remark in a parable. Since the gospel does not in any way indicate the actual fall of Jerusalem, and since the destruction of Jerusalem is predicted in ch. 24, a date before A.D. 70 is the more probable. To select a later date one must believe that 24:1–28 is not prophecy but *vaticinium ex eventu* (prediction based on event, i.e., a literary artifice whereby a past historical incident is presented as still in the future).

Others believe that the opposite is true: any date before A.D. 70 is excluded because of Matthew's dependence upon Mark. Mark, they say, was written later than is traditionally assumed, and if Matthew used and reworked Mark for his gospel, this would place the date considerably later than 70. Besides, it is thought that Matthew reveals in his reworking of Mark that the ecclesiastical situation was more fully developed when Matthew wrote (cf. Matt. 18:15–20; 28:19–20), making a date between 80 and 100 much more probable. Modern scholars add to this line of evidence the belief that Matthew wrote for Greek-speaking Christians outside of Palestine (although most of the readers were of Jewish origin), and this also speaks for a later date. They also are of the opinion that the Judaism explicit in the first gospel is characteristic of the period after the destruction of Jerusalem, when the Jews were still crushed from defeat and the destruction of the temple.

A few scholars have set the date as late as A.D. 115, when it is believed IGNATIUS of Antioch apparently quotes the gospel or is at least familiar with the Matthean traditions. But such argumentation should rather speak of a date at least before A.D. 96 since Clement of Rome apparently knew of the first gospel (see CLEMENT, EPISTLES OF). The use of the gospel by both Clement and Ignatius does not mean that the gospel was written at that time; Matthew could have written much earlier and they quote him much later.

A more reliable date for the composition of Matthew's gospel should be sought in connection with the place of writing. It is not likely that it was written early before the first dispersion of the Christians from Jerusalem (Acts 8:4), for then the church in Jerusalem would not have needed a written gospel. The apostles were present to answer all questions and to impart all authoritative teaching from the Lord. If the testimony of IRENAEUS, who places the writing of Matthew at the time of NERO while Paul and Peter were in Rome, has any validity, it is possible that Matthew may have composed a gospel originally for non-Palestinian converts who did not have access to the apostles and who could be dependent for their knowledge of the words and works of Jesus upon a written document. While the witness of Papias perhaps may be questioned, since there is no evidence of an Aramaic original, it is still possible that such pieces of gospel were extant, and that the writer made a translation or wrote a Greek edition for the Gentile churches. Any Hebrew original would have disappeared at an early time and the Greek gospel would become the traditional gospel of the people.

Many thoughtful scholars believe that the place of composition of Matthew must be found in some area of the Middle E where Judaism and early Christianity existed together and were in close contact, possibly in the initial stages of unity. They believe that the area that suits the requirements best is the territory N of Palestine among the Jews of the DIASPORA and the Gentile converts of the early mission churches. Since ANTIOCH OF SYRIA was a center of early Jewish-Gentile Christianity, this area is a logical choice for the place of writing of the first gospel. Ignatius was in Antioch and his writings reveal he was fond of the gospel. In Antioch both Jews and Gentiles would speak Greek and yet understand the OT. They used the Greek version of the Hebrew Bible and Matthew quotes the OT much through that version.

The old traditional view of the time and place of writing has been that Matthew was the first evangelist to write a gospel and that he wrote in Palestine, possibly in Jerusalem itself, about A.D. 60. Setting the date at the same time but at a different location now seems more plausible. Antioch in Syria, where the Jewish-Gentile church flourished around the year 60, not only accounts for the concerns about the prophecy of the destruction of Jerusalem but also takes into consideration both the Jewish particularism and the Gentile universalism of the first gospel. Matthew's gospel, we must remember, was written in Greek for Greek-speaking Jews by a Greek-speaking Jew, but it also has wide appeal for the Gentile Christians just as Luke's gospel had. Matthew's gospel, therefore, must have been written for a mixed group of Christians outside of Palestine. The church to which it likely was directed is described by Luke in Acts 11:19–26. Although absolute evidence is lacking, Antioch in Syria about A.D. 60 is both a probable and a plausible time and place of writing of the first gospel.

X. Readers and destination. It is almost certain that Matthew wrote for Jewish Christians in order to establish them in their faith in Jesus of Nazareth as the Christ promised in the OT. Where did these Christians live? The quotations from Matthew in patristic writings indicate that the first gospel was no doubt a favorite of the Syrian Jewish church. If the gospel was written in Antioch, as many believe, this setting would bear out the patristic testimony. It would be a mistake, however, to think that Gentiles were excluded. No doubt Matthew had in mind converted Jews, but both converted and unconverted Gentiles would be equally benefited and strengthened in faith. Jewish names and concepts are not explained in the gospel since they would be readily understood. On the one hand, it reflects the unbelief of Israel in Jesus' time, and on the other, it emphasizes the notion that the Gentiles superseded the Jews because the latter had rejected the Messiah. The national Jews needed repentance and the witness of the Messiah, but Matthew's position is no narrow nationalism. Jesus the Messiah is Savior of the Jews, but also of the whole world. To illustrate that his gospel is in no way particularistic, Matthew closes his message with the mandate that the apostles should make disciples of all nations (Matt. 28:19). The gospel is neither anti-Jewish nor anti-Gentile.

The contents of the gospel indicate that while its message is beamed at Greek-speaking Jews who had been converted to Christianity, the gospel also had a message for the Gentiles. While the mission of the Messiah emphasizes the primacy of the Jewish people ("I was sent only to the lost sheep of Israel" [Matt. 15:24]; "Go rather to the lost sheep of Israel" [10:6]) and indicates the Jewish flavor of the gospel, it is clear that the kingdom also is meant for the Gentiles because of the pointed parables condemning the Pharisees and the open door to the Gentile poor and downtrodden. All of this indicates the historical situation of the first gospel as the time of transition or amalgamation of the Jewish and Gentile elements in the early church. Perhaps one can say that the Jewish Christian church was being absorbed into the Gentile church. Matthew's main theme, "Jesus is the Messiah," is followed closely by a second emphasis, "the messianic kingdom for the world."

Matthew's gospel is admirably suited to a church that was still Hebrew but at the same time increasingly aligning itself with the Gentile world. The gospel breathes an atmosphere of messianism, yet it has a message for all the world. The covenant is fulfilled in Abraham and his seed, but in him all the families of the earth are to be blessed (Gen. 12:3). Accordingly, the first readers of the Gospel of Matthew were the amalgam of the Jewish-Gentile church in northern Palestine, Syrian Antioch, and surrounding territories. While it is possible that most of the readers were of Jewish extraction and would feel at home with the OT and Jewish emphasis, the Gentiles also would welcome such a gospel because they, too, accepted the OT. One may imagine that among both Jew and Gentile the lively proclamation of the gospel would not go many miles without some sort of written proof that Jesus was the Messiah, proof from the OT Scriptures. If Jesus was the Messiah, it would have been foretold in the OT. Preaching would give way to the proof of the written gospel (Acts 9:22).

The view that Matthew's readers lived in Palestine and that he wrote from Jerusalem was based on the premise that he had written in Hebrew, but now most scholars are quite certain that he wrote in Greek, and that the readers were not limited to Palestine. All things considered, Antioch in Syria is the most plausible place of writing (see above), and the audience is the Syrian church composed of both Jews and Gentiles. Was not a basic doctrine of Jesus and his apostles that *all* depend on *grace* to be saved? That God is no respecter of persons? For this reason, the readers of the Gospel of Matthew were the believers described in Acts: "Now those who had been scattered by the persecution in connection with Stephen traveled as far as Phoenicia, Cyprus and Antioch, telling the message only to Jews. Some of them, however, men from Cyprus and Cyrene, went to Antioch and began to speak to Greeks also, telling them the good news about the Lord Jesus. The Lord's hand was with them, and a great number of people believed and turned to the Lord" (Acts 11:19–21).

The early Jewish-Gentile church is clearly defined also by the apostle Paul. His statement to the Galatians indicates that the kingdom calls all people and that it is a continuum and culmination of the kingdom of God in the OT (all Christians are Abraham's offspring): "for all of you who were baptized into Christ have clothed yourselves with Christ. There is neither Jew nor Greek, slave nor free, male nor female, for you are all one in Christ Jesus. If you belong to Christ, then you are Abraham's seed, and heirs according to the promise" (Gal. 3:27–29; cf. Eph. 2:11–22).

XI. Language and text. Matthew wrote in the Koine or common Greek that was spoken in the Mediterranean world during the 1st cent. (see GREEK LANGUAGE). This simplified form of Attic Greek was not primarily the language of literature, but a language spoken by the common people. The Gospel of Matthew must have been readily understood by the early Christians, most of whom were ordinary people. The evangelists turned the Koine into a literary vehicle when they committed the oral gospel to writing. Matthew's style is quite elegant, clear, and fluid. His Greek is neither poor Koine nor highly polished Greek. If he used Mark, it seems that he often improved the style and language. Matthew's language is smoother than Mark's but less varied than Luke's style.

By *text* is meant the preservation of Matthew's writing in ancient Greek MSS that are copies of the original autograph of the gospel. Not a single autograph (the author's original document) of any of the Gospels is known to exist, only copies of copies. Since several thousand ancient Greek MSS of the NT have been found, dating from the 2nd cent. onward, plus lectionaries, quotations from early church fathers, and many different translations, the text of the NT may be reliably established. There are, of course, many variant readings (differences in the wording of the various types or families of MSS) that came about through the centuries in the copying of the text, but Matthew's gospel has been affected little. Almost without exception the exact text of Matthew's gospel can be arrived at without great difficulty. The text of Matthew is in splendid condition. Although there may be differences in the wording in certain passages in the versions (simply because the translations were made from different MSS), the more recent English versions are uniform and represent the original text quite accurately. This is due to the fundamental acceptable results of modern textual criticism (judgment or evaluation of the best readings). Amazing discoveries of very ancient Greek texts (which are closer to the originals) during the past hundred years have aided in establishing the text of the Gospels. See TEXT AND MANUSCRIPTS (NT).

Modern English translations have used the most ancient MSS and the more correct readings, and their renderings are considered to be more

Matthew as pictured in a medieval MS in the Georgian language.

accurate than those of older versions. An example of this is the ending of the LORD's PRAYER (Matt. 6:13). The most ancient Greek texts end with the petition, "Deliver us from [the] evil [one]," but the KJV added the words of the familiar doxology: "For thine is the kingdom, and the power, and the glory, forever." The reason for this difference is that the KJV was translated from late Greek copies that preserve what is known as the Byzantine Text, which probably comes from the 4th cent. and tends to be expansive. Textual critics believe the doxology of the Lord's Prayer may have been added because of liturgical considerations from 1 Chr. 29:11. It is another indication that the first gospel was used much in the worship of the early church.

Another example is the KJV wording of Matt. 5:44: "Love your enemies, bless them that curse you, do good to them that hate you, and pray for them which despitefully use you, and persecute you." The best ancient texts read: "Love your enemies and pray for those who persecute you," omitting "bless those who curse you" (added from Lk. 6:28), and "do good to those who hate you" (from Lk. 6:27). One can easily see from such a comparison that while all the words of KJV in Matt. 5:44 are "Scripture," not all of them were included by Matthew.

There are any number of such "conflations" in the Gospels, which resulted from attempts to harmonize them in parallel passages and make them more uniform (even in exact words). Such concerns are the source of many harmless variant readings. The discovery of ancient MSS such as CODEX VATICANUS (B), CODEX SINAITICUS (ℵ or Aleph), CODEX BEZAE (D), and Papyrus 46 (see CHESTER BEATTY PAPYRI), have brought such conflations to light. The text is so well attested by ancient MSS that no fundamental teaching Christian faith and morals depends upon a textual dispute. While the church might debate issues in biblical theology, it is not often that anyone can say the reading of the text clouds the issue.

All interested students of the NT would find it most stimulating and profitable to make a study of the history of the text and the methods of textual criticism, particularly to discover the reasons why variants crept into the text. It is evident that some resulted from copying or repeating from memory and adding phrases from other Gospels, from deliberate changes to clarify the text for the next reader, from intentional changes to satisfy doctrinal concerns, and, as was mentioned above, to harmonize the Gospels. Besides those examples cited, important variants are found Matt. 1:16, dealing with the virgin birth of Jesus; 5:32 and 19:9, which deal with our Lord's teaching on divorce; 5:22, where the phrase "without a cause" is omitted in ancient texts; and several others dealing with less disputed subjects. The fascinating subject of textual study has solved these and many other variations in the NT to the satisfaction of concerned Christians. The results of textual studies have given further evidence that "the word of the Lord stands forever" (1 Pet. 1:25).

(Significant commentaries include J. A. Broadus, *Commentary on the Gospel of Matthew* [1886]; W. C. Allen, *A Critical and Exegetical Commentary on the Gospel according to S. Matthew*, ICC, 3rd ed. [1912]; A. H. McNeile, *The Gospel According to St. Matthew* [1915]; A. Plummer, *An Exegetical Commentary on the Gospel according to S. Matthew*, 2nd ed. [1928]; T. H. Robinson, *The Gospel of Matthew*, MNTC [1928]; R. C. Lenski, *The Interpretation of St. Matthew's Gospel* [1943]; F. L. Filson, *A Commentary on the Gospel according to St. Matthew*, HNTC [1960]; F. W. Beare, *The Gospel according to St. Matthew* [1981]; R. H. Gundry, *Matthew: A Commentary on His Handbook for a Mixed Church under Persecution*, 2nd ed. [1994]; D. A. Hagner, *Matthew*, WBC 33, 2 vols. [1993–95]; W. D. Davies and D. C. Allison, *A Critical and Exegetical Commentary on the Gospel according to Saint Matthew*, ICC, 3 vols. [1988–97]; C. S. Keener, *A Commentary on the Gospel of Matthew* [1999]; F. D. Bruner, *Matthew: A Commentary*, 2 vols. [2004–]; M. J. Wilkins, *Matthew*, NIVAC [2004]; J. Nolland, *The Gospel of Matthew: A Commentary on the Greek Text*, NIGTC [2005]; U. Luz, *Matthew: A Commentary*, Hermeneia, 3 vols. [2001–7]; R. T. France, *The Gospel of Matthew*, NICNT [2007].

(Among many important monographs, see B. W. Bacon, *Studies in Matthew* [1930]; N. B. Stonehouse, *The Witness of Matthew and Mark to Christ* [1958]; G. Bornkamm et al., *Tradition and Interpretation in Matthew* [1963]; R. H. Gundry, *The Use of the Old Testament in St. Matthew's Gospel: With Special Reference to the Messianic Hope* [1967]; M. Goulder, *Midrash and Lection in Matthew* [1974]; J. D. Kingsbury, *Matthew: Structure, Christology,*

Kingdom [1975]; J. P. Meier, *Law and History in Matthew's Gospel* [1976]; D. R. Bauer, *The Structure of Matthew's Gospel: A Study in Literary Design* [1988]; G. Stanton, *A Gospel for a New People: Studies in Matthew* [1992]; P. Luomanen, *Entering the Kingdom of Heaven: A Study on the Structure of Matthew's View of Salvation* [1998]; J. K. Brown, *The Disciples in Narrative Perspective: The Portrayal and Function of the Matthean Disciples* [2002]; W. Carter, *Matthew: Storyteller, Interpreter, Evangelist*, rev. ed. [2004]; M. J. J. Menken, *Matthew's Bible: The Old Testament Text of the Evangelist* [2004]; U. Luz, *Studies in Matthew* [2005]; J. Riches and D. C. Sim, *The Gospel of Matthew in Its Roman Imperial Context* [2005]; J. T. Pennington, *Heaven and Earth in the Gospel of Matthew* [2007]; and the bibliography compiled by W. E. Mills, *The Gospel of Matthew* [2002].)   L. M. PETERSEN

Matthew, Gospel of Pseudo-. See PSEUDO-MATTHEW, GOSPEL OF.

Matthew, Martyrdom of. A late document presupposing the *Acts of Andrew and Matthias* but not a direct sequel (see ANDREW AND MATTHIAS, ACTS OF; cf. PETER AND ANDREW, ACTS OF). In this work the apostle MATTHEW replaces MATTHIAS as ANDREW's companion. It is extant in Greek and Latin, but the Greek MSS at some points differ greatly.

While Matthew is praying Jesus appears in the form of a child and sends him to the city of the man-eaters, bidding him to plant a staff at the gate of the church which he (Matthew) and Andrew founded. He is met by the queen, her son, and her daughter-in-law, all possessed by demons, whom Matthew expels. The bishop and clergy come to meet him, and Matthew preaches and plants the staff. The king at first is pleased, but later turns against Matthew and seeks to burn him to death. The fire, however, melts the images of gold and silver instead, destroys many soldiers, and forces the king to seek Matthew's help. Matthew rebukes the fire, prays, and gives up the ghost.

The body is carried in state to the palace, and there Matthew is seen to ascend to heaven, where he is crowned by the child. The king has the body sunk in the sea in an iron coffin sealed with lead. At dawn the bishop is bidden by a voice to celebrate the EUCHARIST, and Matthew appears between two men in bright apparel, with the child before them. The king repents and is baptized by the bishop, and then the apostle appears and ordains him a priest. On Matthew's departure a voice promises peace and safety to the city. (Text edited by M. Bonnet in *Acta apostolorum apocrypha* 2/1 [1898], 217–62; English trans. of excerpts in M. R. James, *The Apocryphal New Testament* [1953], 460–62l; see also *NTAp*, 2:458–60.)   R. McL. WILSON

Matthew's Bible. See VERSIONS OF THE BIBLE, ENGLISH IV.

Matthias muh-thi′uhs (Ματθίας G3416 [sometimes Ματίας], short from of Ματταθίας G3478, from מַתִּתְיָהוּ H5525, "gift of Yahweh"; see MATTATHIAS, MATTITHIAH). The name of the "twelfth apostle," chosen to take the place of JUDAS ISCARIOT, the traitor (Acts 1:23–26; see A. W. Zwiep, *Judas and the Choice of Matthias* [2004]). Following PETER's proposal (vv. 20–22), two men were put forward who were considered to have the necessary qualifications for apostleship, for they had been followers of Jesus since the time he was baptized by John. (The candidates were likely suggested by the "hundred and twenty" [v. 15], not by the smaller group of the eleven apostles.) Acts 1:22 probably also means that they must have encountered the risen Lord; but this would presumably have been true of all the "hundred and twenty." Human selection was thus involved from the start. To make divine selection clear, the sacred lot was cast after prayer, as had been done frequently in OT days (e.g., 1 Sam. 14:42). To cast URIM AND THUMMIM was the prerogative of the priest under the old covenant (Ezra 2:63), but the early Christians already may have considered themselves a "royal priesthood" (1 Pet. 2:9). After PENTECOST, there is no reference to the casting of LOTS within the church, evidently because the direct guidance of the HOLY SPIRIT was now enjoyed.

Granted Peter's initial thesis that the number of the "sacred college" must be kept at full strength (cf. Matt. 19:28), it was the logical course for a Jew to adopt; Scripture neither blames him nor asserts that PAUL was the true "twelfth man." However, later vacancies (like that created by the execution of JAMES [Acts 12:2]) were not so filled, unless the appearance of James, the Lord's brother, is an instance (12:17). EUSEBIUS says that Matthias was one of the "seventy" (Lk. 10:1). This is possible in view of the "apostolic qualification" mentioned above. Less likely are identifications with Zacchaeus, Nathanael, or Barnabas. Matthias is never mentioned again in the NT. Rival traditions say that he was either martyred in Judea or that he evangelized the Ethiopians. As usual with such shadowy figures, a "Gospel" and "Traditions" were later fathered on him, and samples have been preserved by CLEMENT OF ALEXANDRIA. See ANDREW AND MATTHIAS, ACTS OF; MATTHIAS, GOSPEL (TRADITIONS) OF. R. A. COLE

Matthias, Acts of. See ANDREW AND MATTHIAS, ACTS OF.

Matthias, Gospel (Traditions) of. A *Gospel of Matthias* is mentioned by ORIGEN and other sources. Three (possibly four) quotations from the *Traditions of Matthias* are preserved by CLEMENT OF ALEXANDRIA, and these show affinities with the *Gospel of the Hebrews* and the Coptic *Gospel of Thomas* (see HEBREWS, GOSPEL OF THE; THOMAS, GOSPEL OF). According to Clement and Hippolytus, the Basilidians claimed traditions transmitted by Matthias. The problem is (a) whether the documents mentioned are identical (scholars differ), and (b) whether they are connected with the Basilidians (Clement's quotations are not markedly Gnostic; see *NTAp*, 1:382–86). R. McL. WILSON

Mattithiah mat´uh-thi´uh (מַתִּתְיָהוּ H5525 in 1 Chr. 15:18, 21; 25:3, 21, elsewhere מַתִּתְיָה H5524, both meaning "gift of Yahweh"). This name (in its two Hebrew forms) is one of many in the OT that are built on the noun *mattānâ* H5510 or its cognate *mattat* H5522, both meaning "gift" (and derived from the verb *nātan* H5989, "to give"; the Heb. *n* is often assimilated to a following consonant): MATTAN (NT MATTHAN), MATTANAH, MATTANIAH, MATTATTAH (NT MATTATHA and MATTHAT), MATTENAI (cf. also ELNATHAN, JONATHAN, NATHAN, NATHANAEL, NETHANEL, NETHANIAH). The name Mattithiah (which no doubt could also be spelled *mattatyāhû*; cf. *HALOT*, 2:656, s.v. mat-

tattâ) comes into Greek as MATTATHIAS, with the shorter forms MATTHIAS and (prob.) MATTHEW.

(1) Son of JEDUTHUN; he and his brothers "prophesied, using the harp in thanking and praising the LORD" (1 Chr. 25:3). He was one of the Levite gatekeepers who played the harp when the ARK OF THE COVENANT was brought to Jerusalem (15:18, 20; 16:5). Later he became the head of the fourteenth company of temple musicians appointed by lot under DAVID (25:1).

(2) Firstborn son of Shallum and descendant of LEVI through KORAH; he was a postexilic Levite responsible for baking the offering bread (1 Chr. 9:31).

(3) One of the descendants of Nebo who agreed to put away their foreign wives (Ezra 10:43; called "Mazitias" in 1 Esd. 9:35).

(4) One of the prominent men (not identified as priests) who stood near EZRA when the law was read at the great assembly (Neh. 8:4; 1 Esd. 9:43 [KJV, "Mattathias"; NRSV, "Mattathiah"]). If he was a priest, he may be the same as #2 above.

R. F. GRIBBLE

mattock. A farming implement, with a blade at one end and usually a pick at the other, used to break up the soil. It was especially used on hills, where vines were often grown. The English term is used by modern versions to render Hebrew *ʾēt* H908, which occurs in one passage (1 Sam. 13:20–21; KJV has "coulter," but it uses "matlock" for a different Heb. word in this same passage, and for still other words in 2 Chr. 34:6 and Isa. 7:25).

maw. This English term is used by the KJV once with reference to the stomach of sacrificial animals (Deut. 18:3; NIV, "inner parts"). The Hebrew term (*qēbâ* H7687) occurs in one other passage, where it refers to a woman's belly (Num. 25:8).

Mazda, Mazdaism. See ZOROASTRIANISM.

Mazitias maz´uh-ti´uhs. KJV Apoc. form of MATTITHIAH (1 Esd. 9:35).

Mazzaroth maz´uh-roth (מַזָּרוֹת H4666). Transliteration used by the KJV and other versions to render a Hebrew word that occurs only once (Job

38:32). The context (vv. 31–33) clearly has to do with the stars, and this term is used in parallel with a Hebrew word that probably refers to a constellation (ʿayiš H6568, either the Bear [Ursa Major] or the Lion [Leo]). If Mazzaroth is not a general term for "constellations" (cf. NIV), it may refer to a specific constellation or star cluster (one possibility is the Hyades). The term is sometimes thought to be an alternate form of mazzālôt (pl. of mazzāl H4655), which also occurs only once, apparently with reference to the constellations generally or to the zodiacal signs (2 Ki. 23:5). See ASTRONOMY III.

mazzebah. See MASSEBAH.

meadow. Defined as moist, low-lying grasslands, and associated with lush pastures, meadows are scarcely characteristic of hot, dry PALESTINE. Grassy meadows do occur, however, in rainier uplands as in GALILEE and LEBANON, and in damp patches near springs, wells, streams, and irrigation channels. The presence of the latter often is indicated by the occurrence of ʾābēl H64 in place names (e.g., ABEL MEHOLAH, "meadow of the dance," Jdg. 7:22). In a few passages, English versions use the rendering "meadow" variously for several Hebrew words, such as the rare term kar H4120, "field, pasture" (Ps. 65:13) and the more common nāwâ H5661 (Jer. 25:37 NIV, NJPS). The latter term is often translated "pasture" (see esp. Ps. 23:2). The rendering "pastureland" (NRSV, "pasture land") stands for migrāš H4494, a frequent term (esp. in Josh. 21) referring to a patch of land belonging to a city (but outside its walls) and used for grazing (see also SUBURB). G. R. LEWTHWAITE

Meah mee´uh. KJV transliteration of mēʾâ H4396 with reference to a tower in Jerusalem (Neh. 3:1; 12:39. See HUNDRED, TOWER OF THE.

meal. This English term has two distinct meanings, both of which are found in Bible versions. It most commonly refers to the time or act of eating (from Middle English meel, "appointed time"), or more specifically to the portion of food eaten at such a time. For this sense, see MEALS. The second meaning is its reference to the coarsely ground grains of cereal grass (from Middle English mele, derived in turn from Latin molere, "to grind" [cf. Gk. mylē, "mill"]). The KJV uses it in a number of passages where modern versions commonly have "[fine] flour" (Gen. 18:6 et al.; but cf. also NRSV 1 Ki. 17:12–16 et al.). The NIV sometimes uses "ground meal" where other versions have "dough" (e.g., Num. 15:20–21). See also BREAD; GRAIN; SACRIFICE AND OFFERINGS III.D.2.

meal offering. See SACRIFICE AND OFFERINGS III.D.2.

meals. Time of eating, foods served, manner of eating, and treatment of guests were all important aspects of mealtime in the ANE.
   I. Terminology
   II. Everyday meals
   III. The wayfarer's meals
   IV. Guests at meals
   V. The king's table
   VI. Taboos and restrictions
   VII. Ritual meals
   VIII. Symbolic use of meals in the Bible

I. Terminology. Aside from terms for BANQUET and FEAST, various Hebrew words and phrases referring to the act or time of eating (or to the portion eaten at mealtime) occur in the OT. For example, such words as ʾăruḥâ H786 ("provisions, allowance"), leḥem H4312 ("bread, food"), and maʾăkāl H4407 ("food, fodder") can be rendered "meal" (in the NIV, see respectively Prov. 15:17; 1 Sam. 20:27; Job 33:20). Several expressions with the verb ʾākal H430 ("to eat") are used in the sense of "to have a meal" or the like (e.g., ʾākal leḥem in Gen. 37:25). The phrase ʿēt hāʾōkel ("time of food, mealtime") occurs once (Ruth 2:14).

In the Greek NT one finds parallel uses. For example, the noun brōsis G1111 ("meat, food") can refer to a meal or meal portion (Heb. 12:16). The verb esthiō G2266 ("to eat") is often used with artos G788 ("bread") for the act of having a meal (Matt. 15:2 et al.). But Greek also has the more specific terms ariston G756 ("first [i.e., morning] meal," then "luncheon"; cf. the verb aristaō G753, Jn. 21:12, 15) and deipnon G1279 ("main meal, dinner, supper"; cf. both nouns in Lk. 14:12, translated "luncheon or dinner" in the NIV and other versions).

II. Everyday meals

A. Time of eating. Only two meals a day were usually eaten (Exod. 16:12; 1 Ki. 17:6). The laborer worked until midday before taking his first meal. The noon meal was not important, usually consisting of bread, olives, and sometimes fruit. The chief meal of the day (and prob. the only one for the poor) was served in the early evening, an hour or two before sunset when the duties of the day were over. It was a time of rest, refreshment, and family reunion. After the meal, for an hour or two before bedtime, the men sat around and talked (cf. Jer. 15:17).

B. Place of eating. At family meals in the earliest times the Hebrews usually sat on the ground on mats to eat. Men and women ate together (Ruth 2:14; Job 1:4) except at more formal gatherings (Gen. 18:8–10). Later the Hebrews adopted the Canaanite practice of sitting on chairs or stools and eating from small leather stands. Ordinary homes did not have a room just for dining; at mealtime a broad circular mat or low tables were placed on the floor within reach of all who would dip from the common dish. Larger homes had dining rooms with one side open to the street with adjustable curtains. Passers-by stopped to look in to see who was being entertained and even talked with the guests. The table was a three-sided piece of furniture with open space left for servants to serve the meal. Guests reclined on couches that could accommodate three people. The wealthy homes had large dining halls. Amos denounced the dissolute rich reclining on their couches (Amos 6:4).

Abraham served his guests outdoors (Gen. 18:8). Gideon served an angel under a tree (Jdg. 6:19). Shepherds and laborers ate their meals where they worked. The disciples of Jesus picked ripe grain and ate it one Sabbath as they passed through the fields (Mk. 2:23). Jesus fed the multitude on a hillside (Jn. 6:1–14), and his disciples on a beach after his resurrection (Jn. 21:9–13).

C. Foods served. Bread and water were the mainstay of the common people (Isa. 3:1). Meat was a luxury seldom enjoyed by the poor, though wild game was available (Gen. 25:27–28; 27:3). Meat from specially fattened animals was saved for special occasions (1 Sam. 28:24; Amos 6:4; Lk. 15:23). A lamb sometimes was roasted entire, sometimes stewed in milk (see restriction, Exod. 23:19). Fish was an abundant source of meat. Eggs were available (Isa. 10:14; Lk. 11:12).

Milk, particularly of the goat and camel, was served fresh or made into curds and whey (prob. the dish that was given to Sisera, Jdg. 4:19). Butter and olive oil were important foods. Melons were popular (Num. 11:5). Vegetables were an important part of the diet; beans, lentils, and peas were made into a tasty pottage (Gen. 25:29). Fresh fruit was eaten in season. Figs, raisins, walnuts, almonds were the commonest dried fruits (Gen. 43:11; 1 Sam. 25:18). Relishes (onions, leeks, garlic, lettuce), seasonings (salt, spices), and sweets (usually honey and dates) were greatly desired by the Israelites (Gen. 43:11; Num. 11:5; 1 Ki. 10:10). Locusts were eaten by John the Baptist (Matt. 3:4).

The harvester's fare consisted of bread dipped in vinegar and parched grain (Ruth 2:14). The shepherd carried with him a meal of bread, sometimes fruit and cheese, which he ate at noon while the sheep rested. A soldier's ration consisted of parched grain, bread, and cheese (1 Sam. 17:17, 18; cf. 25:18). See also food.

III. The wayfarer's meals.
Wayfarers often had difficulty finding food. Quail and manna were provided by God in answer to the complaints of the hungry Israelites (Exod. 16:13–16). Hagar

A single bowl located in the center of a mat served as the common dish from which those at the meal would take their portions.

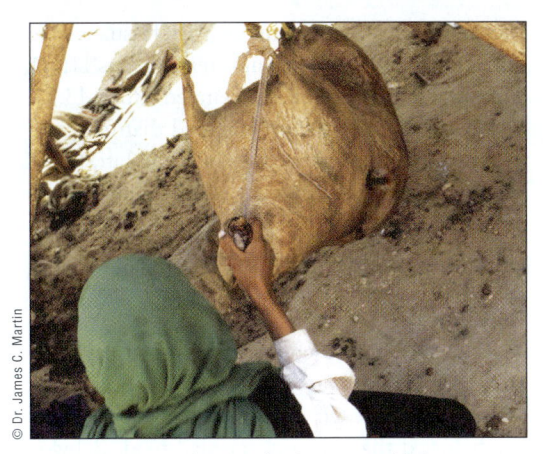

Bedouin woman making curds using a goat-skin bag.

and her son ISHMAEL were sent into the wilderness with only bread and a skin of water (Gen. 21:14). ELIJAH was fed by the ravens (1 Ki. 17:6). Caravan drivers were careful to take generous amounts of food with them, consisting of dried fruits, bread, olives, and cheese. A nomadic code of hospitality developed in the ANE so that a sojourner coming to a stranger's home was assured of food, shelter, and protection from enemies who might be pursuing him. His host knew that one day he might be obliged to ask for similar shelter. JAEL's slaying of SISERA was a violation of the nomadic code (Jdg. 4:17–22; cf. Gen. 18:1–8; 19:1–3; 24:29–33; Jdg. 19:16–21 for other examples of hospitality to travelers). Inns for travelers were a much older institution than most people realize, though usually only the well-to-do trader or traveler could afford them. The brothers of JOSEPH stopped at an inn on the way home from Egypt (Gen. 42:27; 43:21). MOSES and his family stopped at a lodging place on their way back to Egypt (Exod. 4:24). The innkeeper was not subject to the nomadic laws of hospitality, for he required payment for his food and lodging (Lk. 2:7; 10:35).

IV. Guests at meals

A. Duties of host. Proper etiquette was an important part of hospitality in the ANE (Matt. 25:34–35). The host was obligated to protect his guests against enemies (Ps. 23:5). LOT (Gen. 19:8) and GIBEAH (Jdg. 19:23–24) were ready to sacrifice the honor of their daughters in order to protect their guests. The guest was welcomed with a kiss (Lk. 7:45); water was provided to wash his dusty feet (Gen. 18:4; 19:2; Jdg. 19:21; 1 Sam. 25:41; Matt. 15:1–2; Mk. 7:2; Lk. 7:44; Jn. 13:4–5). The guests attended in their best attire, usually white (Eccl. 9:8), or sometimes were provided with garments by their host. They were anointed by their host or by servants (Amos 6:6; Matt. 26:7; Lk. 7:38; Jn. 12:3). Jesus rebuked Simon the Pharisee for ignoring the usual courtesies (Lk. 7:44–46). Sometimes the guests had wreaths placed on their heads (Isa. 28:1; 61:3). They were escorted to the table where they reclined on couches (Esth. 1:6; Ezek. 23:41; Jn. 21:20), seated in order of age or importance (Gen. 43:33; 1 Sam. 9:22; 20:25; Mk. 10:37; Lk. 14:8). Jesus told his disciples not to follow the practice of competing for the highest place at the table (Lk. 14:7–11).

After the guests were seated, servants passed among them to wash the hands. Afterward the host offered a blessing for the food (1 Sam. 9:13). Jesus gave thanks when he fed the multitude (Matt. 14:19; 15:36; Mk. 6:41; 8:6–7; Lk. 9:16). He gave thanks at the LORD'S SUPPER (Matt. 26:26–27; Mk. 14:22–23; Lk. 22:17, 19; 1 Cor. 11:24). He blessed the meal with the EMMAUS disciples (Lk. 24:30). The early Christians thanked God for their meals (Acts 27:35; Rom. 14:6; 1 Cor. 10:30).

B. Serving of food. Guests usually were served by the women of the household (Matt. 8:14–15; Mk. 1:30–31; Lk. 10:40), or by servants in the wealthier homes (1 Ki. 10:5; 2 Chr. 9:4). Forks and other utensils were not used; guests ate with their fingers (Prov. 26:15; Mk. 14:20; Jn. 13:26). Cups and goblets were provided for drinking wine (1 Ki. 10:21). As a special act of respect the master of the house sometimes personally attended his guests. The guest of honor received the choicest and largest portions of food (Gen. 43:34; 1 Sam. 9:24). As an assurance of friendly regard, the host himself would dip a piece of bread in the common dish and hand it to another at the table (Jn. 13:26). Crumbs were thrown under the table to dogs (Matt. 15:27).

C. Entertainment. Banquets and feasts were often accompanied by music (Isa. 5:12), by singing (2 Sam. 19:35; Isa. 5:12; Amos 6:4–6), by dancing

(1 Sam. 30:16; Matt. 14:6; Mk. 6:21–22; Lk. 15:25), by the asking of riddles (Jdg. 14:12–18). In NT times Greek banquets were aesthetic and intellectual gatherings. After eating, the assembled guests talked far into the night on philosophy and politics.

V. The king's table. Ancient oriental rulers gave banquets that are still unmatched for opulence. A tiny lapis-lazuli cylinder seal carved before 3000 B.C. in Mesopotamia shows a banquet of Queen Shub-ad of UR with guests seated on little stools, receiving from servants goblets of wine while other servants are fanning to keep them cool. AKHENATEN of Egypt served in a spacious dining hall with garlands hanging from pillars while slaves cooled the air with fans. He had a summer dining room in a garden on a tiny island on an artificial lake. Egyptians did not eat at the same table with foreigners (Gen. 43:32).

Many people ate at the king's table, including his family, vassals, and favorites (1 Sam. 20:29, 34; 2 Sam. 9:7, 13). Defeated enemies ate at the conqueror's table (2 Ki. 25:29). SOLOMON's table was famous for its lavish service (1 Ki. 10:5) and abundant food (4:27). Sons of loyal friends of DAVID ate at Solomon's table (2:7). Four hundred prophets ate at JEZEBEL's table (18:19). DANIEL and his friends refused the king's food (Dan. 1:5–8). NEHEMIAH had 150 officials at his table (Neh. 5:17). Officials, such as cupbearers, bakers, butlers, and carvers were in charge of the king's table (Gen. 40:1; Neh. 1:11). Singers, dancers, and other entertainers were used to enliven the banquets, which often developed into drunken orgies. The sacred vessels from the Jerusalem temple were used at BELSHAZZAR's drunken debauch (Dan. 5:1–4). Probably the greatest banquet recorded in the Bible was that of Ahasuerus (XERXES) for his nobles and governors which lasted 180 days (Esth. 1:4). ESTHER gave private dinners for the king and HAMAN (5:4–12; 7:1).

VI. Taboos and restrictions. The Hebrews had a number of dietary laws that forbade the eating of certain animals because of UNCLEANNESS (Lev. 11; cf. Acts 10:9–16). The PHARISEES would not eat without washing their hands (Mk. 7:3). In NT times the Jews did not approve of eating with Gentiles or sinners (Matt. 9:11). Moderation in diet was encouraged (Eccl. 10:17). In the NT Christians were not to reject anything God has created (Acts 11:9; 1 Tim. 4:4). Excesses were condemned (Rom. 13:13; Gal. 5:19, 21; 1 Pet. 4:3). Jesus said that food was not the most important thing in life (Matt. 6:25). Christians were not to ask any questions about food set before them at feasts (1 Cor. 10:25–27).

VII. Ritual meals

A. Pagan. The Mesopotamians emphasized that sacrifice was a meal provided for the deities, and Ras Shamra texts (see UGARIT) show that the Canaanites believed that the gods needed food. Babylonians offered wild and domestic animals; they offered cakes of meal, dotted with incense, before their gods as food offerings. Ugaritic worshipers in N SYRIA used food offerings in their worship. JEREMIAH denounced the people for offering cakes to the QUEEN OF HEAVEN (Jer. 7:18). Offerings of food for the dead were common in Mesopotamian and Egyptian cultures. The Greeks offered animal sacrifices, and even the Eleusinian mysteries included the offering of sheaves of grain (see MYSTERY RELIGIONS). The Romans sacrificed great numbers of animals. Gifts of food were brought to the gods at mealtime on special occasions (such as a birthday, wedding, or safe return from a journey).

B. Jewish. Hebrew Scriptures do not equate SACRIFICE with a meal provided for God. The sacrifices of GIDEON (Jdg. 6:19–22) and of MANOAH (13:15–20) were not eaten by the angel of the Lord but were transformed into a holocaust. Israelite sacrifice cannot be satisfactorily explained by calling it a meal offered to a god, though at the popular level it is quite likely that many Israelites thought that sacrifices were a meal in which the Lord took part. The three major festivals of the Hebrews—Passover, Pentecost, and Tabernacles—involved offerings. The prophets protested against the abundance of sacrifices and offerings from a disobedient people (1 Sam. 15:22; Isa. 1:13–17; Amos 5:21–24; Mic. 6:7, 8; Mal. 1:6, 7). Slaves shared in the sacrificial meals (Deut. 12:12).

C. Christian. The NT ritual of the LORD'S SUPPER is a ritual meal derived from the Jewish PASSOVER and instituted by Jesus (1 Cor. 11:23–26). It is observed as a memorial reminder of the sacrificial death of Jesus for our sins. PAUL warned that the Corinthian Christians were making a mockery of the sacred meal (11:20–22).

VIII. Symbolic use of meals in the Bible. In the OT, failure of food is a symbol of God's judgment (Ezek. 4:16; Amos 4:6); fullness of bread symbolizes prosperity (Ezek. 16:49). The Egyptians will be given as food to the beasts and birds, symbolizing judgment (29:5). The psalmist says, "My tears have been my food" (Ps. 42:3), expressing longing for God. Feasting is a symbol of happiness (Prov. 15:15) and of judgment (Jer. 51:39). God will make a great feast at the end of the ages (Isa. 25:6). Solomon speaks of "the bread of wickedness" (Prov. 4:17).

In the NT feasting is a symbol for the coming kingdom (Matt. 8:11; 26:29; Mk. 14:25; Rev. 19:9, 17). Jesus said his food was to do the will of God (Jn. 4:34). He referred to himself as living water (4:10), bread from heaven (6:41), eating his flesh and drinking his blood (6:54–56). God's word is compared to food (Matt. 4:4).

(See further A. C. Bouquet, *Everyday Life in New Testament Times* [1953], 69–79; M. S. and J. L. Miller, *Encyclopedia of Bible Life* [1955], 299–319; E. W. Heaton, *Everyday Life in Old Testament Times* [1956]; R. de Vaux, *Ancient Israel* [1961], 10, 122, 484–517; P. J. King and L. E. Stager, *Life in Biblical Israel* [2001], ch. 2; C. L. Blomberg, *Contagious Holiness: Jesus' Meals with Sinners* [2005].)

F. B. HUEY, JR.

Meani mee-ay´ni. KJV Apoc. form of MAANI (1 Esd. 5:31).

Mearah mee-air´uh (מְעָרָה [not in NIV]; cf. the noun מְעָרָה *H5117*, "cave"). A Sidonian city, listed among the territories that the Israelites had not occupied (Josh. 13:4 KJV, NRSV). The site is unknown, and several emendations of the text have been proposed. The NIV, understanding the first consonant as a preposition (*mē*, i.e., *min H4946*, "from"), has ARAH.

measure. See WEIGHTS AND MEASURES.

measuring line. This expression is used in many English versions as a rendering of two Hebrew phrases, *qāw hammiddâ* (Jer. 31:3; *Ketib qĕwēh*) and *ḥebel middâ* (Zeph. 2:5). Both *qāw H7742* and *ḥebel H2475* can refer to a CORD or LINE, while *middâ H4500* means "size, measure, standard." The word *qāw* by itself can be rendered "measuring line" (cf. NIV, 2 Ki. 21:13; Job 38:5; et al.), and several passages speak of allotting or dividing up land with a *ḥebel* (Ps. 78:55; Amos 7:17; cf. also the beautiful metaphorical expression in Ps. 16:6); the latter term thus also takes on the meaning of "[allotted] plot of land" (e.g., Josh. 17:14) or even "region" (e.g., Deut. 3:4). The use of a cord of definite length for measuring was common (cf. 2 Sam. 8:2; Isa. 44:13). See also MEASURING REED.

measuring reed (rod). The Hebrew expression *qĕnēh hammiddâ* (lit., "reed of the measure") occurs six times in Ezekiel as the prophet gives the dimensions of the future temple (Ezek. 40:3, 5; 42:16–18). The word *qāneh H7866* means "reed" or "stalk," and from the Semitic root is derived the Greek term *kanna* (or *kannē*; cf. also *kanōn G2834*, "rule" [see CANON]), as well as related terms in other Indo-European languages (e.g., English *cane*, through French and Latin). The SEPTUAGINT translation of Ezekiel, however, uses another Greek term for "reed," *kalamos G2812*, which no doubt influenced the writer of Revelation (see Rev. 11:1; 21:15–16). Reeds were commonly used in the ANE as instruments of measurement. The length of such rods would have varied over any given period of time. See MEASURING LINE; WEIGHTS AND MEASURES I.B.

meat. See FOOD.

meat offering. See SACRIFICE AND OFFERINGS III.D.2.

Mebunnai mi-buhn´i (מְבֻנַּי *H4446*, apparently from בָּנָה *H1215*, "to build"). A Hushathite (i.e., from HUSHAH) and one of the Thirty, DAVID's elite guard (2 Sam. 23:27); because he is called SIBBECAI in the parallel passages (2 Sam. 21:18; 1 Chr. 11:29; 20:4; 27:11), some scholars suspect that the name Mebunnai is the result of textual corruption.

Mecherathite mi-ker′uh-th*i*t. See MEKERATHITE.

Meconah mi-koh′nuh (מְכֹנָה H4828, "foundation, abode"). KJV and TNIV Mekonah. A town in JUDAH, listed between ZIKLAG and EN RIMMON in a list of cities settled after the EXILE (Neh. 11:28). It was probably in the NEGEV, but the site is unknown (for the view that Meconah is the same as MADMANNAH, see J. Simons, *The Geographical and Topographical Texts of the Old Testament* [1959], §317.29–30).

Medaba med′uh-buh. KJV Apoc. form of MEDEBA (1 Macc. 9:36).

Medad mee′dad (מֵידָד H4773, "beloved"). An Israelite elder upon whom the Spirit of the Lord came, enabling him to prophesy (Num. 11:26–27). See ELDAD.

Medan mee′dan (מְדָן H4527, "strife"). Son of ABRAHAM and KETURAH and the founder of an Arabian tribe (Gen. 25:2; 1 Chr. 1:32). Since the name is mentioned just before MIDIAN, some think it may be a doublet. Medan is not mentioned anywhere else in the Bible or in any extrabiblical document and therefore remains unidentified, although E. A. Knauf (*ABD*, 4:656) suggests an association with Wadi Mudan in S Midian.

Medanite mee′duh-n*i*t. According to the MT, the Medanites (Heb. *mĕdānim*) sold JOSEPH in Egypt (Gen. 37:36). This name is regarded as an alternate form or a misspelling of *midyānim*, "Midianites" (cf. v. 28). See MIDIAN.

Mede meed. See MEDIA.

Medeba med′uh-buh (מֵידְבָא H4772, perhaps "waters of strength"). An ancient town in MOAB, identified with modern Madeba in Jordan, on a tableland c. 16 mi. SE of the mouth of the JORDAN River and 6 mi. S of HESHBON. The first biblical reference to Medeba is found in a victory song over Moab (Num. 21:30), where Medeba is mentioned as one of the cities taken from SIHON, king of the AMORITES. After the victory of Israel over Sihon (21:21–26), Medeba was assigned to the tribe of REUBEN (Josh. 13:9, 16).

The claim to this land often was disputed by the Reubenites, Ammonites, and Moabites (cf. Denis Baly, *The Geography of the Bible* [1957], 30, 172). The Ammonites (see AMMON), after the disgraceful treatment of DAVID's messengers, united with the Arameans (see ARAM) in a campaign against JOAB and ABISHAI before Medeba, but they were defeated (1 Chr. 19:6–15). According to the MOABITE STONE, Medeba had belonged to OMRI and AHAB, but MESHA king of Moab captured it and had it rebuilt (*ANET*, 320, lines 8, 30). The prophet ISAIAH names Medeba in an oracle against Moab (Isa. 15:2). During Maccabean times (see MACCABEE), Medeba belonged to the NABATEANS. According to 1 Macc. 9:36–42, John son of Mattathias was murdered by a man from Medeba. John's brothers, Jonathan and Simon, avenged their brother's death. After the death of ANTIOCHUS, the city was taken by Hyrcanus and finally was captured by Alexander Jannaeus, although Hyrcanus II promised to restore it to ARETAS, king of ARABIA (cf. Jos. *Ant.* 13.5.4; 13.9.1; 14.1.4). See HASMONEAN II.

In the Byzantine period Medeba was apparently a wealthy city, for several of the mosaic pavements dating from this time are still partially preserved here. Today the fame of Medeba rests upon its mosaic map of the Holy Land, dating from the late 6th cent., but first discovered in 1884 (M. Avi-Yonah, *The Madaba Mosaic Map* [1954]; see CARTOGRAPHY, BIBLICAL). Unfortunately, large portions of the map were damaged or destroyed during the construction of a new church on the old

The Medeba (or Madaba) map, a mosaic that depicts the Holy Land, including a detailed representation of Jerusalem.

site. The mosaic map was included in the pavement of this church. (See *ABD*, 4:656–58; *NEAEHL*, 3:992–1001.)   P. A. Verhoef

Media mee´dee-uh (מָדַי *H4512*; this form, as well as מָדִי *H4513* [only Dan. 11:1], is also used as a gentilic, "Mede[s]"; Aram. מָדַי *H10404*; Gk. Μῆδος *G3597*). The home of the Medes, an ancient Indo-European people of NW Iran who were absorbed by the rise of Persia in the 7th cent. B.C. The Hebrew name appears as Madai, one of the sons of Japheth (Gen. 10:2; 1 Chr. 1:5); Madai is evidently regarded as the ancestor of the Medes. The only sources of knowledge about their geographical distribution in antiquity is found in the annals of the Assyrian rulers who campaigned against them. Their language, although of Indo-European origin and possibly older than Persian, has survived only in loanwords and specific names in Old Persian records. They seem to have settled in the plateau of Iran below the Caspian Sea and considerably NE of the Tigris River. They were shielded somewhat from the Scythians, who shared a related culture, and by the Cimmerians, with whom they appear to have been allied. Ultimately Scythia fell upon the Cimmerians and the nearby kingdom of Urartu (see Ararat), and the Medes were left alone to fend off further aggression.

The origins of Media are obscure; however, the annals of the Assyrian Shalmaneser III mention them. He ruled from 858–824 B.C. and probably discovered them in the region of Ecbatana (Hamadan) around 836. The annals of Shamshi-Adad V (823–811) mention a ruler of Iran who had 1,200 cities N of Lake Urmia. Tiglath-Pileser III (745–727), one of the most methodical of Assyrian strategists, carried out a number of campaigns in Iran penetrating to the foot of Mount Demavend. It appears that during the 8th cent. Media provided horses for the Assyrian army, but the alliance of the Iranian tribes was a constant threat to the settled villages and towns of Mesopotamia. Sargon II (721–705) overcame Hoshea, the ephemeral king of Samaria, and placed the subject peoples "in the towns of the Medes" (2 Ki. 17:5–6; 18:11), which he controlled.

Sargon is known to have taken a certain Dayaukku as prisoner of war and deported him with his family to Hamath in Syria. It has been suspected that this is, in fact, the Deioces mentioned by Herodotus (*Hist.* 1.96) as the founder of the Median royal line, the son of an unknown chieftain. His son Khshathrita (Phraortes) died in a battle with the Assyrians, and his son Uvarkhshatra (Cyaxares) succeeded to his dominion over the three sections of Media (ibid., 1.102) and apparently renewed Median control over the regions round Lake Urmia. Herodotus adds that during this period Cyaxares learned the warfare and military organization of the Scythians and used it with success against Alyattes, king of Sardis, in a long campaign. During this war an eclipse of the sun occurred that greatly terrified the troops of both armies. This astronomical event had been forecast by the Milesian Greek sage Thales and is one of the few dates in Median history that may be pinpointed with accuracy as 28 May 585 B.C.

The effect of Scythian culture is seen in the mixed form of what survives of Median art, which demonstrates strong barbarian motifs. Cyaxares overcame his Scythian overlords and annexed the regions of the Persians and the Mannai to his kingdom apparently using Ecbatana as his capital. In 615 B.C. he had marched on Nineveh but had been repulsed. He turned N and captured Aššus on the Tigris River. The Babylonian king Nabopolassar concluded a treaty with Cyaxares which was sealed by the marriage of Amytis, granddaughter of Cyaxares, with the son and heir of Nabopolassar, Nebuchadnezzar II. In the inscriptions from this period the general term *Umman-manda* is used by

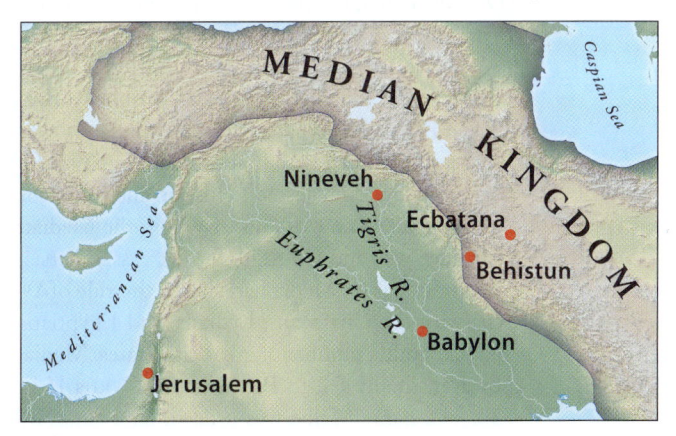

Media.

MEDIATOR

Roman literature, and Luke says that Medes were among those to whom PETER preached on PENTECOST (Acts 2:9).

(See further E. Herzfeld, *Archäologische Mitteilungen aus Iran*, 1 [1929]; F. W. König, *Älteste Geschichte der Meder und Perser* [1934]; G. G. Cameron, *History of Early Iran* [1936]; R. Ghirshman, *Iran* [1961]; E. Porada, *Alt-Iran: Die Kunst in vorislamischer Zeit* [1962]; T. C. Young, Jr., in *CAH*, 4, 2nd ed. [1988], 1–52; E. M. Yamauchi, *Persia and the Bible* [1990], ch. 1; M. Roaf in *Later Mesopotamia and Iran*, ed. J. Curtis [1995], 54–66.)

W. WHITE, JR.

mediator. One who acts as intermediary between parties to reconcile them. In a general sense it means one who interposes, and in so doing, gives some kind of guarantee. By mediating between two persons, the mediator is also to be representative of both sides. Thus, he can give a guarantee in both directions that some kind of agreement can be reached and that justice will be done.

   I. General introduction
      A. Linguistic background
      B. The use of the terms
  II. The special biblical use
      A. The philosophic approach
      B. The prophet as mediator
      C. The priest as mediator
      D. The king as mediator
      E. The modern emphasis
 III. Summary

I. General introduction

A. Linguistic background. The word *mediator* occurs in the English OT once as the rendering of Hebrew *mēlîṣ* H4885 (Job 33:23; this Heb. word occurs also in Gen. 42:33; 2 Chr. 32:31; Isa. 43:27). In the NT it renders Greek *mesitēs* G3542, which is found six times (Gal. 3:19–20; 1 Tim. 2:5; Heb. 8:6; 9:15; 12:24; cf. LXX Job 9:33 [rendering the Heb. ptc. *môṣîaḥ*] and note the verb *mesiteuō* G3541 in Heb. 6:17). The concept of mediation tends to slide over into such others as RECONCILIATION, RANSOM, and ATONEMENT. Actually the sense of reconciliation is more to the fore in the NT passages where the exact Greek word appears. The emphasis

Artistic relief from Persepolis showing typical Median dress (c. 350 B.C.).

the Assyro-Babylonian scribes for Scythians, Cimmerians, and at least in this instance for the Medes (D. J. Wiseman, *Chronicles of Chaldean Kings in the British Museum* [1956], 16).

The hoped-for attack of the Medes upon BABYLON, the subject of Isaiah's prophecy (Isa. 13:17–19), came to pass after the Median power had been combined with that of Persia in 539 B.C. Cyaxares's kingdom passed to his son and successor Arshtivaiga (ASTYAGES), under whom the Median state gave way and fell to its former vassal, Persia. For a brief period Media had shared the rule of W Asia with the Chaldeans, Lydians, and Egyptians and had built a number of great city-states. Media, however, finally fell to Persia under CYRUS II in 550. The name Media was used in later times by the Sassanians and their successors. It appears in seems to be on the efficacy of Christ and his work of salvation, and in the Hebrews passages seems to refer more to the initiator of a new covenant by which reconciliation is established (see COVENANT, THE NEW). In the technical sense, it applies to the finished work of Christ. In it, Christ is mediating between God and human beings, but not always in the reconciling of differences; frequently it is in the sense of his being a channel of communication.

B. The use of the terms. It is still worth noting by way of introduction that *mediation* can be a word of considerable ambiguity, although it is used technically in religion, and especially in the Christian religion. There is the general truth that many things are mediated to mankind in some way or another. One readily sees how life itself is mediated through one's parents; moreover, society and culture give intellectual, moral, and religious convictions. "No man is an island"—everyone has a certain amount of capital with which he operates, mediated to him no matter how much he eventually makes it his own.

This general understanding of the terms may be seen in an even wider context. In religion there is the necessary distinction between natural and supernatural, human and divine, and if there is to be any relationship between these diverse categories of being, some kind of mediation must be assumed. Mediation in the general sense, therefore, especially as it gets closer to a religious understanding, has to do with establishing and maintaining some kind of relationship between God and human beings. It is the assumption of every religion that this gulf, however wide, is bridgeable. People believe they can reach up by way of priests or priestcraft, perhaps by magic. There are official acts and rites that supposedly bring a person into the presence of God. This does not necessarily imply sinfulness; more generally it implies the separation of two different kinds of being. From the other direction, every religion seems to speak of God's reaching down to human beings. What communion is possible? How does the high and holy one condescend to his creatures? How does spirit touch flesh?

In the biblical sense this whole question becomes much more pressing. If man is made in the IMAGE OF GOD, then there need be no fundamental difference between them. Human beings "inbreathed with the breath of God" are not strange to God's presence. The profound and radical problem seen in Scripture is, therefore, not HUMAN NATURE, but the nature of SIN. It is here that the great separation takes place. Not only does sin separate from God, because HOLINESS cannot even "look upon" unholiness, but the nature of sin is so radical, so cosmic, that sinners do not wish to approach God; they no longer want communion with the Holy One. A change in a person's nature can take place so that part of the problem of mediation becomes a creative one, and this is surely by necessity from God's side.

How then may one have a new nature in order that the previous oneness with God may be restored? There is no question that the biblical emphasis is on the GRACE of God; he initiated the process, paid the price, sustained the reconciliation. He alone can give assurance of success. "There is no one righteous, not even one," insists PAUL, echoing the psalmist (Rom. 3:10; Pss. 14:1; 53:1). Not even Israel, the chosen one, does good. All mankind sins continually in rebellion and disobedience. The appeal of the prophets does not restore them; not only are the actions of the Israelites wrong, but their affections are wrong; "their hearts are far from me" (Isa. 29:13). Israel is under the obligation of a series of covenants and even with all of God's help, never makes good. God himself must provide the way; only his mediator can bridge the gap.

Of basic significance, however, is this: COVENANT in the OT is more than contract. As Israel sinned continually, God's arm was still strong to save. Default by one member of a covenant or a contract should render it null and void; the prophetic word, however, is that God will never utterly cast off his people. God keeps the covenant by showing mercy. Indeed, he sustains the covenant until he can rework it in a new covenant. There must be a mediator who will "guarantee it by an oath" (cf. Heb. 6:17 NRSV).

By way of setting or context, therefore, a *mediator*, as the term is generally used, is a "go-between." In religion in general, a person's reaching up and God's reaching down are understandable, but impossible because of sin. In the Bible, specifically, it can be seen that people ought to obey and

Bull head from a Sumerian lyre (Ur, c. 2600 B.C.). Moses functioned as a mediator between God and the people when the Israelites sinned by making a golden calf at Mount Sinai.

therefore, by nature, do not need a mediator; but as a matter of fact, they sin themselves into such a necessity. The solution for this problem, therefore, rests in the act of God, not in the potential in people, so that even Israel, with every support, never made good. Mediator and mediation, therefore, in biblical usage, become a necessity of operation from God's position, not ours. ABRAHAM found a ram in a thicket (Gen. 22:13), the surprising provision made by God. The "lamb was slain from the creation of the world" (Rev. 13:8). God was ready (if one may use a time sequence) for what now appears to have been inevitable. Mediator and mediation in the biblical sense, therefore, are a very special study.

II. The special biblical use

A. A philosophic approach.
It is generally conceded that the approach of the Bible is not philosophic, and this certainly is true as one observes the Greek development of philosophy in the Western world. This is not to say that issues raised in Scripture do not give rise to philosophical problems. There is no question that the Bible presents a "worldview" and that this worldview is supported by persons, teachings, "the mighty acts of God," and the interpretation put on those "acts of God" by the writers of the various biblical books. There is an impressive cohesion and unity in the Bible. What is meant, therefore, is that, whereas there is much philosophic material in the Scriptures, the writers rarely engage in what is strictly called "philosophizing."

The philosophical questions, nevertheless, remain: the nature of God, the move and meaning of history, the hierarchy of values, and basically the necessary relationships between transcendence and immanence. This last is the problem of mediation, and has to be dealt with. How does God touch the world of nature? How do human beings reach up to God? There is in all this the kind of question that became of crucial importance in the development of the LOGOS in Greek philosophy. It started with Thales, probably, and reached its peak with the STOICS, and had the kind of later development in philosophy that may be reflected in the Johannine writings of the NT.

Any complete interpretation of mediation or mediator must face up to the fact that in spite of what has just been said regarding a lack of philosophy, there must be some recognition of hypostatic mediation treated in a variety of ways in the Scriptures. In discussing the word *mediator*, JESUS CHRIST must come to the fore; but this is not to say that similar ideas were not already under treatment before the fulfillment in Jesus Christ. There is no question, as the writer to the Hebrews puts it, that "In the past God spoke to our forefathers through the prophets at many times and in various ways" (Heb. 1:1). This is true of the idea of mediation as it is true of many other subjects.

The OT speaks of WISDOM, or WORD, or SPIRIT, all of which terms can be interpreted as merely ways of speaking, but strangely the terms are frequently used as if they were personal, even though they have to do with the nature of God and may be thought of as ways in which God acts. The terms are frequently used as if there is something, or someone, distinguishable from God, but representing him in his outreach to humanity. In such fashion they are therefore interesting prototypes of what becomes a full-orbed CHRISTOLOGY in the person and work of Christ. These "realities," such as Wisdom, Word, and Spirit, are not merely God's attributes, but become almost personified, especially in the Wisdom Literature of the OT. SERVANT OF THE LORD passages, especially in Isaiah, take on this same character. A hypostasis is a reality between a person and an abstraction—rooted in God's nature, but distinct from him. It is clear, therefore, that the OT is necessarily philosophical in the use of such concepts.

1. Wisdom. Take for example the term *wisdom*. It can be interpreted in the ordinary sense of understanding or broad knowledge. It can be thought of as creative also, or understood as a kind of Tao, the "way of things." It is not so much an attribute of God as it is a clue to God, or something that God has set loose in his world to represent him (cf. Job 28:23–27; Ps. 104:24; Prov. 1:20–33; 3:13–19; and especially 8:22–31). In a poetic way there is an inescapable personification, "Wisdom calls aloud in the street, / she raises her voice in the public squares" (Prov. 1:20).

2. Spirit. The use of *Spirit* is much the same. The development of the idea in the OT is not a systematic one, nor is this surprising, since the OT is surely not a systematic theology. But there is no question that God touches men and women by his Spirit. By the same token, there is no question that God's touching human beings by his Spirit is a mediating act. In a sharper sense, the Spirit is portrayed as appearing in nature (Gen. 1:2; Job 33:4; Ps. 104:29–30). God is creative and supporting in the universe by his Spirit. Again, it is clear that the Spirit is operative in human experience and history (Neh. 9:20; Isa. 4:4; 61:1; Ezek. 37:1–14; 36:27; Zech. 4:6). Thus men are guided and history is controlled and directed by the movement of God's Spirit in the hearts of those who obey him.

On another level the Spirit apparently acts in an eschatological sense. This is not immediately apparent in the OT, but it is established in the NT when the prophet JOEL is quoted on the day of PENTECOST in support of the break-in of the new kingdom: "In the last days, God says, / I will pour out my Spirit on all people. / Your sons and daughters will prophesy, / your young men will see visions, / your old men will dream dreams" (Acts 2:17; cf. Joel 2:28). Frequently the idea of Spirit is used as the inspiring of individuals in prophetic utterances, in artistic skill, and in strength for battle. There is nothing more characteristic in the use of Spirit in the OT than the inspiration of an artist. The OT writers were not puzzled by the psychology of how a great creative idea should come to human beings: it is plainly, in their understanding, a gift of the Spirit of God.

The term HOLY SPIRIT (lit., "Spirit of holiness") occurs three times in the OT: once in the Psalms (Ps. 51:11) and twice in Isaiah (Isa. 63:10–11). It is highly debatable whether this is any reflection of that development of the office of the Holy Spirit which is set forth in the NT, and which reaches definition in the great creeds of the church. In the NT, the person of the Holy Spirit is a member of the TRINITY, and can be understood only insofar as the Trinity is understood, and then over against the Persons of the Father and the Son. The OT emphasis adumbrates the NT doctrine, with an emphasis on the Spirit as essence more than person; power more than personality. Basically God is a Spirit by nature and essence, and the Spirit, as spoken of in the OT, is clearly a reflection of his divine immanence. Yet in all this, God does mediate his person to other persons by spirit touching spirit, and thereby enlightens and quickens with divine energy. The easiest analogy, although not necessarily the best, is the way in which one human being touches another human being. Even though the bodies and the senses are channels of communication, one person may enlighten and inspire another, and communion in friendship and love is possible only when spirit touches spirit.

3. Logos. The word LOGOS is a complex study in itself, but is relevant for brief treatment here as illustrating a means of God's reaching out to his creation. The question is the extent to which it is used in the ordinary sense of the word itself, and the extent to which it is understood in the light of its subtlety and sophistication in the philosophic tradition of the Greeks.

The Logos of God in Scripture refers to Christ and is thus a mediation between God and human beings. God finds ways of speaking and we find ways of hearing. In addition to this, it is by God's command that the world is brought to existence and sustained ("by his powerful word," Heb. 1:3). In mystery and miracle, therefore, God, who is Spirit, crosses the chasm to the world of nature and matter by his creative Word.

B. The prophet as mediator. By way of introduction, it must be recognized that in the history of theology the work of Christ has been classically analyzed into that of Prophet, Priest, and King. The device is a useful one as long as it is remembered that any such outline is a point of departure rather than a rigid control. The outline is a simple one, which is an advantage. It serves well as a basis of operation. In no area is the outline more useful than in an understanding of mediator and mediation as the concepts find fulfillment in the NT, specifically in Jesus Christ.

An added note of interest and of help, which in turn opens up the classification of Prophet, Priest, and King, is the fact that in each case there is a double use. To make this clear, one observes that as Prophet, Jesus not only spoke the Word of God or the words of God, but was in himself the living Word. He said what had to be said "officially," and at the same time manifested what had to be said in terms of life. The same sort of thing is true of the office of Priest. Jesus appears in the Gospels as the fulfillment of OT previews and types (this has its classical explanation in Hebrews), because his is the total fulfillment once and for all. He fulfills the office of Priest, however, not only as the One who makes the offering, but as the One who is the offering. Kingship illustrates the same double thrust. Christ is King in the normal sense of the word: there is no question that he is to rule and to do so eschatologically; his rule will be in power and completeness. At the same time, the evidence is inescapable that Christ the King is also the Suffering Servant, and so, in some sense, he is the King who rules by serving.

From this general introduction, a discussion of Christ as Prophet is now germane. Modern theology has drawn the emphasis on the Living Word as the proper interpretation of Jesus' ministry. This probably is due to the fact that 20th-cent. theology in general has been evading the impact of verbal and plenary INSPIRATION, and this tendency has moved the church away from an authoritative book, away from propositional theology, and away from rules and laws ("moralisms" and "legalisms"), toward a personal encounter with the living Lord. It is not necessary to criticize this emphasis in order to make plain the fact that the other position has been neglected or even discarded. This is a weakness, and certainly an evasion of much that dominates the Gospels, which could and should serve as a guide for life. At the conclusion of the SERMON ON THE MOUNT (and social action in the 20th cent. happily urges the ethic of Jesus' teaching there), Jesus plainly says, "Therefore everyone who hears these words of mine and puts them into practice is like a wise man who built his house on the rock" (Matt. 7:24).

Jesus apparently did not hesitate to underline "these words of mine," and makes the astounding declaration that a man's life stands up or falls down in relation to his *words*. When Jesus had made the requirements of DISCIPLESHIP entirely too stringent for the multitudes, and indeed for some of his closest followers, many turned away. What he was saying to them was indeed a hard saying; and Jesus refused to soften. The question he then set for his disciples was not merely a rhetorical one: "Do you also wish to go away?" (Jn. 6:67 NRSV). Even his disciples could have gone away. It is a nice question whether people really can bear the words of Christ; but Peter's answer is significant: "Lord, to whom shall we go? You have the words of eternal life" (6:68). The emphasis is clearly on the "hard saying" and "the words of eternal life" (6:60, 66–69).

What has been set forth, therefore, by way of these references points up the continuity between the OT and the NT. OT law reaches fulfillment in the teachings of Christ, and the sayings of Christ lay on the Christian the same requirements of obedience; for what he says to human beings mediates what God says to them. Part of the idea of fulfillment includes, of course, interpretation, and Jesus is apparently more interested in content and motive than the OT appears to be. Nevertheless, he did not hesitate to say, as illustrative of this continuity, "Do not think that I have come to abolish the Law or the Prophets; I have not come to abolish them but to fulfill them. I tell you the truth, until heaven and earth disappear, not the smallest letter, not the least stroke of a pen, will by any means disappear from the Law until everything is accomplished. Anyone who breaks one of the least of these commandments and teaches others to do the same will be called least in the kingdom of heaven, but whoever practices and teaches these commands will be called great in the kingdom of heaven" (Matt. 5:17–19). There is no escape from the continuity with the law. There is no escape from even the "iotas" and the "dots." One does not relax these commandments; he "practices them and teaches them." It may be said again that how one "fulfills" the law can be an area of debate, but the law cannot be debated; it is understood at the same time that Jesus and the Gospels give official Christian interpretation to the OT Torah. After all this has been urged, Christ is in the tradition of the prophets, and by way of this high calling mediates the words of God to man.

It is only in the acceptance of Christ's revelatory mediating position with regard to the "words" of God that Christ, the Living Word, may be properly understood. His life is illustrative of what he had come to say. He revealed in the flesh the revelation of God himself, but never apart from the authority and interpretation of the words. To state it another way, there is no escape from the control of the words by way of the Living Word. The two ideas are completely interlocked. It is possible to think of any other man as saying one thing and doing another, as set forth idealistically—what a person ought to do as over against what he is willing and capable of doing; not so with Christ. The living words that come from God through him cannot be divorced from what he showed to be the Word in life.

Nevertheless, the Living Word does mediate God to us. The writer to the Hebrews writes in this fashion: "In the past God spoke to our forefathers through the prophets at many times and in various ways, but in these last days he has spoken to us by his Son.... The Son is the radiance of God's glory and the exact representation of his being" (Heb. 1:1–3). In the Gospel according to John, it is quite evident that the emphasis must be placed on Christ as the Living Word: "I am the way and the truth and the life" (Jn. 14:6). Or again, "Anyone who has seen me has seen the Father" (14:9).

In the Johannine writings generally, this emphasis is the burden of description and definition. The identity between Christ the Word and God himself introduces the philosophical terms of the gospel: "In the beginning was the Word, and the Word was with God, and the Word was God" (Jn. 1:1). This Word was creative (the parallel to the Logos idea in the OT is quite clear), in it was life and light; through it men and women are enlightened, empowered, and brought to a new kind of nature by a new kind of birth (1:2–13). But this was not merely the creative power of the Logos of God's Spirit, for there was more: "The Word became flesh and made his dwelling among us. We have seen his glory, the glory of the One and Only, who came from the Father, full of grace and truth" (1:14). The same idea is picked up again in the First Epistle of John: "That which was from the beginning, which we have heard, which we have seen with our eyes, which we have looked at and our hands have touched—this we proclaim concerning the Word of life. The life appeared; we have seen it and testify to it, and we proclaim to you the eternal life, which was with the Father and has appeared to us. We proclaim to you what we have seen and heard" (1 Jn. 1:1–3).

References to Christ as the Living Word appear again and again in this same fashion throughout the Gospels. It will be evident later that this Word is redemptive as well as revelatory. It is sufficient to make clear at this point only that Christ, as set forth in the Gospels, really does reveal God, not only his will, but also his nature. With regard to the original question of the meaning of mediator and mediation, it is evident that Christ spanned the chasm. He came across from the transcendent God to manifest the GLORY of God, even on the dusty roads of Palestine.

The other ideas of Spirit and Wisdom as developed in the OT are not here separated from Christ the Logos. Wisdom is evident in what Jesus had to say, and the Spirit is needed to take of the things of Christ and show them to us (Jn. 16:15). Even though Christ has come to show how life may be lived, we now live in a variety and complexity unknown in ancient Palestine. How then does the way of God incarnate in Jesus Christ in 1st-cent. Palestine relate to a person in the 20th-cent. civilization? This is the office of the Holy Spirit, who leads mankind into all truth, but he is never to be divorced from the words of Christ and the Living Word. Christ was never married and he never had any children. Has he nothing to say to people who are married and have children? Christ was never attached to a machine on a complex assembly line. Has he nothing to say to a man who is? He was never a slave, nor was he a master. He never suffered the pangs and anxieties of old age. He never traveled by jet plane, and he never bore arms in battle. The mediation, therefore, of the words and the Word requires the mediation of the Holy Spirit. It is at this point that the modern emphasis on existentialism has relevance. The 20th-cent. Christian in a society unimaginable in ancient Palestine or in ancient Rome still obeys the words and Word and may therefore "image God."

The structure is somewhat like this (although there are limitations in finite means and language): the Father is the source and ground of creative and sustaining life. He has spoken in the law, to his OT saints, in the holy nation, in the "mighty acts" of holy history. Thus God "reached" human beings. "I AM WHO I AM" (Exod. 3:14) was at the same time the God of Abraham, Isaac, and Jacob (3:15), and transcendence inspired immanence. Then God's Word became flesh; the Father revealed himself in the Son; the Holy Spirit came upon the church to make known the Son, who revealed the Father. Mediation is inescapably trinitarian.

C. The priest as mediator. In the priestly office, Christ fulfills a double function. He is the "offerer" and is also the offering. When the time came for him to lay down his life he was perfectly clear at this point: "No one takes it from me, but I lay it down of my own accord" (Jn. 10:18). It is essential, therefore, to see what is required of a priest when he offers himself as a sacrifice.

The OT PRIESTS were required to be of the tribe of LEVI. A relationship to the family of MOSES and AARON is indicated. In addition to proper family relationship, there were complex rules and regulations having to do with the priest's physical health and also his physical completeness. Special rules and regulations were laid down regarding his preparation for and his training in his calling. Even his economic support and his dwelling place were under special law. In every regard a man was "set aside" for priesthood.

On the Day of Atonement (Lev. 16) is found the climax of the whole OT approach to God. It is here that in the clearest fashion is depicted the mediatorial office of the priest toward God. As the prophet mediates God's Word to his people, the priest mediates the people's word to God. On the Day of Atonement the whole nation drew near and the priest sought forgiveness for the sins of the whole people. It is easy to see typified here what the NT means when it says that Christ dies for human beings. The Day of Atonement was a community action, and when the priest went into the Holy of Holies, he met God as a representative of God's people and carried out in action what God had set forth as acceptable worship. See ATONEMENT, DAY OF.

At this point, however, the emphasis was on the priest and not on the offering. The preparation of the priest on this day was significant. In order to mediate he must be "right," and the personal preparation he made is assumed to "righten" him to stand in God's presence. He was required to wash his body and to put on clean and fresh garments. So much for the outer person; then he was required to make an offering for his own sins. Cleansed outside and inside, in body and spirit, he was now ready to act as mediator. Only because of his own cleansing might he now make an offering for the cleansing of the people.

The parallel in Jesus to this OT preparation of the high priest is easy to see. On this one thing the Gospels are crystal clear. Christ was indeed the sinless One. Personally he challenged his enemies to find sin in him, and the challenge was not taken. In addition to this, as the writer to the Hebrews makes clear, his identity with his people in his mediating priesthood is much more profound than could have been possible for any priest in the OT dispensation. He "has been tempted in every way, just as we are—yet was without sin"; we do not have a high priest "who is unable to sympathize with our weaknesses" (Heb. 4:15). The book of Hebrews returns to this idea again and again. Finally now, once and for all, there is a High Priest apart from liturgy and ceremonial cleansing who may move people into the presence of God.

Of deeper significance than Jesus' personal preparation and purity is the task itself, which gives enormous weight to mediation and which surely must be its heart and core. He is the mediator supreme in the offering made. When Jesus made his offering on the stage of history, the words of JOHN THE BAPTIST described once and for all his central task. John did not announce the coming of a teacher, nor a healer, nor a social welfare expert, although these are all surely true and have their place in the Gospels and in the theology of the church. These, however, are John's words of announcement: "Look, the Lamb of God!" (Jn. 1:36). No exegesis in those days was required. All his hearers knew what it meant to call Jesus the Lamb of God. In the one simple announcement was summed up the whole sacrificial complexity of the OT TABERNACLE and TEMPLE: the sacrifices, the repeated offerings, the almost endless routines of WORSHIP. Now had appeared the complete sacrifice once and for all. What sinners could not do for themselves God was now doing for them. What endless sacrifices could not secure was now secured by the free gift of grace: "you are to give him the name Jesus, because he will save his people from their sins" (Matt. 1:21).

It is evident that any discussion of Christ as the offerer cannot long stay away from Christ as the offering. The sinless One is clearly called to act as priest (cf. again Lev. 16), but that very description applies to the offering as well. When John announced "the Lamb of God," the first thing that must have come to mind was the care with which the Lamb without blemish was chosen and nurtured for the sacrifice in the OT dispensation. Care was taken also by the priests themselves to insure that the Lamb that was brought for the offering was without blemish. The old hymn rightly reflects what use is made of this in the NT: "There was no other good enough to pay the price of sin."

What begins in this simplicity and in the parallels drawn between the OT and the NT becomes a doctrine of profound concern to the NT. There is

A figure representing the Jewish high priest. Jesus mediates for us in his high priestly role.

the necessity of some price to be paid, but a part of the price has to do with purity of life, perfect obedience, complete commitment; this and much more is required for acceptability in God's sight. It is impossible to speak of this only in terms of mediation; this idea moves over into such other topics as reconciliation, atonement, and the like.

Although Anselm in *Cur Deus Homo* was writing primarily on the INCARNATION and thereby discussing the ATONEMENT by necessity, he was speaking to the point, nevertheless, of this perfection of sacrifice that is acceptable to God. What Anselm established is that there is a necessity for the God-Man. Only man has sinned and cannot pay; only God can pay and he has not sinned. Therefore in the solution of this impasse, a God-Man is required, bearing the debt of man and bearing the power of the forgiving God. When Jesus numbered himself with the transgressors ("God made him who had no sin to be sin for us," 2 Cor. 5:21), in his death he took on himself in his humanity what man had done; nevertheless, in his deity, he was capable of bearing what had been done.

The required OT sacrifices, therefore, are insufficient and incomplete, and the solution is that God had to send his Son in order that what he alone could do would be sufficiently complete. This can be said in a multitude of ways: "Christ died for our sins," "he gave his life a ransom for many," "in that while we were yet sinners, Christ died for us." These and other passages are sufficient in and of themselves, although theological writers are tempted to build arguments on certain texts at the expense of others. Certain definitive ideas, however, seem to run through all the references and must be maintained at all costs: the offering is vicarious, that is, Christ had to do for us what we could not do for ourselves; he died in our place. The offering also must be perfectly holy, for only a perfect sacrifice can answer a sin against God. The offering must, as now suggested, satisfy the demands of God, whether these be the demands of obedience or purity, or in some sense a payment, or in some sense a punishment. And finally, the sacrifice must satisfy the sinners, who must stand in the assurance that they are forgiven. There was great therapy for the OT Jew when he was assured by the priest that his fulfillment of ritual marked him cleansed. The emphasis on belief in the NT has the same therapy available. Where Christianity has been most fruitful and satisfying in human history has been where the mediatorial work of Christ has been believed and accepted.

The Jews were people who accepted the laws of God and God's arrangement for the mediation of the priest as well as the whole complex sacrificial order. In the same sort of simplicity, a Christian is one who "accepts Christ"— so easy to say, so difficult to do. In other words, he finds Christ acceptable. How is this so? Christ as prophet tells him who God is and what God demands. Christ as prophet makes clear how far the sinner is from fulfilling these demands. How then may God and sinners be brought together? What mediation is possible? When one finds Christ "acceptable," or when one "accepts Christ," he simply takes his word for what is accomplished in the priestly act.

The chasm between holy God and sinful man is bridged by the God-Man. One believes that this satisfies God, and knowing that it is satisfying to God, it satisfies the human heart. It must be said that this can hardly do people much good unless they accept it as true. Has it not been clear from the outset that in any religion of the world, from the crudest animism to the highest theism, people find their mediation, their bridge to God, only in what they believe God finds acceptable? No price is too great: even children have been sacrificed. A Christian is one who at the outset, regardless of what else his Christianity demands of him otherwise, believes that he is saved once and for all through the finished work of Jesus Christ. There is for him no other way.

One idea closely related to Christ's priestly office, which is frequently neglected and needs to be refurbished, is that of intercession. Christ makes continual intercession for us at the right hand of the Father (Rom. 8:34; see INTERCESSION OF CHRIST). This, of course, is pictorial language, although it is difficult to see how it can be better said. What needs to be made clear is that Christ's finished work is constantly a reality in God's presence. God continuously saves the sinner through Christ's work. God judges sinners in the light of Christ's redemptive act. God even knows the sinner in, and not through, Christ.

Intercession is popularly thought of as PRAYER, but it is not necessary to read out of this idea that Christ somehow physically or personally stands over against the Father saying prayers. It is not this at all. The writer to the Hebrews lays great emphasis on Christ's relationship to the Father, and the book of Revelation in its own pictorial way says the same. The Lamb that was slain from the foundation of the world is the Lamb of God in the presence of God. In the mystery of the Trinity, all these figures of speech break down. They simply say in a variety of ways, from the time of the cross onward, that what Christ did is now a part of the very life and activity of God. This is not to say that God changes, for to repeat the wonder again, the Lamb was slain from the foundation of the world. But it is to say that God, by the mediatorial act he himself provided, treats sinful man henceforth by way of, or through, or on account of, the sacrifice of Calvary.

This is in a strengthening sense a saving reality. No Christian is alone in his victory or in his defeat in his day-by-day walk before God, or in his evasion of God because of sin. The presence of Christ's work is always before God on the believer's behalf.

D. The king as mediator. Ideas of kingship are so colored and discolored by popular usage that it is difficult to protect the biblical idea of kingship from misuse (see KING, KINGSHIP). It is well to remember the limitations set on kingship in Israel. The prophet SAMUEL resisted the demands of the people because they were wanting a king like the kings of the surrounding nations who were simply oriental potentates, despots, or tyrants. God, however, allowed through Samuel the anointing of a king.

The biblical idea of kingship is made clear by the limitations placed on the first king. In the first place, he was anointed by God, and one anointed by God is appointed by God (1 Sam. 10). In the second place, he was acclaimed by the people, or to turn the phrase somewhat, he was acceptable to them. It is well to remember this in that popular phrase "accepting Christ" (cf. 10:24). Finally, he was called to service. One of the most interesting things about King SAUL was his modesty. After all the excitement of his being appointed by God and acclaimed by the people, he returned to his plow, and it was from his daily tasks that he was called to service. He was clearly God's man for God's people. There are, of course, certain rights and powers in kingship, but they are never divorced from duties (10:25).

It is clear then that a proper king rules as lord, but also as servant. In several passages (2 Sam. 14:17, 20; Ps. 110; Jer. 22:18), the king is set forth as lord; his claims to allegiance are right and proper. In his lordship, however, whether good or bad, he stands for the people and the people are blessed or blamed in him. He holds the mediating position between God and God's people, and in a sense he speaks for God as prophet and acts for the people as a priest. His mediation is so complete that the king is inseparable from the kingdom as God blesses or judges. As the psalmist says, he is the people's "shield" (Pss. 84:9; 89:18). In the NT Christ is God's "Righteous One" and "the author of life" (Acts 3:14, 15). His claims to allegiance are overpowering. It is his expectancy that people should recognize in him that "one greater than Solomon is here" (Matt. 12:42). He did not hesitate to call men into service, even to death. He expected men and women to take seriously and completely the sovereignty of his person (Matt. 10:34–39).

All this by itself may be too much to take from any person, especially from an itinerant rabbi from Palestine, and, of course, the Jew found this hard to accept. The claims of Christ to kingship without the trappings of a king seemed monstrous to Jews expecting a Messiah who would break the power of Rome and rule for the sake of Israel. For those who became believers, however (and the first Christians were Jews), it was the other side of Christ's kingly activity that fulfilled for them the true picture of the king as "the Suffering Servant." Indeed, it is at this point that the gauntlet was thrown down not only for the Jew, but for every person since. This is the true worldliness that stands opposed to Christianity, that is, the acceptance of worldly ideas of kingship, power, and success, as opposed to otherworldliness, which sees true power in complete self-giving, that is, the power of the cross, which as Paul says, can be for many a scandal and foolishness (cf. 1 Cor. 1:18–31).

The Christian accepts the crucified One as the Suffering Servant who rules and to whom eventually every knee shall bow and every tongue confess. But the bowing and the confessing will not be because of the pomp and circumstance of a monarch, but because of the essence and reality of a kingly Person. Today, significantly, only those kings can continue to rule who are willing to be servants to the people, and where kings do not rule, politicians seeking office, whether honestly or hypocritically, must offer themselves as servants. Somehow, the idea has caught.

In the kingship of Christ, therefore, the mediation is clear. God touches his people through the king; the people count on their king to stand for them in God's presence; the king offers himself as a servant of God, and the people accept him in his service. Read in either direction, from man to God or God to man, Christ the king is Christ the mediator.

E. The modern emphasis. The focus on Christ is inescapable, regardless of how the subject of mediator is approached, and there is no question that in the modern emphasis, that focus, by necessity as well as by choice, remains. There is, however, a shift from the old orthodoxy to a different center of operation. Relating this to the rubric of Prophet,

Priest, and King, the old orthodoxy emphasizes the priestly act of Christ, whereas modern theology emphasizes the prophetic and somewhat the kingly office.

This is an outgrowth of the modern emphasis on action, and especially social action. Attention is therefore given to Christ as Prophet in the manner already set forth: the authoritative words and the "Living Word." There is a modern shift of emphasis away from the authority of the words to the existential relationship to the Living Word. This is not to say that the words of Christ are not given attention, but it is to say that they are not given the kind of attention that was formerly given, which rested on the inspiration of Scripture and therefore treated the words of Christ as mediating the will of God.

There is today a heightened appreciation of the ethical question of Christ's teachings and a recognition of the challenge of his ethic over against the life of his day and the modern world. What is missing, however, is any notion that the Bible, or the NT, or even such specifics as the Sermon on the Mount contain or in any way can be treated to produce a "code of ethics." An extreme illustration of the code book approach to behavior was in the quasi-military development of Ignatius Loyola and the Society of Jesus (the Jesuits). This degenerated in time to casuistry, or more popularly, "jesuitism." It was good to believe that God Almighty had mediated to us a way of life that included every possible facet, but it was soon discovered that this approach eventually ran into the ridiculous.

The counter movement may well have run into the ridiculous at the other extreme, but at least it is understood why the shift of emphasis had to be made, and there is, of course, great truth in the recognition of ethical practice as being in some sense existentialist or "situational." As this operates, and the approach is, of course, brief, there was the living Christ of NT times, moving in a Judaistic, Hellenistic, Roman environment, moving among human beings as a revelation of the will of God. The Word had become flesh. It is the function now of the Holy Spirit to mediate directly, albeit on the basis of the NT, the Word of God, as that Word relates to any given person in any given situation. The words of Christ, or even the life of Christ in ancient Palestine, although basic and not irrelevant, nevertheless need the plus factor of the Holy Spirit operating on that Word toward a person's ethical practice. In OT times God spoke through the prophets and "in these last days" he spoke through his Son; and in these days he speaks through his Spirit, who mediates the Living Word to a living situation.

Another modern emphasis, although not as strong as that of the prophetic ministry of Christ, accepts the mediation of Christ as King. Mention is made in the 20th cent. of the idea of Christ as Lord, the ruler of all life. This may be said in many ways, but again the emphasis is on relevance, and now the emphasis is on relevance to the totality of life. Men and women are seeking the Word of God in the broadest possible ways. What does Christ have to say to poverty, war, race, social injustice, international affairs? Christ reiterated in his ministry that he had "come to the lost sheep of the house of Israel." It was only after the coming of the Spirit, Pentecost, and the world vision of Paul, that this original word to the lost sheep of the house of Israel becomes global.

It is a constant temptation of the Christian church to become separatist, and there are good reasons why for the sake of purity there have been constant withdrawal groups in the history of the church. The modern emphasis, however, is on "mission," with the new idea that Christianity must lose itself in human needs in order to find itself. The contemporary conflict between so-called conservatives and liberals is clear enough: does God rule in a person's heart first before he rules in a community, or must the things of God be brought to bear in a community in order to reach a person's heart? This is a false dichotomy and is brought out here merely to point up that the modern emphasis is on community.

What is lacking in the modern emphasis on mediation is an understanding, or an appreciation, or perhaps even better, an acceptance, of the basic transaction that occurred preeminently on the cross of Christ. Christ sacrificed for all eternity his self-giving life. His preaching and healing, his cleansing power, his subsequent resurrection, his continual intercession, and his coming again are all of a piece and are illustrative of his priestly, prophetic, and kingly ministry. (P. T. Forsyth's book title, *The*

Cruciality of the Cross [1909], is not merely a neat play on words.) The cross is the crux, and something had to happen there in the most profound understanding of the word *mediation*.

Nearly all views of the cross have in them some merit. Christ's death was an example of how people ought to stand for their principles. It was an illustration of the love of God. It was surely a victory over sin in the flesh (cf. G. Aulén's *Christus Victor* [1961]). John Bailey is correct here, as elsewhere, when he says that theology must insist on the words "at least." The cross meant "at least all these things," and at some level did mediate light and truth and power. But there is still the question of what was *done*. An offering had to be made, but it had to be an offering acceptable to God. The understanding of the offering is related to the understanding of the offense against God, and no interpretation of Christ's death is complete that does not insist on an offering of life sufficient to satisfy the demands of God; sufficient to pay the price of sin (however this is construed); sufficient to turn away wrath upon the guilt of the sinner; and happily, sufficient to satisfy a person that God himself has provided a way of salvation.

There has to be some acceptance of the theme set forth in 1 Timothy, "For there is one God and one mediator between God and men, the man Christ Jesus, who gave himself as a ransom for all" (1 Tim. 2:5–6). It is easy to make out of this something mechanical, and frequently in medieval times the ransom was treated in a bizarre fashion. The easy way with this and other passages is to throw the loving Christ over against God the judge. Even if such things are impossible it must still be said in some fashion that mediation is dependent on an offering given and accepted. Take, for example, the book of Revelation. There Christ is referred to twenty-nine times as the "Lamb who was slain." The OT background is inescapable as is the necessity of an offering.

Without expecting to plumb the mystery of the godhead, another emphasis must still be made which answers this apparent mechanism in the offering and the receiving of the offering, and which answers this apparent split in the godhead—Christ over against the Father. After Paul has said, "All this is from God, who reconciled us to himself through Christ," he goes on to say, "God was reconciling the world to himself in Christ" (2 Cor. 5:18–19). Both sides of the intellectual impasse are set forth. Christ was provided to make the reconciliation, but God himself was in the act of reconciliation. In simple terms, the judge on the bench pronounced the fine, but came off the bench to pay what he himself had demanded. Christ's mediatorial act, answering the demands of God, was the act of God himself.

III. Summary. The story of the whole Bible is the story of redemption, and redemption rests on the mediatorial work of Jesus Christ. The plot begins with Gen. 3, the FALL. The question then is: What can God Almighty do, or what is God Almighty willing to do, to save his lost creation? Lostness rested on the rebellion and disobedience of one who believed the temptation, "you will be like God" (Gen. 3:5). The action of the story from then on is God's action. He came "seeking," as the simple Genesis narrative portrays, while the sinner went hiding. Found of God, sinners continued their resistance by rationalization and excuse, while God pronounced on them first judgment, then promise.

From that point onward, judgment and grace go hand in hand. Human beings in their sin are not acceptable to God, but God in his grace provides a way of acceptance. The whole sacrificial system of the OT is God-initiated. All the "mighty acts" interrelated with the life of the chosen people speak God's word of judgment and promise, and the words of Scripture accompany the acts for interpretation and understanding. Law and covenant are set in motion, but provision is made for those who break the law and do not keep the covenant. By Word, Wisdom, and Spirit, through law, nation, prophet, or king, God still comes seeking, and sinners are called to accept and respond in obedience.

All this is climaxed in Jesus Christ, who is by definition "the full revelation of God," and however he is approached in study or in personal response, he is the mediator of the new covenant, the arrangement by which God and man at last are one. The act of atonement is the supreme mediatorial act initiated by God, sustained by his power, accepted in its completion, and let loose, finally, as a new force and a new hope in the life of men and women. (See further E. Brunner, *The Mediator* [1934]; V. Taylor, *The Atonement in New Testament Teaching* [1940]; G. S. Duncan, *Jesus Son of Man* [1948]; R. Letham, *The Work of Christ* [1993]; J. H. Armstrong, ed., *The Glory of Christ* [2001].) A. H. LEITCH

medicine. The practice of treating DISEASE. See also HEALING AND HEALTH.

I. Miraculous healing. Cases of divine healing are recorded throughout Bible times. These events were most common in the times of the four Gospels, but also appear in apostolic contexts and are sporadically recorded in the OT. Examples in the latter are the healing of NAAMAN's leprosy (2 Ki. 5:8–14) and of MIRIAM's leprosy (Num. 12:1–15), the restoration of JEROBOAM's withered hand (1 Ki. 13:4–6), and the recovery of HEZEKIAH from what was apparently a severe infection (carbuncle, H-bug, or staphylococcal, 2 Ki. 20:1–11). Raising of the dead is recorded once at the hand of ELIJAH (1 Ki. 17:17–24), and once through ELISHA (2 Ki. 4:1–37). Although in this latter case death may have been due to sunstroke, fulminating meningitis also is possible. Subarachnoid hemorrhage due to rupture of an artery at the base of the brain is another possibility, but this does not occur often in one so young. The four Gospels record some two dozen instances of physical healing of either individuals or groups. In one case ten lepers were healed together. Definite distinction is made between physical sickness and DEMON possession (Mk. 1:32–34).

When claims for faith healing are made today, it frequently is easy to discount them as cases of neurotic illness (psychological illness with apparent physical signs and symptoms), mistakes in diagnosis or prognosis, remissions or temporary improvements that are well known in many incurable diseases, temporary alleviation of symptoms by some means, or the simultaneous pursuit of medical treatment. Most modern claims collapse under this scrutiny. However, the healings of Christ clearly pass these tests. He healed lepers, a man with long-standing paralysis causing wasting, a woman with curvature of the spine, an epileptic, lunatics, and a woman with a gynecological disorder, probably a uterine fibroid (Matt. 9). John is more selective than the other evangelists in his accounts of healing, and these are usually presented to illustrate some spiritual truth, such as the parallel between physical and spiritual blindness, where Christ is set forth as the answer to the latter (Jn. 9). The apostolic miracles also are notable, such as the healing of the man lame from birth (Acts 3).

It is interesting to note that the miracles of healing do not occur evenly throughout Bible times. They are mainly clustered around the times of the exodus, the prophets Elijah and Elisha, and the beginning of the Christian era. This illustrates that their primary function was revelatory. They were used as signs to confirm faith in something new that God was doing.

The belief that healing is "in the atonement"— i.e., that Christ died for all sicknesses and sins—and that there we can claim all physical healing by faith, finds no support in the Scriptures. Professor A. Rendle Short (*The Bible and Modern Medicine: A Survey of Health and Healing in the Old and New Testaments* [1953]) points out that there are a few recorded healings of patients with ailments such as coughs, abscesses, or fractures, from which they were likely to recover anyway. If any group of Christians should have been able to apply faith in this way, it would have been the apostolic Christians, but there are several well-documented cases of illness among them. TIMOTHY suffered from stomach ailments, probably gastroenteritis (1 Tim. 5:23); TROPHIMUS was so ill that he could not travel with Paul (2 Tim. 4:20); EPAPHRODITUS nearly died (Phil. 2:30). In the light of 2 Cor. 12:7–9 and Gal. 4:13–15, it seems inescapable that Paul's "thorn in the flesh" was a physical ailment.

The oft-quoted verse, "This was to fulfill what was spoken through the prophet Isaiah: 'He took up our infirmities and carried our diseases'" (Matt. 8:17), cannot be applied indiscriminately. Although Jesus Christ is "the same yesterday and today and forever" (Heb. 13:8), this does not mean that he acts in the same way under different circumstances and in different ages.

II. Demon possession. Some modern critics would say that the biblical idea of demon possession was the attempt of an unscientific age to explain diseases like epilepsy and the various types of insanity. This view would make Christ either in error himself, or intentionally conforming to the ideas of the day, in both cases giving false and misleading teaching.

Admittedly some of the NT cases do sound like description of modern-day mental illness and epilepsy. In one such case (Matt. 17:15), the Lord is specifically recorded as having cast a demon out of a boy. The clinical descriptions are far from complete, and thus comparison with known diseases must be made with reserve. However, a demonic influence could surely stimulate the motor cortex, the part of the brain initiating movement of limb and other muscles, and thus precipitate an epileptic-like convulsion.

Two cases, interesting in the face of present-day psychiatric knowledge, are those of SAUL and NEBUCHADNEZZAR. The picture given of Saul, in the middle chapters of 1 Samuel, is of a man who periodically had deep depressive moods with dangerous delusions of persecution (paranoia) in which he could be soothed by the playing of a harp. This explanation does not conflict with 1 Sam. 16:14, which states that "an evil spirit from the LORD tormented him." This type of mental illness certainly can be regarded as the evil power acting through a twisted mind, even if it is indirectly by way of the patient's subconscious. This is as far as the writer of 1 Samuel would be able to see. Note also the biblical way of regarding God as finally responsible for everything—his active and permissive will are not distinguished.

Nebuchadnezzar clearly was afflicted with mental illness at the height of his pride, which is described in the latter part of Dan. 4. It has been suggested, probably correctly, that he was suffering from severe melancholia or depression. He may have had a tendency to manic-depression. This is a mental condition in which periods of uncontrollable elation (and high-pressure irrational mental activity) alternate with spells of deep depression. In this case the emphasis was on the depression with only a tendency in the other direction shown, for one cannot blame insanity for his overweening pride—"Is not this the great Babylon I have built as the royal residence, by my mighty power and for the glory of my majesty?" (4:30). In this condition, it is typical that the periods of elation are followed by depths of depression, from which recovery usually occurs.

III. Preventive medicine. A powerful argument for the guiding hand of a supernatural being can be found by studying the sanitary laws of Israel. Compared with the primitive ideas of the surrounding tribes, the children of Israel were centuries ahead. Apart from the refinements that more detailed technical knowledge brings, their preventive medicine compared favorably with that of modern civilizations. It has been suggested that these rules were merely the result of intelligent observation, but the strong tendency for the ancient mind to find a supernatural or magical explanation for natural phenomena argues heavily against this theory. Repeatedly one finds the statement, "The LORD said to Moses." All other explanations are unsatisfactory.

There was a strong emphasis on personal cleanliness. Ceremonial washings were commonplace, and the use of some form of soap has an early origin. The term LYE (Jer. 2:22 NRSV) refers surely to the *natron* or washing soda collected in antiquity from the alkali lakes of Egypt. It was recognized that an uncontaminated WATER supply is essential to a healthy community. Infection of the water supply may lead to typhoid, cholera, and dysentery epidemics. Dead animals in still water were known to contaminate the water, although this did not apply to spring water after the carcass was removed (Lev. 11:29–36).

Model of the double pool of Bethesda in Jerusalem. Here Jesus healed those suffering from disease and illnesses.

It is truly remarkable that each person was held personally responsible for the disposal of his own excreta (Deut. 23:12–14). Foods likely to transmit disease also were restricted, although there was no knowledge of the disease processes involved. The principle of isolation for lepers and of quarantine for other health reasons was important, but also quite out of keeping with then current medical knowledge.

IV. Leprosy in the Bible. The modern disease known as *leprosy* is a condition caused by a rod-shaped bacterium or bacillus called *Mycobacterium leprae*, which belongs to the same family as tuberculosis. Like tuberculosis, it is a long-lasting condition characterized by areas of chronic low grade inflammation. *Nodular leprosy* is characterized by the appearance of nodules in the skin, particularly on the face and on the back of the hands and wrists. Later the three main nerves in the arm are involved, with resultant paralysis. The nodules tend to burst and ulcerate, leading to ugly sores. In *neural leprosy*, the main involvement is that of the peripheral nerves supplying the skin of the limbs. This leads to loss of feeling. In any condition in which this occurs, the anaesthetic (numb) parts become damaged to a surprising degree because the protection of pain sensation is gone. Thus penetrating ulcers form with infection and death of bone, particularly in hands and feet.

There is no description of any disease in ancient literature that fairly definitely sounds like modern leprosy except for a legendary account from China. In studying OT references to leprosy, one must realize that these do not necessarily indicate a carefully classified condition caused by *Mycobacterium leprae* and answering to the above description. The Hebrew word ṣāraʿat *H7669*, translated as "leprosy," apparently is used for a whole group of ugly skin conditions (R. G. Cochrane, medical adviser to the American Leprosy Missions, in a booklet entitled *Biblical Leprosy: A Suggested Interpretation*, 2nd ed. [1963]). That the term refers to conditions completely unrelated by the standards of a dermatology textbook does not mean the Bible is in error. It merely indicates the use of a general term by people who had no detailed scientific knowledge. There is little resemblance between the description of the disease given in Lev. 13 and modern leprosy. In particular, loss of sensation is not mentioned. The regulations of UNCLEANNESS for these patients as far as corporate worship was concerned was good preventive medicine, as it slowed the spread of disease by quarantine.

Dr. Cochrane points out that leprous areas are never white (see Lev. 13:13). This description appears in other references. For instance, in Exod. 4:6 Moses is commanded to put his hand in his bosom, "and when he took it out, it was leprous, like snow" (cf. also Num. 12:10; 2 Ki. 5:27). He suggests that these quotations answer to the description of *leucoderma*, a condition in which there is complete loss of pigment from certain areas of skin with surrounding areas more deeply pigmented than normal. The awful social stigma would be there nevertheless. Interestingly, this condition actually is called "white leprosy" in India.

It is more likely that the various lepers healed by Christ (e.g., Lk. 17:12–19) had the disease known as leprosy today, since the latter was known in Israel at this time. It also seems to fit in better with the hopeless state of these ostracized people as it is described.

V. Circumcision. The rite of CIRCUMCISION was established as a national practice for the descendants of ABRAHAM (Gen. 17). It marked a COVENANT or agreement between God and a people he was setting apart in a special place. The Jews removed the foreskin of their male babies on the eighth day as part of their fulfillment of the law. This was done with a sharp stone (Exod. 4:25) or a sharp knife (Josh. 5:2). PAUL points out that such a covenant brings added responsibility rather than honor. Being a Jew meant nothing in itself, if there was no "circumcision of the heart" (Rom. 2:29), or spiritual surrender of the individual to God.

Today, even in English-speaking lands, circumcision is widely practiced. The advisability of circumcision is one field in which there is room for difference of opinion in the medical profession. Some doctors never advise it, others do as a general rule. There is a minority of babies in which the prepuce is very tight and circumcision should be done. For the rest, in the present writer's opinion, the reasons for and against on medical grounds are practically equal. Although circumcision was widely practiced in the ANE, infant circumcision was apparently limited to Israel; this practice helped the Jews to avoid the licentious puberty rites practiced in some surrounding nations.

VI. Obstetrics in the Bible. The Bible does not profess to be a textbook of science or medicine, but in spite of this few realize how many references occur in the Bible related to CHILDBEARING. The birth of children and attendant circumstances did, in fact, play a prominent part in the lives of OT and NT characters. In fact, it was of such importance that the fertile woman was honored and the barren pitied or even despised. When HAGAR conceived, her childless mistress SARAH was despised in her eyes (Gen. 16:4). Such was RACHEL's distress at her barrenness that she said to JACOB, "Give me children, or I'll die!" (30:1). This feeling of inferiority was carried over into the NT, for ELIZABETH, just before the birth of John the Baptist, said, "The Lord has done this for me.... In these days he has shown his favor and taken away my disgrace among the people" (Lk. 1:25).

Children were regarded, much more directly than often today, as a gift of God (cf. Ruth 4:13; 1 Sam. 2:21; Gen. 4:1; 30:2). Likewise, God was regarded as the cause of sterility. HANNAH's adversary (Elkanah's fertile wife) chided her because "the LORD had closed her womb" (1 Sam. 1:6; cf. also Gen. 16:2; 20:18; 29:31; 30:22). It is interesting to notice on record two undoubtedly miraculous examples of postmenopausal conception: Sarah and Elizabeth (Gen. 18:11; Lk. 1:36).

Back in early times, labor was regarded as an extremely painful experience. The day of desolation of EDOM is described in Jer. 49:22 as the day in which "the hearts of Edom's warriors will be like the heart of a woman in labor." The Lord himself said, "A woman giving birth to a child has pain because her time has come; but when her baby is born she forgets the anguish because of her joy that a child is born into the world" (Jn. 16:21). Apparently it was recognized that women having their first child had a worse time than the others (Jer. 4:31).

The most likely cause of death of a mother soon after the birth of a live child is severe postpartum hemorrhage, which rarely kills today. In OT times it was sometimes friends and relatives apparently who effected the delivery (cf. 1 Sam. 4:20). On other occasions a MIDWIFE was present (Gen. 35:17; 38:28). The Egyptian midwives tried to use the apparently well-recognized fact of the rapid easy labors of the Hebrew women as an excuse for not obeying Pharaoh's command to kill the babes (Exod. 1:19).

Most interesting are the references we have to complicated labor. For instance, the labor of TAMAR is described as follows: "When the time came for her to give birth, there were twin boys in her womb. As she was giving birth, one of them put out his hand; so the midwife took a scarlet thread and tied it on his wrist and said, 'This one came out first.' But when he drew back his hand, his brother came out, and she said, 'So this is how you have broken out!' And he was named Perez. Then his brother, who had the scarlet thread on his wrist, came out and he was given the name Zerah" (Gen. 38:27–30). For the babes to move around this much the mother must have had a large roomy pelvis or the babes must have been very premature (as often with twins), or both. The fact that the first babe appears to have torn the perineum ("you have broken out") is against extreme prematurity. Transverse or oblique lie with hand presentation

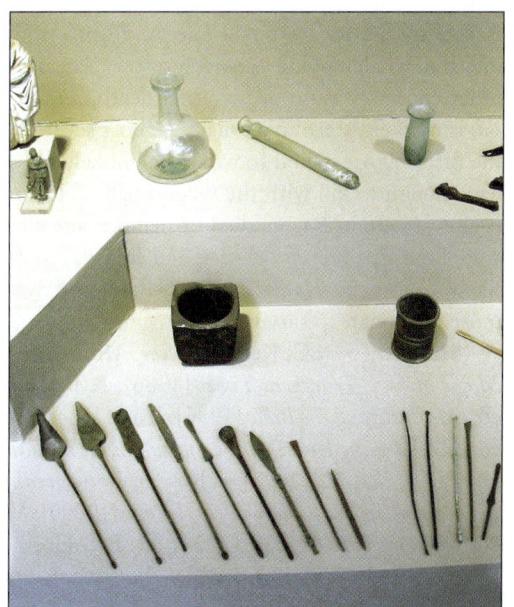

Collection of ancient medical tools found at Ephesus.

occurs in about one in 500 cases and the babe usually has to be turned.

One reads of Jacob's birth, following that of Esau, "After this, his brother came out, with his hand grasping Esau's heel; so he was named Jacob" (Gen. 25:26). It is not clear on a casual reading whether this was another hand presentation (much less likely) or whether the hand episode occurred with both babes born. In any case one must have followed the other very quickly.

Rachel died with the birth of BENJAMIN after hard labor (Gen. 35:16–20). However, the midwife was able to tell her that she was about to have another son, which indicates that it must have been a breech presentation (i.e., the buttocks appeared first). There is no record of difficulty with the birth of Rachel's first son, JOSEPH, which is against the breech lie being caused by a small pelvis difficult for the head to fit into. A breech presentation associated with the death of the mother soon after a live birth is most likely due to *placenta previa*, a condition in which the afterbirth is attached to the inside wall of the womb at a low level. This hinders the head from fitting into the pelvis and the babe swings round into the breech position with the buttocks leading. Such a condition is liable to be associated with hemorrhage both before and after birth, and this could account for the rapid death of Rachel soon after the birth. *Puerperal sepsis* from infection would not kill as quickly as this. The only other common cause of maternal death, *eclampsia*, is unlikely, since this usually is most severe in the first pregnancy, and so would be unlikely to be bad enough to kill with the second babe. Thus it is almost certain Rachel died of hemorrhage also complicating a breech delivery, and this was most likely caused by *placenta previa*. Benjamin was indeed fortunate to survive.

(See further H. C. Kee, *Medicine, Miracle, and Magic in New Testament Times* [1986]; B. Palmer, ed., *Medicine and the Bible* [1986]; I. and W. Jacob, eds., *The Healing Past: Pharmaceuticals in the Biblical and Rabbinic World* [1993]; F. Rosner, *Encyclopedia of Medicine in the Bible and the Talmud* [2000]; V. Nutton, *Ancient Medicine* [2004]; H. F. J. Horstmanshoff and M. Stol, eds., *Magic and Rationality in Ancient Near Eastern and Graeco-Roman Medicine* [2005].)   D. A. BLAIKLOCK

meditation. This English noun occurs a few times in the OT as the rendering of Hebrew *higgāyôn* H2053 (Ps. 19:14) and *śîaḥ* H8490 (Ps. 104:34). More common is the verb *meditate*, which renders primarily the respective cognates *hāgâ* H2047 (Josh. 20:47; Ps. 1:2) and *śîaḥ* H8488 (esp. in Ps. 119, e.g., vv. 15, 23, et al.). (These Hebrew terms occur elsewhere with other meanings.) The KJV uses the verb in the NT as a translation of *meletaō* G3509, "to attend to, practice" (only in 1 Tim. 4:15; cf. also Lk. 21:14 KJV and RSV), which is the word used in the SEPTUAGINT to render the Hebrew verbs mentioned above.

To judge by the use of the terms, meditation seems to have been more a Hebrew than Christian practice. It is a most rewarding act of WORSHIP, of spiritual renewal, of mental refreshing, and of divine communion (see Job 15:4; Ps. 77:3, 6). The first reference concerns ISAAC, who "went out to the field one evening to meditate" and saw REBEKAH coming (Gen. 24:63). The verb here, however, is *śûaḥ* H8452; it occurs nowhere else and its meaning is uncertain (both NRSV and NJPS understand it to mean "walk"). The most familiar passage is Ps. 19:14, "May the words of my mouth and the meditation of my heart / be pleasing in your sight, / O LORD, my Rock and my Redeemer." Also well known is the command given to JOSHUA to meditate on the Book of the Law "day and night" (Josh. 1:8, echoed in Ps. 1:2; cf. 119:97). The godly meditate also on God's CREATION, "on all your works" (Ps. 77:12; cf. 119:27; 145:5).

G. B. FUNDERBURK

Mediterranean. See GREAT SEA.

medium. See DIVINATION; FAMILIAR SPIRIT.

Meeda mi-ee´duh. KJV Apoc. form of MEHIDA (1 Esd. 5:32).

meekness. Mildness and gentleness of character; PATIENCE, HUMILITY. Meekness is one of the most commonly misunderstood terms applied to GODLINESS. It has been interpreted in a variety of ways, from weakness and timidity to strength and self-control. In the OT, the KJV uses the adjective *meek* about a dozen times to render Hebrew

ʿānāw H6705 (Num. 12:3; Ps. 22:26; et al.), but this term in current English often indicates "deficient in spirit or courage," so modern versions prefer such adjectives as "humble, afflicted, poor." The Greek adjective *praus* G4558 occurs a few times, mainly in Matthew (Matt. 5:5 et al.); more common is the noun *prautēs* G4559 (1 Cor. 4:21 et al.).

The meek are specially blessed with divine care and rich rewards. In recording God's rebuke of MIRIAM and AARON for speaking against MOSES, the biblical text states, "Now the man Moses was very meek, more than all men that were on the face of the earth" (Num. 12:3 RSV; the NRSV and NIV have "humble"). DAVID cried, "O LORD, you will hear the desire of the meek" (Ps. 10:17 NRSV; NIV, "afflicted"). ISAIAH prophesied that the messianic King would "decide with equity for the meek of the earth" (Isa. 11:4 NRSV; NIV, "the poor"); moreover, "The meek shall obtain fresh joy in the LORD" (29:19 NRSV; NIV, "the humble"). David offered the oppressed people encouragement by saying that the wicked would soon disappear, "But the meek will inherit the land and enjoy great peace" (Ps. 37:11). The land David referred to was Palestine, but Jesus promised greater possessions: "Blessed are the meek, for they will inherit the earth" (Matt. 5:5). The meek then have access to God's constant protection and boundless love.

Meekness or gentleness in the NT is a natural virtue, a Christian grace, and part of "the fruit of the Spirit" (Gal. 5:22–23). Jesus said, "Take my yoke upon you and learn from me, for I am gentle and humble in heart, and you will find rest for your souls" (Matt. 11:29). PAUL wrote to the Corinthians, "By the meekness and gentleness [*epieikēs* G2117] of Christ, I appeal to you" (2 Cor. 10:1). Paul not only extolled and emulated this virtue of Christ, but commended it to his churches: "As a prisoner for the Lord, then, I urge you to live a life worthy of the calling you have received. Be completely humble and gentle; be patient, bearing with one another in love" (Eph. 4:1–2). He admonished the Colossians to put on the graces of "compassion, kindness, humility, gentleness and patience" (Col. 3:12). Likewise he commends it to Timothy and to Titus (1 Tim. 6:11; Tit. 3:2). JAMES instructs Christians to "welcome with meekness the implanted word" (Jas. 1:21 NRSV; NIV, "humbly"); and recommends to the wise and understanding: "Show by your good life that your works are done with gentleness born of wisdom" (3:13 NRSV; NIV, "humility"). PETER wrote that all Christians should always be prepared to make a defense of their hope "with gentleness and respect" (1 Pet. 3:15). (See *NIDOTTE*, 3:454–64; *NIDNTT*, 2:256–59.)

G. B. FUNDERBURK

Megiddo mi-gid´oh (מְגִדּוֹן H4459 and מְגִדּוֹן H4461 [only Zech. 12:11], derivation uncertain). A major Bronze Age and Israelite city in the JEZREEL Plain. It commands the entrance to the Wadi ʿArah, which served in antiquity as the main pass on the VIA MARIS between the SHARON Plain and the Valley of Jezreel. Near the foot of Megiddo, that route branches out in three main directions: (1) NW past JOKNEAM to the Plain of Acco and the Phoenician coast; (2) NE via ANAHARATH to KINNERETH, HAZOR, and thence to DAMASCUS or the Lebanese BEQAʿ; (3) E to BETH SHAN and from

Megiddo and the Jezreel Valley.

there to TRANSJORDAN and Damascus. Throughout the three millennia of its existence, Megiddo was one of the most strategic points in Palestine, and many crucial battles took place in its immediate vicinity.

I. Identification. The 14th-cent. Jewish scholar Eshtori Haparhi was apparently the first European to propose the location of biblical Megiddo at the Arab village of Lejjun. This latter site had preserved the name of the former village of Roman times that came to be called Legio after the BAR KOKHBA revolt when the sixth Roman legion was stationed there. It formerly had been known as Kephar Othnai (*m. Gittin* 1:5; 7:7; cf. *Kaparkotnei*, Claudius Ptolemaeus, *Geogr.* 5.16.4). The same conclusion was reached by Edward Robinson. C. R. Conder's objections have been refuted successfully by G. A. Smith and others. The excavations at Tell el-Mutesellim, an ancient mound that stands beside Lejjun, have demonstrated that the Megiddo of OT times was located on the tell, while the later village of Kephar Ohtnai (Legio) occupied an area below it (cf. the relationship between Tell el-Ḥusn and Beisan, the ancient mound and Arab village of Beth Shan).

II. Archaeological investigation. Excavations at Tell el-Mutesellim were made by the *Deutsche Orientgesellschaft* from 1903 until 1905 under the direction of Gottlieb Schumacher. He dug exploratory trenches in various areas of the mound and on the slopes along the length of its walls. His main excavation was a deep exploratory cut about 20–25 meters wide that cut across the diameter of the site from N to S. He even uncovered completely a large building near the eastern end of the tell. At one small area in the middle of the large cut, the excavators went clear through the lowest stratum to bedrock. They counted six levels of construction from the Middle Bronze to the Iron Age. Two large buildings were uncovered (Schumacher's *Nordburg* and *Mittelburg*). Sufficient material for establishing their date with certainty has not been published, but it is generally assumed that they were built during the Middle Bronze Age and continued in use during the Late Bronze Age having undergone various repairs and modifications.

Of special interest were two tomb chambers roofed over by corbeled vaults that were discovered under those buildings; these may have been the tombs of the kings of Megiddo during the Late Bronze Age. In the southern section of this excavation, part of an impressive building from the Iron Age also was uncovered (Schumacher's *Palast*). The eastern building was likewise from the Iron Age. Because of the stone pillars discovered in it, Schumacher thought it was a temple containing stelae (*Tempelburg*), but his assumption is unnecessary as such columns were standard in public buildings of that period. The principal segments of the fortification wall that Schumacher uncovered also were from the Iron Age, though portions of older walls also were found. Among the important finds from

Megiddo lies at a key crossroads on what served as an international highway. (View to the NE.)

this excavation, mainly published by C. Watzinger, were seals bearing the inscriptions "belonging to Shema, servant of Jeroboam," and "belonging to Asaph," which came from the palace ruins, as well as a decorated incense stand discovered in the highest level (VI) near the southern end of Schumacher's trench, and a carved proto-Aeolic stone capital that was found in reuse as a building stone in the *Tempelburg* (the first of such capitals to be unearthed in Palestine).

The year 1925 saw the renewal of excavations at Megiddo by an expedition from the Oriental Institute of the University of Chicago. The work continued until 1939 under the consecutive directorship of C. S. Fisher, P. L. O. Guy, and G. Loud. These excavations, which were initiated by J. H. Breasted, comprised the most extensive archaeological endeavor ever conducted on a Palestinian site. The original objective was to uncover every stratum of the tell level by level. The four highest strata of the city from the 9th century B.C. to the Persian Period were completely excavated.

During the last four years of the excavation, work was limited to two principal areas in which earlier levels were reached: in the N at the gate area (A-A) where they went down to level XIII; on the E in the temple area (B-B) where virgin soil was reached (level XX). In two other areas they stopped at what was principally level VI: on the S in the vicinity of Schumacher's *Palast* (C-C), and on the NE in the region connecting areas A-A and B-B (area D-D). On the eastern slope of the tell, which was uncovered mainly to clear a place for the expedition's dump, many burial caves were discovered from all of the various periods of occupation; these contained an abundance of finds that were published in a separate volume and greatly augment the knowledge obtained from the stratified deposits. On this slope seven levels from the early Bronze Age also were uncovered (according to the older terminology of the excavators their beginning was placed in the Chalcolithic period); these were designated as stages I–VII.

The excavators counted a total of twenty strata in the city's history, but some of these were discerned only after the original numbering, and therefore are designated by secondary symbols (e.g., VI A, VI B; IV A, IV B; etc.); there are also levels in which several different building styles can be detected, so the total number of strata actually is closer to twenty-five or more.

The oldest settlement, XX, was founded in the Chalcolithic period during the 4th millennium B.C. This stratum, which includes several phases, is represented only by pits and a few segments of houses, most of them apsidal in form. Levels XIX–XIV belong to the Early Bronze Age. Level XIX, from the first stage of EB, provided the first public building: a small temple surrounded by a thick brick wall. It was discovered in area B-B, which continued to be the city's sacred site throughout the entire Bronze Age, since temples were built there from the end of the 4th millennium until the mid-12th cent. B.C. (level VII). In the stone floor near this earliest temple there were inscribed the forms of men and various animals, apparently in hunting scenes. Stratum XVIII dates to the first phase of EB II (c. 29th cent.). The principal innovation in this level is the stone wall nearly 4–5 meters thick, and which was widened later to c. 8 meters; it was preserved to a height of c. 4 meters. This is the widest wall in the history of the city and resembles in its thickness the brick wall discovered at Khirbet Kerak (Beth-Yerah) which is more or less contemporary. Near the wall a large building was partially uncovered, but not enough of it was revealed to show whether it may have been a temple.

The great wall continued to exist during EB II and III (c. 28th–25th centuries). In stratum XVII (EB II) a large circular "high place" (no. 4017) made of small unhewn stones was built. Level XVI saw the construction of an adjacent temple (no. 4040) that was enclosed within a *temenos* wall. This latter wall was destroyed in level XV by the construction of two additional temples (nos. 5192 and 5269). All three of these sacred shrines have the same general plan (Megaron Type). The central chamber was a broad room containing a rectangular altar built against the S wall; in front of it were two pillars supporting the roof. The entrance from the courtyard was through the N wall opposite the altar, and before it on the outside there were two additional pillars that apparently supported a roof forming a sort of stoa or porch. Beside the central room there was also another, smaller one. The temples continued to exist in level XIV B, that is, until the end of

EB (this interpretation of the sacred area was based on soundings by I. Dunayevsky).

On top of the "high place" and in various other loci, material was discovered which dates to the Middle Bronze I (Intermediate EB-MB). These meager deposits represent that period of decline which followed the destruction of the EB city. The subsequent levels appear to be contemporary with the 12th Egyptian dynasty (c. 1991–1786 B.C.) when the culture of Palestine was the urbanized society of the MB II A. Levels XIII A and B evidently correspond to this phase of Megiddo's history. The statuette base of an Egyptian official named Thuthotep, which was discovered with two other Egyptian stelae in a wall of stratum VII, date to the same period. The wall and gate of level XIII was uncovered in area A-A. They were built of mud bricks on stone foundations; the thickness of the wall was c. 2 meters and was reinforced by salients and recesses. The entryway was a narrow passage that made a 90-degree turn into the city; it was suitable only for pedestrian traffic and for draught animals. Two towers projecting from the line of the wall—inside and outside—protected the openings of the gateway between them. Within the inner tower the chamber for a stairway to the upper story was preserved. On the outside there were steps leading up to the gate; these were built against the wall, which was c. 3 meters wide and was reinforced by a rampart.

Levels XII–X belong to the age of Hyksos domination (18th–17th cent.). By this time Megiddo consisted of the upper city or citadel, and a lower city at the foot of the mound (the existence of such a "suburb" was suspected by the Chicago investigators and confirmed by Yadin's subsequent work). The plan of the buildings was entirely changed and the thickness of the wall base was doubled. In level XII the wall was reinforced by a rampart typical of the early Hyksos age with a narrow stone wall above it. In level X the great gate that served the city until the end of the Bronze Age (stratum VII A) apparently was built. The entrance to this gate was straight, without a turn, in order to facilitate the passage of vehicles. It had the form of a triple entryway guarded by a double row of buttresses protruding from each side. This plan is typical of the Hyksos age, and parallel examples have been found at other sites. Not only in the gate but also in most of the other structures there is a noticeable continuity in layout from level XI (and to some degree even in level XII) up to level VII A, which indicates that there were no appreciable upheavals in the history of the city. In level X a large building called a palace by the excavators because of its size (and the treasure of ornaments and carved ivories that were found in it) was constructed. This building also lasted into level VII A with various modifications and repairs. It was over 50 meters long and the thickness of its outer walls was 2 meters and more.

Level IX was apparently the city conquered by Thutmose III; it had its beginning at the start of the Late Bronze Age. In spite of this conquest there was no perceptible decline in the city, and the period of level VIII (end of the 15th and the 14th cent.) was one of the most flourishing times for Canaanite Megiddo. In the sacred area a new temple of the special "fortified tower" type resembling that at Shechem was built. It had only one long room with a niche at the southern end and an entrance at the N end protected on both sides by two projecting towers; its walls were up to three meters thick, which certainly indicates that it was a tall building. There was a court in front of the temple. This shrine evidently was built during the Amarna period (see Tell el-Amarna), and it remained in existence until level VII A, although it, too, underwent certain alterations and modifications.

The "palace" was repaired and enlarged in level VIII. In one of its rooms was found an extensive treasure that had been hidden under the floor; it bears witness to the wealth of the kings of Megiddo during that age. The collection included gold implements, ivory ornaments, and necklaces of gold and lapis lazuli, etc. The fragment of a clay tablet inscribed in Akkadian cuneiform found by a shepherd at the foot of the excavation dump near the gate probably belongs to this period. The tablet included a few hitherto unknown lines from the seventh tablet of the famed Gilgamesh Epic and, being the first of its kind discovered in Palestine, it furnishes a glimpse into the varied cultural influences at Megiddo during the Amarna Age.

Levels VII B and VII A belong to the 13th and 12th centuries B.C. and no appreciable changes occurred in the layout of the main buildings that continued to exist during these levels from the previous stratum. The most important find from these levels is a collection of more than 200 decorated ivory plaques that are without parallel in Palestinian archaeology. This treasure was found in the western part of the palace in three adjacent rooms, the floors of which were lower than the rest of the structure. Clarification of the stratification of these rooms is of special importance because among the ivories there was a box bearing a hieroglyphic inscription that included the name of RAMSES III. Stratum VII A also produced a bronze stand for a statue of Ramses VI (mid-12th cent.). On the basis of this latter item it is possible to establish that level VII A was destroyed in the last third of the 12th cent.; there was, therefore, a strong Egyptian influence on the city in this period just as there was at nearby Beth Shan.

With the destruction of level VII A the golden age of Canaanite Megiddo came to an end. The principal structures of the city—the gate, the palace, and the temple—were completely destroyed and were never rebuilt. The two phases of level VI date to the 11th cent. B.C. In stratum VI B there were only small, insignificant structures; but a certain degree of resurgence is noticeable in VII A. Near the former palace another large building was erected and the city gate may have been restored partially. According to the pottery found here, the city apparently was still Canaanite, which also seems to be indicated by the thick level of destruction that covered it. It is unknown what caused the great decline in the city between levels VII and VI. The town may have come under PHILISTINE domination since "Philistine" ware also was present in those strata.

The dates of the buildings in levels V and IV still are not settled. At first the opinion of the excavators was accepted: they assigned the "stables" to the reign of SOLOMON, the large buildings that preceded them to that of DAVID, and level V B to the period before David. However, J. W. Crowfoot and K. Kenyon criticized this interpretation and suggested that most of these structures should be dated to the reign of AHAB because of the similarity in style of construction to SAMARIA. Exploratory excavations carried out by Y. Yadin in the vicinity of the northern stables in 1960 and later led him to support this latter suggestion. W. F. Albright and G. E. Wright had discerned that the structures of levels V A and IV B uncovered in various parts of the tell actually belong to one level, although the excavators assigned them to two different strata. (See G. E. Wright, "The Discoveries at Megiddo, 1935–39," *BA* 13 [1950]: 28–46.)

Since in most parts of the tell the Chicago excavators stopped at level IV A, not much is known about the city beneath it. The palace excavated on the southern side of the tell (building no. 1723 and courtyard no. 1693) was partially uncovered by Schumacher. The building itself occupied an area of 28 by 22 meters, and its walls, on an average having a thickness of 2 meters, indicate that the building had a second story. The structure was built entirely of ashlar blocks, and only the inner fill of the walls contained unhewn stones. In front of this building there was a large courtyard surrounded by a wall constructed according to a special method whereby ashlar alternated with unhewn stones. The entryway to the courtyard was in the northern wall, flanked by two projecting towers. Not far from the site of this gate two proto-Aeolic capitals were discovered (embedded in walls of level III); in their original position they may have served as ornamentation for the entrance to the courtyard. The ground plan of this building and of another one situated on the northern side of the tell (as revealed in Yadin's later excavations there) corresponds to that of the typical *bīt ḫilāni*, a royal type structure entered by a portico, of which similar examples are known from Zinjirli.

The main buildings of level IV A, usually referred to as stratum IV, are the large complexes in the SW and the NE portions of the tell. These were built according to a single plan: a long rectangular structure with two parallel lines of columns down the center to support the roof; between the columns stood stones with "troughs" hollowed out of the top. The center "aisle" had a dirt floor while the side "aisles" were of cobblestones. The southern complex included five units; the building fronted on a large courtyard that had a deep, unplastered pit in the center. One alteration in the form of the building was quite noticeable, namely, the addition of another unit on the northern side. In the opinion of the excavators that modification was carried out during the course of the original construction before the building was completed, but this is difficult to accept; it seems more likely that it was made at a time when the complex was being reconstructed after having been destroyed.

The northern complex consisted of three buildings containing twelve units in all, to which an additional unit was later added; this latter stood by itself. The original interpretation of these level IV A structures as stables is *not* supported by Scripture; neither were any objects found in them suggestive of horses or chariotry. J. B. Pritchard has demolished the "stables" theory in a penetrating analysis of all the evidence ("The Megiddo Stables: A Reassessment," in *Near Eastern Archaeology in the Twentieth Century*, ed. J. A. Sanders [1970], 268–76). Subsequently, identical buildings have been found at BEERSHEBA (Tell es-Saba‛) full of storage and other vessels. The masses of pottery vessels were stacked in the *side* "aisles" on the cobblestones. Z. Herzog argues convincingly that the "feeding troughs" were for the pack animals who were tethered in the *center* "aisle" while being loaded and/or unloaded. The Megiddo excavators had admitted many serious objections to the "stable" interpretation. A more careful reading of 1 Ki. 9 would have prevented this archaeological "myth."

A palace was built also during the period of the store city. It stood at the eastern end of the tell near the northern storage complex; part of this structure already had been uncovered by Schumacher, who thought that it was a temple (his *Tempelburg*). The measurements of this structure (no. 338) resemble those of the palace from level IV B, and a walled but somewhat smaller enclosure also was associated with it. At the NW corner of its courtyard a small structure was found (no. 355) reminiscent in plan of the gateway from the palace in level IV B, and the drainage canal passing through the center proves it to be an entryway. The excavators pointed out that this building abutted onto one of the adjacent storage complexes, but since the walls are not structurally joined with it, it is possible that the storehouses were built prior to the gateway. This one resembles in dimensions the earliest phase of the southern storehouses in contrast to all the others. However, one finds it extremely difficult to accept the excavators' interpretation to the effect that a change was made in the building plan during the course of construction; it seems more likely that these additions and alterations were made sometime afterward. The new fort, which was designed to fulfill the function of the previous palace, also was constructed of ashlar stones with unhewn stones between them, and nearby, within walls from levels III and II, five proto-Aeolic capitals were found as well (including the first one discovered by Schumacher); these certainly must have served as ornamentation for the entryways of the building.

The city of storehouses was surrounded by a mighty fortification wall of the salient-and-recess type (first discovered by Schumacher). The city gate associated with this wall is of a layout similar to those of the Bronze Age except there are now four buttresses on each side instead of two or three; a defensive guard tower projects outward on each side of the entryway. Gates of almost exactly the same dimensions have been discovered at both HAZOR and GEZER (cf. below); the same general plan is reflected in the entrance to the temple court as depicted by Ezek. 40:5–16. The fact that the gates at Hazor and Gezer were associated with casemate walls led Yadin to search for traces of such a casemate structure below the salient-and-recesses wall at Megiddo, but no such structures were found either in his own exploratory dig on the N or in the extensive excavations made elsewhere on the mound by the Chicago expedition. It is certain that the complex of "triple gate" (with four buttresses), salient-and-recess wall, and fortified approach ramp all existed together at Megiddo.

The gate was constructed of beautifully formed ashlar stones fitted together according to the system of alternating headers and stretchers. In front of the gate was a spacious plaza surrounded by a wall and leading to an outer gate consisting of two buttresses. A ramp passed through this first entryway and made a 90-degree turn to the left into the main gate.

The question of whether the "store city" with its warehouses was Solomonic or later (perhaps dating to the Omride dynasty) is hotly disputed. Yadin claims that the two palaces of the *bīt ḫilāni* type and a row of beautifully constructed rooms (which he takes to be a casemate wall) attached to the northernmost of them are Solomonic, while the stores and the salient-and-recess wall are from the reign of Ahab. It is hard to see how the triple gate, and the imposing fortified approach way (which matches the one at Gezer where only a casemate wall exists) could be other than contemporary with the triple gates at Hazor and Gezer. One thing is certain: Yadin's assumption that a uniform system of construction (casemate wall and triple gate) existed in the contemporary Solomonic cities of Hazor, Gezer, and Megiddo is subject to serious reservations. The similar gates at all three and the identical casemate walls at Gezer and Hazor do not in any way preclude the possibility that the Solomonic engineers may have elected to encircle Megiddo with a salient-and-recess wall.

As a result of more recent excavations, I. Finkelstein and D. Ussishkin ("Back to Megiddo," *BAR* 20/1 [1994]: 26–43) have argued that levels V A and IV B are not Solomonic but must be dated to the time of Ahab. The chronology of Iron Age strata at Megiddo and other sites continues to be hotly debated.

The city of level IV was destroyed completely and all of its public buildings covered with debris. Therefore between this stratum and the construction of the city in level III there may have been a period of abandonment. Over the ruins of the former royal buildings there arose a series of dwellings, but it must be noted that most of the structures were spread out according to a definite plan that included carefully laid out streets, both straight and intersecting. As mentioned above, the gate of this stratum was only a double entryway, and the salient-and-recess wall continued to exist. The stores and the palace were not rebuilt. On the contrary, two large, public buildings were set up near the city gate, in the same positions as the palaces of the former Canaanite kings. These two new buildings resemble one another in their ground plans; each possessed a large court surrounded by rooms with a double row of rooms on one side. R. Amiran and I. Dunayevsky have demonstrated that these buildings represent a new style of architecture originating in Assyria and bearing close resemblance to the forts at Hazor, Tel Jemmeh, and Lachish.

In stratum II a new fort was built according to a similar plan. The fort stood at the eastern end of the mound, and had been partially excavated by Schumacher. This fort was built on top of fort no. 338 from level IV A. One of the most notable structures of stratum III is the granary that was at least 7 meters deep and 11 meters in diameter, having a circular stairway leading down each side.

The excavators indicate that in levels III and II there is a decided resemblance with regard to structures; there is no destruction layer separating them, and most of the modifications are simply repairs carried out during the course of time. Thus, it would seem that the wall was torn down inasmuch as some of the buildings from level II were set over it. Megiddo was now an unfortified town with a small fortified citadel commanding the surrounding dwellings. The last level at Megiddo (stratum I) represents an unfortified town with no sizable buildings. It belongs to the Persian period (6th–4th centuries B.C.), and with this the long history of the city comes to an end.

One of the most interesting discoveries of the Megiddo excavations is the long water channel dug from within the city to the small spring located

The descent into the Iron Age water system at Megiddo. This protected system provided a safe supply of water in the event of an extended siege.

outside of its walls. The tunnel was constructed in order to facilitate the drawing of water from this spring by the citizens during time of siege. Near the western end of the tell a deep shaft was sunk, c. 25 meters deep, and steps were hewn out of the side by which one could descend into it. From the bottom of this shaft a tunnel c. 70 meters long and 3 meters high led to the spring, and a wall covered the spring blocking the approach to it from the outside. From signs of the quarrying it is clear that the channel was cut simultaneously from both ends in a manner similar to that used for making the SILOAM tunnel at JERUSALEM; and at the meeting point one notes correction for an error of about one meter. The excavators are of the opinion that this channel was hewn at a very late stage in the Bronze Age, but continued its existence into the Israelite period. From Yadin's investigations it seems more likely that both the water tunnel and the beautifully built outside gallery that preceded it were built during the Iron Age.

III. Recorded history. Although the archaeological evidence testifies to Megiddo's existence as early as the 4th millennium, the town's written history does not begin until the 2nd millennium.

The Early Bronze Age (3rd millennium) city was certainly one of the major urban centers of Palestine, and this situation was only temporarily interrupted by the intrusion of the MB I (Kenyon's intermediate EB-MB) settlement. With the beginning of the 12th Egyptian dynasty in the 20th cent. B.C., Megiddo had returned to the status of a strong city state whose culture is in reality a resumption of the Early Bronze civilization. The earliest inscription pertaining to Megiddo is that on the stela of Thut-hotep, which originally must have been set up during level XIII. Its presence at Megiddo bears witness to strong ties with Egypt and may explain the absence of any reference to this city in the famous execration texts (expressing curses on Pharaoh's enemies).

Like the rest of Palestine, Megiddo enjoyed flourishing occupation during the Hyksos Age, but there are, of course, no inscriptions to shed light on this period. When Megiddo again emerges into the light of history, she is at the head of a vast confederacy (mainly inspired by KADESH ON THE ORONTES) to resist Egyptian occupation of Canaan. Pharaoh Thutmose III smashed that effort during his first military campaign; the decisive action took place in the vicinity of Megiddo. The Canaanite allies had hoped to block the Egyptian advance at the passes leading from the Sharon to the Jezreel plains. Pharaoh apparently surprised them by choosing to march through the Wadi ʿArah while they were deployed facing the southern entrance near Taanach and the northern beside Jokneam. Thus the Egyptians were able to set up their camp in the plain before Megiddo near the Qina Brook (see MEGIDDO, WATERS OF). The next day the Canaanites were defeated soundly and fled for refuge to Megiddo. Their escape was assured when the Egyptian troops turned aside from the pursuit to plunder the Canaanite encampments at the foot of the city's lofty mound. Siege was laid to the town and after seven months the besieged princes surrendered. Meanwhile, the Egyptian army had parceled out the agricultural lands of Megiddo and was utilizing them, under the supervision of palace officials for the support of the troops in the field. The wheat was especially notable, over 207,300 sacks besides that used by the army for its daily provision (*ANET*, 234–38).

The Canaanite rulers were sent home ignominiously riding on donkeys; their sons were taken as hostages to Egypt, where they received training at Pharaoh's court that prepared them for future service as royal vassals in their respective homelands. The Leningrad Papyrus no. 1116a bears testimony to the presence of emissaries from Megiddo at Pharaoh's court during the rule of the 18th Egyptian dynasty. Megiddo apparently became the base for an Egyptian garrison that upheld Pharaoh's authority in the Jezreel Valley. This can be inferred from one of the Taanach letters (no. 5) in which a certain Amanhatpa commands the prince at Taanach to send his troops and logistic support to Megiddo. Despite certain difficulties (e.g., the lack of royal titles in the Taanach epistle), this Egyptian possibly is to be identified with Pharaoh Amenhotep II, whose second campaign brought him to the Jezreel Valley in order to quell a revolt at Anaharath (cf. *ANET*, 247a). Upon his return journey he evidently encamped "in the vicinity of Megiddo" long enough to deal with another rebel from Gebathomen.

During the Amarna period Megiddo was ruled by a certain Biridiya, whose name apparently reflects an Indo-Aryan lineage. His epistles date to the end of Amenhotep III's reign and the beginning of AKHENATEN's. They pertain mostly to the tumultuous events associated with the rise and fall of Labʾayu, prince of Shechem, who was actively opposing Egyptian hegemony with the aid of the ʿApiru (see HABIRU). It was a time of confusion: Biridiya complained that the Egyptian administrators were acting in a hostile manner toward him though he himself was carrying out his orders (including the furnishing of thirty head of cattle to Pharaoh's officials; see EA, 243). Perhaps as a result of their mistrust, the Egyptians had removed their garrison from Megiddo, leaving the responsibility for its defense on Biridiya's shoulders; he was on guard day and night, and during the hours of daylight his fields were being harvested under the protection of his foot and chariot forces lest the ʿApiru attack the workmen in the field (EA, 243).

Labʾayu seized control of the towns in the DOTHAN Valley, destroyed the city of SHUNEM at the foot of the Hill of MOREH, and apparently aroused the people of Taanach to expel their own ruler, Yashdata (EA, 250 and 245). The latter sought refuge with Biridiya (EA, 245) whose own town was soon put under siege by Labʾayu. Biridiya pleaded with Pharaoh to reinstate the Egyptian garrison; 100 archers were needed desperately to save the situation (EA, 244). Finally, Pharaoh had ordered Labʾayu's arrest and transport to Egypt, and Biridiya claims that he joined other Canaanite kings in carrying out this order. But the culprit was taken from Megiddo on the way to Acco via Hannathon; there he succeeded in bribing his captor, Suarta of Acco, and of escaping. Biridiya and Yashdata rode out together to apprehend the fugitive but he already had been caught by his enemies (from the land of Gina, i.e., the Jenin Valley) and put to death (EA, 250); Biridiya protested his and Yashdata's innocence of that murder (EA, 245).

The responsibility for harvesting the crops of the ruined Shunem had been laid upon the city-state rulers of the Jezreel Valley, but Biridiya claimed that he alone had been obedient in this regard; he had brought corvée workers from the other side of the valley (Yapū, i.e., JAPHIA, Josh. 19:12) to accomplish the task (EA, 365). The sons of Labʾayu and the ʿApiru soon resumed their nefarious activities (EA, 246), probably until the Egyptians intervened forcibly. The distrust and tension that existed between Acco and Megiddo during the "Labʾayu affair" probably continued to prevail (cf. the letter from Satatna of Acco, EA, 234).

Little can be learned about Megiddo from the subsequent history of the Late Bronze Age. There is one possible reference to the town in a topographical list of Seti I, but the reading is not certain. Papyrus Anastasi I mentions the road to Megiddo from Beth Shan and describes in lurid detail the frightful passage of a lone charioteer through the Wadi ʿArah to the Sharon Plain. The road followed one side of the narrow defile that was much more difficult in those days because of the heavy underbrush and scrub forest. Marauders often were lurking on all sides to catch the unwary Egyptian messenger (*ANET*, 477–78).

In the Iron Age, Megiddo is mentioned among the conquered kings of Josh. 12:21. It was allotted to the tribe of Manasseh, but the Manassites were unable to occupy it or any of the other fortified towns that rimmed the plain of Jezreel (Josh. 17:11; Jdg. 1:27; cf. 1 Chr. 7:29). The allusion to the waters of Megiddo as witnessing DEBORAH's victory over SISERA (Jdg. 5:19) probably refers to the Brook Qina.

Later excavations have shown that both Megiddo and Taanach continued to exist side by side during

This extensive, three-chambered gate structure at Megiddo protected the main entrance into the city (9th or 8th cent. B.C.).

the transition from Canaanite to Israelite occupation; there is no longer any need to suppose (with Albright) that they saw periods of alternate settlement. It would appear that Megiddo became an Israelite city during the wars of David when he wrenched the hitherto unconquered enclaves from the Canaanite and Philistine occupants.

During the reign of Solomon, Megiddo, Hazor, and Gezer were all fortified as part of that king's military network (1 Ki. 9:15), which held the commercial routes of the Levant in an iron grip. Later, Megiddo was included in Solomon's fifth administrative district under the rule of Baana son of Ahilud (4:12).

The city fell to SHISHAK in the fifth year of King REHOBOAM (c. 924 B.C.), as evidenced by its appearance on the Pharaoh's display inscription (no. 27) and the discovery of a fragment of his victory stela at Megiddo. AHAZIAH, king of Judah, who was wounded at the time of Jehu's revolt, fled to Megiddo and died there (2 Ki. 9:27; cf. 2 Chr. 22:9). In the year 733/732 B.C. Megiddo was conquered by TIGLATH-PILESER III, king of Assyria, who made it the capital of an Assyrian administrative district called *Magiddû* that included the Jezreel Valley and GALILEE (the "Galilee of the Nations," cf. Isa. 9:1 [Heb. 8:23]). With the collapse of the Assyrian Empire, Megiddo fell for a short time under the hegemony of the kingdom of Judah, as evidenced by the confrontation between King JOSIAH and Pharaoh NECO that took place in the Valley of Megiddo and culminated in Josiah's death (2 Ki. 23:29; 2 Chr. 35:22). The reign of Josiah was the last period of prosperity at Megiddo. It was evidently during these later stages of Megiddo's history that the ritual mourning for HADAD RIMMON in the plain of Megiddo became so popular (Zech. 12:11), although it may have been a resurgence of pre-Israelite religion.

During the course of the Persian age, the city was abandoned entirely and its role as guardian of the entrance to Wadi ʿArah was taken over by Kefar Othnai (Legio). Megiddo's history as the scene of crucial battles is also reflected in John's Apocalypse, where "the battle on the great day of God Almighty" at the culmination of history is said to take place beside ARMAGEDDON (*Harmagedōn* G762, prob. from *har měgiddô*, "mountain[s] of Megiddo"; Rev. 16:14–16).

(The periodical literature on Megiddo is extensive. Articles by Y. Yadin include "Solomon's City Wall and Gate at Gezer," *IEJ* 18 [1958]: 80–86; "New Light on Solomon's Megiddo," *BA* 22 [1960]: 62–68; "Hazor, Gezer and Megiddo in Solomon's Times," in *The Kingdoms of Israel and Judah*, ed. A. Malamat [1961], 66–109; "Megiddo of the Kings of Israel," *BA* 33 [1970]: 66–96. Important works include the following: H. H. Nelson, *The Battle of Megiddo* [1913]; G. Schumacher, *Tell el-Mutesellim*, 2 vols. [1908–29]; C. S. Fisher, *The Excavation of Armageddon* [1929]; P. L. O. Guy, *New Light from Armageddon* [1931]; R. M. Engberg, *Notes on the Chalithic and Early Bronze Age Pottery of Megiddo* [1935]; R. S. Lamon, *The Megiddo Water System* [1935]; R. S. Lamon and G. M. Shipton, *Megiddo I* [1939]; G. M. Shipton, *Notes on the Megiddo Pottery of Strata VI-XX* [1939]; G. Loud, *Megiddo II* [1948]; J. N. Schofield, "Megiddo," in *Archaeology and Old Testament Study*, ed. D. Winton Thomas [1967], 309–28; A. F. Rainey, *El Amarna Tablets 359–379* [1970], 24–27; Y. Aharoni, "The Stratification of Israelite Megiddo," *JNES* 31 [1972]: 302–11; G. I. Davies, *Megiddo* [1986]; A. Kempinski, *Megiddo: A City-State and Royal Centre in North Israel* [1989]; I. Finkelstein et al., eds., *Megiddo III: The 1992–1996 Seasons* [2000]; T. P. Harrison et al., *Megiddo 3: Final Report on the Stratum VI Excavations* [2004]; *NEAEHL*, 3:1003–24.)

A. F. RAINEY

Megiddo, waters of. A place mentioned in the victory song of DEBORAH (Jdg. 5:19). The allusion is probably to the WADI draining the basin behind MEGIDDO, between it and the hills to the S. THUTMOSE III encamped beside that brook, which was called Qina or Gina (*qi-n*), before attacking Megiddo (*ANET*, 236, 238). The biblical passage suggests that instead of dividing the spoil and receiving a reward for their services, which would have been done on the southern side of the JEZREEL Valley in front of TAANACH and Megiddo, the Canaanite kings were swept away by the torrent KISHON in the center of the plain.

A. F. RAINEY

Megilloth mi-gil´oth. The plural form of *měgillâ H4479*, meaning "scroll" or "roll" (Jer. 36:28–29; Ezek. 3:1–3). The name Megilloth is given to a set of five short OT books, each brief enough to be read publicly at an annual religious festival. The order in some MSS and in editions of the Hebrew Bible follows that of the feasts throughout the year: Song of Songs (Passover), Ruth (Pentecost), Lamentations (the ninth of Ab, commemorating the destruction of the temple), Ecclesiastes (Tabernacles), and Esther (Purim). The grouping of these five books as a collection within the third division of the Hebrew Canon (the Writings; see CANON OF THE OT V.B) seems to have originated after the time of the TALMUD. The Masoretic MSS usually group them together, but their order is not uniform (see C. D. Ginsburg, *Introduction to the Massoretico-Critical Edition of the Hebrew Bible* [1897; repr. 1966], 1–8). S. BARABAS

Mehetabeel mi-het′uh-bee′uhl. KJV alternate form of MEHETABEL (only Neh. 6:10).

Mehetabel mi-het′uh-bel (מְהֵיטַבְאֵל H4541, "God does good [or treats kindly]"). **(1)** Daughter of MATRED and wife of Hadad (Hadar) king of EDOM (Gen. 36:39; 1 Chr. 1:50). See HADAD (PERSON) #3.

(2) Grandfather or ancestor of the false prophet Shemaiah (Neh. 6:10; KJV, "Mehetabeel"). See SHEMAIAH #19.

Mehida mi-hi′duh (מְחִידָא H4694, meaning unknown; on the basis of many Heb. MSS, some scholars prefer the reading מְחִירָא, meaning "bought [as slave]"; cf. MEHIR). Ancestor of a family of temple servants (NETHINIM) who returned from the EXILE with ZERUBBABEL (Ezra 2:52; Neh. 7:54; 1 Esd. 5:32 [KJV, "Meeda"]).

Mehir mee′huhr (מְחִיר H4698, "bought [as slave]"; cf. MEHIDA). Son (or descendant) of Kelub, included in the genealogy of JUDAH (1 Chr. 4:11). His place in the genealogy is unclear.

Meholah. See ABEL MEHOLAH.

Meholathite mi-hoh′luh-thit (מְחֹלָתִי H4716, prob. gentilic of מְחוֹלָה, "dancing"; see ABEL MEHOLAH). A descriptive adjective given to ADRIEL son of BARZILLAI, who married SAUL's daughter, MERAB (1 Sam. 18:19 [NIV, "of Meholah"]; 2 Sam. 21:8). He was probably an inhabitant of Abel Meholah, but some scholars, vocalizing the Hebrew word differently, read Mahlathite, that is, a descendant of MAHLAH, from the tribe of MANASSEH (see *ABD*, 4:681). S. BARABAS

Mehujael mi-hyoo′jay-uhl (מְחוּיָאֵל H4686, prob. "smitten by God"; the second time in the verse, the Qere reading is מְחִיָּאֵל, possibly meaning "God gives life" [cf. *HALOT*, 2:568]). Son of Irad and descendant of CAIN (Gen. 4:18). The name is thought by some to correspond to MAHALALEL in the line of SETH (5:12–17).

Mehuman mi-hyoo′muhn (מְהוּמָן H4540, possibly from Old Pers. *vahumanah*, "intelligent" [see *ABD*, 4:681–82]). One of the seven EUNUCHS sent by Ahasuerus, king of Persia (i.e., XERXES, who reigned 486–465 B.C.), to bring Queen VASHTI to a royal feast (Esth. 1:10). Some have speculated that the name is a variant of MEMUCAN (see v. 14).

Mehunim mi-hyoo′nim. KJV alternate form of MEUNIM.

Me Jarkon mi-jahr′kon (מֵי הַיַּרְקוֹן H4770, "waters of the Jarkon" or "pale waters"). A town (or river?) within the tribal territory of DAN (Josh. 19:46). The text is difficult, and some writers (on the basis of LXX, *apo thalassēs*) emend *mê* to *miyyām*, "from the sea" (i.e., "on the west"). Most scholars, however, associate the name with a stream called Nahr el-ʿAuja, which flows into the Mediterranean a few miles N of JOPPA (but see *SacBr*, 37c). The ancient Hebrew name "pale waters" may well reflect the considerable quantity of organic soil the river carries at certain times, giving it its greenish appearance. See also RAKKON. S. WOUDSTRA

Mekerathite mi-ker′uh-thit (מְכֵרָתִי H4841, gentilic of an otherwise unattested name, מְכֵרָה, meaning "plan"). A descriptive title given to HEPHER, one of DAVID's mighty warriors (1 Chr. 11:36). It is not clear whether Mekerah was a place or an ancestor. Some, however, have proposed that this passage or its parallel (2 Sam. 23:34), or both, have suffered textual corruption.

Mekonah mi-koh´nuh. KJV and TNIV form of MECONAH.

Melatiah mel´uh-ti´uh (מְלַטְיָה H4882, "Yahweh has delivered"). A man from GIBEON who helped rebuild the wall of Jerusalem under NEHEMIAH (Neh. 3:7). For discussion, see JADON.

Melchi mel´ki. See MELKI.

Melchiah mel-ki´uh. KJV alternate form of MALKIJAH.

Melchias mel-ki´uhs. KJV Apoc. form of MALKIJAH.

Melchiel mel´kee-uhl (Μελχιηλ, "God is [my] king"; see MALKIEL). Father of CHARMIS; the latter was one of the governors of BETHULIA to whom JUDITH made an appeal for aid (Jdt. 6:15).

Melchior mel´kee-or. According to late Christian tradition, the name of one of the MAGI who traveled to BETHLEHEM (Matt. 2:1–12).

Melchisedec mel-kis´uh-dek. KJV NT form of MELCHIZEDEK.

Melchi-shua mel´ki-shoo´uh. KJV alternate form of MALKI-SHUA.

Melchizedek mel-kiz´uh-dek (מַלְכִּי־צֶדֶק H4900, "king of righteousness" or "[my] king is righteous[ness]"; Μελχισέδεκ G3519). KJV NT Melchisedec. A priest-king mentioned in three biblical books (Gen. 14:18–20; Ps. 110:4; Heb. 5:6–11; 6:20—7:28) and in several nonbiblical documents.

I. Genesis. In Gen. 14:18–20 Melchizedek is identified as king of SALEM and priest of EL ELYON. After Abram (ABRAHAM) had defeated KEDORLAOMER and the kings who were with him, Melchizedek brought him bread and wine (expressing friendship and perhaps religious kinship) and blessed him. "Then Abram gave him a tenth of everything." Salem is best identified with JERUSALEM on the basis of (1) Ps. 76:2; (2) the early mention of the city as *Uru-salem* or *Uru-salimmu* in the TELL EL-AMARNA letters (14th cent. B.C.) and in Assyrian inscriptions, long before it became an Israelite city; (3) the TARGUMS; and (4) the GENESIS APOCRYPHON.

Most critics regard Melchizedek as a Canaanite priest because both elements of the name he serves (El and Elyon) occur as names of specific deities, the first in UGARIT (M. H. Pope, *El in the Ugaritic Texts* [1955]) and the second in PHOENICIA; an ARAMAIC inscription from SYRIA combines the two into a compound (E. A. Speiser, *Genesis*, AB 1 [1964], 104). In addition, many critics regard both Gen. 14:18–20 and Ps. 110:4 as a piece of syncretism whereby the pre-Davidic kingship and this Canaanite worship of El Elyon were linked with Yahwism and the founding of the Davidic dynasty to foster the emergence of Jerusalem as Israel's cultic center. These views, however, must be rejected, for they presuppose that Scripture is deceptive and that hypothetical reconstructions are more trustworthy.

On the contrary, Scripture equates El Elyon with Yahweh. Melchizedek regarded El Elyon as the creator of matter, the cosmos (Gen. 14:19), a concept foreign to the polytheistic religions of the ANE, which did not distinguish spirit from matter and therefore worshiped the elements of the cosmos. Moreover, it is clear that Abram regarded Melchizedek as worshiping the same God as he. By unhesitatingly giving Melchizedek a tithe of everything (v. 20), the Yahwist Abram not only showed his support of this priest-king and his sanctuary but also publicly demonstrated that he recognized him as a person of higher spiritual rank than he, a patriarchal priest. By contrast, Abram declines a gift from the king of SODOM, thus indicating publicly that he has no theological or spiritual affiliation with him. Also, by referring to Yahweh as El Elyon (v. 22; this feature is not found in the Samaritan, LXX, or Peshitta versions), Abram emphasized to the king of Sodom that his God and Melchizedek's were one and the same. Finally, the OT elsewhere uses this name as an epithet for Yahweh (Pss. 7:17; 47:2; 57:2; 78:56).

II. Psalm 110. In Ps. 110:4 a Davidic king is acclaimed by divine oath "a priest forever, in the

View of the Kidron Valley (looking S, with modern Silwan to left). This is probably the location of the Valley of Shaveh, where Melchizedek went out to meet Abram.

order of Melchizedek." F. F. Bruce has stated: "The background for this acclamation is provided by David's conquest of Jerusalem c. 1000 B.C., by virtue of which David and his house became heirs to Melchizedek's dynasty of priest-kings" (*NBD*, 749). Be that as it may, it is sure that DAVID had in view the One greater than himself when he called him Lord in v. 1 (cf. Mk. 12:35–37). The acclaim must refer to the Lord Jesus, who was Son of God as well as son of David.

III. Hebrews. The writer of Hebrews refers to Ps. 110:4 and applies it to Jesus (Heb. 5:6, 10; 6:20). Then, in order to demonstrate that Christ superseded the Aaronic priesthood, he shows that Melchizedek is a type of Christ by noting that both are identified as king of righteousness as well as king of peace, both are unique ("without beginning of days or end of life"), and both abide as priest continually (Heb. 7:1–3). He then proceeds to show that the order of Melchizedek is superior to the order of AARON because (1) Melchizedek is greater than Abraham (the father of LEVI, from whom Aaron descended), for he blessed Abraham and received tithes from him (vv. 4–10); (2) David predicted that the order of Melchizedek would replace the Levitical priesthood, showing that the latter was imperfect (vv. 11–19); (3) this order has a divine oath behind it (vv. 20–22); and (4) this order is permanent (vv. 23–25). (It is noteworthy that the author of Hebrews does not offer any TYPOLOGY in connection with the bread and wine that Melchizedek brought out to Abraham.)

Attempts to identify Melchizedek with the patriarch SHEM, an angel, a power or virtue or influence of God, the Holy Ghost, the Son of God, the Messiah, etc., are unauthorized additions and irreconcilable with the argument of Hebrews. It is an essential part of this argument that Melchizedek is given no pedigree and that he was a man made like unto the Son of God (cf. W. Smith, *A Dictionary of the Bible* [1863], 2:315).

IV. Extrabiblical sources. PHILO JUDAEUS (*Leg.* 3.25–26) refers to Melchizedek simply as a peaceable and righteous or lawful king. In contrast, a midrashic document found among the DEAD SEA SCROLLS (11QMelch=11Q13) depicts Melchizedek as an eschatological judge (comparable to the role of the archangel MICHAEL) who will destroy BELIAL in the end times. Finally, *Melchizedek* is the title of a fragmentary gnostic tractate preserved in

Coptic (originally composed in Greek, prob. in the 3rd cent. A.D.) that is part of the NAG HAMMADI LIBRARY (NHC IX, 1); it apparently identifies Jesus as Melchizedek redivivus, an eschatological high priest and warrior.

(In addition to the standard commentaries on Genesis, Psalms, and Hebrews, see the bibliography in M. de Jonge and A. S. van der Woude, "11Q Melchizedek and the New Testament from Qumran Cave 11," *NTS* 12 [1966]: 318 n. 3; H. H. Rowley, "Melchizedek and Zadok," in *Festschrift für A. Bertholet*, ed. W. Baumgartner et al. [1950], 161ff.; A. R. Johnson, *Sacral Kingship in Ancient Israel* (1955), 31–46, 120–22; O. Cullmann, *The Christology of the New Testament* [1959], 38ff.; B. A. Pearson, *Gnosticism, Judaism, and Egyptian Christianity* [1990], 108–23; *NHL*, 438–44; *DDD*, 560–63.) B. K. WALTKE

Melea mee′lee-uh (Μελεά *G3507*, perhaps from מַלְאָה *H4852*, "fulness"). Son of Menna, included in Luke's GENEALOGY OF JESUS CHRIST (Lk. 3:31).

Melech mee′lik (מֶלֶךְ *H4890*, "king," possibly short form of מַלְכִּיָּהוּ *H4899*, "Yahweh is [my] king"; see MALKIJAH). TNIV Melek. Son of Micah and descendant of SAUL through JONATHAN and MERIB-BAAL, included in the genealogy of BENJAMIN (1 Chr. 8:35; also 9:41).

Melek mee′lik. TNIV form of MELECH.

Melicu mel′i-kyoo. KJV form of MALLUCH (only Neh. 12:14).

Melita mel′i-tuh. KJV form of MALTA.

Melito mel′i-toh (Μελίτων). Bishop of SARDIS in the 2nd cent. A.D. EUSEBIUS refers to him several times and gives a list of his numerous writings (*Eccl. Hist.* 4.26.2). One of them is *Peri Pascha*, a polemical treatise that sets forth Christ (who is "by nature God and man") as the new and true PASSOVER (text and English trans. by S. G. Hall, *On Pascha and Fragments* [1979]; see also L. H. Cohick, *The Peri Pascha Attributed to Melito of Sardis: Setting, Purpose, and Sources* [2000]). Melito had an interest in the CANON OF THE OT, referring to it as the "old covenant" (Eusebius has preserved his list, *Eccl. Hist.* 4.26.13–145). A Latin work known as *Narrative of Melito* (an account of the death and assumption of Mary) was wrongly ascribed to Melito of Sardis.

Melki mel′ki (Μελχί *G3518*, from מַלְכִּי, possibly short form of מַלְכִּיָּהוּ *H4899*, "Yahweh is [my] king"; see MALKIJAH). The name of two men included in Luke's GENEALOGY OF JESUS CHRIST: Melki son of Jannai and Melki son of Addi (Lk. 3:14, 28).

melon. The valued fruit of a tendril-bearing vine (of the family *Cucurbitaceae*, which includes the CUCUMBER and the pumpkin). Melons were among the foods of Egypt that the Israelites missed in the desert (Num. 11:5; Heb. ʾăbaṭṭiaḥ *H19*). Does this refer to sweet melon (muskmelon, *Cucumis melo*) or watermelon (*Citrullus vulgaris*)? Probably the latter, but both grew in Egypt; both were delicious and would have been invaluable in the wilderness. A good watermelon could weigh 30 lbs., and a large sweet melon 6–7 lbs. The Hebrew word *miqšâ H5252* (Isa. 1:8; Jer. 10:5) possibly refers to a melon patch (so NIV, but most versions understand it to mean "cucumber field"). W. E. SHEWELL-COOPER

Melzar mel′zahr (מֶלְצַר *H4915*). According to the KJV, Melzar was the name of the Babylonian official in charge of DANIEL and his friends (Dan. 1:11, 16). In fact, however, the term is a common noun (from Akk. *maṣṣāru*) meaning "guard" or "warden."

mem maym (from מַיִם *H4784*, "water[s]"). The thirteenth letter of the Hebrew ALPHABET (מ), with a numerical value of forty. It is named for the shape of the letter, which in its older form seems to be a stylized picture of running water. Its sound corresponds to that of English *m*.

member. A body part; also, one of the persons that compose a group. No Hebrew term corresponds precisely to English *member*, but modern versions use it occasionally in idiomatic expressions (e.g., "the members of his household," Gen. 36:6; in the KJV, see Deut. 23:1; Job 17:7; Ps. 139:16). In the NT, by contrast, the Greek noun *melos G3517* occurs more than twenty times. This term can be used literally of a body part, such as the eye or the hand (Matt. 5:29–30), but usually it has a derived sense. The parts of the body are not to be an instrument of wickedness but of righteousness (Rom. 6:13, 19; cf. 7:5, 23; Jas. 4:1). The "members that are upon the earth" (NIV, "whatever in you is earthly") are to be put to death (Col. 3:5). Even the tongue, though a "small member," can be "a world of evil" (Jas. 3:5–6).

A different metaphor is that of Christians viewed as members of the BODY OF CHRIST. As such, believers must not unite themselves with prostitutes (1 Cor. 6:15). For the same reason, they are to "speak truthfully" to their neighbors (Eph. 4:25). Since Christian husbands are members of Christ's body, they must love their wives as their own bodies (Eph. 5:28–30). Moreover, the body illustrates our function in the CHURCH (Rom. 12:4–5; 1 Cor. 12:12–27). God has arranged the physical body "so that there should be no division in the body, but that its parts should have equal concern for each other. If one part suffers, every part suffers with it; if one part is honored, every part rejoices with it" (1 Cor. 12:25–26). Similarly, believers must honor and care for each other. W. G. BROWN

Memmius, Quintus mem´ee-uhs, kwin´tuhs (Κόιντος Μέμμιος). A Roman envoy who, with Titus MANIUS, bore a letter to the Jews after defeating LYSIAS in battle in 164 B.C. and offered to negotiate in their behalf with ANTIOCHUS Epiphanes in Antioch (2 Macc. 11:34). Neither of the men is otherwise known to history.

memorial. An object or a ceremony that commemorates an event or keeps its remembrance alive. One of the Hebrew words translated "memorial," *ʾazkārâ H260*, is a sacrificial term describing the act that brings the offerer into remembrance before God, or God into remembrance with the offerer (cf. Num. 5:26 et al.; the cognate verb *zākar H2349*, "to remember," can be used in the hiphil stem in the sense of "bring a memorial offering," Isa. 66:3). The related noun *zikkārôn H2355*, a more general term meaning "reminder," can be used of an offering (Num. 5:15), but also of a memorial made of stones (Josh. 4:7), of a written record to be remembered (Exod. 5:15; Mal. 3:16; see BOOK OF REMEMBRANCE), and of a celebration (Lev. 23:24).

The object of memorials is to preserve and perpetuate the most valuable in persons and incidents (cf. Exod. 13:8–10). SOLOMON said, "The memory [*zēker H2352*] of the righteous will be a blessing" (Prov. 10:7). Contrarily for the wicked, "the memory of him perishes from the earth" (Job 18:17; cf. Pss. 9:6; 109:15; Eccl. 9:5; Neh. 2:20).

That which qualifies for memorial is the worthily unusual—persons, incidents, or things, usually epoch-making. Memorials are direction markers in history, indicating trends in the course of events. When the Hebrews discovered that there was one living God who participated in human affairs, and with whom COVENANT could be made, his name became a memorial. An apocalyptic psalmist said, "O LORD, we wait for thee; thy memorial name [NIV, your name and renown] is the desire of our soul" (Isa. 26:8 RSV). Also, "the law of the LORD" was to be memorialized (Exod. 13:9). Great acts of God are preserved in memorials: the CREATION (20:11); the deliverance from Egyptian bondage (13:8); and Christ's death on the cross (1 Cor. 11:24–26; Gk. *anamnēsis G390*, "remembrance"). True worship and good deeds were objects of memorials: Israelite worship (Lev. 2:2; Num. 31:54); Mary's anointing Jesus (Matt. 26:13; Mk. 14:9; Gk. *mnēmosynon G3649*); and Cornelius's worship and neighborly service (Acts 10:4). These and others are recalled by the various memorials that perpetuate them.

Memorials are to aid a person's memory in preserving what is most cherished. Maybe it is a subconscious sense of immortality that has always prompted human beings to try in some way to survive the grave. Prehistoric men drew pictures on their cave walls, and throughout history people have marked the graves of their loved ones. Stone is one of the oldest means of memorials. Rulers of Egypt, Babylonia, Assyria, Hatti, Persia, Greece, and Rome have left their memorials in pyramids, obelisks, cliffs, statues, slabs, and other stone forms. MOSES had the names of the twelve sons of Israel engraved on two onyx stones as a memorial (Exod. 28:9–12); and the TEN COMMANDMENTS were put on stone (34:1). Later, JOSHUA "copied on stones the law of Moses" (Josh. 8:32). Another medium was the use of BOOKS, whether of parchment, papyrus, or paper. It is a mark of divinely inspired genius that Moses began the book that resulted in the Bible, a memorial of divine revelation and human response (Exod. 17:14; 24:4). Eventually the Bible became the most durable, inclusive, and influential memorial in history.

Other memorials were religious activities. Israelite priests presented cereal offerings, burned with incense, "as a memorial portion" (Lev. 2:2). Gold offerings were made "as a memorial for the Israelites before the Lord" (Num. 31:54). The angel said to Cornelius, "Your prayers and gifts to the poor have come up as a memorial offering before God" (Acts 10:4). Memorial days, particularly those associated with worship and feasts, have been most meaningful. Two paramount memorial feasts of Bible record are the Passover and the Lord's Supper. Moses said, "This day [Nisan 15] shall be for you a memorial day, and you shall keep it as a feast to the Lord" (Exod. 12:14 RSV). Instituting the Lord's Supper, Jesus said, "This is my body, which is for you; do this in remembrance of me" (1 Cor. 11:24). The fourth commandment is, "Remember the Sabbath day by keeping it holy" (Exod. 20:8). See also remember. G. B. Funderburk

Memphis mem′fis (from Gk. Μέμφις; Heb. נֹף H5862 and מֹף H5132 [only Hos. 9:6]). KJV Noph (except. Hos. 9:6). A city of Egypt, on the W bank of the Nile, some 13 mi. S of Cairo, in an area including the modern village of Mit Rahineh. The city was first called *inb-ḥd*, "the white wall," but later was known as *mn-nfr* (Mennefer), after the pyramid of Pepi I of the 6th dynasty. From this name are derived the Hebrew forms as well as Greek *Memphis*, by which the city is now commonly known. Memphis was also called in Akkadian *Hikuptah* (from *ḥ[t]-kʾ-ptḥ*, "the house of the spirit of Ptah"), from which later the name *Aigyptos*, "Egypt," developed.

General history. According to legend, Memphis was the first capital of united Egypt, being built by the traditional unifier and first king, Menes. It remained the capital until the end of the Old Kingdom (c. 2200 B.C.). After it lost the seat of government it was still a city of importance, particularly in religion, and kings of later times built temples and other structures there. In 670 B.C. the city was captured by the Assyrians. During the Persian period it was a cosmopolitan city and was visited by the Greek historian Herodotus. Little of its late history is known; after the Muslim conquest the ruins of Memphis were used for the construction of Fostat, which later became Cairo.

Archaeological history. Excavations were conducted here in 1909–13 by Flinders Petrie around the acropolis and the temple of Ptah. Later (1915–19, 1921–22), C. S. Fisher excavated the palace of Merneptah. These earlier excavations also revealed part of a temple of Ramses II (1301–1234 B.C.), a chapel of Seti I (1313–1301), some tombs dated c. 800, and remains of the embalming house of the Apis bulls, with inscriptions of Neco, Apries (Hophra), and Sheshonk (Shishak). Further work by the Pennsylvania University Museum and the Egyptian Department of Antiquities in 1954–56 was carried out in the area of the enclosure wall of Ptah. In 1980, the Egyptian Exploration Society began an archaeological survey of Memphis that continues to the present.

Religious importance. The supreme god of Memphis was Ptah, a creator-god, patron of arts and crafts, depicted usually in the form of a man wearing the straight beard, having a smooth (hairless?) head, and holding the *wʾs*-scepter, the symbol of dominion. A late stela, dating from the time of Shabaka, c. 700 B.C., preserves an early text of Memphite theology, which affirms that Ptah created everything, essentially by the simple processes of thought and speech. At Memphis the divine triad consisted of Ptah, his wife, the lioness-headed Sekhmet, and their son, Nefertem. The Apis bull, also worshiped here, is shown with the solar disc and uraeus serpent

Sphinx of Ramses II at Memphis.

between its horns. It was regarded as an incarnation of Ptah and Osiris (the latter also combined with Apis to make Serapis). See Egypt VII.A.

Other Memphite remains. To the W of the city site is a vast cemetery at Saqqara, with royal tombs, or cenotaphs, of rulers of the first two dynasties. From the third dynasty there is the world's "first monumental architecture in stone," the step-pyramid of King Djoser. The fourth dynasty royal inhabitants of Memphis created at Giza the most impressive group of tomb structures known, the Giza pyramids; around these clustered the lesser tombs of royal retainers and officials. The fifth dynasty kings built their sun temples and pyramids at Abusir, between Saqqara and Giza. At Saqqara, dynasties five and six provided excellent examples of scenes of daily life executed in painted relief on the walls of rooms of funerary complexes of officials such as Ptahhotep, Ti, Mereruka, and Kagemni. Here were the royal pyramids of those dynasties, such as that of Pepi I, mentioned above as the source of the name of Memphis. The pyramids of dynasties five and six are especially significant because of the religious spells, the Pyramid Texts, inscribed upon their walls. Also of importance at Saqqara is the Serapeum, the burial place of the Apis bulls, whose monuments range in date from dynasty eighteen to the end of the Ptolemaic period.

Biblical associations. In the Bible the name Memphis appears only eight times, all in the OT prophets. Hosea prophesied that the Israelites would return to Egypt and that Memphis would bury them (Hos. 9:6). In Isa. 19:13 ("an oracle concerning Egypt"; see v. 1), the Lord declares that "the leaders of Memphis are deceived; / the cornerstones of her peoples have led Egypt astray." In Jer. 2:16 the prophet states that as a consequence of apostasy and false worship Israel has suffered at the hands of the Egyptians: "Also, the men of Tahpanhes and Memphis / have shaved the crown of your head." After the murder of Gedaliah by Ishmael, the Israelite remnant fled to Egypt in fear of possible reprisals by the Babylonians, in spite of the warnings of Jeremiah (cf. 43:5–7).

In Egypt the Hebrew refugees were further admonished by the Lord. Jeremiah 44 contains a prophetic message addressed to "all the Jews living in Lower Egypt—in Migdol, Tahpanhes and Memphis—and in Upper Egypt" (44:1). Chapter 46 is largely a prophecy against Egypt; the report of war was to be published in her cities, including Memphis: "Take your positions and get ready, / for the sword devours those around you" (46:14). Perhaps the most striking predictions concerning Memphis are in Ezek. 30:13, where the Lord declares, "I will destroy the idols / and put an end to the images in Memphis," while the prophet Jeremiah stated that the city "will be laid waste and lie in ruins without inhabitant" (Jer. 46:19). The ruins of Memphis give silent witness to the fulfillment of these prophecies, and the scarcity of statues of Egyptian deities is quite marked, particularly in view of the long history of the building of temples at this city.

(See further J. Capart and M. Werbrouck, *Memphis à l'ombre des pyramides* [1930]; A. Badawi, *Memphis als zweite Landeshauptstadt im neuen Reich* [1948]; M. Dimick, *Memphis: The City of the White Wall* [1956]; R. Anthes, *Mit Rahineh 1955* [1959]; idem, *Mit Rahineh 1956* [1965]; J. Kamil, *Sakkara and Memphis: A Guide to the Necropolis and the Ancient Capital*, 2nd ed. [1985]; D. G. Jeffreys, *The Survey of Memphis* [1985]; D. J. Thompson, *Memphis under the Ptolemies* [1988]; C. Maystre, *Les grands prêtres de Ptah de Memphis* [1992]; L. Giddy, *The Survey of Memphis II* [1999].)   C. E. DeVries

Memphitic Version. See versions of the Bible, ancient, IV.C.

Memra mem´ruh. See Logos II.B.

Memucan mi-my*oo*´kuhn (מְמוּכָן *H4925*, derivation uncertain; cf. H. S. Gehman in *JBL* 43 [1924]: 325). TNIV Mamukan. One of "the seven nobles of Persia and Media who had special access to the king and were highest in the kingdom" (Esth. 1:14, 16, 21). Memucan served as their spokesman, and Queen Vashti was banished by Ahasuerus (Xerxes) on their advice.

Menahem men´uh-hem (מְנַחֵם *H4968*, "comforter"). Son of Gadi; he usurped the throne and became one of the last kings of Israel (2 Ki. 15:14–22). The name Menahem is found in various epigraphical sources (*IPN*, 222); Sennacherib mentions a Menahem of Samsimuruna in Palestine (Taylor Prism, *ANET*, 287).

I. Career. Aside from his father's name, Gadi, we know nothing of his antecedents. He was at Tirzah when Shallum assassinated Zechariah, the last of Jehu's dynasty; a month later, he in turn killed Shallum and assumed the kingship (2 Ki. 15:10–14). M. Unger (*Israel and the Aramaeans* [1957], 97ff.) suggests that he was an army commander who, like Omri, avenged his master. The book of Kings records: (1) the scandal of Menahem's sack of Tiphsah (v. 16); (2) the formal notice of Menahem's reign (vv. 17–18); (3) the heavy tribute to Pul (Tiglath-Pileser III, vv. 19–20); (4) the formal notice of Menahem's death in the fiftieth year of Azariah (Uzziah, vv. 21–22).

II. Chronology. The synchronisms in 2 Ki. 15:17, 23 date Menahem's reign from the thirty-ninth to the fiftieth year of Uzziah, that is, a period of ten years plus his accession year (this shows that Israel used the accession year system by this time, also that the regnal years in Israel and Judah did not coincide; otherwise the tenth of Menahem would have covered Uzziah's forty-ninth). Tiglath-Pileser became king of Assyria in 745 B.C. and king of Babylon (under the name Pulu) in 727, the year before his death; this is proved by a correlation of the Babylonian Chronicle with a Babylonian king list. A passage in the Annals of Tiglath-Pileser records tribute paid by "Menihimmu of Samarina"; this event generally had been dated to 738, as the next section of the Annals covers the events of his ninth year. W. F. Albright (in *BASOR* 100 [Dec. 1945]: 16–22) accordingly takes 738 as the earliest date for Menahem's death, but E. R. Thiele (*The Mysterious Numbers of the Hebrew Kings*, 3rd ed. [1983], ch. 7) has shown that the relevant passage could well refer to Tiglath-Pileser's third year (743) or to any intermediate year (cf. A. Poebel in *JNES* 2 [1943]: 89 n. 23).

Consistently with the above, Thiele (*Mysterious Numbers*, 124) derives the dates 752–742. Albright follows a different method, avoiding Thiele's extended coregency of Amaziah and Uzziah; he dates Uzziah 783–742, and Menahem 745–738. This involves rejecting a synchronism in 2 Ki. 15:1, but elsewhere rejecting the lengths of reign and

Panel depicting Tiglath-Pileser III (from Nimrud, c. 728 B.C.). Menahem king of Judah was forced to pay tribute to this Assyrian conqueror.

working by the synchronisms. Some older systems put Menahem's reign earlier to make room for the years given for the remaining kings (15:23, 27; 17:1); but it is now clear that the Assyrian cross-reference is incontrovertible, and another explanation must be found (see Pekah).

III. Tiphsah. A very abrupt statement (2 Ki. 15:16) records that, after ousting Shallum, Menahem sacked "Tiphsah" and ravaged the district with a brutality unprecedented among Israelites, though it had been practiced by Syrians (8:12) and Ammonites (Amos 1:13). The name is that of a town on the upper Euphrates (Gk. *Thapsakos*), but this cannot be meant. Lucian appears to have been the first to emend to Tappuah; the assumed textual corruption (from *w* to *s*), would be plausible for the early Hebrew alphabet. J. A. Montgomery (*A Critical and Exegetical Commentary on the Book of Kings*, ICC [1951], 450) objects that "such a barbarous raid is incomprehensible between neighbouring cities"; the distance was some 15 mi., with Shechem between. The words "from Tirzah" suggest their proximity, though the language might mean rather that Menahem was not yet in control of Samaria. In the last years of Israel, "no man spares his brother" (Isa. 9:19 RSV).

IV. Relations with Assyria. If Menahem became king in 752/1, there was a recession of Assyrian power during his early years, and he paid tribute to Tiglath-Pileser toward the end of his reign; or if Albright's chronology is followed, a principal argument for it would be the interpretation of the Assyrian record as referring to Menahem's last year, 738. A figure of 1,000 talents is mentioned in 2 Ki. 15:19, representing fifty shekels for every wealthy man (v. 20), or approximately 60,000 people. This was the price of a slave in Assyria; it makes an interesting comparison with the thirty shekels of Zech. 11:12. The statement is valuable evidence as to the population of Israel, and incidentally concerning the keeping of fairly accurate records at court. A similar tribute was extracted by Tiglath-Pileser again when he overthrew Pekah (*ANET*, 284), and by SENNACHERIB from HEZEKIAH (*ANET*, 288); Adadnirari took 2,300 talents from DAMASCUS in 806 with twenty talents of gold (*ANET*, 281–82); but this was not, apparently, exacted from the people.

The question arises whether this tribute was altogether imposed; Kings implies that Menahem was bargaining for special protection "to strengthen his own hold on the kingdom." This has led some authorities to date the event to Menahem's early years; but apart from the chronological problems of such a view, taxation at the end of the reign would help explain Pekah's revolt and successful instigation of an anti-Assyrian policy. Menahem may have been facing internal disaffection, or he may have sought, in view of the resurgence of Assyria, to secure himself by vassalage rather than take his chance with the states of ARAM and PHOENICIA. Hosea may refer to this policy, which could be regarded as dating from Jehu's time (Hos. 5:13; 8:9). (See further H. Tadmor in *Studies in the Bible*, ed. C. Rabin [1961], 248–66; C. Schedl in *VT* 12 [1962]: 101–7; V. Pavlovský and E. Vogt in *Bib* 45 [1964]: 326–37; T. R. Hobbs in *ABD*, 4:692–93.)   J. LILLEY

Menan mee´nan. KJV form of MENNA.

mene, mene, tekel, parsin (upharsin) mee´nee, mee´nee, tek´uhl, pahr´sin, yoo-fahr´sin (Aram. מְנֵי מְנֵא תְּקֵל וּפַרְסִין, from מְנָא *H10428*, תְּקֵל *H10770*, פְּרַס *H10593*). An inscription that appeared on the wall of the palace of BELSHAZZAR at BABYLON (Dan. 5:25–28).

I. The text. The handwriting probably employed the local unvocalized ARAMAIC in cursive script. It is, however, possible that ideographs in Neo-Babylonian CUNEIFORM script were used. Some vocalize the initial word as *menâ*, "he has weighed" or "weigh out"; others argue that the second *mene* is dittography and a later addition to the text (it is missing in Theodotion's Gk. version; cf. Jos. *Ant.* 10.11.3). However, the interpretation given in Dan. 5:27–28 presupposes the MT (so Otto Eissfeldt in *ZAW* 63 [1951]: 105). Most revocalizations of the text and discussions—as that which considers that the second *mene* has been added to bring a parallel with the four kingdoms of Dan. 2 and 7—are in effect questions of interpretation.

II. The reading. The fact that the king was disturbed as the hand wrote across the wall was almost certainly due to the unique manner and timing, which would remind a Babylonian of the so-called *šiṭir šame* or "writing of heaven," considered an augury. That the leading scholars of Babylon failed to read and interpret was not due to its illegibility or to the use of an unknown or esoteric script or language, since DANIEL made an interpretation on the basis of Aramaic. The problem was one of both reading (vocalization) and interpretation, and in both of these many variations were possible.

The text could be understood as meaning, "Mina, mina, shekel, and half-shekels." This series of WEIGHTS was approximately equivalent to our "pound, pound, ounce, half-ounce" (though at that time the mina weighed 1 lb. 1 oz. = 60 shekels). Such a reading must have offered many speculative possibilities to the Babylonians versed in arithmetical, algebraic, and astronomical methods, especially as numbers or words were sometimes used as symbols in certain types of omen texts. The "Peres" (*pĕrēs*, Dan. 5:28) is attested as a "half-shekel" both at Babylon and in the ALALAKH tablets from SYRIA in the 14th cent. B.C. The form *parsin* could be a plural (or even dual) referring to two half-shekels. (The *u-* represents the conjunction "and.")

Another reading would be, "Counted, counted, weighed, and assessed." These words might be a popular proverbial saying involving wordplay on the former reading or even a technical legal phrase denoting the completion of a contract and the final demand for fulfilling its terms.

III. Interpretation. Daniel's successful interpretation accepted both ways of reading the words and the revocalization, *měnâ H10431*, "he numbered." He had already stated his belief that it was the Most High God who gives kingship (Dan. 5:18) and removes it (v. 19). God alone rules in the kingdom of men as of heaven and sets whom he will over earthly realms (v. 21). So Daniel interpreted *měnê* to include the numbering of the days of a reign and of life (Ps. 90:12) and thus the inevitable end of it. The term *těqēl* was taken by Daniel to mean, "you have been weighed," from the verb *těqal H10769*; the cognate verb in Akkadian (Babylonian) is used to denote what is owed, and must be paid, in a debt. Daniel then equated *pěrēs* with the Akkadian verb *parāsu*, meaning to "divide" and thus "decide, pass judgment." So he sees the kingdom as about to be divided up and given to the combined Medes and Persians; the latter term (*pāras H10594*) is a wordplay on *pěrēs*. Daniel's interpretation followed common Jewish exegetical practice and won immediate acceptance as credible. The advance of the combined Medo-Persian army was already common knowledge, since at least two weeks earlier they had breached the Babylonian defenses at Opis. See MEDIA; PERSIA.

Daniel's interpretation demands that the kingdom found wanting and to be superseded by the Medes and Persians was the Chaldean Dynasty founded by NABOPOLASSAR in 626 B.C., of which the last ruler was NABONIDUS with his son and coregent Belshazzar. A number of interpreters since C. Clermont-Ganneau (*Journale asiatique* ser. 8, no. 7 [1886]: 36–67) have therefore sought to equate each of the words in the writing with kings of this dynasty. Thus "mina, [mina,] shekel, and half-shekel" is interpreted by Clairmont-Ganneau as Nebuchadnezzar / - / Belshazzar / Medes-Persians; by E. G. Kraeling (in *JBL* 63 [1944]: 11–14) as Evil-Merodach / Neriglissar / Labashi-Marduk / Nabonidus + Belshazzar; by D. N. Freedman (in *BASOR* 145 [Feb. 1957]: 31–32) as Nebuchadnezzar / - / Evil-Merodach / Belshazzar. It would be equally possible to consider the two great rulers of the dynasty Nabopolassar and NEBUCHADNEZZAR II as the minas and Nabonidus as the shekel, with Belshazzar, who only had part of the royal powers, as the "half-shekel." The important aspect of the interpretation must remain Daniel's insistence on the termination of the power of Babylon at the hands of the Medo-Persians. (See further J. J. Collins, *Daniel*, Hermeneia [1993], 250–52.)

D. J. WISEMAN

Menelaus men´uh-lay´uhs (Μενέλαος). A brother of Simon the Benjamite (2 Macc. 4:23) who usurped the high priesthood in the Maccabean era (JOSEPHUS, in *Ant*. 12.5.1, unreliably identifies Menelaus as brother of JASON and ONIAS III). In the reign of ANTIOCHUS Epiphanes, Menelaus was sent by the high priest Jason (who had himself undermined Onias) to ANTIOCH OF SYRIA (171 B.C.) to carry promised tribute to the king; instead of executing his commission, however, he offered a higher bid for the high priesthood and was authorized to supplant Jason (2 Macc. 4:23–24). See discussion under MACCABEE.

Upon Menelaus's return to Jerusalem, the high priest Jason fled (2 Macc. 4:25–26). But Menelaus, failing to pay Antiochus the money, was called to account (vv. 27–28). Reporting to Antioch, he did more bribing. The not altogether trustworthy Maccabean account states that Menelaus stole the temple vessels, which he offered to Antiochus's deputy, Andronicus, and then urged the latter to murder Onias, who had condemned and exposed Menelaus for his sacrilege (vv. 31–34). When details of the atrocity were reported to Antiochus, Andronicus was executed; but Menelaus came through unscathed (vv. 35–38).

Menelaus had left his brother LYSIMACHUS as deputy in Jerusalem (2 Macc. 4:29). The latter's actions brought on a bloody riot in which he was mobbed and killed (vv. 39–42). The news reached Antiochus when he was at TYRE; and the wily Menelaus bribed Ptolemy, an influential courtier, to gain favor for him with the king, the result being acquittal for Menelaus and execution for his accusers (2 Macc. 4:43–50).

The reported death of Antiochus in Egypt brought back the fugitive Jason with allies who forced Menelaus to flee. When the king returned, he massacred Jerusalem's citizens and plundered the temple with the aid of the scoundrel Menelaus (2 Macc. 5:5–23). Menelaus is later mentioned in a letter from Antiochus's son and successor, Eupator (11:29, 32). In 162 B.C., apparently no longer high priest, he was condemned by Eupator. The death of Menelaus was as unique as his career was notorious: he was flung from the top of a tower into some ashes below (13:1–7). (See *HJP*, rev. ed. [1973–87], 1:148–51; J. C. VanderKam, *From Joshua to Caiaphas: High Priests after the Exile* [2004], 203–26.)

R. F. GRIBBLE

Menestheus mi-nes′thee-uhs (Μενεσθεύς). The father of Apollonius; the latter governed COELE-SYRIA and PHOENICIA under ANTIOCHUS Epiphanes (2 Macc. 4:4 [by emendation from the Latin] and 21). Some think this Apollonius may be the same as an official of SELEUCUS IV mentioned by Polybius (*Hist.* 31.13.2–3).

Meni muh-nee′ (מְנִי *H4972*, from מָנָה *H4948*, "to count, consign"). The name of a pagan deity mentioned in Isa. 65:11, "But as for you who forsake the LORD / and forget my holy mountain, / who spread a table for Fortune [Gad] / and fill bowls of mixed wine for Destiny [Meni]." (The KJV renders the names as common nouns, respectively "troop" and "number.") See GAD (DEITY). In the rites referred to in this verse a table was spread, furnished with food as a meal for the gods. With a wordplay, the next verse says, "I will destine [Heb. *māniti*] you for the sword." Gad and Meni were worshiped by apostate Jews. It is possible that they were Babylonian deities, but the evidence points to W Asia as the natural environment of this cult. (See *DDD*, 566–68.)

S. BARABAS

Menna men′uh (Μεννά *G3527*). Son of Mattatha, included in Luke's GENEALOGY OF JESUS CHRIST (Lk. 3:31; KJV, "Menan").

menorah muh-nor′uh. See CANDLESTICK, GOLDEN.

Menuchah, Menuhah min-yoo′hah. See NOHAH #2.

Menuhoth min-yoo′hoth (מְנֻחוֹת, "resting places"). A clan descended from CALEB through HUR (1 Chr. 2:52 NRSV). The name is probably a variant of MANAHATHITES (v. 54; see *ABD*, 4:695–96).

Meonenim, plain of mee-on′uh-nim (מְעוֹנְנִים, from עָנַן *H6726*, "to practice soothsaying"). A place mentioned once in the KJV (Jdg. 9:37). However, the reference is probably to a tree. See DIVINERS' OAK.

Meonothai mee-on′oh-thi (מְעוֹנֹתַי *H5065*, "my dwellings"). Son of OTHNIEL, nephew of CALEB, descendant of JUDAH, and father of OPHRAH (1 Chr. 4:13–14). The MT lacks the name Meonothai in v. 13, but the context seems to require it, and most versions supply it on the basis of the Lucianic recension of the SEPTUAGINT as well as the VULGATE.

Mephaath mi fay′ath (מֵיפַעַת *H4789*, possibly "shining, radiant"). A town within the tribal territory of REUBEN, listed between KEDEMOTH and KIRIATHAIM (Josh. 13:18); it became a Levitical city assigned to the descendants of MERAR (Josh. 21:37; 1 Chr. 6:79). Apparently it was later conquered by MOAB (Jer. 48:21). The location of Mephaath is uncertain. Proposed identifications include modern Tell Jawah (c. 6 mi. S of Amman), Khirbet Nefaʿah (c. 5 mi. S of Amman), and Umm er-Rasas (c. 18 mi. SE of MEDEBA). A medieval church in the latter site contains a Mosaic with the name Kastron Mefaa (see *ABD*, 4:696).

Mephibosheth mi-fib′oh-sheth (מְפִיבֹשֶׁת *H5136*, "from the mouth of shame"; apparently a deliberate scribal distortion of מְרִיב בַּעַל *H5311* [1 Chr. 8:34; 9:40]; see MERIB-BAAL). **(1)** Son of SAUL by his concubine RIZPAH (2 Sam. 21:8). Saul had tried to exterminate the Gibeonites (21:2), who had tricked JOSHUA into a pledge of protection when Israel had invaded Palestine (Josh. 9; see GIBEON). In answer to DAVID's offer to atone for Saul's bloody deed in order to secure the Gibeonites' blessing on Israel, they demanded the hanging of seven of Saul's sons (2 Sam. 21:3–6). This Mephibosheth was one of the seven (21:8). Possibly his original name was Mephibaal; see #2 below.

(2) Son of JONATHAN and grandson of Saul (2 Sam. 4:4). In the Chronicler's genealogies he is called MERIB-BAAL (1 Chr. 8:34; 9:40), probably his original name (and perhaps also the original name of #1 above). When the name BAAL (meaning "lord") took on pagan associations, the scribes apparently substituted it with the word *bōšet* H1425, meaning "shame" (see ISH-BOSHETH). Why the first element of the name was also changed (from "Merib" to "Mephi") is unexplained; some attribute it to a confusion with the name of Saul's son, which may have originally been "Mephibaal."

When Mephibosheth was five years old, both his father and grandfather were killed at GILBOA (2 Sam. 1:4; 1 Chr. 10). His nurse, hearing of the defeat and fearful of the advancing PHILISTINES, fled with the boy in such haste as to occasion a crippling fall, leaving him lame in both feet. This began a train of sorrows to which the young prince was heir during his melancholy life.

In GILEAD, at LO DEBAR, Mephibosheth found refuge with MAKIR (2 Sam. 9:4). Through ZIBA, a prosperous former steward in Saul's house, David learned that a son of Jonathan was living (v. 3). Summoned to Jerusalem by David, Mephibosheth (with his son Mica) ate at the king's table continually (v. 12). Saul's estate was given to Mephibosheth; and Ziba and his household were made steward and servants to him.

When, on the occasion of ABSALOM's rebellion, David fled from his capital (2 Sam. 15), Ziba met his company at the MOUNT OF OLIVES with provisions (16:1). Ziba reported that Mephibosheth had remained in Jerusalem in hope of kingship. David seems to have been dubious; but he forthwith consigned Mephibosheth's property to the informant (16:1–4). After Absalom's rebellion was quashed, David challenged Mephibosheth's loyalty, but the latter alleged that Ziba had slandered him. And his sincere grief, as shown in his unkempt appearance since David's flight, lent credence to his good faith (see 19:24–30). David cut the knot by dividing the land between Mephibosheth and Ziba (19:29). Later he spared Mephibosheth's life (21:7).

R. F. GRIBBLE

Merab mee´rab (מֵרָב H5266, possibly "abundance" or "chief"). Older daughter of king SAUL (1 Sam. 14:49). Merab was promised to DAVID (18:17), but when the time came for David to marry the girl, for some unknown reason she was given to ADRIEL the Meholathite (v. 19). It seems likely that the reason lay in Saul's neurotic behavior in all his dealings with his rival David. Merab bore five sons to Adriel (2 Sam. 21:8, where the MT, surely by mistake, has MICHAL, the name of Saul's younger daughter; most modern versions read Merab, following some Heb. and Gk. MSS).

E. B. SMICK

Meraiah mi-ray´yuh (מְרָיָה H5316, perhaps short form of אֲמַרְיָה H618, "Yahweh has said" [see AMARIAH], or derived from מָרָה H5286, "to be stubborn" [see MERAIOTH]). The head of the priestly family of Seraiah in the time of the high priest JOIAKIM (Neh. 12:12). EZRA belonged to the same family (Ezra 7:1).

Meraimoth mi-ray´moth (Lat. *Marimoth*). Son of Arna and ancestor of ZADOK and EZRA (2 Esd. 1:2; KJV, "Marimoth"; RSV, "Meraioth"). See MERAIOTH.

Meraioth mi-ray´yoth (מְרָיוֹת H5318; possibly "obstinate"). **(1)** Son of Zerahiah, descendant of LEVI through ELEAZAR, and ancestor of ZADOK and EZRA (1 Chr. 6:6–7, 52; Ezra 7:3; cf 2 Esd. 1:2 RSV [KJV, "Marimoth"; NRSV, "Meraimoth"]).

(2) Son of AHITUB and ancestor of Azariah and Seraiah; the latter two had supervisory responsibilities in "the house of God" (1 Chr. 9:11; Neh. 11:11).

(3) A priestly family in the days of the high priest JOIAKIM (Neh. 12:15 KJV and other versions, following MT; the NIV, on the basis of some Gk. MSS, reads MEREMOTH, as in v. 3).

Meran mer´uhn KJV Apoc. form of MERRAN (Bar. 3:23).

Merari mi-rah´ri (מְרָרִי H5356, "bitter" or "strong" or "blessing"; see C. H. Gordon, *Ugaritic Textbook* [1965], no. 1556, and L. Kutler in *UF* 16 [1984]: 111–18; the same form [מְרָרִי H5357] is used as a gentilic, "Merarite," in Num. 26:57 and perhaps elsewhere). **(1)** Third son of LEVI and eponymous ancestor of the Merarites, an important Levitical family (Gen. 46:11; Exod. 6:16; 1 Chr. 6:16). He had two sons, MAHLI and MUSHI (Exod. 6:19;

1 Chr. 6:19; 23:21). The clans of the Mahlites and Mushites (Num. 3:20, 33; 26:58) were charged with carrying the frames, the bars, pillars, bases, and accessories of the TABERNACLE (3:36–37; 4:31–33; 7:8; 10:17; Josh. 21:7, 34, 40). After the conquest, the Merarites were allotted twelve Levitical towns from the tribes of Reuben, Gad, and Zebulun (Josh. 21:7, 34–40; 1 Chr. 6:63, 77–81). Numerous references to Merari's family in the Chronicles show their importance as workers in the TEMPLE in late OT times (1 Chr. 6; 9; 15; 23; 24; 26; 2 Chr. 29; 34; cf. also Ezra 8:19).

(2) Son of Ox and father of JUDITH (Jdt. 8:1; 16:6). E. B. SMICK

Merathaim mer′uh-thay′im (מְרָתַיִם *H5361*, dual [emphatic?] form derived from מָרָה *H5286*, "to be obstinate"). A symbolic name for BABYLON in Jer. 50:21. Meaning something like "doubly bitter" or "twice rebellious," the name appears to be a wordplay on *nār marratum* ("bitter river"), a large lagoon or marshy area formed by the convergence of the TIGRIS and EUPHRATES in S Babylonia. See also PEKOD.

merchandise. The goods or wares that are bought and sold in business. This term is used variously in the English versions to render a variety of terms, such as Hebrew *meker H4836* (Neh. 13:16) and ʿ*izbônîm H6442* (Ezek. 27:12 and several other times in this chapter, along with its synonym *maʿărāb H5114*, "goods for barter," rendered "wares" by NIV but "merchandise" by NRSV, v. 13 et al.). The KJV uses the term a few times in the NT to render, for example, Greek *emporia G1865*, "business" (Matt. 22:5) and *gomos G1203*, "cargo" (Rev. 18:11–12). See also MERCHANT; TRADE, COMMERCE, AND BUSINESS.

merchant. A trader; someone who buys and sells commodities for profit. The participle of the Hebrew verb *sāḥar H6086* is used fifteen times, chiefly of international merchants (e.g., Gen. 37:28; Prov. 31:14), whereas the participle of *rākal H8217*, which occurs with similar frequency, seems to be a more general term (Neh. 3:31; Ezek. 17:4; Nah. 3:16). The term *kĕnaʿănî H1050* means "Canaanite," but a different word with the same form (*kĕnaʿănî H4051*) clearly refers to traders in at least two passages (Job 41:6; Prov. 31:24; possibly also Zech. 14:21); note also *kĕnaʿan H4047* (Ezek. 16:29; 17:4; Hos. 12:7; Zeph. 1:11) and *kinʿān H4048* (Isa. 23:8). The Canaanites, and in particular the Phoenicians, were so famous for their trading that the name for the inhabitants of Canaan took on this additional meaning (see CANAAN; PHOENICIA).

In NEHEMIAH's time different classes of merchants had their own quarters in Jerusalem. Thus

In NT times, merchandise shipped into Palestine was temporarily stored in vaults like these at Caesarea.

goldsmiths and grocers had one location, and fishmongers another (Neh. 3:32; 13:16). The NT makes reference to merchants (Gk. *emporos G1867*) in a parable of Jesus and several times in Revelation (Matt. 13:45; Rev. 18:3 et al.). See also TRADE, COMMERCE, AND BUSINESS.   J. L. KELSO

Mercurius muhr-kyoor´ee-uhs. That is, Mercury. KJV rendering of Greek *Hermēs G2259* (Acts 14:12). See HERMES (DEITY).

Statuette of Mercury, the messenger god.

mercy. Compassion or leniency shown to another, especially an offender.

I. Definition. Present usage identifies mercy with COMPASSION, in the sense of a willingness to forgive an offender or adversary and, more generally, a disposition to spare or help another. This disposition, although inwardly felt, manifests itself outwardly in some kind of action. It is evident that mercy combines a strong emotional element, usually identified as pity, compassion, or LOVE, with some practical demonstration of KINDNESS in response to the condition or needs of the object of mercy. In defining the word *mercy*, as employed by various English versions, one must consider a variety of Hebrew and Greek terms. Such a consideration will not only illuminate the richness of mercy vocabulary, but will also demonstrate something of the difficulty experienced by translations in past attempts at uniformity in handling the subject.

II. Mercy in the OT. The most common Hebrew words expressing the idea of mercy are the verb *rāḥam H8163*, "to show mercy, have compassion" (1 Ki. 8:50 et al.) and the noun *raḥămîm H8171*, an intensive plural form meaning "love, compassion" (Gen. 43:14 et al.). These terms are apparently derived from the noun *reḥem H8167*, "womb" (e.g., Gen. 49:25), which probably could be used metaphorically in a sense approaching that of "heart" (cf. Job 24:20). Thus the term *raḥămîm* could be used with the verb *kāmar H4023* (niphal), "to be agitated, stirred" (possibly "to become warm, tender") to indicate the arousal of the feelings of the heart (Gen. 43:30 [KJV, "his bowels did yearn"]; 1 Ki. 3:26; Hos. 11:8).

As a denominative piel verb, *rāḥam* can describe the attitude of God in response to the misery of his people (2 Ki. 13:23, where it is based both on their condition and on God's remembrance of his covenant), or simply the sovereign attitude of God in response to his will (Exod. 33:19, with which cf. Rom. 9:15). When a person is the subject, this physically felt emotion most naturally expresses itself in the context of family or fraternal ties. It is the expected reaction of a mother toward her sucking child (Isa. 49:15), of a father toward his dear son (Jer. 31:20), of a lover toward his betrothed (Hos. 2:23 [MT v. 25]). Where no such tie exists, as in the case of a conqueror who shows compassion toward the conquered, the Bible uniformly attributes the real motivation to God, whose action behind the scenes creates compassion in an otherwise uncompassionate individual (cf. Isa. 13:18; Jer. 6:23; 21:7; cf. 1 Ki. 8:50; Jer. 42:12).

The noun *raḥămîm* indicates that emotion of pity, compassion, or love which is activated in each of the relationships noted above. It is a quality extended to the redeemed as one of Yahweh's benefits (Ps. 103:4), as well as a characteristic of God in light of which the rebellious may make their plea (Dan. 9:9). It is mercy that gives a covenant-believer hope for continued relationship with his God, and, in fact, it is this quality which the believer is commanded to exemplify in his relationships with others, particularly those in special need (Zech. 7:9–10). This latter prophetic commandment points back to the true cause of mercy, that is, the pitiable condition of the one in need.

A second Hebrew word, *ḥesed H2876*, is consistently rendered "mercy" by the KJV, but seldom by modern versions. The NRSV uses the phrase "steadfast love," a change reflecting widespread acceptance of the work of Nelson Glueck, whose 1927 dissertation argued that the Hebrew term was connected with COVENANT terminology (English trans., *Ḥesed in the Bible* [1967]; for a contrary view, see S. Romerowski in *VT* 60 [1990]: 89–103). Glueck sought to show that it included, at least in earlier material, the element of loyalty, devotion, or faithfulness to the demands of a covenant (Exod. 20:6; Josh. 2:12–14). In the later writings, however, it moves beyond this sense of obligation and is charged with an indefinable but clearly emotional content. This manifestation of kindness and goodness, compassion and sympathy, both as demonstrated by God (Jer. 3:13) and as required of human beings (Zech. 7:9), makes *ḥesed* almost indistinguishable from *raḥămîm* (in the last reference mentioned, they occur in parallel). See also LOVINGKINDNESS.

A third shade of meaning connected with the concept of mercy is seen in the Hebrew verb *ḥānan H2858*, "to be gracious, show mercy" (Pss. 57:1; 123:2–3; et al.). The root idea is found in the frequently used noun *ḥēn H2834*, "favor, grace, acceptance," often in the expression "find favor in the eyes of" (Gen. 6:8 et al.). Although it is still the condition of the suppliant to which appeal is made (cf. Job 19:21, where *ḥānan* is translated "Have pity on me"), the emphasis is on the success granted to the one in need. That such response is not limited to God is shown by biblical exhortations to show favor or be kind to the poor, the needy, widows, and orphans (Pss. 37:21, 26; 112:5; Prov. 14:21, 31; 19:17; 28:8, all in wisdom context). The sense of pitying or sparing is even more explicit in Deut. 7:2, where the Israelites are commanded, "Make no treaty covenant with them, and show them no mercy." See also GRACE.

Other Hebrew terms expressing the idea of mercy or compassion include the verbs *ḥûs H2571* and *ḥāmal H2798* (e.g., Jer. 13:14, where both occur in conjunction with *rāḥam*). (See further W. F. Lofthouse in *ZAW* 41 [1933]: 29–35; N. H. Snaith, *The Distinctive Ideas in the Old Testament* [1944], 95; W. L. Reed in *JBL* 73 [1954]: 36–41; A. R. Johnson in *Interpretationes ad Vetus Testamentum pertinentes Sigmundo Mowinckel* [1955], 100–112; W. Eichrodt, *Theology of the Old Testament* [1961], 1:232–39; *NIDOTTE*, 2:50–52, 174–75, 203–6, 211–18; 3:1093–95.)

III. Mercy in the NT. The common Greek term for "mercy," *eleos G1799*, is consistently used by the SEPTUAGINT to render Hebrew *ḥesed* (e.g., Gen. 24:12); its cognate verb, *eleeō G1796*, translates mainly *ḥānan* (Gen. 33:5), although in the prophets it is usually the rendering of *rāḥam* (piel, Hos. 1:6). Both of these Greek terms stand normally in the Gospels for compassion in a sense similar to that of *raḥămîm*. Matthew and Luke, in particular, present several kinds of human need, each with appeals to Jesus based on his mercy. Blind men cry for sight (Matt. 9:27; 20:30–31; Mk. 10:47–48; Lk. 18:38–39); a Canaanite woman appeals on behalf of her daughter (Matt. 15:22); a father seeks peace for his possessed son (Matt. 17:15); and ten lepers plead for their cleansing (Lk. 17:13). It is to the mercy, or compassion, of Abraham, that the rich man appeals (16:24), and it is that same attribute in the Good Samaritan which Jesus commends (10:37). It is perhaps this same kind of compassion for the needy that Jesus listed as one of "the more important matters of the law" so neglected by some PHARISEES (Matt. 23:23). By contrast, to be "merciful" (*eleēmōn G1798*) was to be a mark of the subject of Jesus' kingdom, as shown in the familiar BEATITUDE (5:7).

Mercy in the sense of *ḥesed* (insofar as this term may indicate the covenant faithfulness owed to one another in mutual relationships) is also found in the Gospels, especially in the uses of *eleos* employed in Mary's MAGNIFICAT (Lk. 1:50, 54) and in Zechariah's BENEDICTUS (1:72, 78). Such usage, however, is never seen as mere legal obligation. Rather, it is an internalizing of the obligations of the covenant, so strongly proclaimed in the prophetic KERYGMA (Hos. 6:6), that Jesus urged on the covenant people of his day (Matt. 9:13; 12:7). It was only as the Pharisees learned the true meaning of *ḥesed*, a meaning intimately connected with *raḥămim*, that they could accept the meeting of human need and a redemptive ministry to sinful human beings as the true fulfillment of covenant obligation.

In the Epistles, *eleos* has come to have almost the same meaning as *charis* **G5921**, "grace" (cf. the salutations, such as 1 Tim. 1:2; 2 Jn. 3; Jude 2). If there is a difference, it is probably that suggested by R. C. Trench (*Synonyms of the New Testament*, 9th ed. [1880], 163–64): the latter term is God's free grace extended to sinners as they are guilty, whereas *eleos* is God's love extended to them as they are miserable. Further, *eleos* is the active agent of God's love (Eph. 2:4); it reaches out to the disobedient (Rom. 11:32, but note the covenant context both here and in Rom. 9:15–16, 18, 23); it is the basis of special ministries or abilities (2 Cor. 4:1); and it enables the sinner to become a trusted saint (1 Cor. 7:25). Finally, mercy is that indispensable gift which is required on the final day for a person who must stand before a holy God (2 Tim. 1:18).

A less frequent word, *oiktirmos* **G3880**, is normally the LXX rendering of *raḥămim* and conveys the same sense. Under the influence of the Hebrew term, the Greek almost always occurs in the plural both in the LXX and in the NT (e.g., referring to God's concerns, Rom. 12:1; 2 Cor. 1:3). The verbal form *oiktirō* **G3882** is used in the NT only once and as part of an OT quotation, where it is obviously parallel to *eleeō* (Rom. 9:15, citing Exod. 3:19). When applied to human emotions, the plural *oiktirmoi* clearly shows the same physical seat of deep concern that was noted earlier in *raḥămim*, a thought especially evident in its relationship to *splanchna* (pl. of *splanchnon* **G5073**), meaning "the inward parts" (KJV, BOWELS) as the seat of the affections (Col. 3:12; Phil. 2:1; in the latter passage the two terms probably form a hendiadys and thus the construction corresponds to that of the Colossians passage). It should be added that in the NT the notion of divine mercy is often expressed by other concepts, such as ATONEMENT and FORGIVENESS. (See further C. H. Dodd, *The Bible and the Greeks* [1954], 55–69; *TDNT*, 2:477–87; 5:159–61; *NIDNTT*, 2:593–601.)

IV. Summary. Mercy in biblical usage, therefore, is many-faceted. Basic to the concept is God's care for human beings in their wretchedness and creatureliness. This emotionally based response manifests itself in his redemptive acts. The person responding to God sees in himself one who has received mercy; therefore he in turn must show mercy to others.

C. E. ARMERDING

mercy seat. Traditional rendering of Hebrew *kappōret* **H4114** (from the verb *kāpar* **H4105** piel, "to cover [sin], make atonement, effect reconciliation"). Specifically the term refers to the lid or gold plate measuring 2.5 by 1.5 cubits (approx. 3.75 x 2.25 ft.) covering the ARK OF THE COVENANT. Resting on top of this plate were two CHERUBIM placed facing each other with outspread wings (Exod. 25:17, 22). The Hebrew word is best rendered "propitiatory." The paraphrase "mercy seat" by Tyndale was adopted from Luther's rendering (*Gnadenstuhl*, apparently on the basis of the Gk. and Lat. versions; see Martin Noth, *Das Zweite Buch Moses in das Alte Testament Deutsch* [1959], 164–67; cf. English trans., *Exodus* [1962], 204). Even though the word refers to a lid, it is quite apparent from the Levitical ritual on the Day of Atonement that its meaning preserves the idea of PROPITIATION (cf. also the LXX rendering *hilastērion* **G2663**, also used

Model showing the position of the mercy seat in the tabernacle.

in Heb. 9:5). The NIV appropriately translates "atonement cover." See also ATONEMENT; ATONEMENT, DAY OF.

The mercy seat seems to be the nearest approximation of the presence of God among the Israelites. They were not permitted to make a material representation of God. The pillar of cloud by day and the pillar of fire by night, which represented God's presence among them, hovered over the mercy seat where the high priest sprinkled the blood for the congregation of Israel on the Day of Atonement (see PILLAR OF FIRE AND CLOUD). Apparently it was not the lid or the cherubim but the space between the cherubim that represented God's presence among them. This space could not be confined nor controlled by man. In this manner the mercy seat conveyed to the Israelites, without a material representation, the idea that God was in their midst. — S. J. SCHULTZ

Mered mee'rid (מֶרֶד *H5279*, "rebellious" or "daring"). Son of Ezrah, included in the genealogy of JUDAH (1 Chr. 4:17–18). Mered had two wives, one of them an unnamed Judean woman, and the other an Egyptian named BITHIAH, who is described as "Pharaoh's daughter." Each of his wives bore him three children.

Meremoth mer'uh-moth (מְרֵמוֹת *H5329*, derivation uncertain). **(1)** Son of Uriah; he was a priest commissioned to handle "the silver and gold and the sacred articles" that EZRA brought to Jerusalem (Ezra 8:33; 1 Esd. 8:62 [KJV, "Marmoth"]). He may be the same Meremoth—also described as son of Uriah (and grandson of Hakkoz), but not called a priest—who repaired a section of the wall adjacent to the house of Eliashib and a section next to the Fish Gate (Neh. 3:4, 21). This identification, however, seems to be at odds with the information that the descendants of Hakkoz were unable to find their names in the genealogical records and thus were excluded from the priesthood (Ezra 2:61–62; Neh. 7:63–64). Such an identification, moreover, may indicate that the chronological order of Ezra and NEHEMIAH should be reversed. Some scholars thus argue that the Meremoth who helped repair the wall was a different person, possibly a layman. (See E. Yamauchi in *EBC*, 4:584; cf. also the discussion by R. H. Shearer in *ABD*, 4:699–700.)

(2) A priest (or priestly family) who returned from Babylon with ZERUBBABEL (Neh. 12:3). Later, in the days of the high priest JOIAKIM, the head of Meremoth's family was Helkai (v. 15 NIV, following some Gk. MSS; the MT has MERAIOTH).

(3) One of the priests who sealed Nehemiah's covenant (Neh. 10:5); he is probably to be identified with #1 or #2 above.

(4) One of the descendants of Bani who agreed to put away their foreign wives (Ezra 10:36).
— E. B. SMICK

Merenptah muhr'enp-tah'. Variant form of MERNEPTAH.

Meres mee'reez (מֶרֶס *H5332*, meaning uncertain). One of "the seven nobles of Persia and Media who had special access to the king and were highest in the kingdom" (Esth. 1:14). Queen VASHTI was banished by Ahasuerus (XERXES) on their advice.

Meribah mer'i-bah (מְרִיבָה *H5313*, "contention"). A name applied to two different places where water was brought miraculously from rock to satisfy thirsty Israelites in the wilderness. The first place, which bears the double name "Massah and Meribah," was near REPHIDIM and Mount HOREB in the Desert of SINAI, and the incident took place when Israel was less than two months out of Egypt (Exod. 17:7; the names Massah ["testing"] and Meribah ["contention"] are used in parallelism in Deut. 33:8 and Ps. 95:8). Another incident took place in S Palestine at KADESH BARNEA nearly thirty-nine years later; this place is referred to as "the waters of Meribah" (Num. 20:13, 24; Pss. 81:7; 106:32) or "the waters of Meribah Kadesh" (Num. 27:14; Deut. 32:51; Ezek. 47:19; 48:28; NRSV, "Meribath-kadesh"). See discussion under MASSAH.

Meribath-kadesh mer'i-buhth-kay'dish. See MERIBAH.

Merib-Baal mer'ib-bay'uhl (מְרִיב בַּעַל *H5311* [also מְרִי־בַעַל, 1 Chr. 9:40b], possibly "Baal is [my] contender [*or* advocate]"; but see other suggestions in J. D. Fowler, *Theophoric Personal Names in*

Ancient Hebrew [1988], 61). Son of Jonathan and grandson of Saul (1 Chr. 8:34; 9:40). See Mephibosheth #2.

Merkabah mysticism muhr´kuh-buh. Also Merkavah. A form of Jewish speculation that focused on God's throne as a chariot ascending into heaven (from Heb. *merkābâ H5324*, "chariot"). It was in part derived from Ezekiel's vision of the cloud of fire, the four living creatures, and the four wheels (Ezek. 1). Merkabah mysticism is the subject of various rabbinic esoteric writings, particularly the Hekhalot (heavenly palaces) literature, including *3 Enoch* (for the latter, see *OTP*, 1:229–53). It influenced the later Kabbalah, a medieval theosophy. (See D. J. Halperin, *The Merkabah in Rabbinic Literature* [1980]; H. L. Strack and G. Stemberger, *Introduction to the Talmud and Midrash* [1992], 374–82.)

Merneptah muhr´nep-tah´. Also Merenptah (and other spellings). Son and successor of Ramses II. Although not mentioned in the OT, Merneptah is of significance for biblical studies. He ascended the throne of Egypt when he was around sixty years old, c. 1224 (or 1213) B.C., and ruled ten years. Accordingly, some scholars who adopt a very late date for the Israelite exodus have regarded Merneptah as the pharaoh who ruled Egypt at the time of this event. See exodus, the. His mortuary temple, on the W bank at Thebes, not far from the Rameseum, is in ruins, but W. M. F. Petrie recovered many artistic and structural elements of it. The most famous object found there is a large granite stela, originally of Amenhotep III but reused by Merneptah and dated to the latter's fifth year. This monument is often referred to as the Israel Stela because it mentions several victories in Canaan, including the claim: "Israel is laid waste; his seed is not" (*ANET*, 376–78; see G. Ahlström and D. Edelman in *JNES* 44 [1985]: 59–61; M. G. Hasel in *The Near East in the Southwest: Essays in Honor of William G. Dever*, ed. B. A. Nakhai, AASOR 58 [2003], 19–44). According to most scholars, this statement requires that the Israelites had occupied Palestine prior to the accession of Merneptah. During his reign, Merneptah faced and repelled a Libyan invasion. His mummy, which has been

The Merneptah Stela, also known as the "Israel Stela" (from Thebes, c. 1230 B.C.). The inscription is a poetic eulogy of Merneptah's victories and includes the statement, "Israel is laid waste; his seed is not."

recovered, shows that he had been in very poor health during the last years of his life (see J. Harris and K. Weeks, *X-Raying the Pharaohs* [1973], 157).

C. E. DeVries

Merodach mi-roh´dak (מְרֹדָךְ *H5281*). Hebrew form of Akkadian Marduk, the Babylonian god (Jer. 50:2 KJV and other versions). Merodach is the divine element in the names Evil-Merodach (2 Ki. 25:27; Jer. 52:31), Merodach-Baladan (2 Ki. 20:12; Isa. 39:1), and possibly Mordecai (Ezra 2:2 et al.).

Merodach-Baladan mi-roh´dak-bal´uh-duhn (בְּרֹאדַךְ בַּלְאֲדָן *H5282* [מְרֹדַךְ־בַּלְאֲדָן] in 2 Ki. 20:12], from Akk. *Marduk-apla-iddin[na]*, "Marduk has given a son," the name also of a 12th-cent. B.C. Kassite king). TNIV Marduk-Baladan. A Babylonian king at the time of King HEZEKIAH of Judah (2 Ki. 20:12 [KJV, "Berodach-baladan"]; Isa. 39:1). According to the biblical record, Merodach-Baladan sent an embassy to Hezekiah when the latter was sick, although probably his real motive was to encourage revolt against ASSYRIA. The prophet ISAIAH opposed and frustrated this plan, and the Babylonians themselves forestalled the plot by setting up Marduk-zākiršumi as king in 703 B.C.

Merodach-Baladan claimed descent from Eriba-Marduk, king of Babylon c. 800 B.C., and was first mentioned in the inscriptions of TIGLATH-PILESER III, king of Assyria. When the latter entered BABYLON in 731, Merodach-Baladan brought gifts to him and supported the Assyrians. In 721, under the rule of another Assyrian king, SARGON II, Merodach-Baladan usurped the Babylonian throne. Although the Assyrians reacted, Merodach-Baladan stayed on the throne until 710, when Sargon entered Babylon unopposed. Even then, he remained as local ruler and did not oppose Sargon during the rest of his reign.

After the death of Sargon, Merodach-Baladan again revolted and ruled for a short period in 703, but when SENNACHERIB seized Babylon, he retreated to his homeland. Sennacherib defeated the rebels and entered Babylon, where he placed Bel-ibni on the throne. Eventually this throne was occupied by Sennacherib's son, Ashur-nadin-shumi. When Sennacherib attacked the coastal cities of ELAM, where Merodach-Baladan had fled, no mention was made of him, but his son Nabushumishkun was taken prisoner by Sennacherib in the battle of Halulê. Merodach-Baladan died in Elam before Sennacherib entered the area in 694. This Babylonian king is remembered as a clever and ambitious ruler who bitterly opposed the influence of Assyria in Babylon. (See J. A. Brinkman in *Studies Presented to A. Leo Oppenheim*, ed. R. D. Biggs and J. A. Brinkman [1964], 6–53; G. Roux, *Ancient Iraq* [1964], 258–66; J. A. Brinkman in *CAH* 3/2, 2nd ed. [1991], 1–70, esp. 15–35.)   L. WALKER

Merom, Waters of mee'rom (מֵרוֹם *H5295*, "high place"). A place near which the Israelites defeated the combined forces of the kings of GALILEE (Josh. 11:5, 7). Merom was most certainly a town in Upper Galilee, as evidenced by the ancient extra-biblical sources. THUTMOSE III's list of Galilean towns included *mrmʾim* (no. 85). In a series of reliefs from the eighth year of RAMSES II, *mrm* is associated with the mountain of BETH ANATH and KANAH (of Asher), all of which are in Upper Galilee. During his campaign in the same region TIGLATH-PILESER II (733 B.C.) conquered a place called Marum (*ANET*, 283b).

EUSEBIUS seems unaware of the real location for Merom. His allusion (*Onom.* 128.4–6, 12–13) to a village called *Merrous* 12 Rom. mi. from Sebaste (SAMARIA) near Dothaim (DOTHAN) probably is nothing but a remark made in passing. The view of H. Reland (*Palaestine ex monumentis veteribus illustrata* [1714], 261–64) that the Waters of Merom are to be identified with Lake Hula has nothing to commend it. This lake was known in Roman times as *Semechōnitis* (Jos. *War* 3.10.7 §515 et al.; cf. *smkw*, *y. Kil.* 9:32c [bottom], and *sybky*, *y. B. Bat.* 5:15a). It was renowned as one of the seven lakes of the Holy Land and further identified as *ymʾ dḥwltʾ*, "The Lake of Ḥulta" (*y. Kil.* 9:32), after the valley region to the N of the lake. This latter was called *Oulatha* by Josephus (*Ant.* 15.10.3 §360), and the name was preserved until modern times in the Arabic, Baḥeiret el-Ḥuleh.

The generally accepted identification of Merom with the village of Meirun at the foot of the Jebel Jarmaq also has its problems. The place was an important center in NT times, and later, under the name *myrwn*, was well known for its excellent olive oil (*y. Šebiʿit* 9:38b [bottom]). Josephus claims to have fortified it against the impending Roman attack on Galilee (mentioned by him under various names, e.g. *Amrōth*, *Life* 37 §188]; *Mērō*, *War* 2.20.6 §573). Elsewhere he reckoned it as the western limit of Upper Galilee (*Mērōth*, *War* 3.3.1 §40). It is possible that Josephus is referring to this same town when he places Joshua's victory at *Bērōthē*, "a city of the upper Galilee, not far from Kadesh, another place in the Galilee region" (*Ant.* 5.1.18 §63), but it is far from certain.

After the destruction of the temple in A.D. 70, Meirun (Meiron) became the home of priests from the course of JEHOIARIB (*t. Demai* 4:13; cf. 1 Chr. 24:7). The ruins of an ancient synagogue, various important rabbinic burials, and abundant Hellenistic-Roman pottery attest to the authenticity of Meirun as an important town of the early centuries of our era. M. Avi-Yonah, however, doubts that Josephus is referring to this Meirun; he now holds that the Meirun of Roman times was near Marun er-Ras (*The Holy Land* [1966], 133). If Josephus is excluded, then the earliest recorded suggestion to equate Meirun with the biblical Merom is evidently that of Rabbi Tanhum Yerushalmi in his 13th-cent. commentary (see Josh. 11:5). W. F. Albright (*BASOR* 35 [Oct. 1929]: 8) found Late Bronze and Early Iron sherds on the slopes below the synagogue ruins and thus accepted the identification of Meirun as Merom. But J. Garstang (*Joshua-Judges* [1931], 183–98) rightly observed that all roads leading into Upper Galilee met at Bint Umm el-Jebeil near the foot of Jebel Marun. On this mountain stands the village of Marun er-Ras.

Y. Aharoni (*The Land of the Bible: A Historical Geography*, rev. ed. [1979], 225–26) has proposed to identify the biblical Merom with Tell el-Khirbeh, an impressive site S of Marun er-Ras on the Israel-Lebanon border. The Waters of Merom may be identified either with the perennial spring at the foot of the tell or, what is more likely, with the numerous wells in the several branches of the Wadi Farʿah.

One of the rulers called out to join the king of HAZOR was, according to the Hebrew text, the king of MADON (Josh. 11:1; 12:19). Scholars have usually identified that town with Khirbet Madin on the southern slope of Qarn Ḥaṭṭin (Horns of Hattin). However, the SEPTUAGINT reads *Marrōn* in 11:1, and it certainly would be strange if the king of Merom was not present at that battle. The name is missing in the LXX of 12:19, but cf. v. 20 and see SHIMRON (PLACE). Furthermore, B. Mazar (in *Yerushalayim* 4 [1952]: 13–20 [Heb.]) has presented arguments for identifying the impressive Bronze and Iron Age ruins on Qarn Ḥaṭṭin with the *šmš-ʾtm*, "Shemesh-Adam," of Amenhotep II's inscription. (Some identify Meron itself with Qarn Ḥaṭṭin.)

The fixing of Merom in the vicinity of Jebel Marun harmonizes nicely with all of the sources in which the city is mentioned and provides a reasonable topographical explanation for Joshua's battle. First of all, Merom is situated on the main road from ACCO, via GATH (perhaps Thutmose II's no. 93 and/or the "Gath-asher" of two topographical lists from the time of Ramses II) and Tell er-Ruweisa (possibly BETH SHEMESH of Naphtali, Josh. 19:38; Jdg. 1:33), to KADESH of Galilee. The respective columns of Ramses II and Tiglath-Pileser would have passed this way, the former going N, the latter S. The king of ACSHAPH must certainly have come up this way from the plain of Acco to Merom.

It also is understandable why the Canaanites fled after their defeat, not toward Acco but rather to MISREPHOTH MAIM. The Israelites had cut off the route between Merom and the southern portion of the plain of Acco when they came up to make their attack; therefore, the Canaanites were forced to retreat due westward by way of Iqrit and Abdon to the coast. Apparently, the Israelites also had blocked the northeasterly route to Kadesh and thence to Hazor, so that some of the defeated enemies had to retreat due N. These latter fugitives split up near BETH ANATH, part of them going NE to the MIZPAH Valley and the rest turning NW toward TYRE and SIDON. Tell el-Khirbeh was a strong Canaanite fort on the S boundary of Canaanite Galilee. It was the logical point at which to assemble if one wanted to curb the Israelite advance northward. It also was a natural meeting place for the allies coming from the plain of Acco and from Hazor.

As a result of Joshua's victory, the Israelites were able to conquer the cities whose kings fell at Merom, and none of these towns appears in the list of unconquered towns in Jdg. 1. All of them except Merom appear among the towns assigned to the northern tribes in the book of Joshua. (See further A. Neubauer, *La géographie du Talmud* [1868], 228–30; W. Oehlers in *ZDPV* 28 [1905]: 49–74; G. Dalman in *ZDPV* 29 [1906]: 195–99; S. Klein, *Beiträge zur Geographie und Geschichte Galiläas* [1909], 23–25; G. A. Smith, *The Historical Geography of the Holy Land*, 25th ed. [1931], 425, 480 n. 5.)
A. F. RAINEY

Meron mee´ron. See SHIMRON.

Meronoth mi-ron´oth. See MERONOTHITE.

Meronothite mi-ron´oh-thit (מְרֹנֹתִי *H5331*, gentilic of the unattested name מְרֹנֹת). The designation of two men in the OT: JEHDEIAH, a member of DAVID's household (1 Chr. 27:30), and JADON, who helped NEHEMIAH repair the wall of Jerusalem

(Neh. 3:7; NIV, "of Meronoth"). The latter passage suggests that Meronoth was near GIBEON and that it was closely connected with (or perhaps even an alternate name for) MIZPAH, but the exact location is unconfirmed.

Meroz mee´roz (מֵרוֹז H5292, derivation uncertain). A place in or near the Valley of ESDRAELON. DEBORAH in her song of victory called a curse upon the town of Meroz for not sending help in the battle against SISERA (Jdg. 5:23). E. G. Kraeling suggests that Meroz was not Israelite but rather a "Canaanite city in a covenant obligation with a Hebrew tribe, probably that of Manasseh" (*Rand McNally Bible Atlas*, 2nd ed. [1962], 154). A Hebrew city would probably not have been cursed, since that implies extermination; but a Canaanite city would have had a problem fighting Canaanites. Although several identifications have been proposed, the location of Meroz is unknown; however, it must have been very near the scene of battle by the KISHON River.

E. B. SMICK

Merran mer´uhn (Μερραν). A place whose merchants are mentioned alongside those of TEMAN as people who "have not learned the way to wisdom" (Bar. 3:23; KJV "Meran"). Many scholars believe that the original Hebrew had *mdyn* (MIDIAN) and that the Greek translator misread the *d* as *r*.

Meruth mee´ruhth. KJV Apoc. variant of IMMER (1 Esd. 5:24).

Mesaloth mes´uh-loth (Μαισαλωθ). A town in ARBELA captured by BACCHIDES and ALCIMUS in their march on Judah (1 Macc. 9:2; KJV, "Masaloth"). The site is unknown.

Mesech mee´sik. KJV alternate form of MESHECH (only Ps. 120:5).

Mesha mee´shuh (מֵשָׁא H5392 [Gen. 10:30] and מֵישָׁא H4791 [1 Chr. 8:9], derivation uncertain; מֵישַׁע H4795 [2 Ki. 3:4] and מֵישָׁע H4796 [1 Chr. 2:42], "helper, savior"). **(1)** A place "in the east country" (prob. ARABIA) that, along with SEPHAR, served to delimit the territory occupied by the sons of JOKTAN, a descendant of SHEM through EBER (Gen. 10:30). Some have identified it with the MASSA of the Ishmaelite group (25:14).

(2) Firstborn son of CALEB and descendant of JUDAH (1 Chr. 2:42). The Hebrew text is difficult. See MARESHAH (PERSON).

(3) Son of SHAHARAIM and descendant of BENJAMIN; a family head (1 Chr. 8:9). Mesha was one of seven children that were born to Shaharaim in MOAB by his wife HODESH after he had divorced Hushim and Baara (v. 8).

(4) King of MOAB during the days of AHAB and his sons (2 Ki. 3:4, which also describes Mesha as a sheep breeder). In the famous MOABITE STONE, Mesha identifies himself as a Dibonite (see DIBON) and as the son of Chemosh[-yat], and says that his father had reigned thirty years before him (*ANET*, 320; the component *-yat* is restored from a fragmentary inscription found in KERAK). See CHEMOSH.

From the time of DAVID (2 Sam. 8:2), Moab was subject to Israel until the divided kingdom, when several peoples including Moab rebelled. But the mighty OMRI of the N kingdom brought Moab again into subjection. After the country had been tributary to Israel for some forty years, the forceful King Mesha sought independence. The biblical record indicates that the tribute laid upon Mesha's people was exorbitant—an annual levy of 100,000 lambs and the wool of 100,000 rams (2 Ki. 3:4). The date of the successful coup presents some difficulties to the present-day reader. It is clear that Mesha's rebellion occurred after Ahab died. JOSEPHUS (*Ant.* 9.2.1) locates it "in the second year of Ahaziah," which could be correct.

According to Mesha's record on the Moabite Stone, it was after forty years of subjection to Israel, in the middle of the reign of Omri's son (Ahab), that deliverance was effected. According to biblical chronology, Ahab and Omri together reigned only thirty-four years. The forty years may be a magnification of Mesha's glory as deliverer; or it may be thought a round number; or Omri's "son" may have been his grandson, either AHAZIAH or Joram (see JEHORAM). Whatever the exact date of Mesha's rebellion, it was during the reign of Ahab's second son, Joram, that the attempt was made to recover Moab to Israel (see 2 Ki. 1:17; 3:5–6). (See further M. Noth, *History of Israel* [1960], 157, 244–45; M. Cogan and H. Tadmor, *II Kings*, AB 11 [1988], 50–52.)

of Joed (Neh. 11:7). Some scholars believe that one list or the other is in error. Given the genealogical and chronological discrepancies, it is possible that different people are meant. More likely, Sallu could be understood as an eponym or family name.

(6) Son of Shephatiah, listed among the Benjamites who resettled in Jerusalem (1 Chr. 9:8).

(7) Son of ZADOK and grandfather of AZARIAH; the latter is listed among the priests who resettled in Jerusalem and is described as "the official in charge of the house of God" (1 Chr. 9:11; Neh. 11:11 [the latter has SERAIAH instead of Azariah]). This Meshullam is probably the same as SHULLAM in the parallel lists (1 Chr. 6:12–13; Ezra 7:2).

(8) Son of Meshillemith and ancestor of Maasai; the latter is listed among the priests who resettled in Jerusalem (1 Chr. 9:12).

(9) A Levite descended from KOHATH who served as one of the overseers in repairing the house of the Lord during the reign of JOSIAH (2 Chr. 34:12).

(10) One of a group of leaders sent by EZRA to Iddo to get attendants for the house of God (Ezra 8:16; 1 Esd. 8:44 [KJV, "Mosollamon"]).

(11) One of the men who apparently challenged Ezra's instruction that those who had married foreign women should divorce them (Ezra 10:15; cf. 1 Esd. 9:14 [KJV, "Mosollam"]). The Hebrew text, however, can be understood differently. See discussion under JAHZEIAH.

(12) One of the descendants of Bani who agreed to put away their foreign wives (Ezra 10:29; called "Olamus" in the parallel passage, 1 Esd. 9:30).

(13) Son of Berekiah; he is mentioned as having made repairs to two sections of the wall of Jerusalem (Neh. 3:4, 30). Meshullam's daughter was given in marriage to Jehohanan son of TOBIAH, NEHEMIAH's opponent (6:18).

(14) Son of Besodiah; he and JOIADA son of Paseah repaired the Jeshanah Gate (Neh. 3:6). See OLD GATE.

(15) One of the prominent men who stood near EZRA when the law was read at the great assembly (Neh. 8:4; not mentioned in the parallel, 1 Esd. 9:44).

(16–17) The name of one of the priests and of one of the lay Israelite leaders who signed the covenant of Nehemiah (Neh. 10:7, 20). Perhaps either of these men should be identified with one of the individuals mentioned above.

(18–19) The name of two heads of priestly families (respectively the family of Ezra and the family of Ginnethon) in the time of the high priest JOIAKIM (Neh. 12:13, 16).

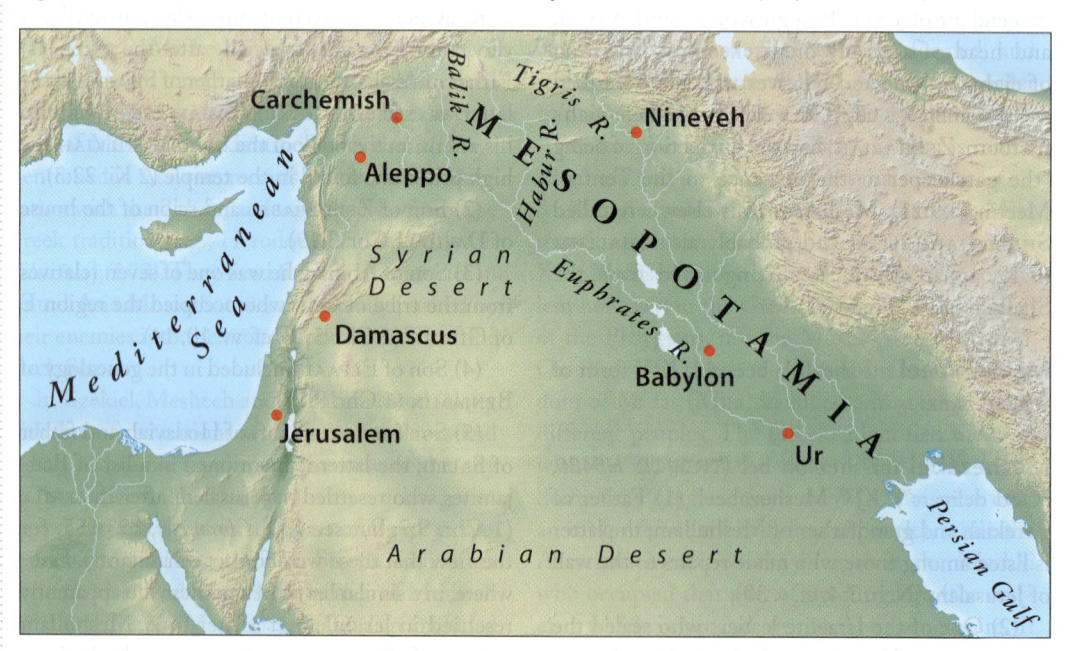

Mesopotamia.

Aerial view of the northern Euphrates River (looking E).

(20) One of the Levitical "gatekeepers who guarded the storerooms at the gates" (Neh. 12:25).

(21) A leader of Judah who took part in the procession at the dedication of the wall (Neh. 12:34). Perhaps he should be identified with #17 above.

C. P. Gray

Meshullemeth mi-shool´uh-mith (מְשֻׁלֶּמֶת *H5455*, fem. of Meshullam). Daughter of Haruz, from Jotbah; she was married to King Manasseh and gave birth to Amon (2 Ki. 21:19). If Jotbah was the town in Galilee later known as Jotapata, the marriage may have been arranged to strengthen ties with the northern kingdom; others think Jotbah was the same as Jotbathah, near the Gulf of Aqabah (consistent with the possibility that Haruz was an Arabic name), which would suggest an alliance with Arabs or Edomites (cf. M. Cogan and H. Tadmor, *II Kings*, AB 11 [1988], 275).

Mesobaite mi-soh´bay-it. KJV form of Mezobaite.

Mesopotamia mes´uh-puh-tay´mee-uh (Μεσοποταμία *G3544*, "between rivers," used by the LXX to render אֲרַם נַהֲרַיִם *H808*, "Aram of the [two] rivers," and פַּדַּן אֲרָם *H7020*, possibly "open country of Aram"). The land around and between the Tigris and Euphrates Rivers. This term is used in most English versions to render the name Aram Naharaim (Gen. 24:10; Deut. 23:4; Jdg. 3:8; 1 Chr. 19:6; Ps. 60 [title]). It occurs also in the KJV and RSV at Jdg. 3:10, where the Hebrew has only the name Aram; the context makes it clear, however, that this is the same place mentioned in v. 8. See Aram (country). Mesopotamia could refer to anything from modern Eastern Turkey to the Persian Gulf. When it is used in the Bible, usually the northern parts are understood.

According to Gen. 24:10, Abraham's servant went to Mesopotamia to find a wife for Isaac and came to the town of Nahor, a place mentioned in the Mari texts and located near the Balikh tributary of the Euphrates (see Nahor #3). Balaam's home town of Pethor of Mesopotamia (Deut. 23:4) is in the same vicinity.

The judgeship of Othniel was occasioned by the aggression and oppression of Cushan-Rishathaim, a king of Mesopotamia (Jdg. 3:8). The king's name has not yet been attested nor is any definition of his realm certain. Mesopotamia was the Ammonites' source of chariots and horsemen when they battled with David (1 Chr. 19:6–7). The context of the name Aram Naharaim in the title of Ps. 60 connects this passage with 2 Sam. 8:5.

Mesopotamia has gone under various names throughout its long history. In the beginning it was mostly SUMER in the extreme S, AKKAD in the middle, and Subartu in the NW. In the 2nd millennium B.C., BABYLON was the power in the lower half and Mitanni in the N. With the turn of the millennium, ASSYRIA in the N gained control of the whole but lost it again to Neo-Babylonia in 587 B.C. This was followed by the Persian, Hellenistic, and Roman rules. The Greek name occurs twice in the NT (Acts 2:9; 7:2). Today most of Mesopotamia is in Iraq, with small parts in Syria and Turkey.

(See further M. A. Beek, *Atlas of Mesopotamia* [1962]; A. L. Oppenheim, *Ancient Mesopotamia*, rev. ed. [1977]; G. Roux, *Ancient Iraq*, 3rd ed. [1992]; K. R. Nemet-Nejat, *Daily Life in Ancient Mesopotamia* [1998]; K. L. Younger, Jr., and M. W. Chavalas, eds., *Mesopotamia and the Bible: Comparative Explorations* [2002]; E. Ascalone, *Mesopotamia: Assyrians, Sumerians, Babylonians* [2007]; *ABD*, 4:714–77; *CANE*, 2:807–979.)

R. L. ALDEN

messenger. This English term is usually the rendering of Hebrew *mal'āk H4855* and Greek *angelos G34* or *apostolos G693* (see ANGEL; APOSTLE). It may refer to a bearer of news, as when JOB was told of the disasters that fell on his property and family (Job 1:13–19) or when DAVID was notified of ABSALOM's rebellion (2 Sam. 15:13). A messenger may be a bringer of requests, as from MOSES to the king of EDOM (Num. 20:14) or to SIHON (Num. 21:21; Deut. 2:26) to go through their country, or from David when his men asked toll from NABAL for having protected him (1 Sam. 25:14).

The messengers might be spies, as in JERICHO (Josh. 6:17, 25; cf. 2:1; Jas. 2:25); or they might summon, as when MICAIAH was ordered to appear before the kings (1 Ki. 22:13; 2 Chr. 18:12), or when men of war from several tribes were called to help GIDEON (Jdg. 6:35). Messengers also might be deputies, as from ELISHA to NAAMAN (2 Ki. 5:10), or from AHAB to kill Elisha (6:32). They might even be envoys, as from David to announce to the men of JABESH GILEAD his kingship (2 Sam. 2:5), or to threaten EIJLAH (1 Ki. 19:2), or to TIGLATH-PILESER to ask help of the Assyrian monarch (2 Ki. 16:7) or to So of Egypt from HOSHEA (2 Ki. 17:4). Such envoys were important (cf. Nah. 2:13), and a good one was refreshing (Prov. 25:13; cf. 13:17).

A messenger of God might be a teaching priest (Mal. 2:7). He is synonymous with a prophet in the summary of the divine appeal (2 Chr. 6:15–16), as was JOHN THE BAPTIST (Mal. 3:1 quoted in Matt. 11:10), though Christ is the messenger of the covenant (Mal. 3:1). A messenger might be an appointee of the churches, as in the collection for the Jerusalem saints (2 Cor. 8:23) or a church gift to the apostle (Phil. 4:18).

Occasionally, the term *messenger* is used metaphorically: "A king's wrath is a messenger of death" (Prov. 16:14), and PAUL's ailment was a "messenger of Satan" (2 Cor. 12:7).

W. G. BROWN

Messiah muh-si'uh (מָשִׁיחַ *H5431*, "anointed one," from מָשַׁח *H5417*, "to smear over, anoint"; almost always rendered by the LXX with χριστός *G5986*, a verbal adj. from χρίω *G5987*, "to rub, anoint"; the Gk. NT, in addition, uses twice the transliteration Μεσσίας *G3549* [Jn. 1:41; 4:25]). The KJV uses this term in only one passage in the OT (Dan. 9:25–26), and the variant form "Messias" in two NT passages that have the Greek transliteration *Messias* (Jn. 1:41; 4:25); the RSV and the NIV use "Messiah" only in the two verses in John. By contrast, the NRSV and the TNIV use the term over sixty times in the NT to render Greek *Christos*, presumably when the translators believe that this Greek word functions as a title (e.g., Matt. 1:1; Mk. 14:61; Lk. 2:11; Jn. 1:20; Acts 2:31; Rom. 9:5; Rev. 11:15); the rendering "Christ" is then reserved for the many passages where it functions as a name. Some other modern versions follow the same approach, although it is admittedly difficult to draw the distinction in many instances. It is sometimes argued that even the combination JESUS CHRIST should be rendered "Jesus the Messiah." An understanding of the term Messiah/Christ requires an appreciation for the cultic use of OIL in the ANE. See also ANOINT.

    I. The practice of anointing outside Israel
   II. The practice of anointing in Israel
   III. The anointing of priests
   IV. The anointing of kings
   V. Charismatic kingship

VI. The ideal king
VII. Messianic texts
VIII. The extracanonical literature
IX. Christ in the NT
   A. Son of Man
   B. Son of God
   C. Kyrios
   D. Jesus—Savior

I. The practice of anointing outside Israel. Oil played an important part in the ancient world. It was used for lighting, cooking, washing (as a substitute for soap), for cosmetic purposes; it could also serve as an expression of joy. Plato describes it as "beneficial to human hair and to the human body generally" (*Protagoras* 334 b-c). Oil also was used as a medicine and in religious rites. Sacred anointing was practiced on people as well as on objects: "To oil a cult object is one of the commonest acts of worship" (*OCD* [1949], 619; cf. J. G. Frazer, *The Golden Bough, Part 4: Adonis, Attis, Osiris*, 2nd ed. [1907], 31–32). The anointing of the statues of the gods was a common practice in Egypt, Babylon, Rome, and elsewhere. Such cultic acts served the purpose of cleansing, consecration, and veneration at the same time.

From the TELL EL-AMARNA tablets it would appear that PHARAOHS' viceroys received anointing on taking office (cf. tablet 51). Whether this applied to the pharaohs themselves cannot be established with any degree of certainty. That the pharaohs were anointed at certain solemn occasions is suggested by tablet 34: "I have sent ... good oil, to pour upon thy (head) whilst thou sittest upon the throne of thy kingdom." There is some indication that kings received anointing in their capacity as priests. J. G. Frazer has shown that priests used to be anointed at an installation ceremony (*The Golden Bough, Part 2: Taboo and the Perils of the Soul* [1911], 14–15). Thus the ancient Hebrew custom of the use of oil for purposes of consecration is a practice which has many analogies outside Israel.

II. The practice of anointing in Israel. The OT makes frequent reference to the cosmetic value of oil (cf. Ezek. 16:9; Ruth 3:3; Cant. 1:3; 4:10). It also knows of oil as a medicine (cf. Isa. 1:6; 2 Chr. 28:15). That oil enhances joy and happiness appears to be an accepted view (cf. Ps. 45:7; Eccl. 9:8; Isa. 61:3). To refrain from the use of oil was an indication of mourning (cf. 2 Sam. 14:2; Dan. 10:3). Oil was used widely in cultic rites for the anointing of objects and persons. When JACOB poured oil upon the stone at BETHEL (Gen. 28:18), this act was later explained as a sacral act (cf. 31:13).

The book of Exodus provides a prescription for the ingredients of the oil of anointing: liquid myrrh, cinnamon, aromatic cane, cassia, and olive oil (Exod. 30:23–25). These substances were blended skillfully with the art of the "perfumer." The act of consecration required the anointing of every object appertaining to worship: "the Tent of Meeting, the ark of the Testimony, the table and all its articles, the lampstand and its accessories, the altar of incense, the altar of burnt offering and all its utensils, and the basin with its stand." All these items acquired a special sanctity by reason of anointing, so that "whatever touches them will be holy" (vv. 26–29). What applied to objects applied also to persons: AARON and his sons were to be consecrated to the priesthood by means of anointing (vv. 30–31). The recipe prescribed for cultic purposes was not to be repeated for any other use and was not to be "poured upon the bodies of ordinary men" (30:32 RSV).

III. The anointing of priests. The anointing to the priesthood extended to all descendants of the house of Aaron (Exod. 30:30). The consecration ceremony was performed by MOSES. According to another tradition Moses consecrated Aaron and his sons with the oil of anointing and the blood of sacrifice (Lev. 8:30). The question whether the rite of anointing to the priesthood was practiced from generation to generation and whether it applied to all priests cannot be answered with any certainty.

According to rabbinic tradition only the high priest or the son of a high priest was anointed with the oil of unction (cf. Maimonides, *Sefer Abodah* 1.7). This custom persisted only until the time of Josiah. After that time appointment to the high priesthood was by investiture of the appropriate garments: eight pieces for the high priest and four in the case of the common priests (cf. *m. Yoma* 7:5). The MISHNAH seems to distinguish between the ordinary priests and the anointed priest (i.e., the high priest; cf. *m. Šebuʿot* 1:7; *m. Megillah* 1:9; *m. Horayot* 3:4). There may be a reliable tradition behind these views, though this has sometimes been contradicted by Christian scholars (cf. David Jennings, *Jewish Antiquities* [1837], 125–26). Maimonides, on the basis of Jewish tradition, makes the definitive statement: "In the days of the Second Temple, when there was no anointing with oil, the High Priest would be consecrated only by putting on of vestments" (*Sefer Abodah* 1.8). It was also the custom to anoint a priest who would lead into battle (cf. *m. Soṭah* 8:1; *m. Makkot* 2:6).

It is difficult to ascertain the historical accuracy of the tradition. It may have been an exegetical conclusion based on Deut. 20:2–4, which provides for a speech by a priest on the eve of war. Shields used to be anointed in preparation for war (cf. 2 Sam. 1:21; Isa. 21:5). The practice may be taken either as a cultic act or a warrior's device to make the metal slippery or, if leather, more resistant. It is evident that the act of anointing was an ancient custom and carried definite cultic and sacral meaning. A person thus anointed was set apart and was consecrated for a special task, usually a sacred task. In the case of the priesthood such anointing carried perpetual validity (Exod. 40:15).

IV. The anointing of kings. For the rite of anointing of kings there is ample OT evidence. Saul, David, Solomon, Joash, and others were consecrated to the kingship by anointing with oil. For this reason "the anointed of the Lord" (1 Sam. 24:6; cf. 12:3, 5, et al.) was a phrase synonymous with "the king." Anointing conveyed sanctity to the person who now stood under the special protection of the God of Israel (cf. 24:5–6). This rite of commissioning to high office was not only symbolic of the gifts requisite for that office but was regarded as a charismatic bestowal of such gifts (cf. 1 Sam. 16:13; Isa. 61:1).

There appears to have been a rival claim to the prerogative of performing the rite between prophet and priest. In the case of Saul and David it was Samuel the prophet who performed the act of anointing (1 Sam. 10:1; 16:13). In the case of Solomon it was Zadok the priest who performed the rite, while Nathan was only one of the witnesses (cf. 1 Ki. 1:39). In the case of Jehu it was

An alabaster oil jar for holding special ointments of the Egyptian 18th dynasty (c. 1500 B.C.). Refined oil was used to anoint leaders set aside for special assignments.

a young prophet who acted on behalf of Elisha (2 Ki. 9:1–10). This was clearly a case of emergency necessitated by the conspiracy against the house of Ahab. The circumstances of the crowning of Joash are equally complex. In this case it is again Jehoiada the priest who performs the rite (2 Ki. 11:12). It would seem that with the establishment of the national cult the privilege of anointing became vested in the priesthood.

According to the rabbis only kings descended from the house of David received anointing. Even this practice was limited to an heir who was not in the direct line. "A king whose father had been a king was not anointed, for the kingdom was always his as an heir" (Maimonides, *Sefer Abodah* 1.11). According to the same authority, anointing took place when there was a dispute concerning the legitimate heir in order to end the quarrel. It is always difficult to assess the historic value of rabbinic tradition but it frequently transmits data otherwise unknown. The rabbis have also preserved the tradition concerning the manner of anointing: kings were anointed by pouring oil upon the head in a circle to form a crown. By contrast, the high priest was anointed by pouring oil upon his head and rubbing it upon his forehead crosswise like the Greek letter X (ibid. 1.9). Originally this sign would have been a cross (Ezek. 9:4, 6, where the MARK stands for the last letter in the ancient Hebrew ALPHABET). (See also *NIDOTTE*, 2:1123–27.)

V. Charismatic kingship. Some scholars work on the principle of direct correspondence between ancient Israel and the adjacent cultures. Canaanite culture especially is regarded as the formative principle in the social and religious makeup of the Hebrews. There is no denying that the invading tribes assimilated some pagan features peculiar to the indigenous population. To assume complete similarity, however, is to deny the peculiar genius of the Hebrew people. For example, it is more than doubtful whether the position of kings in the ANE was at any time acceptable among Israelites. In Egypt kings were regarded as divine incarnations and were worshiped as gods. In Babylon kings were divinized and thus constituted the link between the gods and ordinary mortals. In Canaan there was a close connection between the kings and the FERTILITY CULTS. There is no evidence for anything like it in Israel.

Even a radical scholar like S. Mowinckel (*He That Cometh* [1956], ch. 3) admits that under the influence of Yahweh worship "the king-ideology" of the ANE underwent important modifications. It is evident that the desert tradition of the BEDOUIN chieftain persisted long after settlement in the land of Canaan. There is no trace of direct evidence that Israelite kings ever claimed or were ever accorded divine honors. Even Mowinckel concedes that the Hebrew king was *primus inter pares*. The fact that the Israelite king was an ordinary mortal and chosen from among his brethren did not preclude special charismatic gifts requisite to his office. As the anointed of the Lord, he was looked upon as endowed with the Spirit of Yahweh (cf. 1 Sam. 10:1–13; 11:6; 16:13). David is credited with the charisma of leadership (cf. Ps. 89:20–29); Solomon is regarded as specially equipped with the gift of wisdom (cf. 1 Ki. 3:10–14). This is in accordance with the biblical view that God equips those whom he calls to his service.

In the last resort, all human wisdom and all skill derives from Yahweh, who is the source of all knowledge. Thus BEZALEL, the son of Uri, was filled with the Spirit of God to work in every craft (Exod. 31:3–5); by the Spirit of God the judges led and ruled over his people (Jdg. 3:10; 6:34; 11:29; et al.). Even a foreign king like CYRUS acts by the influence of the Spirit of the Lord (Ezra 1:1). In this sense the king is not an ordinary mortal. Being the consecrated and anointed servant of Yahweh, he acts as divine plenipotentiary and is therefore God's viceroy. At the same time, he is never without supervision — the prophet's eye is upon him most of the time (cf. 2 Sam. 12:1–12; 1 Ki. 21:18–19; 22:13; 2 Ki. 19:20–31). Mowinckel exaggerates the importance and the "sacrosanct" position of the Israelite kings. H. Frankfort's view (*Kingship and the Gods* [1948], 337ff.) is more true to fact: Hebrew kingship "lacks sanctity." He holds that the relation between the Hebrew monarch and his people "was as nearly secular as is possible in a society wherein religion is a living force."

VI. The ideal king. Ideally speaking, Israel's kings were meant to be true shepherds of their people and to act in God's stead (cf. Jer. 23:2, 5, with Isa. 40:11). In history, ideals never quite materialize. The warning contained in Deut. 17:16–20 served only too often as a reminder of the true state of affairs; kings who multiplied horses and wives entered into selfish alliances with former enemies, lifted themselves above their brethren, and turned aside from God's commandments.

The messianic hope was born from the recognition that no human king is able to fulfill the high ideal. The ideal king must be more than an ordinary mortal. Together with the eschatological hope there was the historic association with the covenantal promises made to David (cf. 1 Sam. 7:1–17). The COVENANT relationship and the promises that go with it make the messianic hope a sheer necessity. If God's purpose is not to be defeated, the true Messiah (= King) as God's authentic Servant is the only answer. The remedy is centered upon a person and not upon an abstract doctrine or an ideal system. There can be no messianic kingdom without God's anointed King.

At this point HISTORY and ESCHATOLOGY become strangely intertwined: the Messiah's pedigree goes back to the promises to David. The ideal King has his roots in history, hence the reference to "the Root of Jesse" (Isa. 11:10). His name "Branch" carries the same Davidic connotation (cf. Jer. 23:5; 33:15; Zech. 3:8; 6:12). At the same time he is endowed with "names" (= functions) that place him beyond ordinary mortals (Isa. 9:6). Mowinckel holds that these extraordinary names can be illustrated from Egyptian sources and represent nothing more than the coronation ritual. He believes that at this point the Messiah is not yet a supernatural being. He does not yet come from above, but is an ordinary man endowed with power to restore the Davidic kingdom. His endowment with divine strength is only because the Spirit of Yahweh rests upon him. The question why the prophet should use such names in contexts that have nothing to do with the coronation ritual is not answered by this interpretation. More conservative scholars will be quick to reject Mowinckel's arguments.

VII. Messianic texts. That the OT contains messianic passages is accepted by most scholars. They differ, however, regarding their age and significance. Mowinckel would allow only two texts as preexilic (Isa. 7:10–17; 9:1–6). All other texts he puts down as belonging to a later time. Messianism is for him a purely national and political phenomenon, so that all these texts are concerned with the restoration of the Davidic line. The Scandinavian school makes much of the "royal psalms," which are used in support of the theory that kingship and divinity were closely related and that the king occupied a central position in the cult. The annual enthronement of the king as the viceroy of God was allegedly the main cultic festival and was closely connected with the fertility rites of the ANE. Three passages (2 Sam. 21:1–14; Pss. 45; 72) are singled out as chief evidence for a New Year enthronement festival in which the king took the place of Yahweh.

Some allowance has already been made for the influence of pagan customs upon the religious life of ancient Israel. The OT provides all the evidence for this fact: AHAZ, king of Judah, burned his son as an offering (2 Ki. 16:3); MANASSEH, another Judean king, practiced all the abominations of the pagan cults and built altars to BAAL and ASHERAH (21:3, 6–7). The question one must ask is this: do these practices constitute Israel's faith or are these aberrations? The answer is obvious; the Pentateuch, the Prophets, the Historical Books, the HAGIOGRAPHA, all unanimously condemn, deplore, and execrate these lapses into paganism. This struggle between paganism and Yahweh worship dominates the OT and constitutes a recurring theme. One must therefore work on the principle that whatever ancient material was used by the OT writers, their main concern was to put every document to the service of Yahweh worship. At least some of the messianic texts come from preexilic times and point to the fact that the messianic hope is older than the fall of the Davidic dynasty. This is an important point that must be given full weight.

OT messianism is the logical result of the claim that Yahweh is Lord of heaven and earth. Political and social distress were contributing factors, but the main reason for the messianic hope derives from faith in Yahweh as the covenant-keeping God. The tension between historic experience and faith in the omnipotence of the benevolent God of the patriarchs can find no solution except in messianic fulfillment. There is certainly an unevenness in the messianic vision: sometimes the Messiah is seen as the Prince of Peace (Isa. 9:6), at other times he is described as the slayer of the wicked (11:4), but at all times he is the One who acts in the power and under the guidance of the God of Israel.

There are occasions when the ideal King of the house of David recedes in the background and his place is taken by a supernatural being entering history from another realm (cf. Dan. 7:13–14). The church has inherited from Hebrew tradition the messianic interpretation of most texts. A case in point is the reference to SHILOH in Gen. 49:10 (KJV, NIV mg.), a name that the TARGUMS and other rabbinic sources identify with the Messiah. The twelve tribes of Israel are described as gathering around the golden bed of the dying patriarch Jacob who, with his last breath, prophesied the messianic end. This is how *Targum Pseudo-Jonathan* renders the text: "Kings shall not cease, nor rulers from the house of Judah ... till the time that the King, the Messiah, shall come, the youngest of his sons; and on account of him shall the nations flow together. How beautiful is the King, the Messiah, who will arise from the house of Judah!" The messianic exegesis of this text and endowment of the Messiah with the name of Shiloh as his *nomen proprium* (cf. Str-B, 1:65) must be much older than the church, for the rabbis were not likely to play into the hands of the Christians.

The words of Gen. 49:10 have been used by the church as an example of fulfilled prophecy. Luther called it the "golden text" and chides the rabbis for failing to see its fulfillment in the person of Jesus Christ. Some scholars, however, understand the words as no more than a *vaticinium ex eventu* in reference to King David. Another text, Gen. 3:15, traditionally known as the *protevangelium* (initial proclamation of the gospel), was described by Luther as the first comfort, the source of all mercy, and the fountainhead of all promises. This passage can be read on two levels: as the natural enmity between man and the serpent, or else typologically as Christ's ultimate victory over evil; it depends on the perspective of the reader. A similar situation arises in respect to the translation of the word ʿ*almâ H6625* as "virgin" (Isa. 7:14; cf. Matt. 1:23).

Dealing with messianic passages, one must keep in mind the difference in the historic perspective, the context of the original text, and the typological use in the NT (see TYPOLOGY). "The identity of prophecy and fulfilment is not direct but an indirect one" (G. F. Oehler, *Theology of the Old Testament* [1883], 491). NT writers see the OT from the perspective of the messianic event, they thus see, in Woollcombe's words, a pattern "converging on a central motif"; it is in the light of this fact that "the evidence of God's consistent purpose in history" can be seen (G. W. H. Lampe and K. J. Woollcombe, *Essays in Typology* [1957], 68).

Other passages carry indisputable messianic import: Isa. 4:2, the branch of the LORD; 7:10–17, the promise of Immanuel; 9:1–7, the birth of the son; 11:1–10, the great messianic vision; 32:1–8, the righteous king; 55:3–4, the everlasting covenant with David; Jer. 23:5–6, the Lord our righteousness (cf. 33:14–16; 30:9, 21–22); 31:31–34, the new covenant; Ezek. 34:23–24, the shepherd of Israel; 37:20–28, the everlasting covenant (Mowinckel includes Ezek. 17:22–24 in the messianic passages as a reference to the house of David); Hos. 3:4–5, Israel's return in the latter days; Amos 9:11, the raising of the fallen booth of David; Mic. 5:1–4, Bethlehem Ephratha (Mowinckel regards Mic. 4:8 as a messianic reference); Zech. 9:9–10, the triumphant entry of the messianic king.

Egyptian scepter or ruler's staff (from Saqqara). "The scepter will not depart from Judah, / nor the ruler's staff from between his feet, / until he comes to whom it belongs / and the obedience of the nations is his" (Gen. 49:10).

There are numerous other passages that are capable of messianic interpretation and are used in the NT in connection with messianic fulfillment: Deut. 18:18–19 (Acts 3:22–23; 7:37); Ps. 2:1–2 (Acts 4:25–26; cf. 13:33; Matt. 3:17; Acts 13:33; Heb. 1:5; 5:5; 2 Pet. 1:17; et al.); Ps. 110:1, 4 (Matt. 22:44 and parallels; Acts 2:34; Heb. 5:6, 10; 6:20; 7:11, 15, 21); Ps. 118:22–23 (Matt. 21:42; Acts 4:11; 1 Pet. 2:7). The PSALMS are important for an understanding of the messianic pattern, and not a few of them are cited in the NT in connection with the life of the Messiah: Pss. 8; 22; 34:21; 41:10; 45; 69; 72 (cf. also Isa. 28:16, cited in Rom. 9:33; 10:11; 1 Pet. 2:4). In addition are to be noted the great SERVANT OF THE LORD passages in Isaiah: Isa. 42:1–4; 49:1–6; 50:4–9; 52:13—53:12. The latter section plays an especially important part both in the NT and in the history of Christian theology.

Even these by no means exhaust the messianic pattern provided by the OT. Many other passages, such as Joel 2:28–29, used by PETER in his first sermon at PENTECOST (Acts 2:17–21), and the great chapters of the latter part of Isaiah (e.g., Isa. 61:1–2; cf. Lk. 4:18–19; 7:22), are part of the OT heritage bequeathed to the NT. Paul uses Isa. 25:8 in his great chapter on the RESURRECTION (1 Cor. 15:54). The Gospels apply Mal. 3:1 to the preparatory work of John the Baptist (Matt. 11:10; Mk. 1:2; Lk. 1:17; 7:27). To these one must add the endless allusions to OT texts that are built into the messianic story of the NT. See QUOTATIONS IN THE NT.

The two Testaments are interdependent and the one cannot be understood without the other. At the same time one must not seek a detailed blueprint in the OT that would preempt the messianic event. The relation is rather between expectancy and fulfillment.

VIII. The extracanonical literature. The Apocrypha and Pseudepigrapha fill the gap of the intertestamental period. The contribution of this literature to the messianic expectation may be variously assessed. Some scholars stress the APOCALYPTIC features in the NT and see a close relationship between it and the Pseudepigrapha; others hold that both depend upon OT material. Frequently the choice lies between the book of Daniel and *1–3 Enoch* (see Enoch, Books of), especially with regard to the Son of Man concept.

The Apocrypha do not seem to show the same intense interest in the messianic hope as do the Pseudepigrapha. It is widely held that certain turns of phrase in the NT reveal familiarity with some of the apocryphal books (such as Tobit, Sirach, and Wisdom of Solomon). The case with the Pseudepigrapha is different. Messianic concepts are highly developed and play a vital part in the message these books try to convey. Especially *1 Enoch* is infused with a great messianic hope. It spells out judgment over Israel's enemies; it foretells the founding of the new Jerusalem; it envisions the conversion of the Gentiles; it tells of the resurrection of the righteous, climaxing its vision with the advent of the Messiah. R. H. Charles regards this work as the most important pseudepigraphic writing in the history of theological development during the 2nd and 1st centuries B.C. (*APOT*, 2:163). It depicts the Messiah as a Lamb with horns on its head over whom the Lord of the sheep rejoices (*1 En.* 90.38). The titles given to the Messiah in this book are noteworthy, for these bring one close to NT nomenclature: the Anointed One (48.10; 52.4); the Righteous One (38.2; 46.3; 53.6; cf. Acts 3:14; 7:52; 22:14; 1 Jn. 2:1); the Elect One (*1 En.* 40.5; 45.3–4; 49.2, 4; 51.3, 5; cf. Lk. 23:35; 1 Pet. 2:4); the Son of Man (*1 En.* 46.3–4; 48.2; 62.9, 14; 63.11; 69.26–27; 70.1; 71.1).

Functions assigned to the Messiah are even more striking than the titles. The Messiah is described as the judge of the world, as the revealer of all things, and as the champion and ruler of the righteous. Part of the Messiah's task is to raise the righteous from the dead (cf. *1 En.* 51.1; 61.5). For the first time in Jewish literature the Son of Man is spoken of with the demonstrative "this," which Charles regards as significant for the messianic title. Scholars regard the book as composite in nature, and Klausner has shown how the material and spiritual understanding of the messianic age are here placed side by side without any effort at reconciliation. The same observation applies to the person of the Messiah: sometimes he is presented as one among equals; at other times he is placed in a position of preeminence. Klausner's assessment of *1 Enoch* matches that by Charles: "the messianic book *par excellence* of Judaism in the period of the Second Temple" (J. Klausner, *The Messianic Idea in Israel* [1956], 301).

Other books of the Pseudepigrapha are also important. The Testaments of the Twelve Patriarchs show remarkable universalist tendencies; *2 Baruch* (see Baruch, Apocalypse of (Syriac)) points to the messianic kingdom and stresses the RESURRECTION of the body; *4 Ezra* (see Esdras, Second) envisions Messiah's triumph over his enemies. That there is a connection between this literature and the NT cannot be denied, but the connection seems to be more ideological than literary. The question of whether there was direct borrowing has been widely discussed. In spite of certain philological affinities, the connection seems to be mainly of a theological nature peculiar to certain circles in Judaism.

From the testimony of Suetonius about Jewish messianic hopes (*The Life of Vespasian* 4) and Josephus's veiled reference to the defenders of Jerusalem (*War* 6.5.2) one can gauge the deep-rooted messianic expectations that inspired the nation. This finds corroboration in the Qumran documents, though the messianic doctrine of the desert sect is not quite clear (see Dead Sea Scrolls). We do not know the relationship of the two Messiahs of Aaron and Israel to each other (cf. 1QS IX,11), nor do we know the messianic significance of the Teacher of Righteousness. There are other messianic allusions in the texts: some have surmised, for example, that the "man" in 1QS IV, 18 is identical with the "prophet" in IX, 11. G. Vermès (*Discovery in the Judean Desert* [1956], 221) identifies the "man" with two passages in *T. 12 Pat.* and with Zech. 12:7 and Lam. 3:1. A similar reference to the "man" occurs in the Thanksgiving Hymns in an unmistakable messianic context where he is described as "a Marvellous Mighty Counsellor" (G. Vermès, *The Dead Sea Scrolls in English* [1968], 157; 1QH^a III, 4 [Sukenik] = XI, 10).

Another hymn, with its reference to the "bud," the "shoot," and the "everlasting Plant" that "shall cover the whole [earth] with its shadow" (Vermès, *Dead Sea Scrolls in English*, 171; 1QH^a VI, 15 [Sukenik] = XIV, 15), is equally suggestive of messianic hope derived from the OT. Vermès (*Discovery*, 222) points to the prophetic, sacerdotal, and royal qualities of the Messiah that are exhibited in the Qumran scrolls, bringing them close to the Jewish and Christian cycle of ideas. This proves the pervasive messianic hopes in ancient Israel. The NT was written in an atmosphere of widespread messianic expectation, not only in Judaism but outside Israel as well. Klausner holds that Virgil's fourth *Eclogue*, which speaks of the birth of the child who would bring peace to the world, was written under the influence of the Jewish Sibyl and reflects the influence of Hebrew messianism upon non-Jews. The question is not who borrowed from whom, but in what way did the diverse messianic ideas influence the central Personality of the NT, namely Jesus Christ himself?

IX. Christ in the NT. *1 Enoch* concludes with the promise of God: "For I and my son will unite with them for ever in the paths of righteousness in their lives; and ye shall have peace: rejoice ye children of uprightness. Amen" (105.2). This sounds remarkably like NT theology, yet it is not. *1 Enoch*'s message is salvation for the righteous, whereas Jesus addressed himself to sinners (cf. Matt. 9:13). Further, the reference to the "Son" is only an echo of Ps. 2 (cf. 4 Ezra 7:28; 13:32, 37, 52; 14:9). Above all, the Messiah in *1 Enoch* knows no suffering: he occupies God's throne (51.3), executes judgment in heaven, and triumphs upon earth. One may conclude that the NT owes to the intertestamental literature some of the messianic imagery and phraseology, but not the central Christological features. These were formed upon reflection on the life, death, and resurrection of Jesus of Nazareth in conjunction with his teaching.

A. Son of Man. Scholars tend to regard the frequent references to the SON OF MAN in the Gospels as an honorific title that the early church gave to the Messiah. For the origin they go to the Pseudepigrapha or to the book of Daniel (Dan. 7:13). This title for the Messiah is peculiar to the Gospels, where it occurs eighty-one times, and only four times in the rest of the NT (Acts 7:56; Heb. 2:6; Rev. 1:13; 14:14).

It is noted that in the Gospels this title is never used except by Jesus himself, and always as a self-designation. There is therefore no need to ascribe the title to the early church except on the supposition of some radical scholars (Bousset, Bultmann, and others) who deny to Jesus a messianic consciousness. These scholars point to Mk. 8:38 and Lk. 12:8 as evidence that Jesus did not identify himself with the Son of Man but looked upon himself as his messenger, with the task of announcing the closeness of his coming. They therefore maintain that the identification of Jesus with the Son of Man took place at a later stage as a result of the Easter experience. It is difficult to see why the Gospels, which on their own premise are typical church documents, should leave such a glaring discrepancy out of sheer reverence for an unwritten tradition, while at the same time distorting the facts of history. It is much more natural to accept the Son of Man title as the peculiar self-description on the part of Jesus as presented by the Gospels (cf. Matt. 8:20; Mk. 2:10, 28).

The question arises, what did Jesus mean by this description? Some scholars hold that the Son of Man passages resulted from a misunderstanding of the Aramaic idiom, which uses the corresponding expression *br nš* (or *br nš'*) with the meaning "man" pure and simple. Only later, when the phrase had to be rendered in Greek, was it translated literally as *ho huios tou anthrōpou* instead of simply *anthrōpos*. In this way Son of Man became a messianic title. Another suggestion that amounts to the same thing is that Jesus used the phrase as a substitute for "I" and that therefore it carried no special significance.

This view would exclude any identification with the apocalyptic Son of Man idea one meets in the Pseudepigrapha and in the book of Daniel. The corollary would seem to be that Jesus made no claim to messiahship at all. This is supposedly corroborated from Jewish sources, which blame Jesus for all sorts of crimes but never for claiming to be the Messiah (W. Kramer, *Christ, Lord, Son of God* [1966]). But this contention rests upon a misunderstanding, for claim to messiahship was never regarded a crime. That this is the case can be seen from the rabbinic attitude to Simeon surnamed BAR KOKHBA ("Son of a Star"): after the failure of his revolt against Rome, he was nicknamed Bar Koziba, "the Son of Lies" (a title that sounded like his own patronymic, Bar Kosiba, discovered in the Qumran documents). He became a "false messiah" only after he had failed.

Jesus' conflict with the PHARISEES was not because of the messianic overtones in his message but because of his attitude to the law: a messiah who appeared to treat the law lightly could be only a false messiah. The question raised by some concerning the reason for Jesus' concealment behind a pseudonym raises no real difficulty. Messiahship was too explosive a concept to be bandied about freely. M. de Jonge's contention that the term "anointed" had yet no fixed meaning and simply denoted divine appointment is contradicted by the documents already cited.

B. Son of God. In the OT Israel is described as God's firstborn (Exod. 4:22) and is called his son (Hos. 11:1). There is therefore precedent for calling the Messiah "Son of God" (cf. Ps. 2), for he is Israel's representative *par excellence*. In Jn. 10:34–36, Jesus argues on the principle of *argumentum a minori ad majus*: if Israel's judges and kings were called "gods" and sons of the Most High (cf. Ps. 82:6), how much more does this term apply to him whom the Father has set apart (the verb *hagiazō G39* may be an intended reference to "anointing") and sent into the world. Only in the fourth gospel does Jesus appear to call himself by the title "Son of God" (Jn. 10:36; 11:4; cf. 5:25; 8:36; et al.). In the synoptics the phrase is applied to Jesus indirectly. He is called Son of God by the demoniacs (Mk. 3:11; 5:7); by the centurion at the cross (15:39); by Peter according to the Matthean version (Matt. 16:16; cf. Mk. 8:29; Lk. 9:20).

The question regarding the Messiah's pedigree was obviously a matter of theological discussion: according to Mk. 12:35–37, Jesus raises the question with the scribes; according to Matt. 22:41–46 and Lk. 20:41–44, the discussion is with the Pharisees. The reference to Ps. 110:1 is intended to indicate that the Messiah's descent exceeds the dynastic claim. Christ is more than the Son of David.

It has been noticed that Paul uses the title Son of God infrequently, but that he does so in crucial contexts. The appellation he more frequently uses is Jesus Christ or Christ Jesus. Werner Kramer observes that the sonship of the Messiah occurs in texts where reference is made to God the Father; the Father sends his Son (Rom. 8:3); the Son's Spirit in our hearts cries, "Abba, Father" (Gal. 4:6; cf. Phil. 4:4–6). The gospel of God is the gospel concerning his Son, who was descended from David according to the flesh and designated Son of God according to the Spirit of holiness (Rom. 1:1–4). For Paul, Son of God is essentially a Christological description expressing "the Son's solidarity with God." The other passages convey the same conception. The Father spared not his Son but gave him up for us (8:32). It is thanks to the Son that one can call God Father (8:15). Only because Jesus as Son is heir are believers made sons by ADOPTION (Gal. 4:1–7). The heathen through the preaching of the gospel have turned from idols to serve the true and living God, and are now waiting for his Son from heaven who is none other than Jesus raised from the dead (1 Thess. 1:9–10).

In the Johannine literature the title Son of God is widely used. In the first epistle it recurs with frequent regularity and dominates the Christological perspective; to be a Christian means to have fellowship with the Father and his Son Jesus Christ (1 Jn. 1:3). To deny that Jesus is the Christ is tantamount to denying both Father and Son (2:22–23). To confess that Jesus is the Son of God is to abide in God (4:15). The last chapter of the first epistle makes every possible emphasis upon the principle that Sonship is the mark of messiahship.

The same is the case with the fourth gospel, where Son of God is synonymous with Messiah and occurs more frequently than any other title. E. Haenchen maintains that the same equation, Messiah=Son of Man=Son of God, applies to Mark's gospel (*Der Weg Jesu* [1966], 36, 133, 498). The same may be said of the rest of the NT. There is, however, a difference in the distribution of the use of the title determined by Christological emphasis.

It is a mistake to seek the origin of the title Son of God in pagan religions. G. Dalman (*The Words of Jesus* [1902], 276–80) suggests an easy transition from the Servant passages in Isaiah via the Septuagint. This is corroborated by other scholars: the LXX translates ʿ*ebed H6269* with *pais G4090*, a fact which Georg Bertram regards as a *praeparatio evangelica* (*VT* 7 [1957]: 232–33). The Targum translates Hebrew ʿ*ebed* into the Aramaic ʿ*bdy mšyḥ*ʾ, "my servant Messiah" (Isa. 42:1; 43:10; 52:13; Zech. 3:8). From the LXX the NT inherited the tradition of using Greek *pais*, which may mean either "child" or "servant" (cf. Acts 3:13, 26; 4:25–26, 30; cf. also Matt. 8:6, 8, 13; 12:18; 14:2; Mk. 14:54, 65; Jn. 18:36). In Wisdom of Solomon *pais* stands for *huios* (cf. Wisd. 2:13, 16). The ambiguity that arises from this double meaning is not sufficient to explain the phrase "Son of God" as used in the NT.

This point is illustrated by the parable of the vineyard, where *ho huios agapētos* ("the beloved son") as heir is not just one among other servants; he is not even *primus inter pares* but rather stands in a unique position (cf. Mk. 12:6; cf. Matt. 3:17). The uniqueness is not vested in function but in status. He is the Son whom the tenants are expected to revere. At the same time the Son of God does not exist in isolation; he is the firstborn among many brethren (Rom. 8:29). This twofold connection—the *prōtotokos G4758*, "firstborn," of Mary (Lk. 2:7) and the *monogenēs G3666*, "only [begotten]," of God (Jn. 3:16; 1 Jn. 4:9)—expresses the Messiah's position. He is the link between heaven and earth. His preeminence in Pauline terms lies in the fact that he is both the *prōtotokos* of all creation and the *prōtotokos* from the dead (Col. 1:15, 18). He is thus the Head of the body, the church, and the *prōtotokos* of those who are enrolled in heaven (Heb. 12:23).

Closeness to the Father is the basic meaning of Son of God. It is for this reason that the Son is able to reveal the Father (Matt. 11:27; cf. Lk. 10:32). Our Lord's characteristic use of such phrases as "your Father," "our Father," "my Father," is behind the title Son of God. This close relationship to his Father in heaven is even more pronounced in the fourth gospel. The phrase "the Father and I" expresses the intimacy of the relationship (cf. Jn. 5:43; 8:38, 40; 10:32; 12:49; 15:15; et al.). In the Johannine gospel Jesus is both the son of Joseph (1:45) and the Son of God (1:34, 49). There appears to be no discrepancy in these two statements. It is obvious that sonship must not be understood in a crude pagan way. This bears out Dalman's contention that the Hebrew concept of "son" does not "denote an extensive circle of relationships" (*Words of Jesus*, 288; cf. also W. Grundmann in *NTS* 1 [1965]: 42ff.). It is rather the *intensive* relationship between Jesus and his Father in heaven which marks him as *the* Son.

C. Kyrios. The most characteristic title ascribed to the Messiah in the NT is *kyrios G3261*, meaning LORD. It carries a certain ambiguity, for it is both an address to men and to God. For this reason there is a division of opinion as to the original meaning of the term. In the Gospels it seems to be treated as equivalent to *didaskalos G1437* ("teacher"), *epistatēs G2181* ("master"), and *rhabbi G4806* (Matt. 8:25 = Mk. 4:38 = Lk. 8:24; Matt. 17:4 = Lk. 9:33 = Mk. 9:5). Some therefore argue that *kyrios* is a translation either of Hebrew *rabbi* or Aramaic *mari* (both meaning "my master") and is meant to be taken as an address of respect, but that *kyrios* acquired a different meaning in Greek-speaking communities acquainted with Hellenistic cults and EMPEROR WORSHIP.

These scholars maintain that the deification of Jesus as the supernatural Messiah could have taken place only outside Israel, that is, in a Hellenistic environment (W. Bousset, R. Bultmann, W. Kramer). At the same time it is admitted that there are traces of a pre-Pauline use of the term *kyrios*, and this in a liturgical context, chiefly in connection with the LORD'S SUPPER (W. Kramer). This fact would seem to contradict a Hellenistic origin. Oscar Cullmann has shown beyond contradiction that *mar*, not as a courtesy title, but as a Christological confession, derives from the most primitive time of the church while still upon Jewish soil (see

The Christology of the New Testament [1959], part 3). The phrase MARANATHA has come down untranslated from a time when ARAMAIC was still the mother tongue of the church (1 Cor. 16:22). The fact that the phrase belongs to a liturgical setting (cf. *Didache* 10.6) shows that *māran* ("our Lord") was used in a Christological sense. The question as to whether the phrase should be read *māran ʾātāʾ* ("our Lord comes/has come") or *māranāʾ tāʾ* ("our Lord, come!") is solved in favor of the latter by the NT itself, for Rev. 22:20 provides the Greek translation *erchou, kyrie Iēsou*, "Come, Lord Jesus!"—*maranatha* is in the form of a prayer.

Some have argued that this liturgical phrase does not necessarily prove Palestinian origin, but this position cannot be taken seriously. There is early proof for a Christological meaning of the title *kyrios*. Furthermore, there are good grounds for believing that Phil. 2:6–11 is a Christological hymn going back to an Aramaic source (E. Lohmeyer). If this is the case, there is added reason to accept a high pre-Pauline Christology. That the Messiah was given "the name that is above every name" (v. 9) brings him close to the *Tetragrammaton* (YHWH). This connection can be seen from what follows: "that at the name of Jesus every knee should bow ... and every tongue confess that Jesus Christ is Lord, to the glory of God the Father" (vv. 10–11). What Isaiah says of Yahweh (Isa. 45:23) is said of the Messiah.

There is therefore no need to take seriously the contention that the *kyrios* concept entered the NT from the outside. In fact, the Kyrios-cult of Hellenism and Caesar worship was challenged by the proclamation that Jesus is Lord. The Lordship of Jesus the Messiah was the essential KERYGMA of the church. The root for this claim stemmed from the authority Jesus exercised during his ministry. His authority was confirmed by the fact of the resurrection. That the Messiah is the legitimate king of Israel is an ancient Jewish tradition (cf. Str-B, 3:146–47, 472; G. Dalman, *Jesus-Jeshua* [1929], 198). Cullmann draws attention to the importance attached to Ps. 110 in the NT. It is quoted or alluded to some twenty times (Matt. 22:44; 26:64; Mk. 12:36; 14:62; 16:19; Lk. 20:42–43; 22:69; Acts 2:34–35; 5:31; 7:55; Rom. 8:34; 1 Cor. 15:25; Col. 3:11; Eph. 1:20; Heb. 1:3; 8:1; 10:12–13; 1 Pet. 3:22; Rev. 3:21) and is used to prove the absolute authority of the Messiah.

Cullmann regards the confession that Jesus is Lord as the most ancient Christian statement of faith. That God has made Jesus both "Lord and Christ" (Acts 2:36) was a challenge not only to the Jewish people but to the whole order of the ancient world. Accordingly, the purpose of the book of Revelation is to challenge all other authority with the proclamation that Jesus Christ as the firstborn of the dead is the only ruler of the kings on earth (Rev. 1:5).

The *kyriotēs* G3262 ("lordship, dominion, authority") of Jesus as Messiah is all-embracing: all authority is given to him (*exousia* G2026, Matt. 28:18). It exceeds Christ's lordship upon earth and assumes cosmic significance (cf. Col. 1:16–20). This is at the heart of PAULINE THEOLOGY: Christ is not only the Lord of the church but also the Head of all rule and authority (*hē kephalē pasēs archēs kai exousias*, Col. 2:10). This fact may not be immediately apparent by reason of the interval between his exaltation and his PAROUSIA (Rom. 8:19, 23; 1 Cor. 1:7; Gal. 5:5; cf. Heb. 2:8; 10:13), but because the Messiah is already at the right hand of God, he will in the end assert his dominion over all creation (Rom. 8:34; Col. 3:1). Not only will the rulers of the earth ultimately surrender, but even death itself, the last enemy, will be vanquished (1 Cor. 15:25). The fact that the Messiah is at the right hand of God is a source of endless comfort to the embattled church and gives it the courage to acclaim him Lord (cf. Acts 7:56; Heb. 1:3, 13; 8:1; 10:12; 12:2).

The Messiah's lordship is not a matter of impersonal and autocratic rule to which the believer submits under duress. Jesus did not impose his lordship; he came not to rule but to serve and to give his life for others (Matt. 20:28). His obedience to death, even the death on a cross (Phil. 2:8), marks him as the Servant first and foremost. That the Son of God should die for sinners is the startling discovery underlying the gospel (cf. Rom. 5:6–11; Heb. 12:1–2). The profession that Jesus is Lord is the disciples' response to God's love in Christ. The Pauline letters are dominated by the phrases "in the Lord" and "in Christ (Jesus)." To be *in* Christ means first the willing and joyful acceptance of his lordship over the totality of one's own life: "I no longer live, but Christ lives in me; ... who loved me and gave himself for me" (Gal. 2:20). The test of discipleship is in the possessive pronoun: Jesus Christ my Lord (Phil. 3:8).

D. Jesus—Savior. Compared with the ascription *kyrios*, the title *sōtēr G5400* occurs only infrequently. This comes as a surprise, for Savior has a long-standing OT tradition and best describes the messianic function. It is to be noted that *sōtēr* as a messianic title occurs mainly in the later NT writings. Cullmann (*Christology*, 241) concludes that Jesus never called himself, nor did any one else call him, by this address during his ministry. He admits, however, a pre-Pauline tradition (Phil. 3:20).

There is a linguistic reason for the lack of evidence in the earliest sources of the NT: the expression "Jesus Savior" is possible in Greek (cf. Acts 13:23, as well as the cryptogram ΙΧΘΥΣ, "fish," representing *Iēsous Christos Theou Huios Sōtēr*), but in Hebrew it would create a tautology. The name JESUS is the Greek equivalent of the later Hebrew form of JOSHUA, *yēšûaʿ H3800*, from the verb *yāšaʿ H3828*, "to save." Thus "Jesus Savior" in Hebrew is *yēšûaʿ môšîaʿ*, which might be perceived as a linguistic infelicity (although Aramaic would use a different root for "save").

The name Yeshua/Jesus is not peculiarly messianic but it is emphatically Yahwistic: it is an abbreviated form of *yĕhôšuaʿ H3397*, "Yahweh is salvation," a name well known in the OT (in addition to Joshua ben Nun, cf. Ezra 3:2; Neh. 8:17; Hag. 1:1; Zech. 3:1; et al.) and common in NT times (cf. Col. 4:11; Josephus records a number of men with the name). But for the Aramaic-speaking church the name Yeshua given to the Messiah carried special significance. Its etymological meaning is noted in Matt. 1:21: "you are to give him the name Jesus [*yēšûaʿ*] because he will save [*yôšîaʿ*] his people from their sins." Other NT writers are equally aware that the name means Savior or Salvation (cf. Jn. 1:29; Acts 13:23; in Heb. 4:8 and possibly in Acts 7:45, an allusive comparison is made between Jesus and Joshua).

The title *sōtēr* most frequently occurs in conjunction with the saving acts of God through the Messiah, as Cullmann observes (cf. Acts 5:31; 13:23; 1 Tim. 1:1; 2:3–4; 4:10; Tit. 1:3–4; 3:4–5; 1 Jn. 4:14; Jude 25). The OT regards saviorhood as God's divine prerogative (cf. Isa. 43:3, 11; 45:15, 21; Jer. 14:8; Hos. 13:4; et al.). But God performs his saving acts by sending saviors to act as his plenipotentiaries (cf. 2 Ki. 13:5; Neh. 9:27; Isa. 19:20; Obad. 21). In this sense Cyrus, though a pagan king, is understood to be God's shepherd (Isa. 44:28) and his anointed (45:1). The Messiah as *sōtēr* therefore stands in the line of a long tradition, but with a difference: in the NT the distinction

Catholic priests in Jerusalem celebrating Palm Sunday, when the Messiah entered Jerusalem triumphantly.

between God and Messiah disappears (cf. Tit. 1:3, God our Savior; v. 4, Christ Jesus our Savior). The identification is so close that in some passages it is a matter of guessing whether God or Jesus Christ is meant (cf. Tit. 3:4, 6; 2 Pet. 1:1).

A. T. Hanson allows that both STEPHEN and the author of Hebrews appear to identify Jesus with the theophanies of the OT (*Jesus Christ in the Old Testament* [1965], 164). The same would apply to John and Paul, who see the eternal LOGOS operative in OT history. There can be no doubt that the preexistence of the Messiah is an established NT doctrine (cf. Jn. 1:1–14; Col. 1:15–20; Heb. 1:3).

Some of the *egō eimi* ("I am") passages, particularly Jn. 8:58, appear to be a deliberate allusion to the name of Yahweh. This conclusion is corroborated by a rabbinic practice of circumlocution for the Tetragrammaton: the imprecation ʾānnāʾ yhwh (Ps. 118:25) was paraphrased as ʾănî wĕhûʾ, meaning literally "I and he" or "I, like him" (*m. Sukkah* 4:5; cf. also C. G. Montefiore and H. Loewe, *A Rabbinic Anthology* [1938], 13, 279). John's gospel seems to be aware of the tradition and uses the phrase in order to indicate the Messiah's intimacy with Yahweh (cf. C. H. Dodd, *The Interpretation of the Fourth Gospel* [1953], 93–96).

One is led to conclude that a high CHRISTOLOGY is deeply embedded in the NT tradition and that titles like Son of Man, Son of God, and Savior are intended to emphasize Messiah's unique and representative position both with regard to mankind and to God. In the last resort, this is the messianic secret: Jesus is the Christ (Mk. 8:27–30), but for the earliest believers this was tantamount to a position extraordinary in relation to God (cf. Matt. 16:16).

It must be admitted that in the popular sense, as conceived by Jewish tradition, Jesus is not the Messiah. The unique position accorded to him in the NT is contrary to all Jewish views. Son of God, says Dalman, "was not a common Messianic title" (*Words of Jesus*, 272). Though Christ was the Son of David (Rom. 1:3), the Fulfiller of prophecy (Jn. 1:45), the Redeemer of Israel (Lk. 1:68–69), yet he did not easily fit into Jewish preconceived messianic expectations. In this one respect E. Stauffer is right: Jesus is a different Messiah than expected by Jewry (*NovT* 1 [1956]: 102). To start with, he had no official standing; he was never anointed, except by the Holy Spirit (cf. Mk. 1:9–11; Lk. 4:16–21; Isa. 61:1–2). It is part of the revolutionary effect of the gospel that messiahship was transformed under the impact of the life, death, and resurrection of Jesus Christ. This transformation took place in two directions: in respect to the Gentiles and in respect to God. Jesus is not only the Messiah of Israel, but also the Savior of the world (Jn. 4:42; 1 Jn. 4:14); he is not only the Son of David, but also the Son of God (Mk. 12:35–37).

(In addition to the works mentioned in the body of this article, see E. G. Jay, *Son of Man—Son of God* [1965]; S. H. Levey, *The Messiah: An Aramaic Interpretation* [1974]; T. N. D. Mettinger, *King and Messiah: The Civil and Sacral Legitimation of the Israelite Kings* [1976]; H. Cazelles, *Le Messie de la Bible: Christologie de l'Ancien Testament* [1978]; J. Neusner, *Messiah in Context: Israel's History and Destiny in Formative Judaism* [1984]; M. de Jonge, *Jesus, the Servant-Messiah* [1992]; M. Bockmuehl, *This Jesus: Martyr, Lord, Messiah* [1994]; W. C. Kaiser, Jr., *The Messiah in the Old Testament* [1995]; R. S. Hess and M. D. Carroll R., eds., *Israel's Messiah in the Bible and the Dead Sea Scrolls* [2003]; A. Chester, *Messiah and Exaltation: Jewish Messianic and Visionary Traditions and New Testament Christology* [2007].)

J. Jocz

Messianic Banquet. A term used sometimes to refer to "the wedding supper of the Lamb" (Rev. 19:9) or more generally to the festivities of the end time, which are often symbolized by means of a meal. In the ANE, it was not uncommon for kings to celebrate a military victory by providing a great banquet (cf. 1 Chr. 12:38–40; 3 Macc. 6:30–41), and this notion was transferred to the gods in some myths (e.g., *ANET*, 69a). It was only natural that the symbol should be used to depict Yahweh's eschatological celebration. Thus Isaiah promises that "the LORD Almighty will prepare / a feast of rich food for all peoples, / a banquet of aged wine— / the best of meats and the finest of wines," at which times he "will wipe away the tears from all faces" (Isa. 25:6, 8; cf. Rev. 21:4).

The theme becomes prominent in APOCALYPTIC LITERATURE and is picked up in the NT. Jesus promises that those "who hunger now … will be satisfied" (Lk. 6:21); he also compares the kingdom of heaven to "a king who prepared a wedding banquet for his son" (Matt. 22:1; cf. Lk. 14:16). The imagery is especially prominent in the book of Revelation. After the destruction of BABYLON (Rev. 18), John heard a sound "like the roar of rushing waters and like loud peals of thunder, shouting: 'Hallelujah! / For our Lord God Almighty reigns. / Let us rejoice and be glad / and give him glory! / For the wedding of the Lamb has come, / and his bride has made herself ready" (19:6–7). (Cf. *ABD*, 4:788–91.) See CHURCH I.G; ESCHATOLOGY; SECOND COMING.

messianic secret. A term used in biblical scholarship to refer to those passages in the Gospels where Jesus tells his followers not to publicize his miracles (or other extraordinary details). This feature is especially prominent in Mark (e.g., Mk. 1:43–44; 5:43; 7:36; 8:30; 9:9), and it has led to considerable debate regarding its significance.

In 1901, Wilhelm Wrede devoted a monograph to this topic, arguing that Jesus did not in fact issue such prohibitions (*Das Messiasgeheimnis in den Evangelien: Zugleich ein Beitrag zum Verständnis des Markusevangeliums*; English trans., *The Messianic Secret* [1971]). In Wrede's view, (1) the earliest Christians believed that Jesus had become the MESSIAH at the time of the resurrection; (2) only later was messiaship thought to apply to Jesus' earthly life; (3) but the church was not aware that Jesus had made any messianic claims during his life; (4) therefore, the element of secrecy was invented and added to the tradition in order to account for the lack of evidence that Jesus had proclaimed himself as the Messiah. (Mark found this feature in the tradition and incorporated it in his gospel.)

Wrede's theory, though generally rejected in its original form, has exerted profound influence in NT scholarship, mainly because it showed that the secrecy motif required some kind of theological explanation. Most scholars accept (though usually in modified form) one or another feature of Wrede's explanation, but no clear consensus has emerged (see, e.g., C. M. Tuckett, ed., *The Messianic Secret* [1983]; H. Räisänen, *The "Messianic Secret" in Mark* [1990]). The basic historicity of the Markan account is defended by some prominent writers (see esp. the able treatment by N. B. Stonehouse, *The Witness of Matthew and Mark to Christ* [1944], ch. 3; and cf. the brief discussion by V. Taylor, *The Gospel according to St. Mark*, 2nd ed. [1966], 122–24).

Messias muh-si′uhs. KJV NT form of MESSIAH.

Messos, Apocalypse of. See ALLOGENES SUPREME.

metals and metallurgy. Metals comprise a large group of chemical elements that are distinguished from nonmetallic substances by their high conductivity for electricity and heat, properties resulting from the presence of "conduction" electrons that are free to move about within a metal, not being bound by specific atoms. Metals are also characterized by their high reflectivity for light. A polished sheet of metal, called a *speculum*, was used in ancient times as a mirror (cf. 1 Cor. 13:12). However, the widespread use of metals in ancient times, and to a considerable extent today, is dependent upon other properties that permit them to be shaped by hammering, melted and cast into molds, and alloyed with other metals. Alloying is carried out to increase strength and improve other properties.

The metals used in prebiblical and biblical times were almost entirely COPPER, GOLD, IRON, LEAD, TIN, and SILVER, although mercury and zinc also were used. Some of the properties of these metals are:

Metal	Chemical Symbol	Density	Melting Point
Copper	Cu	8.9	1083°C
Gold	Au	19.3	1063
Iron	Fe	7.9	1540
Lead	Pb	11.3	327
Mercury	Hg	13.6	−39
Silver	Ag	10.5	961
Tin	Sn	7.3	232
Zinc	Zn	7.1	420

Of these metals, copper and gold commonly occur in the native state, with gold almost certainly the first metal known to and used by man. It is too soft to be used for weapons or tools, but much used for jewelry and decorative purposes. Native copper is also soft, but it was found that it hardened appreciably when hammered and so was used for making weapons such as daggers and tools such as sickles. The common use of copper c. 4500 heralded the Chalcolithic age (copper-stone age). Although iron is the most abundant metal on earth, it is rarely found in its elemental (free) state, and the technology needed to remove its impurities was not fully developed until late in the 2nd millennium. However, the majority of meteorites, which are extraterrestrial bodies, are mainly iron with some nickel, and this material was used before 4000 B.C., as were gold and copper.

Silver also is found in the native state, and its use by man for jewelry and decorative purposes began c. 4000. The use of lead, tin, mercury, and zinc was dependent upon metallurgical discoveries relating to their smelting, refining, alloying, and working, as was the extension of the use of copper as the copper-tin alloy, BRONZE. This was also the case much later for BRASS, a copper-zinc alloy, and for the common use of iron.

Metallurgy is the science and technology of metals. It covers the processes of producing metals by extracting them from their ores, the refining and purification of these ores, and the working of them mechanically or alloying them to adapt them for various uses. The development of metallurgy during the pre-Christian era can be summarized as follows (all dates are B.C.):

Before 4000: native gold, copper, and meteoric iron hammered into shape, with the copper and iron hardened; melting, casting, and annealing of copper.

4000–3000: native silver hammered into shape; reduction of oxidized ores of copper (e.g. MALACHITE) and lead; smelting of natural mixed ores to produce copper alloys, including bronze; melting and casting of copper alloys; accidental reduction of oxidized ores of iron.

3000–2000: smelting of copper sulphides and tin oxides with metallic tin becoming an important item of trade; production of sponge iron; extraction of silver by cupellation with lead; making of gold leaf and metal wire.

2000–1000: bellows used in furnaces; iron reduced from ore and forged without melting to produce wrought iron—important by the year 1600; steel made by carburization in a hearth and by 1200 hardened by quenching; brass made from copper and zinc ores c. 1500 (not important until about 200); high-tin bronze (speculum) for mirrors.

1000 to the Christian era: vast expansion in production of metals, particularly iron; iron and steel welded into composite tools and weapons; mercury distilled from ores; separation of gold by amalgamation with mercury; stamping of coins (c. 700); more general use of bronze.

Much of this progressive development of metallurgy took place in the E Mediterranean and ANE region. However, a great deal of it was unknown to the slaves who escaped from Egypt under the leadership of MOSES (Exod. 12:51) during the 13th cent. At this time the production of iron was widespread in regions to the N, such as Anatolia (see ASIA MINOR), with the beginning of the Iron Age generally being placed c. 1200. That a group with such little knowledge of the science and technology of metals should have developed into the nation of Israel by the early part of the 10th cent. under DAVID, and subsequently become skilled in metal craft under SOLOMON (1 Ki. 10:16–23), is remarkable.

Entrances to horizontal mineshafts in Timnah. Copper was mined from these hills in the Desert of Paran.

Two contributing factors were the recognition, by David, of the importance of metalliferous ore deposits as a basis for national prosperity and strength, as shown by his conquest of EDOM with its deposits of iron and copper (2 Sam. 8:14), and the recognition, by Solomon, that experts had to be brought in from other more advanced cultures (1 Ki. 7:13–14). Assimilation of other cultures and expertise may have taken place by intermarriage, although this was contrary to instruction (Deut. 7:3). Unfortunately Solomon was not wise in the use of his power, and his expenditure was far too great in relation to the relatively limited, if important, natural resources at his disposal. This led to a dissipation of much of what David had gained, and was a primary cause leading to the breakup of the kingdom under his successor.

Metallurgy of gold. The gold of the ANE occurs in the native state, with that used by early humans recovered from stream sands and gravels where the gold is present as small flakes, or sometimes as nuggets. This gold was recovered by washing away the other mineral grains of the sand, which have a density about one sixth that of gold. Washing also was used to separate gold mined from veins, after the ore had been ground to a small size (see MINES, MINING).

The washing of gold ores is depicted on Egyptian monuments of the 1st dynasty (c. 2900). The simplest and earliest means of washing was by hand, in pans. Other means used included washing the stream sand or crushed ore over a sloping table or by sending the material down an inclined sluice with transverse ripple bars behind which the gold collected. The legend of the Golden Fleece was based on an expedition (c. 1200) to ARMENIA to obtain alluvial gold by washing gold-bearing sands over sheepskins.

By Roman times native gold (as well as silver) was extracted from ore by means of mercury, the process being called amalgamation. The ores are crushed in water and mixed with mercury while being agitated. The metallic gold (or silver) adheres to the mercury (quicksilver) and particles of the amalgam adhere to one another. These aggregates become large enough and heavy enough to sink in running water, which washes away the other mineral particles. This is much more efficient than just washing gold-bearing material with water. The amalgam is separated by heating in retorts. The mercury is driven off as a vapor, condensed, and reused, while the gold is melted and cast.

Whatever means of separation used, the gold generally contains other metallic elements. An

The upper register of this tomb painting from Egypt shows men smelting metal during the New Kingdom period (Tomb of Rekhmine near the Valley of the Kings, c. 1500 B.C.).

early method of refining was heating the gold with lead, salt, and barley bran, which act respectively as scorifier, flux, and reducing agent. This was done in an airtight clay crucible that remained in a hot fire for five days. By this time only the gold remained, with the other components of the charge absorbed by the clay of the crucible. Sometimes tin was added to the charge to harden the gold. The separation of base metals, such as copper and tin, also was carried out from a very early time by the method of cupellation. The gold to be purified is melted with lead, which is oxidized by the oxygen of the air. The molten lead oxide forms a slag into which the base metals go and with which they are separated off from the refined gold (cf. 1 Chr. 28:18; Mal. 3:3). However, any silver remained. From c. 600 onward this silver was separated from the gold by heating in a crucible with salt. The silver is converted to silver chloride, which passes into the molten slag, leaving the gold.

Methods of working gold were developed in ancient times. Soldering with gold-copper alloys was known before 3000, and before 2500 most jewelry techniques, such as inlay, stamping, repoussé, and granulation, were known. Gold was hammered into thin gold leaf and wire made by cutting sheet. These various techniques were used more than 1,000 years later by the children of Israel (e.g. Exod. 25:31; 39:3).

Metallurgy of copper. Native copper often occurs as large lumps. Though soft, it is hardened appreciably when hammered, and the first fabricated metallic articles used for other than adornment (prob. as early as 8000 B.C.) were made of copper. More than 2,000 years later it was found that copper could be melted (at 1083°C) and cast into desired shapes.

The reduction of copper ores to metallic copper in a red-hot charcoal fire was, almost certainly, a repeated campfire accident, possibly where brightly colored oxidized minerals of copper (turquoise, malachite) were being mined for ornamental and decorative purposes. The next step was to make a hole in the hearth to collect the molten metal and to line this with clay, a material that pottery manufacture had demonstrated to be fire-resistant. Subsequently rudimentary furnaces, enclosed by stones, evolved.

The copper ore initially smelted was the weathered, oxidized portion of the lode that cropped out at the surface and could be mined using wooden shovels, antler picks, and flint hammers. The copper produced from such weathered surface outcrops in the ANE before 2500 contained only 0.5 percent impurities. Subsequently the realization that there was copper in the deeper, unweathered parts of the rock mass led to the mining of less pure ore and the production of copper with 2–3 percent impurities. However, this metal was both harder and much easier to cast than the purer metal. Its production was the first step toward the deliberate mixing of ores and the production of various alloys of copper, of which bronze was the most important.

Bronze was made by smelting copper and tin ores together with charcoal, using a forced draught. This was created, before 1800, with the lungs; later bellows were used. The draught was through a nonflammable clay nozzle, with the molten metal collected in a clay crucible and then cast into ingots, or directly into molds. Later bronze was made from copper and tin previously reduced from their ores. The copper-zinc alloy, brass, was initially produced by heating copper with charcoal and smithsonite, the naturally occurring zinc carbonate. Later it was made from copper and zinc, both previously reduced from their ores.

Metallurgy of lead. Lead is reduced easily from its ores, particularly the oxidized ores such as lead carbonate (cerussite). The earliest method of smelting, which may have been the first metallurgical process used, was to place the ore with wood in a hole in the ground and fire it. The lead that was produced then ran along a gutter to a second hole, where it was collected. In the case of the chief lead ore, galena (lead sulphide), roasting is carried out in an oxidizing atmosphere. At a moderate temperature lead oxide and lead sulphate are formed from the lead sulphide. With increased temperature, and assisted by the addition of a small amount of flux (e.g., quicklime), the remaining lead sulphide reacts with the two oxidized products to produce lead and the gas sulphur dioxide. Any copper, antimony, or bismuth are oxidized and form a scum on the surface, mixed with a little lead oxide (litharge). This is taken off. The metal is desilvered by cupellation.

Metallurgy of silver. The earliest source of silver was native silver, which occurs mainly in an upper, secondarily enriched zone of silver lodes, as at Laurion, Greece. Subsequently silver was extracted from its ores by smelting with lead in a simple furnace, often following a preparatory roasting in the open air. The resultant lead-silver alloy is melted on a flat dish (cupel) of bone ash or marl. The lead, together with any other base metal impurities, is oxidized

A smelting furnace at Timnah that was used to change copper ore into usable metal.

by an air blast directed at the surface of the molten metal. The impurities are skimmed off (DROSS, Ezek. 22:18) and the last portions of the oxidized impurities are absorbed by the porous cupel. Only the silver, free from base metals, but containing any gold or platinum that may have been present, remains. This process of cupellation is thought to have been used by the Babylonians.

Metallurgy of tin. Almost the sole ore of tin is cassiterite (tin oxide). This is an uncommon mineral in the ANE, but a metal in which PHOENICIA traded (cf. Ezek. 27:12), particularly with Cornwall, England. Cassiterite was smelted in a hole in the ground by means of a charcoal fire and a forced draught. The tin oxide reacts with the carbon of the charcoal, producing tin and carbon monoxide gas. To assist in obtaining the temperature needed, the furnace probably had alternate small amounts of ore and burning charcoal added while the forced draught was in operation.

Metallurgy of iron. The earliest metallurgical working of iron was cold hammering of meteoric iron with flint tools. Ornaments were fabricated and weapons and tools made. Native iron probably was first reduced from its ores in large camp fires adjacent to rocks containing the oxides of iron-magnetite, haematite, and limonite. This accidentally smelted product would have been a dark spongy mass, not at first recognized as a metal, while remnants of unreduced ore would have rendered the mass non-malleable, and so useless. Only when air was excluded during cooling, following a sufficiently high fire temperature (800–900°C), would a coherent lump of metal have been produced. Hammering, aided by heat, welded such small pieces of sponge iron into larger pieces and hardening took place if heating was followed by sudden quenching in water.

The slowness of the ancients to make this discovery, which cleared the way for the massive use of iron and opened the door to the Iron Age, probably resulted from their experience with copper, a metal that softened when heated and was unaffected by quenching. However, once the secret of producing hard wrought iron was discovered, it was jealously guarded, in turn by the HITTITES of Asia Minor, and then by their conquerors, the PHILISTINES (cf. 1 Sam. 13:19–20). The method involved using forced draught in pits or primitive furnaces in which the iron ore was reduced to metallic iron by charcoal. Then the glowing ball was pulled out of the furnace (cf. Deut. 4:20; 1 Ki. 8:51; Jer. 11:4) and while still white hot hammered vigorously (forged), both to expel slag and to weld the hot metal into a coherent mass. The iron was not melted, and the product was wrought iron.

Accidentally, and later by design, ordinary iron was subjected to carburization when it was reheated in a charcoal forge. In this way additional carbon was absorbed with the resultant product being steel. These methods used by the ancients, with modifications and improvements of equipment and technique, produced all the iron up to the 14th cent. Only then was liquid pig iron (requiring temperatures in excess of 1500°C) and cast iron produced.

Metallurgy of zinc. The preparation of the metal zinc referred to as mock silver, by heating the oxide with coal, was described about 7 B.C. However, the zinc of brass almost certainly came from smelting smithsonite (zinc carbonate) with charcoal and with copper. Smithsonite was known from the silver mines of Laurion, Greece.

Metallurgy of mercury. The mercury used for separation of gold from its gangue was made, as at present, by roasting cinnabar, the naturally occurring mercury sulphide, in a current of air. The mercury vapor is carried on with the air and the liberated sulphur dioxide and is condensed by cooling. The cinnabar would have been obtained from Spain or Italy.

(See further T. A. Richard, *Man and Metals: A History of Mining in Relation to the Development of Civilization*, 2 vols. [1932]; J. R. Partington, *A Textbook of Inorganic Chemistry*, 6th ed. [1950], 776–80, 786–89; R. F. Tylecote, *A History of Metallurgy*, 2nd ed. [1992]; R. W. Cahn and P. Haasen, eds., *Physical Metallurgy*, 4th ed., 3 vols. [1996]; A. Hauptmann et al., *The Beginnings of Metallurgy* [1999].) D. R. BOWES

Meterus muh-tee´ruhs. KJV form of BAITERUS (1 Esd. 5:17).

Metheg Ammah mee´thig-am´uh (מֶ֫תֶג הָאַמָּה H5497, "bridle of the forearm [*or* cubit]" or "bridle of the canal" or, less likely, "bridle [*i.e.*, jurisdiction]

of the mother [city]"). Also Metheg-ammah. An otherwise unknown town that DAVID took from the control of the PHILISTINES (2 Sam. 8:1). Instead of this name, the parallel passage has "Gath and its surrounding villages" (1 Chr. 18:1), leading some to speculate that GATH was considered the "mother city" of the Philistines (cf. ASV and see 2 Sam. 20:19, which has the usual word for "mother," ʾēm H562; the form ʾammâ, however, never means "mother" in the OT). Some argue that the words should be translated as common nouns, referring to one cubit's length of a bridle and symbolizing either friendship or surrender (cf. LXX, tēn aphōrismenēn, "what was marked off," perhaps a reference to tribute, leading to the Vulgate's rendering *frenum tributi*, "bridle of tribute"; see ABD, 4:800).

S. WOUDSTRA

Methusael mi-th*oo*′say-uhl. KJV form of METH-USHAEL.

Methuselah mi-th*oo*′suh-luh (מְתוּשֶׁלַח H5500, possibly "man of the javelin" or "man of [the god] Shalach" [see ABD, 4:800–801]; Μαθουσαλά G3417). Son of ENOCH, descendant of SETH, and grandfather of NOAH (Gen. 5:21–22, 25–27; 1 Chr. 1:3; included in Luke's GENEALOGY OF JESUS CHRIST, Lk. 3:37). In the antedeluvian age of unusual longevity, Methuselah lived 969 years, longer than any other (Gen. 5:27). Some have thought his name ("man of the javelin") implies that he was a violent man, suggesting the wickedness of the generations just before the flood, but such a name would equally fit a hunter. Still others feel the element *šelaḥ* is a divine proper name indicating idolatry. The name Methuselah in the line of Seth seems to correspond to METHU-SHAEL in the line of CAIN, but the connection, if any, is difficult to ascertain. In later APOCALYPTIC LITERATURE, Methuselah plays an important role (e.g., *1 Enoch* 81–85).

E. B. SMICK

Methushael mi-th*oo*′shay-uhl (מְתוּשָׁאֵל H5499, possibly "man of God [*or* of request *or* of SHEOL]"; see ABD, 4: 801). KJV Methusael. Son of MEHU-JAEL, descendant of CAIN, and father of LAMECH (Gen. 4:18). Some have speculated that Methushael and METHUSELAH represent different traditions arising from the same name.

Meunim mi-yoo′nim (מְעוּנִים H5064, apparently the gentilic plural of a name such as מָעוֹן H5062; see MAON. In the NIV, the Hebrew term is rendered "Meunim" only twice, namely, in parallel passages that list the descendants of temple servants (NETHINIM) who returned from the EXILE (Ezra 2:50 [KJV, "Mehunim"]; Neh. 7:52; cf. 1 Esd. 5:31 [NRSV, "Maani"; KJV, "Meani"]). Apparently, the NIV regards Meunim here as a personal name referring to the ancestor of that family. It is possible, however, that in these passages, as elsewhere, the name is that of a non-Israelite people group. See MEUNITES.

Meunites mi-yoo′nits (מְעוּנִים H5064, apparently the gentilic plural of a name such as מָעוֹן H5062; see MAON). Also MEUNIM (for no obvious reason, the NRSV has "Meunim" in 1 Chr. 4:41, but "Meunites" in 2 Chr. 20:1; 26:7). A minor desert tribe of uncertain origin. This people group occupied an area SE of the DEAD SEA on the eastern border of EDOM whose chief city was Maʿan (about 12 mi. SE of PETRA). The Meunites were not Edomites, but apparently had such close relations with the people of Mount SEIR that they were in danger of being identified with them. It is possible, but disputed by some, that the Meunites were the same as the MAONITES who oppressed the Israelites in the time of the judges (Jdg. 10:12).

The Simeonites seem to have dispossessed one group of the Meunites and occupied their territory (1 Chr. 4:41; the KJV here understands the name as a common noun, *hammeʿônîm*, "the habitations"). On another occasion some of the Meunites joined forces with the Moabites and Ammonites to attack Judah (2 Chr. 20:1, where the MT reads "Ammonites" [cf. KJV], which seems redundant in context; most scholars emend to "Meunites" on the basis of the LXX and of 26:7 [KJV, "Mehunims"]). The combined armies moved around the S end of the Dead Sea and had gotten as far as EN GEDI before word reached the ears of the king of Judah. JEHOSHAPHAT was quite disturbed, but gathered an army and met them at the Pass of ZIZ. The battle, however, never took place, for the invading army practically annihilated itself because of internal dissension. All that the men of Judah had to do was gather up the spoil. The mention of Mount Seir in this passage does not refer to the Edomites (they did not participate in this invasion), but rather to the direction from which the coalition army came.

In the reign of King Uzziah (c. 783–742 B.C.) the Meunites are mentioned, along with the Philistines and Arabians, as being troublesome to Judah again (2 Chr. 26:7; in v. 8 some scholars emend "Ammonites" to "Meunites" on the basis of the LXX). The passage records that Uzziah was successful in his campaign against them, and it is thought that he may have taken a number of them prisoners and given them to the temple priests as servants (cf. Num. 31:30; Josh. 9:27; Ezra 8:20; and see Nethinim). This assumption would help to explain the presence of descendants from the Meunites among the temple servants who returned after the exile (Ezra 2:50; Neh. 7:52), although some think that the reference here is to descendants of Caleb associated with the town of Maon. See Maon (place). In these passages, however, the NIV and the NRSV have "Meunim," as though it were the name of an ancestor.

It should be added that in two occurrences (1 Chr. 4:41; Ezra 2:50), the Hebrew consonantal text (Ketib) reads *meʿînîm*, "Meinites"; moreover, in all the Chronicles passages the Septuagint has *Minaioi*. On this basis, it has been argued that two of the texts (1 Chr. 4:41 and 2 Chr. 26:7–8) refer to the Mineans, a tribe from the S Arabian area of Maʿin that colonized some Mediterranean cities, such as Gaza, around 400 B.C. (E. A. Knauf in *ABD*, 4:801–2, s.v. "Meunim"); but such an identification would mean that the Chronicler transferred his own historical setting back to earlier times. Others have proposed that the Meunites should be identified with the Muʾnayya mentioned by Tiglath-Pileser III (see I. Ephʿal, *The Ancient Arabs: Nomads on the Borders of the Fertile Crescent 9th-5th Centuries B.C.* [1982], 219–20.)

C. P. Gray

Meuzal mee-yoo´zuhl. KJV marginal reading for Hebrew *meʾûzāl*, a word of uncertain meaning (Ezek. 27:29). See Uzal.

Me-Zahab mee´zuh-hab (מֵי זָהָב *H4771*, "waters of gold"). Grandfather of Mehetabel, who was the wife of Hadad (Hadar) king of Edom (Gen. 36:39; 1 Chr. 1:50). See Hadad (person). The name, however, would seem to refer to a place. The description of Matred as the daughter of Me-Zahab might mean that the latter was Matred's native city (cf. *ABD*, 4:804–5).

Mezobaite mi-zoh´bay-*it* (מְצֹבָיָה *H5168*, derivation uncertain). KJV Mesobaite. A descriptive title identifying Jaaziel, one of David's mighty warriors (1 Chr. 11:47). If the adjective is a gentilic of *ṣôbâ H7420*, the form is anomalous, so many scholars conjecture that the original was *miṣṣōbah*, "from Zobah" (cf. 2 Sam. 23:36). Several of David's warriors in the latter part of the list seem to have come from Transjordan, so it is indeed possible that Jaaziel was an Aramean from the kingdom of Zobah.

mezuzah muh-zoo´zuh. Plural *mezuzot*. This term does not occur in English versions of the Bible. It is a transliteration of Hebrew *mĕzûzâ H4647* ("doorpost"), used, for example, for the doorframes of ordinary houses where the blood of the Passover sacrifice was sprinkled (Exod. 12:7, 22–23),

Mezuzah fixed to the door frame of a modern home.

or where the law was to be written (Deut. 6:9; 11:20; cf. Prov. 8:34; Ezek. 43:12). The doorposts of a building, like the THRESHOLD, evidently had a special significance, bordering on sacredness. In the course of time the term *mezuzah* came to mean the small container of portions of Scripture which orthodox Jews still attach to the doorposts of their home (Deut. 6:9; 11:20).   J. ARTHUR THOMPSON

Miamin mi′uh-min. KJV alternate form of MIJAMIN.

Mibhar mib′hahr (מִבְחָר *H4437*, "choice, special"). Son of Hagri; he is included in the list of DAVID's mighty warriors (1 Chr. 11:38). The name does not appear in the parallel passage (2 Sam. 23:36); see discussion under HAGRI.

Mibsam mib′sam (מִבְשָׂם *H4452*, "fragrant"; cf. BASEMATH, IBSAM). (1) Son of ISHMAEL and grandson of ABRAHAM (Gen. 25:13; 1 Chr. 1:29). The twelve sons of Ishmael became the eponymous ancestors of tribes in N ARABIA (F. V. Winnett, "The Arabian Genealogies in Genesis," in *Translating and Understanding the Old Testament*, ed. H. T. Frank and W. L. Reed [1970], 171–96, esp. 193–96). See also below, #2.

(2) Son of SHAUL or, more likely, of SHALLUM; included in the genealogy of SIMEON (1 Chr. 4:25). Because the name MISHMA occurs in connection with both this Mibsam and #1 above, some scholars speculate that #1 and #2 refer to the same clan. According to this view, the Ishmaelite or Arabian clans of Mibsam and Mishma inhabited the NEGEV; when the tribe of Simeon occupied this region, these clans somehow became integrated into the Simeonite genealogy (cf. *ABD*, 4:805).

Mibzar mib′zahr (מִבְצָר *H4449*, possibly "fortress"). Descendant of ESAU, listed among the clan chiefs of EDOM (Gen. 36:42; 1 Chr. 1:53). His name may have been preserved in an ancient locality. EUSEBIUS (*Onom.* 124.20–21) identifies it with *Mabsara*, a large village subject to PETRA and still in existence in his time. Others have suggested BOZRA.

Mica mi′kuh (מִיכָא *H4775*, short form of מִיכָיְהוּ *H4780*, "who is like Yahweh?"; cf. MICAH, MICAIAH, MICHAEL). KJV also Micha; TNIV Mika. (1) Son of MEPHIBOSHETH (2 Sam. 9:12). See MICAH #2.

(2) Son of Zicri (or Zabdi), descendant of ASAPH, and father of MATTANIAH; the latter is listed among the Levites who resettled in Jerusalem after the EXILE and is described as being responsible for leading in thanksgiving and prayer (1 Chr. 9:15 [KJV, "Micah"]; Neh. 11:17; in the latter reference, the name is spelled *mîkâ*). One of his descendants, UZZI son of Bani, became chief officer of the Levites (Neh. 11:22). This Mica is probably the same as MICAIAH son of Zaccur, whose descendant, ZECHARIAH son of Jonathan, participated in the procession at the dedication of the wall (12:35).

(3) A Levite who affixed his seal to the covenant of NEHEMIAH (Neh. 10:11). Because of the chronological differences, this Mica cannot be the same as #2 above, but some have speculated that the list is not authentic, that it is composed of names from other records, and that therefore Mica #2 was wrongly incorporated into the list of signatories (cf. *ABD*, 4:806).

Micah mi′kuh (מִיכָה *H4777*, short form of מִיכָיְהוּ *H4780*, "who is like Yahweh?"; cf. MICA, MICAIAH, MICHAEL). KJV also Michah. (1) An Ephraimite who set up an idolatrous shrine, and whose idols were used by the Danites when they resettled in LAISH (Jdg. 17–18; the first two occurrences of his name are given in the full form, *mîkāyāhû* [17:1, 4], but elsewhere *mîkâ*). Micah had stolen 1,100 pieces of silver from his mother, who pronounced a curse on the thief. He then returned the money to her, and she used 200 pieces of the silver to make "a carved image and a cast idol" (17:3; NRSV, "an idol of cast metal"), which were put in Micah's house. Micah also made an EPHOD and some TERAPHIM, and even made one of his sons priest of this shrine. Some time later, a Levite from BETHLEHEM (prob. the one identified as JONATHAN son of GERSHOM in 18:30), who was searching for a new place to live, stopped in Micah's house. In return for a salary and provisions, the Levite became Micah's priest. When five Danites in search of a new home for their tribe obtained a favorable oracle from the Levite, they returned with 600 armed men and offered him employment as priest in their new tribal territory.

They took with them Micah's ephod, teraphim, and the carved image. Micah was helpless to prevent this action. He pursued after them, but was warned that interference would cost him his goods and his life. Micah's idols became a shrine in the city of Laish. See DAN (PERSON AND TRIBE); DAN (PLACE). The story of Micah serves as striking evidence of the truth repeated several times in the book of Judges: "In those days Israel had no king; everyone did as he saw fit" (17:6).

(2) Son of MERIB-BAAL (MEPHIBOSHETH) and descendant of King SAUL through JONATHAN; he had four sons (1 Chr. 8:34–35; 9:40–41). He is also called MICA (2 Sam. 9:12).

(3) Son of Shimei, descendant of REUBEN through Joel, and ancestor of Beerah; the latter was a Reubenite leader who was taken into exile by the Assyrians under TIGLATH-PILESER (1 Chr. 5:4–6).

(4) Son of Uzziel and descendant of LEVI; he served during the latter part of DAVID's reign (1 Chr. 23:20; 24:24–25).

(5) Son of Imlah (2 Chr. 18:14 Heb.); see MICAIAH #2.

(6) Father of Abdon, who was one of JOSIAH's messengers to HULDAH (2 Chr. 34:20); also called MICAIAH (2 Ki. 22:12).

(7) Son of Zicri (or Zabdi) and father of Mattaniah (1 Chr. 9:15 KJV; Neh. 11:17 Heb.); see MICA #2.

(8) Micah the MORASTHITE, prophet (Jer. 26:18; Mic. 1:1). See MICAH, BOOK OF.

A. K. HELMBOLD

Micah, Book of. Sixth book of the Minor Prophets. It is mentioned by Ben Sirach in a way that attests its early acceptance as part of sacred Scripture (Sir. 48:10).

I. Background. The prophet Micah ministered during the reigns of JOTHAM (742–735 B.C.), AHAZ (735–715), and HEZEKIAH (715–687; cf. Jer. 26:18). Since Mic. 6 is addressed to "Israel" and ch. 1 speaks of the downfall of SAMARIA, Micah's career evidently began sometime before the year 722. The great world power and constant threat to the security of the Hebrews was ASSYRIA, ruled by TIGLATH-PILESER III (745–727), SHALMA-NESER V (727–722), SARGON II (722–705), and SENNACHERIB (705–681). During the early part of Micah's life, the Syro-Ephraimitic war between Judah on the one side and the coalition of Israel and SYRIA (ARAM) on the other was waged. Part of the reason for the war was the refusal of Ahaz to join the alliance against Tiglath-Pileser. Micah saw the defeat of the northern kingdom and fall of Samaria to Assyria in 722/721. The close of his ministry probably came before the invasion of Sennacherib (2 Ki. 18:13), who besieged JERUSALEM in 701, a siege which occasioned the construction of the SILOAM tunnel.

Micah lived in Moresheth (see below, section III) (Mic. 1:1; Jer. 26:18), on the border between Judah and a "no-man's land" contested by Egypt, Assyria, and the Philistines. The latter's uprisings against Assyria in the period 721–711 were in full view. The incursions of Sargon II into the area between 715 and 711 may be referred to in Mic. 1:10–16. By paying tribute to the Assyrians, Ahaz had maintained an uneasy peace. During UZZIAH's long reign (ending in 742) and following, there was a period of comparative economic prosperity, occasioned in part by Judean control of an overland trade route to the port of ELATH (cf. 2 Ki. 14:7). This prosperity concentrated wealth and its concomitant power in the hands of a few and brought with it social injustices that the prophet castigated. It seems likely that the religious reforms instituted by King Hezekiah must have taken place near the end of Micah's recorded ministry, or that the reforms affected only the cult and had little impact upon the personal and social lives of the Judeans.

II. Unity. One of the first scholars to question the unity of Micah was Bernhard Stade (in *ZAW* 1 [1881]: 161–72, and 4 [1884]: 291–97), who contended that nothing beyond Mic. 3 was written by the prophet. Most modern scholars believe that chs. 4–7 are two (or more) miscellaneous collections later added as supplements, and are probably postexilic. Many modern scholars think there are genuine Michaean elements in chs. 4–7, but disagree on their extent. For example, W. J. Harrelson thinks a "good part" comes from Micah (*Interpreting the Old Testament* [1964], 361).

Contrary to common opinion, S. Sandmel says all of ch. 7 is from Micah, observing that the hopeful tone of vv. 7–20 is against a late date (*The Hebrew Scriptures: An Introduction to Their Literature and Religious Ideas* [1963], 103). However, most scholars think that 7:7–20 (or 7:8–20) is probably exilic or later. The lack of agreement among critical scholars leaves their conclusions open to question.

There are substantial arguments for the unity of the book: (1) Three separate oracles are introduced by the word "hear" (Mic. 1:2; 3:1; 6:1). (2) The shifts in subject matter—thought by the critical scholars to indicate composite authorship—are explainable on the basis of the book's being a collection of fragments of oracles of the prophet rather than records of extended discourse. (3) The same image of the shepherd is found throughout the book (2:12; 3:2–3; 4:6; 5:3–5; 7:14). (4) The literary device of "interruption-answer" is found in each section (2:5, 12; 3:1; 6:6–8; 7:14–15). (5) There are frequent historical allusions or references throughout. (6) At least twenty-four passages from the other 8th-cent. prophets, Hosea, Amos, and Isaiah, as well as two from Joel (who may also be 8th cent.), are paralleled in Mic. 4–7, arguing for its composition in that century. Arguments against Micah's unity based on the usage of Isa. 40–66 in Mic. 4–7 are dubious because they beg the question of the date of Isa. 40–66 (cf. J. H. Raven, *Old Testament Introduction* [1906], 229–30).

III. Authorship. The prophet Micah was a native of MORESHETH (Mic. 1:1; Jer. 26:18), perhaps identical with MORESHETH GATH, a dependency of GATH (Mic. 1:14; cf. LXX, *klēronomias Geth*). Some have equated it with the ancient Greek place name, Marisa. The site is located in the area about modern Beit Jibrin, some 25 mi. SW of Jerusalem. JEROME located it just E of Jibrin; others have located it at Tell el-Judeideh (cf. E. G. Kraeling, *Rand McNally Bible Atlas*, 2nd ed. [1962], 301), or at Tell el-Menshiyeh, 6.5 mi. W of Beit Jibrin (cf. E. A. Leslie in *IDB*, 3:369). Moresheth is mentioned in Josh. 15:44; 2 Chr. 11:8; 14:9, 10; 20:37. Its location made it a frontier outpost, with military movements easily observable in the area. The Assyrians marched through in 734, 711, and 701, and met the Egyptians at nearby RAPHIA in 719. Hence, Micah's outlook was not that of an isolationist, but of one vitally concerned about his nation's foreign affairs. As a native of the SHEPHELAH, he felt keenly the plight of poor country people.

Micah was a man of courage, conviction, and rare personal faith. His attributes have been summed up as follows: "Strict morality, unbending devotion to justice both in law and in action, sympathy with the poor, these are Micah's characteristics" (W. Nowack, *Die kleinen Propheten* [1897], 254). His main concern was the social injustice prevalent in his day. Such injustice, however, could be removed only by a religious revival. If men do not return to the Lord, there will be a visitation of God's avengers. Final hope is offered in the coming of the Messiah from BETHLEHEM.

IV. Date. Scholars disagree as to the exact dates of Micah's ministry. According to Mic. 1:1, he prophesied "during the reigns of Jotham, Ahaz and Hezekiah, kings of Judah." Other than this general information (which some hold to be a later addition by a postexilic editor), the evidence is scanty and inferential. The content of ch. 6 would seem to indicate a date before 722 for that oracle. Jeremiah's quotation of Mic. 3 (Jer. 26:18–19) would date that section during Hezekiah's reign. Micah's description of the prevailing corruption and immorality would fit conditions in the reign of Ahaz (735–715). It seems likely that the bulk of his recorded prophetic oracles were uttered in the period 725–710. Unless Hezekiah's reforms left social conditions untouched, his ministry must be placed before that revival. He prophesied against both the northern and southern kingdoms, but was chiefly concerned with the latter.

V. Occasion and purpose. Stemming from the poorer class, Micah was acutely aware of the injustices and avarice of the rich. While he was interested in the political affairs of his nation, it was only as they were connected with the religious and moral situation that Micah spoke to them. His message can be epitomized in his own words: "But as for me, I am filled with power, with the Spirit of the LORD, and with justice and might, to declare

A general view of the region around Bethlehem, where Micah prophesied that Messiah would be born (Mic. 5:2).

to Jacob his transgression, to Israel his sin" (Mic. 3:8). It is because of the sins of his people that God sends the Assyrians as his scourge. God's punishment is to be followed by a period of unparalleled blessing connected with the coming of the MESSIAH. For Micah, faith in Yahweh must issue in social justice and personal holiness because Yahweh is righteous and sovereign. The refusal of Ahaz to seek a sign (Isa. 7:12) and Hezekiah's payment of tribute to Assyria (2 Ki. 18:14–16) are examples of the lack of faith in Yahweh's protection on the part of the kings, a lack also evident among the commoners. Micah set forth God's complaint against his people (cf. Mic. 6) and announced certain punishment. However, God's mercy will finally prevail (cf. ch. 7).

VI. Text. Much of the Hebrew text of Micah seems to be quite well preserved, and the antiquity of the textual form preserved in the Masoretic tradition is confirmed by the Minor Prophets Scroll discovered at Wadi Murabbaʿat (Mur 88=MurXII) and by the Greek Minor Prophets Scroll discovered at Naḥal Ḥever (8ḤevXIIgr). Nevertheless, some passages in the book present significant textual difficulties, and the ancient versions, especially the SEPTUAGINT, are helpful in reconstructing the original text.

VII. Special problems. Three special problems stand out in the study of the book of Micah. First, because of the abrupt transition, many scholars think Mic. 2:12–13 is out of place or is an interpolation. Among the explanations offered are the following: (a) These are the words of false prophets of hope (Ibn Ezra, Michaelis), or they are a marginal note by Micah or someone else giving the teaching of the false prophets (Ewald), or an interruption of Micah by a false prophet (Van Orelli). However, it would seem unique for a false prophet to admit the exile—they were prophets of false hopes. (b) The passage is a late, postexilic composition (J. M. P. Smith). (c) The passage is genuine and belongs in the context. (d) It continues the threat of v. 10, that is, Jacob is assembled for punishment (Kimchi, Ephraem Syrus, Theodoret, Calvin, Van Hoonaker). (e) The passage is genuine but out of place (Van Ryssel, Koenig, Driver). The simplest explanation seems to be that the passage is Micah's quotation of a false prophet who may be speaking of the remnant left by the Assyrians after 722.

The second problem is that of the relationship of the oracle found in Mic. 4:1–3 to the identical passage in Isa. 2:2–4. Most older scholars felt that Micah had borrowed from Isaiah. There is enough difference in the context and in the extent of the oracle to argue that both prophets made use of a "floating oracle" by an earlier prophet of hope. In Micah the oracle fits the context better than in Isaiah.

The third problem is the occurrence of the word BABYLON in Mic. 4:10. Those who deny the predictive element in prophecy explain the passage either as coming from a late date (after 605, when NEBUCHADNEZZAR's power was evident), or as a metonymy (with "Babylon" standing for Assyria).

VIII. Content and outline. Most scholars divide Micah into three major sections:
 A. Yahweh's judgment upon Israel and Judah (Mic. 1–3)
  1. Judgment upon Samaria and Judah (ch. 1)
  2. Woe pronounced upon oppressors (2:1–11)
  3. Mercy upon a remnant (2:12–13; perhaps an interruption?)
  4. Denunciation of the heads of Jacob (ch. 3)
 B. The vision of a glorious future (chs. 4–5)
  1. The character of the messianic kingdom (4:1–5)
  2. The establishment of the kingdom (4:6—5:1)
  3. The coming of the Davidic ruler (5:2–4)
  4. Judah blessed and judged in the kingdom (5:5–15)
 C. Yahweh's controversy with his people and the promise of future blessings (ch. 6–7)
  1. The requirements of Yahweh's covenant (6:1–8)
  2. The sins of Judah denounced (6:9–16)
  3. The prophet's lamentation over social sins (7:1–6)
  4. The prophet's faith expressed in a liturgy of confession and trust (7:7–20)

Micah singled out the leaders, the civil rulers, and the false prophets for special denunciation (Mic. 3:1–7). He was concerned with Samaria and Jerusalem, the capitals of the northern and southern kingdoms, for there power was centralized, and from these centers injustice flowed forth. Among the sins he castigated were the following: (a) Idolatry was to be destroyed (Mic. 1:1–7, cf. 2 Ki. 16:10–18). (b) The nobility were seizing the fields of the poor (Mic. 2:2). (c) They disregarded inheritance rights (Mic. 2:4–5; cf. Lev. 25:8–13; Num. 27:11; Deut. 27:17). (d) Even tourists were robbed (Mic. 2:8). (e) Widows were evicted (Mic. 2:9; cf. Exod. 22:22; Deut. 27:19; Isa. 1:17). (f) The ultimate in sin was the practice of human sacrifice (Mic. 6:7; cf. 2 Ki. 16:3–4). This rite was not unknown in the time of Ahaz, nor during the reign of MANASSEH, whose accession probably was after Micah's lifetime.

The preaching of AMOS, HOSEA, and ISAIAH is summarized in the famous saying of Mic. 6:8: "He has showed you, O man, what is good. And what does the LORD require of you? To act justly and to love mercy and to walk humbly with your God." Amos was the prophet of justice (Amos 5:24), Hosea spoke of mercy (Hos. 6:6), while Isaiah called upon his people to live in communion with Yahweh (Isa. 6:5). Probably the most outstanding example of the so-called *rib* or lawsuit oracle (from the Heb. verb *rib H8189*, "to dispute, plead a case") is found in Mic. 6:1–8. The *rib* pattern may be based on the formal features of human covenants. Heaven and earth are called to witness (Deut. 32:1, 5; Ps. 50:4; Isa. 1:2; Ezek. 6:2–3).

Among the predictive passages in the book are Mic. 1:3–5 and 3:12, both foretelling the destruction of Jerusalem, and 4:10, which promises the rescue of God's people from Babylon. The passage in 5:2 promising the ruler to come from BETHLEHEM should perhaps be interpreted as referring to the dynasty of DAVID rather than to a geographical location. One notable feature of the content of the book is the long passage in 1:10–16, which is replete with typical Hebrew paronamasia (for attempts at rendering these paronomasiae into English, see esp. F. W. Farrar, *The Minor Prophets* [1890]; J. Moffatt, *A New Translation of the Bible* [1930]; and L. Smith in *Int* 6 [1952]: 210–27).

(Important commentaries include J. Calvin, *Commentaries on the Twelve Minor Prophets*, 5 vols. [1846–49, orig. 1557], 149–409; G. A. Smith, *The Book of the Twelve Prophets* [1896]; J. M. P. Smith, *A Critical and Exegetical Commentary on Micah* [bound with other minor prophets], ICC [1911]; G. L. Robinson, *The Twelve Minor Prophets* [1926]; T. F. K. Laetsch, *The Minor Prophets* [1956]; L. C. Allen, *Joel, Obadiah, Jonah, and Micah*, NICOT [1976]; J. L. Mays, *Micah*, OTL [1976]; D. R.

Hillers, *Micah*, Hermeneia [1984]; R. L. Smith, *Micah-Malachi*, WBC 32 [1984]; H. W. Wolff, *Micah: A Commentary* [1990]; T. J. Findley, *Joel, Obadiah, Micah* [1996]; B. K. Waltke in *The Minor Prophets: An Exegetical and Expository Commentary*, ed. T. McComiskey [1992–98], 2:591–764; R. Kessler, *Micha*, HTKAT [1999]; K. L. Barker and W. Bailey, *Micah, Nahum, Habakkuk, Zephaniah*, NAC 20 [1998]; W. McKane, *The Book of Micah: Introduction and Commentary* [1998]; F. I. Andersen and D. N. Freedman, *Micah: A New Translation with Introduction and Commentary*, AB 24E [2000]; B. K. Waltke, *A Commentary on Micah* [2007]. See also B. Renaud, *La formation du livre de Michée: tradition et actualisation* [1977]; D. G. Hagstrom, *The Coherence of the Book of Micah: A Literary Analysis* [1988]; C. S. Shaw, *The Speeches of Micah: A Rhetorical-Historical Analysis* [1993]; E. Ben Zvi, *Micah*, FOTL 21B [2000]; M. R. Jacobs, *The Conceptual Coherence of the Book of Micah* [2001]; J. A. Wagenaar, *Judgement and Salvation: The Composition and Redaction of Micah 2–5* [2001]; and the bibliography compiled by W. E. Mills, *Jonah-Micah* [2002].)

A. K. Helmbold

Micaiah mi-kay′yuh (מִיכָיָה *H4779* [2 Ki. 22:12; Neh. 12:35, 41], מִיכָיְהוּ *H4780* [2 Chr. 17:7], elsewhere מִיכָיְהוּ *H4781*, "who is like Yahweh?"; cf. Mica, Micah, Michael). KJV also Michaiah. **(1)** An Ephraimite (Jdg. 17:1, 4, Heb.); see Micah #1.

(2) Son of Imlah, prophet (1 Ki. 22:8–26; 2 Chr. 18:7–25 [in v. 14 the Heb. has the short form *mikâ*]). This man performed a deed which took great courage and unwavering faith in the Lord as God. Ahab and his idolatrous wife Jezebel were determined to suppress those who called for the worship of Yahweh only. About this time Ahab sought to regain control of the frontier city Ramoth Gilead from his old enemy Ben-Hadad, the Aramean. For that purpose he sought and needed the assistance of Jehoshaphat king of Judah. On the occasion of a formal state visit, Ahab put the question bluntly to the Judean king and was given an affirmative answer, but with the condition that they inquire of the Lord his will in the matter (1 Ki. 22:4–5). The king of Israel obligingly gathered 400 prophets, presumably prophets of the Lord (Yahweh) and asked, "Shall I go to war against Ramoth Gilead, or shall I refrain?" They all gave this wicked man the answer he wanted to hear, "Go ... for the Lord will give it into the king's hand" (v. 6). One of them even acted out the victory with a set of iron horns (v. 11).

Jehoshaphat sensed their perfidy and asked for a true prophet of the Lord. Ahab responded, "There is still one man through whom we can inquire of the Lord, but I hate him because he never prophesies anything good about me, but always bad" (1 Ki. 22:8). Jehoshaphat insisted, so Micaiah was summoned. The messenger warned Micaiah to conform, but the prophet responded (as Luther would many centuries later at Worms), "As surely as the Lord lives, I can tell him only what the Lord tells me" (v. 14).

When questioned, this true prophet began by giving an affirmative answer in obvious contempt (1 Ki. 22:15). Ahab sensed that he was being mocked and called for the truth, whence Micaiah painted two word pictures in unmistakable clarity. The first showed Israel as a scattered flock without a shepherd, and the second depicted the council of heaven with the Lord seated on his throne and before all the host of heaven, one of whom volunteered to become a lying spirit in the mouth of Ahab's prophets. (The picture is similar to Job 1–2, where Satan, the Accuser, stands before the Lord and presses for permission to attack Job.) The prophecy had such forcefulness that the same false prophet who had demonstrated with iron horns, Zedekiah son of Kenaanah, smote Micaiah on the cheek and accused him of being the false one. Jehoshaphat, a good but weak man, said nothing; but Ahab had had enough and might well have taken the bold prophet's life if Jehoshaphat had not been present. Instead he returned Micaiah to prison to be fed on bread and water. As Micaiah was led away he drove his darts of truth in deeper by warning that if Ahab came back from the battle alive then the Lord had not spoken by him (v. 28).

Although Ahab had rejected Micaiah's words by declaring he would come again in peace (1 Ki. 22:27), yet the words so lingered in his mind that he disguised himself as he went into battle. The Scripture makes clear that wholly by the Lord these words were fulfilled. The Arameans could not find

Ahab to kill him, but an archer simply shot an unaimed arrow into the air and when it descended it hit Ahab in a small unprotected spot between his scale armor and breastplate. The king fell mortally wounded, and Micaiah's prophecy was vindicated (cf. Deut. 18:22). (See E. J. Young, *My Servants the Prophets* [1961], 136–42.)

(3) Mother of King ABIJAH of Judah (2 Chr. 13:2 NRSV; KJV, "Michaiah"; NIV, "Maacah," following some versional evidence). See MAACAH #9.

(4) One of five officials sent by King JEHOSHAPHAT "to teach in the towns of Judah" (2 Chr. 17:7).

(5) Son of Zaccur and father of Mattaniah; his descendant, ZECHARIAH son of Jonathan, participated in the procession at the dedication of the wall (Neh. 12:35). See MICA #2.

(6) A priest who played the trumpet at the dedication of the wall (Neh. 12:41).

(7) Father of Acbor; the latter was one of JOSIAH's messengers to HULDAH (2 Ki. 22:12); also called MICAH (2 Chr. 34:20).

(8) Son of GEMARIAH, grandson of SHAPHAN, and a contemporary of JEREMIAH (Jer. 36:11, 13). Micaiah carried Jeremiah's message to the princes gathered at the palace of King JEHOIAKIM. The princes then called for the sermon to be read to them. Some have proposed that this Micaiah is the same as #7 above (see the discussion in *ABD*, 4:810–11).   E. B. SMICK

mice. See MOUSE.

Micha m*i*´kuh. KJV alternate form of MICAH.

Michael m*i*´kay-uhl, m*i*´kuhl (מִיכָאֵל *H4776*, "who is like God?" [cf. MICAIAH]; Μιχαήλ *G3640*). **(1)** Father of Sethur, who was one of the twelve spies sent out to reconnoiter the Promised Land; he represented the tribe of ASHER (Num. 13:13).

(2) Son of Abihail; he was one of seven relatives from the tribe of GAD who occupied the region E of GILEAD (1 Chr. 5:13; cf. vv. 10, 14).

(3) Son of Jeshishai and ancestor of #2 above (1 Chr. 5:14).

(4) Son of Baaseiah, descendant of LEVI through GERSHON, and great-grandfather of ASAPH the singer (1 Chr. 6:40).

(5) Son of Izrahiah and descendant of ISSACHAR; a military chief (1 Chr. 7:3).

(6) Son of Beriah and descendant of BENJAMIN, listed among the heads of families living in postexilic Jerusalem (1 Chr. 8:16; cf. v. 28). His father and uncle, however, are described as "heads of families of those living in Aijalon and who drove out the inhabitants of Gath" (v. 13).

(7) One of several warriors from the tribe of MANASSEH who joined DAVID at ZIKLAG; they are described as "leaders of units of a thousand" (1 Chr. 12:20).

(8) Father of Omri; the latter was an officer over the tribe of ISSACHAR during the reign of David (1 Chr. 27:18).

(9) Son of JEHOSHAPHAT, king of Judah (1 Chr. 21:2). He and his brothers received a very generous inheritance (v. 3). Jehoshaphat's firstborn, JEHORAM, killed all his brothers when he became king (v. 4).

(10) Descendant of Shephatiah; his son Zebadiah was one of the family heads who returned to Jerusalem with EZRA (Ezra 8:8; 1 Esd. 8:34).

(11) An angel. See MICHAEL THE ARCHANGEL.

J. E. ROSSCUP

Michael the archangel m*i*´kay-uhl, m*i*´kuhl (מִיכָאֵל *H4776*, "who is like God?" [cf. MICAIAH]; Μιχαήλ *G3640*). The book of DANIEL refers to Michael as a (great) prince (Dan. 10:13, 21; 12:1). The NT refers to him as "the archangel Michael" (Jude 9) and elsewhere speaks of "Michael and his angels" (Rev. 12:7). See ANGEL. Paul does not expressly mention Michael but makes reference to "the archangel" (1 Thess. 4:16; the Bible never uses the pl. "archangels"). The Bible also names GABRIEL as an important angel (Dan. 8:16; 9:21; Lk. 1:19, 26). The pseudepigraphic book of *1 Enoch* names Michael, Gabriel, Raphael, and Uriel (9.1; 40.9), and numbers archangels at seven (20.1–7; cf. Tob. 12:15). Among the DEAD SEA SCROLLS, the *War Scroll* gives attention to Michael and other angels (e.g., 1QM IX, 15–16; for other extrabiblical references, see *ABD*, 4:811).

Daniel distinctly relates Michael to Israel as prince and guardian over the destinies of that nation (Dan. 10:21; 12:1). During Israel's unprecedented "time of distress" (12:1; cf. Jer. 30:7; Matt. 24:21),

Michael will be active for her welfare when Satan is seeking to destroy her (Rev. 12:7–9). This seems to be at the outset of the last part of the tribulation period. J. A. Seiss likens Michael to a general who has his officers and soldiers, though all are under the king, who in this case is Christ (*The Apocalypse*, 15th ed. [n.d.], 305–7; there is no proof that Michael is Christ, as some contend).

Jude 9 speaks of Michael resisting the devil, but committing the judgment of him to the Lord. The dispute involved the body of Moses. Specific background for this, nowhere mentioned in the OT, may have been known by 1st-cent. readers because of written or oral traditions. Origen (*On First Principles* 3.2.1) supposed it was taken from a pseudepigraphical writing, "The Ascension of Moses" (see Moses, Assumption of). R. H. Charles lists other parallels between this work and Jude (*APOT*, 2:412–13). If Jude did use such a source, the Spirit enabled him to discern as fact what really was true in it. One explanation of Jude 9 is that the devil sought to deny honorable burial to Moses' body when he died (Deut. 34) on the ground that he was a murderer (Exod. 2), and that Michael contended for the body (see other traditions cited by R. Wolff, *The General Epistles of James and Jude* [1970]).

The Jehovah's Witnesses group claims that Christ is not God but only an exalted angel, namely Michael. E. W. Hengstenberg (*Christology of the Old Testament*, 2nd ed., 4 vols. [1858–68], 4:266–71) and some other Protestants have identified Michael with the glorious man dressed in linen (Dan. 10:5–6) and also with the "angel of the Lord" and then Christ. They, however, uphold the deity of Christ. Hengstenberg distinguished the one who *appears* in linen (10:5) from the one who *speaks* to Daniel (10:10–14), equating the latter with Gabriel. C. F. Keil reasons—on what this writer considers better grounds—that the one in linen is more naturally also the one who speaks (KD, *Daniel*, 411–14). From this he goes on to view this one in linen, distinct from Michael (10:13, 21), as the angel of the Lord seen in other OT passages (Gen. 18:22; 19:1; Zech. 3:1–10; et al.). The description here fits that of the Lord (Ezek. 1:26–28; Rev. 1:13–16). So to Keil and a host of others he is the preincarnate Christ, while Michael is a high angel. Another possibility, followed by O. Zöckler (in J. P. Lange, *A Commentary on the Holy Scriptures*, 25 vols. [1865–80], 7:232–33) and many scholars, is that the one in linen is an angel of high rank who cannot be identified by name—not the angel Michael and not Christ. (See further E. W. Hengstenberg, *Christology of the Old Testament* [1854–56], 4:266–271; *DDD*, 569–72.)

J. E. Rosscup

Michah mi′kuh. KJV alternate form of Micah.

Michaiah mi-kay′yuh. KJV alternate form of Micaiah.

Michal mi′kuhl (מִיכַל H4783, short form of מִיכָאֵל H4776, "who is like God?" [see Michael]). Younger daughter of Saul and wife of David. After the slaying of Goliath, David's growing popularity with the people so angered Saul (1 Sam. 18:6–7) that the king began to seek ways of destroying him. Saul's scheming mind first hit upon the idea of offering him Merab, his oldest daughter in marriage, hinting that all the dowry he would require would be his valor in fighting the Philistines, but secretly hoping that David would fall by the hand of the enemy (18:17–18). David did not take the hint, but excused himself on the ground of his lack of wealth and his family status. The king did not press the matter and Merab was given to Adriel, but Saul continued to scheme.

Then one day, when the news came to him that Michal, his younger daughter, loved David, an idea took fire in his brain (1 Sam. 18:20–21). He offered Michal in marriage to him, stipulating that the requirement would be the foreskins of one hundred Philistines. Saul was confident that his rival would be slain, but instead, David killed two hundred Philistines. He merely gained greater popularity out of the affair, married Michal, and continued to annoy the king. The young couple seemed suited to each other, and when Saul conceived another dastardly plan to kill David, Michal shrewdly thwarted her father's scheme and saved David's life (19:10–17). When David finally was forced to flee for his life and became an outlaw with a price on his head, Saul gave Michal to Paltiel, son of Laish (25:44).

Years later, when Saul was dead and David was negotiating with ABNER to obtain the entire kingdom, his first requirement was that Michal should be returned to him (2 Sam. 3:12–16). Abner complied with his request, and despite the grief of Paltiel, Michal again became the wife of David. It seemed that the old rapport between the two was gone. It is possible that to David, who was now a successful man with many wives and enormous responsibility, she was no longer attractive. It may be that the inevitable difference between the boy-husband of Michal's earlier years and the mature and occupied warrior of her later life was too much for her to take. Suffice it to say that her stinging criticism in the episode of moving the ARK OF THE COVENANT to Jerusalem (6:16, 20–23) destroyed what little regard he may have had left for her in his heart. Michal's romance with David, its bright beginning and its sorrowful ending, is a telling reflection of the fortunes of the house of Saul as found in 1 and 2 Samuel. In addition, she suffered the worst fate a Hebrew woman could sustain—she died childless. The only other mention of her name is probably the error of a scribe who mistakenly wrote Michal when he should have written Merab (21:8 KJV). (On the literary qualities of the story see R. Alter, *The Art of Biblical Narrative* [1981], 118–26; J. P. Fokkelman, *Narrative Art and Poetry in the Books of Samuel*, 4 vols. [1981–93], 2:209–47.)   C. P. GRAY

Micheas mik′ee-uhs. KJV Apoc. form of MICAH (2 Esd. 1:39).

Michmas, Michmash mik′mas, mik′mash. See MICMASH.

Michmethah, Michmethath mik′mu-thuh, -thath. See MICMETHATH.

Michri mik′ri. See MICRI.

michtam mik′tam. KJV form of MIKTAM.

Micmash mik′mash (מִכְמָס H4820 [only Ezra 2:27; Neh. 7:31] and מִכְמָשׁ H4825, possibly "hidden place"). TNIV Mikmash; other versions have Michmas or Michmash (the final consonant in both Hebrew forms is properly represented in English with *s* and not with *sh*, but the latter has become traditional). The name of a town and of a pass c. 6 mi. SE of BETHEL. The town apparently was not a large enough town to warrant mention in the list of Benjamite cities. Its only real claim to fame is in the battle that was fought there by SAUL and JONATHAN against the PHILISTINES (1 Sam. 13:1—14:35). The town does receive mention in the postexilic period. EZRA records that 122 men of Micmash returned from exile (Ezra 2:27; cf. Neh. 7:31; 11:31; the parallel in 1 Esd. 5:21 has *Makalōn*, "Macalon," perhaps through the misreading of a Gk. uncial M for ΑΛ). After the siege of BETHBASI, Jonathan MACCABEE settled in Micmash, which may have served as a competitor with JERUSALEM for the allegiance of the people (1 Macc. 9:73; cf. Jos. *Ant.* 13.1.6).

Biblical Micmash is modern Khirbet el-Hara el-Fawqa, just N of the Arab town of Mukhmas. It is reached by the road that goes E from the main highway at RAMAH. South of Mukhmas less than a mile is the narrow canyon of the Wadi es-Suweinit, a deep ravine that joins the Wadi Qelt and empties into the Jordan near JERICHO. To the SW of Micmash is GEBA, situated on another hill.

A knowledge of this geography is helpful in understanding the battle of Micmash as recorded in 1 Sam. 13–14. Saul had been camped at Micmash with 2,000 soldiers while his son Jonathan was at GIBEAH (perhaps here one should read GEBA, less than 2 mi. SW of Micmash) with another 1,000. Jonathan had reached Geba after routing the Philistines. When they retaliated by rushing on Micmash, Saul fled eastward to GILGAL and his

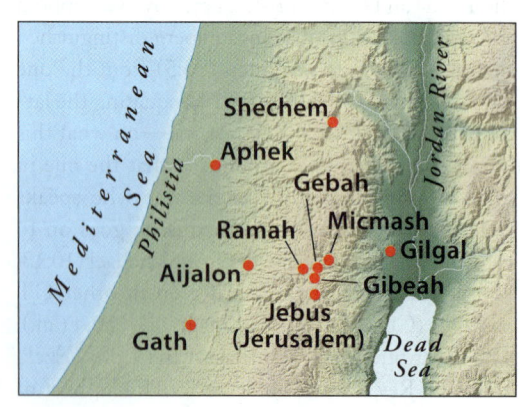

Micmash.

Jonathan, creeping through the canyon of Wadi es-Suweinit in the distance (view to the ESE), surprised the Philistine outpost at Micmash (foreground).

men scattered—some even across the Jordan. The Philistines did not pursue, but waited at the pass of Micmash, which was easily defended. At Gilgal, SAMUEL shamed Saul into going back and fighting. So with 600 men out of the original 2,000, Saul joined forces with Jonathan at Geba (13:15). The Philistines accepted the challenge and split into three companies, with a garrison guarding the pass at Micmash (13:17–23).

The weak character of Saul continues to show as he remains under the pomegranate tree (1 Sam. 14:2) while Jonathan plots to defeat the Philistines. Jonathan took his armor-bearer, made his way across the pass, and scaled the precipitous N wall in front of Micmash. The two of them made a surprise attack on the garrison and killed twenty men (14:14). This threw the whole Philistine army into panic and they raced westward to escape. It was then that Saul and his men joined in the chase and "the LORD rescued Israel that day, and the battle moved on beyond Beth Aven" (14:23). There were Philistine casualties all the way from Micmash to AIJALON (14:31). All the geographical details of the battle fit the area around Mukhmas; the land is rough and hilly, and the pass or canyon leading SE fits the description in the Bible, as well as that in JOSEPHUS (*Ant.* 6.6.2).

In a vivid account of an Assyrian or Syro-Ephraimitic attack on Jerusalem, Isaiah mentions Micmash. "They enter Aiath; / they pass through Migron; / they store supplies at Micmash. / They go over the pass, and say, / 'We will camp overnight at Geba.' / Ramah trembles; / Gibeah of Saul flees" (Isa. 10:28–29). Perhaps to facilitate mobility, the heavy noncombat equipment was stored some distance from the Assyrians' objective. (See E. Kraeling, *Bible Atlas* [1956], 180–82; P. K. McCarter, Jr., *I Samuel*, AB 8 [1980], 224–42, esp. map on 231; *ABD*, 4:814–15.)

R. L. ALDEN

Micmethath mik´muh-thath (מִכְמְתָת *H4826* [used with the definite article], meaning unknown). KJV Michmetha; NRSV Michmethath. A town or geographical feature that served to define the boundary between the tribes of EPHRAIM and MANASSEH (Josh. 16:6; 17:7). The latter passage locates Micmethath E of SHECHEM, but its location is uncertain. Proposals include Khirbet Makhneh el-Foqa (Y. Aharoni, *The Land of the Bible: A Historical Geography*, rev. ed. [1979], 257; this site, however, is c. 2.5 mi. SSW of Shechem), Khirbet Juleijil (L. H. Grollenberg, *Atlas of the Bible* [1965], 157 and map 11 on p. 59), and others (cf. Z. Kallai, *Historical Geography of the Bible* [1986], 150–51).

S. WOUDSTRA

Micri mik′ri (מִכְרִי *H4840*, perhaps "recompense"). Also Michri; TNIV Mikri. Descendant of BENJAMIN and grandfather (or more distant ancestor) of Elah; the latter is listed among the first Benjamites who resettled in Jerusalem (1 Chr. 9:8; LXX *Machir*, cf. MAKIR).

Middin mid′uhn (מִדִּין *H4516*, meaning unknown). A town allotted to the tribe of JUDAH in the desert (Josh. 15:61). It was apparently between BETH ARABAH and SECACAH, but its location is uncertain. Many identify it with modern Khirbet Abu Tabaq, some 10.5 mi. ESE of JERUSALEM, in el-Buqeʿah (the Valley of ACHOR). See SALT, CITY OF.

Middle Gate. A gate in JERUSALEM where the officials of NEBUCHADNEZZAR gathered after they had captured the city (Jer. 39:3; the LXX reads "Middle Gate" also in 2 Chr. 23:5, where the Heb. has FOUNDATION GATE). Nothing else is known about the Middle Gate, although its name possibly suggests that it was located at some point between the upper and lower sections of Jerusalem.

Midian mid′ee-uhn (מִדְיָן *H4518*, derivation unknown; gentilic מִדְיָנִי *H4520*, "Midianite"). Son of ABRAHAM and KETURAH, and eponymous ancestor of a people group that lived E and SE of CANAAN.

I. The biblical record. The name of the country and the people who comprised it come from a forefather named Midian. After SARAH and HAGAR, Abraham took another wife whose name was Keturah. She bore him Zimran, Jokshan, Medan, Midian, Ishbak, and Shuah (Gen. 25:1–2; 1 Chr. 1:32). The sons of Midian were Ephah, Epher, Hanoch, Abida, and Eldaah (Gen. 25:4, 1 Chr. 1:33). Abraham sent all his concubines' sons away "to the land of the east" (Gen. 25:6). Nothing else is known about the person Midian. See also MEDAN.

Midian as the name of a country or people occurs first in Gen. 36:35, which records that an Edomite king, Hadad son of Bedad, "defeated Midian in the country of Moab." We also read that the traders who took JOSEPH out of the pit and sold him to the Ishmaelites were Midianites (37:28, cf. v. 36, where the Heb. has *mĕdānim*, "Medanites," probably an alternate form or a misspelling of *midyānim*). The land of Midian played an important part in the life of MOSES, who fled there from PHARAOH (Exod. 2:15). He met and eventually was employed by Reuel (or JETHRO), a priest of Midian who had seven daughters (2:16–22). One of these Midianite women, ZIPPORAH, became his wife. It was while Moses was watching Jethro's flocks that he came to Horeb, the mountain of God (3:1; see SINAI, MOUNT).

Mention of Midian does not occur again until the wilderness wanderings, when the Israelites passed through MOAB, which bordered on Midian. To protect themselves, the elders of Moab and Midian hired BALAAM to pronounce a curse on Israel (Num. 22:4–7). Relations between Israel and Midian further deteriorated after a Hebrew man married a Midianite woman (25:6). This caused a plague which ceased only when the offenders were killed. The summary comment of Moses on Midian was, "Treat the Midianites as enemies and kill them, because they treated you as enemies when they deceived you in the affair of Peor and their sister Cozbi, the daughter of a Midianite leader, the woman who was killed when the plague came as a result of Peor" (25:17–18). The Lord further instructed the Israelites to take vengeance on Midian (31:1–4). Even though five chapters of genealogy and legislation intervene between this and the previous episode, it seems to come as a result of that international marriage. Israel was victorious in the battle that God prompted them to begin. They slew every male and five Midianite kings, Evi, Rekem, Zur, Hur, and Reba (31:7–8; cf. Jdg. 13:21). They also killed Balaam. The people spared all the women, but Moses ordered that only the unmarried of them should live (Num. 31:14–18).

The Lord raised up GIDEON the judge in order to overthrow the Midianite yoke that had been on Israel for seven years (Jdg. 6:1). The Midianites clearly were waging an offensive war, for they had moved across to the W bank of the JORDAN and were encamped in the Valley of JEZREEL (6:33). It was in that valley that the Lord routed the enemy with Gideon and one hundred torch-bearing trumpeters (7:19–25). Two of the Midianite princes, ZEBAH AND ZALMUNNA, played a major role in the sequel to the battle in Jdg. 8. Oreb and Zeeb had been captured and killed, but these other two escaped to TRANSJORDAN. Gideon received no support nor encouragement from the towns of Succoth or Penuel and so cursed and punished them when he finally returned triumphantly (8:16–17). This victory over the Midianites at Jezreel was memorialized by the prophet Isaiah. "The LORD Almighty will lash them with a whip, / as when he struck down Midian at the rock of Oreb" (Isa. 10:26; cf. 9:4; Ps. 83:9; Hab. 3:7).

II. The land of Midian. The boundaries of the land of Midian are very indefinite. The general comment of Gen. 25:6 that it was simply to the E could mean anything or everything all the way from Mount HERMON to the EUPHRATES and S to the Arabian peninsula, and perhaps include the Sinai peninsula. All of this is rugged desert country. Most scholars limit the term *Midian* to N Hejaz, that part of ARABIA E of the Gulf of AQABAH. The ancient geographer Ptolemy knew of a *Madiana* (*Geogr.* 6.7.27), which is probably the *Madiam* mentioned by EUSEBIUS (*Onom.* 136.31). It may be the modern el-Bed, 26 mi. E of the Gulf of Aqabah. The city *Madianē* mentioned by JOSEPHUS was on the coast of this same gulf (part of the RED SEA, *Ant.* 2.11.1 §257).

III. The people of Midian. Although the Midianites were descendants of Abraham through his wife Keturah, they never were considered part of the COVENANT people of God. The hospitality of Jethro to Moses is commendable, but beyond that the Midianites were a people hostile to Israel.

Being desert people, their existence was nomadic. When some of them picked up Joseph, it was typical of their way of life—trading, traveling, and troubling others. Most BEDOUIN know no boundaries, and apparently these Midianites knew none either (although some scholars believe that the Midianite society was well organized and predated bedouin culture; cf. G. Mendenhall in *ABD*, 4:815–18). They were present as far N as Moab according to Gen. 36:35. If Horeb is in SINAI, then they were SW of ELATH (Num. 10:29). They were "beyond the Jordan" in the vicinity of the plains of Moab (Num. 25; 31). They could be found even in the area S of GALILEE in Cisjordan when Gideon routed them (Jdg. 6–8). Recent archaeological evidence, however, suggests that the Midianites built an impressive culture in the Hejaz beginning in the 13th cent. B.C. Surveys of the region have revealed numerous towns, including walled cities, painted pottery, irrigation systems, and mining. It is thought that the Midianites must have traded with Egypt, Asia Minor, and the Aegean.

Twice in the book of Judges, Moses' father-in-law is called a KENITE (Jdg. 1:16; 4:11). Viewpoints differ as to the relationship between Midianites and Kenites. Some say they are synonymous terms, others that the Kenites were a part or a clan of the Midianites (cf. Num. 24:21). The etymology or origin of the name *Kenite* is uncertain, although many think it means "smith." The Kenites lasted much longer than the Midianites. They receive mention in the times of DAVID (1 Sam. 27:10; 30:29) and even into the times of JEREMIAH (Jer. 35; cf. 1 Chr. 2:55). There they are a religious order. On the other hand, Moses apparently made the Midianites

The general location of the Midianites.

extinct when he slaughtered all but the young girls (Num. 31:13–20).

IV. Archaeology and Midian. Since nomads build no cities, and since no Midianite city name is even known, archaeologists have little with which to work. Surveys of N Arabia have been made, but

A worship site at the copper mines of Timnah dedicated to the Midianite and Egyptian deity Hathor.

nothing noteworthy has come to light. The only relationship one can draw is between the name of the Haiappu tribe in the lists of Tiglath-Pileser III and Ephah, one of the sons of Midian (Gen. 25:4). According to the Assyrian record, that tribe paid taxes in gold, silver, camels, and spices. Isaiah connects the names Midian, Ephah, and Sheba (Isa. 60:6); in the Assyrian record the Haiappu occur with the Sabeans (i.e., Sheba). (See further J. Montgomery, *Arabia and the Bible* [1934]; H. H. Rowley, *From Joseph to Joshua* [1948], 152–53; J. F. A. Sawyer and D. J. A. Clines, eds., *Midian, Moab, and Edom: The History and Archaeology of Late Bronze and Iron Age Jordan and North-west Arabia* [1983]; E. A. Knauf, *Midian: Untersuchungen zur Geschichte Palästinas und Nordarabiens am Ende des 2. Jahrtausends v. Chr.* [1988].) R. L. Alden

midrash mid´rash. Plural *midrashim*. The Hebrew term *midrāš* H4535 ("study, writing, story," from the verb *dāraš* H2011, "to search, examine, inquire") occurs only twice in the OT. Reference is made to the midrash (NIV, "annotations") of the prophet Iddo for additional information concerning Abijah (2 Chr. 13:22; NRSV, "story") and to the midrash on "the book of the kings" (24:27; NRSV, "Commentary"). These midrashim may have been historical records themselves or commentaries on the historical narratives, but the precise meaning is debated (for the options, see *ABD*, 4:818–19).

The term is very common, however, in rabbinic literature, where it refers to the elucidation and exposition of the Bible. This type of exegesis is dated back to Ezra, who "had devoted himself to the study [*lidrôš*] and observance of the Law of the Lord, and to teaching its decrees and laws in Israel" (Ezra 7:10). When the exiles returned from Babylonia, they accepted the Torah as their sole authority, and it became necessary to interpret the law in terms of the specifics of new situations. (The understanding of midrash as an attempt to actualize the biblical text and make it relevant is emphasized by R. Bloch in *DBSup* 5:1263–80. Various other definitions have been offered, and unfortunately the term is often used very loosely.) Furthermore, if the Torah alone was binding, all traditional customs and practices had to receive the sanction of the written law to have authority. Later, when the literalists (the Sadducees) sought to deny the validity of the oral law (see Mishnah), those who sought justification for the oral law (the Pharisees) did so through expositions (midrashim) of the written law.

The term *midrash* (esp. when capitalized) can also refer more specifically to a type of literature consisting of biblical exposition. Thus the Midrashim are rabbinic commentaries on the Bible. These works sometimes address detailed issues of exegesis, but their primary purpose is religious edification. There are two types of Midrashim: halakic (or halachic) and haggadic. The Hebrew noun *hălākâ* (lit., "walk") refers to "law, ruling, tradition" (see Halakah); thus the halakic Midrashim sought to explain more fully the biblical law, applying the principle of the biblical legislation to particulars, resolving apparent contradictions, and so on. The term *haggādâ* means "story, narration," and the haggadic Midrashim used a freer method of interpretation, focusing on ethics and devotion (see Haggadah). The latter is rather homiletical in that it seeks to exhort rather than legislate. It is important to note, however, that both halakic and haggadic material are found in almost all the Midrashim.

These expositions were transmitted orally for generations before they were written down. The earliest written halakic Midrashim can be dated to the second cent. A.D. The most important among them are the *Mekilta de Rabbi Ishmael* (Aram. *měkiltāʾ* means "collection of [halakic] rules, treatise"), which deals with portions of Exodus; the *Sifra* (or *Sipra*, "book"), which comments on every verse of Leviticus; and the *Sifre* (or *Sipre*, "books"), two works that cover most of Numbers and Deuteronomy. The most important haggadic Midrashim are *Midrash Rabba* (a collection that includes expositions of the whole PENTATEUCH and the five MEGILLOTH: Canticles, Ruth, Lamentations, Ecclesiastes, Esther); the *Tanḥuma* (homilies to the whole Pentateuch); and the *Pesikta de Rab Kanana* (homilies concerning the holy days and other special occasions). These writings became source books of preaching for the rabbis.

(See further A. G. Wright, *The Literary Genre Midrash* [1967]; G. G. Porton, *Understanding Rabbinic Midrash: Text and Commentary* [1985]; H. L. Strack and G. Stemberger, *Introduction to the Talmud and Midrash* [1992], part 3; A. Yadin, *Scripture as Logos: Rabbi Ishmael and the Origins of Midrash* [2004]; J. Neusner and A. J. Avery-Peck, eds., *Encyclopaedia of Midrash: Biblical Interpretation in Formative Judaism*, 2 vols. [2005].) W. B. COKER

midwife. A woman who helps in childbirth (Heb. *měyalledet*, piel ptc. of *yālad* H3528, "to give birth"). A midwife may often have been an older relative or friend of the family. Some of her duties included cutting the umbilical cord, washing the baby with water, rubbing it with salt, and wrapping it in swaddling clothes (cf. Ezek. 16:4). A midwife was with RACHEL at the birth of BENJAMIN (Gen. 35:17–18). When twins were born to TAMAR, the midwife put a scarlet thread on the firstborn so that it might be known which was the older (38:28). The pharaoh of Egypt ordered the midwives, Shiphrah and Puah, to kill the Hebrew boy babies, but to let the girls live (Exod. 1:15–16). The midwives disobeyed the king, however, and when rebuked replied, "Hebrew women are not like Egyptian women; they are vigorous and give birth before the midwives arrive" (v. 19). The "birthstool" referred to in this passage is illustrated on the walls of the palace of Luxor, in Upper Egypt, where a painting shows Queen Mautmes sitting on a stool giving birth to a child while two midwives chafe her hands (however, see BIRTHSTOOL). Midwives probably are referred to also in 1 Sam. 4:20 and Ruth 4:14–15. J. L. KELSO

Migdal Eder mig´duhl-ee´duhr. See EDER (PLACE) #1.

Migdal El mig´duhl-el´ (מִגְדַּל־אֵל H4466, "tower of God"). Also Migdal-el. A fortified city within the tribal territory of NAPHTALI (Josh. 19:38). It was apparently in the vicinity of IRON in N GALILEE, but its precise location is unknown.

Migdal Gad mig´duhl-gad´ (מִגְדַּל־גָּד H4467, "tower of Gad [fortune]"). A town in the SHEPHELAH, within the tribal territory of JUDAH (Josh. 15:37). It is tentatively identified with Khirbet el-Mejdeleh, about 4 mi. SE of LACHISCH.

Migdol mig´dol (מִגְדֹּל H4465, "tower, fort"). A place name in the NE part of the NILE delta. Twice in Jeremiah, Migdol heads a short list of places in Egypt where Jews sought refuge (Jer. 44:1; 46:14); and twice in Ezekiel, Migdol is the N or NE extremity of Egypt, while Aswan (SYENE) marks its S limit (Ezek. 29:10; 30:6; KJV, "tower of Syene"), true to conditions in the 26th dynasty. This Migdol is the Magdolo of the Antonine Itinerary, being generally identified with Tell el Ḥer, some 12.5 mi. NE of Qantara on the ancient road from Egypt to Palestine. In Egyptian sources, it is most probably the Migdol of Sethos I (Karnak war scenes) and of other sources (see A. H. Gardiner in *JEA* 6 [1920]: 107–10).

In the PENTATEUCH, however, we read that the Israelites, after turning back from the wilderness, encamped "between Migdol and the sea" (Exod. 14:2; cf. Num. 33:7), and then crossed the latter from W to E into the wilderness again. This seems to require a Migdol differently sited from Tell el Ḥer (which is E of all likely candidates for the RED SEA or "Sea of Reeds"), especially as Lake Serbonis farther NE lies along the "way of the land of the Philistines" and so may be excluded. It is, therefore, probable that Migdol here is simply another fort—*migdāl* H4463 is a common word—SE of Daphnai and W of the Sea of Reeds (Lake Ballah region?). If so, it has not yet been identified in Egyptian sources, but could turn up in new documents. See also EXODUS, THE. K. A. KITCHEN

mighty men. This expression is often used to render Hebrew *gibbôrîm* (pl. of *gibbôr* H1475, "strong, valiant; man, warrior, champion"). The word first appears in Gen. 6:4 with reference to the NEPHILIM (NIV and NRSV, "heroes"). It can be used of fighting men in general (e.g., 2 Sam. 10:7), but also more especially of warriors notable for their valor (17:8). The names and exploits of three such men and those of DAVID's "Thirty" are recorded in 2 Sam. 23:8–39 and 1 Chr. 11:10–47.

S. WOUDSTRA

migration. See BIRD MIGRATION.

Migron mig´ron (מִגְרוֹן H4491, prob. "threshing floor"). A locality in the outskirts of GIBEAH where SAUL at one time camped under a pomegranate tree (1 Sam. 14:2). The Gibeah referred to in this passage is either the modern Tell el-Full (3 mi. N of the temple terrace in JERUSALEM) or Jeba‘ (an additional 2 mi. NE). A place by the name of Migron is mentioned also in Isa. 10:28 as being in the line of march of the Assyrian army, suggesting it is N of MICMASH. An unresolved question is whether these two Migrons are the same place, for the one mentioned in Samuel is located S of the pass of Micmash. Both verses are ambiguous, however, and the likelihood is that they refer to the same place (the Migron mentioned in Isaiah does not necessarily have to be located N of the pass). In any case, the precise location of Migron is unknown. Tentative identifications include Tell Maryam (just SW of Micmash) and Wadi es-Suweiniṭ (for the latter, see P. M. Arnold in *ABD*, 4:822–23, who thinks the name comes from the verb *nāgar* H5599, niphal "gush forth"). S. WOUDSTRA

Mijamin mij´uh-min (מִיָּמִין H4785, a contraction of מִנְיָמִין H4975, "from the right" [i.e., "favored"] or perhaps "from the south"; cf. BENJAMIN, MINIAMIN). KJV also Miamin. **(1)** A priest who received the sixth lot of the twenty-four divisions in DAVID's time (1 Chr. 24:9).

(2) One of the descendants of Parosh who agreed to put away their foreign wives (Ezra 10:25; 1 Esd. 9:26 [KJV, "Maelus"]).

The views from Tell el-Ful (prob. Gibeah of Benjamin) looking toward the area of Migron.

(3) A priest who affixed his seal to the covenant of NEHEMIAH (Neh. 10:7).

(4) One of the priestly leaders who had returned from the EXILE with ZERUBBABEL (Neh. 12:5). He was possibly an ancestor of #3 above, and both of these priests may have belonged to the priestly order of #1 above (see the discussion in KD, *Ezra, Nehemiah, and Esther*, 266–71). E. B. SMICK

Mika mi'kuh. TNIV form of MICA.

Mikloth mik'loth (מִקְלוֹת *H5235*, perhaps from מַקֵּל *H5234*, "branch, staff," or from קוֹל *H7754*, "voice"). (1) Son of JEIEL and descendant of BENJAMIN; his brother NER was the grandfather of SAUL (1 Chr. 8:31; 9:37–38).

(2) The leader of a division in the army of DAVID (1 Chr. 27:4). On the basis of the SEPTUAGINT, and in conformity with the pattern in this passage, many scholars omit the reference to Mikloth (e.g., RSV, "Dodai the Ahohite was in charge of the division of the second month; in his division were twenty-four thousand").

Mikmash mik'mash. TNIV form of MICMASH.

Mikneiah mik-nee'yah (מִקְנֵיָהוּ *H5240*, "possession of Yahweh"). A Levite and one of the gatekeepers assigned to be a musician when DAVID made preparation to transfer the ARK OF THE COVENANT to Jerusalem (1 Chr. 15:18). He is called one of the brothers of the "second order" (NRSV; NIV, "next in rank") who followed HEMAN, ASAPH, and ETHAN. Mikneiah and some others "were to play the harps, directing according to *sheminith*" (v. 21; see MUSIC VI.C).

Mikri mik'ri. TNIV form of MICRI.

miktam mik'tam (מִכְתָּם *H4846*). Also *michtam* (sometimes capitalized). Apparently a musical (or liturgical) term found in the superscription of six psalms (Pss. 16 and 56–60; in addition, *miktāb H4844*, "writing," is sometimes emended to *miktām* in Isa. 38:9). Some think it means nothing more than "inscription" or "epigram" (*HALOT*, 2:582–83); others relate it to a Semitic root meaning "to cover" and deduce that these psalms deal with ATONEMENT for sin. An ancient proposal is that the term derives from *ketem H4188*, "gold," and that it refers either to a golden inscription or, figuratively, to the precious quality of the poem (see P. D. Miller in *Congress Volume: Vienna, 1980* [1981], 311–32, esp. 312–14). See MUSIC VI.A; PSALMS VI.A.

Milalai mil'uh-li (מִלֲלַי *H4912*, perhaps short form of מְלַלְיָה, "Yahweh has spoken"). A priestly musician who participated in the dedication of the rebuilt wall of Jerusalem under EZRA (Neh. 12:36; his name is one of several omitted in the LXX).

Milcah mil'kuh (מִלְכָּה *H4894*, "queen, princess"). TNIV Milkah. (1) Daughter of HARAN, sister of LOT (and ISCAH), and wife of NAHOR, who was her uncle (Gen. 11:29; cf. v. 27). ABRAHAM was also Milcah's uncle. Her offspring are mentioned in Gen. 22:20–23; one of them was BETHUEL, the father of REBEKAH and LABAN (22:22–23; 24:15, 24, 29, 47).

(2) One of five daughters of ZELOPHEHAD of the tribe of MANASSEH (Num. 26:33). Since Zelophehad had no sons, his daughters requested ELEAZAR the priest that they be allowed to inherit their father's property, and the request was granted on condition that they marry into their father's tribe (27:1–11; 36:11; Josh. 17:3–4). This decision was very important and became a precedent.

Milcom mil'kuhm (מִלְכֹּם *H4904*, "king"). TNIV Milkom. The national god of the Ammonites (see AMMON). Most scholars believe he is to be identified with MOLECH (cf. 1 Ki. 11:5 with v. 7). The Hebrew form *milkōm* occurs only three times (always rendered "Molech" by the NIV): (1) Milcom was one of the foreign gods for whom SOLOMON built a high place on the MOUNT OF OLIVES (1 Ki. 11:5); (2) he was worshiped by many Israelites (v. 33); (3) he was later desecrated by JOSIAH (2 Ki. 23:13; see further *DDD*, 575–76). In addition, the form *malkām* ("their king") occurs in the MT in some passages where most scholars believe that the context requires a reference to Milcom (2 Sam. 12:30=1 Chr. 20:2; Jer. 49:1, 3; Zeph. 1:5). See MALCAM #2.

mildew. A common species of fungus that attacked the crops of Palestine; it is produced by dampness.

The Hebrew term *yērāqôn H3766*, in its meaning "rust" or "mildew," always occurs in combination with *šiddāpôn H8730*, "blight, scorching." These conditions were interpreted as God's punishment upon the disobedient (Deut. 28:22; Amos 4:9; Hag. 2:17), and SOLOMON prayed for deliverance from them (1 Ki. 8:37; 2 Chr. 6:28). The NIV uses "mildew" also as the rendering of Hebrew *ṣāraʿat H7669* (which refers to a variety of skin diseases), when this word occurs in connection with objects, such as clothing (Lev. 13:47–59) and walls (14:34–57).

S. BARABAS

mile. See WEIGHTS AND MEASURES I.G.

Miletus m*i*-lee´tuhs (Μίλητος *G3626*). Also Miletos. Ancient and important Ionian city in ASIA MINOR, in the region of CARIA, on the shore of the Mediterranean near the mouth of the river Maeander. It was colonized first by Cretans, and later by Greeks (see CRETE; GREECE). During the great period of colonization (750–550 B.C.), when the Greeks extended their influence to every corner of the Mediterranean area, Miletus was most active, being credited with the establishment of about ninety colonies, chiefly in the Black Sea region, among them Abydos, Cyzicus, and Sinope. It also led the way in the Greek penetration of Egypt, being largely responsible for the founding of Naucratis in the 7th cent. B.C., the first permanent Greek settlement in the country.

Situated favorably, with four good harbors, Miletus became a great sea power and dominated the Black Sea trade, from which it became exceedingly wealthy. Luxury items from Miletus played a part in Athenian economic activity in the 6th cent. The kings of LYDIA found a strong rival in Miletus, until a treaty was concluded in which the latter evidently acknowledged Lydian rule, but enjoyed a privileged position especially under Croesus. This relationship continued after the Persian conquest in the mid-6th cent.

Throughout this same time Miletus was distinguished for its literary and scientific accomplishments. It was the home of the first Greek philosopher, Thales, who sought to understand the world in terms of one basic substance, water. His successors, Anaximander and Anaximenes, belonged to the so-called Milesian school of philosophy, which sought to explain things without recourse to supernatural intervention. Anaximander is distinguished as the first person to draw a map of the world. Toward the end of the 6th cent., Hecataeus founded a school of antiquarian historians known as the logographers, which had a great influence on the development and work of HERODOTUS, acknowledged as the "Father

Remains of a lighthouse at Miletus, a city that dominated Aegean Sea traffic from its harbor.

of History." Until 500 B.C., Miletus was the greatest of the eastern Greek cities.

This period of material and cultural prosperity came to an end with the involvement of Miletus in the Ionian revolt, beginning in 499 B.C. Persia proved too strong, and after the naval disaster at Lade (in 494) the city was captured and the inhabitants sold into slavery. Then began a slow recovery. The city was rebuilt on a new grid plan invented at this very time by a native son, Hippodamus. It became part of the Athenian confederacy in about 450, and in 412 revolted and ultimately fell again under Persia. Toward the end of the 4th cent. it was conquered and rebuilt by ALEXANDER THE GREAT. Under the Hellenistic kings it retained some importance as a commercial town, and some great buildings were raised by these rulers.

In 133 B.C. the city passed into Roman hands as part of the province of ASIA and subsequently received special attention from AUGUSTUS and TRAJAN because of its commercial importance. However, the harbors slowly silted up, and the city became a typical small Roman provincial town. In A.D. 263 the Goths came and destroyed the great temple of ARTEMIS. By the time of Justinian (6th cent. A.D.) it was a small village, and it is now deserted. Excavations and investigations have been in progress from the 16th cent. on, and today the classical town may be seen, containing extensive remains of both private and public buildings covering the period from the 5th cent. B.C. to Roman imperial times.

The apostle PAUL stopped at Miletus on his journey from Greece to Jerusalem, and spoke to the elders of the Ephesian church whom he asked to meet him there (Acts 20:15, 17). In 2 Tim. 4:20 (KJV, "Miletum") he mentions leaving TROPHIMUS in Miletus to recover from an illness. The city, however, played little part in the history of Christianity, though it had a bishopric in the 5th cent. (See further G. Kleiner in *Princeton Encyclopedia of Classical Sites*, ed. R. Stillwell et al. [1976], 578–82, s.v. "Miletos"; E. M. Yamauchi, *The Archaeology of New Testament Cities in Western Asia Minor* [1980], ch. 8; N. Ehrhardt, *Milet und seine Kolonien: Vergleichende Untersuchung der kultischen und politischen Einrichtungen* [1983]; *ABD*, 4:825–26.)

R. C. STONE

milk. See FOOD.

Milkah mil′kuh. TNIV form of MILCAH.

Milkom mil′kuhm. TNIV form of MILCOM.

mill, millstone. A mill is an apparatus, consisting of two stones, used to grind GRAIN into flour. Hand mills (Heb. *rēḥayim* H8160, a dual form, Exod. 11:15 et al.) were of several types. The earliest used, called the saddle quern, consisted of a rough, base stone and a rubbing stone. The base stone (called in the OT *pelaḥ taḥtit*, Job 41:24), varied from 18 to 30 in. in length and 10 to 15 in. in breadth and usually was slightly concave, having one end thicker than the other. The upper or rubbing stone (*pelaḥ rekeb*, Jdg. 9:53) varied from 6 to 15 in. in length, was narrow and tapered for gripping at both ends, and had one slightly convex surface for grinding. It was rubbed back and forth over grain placed on the base stone. Only a small portion of grain could be ground at one time. This upper stone was the type which killed ABIMELECH when it was dropped on his head (Jdg. 9:53; 2 Sam. 11:21).

The other type of mill (Gk. *mylos* G3685) consisted of two round stones, each about 18 to 24 in. in diameter. The lower one was fixed and had a center wooden peg over which the upper stone was placed. A central, funnel-shaped hole received the peg and also served for feeding grain into the mill. The upper stone was turned back and forth on the lower by use of a wooden handle on its outside

A basalt millstone typical of those found throughout the Holy Land.

edge. A variation of this type of mill used a bottom stone convex in shape and a top concave, fitting over the lower. The ground grain sifted out from the lower edges of the upper stone. Small mills could be operated by one person, but larger ones required two (Matt. 24:41). The type of stone used, whether for the saddle quern or the round mill, was usually black basalt, rough and porous, constantly presenting good cutting edges. (For the claim that small rotary hand mills were developed only in the Middle Ages, see *ABD*, 4:831–32.)

A third type of mill was larger and normally required animal power. A millstone 4–5 ft. in diameter was rolled on edge by means of a lever arrangement, in a circular pattern on top of a still larger base stone on which grain was spread. This type of mill could supply flour for a community. It was probably this size mill at which SAMSON was made to grind by the Philistines (Jdg. 16:21).

Saddle querns were in use from early times. SARAH must have used one in preparing the three measures of "fine flour" for ABRAHAM's visitors (Gen. 18:6). The figure of an Egyptian woman grinding with a saddle quern, dating from the Old Kingdom period, has been preserved (*ANEP*, 46, fig. 149). Grinding was the task of servants (Exod. 11:5) and of women (Isa. 47:2). The law prohibited taking either the family's mill or upper millstone in pledge (Deut. 24:6).

(See further W. M. Thompson, *The Land and the Book* [1907], 218–19, 455; G. A. Barton, *Archaeology and the Bible*, 7th ed. [1937], 176–77, pl. 34; G. Loud, *Megiddo II* [1948], pl. 264:11; L. A. Moritz, *Grain-mills and Flour in Classical Antiquity* [1958]; P. J. King and L. E. Stager, *Life in Biblical Israel* [2001], 94–95.) L. J. WOOD

millennium muh-len'ee-uhm. A Latin word meaning "a thousand years." In biblical and theological studies, "the millennium" refers to the 1,000-year period during which SATAN is bound, and during which Christ reigns with those who have come to life at the first RESURRECTION (Rev. 20:1–7). This period of time appears to follow the destruction of the enemies of God (ch. 19). The 1,000 years begin with the binding and confinement of Satan in the ABYSS (20:1–3; KJV, "the bottomless pit"), the resurrection and reward of the martyred dead of the period immediately preceding (20:4), and the beginning of the reign of Christ on earth as King of kings and Lord of lords. The millennium ends when Satan is loosed and organizes a rebellion against Christ that is crushed by fiery destruction from heaven (20:9). The casting of Satan into the LAKE OF FIRE, the resurrection and judgment of the wicked dead, and the creation of a new heaven and earth follow the millennium.

PREMILLENNIALISM understands these prophecies of the millennium as subject to future fulfillment in keeping with many OT passages picturing a kingdom of righteousness and peace on earth ruled over by the son of David. (See N. West, *The Thousand Years in Both Testaments* [1880]; W. E. Blackstone, *Jesus Is Coming* [1917]; D. H. Kromminga, *The Millennium in The Church* [1945]; C. Feinberg, *Premillennialism or Amillennialism?* 2nd ed. [1954]; D. K. Campbell and J. L. Townsend, eds., *A Case for Premillennialism: A New Consensus* [1992].)

POSTMILLENNIALISM holds that the millennium will be fulfilled somewhat symbolically during the last 1,000 years of this present age, when Christ will reign spiritually in his church. (See D. Brown, *Christ's Second Coming: Will It Be Premillennial?* [1919]; J. H. Snowden, *The Coming of the Lord: Will It Be Premillennial?* [1919]; L. Boettner, *The Millennium* [1957]; K. L. Gentry, Jr., *He Shall Have Dominion: A Postmillennial Eschatology* [1992].)

According to AMILLENNIALISM, the millennium begins at the first advent of Christ and finds its fulfillment in the reign of Christ spiritually in the hearts of believers on earth, though some find it in the INTERMEDIATE STATE after death. (See F. E. Hamilton, *The Basis of Millennial Faith* [1942]; G. L. Murray, *Millennial Studies: A Search for Truth* [1948]; K. Riddlebarger, *A Case for Amillennialism: Understanding the End Times* [2003].)

(For general treatments of the various interpretations, note S. J. Grenz, *The Millennial Maze: Sorting Out Evangelical Options* [1992]; R. G. Kyle, *Awaiting the Millennium: A History of End-Time Thinking* [1998].) See also ESCHATOLOGY III.J; SECOND COMING. J. F. WALVOORD

millet. This English term is used to render Hebrew *dōḥan H1893*, which occurs only once in a reference to several ingredients used to make bread (Ezek. 4:9). Of all the grains used for food, millet (*Panicum miliaceum*) is the smallest. It is borne in large numbers on a stalk (hence the name, from *milia*, "thousands"). The stalks are similar to rye, but they are heavier croppers. This annual plant grows two feet high. It is used now in Europe and the USA as bird seed. When made into flour for bread, the result is unappetizing—no wonder this was part of the prophet's fare as an indication of food shortage (see *FFB*, 141–42). There is an Italian millet, *Setacia italica*, but this was not grown in Palestine. Some argue that the Hebrew word refers to sorghum (*Sorghum vulgare*, similar to Indian corn). The NRSV uses English *millet* also to render Hebrew *pannag* H7154 (Ezek. 27:17; see PANNAG).

W. E. SHEWELL-COOPER

Millo mil′oh (מִלּוֹא H4864, "filling, mound"). **(1)** A fortification or citadel near JERUSALEM, constructed by SOLOMON with forced labor (1 Ki. 9:15, 24; 11:27). The NIV translates the Hebrew term as a common noun, "supporting terraces" (TNIV simply "terraces"). Apparently Solomon added to an existing Millo, for DAVID is said to have built the city of Jerusalem "around from the Millo inward" (2 Sam. 5:9 NRSV; cf. 1 Chr. 11:8). The Millo formed a prominent part of the works of defense set up by King HEZEKIAH for the protection of the city (2 Chr. 32:5). The BETH MILLO where King JOASH was assassinated (2 Ki. 12:20; KJV and other versions have "the house of Millo") is thought to have been a well-known building in this area. (See J. Simons, *Jerusalem in the Old Testament* [1952], 131–44; W. H. Mare, *The Archaeology of the Jerusalem Area* [1987], 65–66.)

(2) The place where ABIMELECH was crowned king is called "the house of Millo" in the KJV (Jdg. 9:6, 20). See BETH MILLO #1. S. WOUDSTRA

mina min′uh (מָנֶה H4949; μνᾶ G3641). In the OT, a measure of weight consisting of about 50–60 shekels (Ezek. 45:12 et al.), and thus weighing approximately 600–700 grams (see WEIGHTS AND MEASURES IV). In the NT, the word refers to a coin worth one hundred denarii (Lk. 19:13–24), approximately three months' wages for a laborer (see DENARIUS).

These weights made of hematite date to the early 2nd millennium B.C. The largest weight in the group is the mina. (The smallest weighs three shekels.)

Minaeans. See MINEANS.

mind. The seat of the mental faculties; the part of the individual that thinks, reasons, and feels.

I. Problem of terminology. Biblical conceptions of psychology lack analytical and technical precision. Both OT and NT focus attention on the human being's concrete and total relationship to God, and where psychological terms do appear their intention seems to be emphasis rather than a concern to divide or compartmentalize human activity. For this reason, no consistent pattern of terminology can be determined in either Testament.

In some cases, our English versions idiomatically render the Hebrew text with the word "mind" even in passages where no Hebrew equivalent is found (cf. Gen. 37:11). Otherwise, it is used in the OT to render a variety of terms, such as Hebrew *yēṣer* H3671, "thought, tendency" (Isa. 26:3); *rûaḥ* H8120, "spirit" (Num. 16:28 NIV); and especially *lēb* H4213 and *lēbāb* H4222, "heart" (Deut. 28:65; Ezek. 38:10). In the NT, the faculty of cognition or thought is variously referred to by such terms as *nous* G3808, "mind, intellect" (Rom. 7:25); *kardia* G2840, "heart" (in imitation of the Heb.; cf. Matt. 13:15, citing Isa. 6:10 LXX); *psychē* G6034, "soul" (Phil. 1:27); *dianoia* G1379, "thought, understanding" (2 Pet. 3:1); *gnōmē* G1191, "thought, will" (Rev. 17:13); *ennoia* G1936, "notion, intent" (1 Pet. 4:1); and *phronēma* G5859, "mind-set, purpose" (Rom. 8:7). See also HEART; SOUL; SPIRIT.

What becomes obvious as one surveys the complexity of biblical terminology is that no one term occupies an exclusive meaning, nor is one term alone used to indicate the faculty of reflection or cognition. It is equally clear because of this constellation of terms that HUMAN NATURE defies precise definition. All these terms call attention to the inner being as over against a person's objective, physical manifestation. This is not meant to imply a depreciation of the BODY in biblical theology, but there is an antithesis between the FLESH (*sarx G4922*) and that inner self or the mind that controls the self. "So then, I myself in my mind am a slave to God's law, but in the sinful nature [flesh] a slave to the law of sin" (Rom. 7:25).

II. Cognitive concreteness. Although the Hebrew mentality is often regarded as strikingly different from the Greek, it should be emphasized that NT terminology and concepts are closely related to the OT in connotation. To the Hebrew mind, the process of thought was more existential than abstract (although some scholars would argue that the examples that follow reflect simple metaphorical shifts and do not necessarily point to a different way of thinking). This point is illustrated sometimes by the Hebrew word for "meditate," *hāgâ H2047*, which literally means "to murmur" or the like (cf. Josh. 1:8; Pss. 1:2; 63:6; Isa. 33:18). Even the Hebrew term *śiaḥ H8488*, which can be translated both "to meditate" and "to utter a complaint," portrays action rather than passive contemplation (cf. Ps. 119:15, 23 et al.; 55:17 NRSV et al.). This cognitive concreteness often is obscured by our English translations. For instance, the RSV renders Gen. 31:20 as "Jacob outwitted Laban," whereas a literal rendering of the text would read, "Jacob stole the mind [heart] of Laban."

But it is especially in the area of ETHICS that we see the distinction between abstraction and concreteness. The high ideal, ethically speaking, is not mere contemplation of the *good* or the *beautiful*, but it is rather "to do justice or righteousness" (cf. Gen. 18:19; 1 Ki. 10:9; Ps. 10:18; Isa. 56:1; Jer. 5:1; Ezek. 45:9; Mic. 6:8). When a person "meditates," his lips move; when he "thinks" of righteousness, he does justice. There is little or no evidence for a philosophical idealism that identifies thinking with being in the Platonic sense; however, there is a realism, particularly about the OT, that does imply that *thought* and *being* are identical (cf. Prov. 4:23; 23:16–17). Although the Hebrew text of Prov. 23:7 is obscure, the KJV captures this Hebrew nuance, "As he thinketh in his heart [mind], so is he."

III. The mind and human nature. It has been indicated that neither the OT nor the NT is concerned about dissecting man into constituent parts, elements, or faculties. The being of a person is a united whole, and his reflective or cognitive faculties are never isolated from his total being. On the one hand, the Bible locates the center of a person's being in those physical organs where he or she existentially grasps the reality of God and the world. In the OT, the bowels, liver, heart, and even the womb are identified with this psychosomatic center (cf. Gen. 43:30; 1 Ki. 3:26; Ps. 109:18; Lam. 1:20; 2:11; 2 Cor. 6:12; Phil. 1:8; 2:1; Col. 3:12; Phlm. 7, 12, 20).

At the same time, the Bible does specifically call attention to human beings as thinking creatures. In the OT, the heart functions emotionally and volitionally as well as cognitively. The NT, however, provides a wider spectrum from which to view people as thinking beings. The term *nous* is primarily a Pauline term, and J. Behm suggests that "there is no connection with the philosophical or mystico-religious use. *Nous* is not the divine or the divinely related element in man" (*TDNT*, 4:958). (For non-Pauline examples cf. Lk. 24:45; Rev. 13:18; 17:9.) For PAUL the *nous* can become "senseless" when turned away from God (Rom. 1:28). Or it can be the means by which the Christian community expresses its oneness in Christ. So Paul exhorts the church to be of one *nous* (1 Cor. 1:10). A less frequently used term is *noēma G3784*, which occurs in both positive and negative contexts (Phil. 4:7; 2 Cor. 3:14). *Dianoia* occurs rather infrequently but is common to most of the NT writers. It usually conveys the idea of "understanding" (cf. Mk. 12:30; Lk. 1:51; Eph. 4:18; 1 Pet. 1:13; 1 Jn. 5:20).

At the heart of the NT understanding of CONVERSION and REPENTANCE is the term closely related to the concept of the mind, *metanoia G3567* (verb *metanoeō G3566*). Literally this term means "change of mind" but it also connotes an emotive element (cf. Lk. 13:3, 5; Acts 2:38; 2 Cor. 7:9–10). Generally speaking, the Bible knows the mind only in its actuality as being controlled by Christ expressed in the unity of the Christian community or as alienated from the "knowledge of God" and under the power of the devil or sin (cf. Rom. 8:6–7; 12:1–2; 1 Cor. 2:14–16; 15:34; 2 Cor. 4:4).

(See further J. Laidlaw, *The Bible Doctrine of Man* [1905]; H. W. Robinson, *The Christian Doctrine of Man* [1926]; D. R. G. Owen, *Body and Soul* [1956]; A. B. Come, *Human Spirit and Holy Spirit* [1959]; G. C. Berkouwer, *Man: The Image of God* [1962]; W. N. Pittenger, *The Christian Understanding of Human Nature* [1964]; D. W. Mork, *The Biblical Meaning of Man* [1967]; L. Verduin, *Somewhat Less than God* [1970]; H. H. Wolff, *Anthropology of the Old Testament* [1974]; J. P. Moreland and S. B. Rae, *Body and Soul: Human Nature and the Crisis in Ethics* [2000]; M. Carasik, *Theologies of the Mind in Biblical Israel* [2006]; *NIDOTTE*, 2:748–54; *NIDNTT*, 2:616–20.)   D. M. LAKE

mine, mining. Excavation for minerals began long before historic times, when Neolithic miners obtained FLINT for use in weapons and implements and gathered SALT, activities that played an important part in determining the course of TRADE in the ancient world. Initially both minerals would have been scraped from the surface, or, in the case of flint, removed from a bank of CHALK. Subsequently the quarrying and underground extraction of flint would have been stimulated by the discovery that freshly extracted flint was more easily chipped than surface stones as it contained some ground water. Also mined by Neolithic man was red and yellow ochre for use as pigments.

The mining methods used in the Neolithic period were little improved upon in many of the metal mines, worked by slaves, that supplied mineral wealth to the empires of Egypt, Assyria, Greece, and Rome. However, the range of materials mined increased. The METALS of the pre-Christian era — COPPER, GOLD, IRON, LEAD, SILVER, TIN, and to a lesser extent mercury and zinc — were all mined, in their native state in the case of copper, gold, and silver, or as other ores, except in the case of gold. Early mining of other minerals took place in the ANE, particularly for gems and ornamental material. The ancient Egyptians sank hundreds of shafts in the search for EMERALDS on the coast of the RED SEA, but TURQUOISE was probably the first material used in jewelry to be mined extensively (see JEWELS AND PRECIOUS STONES). This work was carried out on the SINAI Peninsula, an operation that led people to live in places that otherwise would be uninhabited and to build roads or tracks that otherwise would not have been made. However, these mining tracks were of considerable use to the Israelites during the exodus from Egypt.

The wealth and exploits of the various empires and states of the ANE were closely linked to the exploitation of metallic ore deposits by mining. Gold, which is widely distributed and found in relics in many countries, was abundant and mined to a considerable extent in Egypt, and formed the basis of this nation's wealth during the height of its powers. The rise of Israel to a nation was related to the annexing of EDOM, with its copper and iron deposits, by DAVID (2 Sam. 8:14), and their exploitation both during his reign and the subsequent reign of SOLOMON (1 Ki. 4–10). The history and power of the city-state of ATHENS is closely linked with the silver mines of Laurion and of their exploitation. In the 4th cent. B.C., the wealth and exploits of Philip of Macedon, and then of his son ALEXANDER THE GREAT, were linked with the gold mining of the Mount Pangeus district near PHILIPPI, where the output was so high that the Greeks believed that the gold regenerated itself as it was gathered.

The mining of copper in CYPRUS made the island a prized possession successively of the

This artistic replica shows Egyptian slaves using foot bellows to smelt copper ore.

Egyptians, Assyrians, Phoenicians, Greeks, Persians, and Romans. Even the mining of tin in Cornwall, England, had a considerable bearing on the history of the ANE because of the trade by the Phoenicians in this metal needed for making bronze (see PHOENICIA). The iron of Anatolia (see ASIA MINOR) and ARMENIA was closely linked with the successive power of the HITTITES (c. 1400–1200 B.C.) and then the PHILISTINES.

The methods and conditions of mining in the pre-Christian era are illustrated by mining for gold in ancient Egypt, for turquoise and copper in the Sinai Peninsula, and for silver in Greece.

(1) *Gold in ancient Egypt.* Alluvial mining by washing river sands and gravels produced the earliest gold before 4000 B.C. This placer gold then was traced back to the source veins that were mined, particularly in the Northern Sudan (the ancient Nubia, a name thought to have been derived from the Egyptian *nub*, meaning gold). There were several producing districts in the desert between the 18th and 23rd latitudes and between the Nile and the Red Sea. Gold also came from the Coptos region to the N, also between the Nile and the Red Sea.

Underground mining was carried out on a series of adit levels and using slave labor. The harder rock was cracked by making wood fires against the rock face and then throwing water on the hot rocks. Hammers were used to reduce the size of the pieces before being carried out of the mines to be further reduced in size in stone mortars and then in stone hand mills. The rock dust was then washed on a sloping board, the sand being washed off and the heavy gold flakes remaining.

(2) *Turquoise and copper on the Sinai Peninsula.* Turquoise of a period earlier than 3400 B.C. is known from Egypt. Whether it was mined by Egyptians on the Sinai Peninsula or obtained by barter from the BEDOUINS of that region is not known. However, references to mining at the NE end of the Red Sea are among the earliest inscriptions in Egypt and pictorial records of mining covering the period 3200 to 1150 were found on sandstone cliffs in the Wadi Maghara, on the Sinai Peninsula. Here turquoise and MALACHITE, both minerals of copper, were mined, initially for decorative purposes and jewelry and, in the case of malachite, as a green face paint and as a paint for the eyes to lessen the glare of sunlight.

The early workings were mainly for turquoise, which was extracted with the aid of flint tools, the nodules of turquoise being separated from the encasing friable sandstone by hammering. When it was discovered, probably by accident, that malachite would smelt to copper in a charcoal (camp) fire, this mineral was mined and copper wedges and chisels made for use in the mining of turquoise. Later, malachite was mined to obtain copper to send back to the main part of Egypt. A room-and-pillar method of mining was used with individual chambers up to 24 ft. long and 6 ft. across. These copper deposits are not of the type associated with ores of tin, and this may explain why Egypt lagged behind other countries in the use of BRONZE, the copper-tin alloy.

(3) *Silver in Greece.* The silver mines of Laurion, about 25 mi. S of Athens, probably were being worked by 1000 B.C., and they provided much of the wealth of the city-state of Athens some 500 years later. The ore mined was mainly lead sulphide (galena), which contained 30 to 300 ounces of silver per ton of lead, the silver being extracted by metallurgical processes. There are associated minerals of iron and zinc. Most of the ore occurs in a limestone near its contact with a schist, a foliated rock of metamorphic origin. The earliest mining was done where the ore body cropped out at the surface and was oxidized. Here there was native silver as well as carbonates of lead, zinc, and iron. Cuts or passages were made in the hillside, and these were the *laurai* (lanes) that gave Laurion its name.

Ore at deeper levels was of sulphide minerals, mainly the argentiferous galena, and occurring mainly as tabular masses, up to 35 ft. thick, at the limestone-schist contact. More than 2,000 shafts were sunk, the deepest being to 386 ft. below the surface. The main shafts were 6 by 4 ft., with footholds to assist climbing, but the underground passages were generally only 2–3 ft. high and across. The mining was carried out by slaves in chains, using the pillar-and-stall type of stope, with patches of poor ore being left as pillars. In smaller stopes dry stone constructions supported overhanging rock. Timber was not commonly used. Because the passages were small, ventilation was poor, and mining by fire-setting followed by quenching with water could not have been used. However, fires were used to assist the movement of air in the shafts.

Each slave, who had a lamp made of baked clay containing enough oil to burn ten hours, broke about 25 tons of rock a month using a hammer, chisel, pick, and shovel, the metallic parts of which were of hammered and tempered iron. The broken ore and waste were passed from man to man in panniers of hide or grass, then taken to the surface. Here it was crushed in stone mortars and iron pestles, then sieved on to large (70 by 40 ft.) washing tables constructed of masonry faced with mortar. The flow of water carried away the lighter gangue and left behind the ore, which was then gathered, smelted, and treated using various other metallurgical processes (see METALS AND METALLURGY).

(See further T. A. Rickard, *Man and Metals: A History of Mining in Relation to the Development of Civilization*, 2 vols [1932]; C. E. Gregory, *A Concise History of Mining* [1980]; R. Shepherd, *Ancient Mining* [1993]; P. T. Craddock, *Early Metal Mining and Production* [1995]; M. Lynch, *Mining in World History* [2002].) D. R. BOWES

Mineans min-ee′uhnz. Also Minaeans. A Semitic people of the kingdom of Maʿin in SW ARABIA, probably not mentioned in the Bible (but see MEUNITES). The Minean kingdom was centered in the Jauf, a region in the NE corner of modern Yemen, just N of ancient SHEBA. Intensive cultivation by irrigation canals and control of the principal caravan route supported a number of cities there. Strabo lists the Mineans as one of the four major peoples of Arabia in his day and says the name of their capital was Karna. Minean inscriptions (*ANET*, 508–10) give it as QRNW (vocalized as *Qarnāwu*), modern Maʿin. These also show that Maʿin was founded by the kings of Hadhramaut (see HAZARMAVETH) c. 400 B.C. It reached its zenith c. 200–75 B.C., and was conquered by Qataban c. 50–25 B.C. (W. F. Albright, "The Chronology of the Minaean Kings of Arabia," *BASOR* 129 [1953]: 20–24.) J. REA

mineral. A substance having a definite chemical composition and atomic structure and formed by the inorganic processes of nature. Minerals exhibit various properties, such as color, luster, crystal form, cleavage, fracture, hardness, and density, which are used for identification and which exercise control on the commercial and industrial uses of the particular mineral. Small impurities in some minerals can result in varieties showing vastly different colors; for example, varieties of corundum (aluminum oxide) include ruby (red), sapphire (blue), and oriental emerald (green).

However, the possession of a definite chemical composition does not in every case suffice to fix a mineral species. Two (or more) minerals, such as diamond and graphite, which are carbon, can have the same chemical composition, but very different physical properties. This results from the way in which the constituent atoms are arranged. Where this internal atomic structure is expressed in the external form, the mineral is bounded by flat surfaces and is referred to as a CRYSTAL. From earliest times some minerals that occur as crystals have been sought after for their beauty, particularly their form and striking color (e.g., sapphire), or variegated colors (e.g., agate). Such precious or semiprecious stones were prized from earliest times (cf. Gen. 2:12), used for ecclesiastical vestments and regalia (cf. Exod. 28), for trade (cf. Job 28:15–19), and to portray the nature of things to be (cf. Rev. 21:18–20). See JEWELS AND PRECIOUS STONES. Other materials of the mineral kingdom were, and are, used in everyday life—for example, clay (Jer. 18:4) and copper (Ezra 8:27) for liquid containers, iron for tools (2 Sam. 12:31) and for vehicles (Jdg. 4:3), and the soil (Matt. 13:8) for growing crops. See separate articles for individual minerals.

D. R. BOWES

Miniamin min′yuh-min (מִנְיָמִין *H4975*, "from the right" [i.e., "favored"] or perhaps "from the south"; cf. BENJAMIN, MIJANIM). (1) A Levite who faithfully assisted KORE in distributing the contributions made to the temple during the reign of HEZEKIAH (2 Chr. 31:15).

(2) The ancestor of a priestly family in the days of JOAKIM; both this family and that of MOADIAH were headed by Piltai (Neh. 12:17).

(3) A priest who played the trumpet at the dedication of the wall (Neh. 12:41). E. B. SMICK

ministry. The duties and functions of those who serve God.

    I. Biblical terms for ministry
        A. In the OT
        B. In the NT
    II. Christ and ministry
        A. Christ the pattern for ministry
        B. The continuation of Christ's ministry
    III. The nature and purpose of ministry
        A. Ministry as mission
        B. Ministry as service
        C. Ministry as priesthood
        D. The purpose of ministry
    IV. Spiritual gifts and ministry
        A. The primacy of the Holy Spirit in ministry
        B. The charismatic character of ministry
        C. Varieties of spiritual gifts
    V. The organized ministry
        A. Presbyters or bishops
        B. Deacons

I. Biblical terms for ministry

A. In the OT. In keeping with its sacerdotal system, the OT distinguishes between the religious ministrations of cultic professionals on the one hand, and the laity on the other. The Hebrew verb *šārat H9250* ("to wait on, serve, minister"), usually rendered in the SEPTUAGINT with *leitourgeō G3310*, usually designates the duties performed by PRIESTS AND LEVITES in relation to God (Exod. 28:43; 29:30; Num. 3:6, 31; 8:26; 18:2; Deut. 10:8; 17:12; 18:5; 21:5; 1 Ki. 8:11; 1 Chr. 15:2; Jer. 33:21). The verb *ʿābad H6268* (often *latreuō G3302* in the LXX) refers to religious service rendered by the entire congregation or an individual (Exod. 3:12; 4:23; 7:16; 8:1; 2 Sam. 15:8; Job 21:15; Ps. 22:30; Mal. 3:14). It should be noted that where the noun *leitourgia G3311* occurs in the LXX, it nearly always represents *ʿăbōdâ H6275* (possibly because no abstract noun had been formed from *šārat*). (See further *NIDOTTE*, 3:304–9; 4:256–57.)

B. In the NT. When we turn to the NT, we are struck immediately by the obliteration of the OT distinction between professional and nonprofessional religious service, for here sacerdotalism has yielded to a universal priesthood constituted by Christ and shared alike by all who are united to him in the bonds of a living faith (Phil. 2:17; 1 Pet. 2:5, 9; Rev. 1:5–6; 5:10; 20:6). Since there is no longer any elite priestly caste, but ministry is essentially and equally the privileged vocation of all, priestly language generally is applied to the body of believers as a whole.

The NT employs a variety of terms in connection with differing types and functions of ministry, both general and particular. Although each term has its own special shade of meaning, there is considerable overlapping in usage, so that even from a single point of view any number of these terms may be used to designate a particular ministration, or the one who performs it.

(1) The most common NT term for ministry is *diakoneō G1354* with its cognates. Originally signifying the service of a table waiter (cf. Lk. 12:37; 17:8; Jn. 12:2), in classical Greek the word generally has a menial connotation. In the NT, however, where the root idea is supplying beneficial service, *diakoneō* is dignified by the highest associations and employed with a wide range of application. Christian apostles are ministers of Christ (1 Cor. 3:5; 1 Tim. 1:12), while even heathen magistrates are ministers of God (Rom. 13:4). Angels are ministering spirits sent forth to serve the heirs of salvation (Heb. 1:14). PAUL says that Christ became a minister to the circumcised (Rom. 15:8), while Jesus described himself as "one who serves" (Lk. 22:27). By contrast with the old ministry of the law which was a ministry of condemnation, a new ministry of the Spirit has now been inaugurated as a ministry of righteousness (2 Cor. 3:7–9).

In relation to the Christian community *diakonein* is used to denote: (a) discipleship in general (Jn. 12:26); (b) the full sweep of ministrations and activities by means of which Christ's work is carried on in the church and in the world (Acts 21:19; 1 Cor. 16:15; Eph. 4:11; Col. 4:17; 2 Tim. 4:5); (c) the preaching and teaching of the Word (Acts 6:4); (d) a special divine "gift" for various spiritual and temporal services (Rom. 12:7; 1 Cor. 12:5); (e) specific benevolent ministries such as the distribution of welfare assistance in the church at Jerusalem (Acts 6:1), and contributions from Gentile churches for impoverished believers at Jerusalem

(2 Cor. 8:4); (f) personal services like those which Tychicus rendered to Paul (Eph. 6:21); (g) the office of DEACON (Phil. 1:1; 1 Tim. 3:8, 12).

(2) Closely allied to *diakoneō* is *hypēreteō* G5676, which in secular Greek originally designated the labor of an under-rower in a galley, but which in the NT refers simply to the work of assisting a superior. Insofar as the term has any special connotation in apostolic literature, it seems to suggest subordination. The noun *hypēretēs* G5677 is used of attendants in the high priest's household (Matt. 26:58; Mk. 14:54, 65), and of inferior officials of the SANHEDRIN (Matt. 5:25; Jn. 7:32, 45–46; 18:3, 12, 22; Acts 5:22, 26). LUKE also uses it to designate the *ḥazzan* of the SYNAGOGUE at NAZARETH, an attendant similar to a verger, who had custody of the sacred scrolls read in public worship (Lk. 4:20); also of John Mark (see MARK, JOHN) as assistant to Paul and BARNABAS on their first missionary excursion (Acts 13:5); and of those whom Jesus sent out to preach the Word (Lk. 9:2). When reporting Paul's sermon in ANTIOCH OF PISIDIA, Luke employs the verb in connection with DAVID's service to God (Acts 13:36). Jesus referred to his followers as *hypēretai* (Jn. 18:36), and Paul proudly claimed the same relationship to Christ (Acts 26:16; 1 Cor. 4:1).

(3) Of weighty importance for any study of Christian ministry is *douleuō* G1526 and its cognate noun *doulos* G1528. Frequently translated "servant" in English versions, the force of *doulos* in the original is thereby lost, for the word means "slave" or "bondslave." Where the emphasis rests on divine lordship, with the correlative concepts of ownership and sovereignty, a person's service accordingly is viewed in terms of SLAVERY (Matt. 6:24; Lk. 16:13; 1 Thess. 1:9). Christians generally, also their leaders and even apostles, therefore function as slaves of God and of Christ in fulfilling their divine vocation (Acts 4:29; 1 Cor. 7:22; Gal. 1:10; Col. 4:12; 2 Tim. 2:24; 1 Pet. 2:16; cf. Rom. 6:22). In the opening salutation of his epistles, Paul more than once identifies himself as a slave of Christ (Rom. 1:1; Phil. 1:1; Tit. 1:1), a characteristic common to other apostolic authors (Jas. 1:1; Jude 1). Elsewhere, in a passage of intense emotion, Paul uses the kindred verb *douloō* G1530 ("enslave") to testify that in his ministry he willingly made himself a slave to all, in order that he might win more to Christ (1 Cor. 9:19). Most remarkable of all, in sounding the depths of the divine self-humiliation that shaped the pattern of the INCARNATION, the same apostle does not shrink from declaring that to accomplish his ministry of redemption Christ assumed "the form of a slave, being born in human likeness" (Phil. 2:7 NRSV).

(4) It was observed above that the LXX almost exclusively restricts *leitourgeō* to professional religious service. In the NT this verb and its correlates occur only fifteen times in Luke, Paul, and Hebrews, but nowhere else (*diakoneō* and cognates have now supplanted them), and never denote a literal priestly function in regard to Christian ministry. They are retained to designate the work of the Jewish priesthood (Lk. 1:23; Heb. 9:21), angelic ministrations on behalf of believers (1:14), and the priestly ministry of the ascended Christ in heaven (8:2, 6). By contrast with the LXX, and in harmony with its doctrine of the universal priesthood of believers, the NT extends the usage of these terms indiscriminately and figuratively to include the worship of prophets and teachers (Acts 13:2), Paul's ministry of the gospel to Gentiles (Rom. 15:16), the self-sacrificing service of the Philippians (Phil. 2:17), the care of EPAPHRODITUS for Paul's physical needs (2:25), the relief offering for the Jerusalem church (Rom. 15:27), and even civil authorities (13:6).

(5) One other word, *latreuō*, deserves mention. At first signifying remunerative service (the

Coptic priests worshiping at the Church of the Holy Sepulchre in Jerusalem.

opposite of *douleuō*, the nonremunerative service of a slave), this verb was expanded to include service rendered to God. In the LXX it designates the people's service to God in contrast to the special service of the priestly caste (*leitourgeō*). A technical NT term for the performance of religious duties, especially of a cultic nature, this verb and its correlate noun *latreia* designate divine worship in the strict sense of adoration, prayer, and sacrificial offerings (Matt. 4:10; Acts 7:7, 42; Rom. 9:4; Heb. 9:1–14; 10:2; Rev. 7:15; 22:3). They also are used in a general figurative sense for the whole life of righteous devotion, which in its rich and manifold expression finds favor with God (Lk. 1:74; Acts 24:14; 27:23; Rom. 1:9; 12:1; Phil. 3:3; 2 Tim. 1:3). (See further *NIDNTT*, 3:544–53.)

II. Christ and ministry

A. Christ the pattern for ministry. Christian ministry in all of its modes and manifestations must be traced ultimately to the ministry of Christ. From the outset the church perceived that the public career of Jesus is most aptly described by the term *ministry*, and it is within this framework that the gospel records in their entirety are set. The reference to Jesus in prayer by the early church as the "holy servant" of God (Acts 4:27, 30) recalls the prophetic description of the Messiah as the Servant of the Lord (Yahweh), whose self-sacrificing career fulfills God's redemptive purpose for his people (Isa. 40–66; Zech. 3:8–10). The angel who revealed Jesus' approaching birth to Joseph declared that his essential work would be the unique ministry of saving his people from their sins (Matt. 1:21). Paul conceives of the incarnation as Christ's vesting himself in the form of a slave (Phil. 2:7).

It was thus that Jesus understood his vocation. This concept of a Servant-Messiah, however, set him immediately on a collision course with prevailing messianic expectations which, embellished with symbols of earthly pomp and dominion, focused on the political elevation of Israel over all nations, especially its oppressors. The temptation (Matt. 4:1–11), the abortive coronation scheme after the feeding of the 5,000 (Jn. 6:1–15), Peter's rebuke at Caesarea Philippi (Mk. 8:27–33), and the popular acclaim at the triumphal entry (Matt. 21:1–11) represent unsuccessful bids for Jesus' acceptance of the conventional messianic image (cf. T. W. Manson, *The Church's Ministry* [1948], 17–18). Jesus' commission as Messiah was a divine investiture for ministry to the whole spectrum of human need, whose remedy in every particular lies in the all-embracing term "salvation." His decisive and unswerving commitment to this self-sacrificing career shines through many of his recorded sayings, but nowhere is it more clearly epitomized than in the words, "For even the Son of Man did not come to be served, but to serve, and to give his life as a ransom for many" (Mk. 10:45; cf. Lk. 22:27). His washing of the disciples' feet in the Upper Room was a dramatic vignette of the unselfish life of ministry now rushing to its close (Jn. 13:1–11).

Ministry describes the whole range of Jesus' messianic activities: preaching, teaching, various types of miracles, including healing the sick and raising the dead, forgiveness of sins, institution of the sacraments, etc. It extends even further to include his passion and death (Mk. 10:45). So far from being an innovation or disfigurement, the cross is of a piece with the preceding ministry, the scandalous yet crowning consummation that invests his messianic career with ultimate and eternal significance. His whole service on behalf of sinful and suffering humanity is telescoped in his sacrificial death. The Servant-Messiah mounts the throne of universal empire by laying down his life as a ransom for the citizens of his kingdom.

This perfect example of humble, self-denying service becomes, in turn, the norm and pattern for all of Christ's followers whom he calls to share his own destiny. Discipleship is service (Jn. 12:26; cf. Acts 20:18–35; Rom. 12:1; 2 Cor. 3–7). As the Father sent the Son into the world for ministry, so the Son sends his followers into the same world for ministry (Jn. 17:18; 20:21). Whereas the world calculates greatness on the scale of lordly dominion and authority, the only greatness Christ recognizes in his kingdom is lowliness of service: "whoever wants to become great among you must be your servant, and whoever wants to be first must be slave of all" (Mk. 10:43–44). The point is not that service is the avenue to honor; service is itself honor.

B. The continuation of Christ's ministry. The ministry of Christ did not terminate abruptly with the completion of his earthly career in the resurrection and ascension. The NT indicates its continuation along two different but parallel lines. There is, first, his ministry in heaven where he rules over all things for his CHURCH (Eph. 1:20–23), represents and intercedes for his people as their priest before the throne of God (Heb. 7:25; 1 Jn. 2:2), and is preparing a place for them to dwell with him forever (Jn. 14:1–3).

Christ also continues his ministry on earth through his body, the church, in which he is permanently present in the person of the HOLY SPIRIT (Jn. 14:15–17; 1 Cor. 12:4–11; Eph. 1:22–23; 4:1–16; cf. Matt. 28:18–20). The church is a living organism created by the Spirit for Christ's use in carrying out his redemptive purpose in the world, just as his physical body was fashioned by the same Spirit for his ministry during the earthly period of the incarnation (Lk. 1:31, 34, 35). See BODY OF CHRIST.

All Christian ministry at its source and in its manifold expressions is a continuation of the ministry of Jesus across the age-long sweep of history. There is truth, therefore, in the view of the church and its ministry as an extension of the incarnation (though G. W. Bromiley labels the conception as "hazardous"; see his *Christian Ministry* [1959], 16). The church has no independent ministry of its own, but one which is in every respect derivative. It has received its ministry from Christ. It learns its ministry from Christ. It discharges its ministry in the name of Christ and on his behalf. Whether it is the preaching of the Word, the administration of the sacraments, the relief of human distress, or the exercise of discipline, it is the personal, determinative action of Christ that lies behind and assumes tangible expression in the ministry of the church.

It should not be assumed, however, that this continuing ministry in the church is wholly identical with Jesus' ministry in Galilee and Judea 2,000 years ago. That ministry was unique and formative, the single root from which the continuing ministry has sprung and to which it must ever return for its energy and dynamic. Through its ongoing service the church communicates to each new generation the saving grace first released through the life, death, and resurrection of the Servant-Messiah. It does so only as the organic instrument of the living Lord who in the Spirit is ever present with and within his body.

This truth is further attested in the NT by its ascription to the ascended Christ of many of the titles by which varieties and orders of ministry in the church are designated. He is called apostle (Heb. 3:1; cf. Mk. 9:37; Lk. 10:16; Jn. 5:36; 6:29; 7:29; 8:42; 10:36; 11:42; 17:3–4); teacher (Mk. 4:38; 9:17, 38); bishop (1 Pet. 2:25); shepherd, translated "pastor" when used of ministers (1 Pet. 2:25; cf. Matt. 26:31; Mk. 14:27; Jn. 10:11–16; cf. 1 Pet. 5:4); and deacon or servant (Rom. 15:8; cf. Lk. 22:27).

The church, then, is absorbed into the ministry of Christ. This is to say that ministry is not the privilege and responsibility of an elite corps of ecclesiastical dignitaries, but belongs equally and alike to every member of Christ's body. No one can share in authentic Christian ministry unless by faith he first lays hold for himself on the saving benefits of Christ's own ministry. The moment a person does that, there falls upon him the solemn, binding obligation of helping to advance God's gracious design in Christ to earth's outmost frontiers.

Christian discipleship is ministry. The accomplishment of God's purpose for the world in Christ is never to be construed as itself necessitating the ministry of the church and its individual members. "The necessity of the Church's ministry is the necessity of its incorporation into Christ, not its indispensability for the fulfillment of the divine purpose" (Bromiley, *Christian Ministry*, 27). Only Christ is the true Minister, and his ministry alone is original, ultimate, indispensable.

III. The nature and purpose of ministry

A. Ministry as mission. All ministry, whether of Christ or the church, is divine in its origin and sanction. In the fourth gospel Jesus characteristically refers to himself as having been sent by God, thereby claiming both a general divine commission and specific divine authority for utterances and actions that sometimes outraged the religious scruples of his contemporaries (Jn. 5:36–37; 6:29–60; 7:28–29; cf. Matt. 15:24; Mk. 9:37; Lk. 9:48; 10:16). He employs the same language when commissioning his disciples to carry on his ministry after his ascension (Jn. 20:21). The church's ministry is a mission, and in rendering its service to the world the church demonstrates its obedience to the command of its Lord (Matt. 28:18–20).

B. Ministry as service. To describe the church's ministry, the NT writers chose out of various possibilities the word *diakonia*, a familiar term for lowly service, which they apply indiscriminately to the service of all believers alike. The comprehensiveness of this term is brought out by its wealth of associations in the NT. Apostles and their coworkers are servants (*diakonoi*) of God (2 Cor. 6:4; 1 Thess. 3:2), of Christ (2 Cor. 11:23; Col. 1:7; 1 Tim. 4:6), of a new covenant (2 Cor. 3:6), of the gospel (Eph. 3:7; Col. 1:23), of the church (1:24, 25), or in an absolute sense (1 Cor. 3:5; Eph. 6:21; Col. 4:7). Ministry likewise is a *diakonia* of apostleship (Acts 1:17, 25), of the Word (Acts 6:4), of the Spirit (2 Cor. 3:8), of righteousness (3:9), of reconciliation (5:18), of serving tables (Acts 6:2), and of financial aid for fellow believers in distress (2 Cor. 8:4; cf. 8:19–20). It is received from the Lord (Col. 4:17), who calls all his followers to participate in it (Eph. 4:12). It should be noted that Christian ministry is not exclusively oriented to the spiritual, but encompasses the physical dimensions of life as well (cf. Rom. 15:25).

The spirit of HUMILITY that animates Christian ministry, already evident in the term *diakonia*, is intensified when believers are called "slaves" of Christ and of God (Acts 4:29; 1 Cor. 7:22; 1 Pet. 2:16; cf. Rom. 12:11; 1 Thess. 1:9). No ground for human vanity and pride remains when even apostles bear the name of slave (Rom. 1:1; Jas. 1:1; Jude 1). Yet where gratitude reigns in hearts redeemed by the Lord who took the lowest place of service in love (Phil. 2:7–8), offering his life as a ransom for his own people (Mk. 10:45), even the calling to be his slave is gladly embraced as the noblest, most privileged vocation of all.

C. Ministry as priesthood. Christian ministry further has a priestly character and function. It is hardly accidental that the NT, while retaining the term "priest" (*hiereus G2636*) for Jewish and pagan priests, nowhere applies this term to any single class of Christian ministers. The only priests so designated by the NT are the saints, all believers in Christ (1 Pet. 2:5, 9; Rev. 1:6; 5:10; 20:6). Herein lies a fundamental distinction between Christianity and ancient pagan cults, and one of the greatest spiritual advances of the Christian dispensation over the OT. There is only one priesthood, that of Christ himself, and he shares it equally with all the members of his body. It is a corporate rather than an individual possession. In their priestly ministrations, individual Christians function as representatives of the whole community and on its behalf.

Equally significant is the deliberate restraint with which the NT applies sacrificial language to Christian ministry. As priests, believers offer sacrifices of praise (Heb. 13:15), of service (Phil. 2:17; Heb. 13:16), and of self-dedication (Rom. 12:1), but never do they offer SACRIFICES for sin. The solitary sacrifice for sin which the NT allows is the self-sacrifice of Christ, offered once for all (Heb. 10:12, 26–27). It is only by means of the great Head of the church that the union with the all-meritorious sacrifice of lesser sacrifices of worship and service offered by the members of Christ's body are rendered acceptable to God. The priestly and sacrificial system of the OT stands forever abrogated by the sacrifice and priesthood of Christ in which it has been perfectly fulfilled (Heb. 5:1–10).

D. The purpose of ministry. Christian ministry, like all creation, is intended primarily for the glory of God (1 Pet. 4:10–11). To achieve this end it serves a dual purpose. In relation to the unbelieving world, Christian ministry, even in its humanitarian expressions, is essentially evangelistic and missionary, looking to the numerical and geographical expansion of the body of Christ, until in its human composition it is complete. Ministry also serves a reflexive purpose in relation to the church itself. Enumerating various gifts conferred on the church by its ascended Lord, Paul asserts that they are "to prepare God's people for works of service, so that the body of Christ may be built up [*oikodomē G3869*, edification]" (Eph. 4:12; cf. Acts 9:31; Rom. 14:19; 1 Cor. 14:5, 12, 26; Eph. 4:16). Commonly misconstrued as the stimulation of pleasant religious feelings, edification means inner spiritual strengthening and growth. Within the church, ministry is didactic and pastoral, seeking to develop believers into mature disciples, who as robust, healthy, and vigorous members of the body of Christ render it a more effective instrument for his service. Both forms of ministry, however, converge on a common goal: the upbuilding of the body of Christ—in the one case, by the accession of new members, and in the other, by advancing and enriching the spiritual life of present members.

IV. Spiritual gifts and ministry

A. The primacy of the Holy Spirit in ministry. A focal point in Jesus' upper room discourse and postresurrection teaching concerns the advent of the HOLY SPIRIT, whom he promised to send from the Father, and in whom he would be present with his followers until the close of the age (Jn. 14:16–17, 26; 15:26; 16:7–15; 20:22; Acts 1:4–5, 8; cf. Lk. 24:49). These passages set forth the primacy of the Holy Spirit in the continuing ministry of the risen and ascended Lord through his body, the church. This executive operation of the Holy Spirit furnishes a double continuity with the ministry of Christ. On the one hand, he mediates the presence and power of the living Lord, while on the other hand the incarnate ministry of Jesus himself was conducted in the power and under the control of the Spirit (Lk. 4:14–15; Acts 10:38).

The book of Acts abundantly documents the reality of the Spirit's dominant role in the concrete experience of the apostolic church (Acts 2:1–4; 4:8, 31; 5:1–11, 32; 6:3–10; 9:31; 10:19; 13:2, 4; 15:28; 16:6, 7; 19:6, 21; 20:28). The Spirit equips and empowers the church for ministry, then channels its many varieties of service to their divine goal in the expansion and spiritual enrichment of the church. While to the body of Christ has been entrusted an external ministry of evangelistic and pastoral dimensions, in the inner spiritual regions it is the living Christ who executes all ministry in the person of his Spirit. Christian ministry came of age at Pentecost (Acts 1:4–5, 8; Eph. 4:8–13).

B. The charismatic character of ministry. The NT identifies all forms of ministry as divine "gifts" (*charisma* G5922, "grace-gift") of the ascended Lord who bestows them on the church through his Spirit (Eph. 4:7–12). These gifts, which are wholly of GRACE—the same grace which is the source of the believer's justification—display the following characteristics:

1. Necessity. Possession of a supernatural endowment of the Spirit is indispensable for effective ministry. The NT envisions no possibility of service

Worshipers at the Church of the Holy Sepulchre celebrating the presence of the Holy Spirit among them.

whatever apart from the Spirit's gifts. It is misleading, therefore, to distinguish between so-called "charismatic ministries" (prophecy, tongues, miracles, etc.) and "noncharismatic" ministerial orders (elder and deacon). All of the essential functions associated with ministerial orders in the NT are included in the Pauline catalogues of spiritual gifts (Rom. 12:6–8; 1 Cor. 12:4–11, 28–31; 14:1–5; Eph. 4:11–12). The same apostle further regarded elders, who presumably held their office by some manner of human selection and ordination, as appointed by the Holy Spirit (Acts 20:28). Since the apostolic church required satisfactory evidence that a person was filled with the Holy Spirit before entrusting him with the most ordinary service (6:3), one may assume that candidates for official ministerial orders were chosen from among those persons in whom the Spirit's gifts were most conspicuous. In any event, all ministry is charismatic, so that it is the Spirit's gifts which decisively qualify believers for service.

2. Diversity. All gifts originate with the same Spirit; however, they display a diversity that accords with the division of labor within the body of Christ

(1 Cor. 12:4–11). The grace of the Spirit assumes many varieties of forms and flows through many different channels. Although useful in their own right, not all gifts are of equal value. Paul regarded tongues, for example, as inferior to prophecy (1 Cor. 14:1–5), while esteeming LOVE as the highest gift of all (ch. 13, which follows without interruption the detailed discussion of gifts in ch. 12). See SPIRITUAL GIFTS.

3. Universality. Just as every organ in the human body performs its own unique function, so every member of the body of Christ has his or her special contribution to make to the well-being and usefulness of the whole (1 Cor. 12:7; Eph. 4:7, 16; 1 Pet. 4:10). The NT is entirely innocent of the common distinction between clergy and laity, which regards the clergy as "ministers" and the laity as mere spectators. The term *laity* (from Gk. *laos* G3295, "people") refers to "the people of God" and embraces all members of Christ's body, while all members are his servants. In sovereign freedom the Spirit distributes to individual believers the gifts that render their service possible (1 Cor. 12:11). While the same believer may possess multiple endowments (2 Tim. 1:11), there is no monopoly of the Spirit's gifts. Every believer has one gift or more, held in trust for the common good.

4. Sufficiency. All ministry is designed to build up the body of Christ in living union with its Head (1 Cor. 14:3–5; Eph. 4:11–12). Determined in accordance with this purpose, the Spirit's gifts are by their very nature and bestowal the pledge and guarantee of its fulfillment. Nothing else is needed. Drawing on its vast wealth of spiritual resources, the ministering church advances toward its completeness in Christ.

C. Varieties of spiritual gifts. Of the several passages in which Paul catalogues the Spirit's gifts, three deserve special notice. Romans 12:6–8 lists prophecy, service (*diakonia*), teaching, exhortation, liberality, leadership, and acts of mercy. First Corinthians 12:28–31 mentions apostles, prophets, teachers, workers of miracles, healers, helpers, administrators, speakers in tongues, and interpreters of tongues. Ephesians 4:11–12 specifies apostles, prophets, evangelists, and pastors and teachers.

1. Apostles. The most important group of persons mentioned in these lists were the apostles. The term APOSTLE is used first of the Twelve whom Jesus chose and personally trained as apprentices through intimate association with himself for their career of preaching the gospel (Mk. 3:13–19; 6:30). These two features—appointment by Jesus in the days of his flesh and companionship with him throughout his entire ministry—were the distinguishing marks of the Twelve.

Others also bore the name of apostle: MATTHIAS, who by divine direction was chosen to replace JUDAS ISCARIOT (Acts 1:15–26); PAUL, who claimed direct appointment to apostleship by the risen Lord (Rom. 1:1–5; Gal. 1:1); JAMES the brother of Jesus and head of the Jerusalem church, who also presided over the first general church council even though Peter and Paul were present (Acts 15); BARNABAS (14:14; 1 Cor. 9:6); ANDRONICUS and JUNIAS (Rom. 16:7); possibly APOLLOS (1 Cor. 4:6–9); and perhaps SILAS (1 Thess. 1:1; 2:6). Paul calls EPAPHRODITUS an "apostle" of the Philippian church (Phil. 2:25), and further refers to other "apostles of the churches" (2 Cor. 8:23). In the last two instances *apostolos* G693 frequently is translated "messenger"; however, since the NT elsewhere does not use the term of ordinary messengers, this rendering may be questioned. False apostles also are mentioned (2 Cor. 11:13; Rev. 2:2), whose fraudulent claims may have been exposed by their failure to show the signs of an apostle (2 Cor. 12:12).

Essential to apostleship is the idea of mission (*apostellō* G690, "to send"). The NT apostles were primarily pioneer preachers of the gospel and the original authoritative witnesses to Christ who traveled throughout the Jewish and Gentile world establishing congregations of new converts. Occupying unique positions of leadership and authority, they further superintended the work of the churches, commissioned local officers, administered discipline, and settled issues of general dispute (Acts 14:23; ch. 15). Nearly all of the NT books were written by apostles, and the few that were not came from the hands of their intimate associates and evidently received apostolic endorsement.

2. Evangelists. Also itinerant missionary preachers, EVANGELISTS seem to have differed from apostles very little, except for their lower rank and authority, possibly because they lacked the unique qualifications for apostleship. PHILIP, one of the "Seven" who became an evangelist (Acts 6:5; 21:8), first introduced the gospel to SAMARIA (8:4–13). Paul exhorted TIMOTHY to fulfill his ministry by doing the work of an evangelist (2 Tim. 4:5).

3. Prophets. Second in importance only to the apostles, with whom they were sometimes classed, were the PROPHETS (Eph. 2:20; 3:5). Jesus promised to send prophets (Matt. 23:34), and the NT shows that his promise was fulfilled. Although they received direct REVELATION from God (1 Cor. 14:30), prophets were not channels of new truth for the church but inspired preachers of the Word whose deliverances provided upbuilding, encouragement, and consolation (14:3). They did occasionally, however, forecast future events (Acts 11:27–28; 21:10–11). They were required to speak only what was revealed to them (Rom. 12:6), and their words must agree with the authoritative apostolic teaching (1 Cor. 14:37–38).

Any believer might receive this gift, and Paul encouraged all the Corinthians to seek it (1 Cor. 14:1). Generally spontaneous and occasional (Acts 19:6), it was more permanently bestowed on some who formed a special group of prophets, anyone or several of whom might speak in turn at regular services of worship (1 Cor. 14:29–33). Those specifically mentioned include AGABUS (Acts 11:28; 21:10); Simeon called NIGER, LUCIUS, and MANAEN at Antioch, along with Barnabas and Paul (13:1); Judas and Silas (15:32); and the four daughters of PHILIP (21:9). False prophets also circulated in the church, as Jesus had forewarned (Matt. 7:15); hence, believers were admonished to test prophetic teaching for its consistency with the essential faith of the gospel (1 Jn. 4:1–3). A specific impostor, a woman named JEZEBEL (most likely a symbolical name), corrupted the church at THYATIRA with her pernicious doctrine (Rev. 2:20). The gift of prophecy is especially prominent in 1 Corinthians because its practice in CORINTH was badly abused and in need of correction.

4. Teachers and pastors. That persons who had the gift of teaching were highly esteemed in the apostolic church is evident from their association with apostles and prophets (*didaskalos G1437*, Acts 13:1; 1 Cor. 14:28; cf. 1 Tim. 2:7; 2 Tim. 1:11). Including women in their number (Tit. 2:3–5), they gave instruction in matters of Christian faith and ethical duty. In the Gentile churches especially they trained converts from paganism in the knowledge and interpretation of the OT, while they also expounded the words of Jesus and the apostolic doctrine contained in the growing body of tradition. They sometimes actively participated in the services of worship (1 Cor. 14:26), but much of their ministry was conducted more informally among groups of believers. In Eph. 4:11 teachers are also called "pastors" (*poimēn G4478*, "shepherd"), a term that suggests general oversight of a local congregation as well as instruction.

5. Other gifts. The exact nature of some of these gifts of the Spirit is uncertain. "Administrators" apparently shared in the management of local congregational affairs. "Helpers" likely attended to benevolent service among the sick, the poor, the persecuted, etc. Persons having the gift of "tongues" employed it in prayer, singing, and thanksgiving (1 Cor. 14:14–17). Gifts of "healing" and other miraculous powers also were found in the apostolic church.

V. The organized ministry. Perhaps no subject in the history of the Christian church has been more greatly vexed by confusion, discord, and bitter strife than that of ministerial order. The problem is a vastly complicated one. For one thing, the NT presents a picture of local communities of believers in different stages of development and with few fixed structures of ministry. Then, too, the NT evidence is in many important particulars incomplete or altogether missing, while information from the early postapostolic period is likewise scanty and not always reliable. High-sounding pronouncements on many aspects of this subject tend to be fragile and brittle, revealing more about the author's own views than the practice of the primitive church. One must, therefore, proceed with caution and humility, not vainly boasting a knowledge which is not ours.

This much is certain. In the formative years of the church its ministry exhibited amazing variety and adaptability. Emerging at PENTECOST as a non-schismatic Jewish sect, the church naturally modeled its ministry in part on patterns borrowed from the SYNAGOGUE. The creative Spirit of the risen Lord inhabiting his body also fashioned within it from the beginning new organs and channels of ministry through which to communicate the life-giving grace of God to men.

From the early chapters of Acts it is evident that at the first the apostles directed the life of the infant church. They were soon joined in their ministry by evangelists and prophets who assisted them in spreading the gospel far and wide. As new communities of Christians sprang up in Judea, Samaria, and throughout the Gentile world, the need emerged for official structures of ministry to direct the affairs of local churches. The NT generally employs three terms to designate the two official orders of ministry which were established: ELDER, BISHOP, and DEACON. It always must be remembered that alongside of these orders there existed a veritable constellation of other local and itinerant ministries, all alike Christ's gifts to his church through his indwelling Spirit. See also CHURCH GOVERNMENT IN THE APOSTOLIC AGE.

A. Presbyters or bishops. There is no record to indicate when the office of "elder" (*presbyteros* G4565) was instituted. Elders are found early in the Christian communities of Judea (Acts 11:30), while Paul and Barnabas appointed elders in charge of the congregations they established on their first missionary journey (14:23). This office was borrowed, though modified, from the Jewish synagogue, where a company of elders ruled the religious and civil life of the community. Primarily custodians of the Mosaic law, these Jewish elders taught and interpreted its precepts and administered punishments to its offenders.

The NT also designates Christian elders by the name "bishop" (*episkopos* G2176, "overseer"). Although sometimes disputed, the evidence overwhelmingly supports this identification. (1) In Acts 20:17, Paul summons the elders of the church at EPHESUS, while in v. 28 he calls these same men "bishops." (2) In Phil. 1:1, Paul extends formal greetings to all the Christians at Philippi, along with their bishops and deacons, but he takes no notice of elders. This omission is inexplicable unless bishops and elders were identical. (3) In 1 Tim. 3:1–13, Paul sets forth the qualifications of bishops and deacons, but not elders, in considerable detail. Yet he specifically mentions elders in ch. 5, where he ascribes to them the same functions of ruling and teaching which in the earlier passage are attributed to bishops (cf. 3:4–5; 5:17). (4) In Tit. 1:5–6, after commanding TITUS to appoint elders in all the churches in CRETE, Paul counsels him to restrict his choice of elders to men who are "blameless." He then explains this requirement by adding, "For a bishop ... must be blameless" (v. 7 NRSV), a pointless argument if the two terms do not designate the same office.

Elder and *bishop*, then, are synonymous, but whereas the former term indicates the great dignity surrounding this office, the latter signifies its function of rule or oversight. In the NT oversight is especially related to the figure of the shepherd who feeds and cares for his flock. It is therefore natural that pastoral language is interwoven with the use of the term *bishop* (Acts 20:28; cf. Jn. 21:15–17). In their pastoral oversight of congregational life, elders reflect Christ's own office as the Shepherd and Bishop of souls (1 Pet. 2:25; cf. John 10:11–16; Heb. 13:20; 1 Pet. 4:4), and rule with his authority.

The comprehensive character of their office involved elders in a wide variety of duties. They engaged in the ministry of preaching and teaching the Word (1 Tim. 5:17). Not all of them did so, but the view that distinguishes between "teaching" and "ruling" elders, as if they formed two separate classes, has no clear textual basis. Elders also guarded the churches against false doctrine (Tit. 1:9), rendered pastoral service (Jas. 5:14), and administered ecclesiastical discipline. Their participation in the Jerusalem Council along with the apostles (Acts 15) indicates that their authority, though essentially local, extended to the whole church. They are charged not to rule in lordly fashion nor for financial gain, but to exercise their authority with humility (1 Pet. 4:1–5).

Likely they conducted WORSHIP, although anyone in the congregation possessing a suitable gift of the Spirit might participate in the service (1 Cor. 14:26). Little is said in the NT about sacramental duties, but since both SACRAMENTS were closely tied to the ministry of the Word and worship (Matt. 28:19; Acts 2:41–42; 8:35–38; 20:7; 1 Cor. 11:17–26), one may assume that in the absence of an apostle, evangelist, or prophet, elders were largely responsible for their administration. Clement of Rome, writing near the end of the 1st cent., says specifically that they officiated at the EUCHARIST. Local churches apparently appointed their own elders, who were then ordained by other elders in a solemn ceremony of laying on of hands (1 Tim. 4:14), although one cannot be absolutely sure of either of these things. Presumably the elders of the apostolic church were the equivalent of pastors today. It is especially notable that the apostles Peter and John both refer to themselves by this name (1 Pet. 5:1; 2 John 1; 3 Jn. 1).

B. Deacons. Forming a subordinate order of ministry were the deacons (*diakonos* G1356, Phil. 1:1; 1 Tim. 3:8–10). Not copied from any Jewish or Gentile prototype, this office was a wholly new creation of the Christian church. Its origin frequently is traced to the "Seven" who were appointed to administer the distribution of welfare in the Jerusalem church (Acts 6:1–6). Nowhere are the Seven called "deacons," while the word *diakonia* is used in this passage to contrast their ministry of serving tables with the apostles' ministry of the Word. Moreover, two of their number, STEPHEN and PHILIP, soon distinguished themselves as highly gifted preachers (6:8–10; 8:4–8; 21:8). Alfred Plummer summed up the situation well: "To call the 'Seven' the first deacons is a conjecture which can be neither proved nor disproved." While there is no evidence to link the Seven with the deacons of Philippians and 1 Timothy, their appointment may have provided the basic pattern for the later office.

The specific functions of the deacons are beclouded by nearly as much uncertainty as their origin, and their duties must be inferred from the nature of their qualifications. They were required to be of serious mind and character, honest in speech, temperate, free from greed for money, and to "keep hold of the deep truths of the faith with a clear conscience" (1 Tim. 3:8–9). This list of qualifications, together with the natural associations of the word *diakonia*, suggests that household visitation and administration of local benevolence funds were among their responsibilities. At a later date this was certainly so. It is further known that in the postapostolic church deacons served as personal assistants to the bishops in conducting worship, especially at the Eucharist, and in the management of church affairs. It is possible from 1 Tim. 3:11 to infer that women also held this office, and Rom. 16:1 describes PHOEBE as a *diakonos* of the church at CENCHREA. The masculine form of the noun may signify that it is a common noun, meaning "servant," and not an official title. In any event, deaconesses do not appear to have been prevalent until the 3rd cent. The NT nowhere indicates the manner in which deacons were appointed to office, but as in the case of the Seven, they may have been chosen by the local congregation and ordained by the laying on of hands.

In view of the NT evidence, there seems to be no reasonable doubt that the apostolic church had only two official *orders* of local ministry: presbyter-bishop and deacon. The ministry exercised by these orders assumed three *forms*: Word, rule, and service. To this threefold ministry the body of Christ, equipped and empowered by his indwelling Spirit, is unceasingly summoned by its living Head until his return in glory.

(In addition to the works mentioned in the body of the article, see F. J. A. Hort, *The Christian Ecclesia* [1897]; J. B. Lightfoot, *The Christian Ministry* [1901], also found as an appendix in his *Philippians*, rev. ed. [1890], 181–269; T. M. Lindsay, *The Church and Its Ministry in the Early Centuries* [1902]; W. Lowrie, *The Church and Its Organization in Primitive and Catholic Times* [1904]; A. von Harnack, *The Constitution and Law of the Church in the First Two Centuries* [1910]; H. B. Swete, ed., *Early History of the Church and Ministry* [1918]; B. H. Streeter, *The Primitive Church* [1929]; K. E. Kirk, ed., *The Apostolic Ministry* [1946]; S. Neill, ed., *The Ministry of the Church* [1947]; G. W. H. Lampe, *Some Aspects of the New Testament Ministry* [1949]; T. F. Torrance, *Royal Priesthood* [1955]; A. Ehrhardt, *The Apostolic Ministry* [1958]; A. T. Hanson, *The Pioneer Ministry* [1961]; E. Schweizer, *Church Order in the New Testament* [1961]; L. Morris, *Ministers of God* [1964]; R. S. Paul, *Ministry* [1965]; K. H. Rengstorf, *Apostolate and Ministry* [1969]; C. K. Barrett, *Church, Ministry and Sacraments in the New*

Testament [1985]; D. A. Carson, ed., *The Church in the Bible and the World* [1987]; D. L. Bartlett, *Ministry in the New Testament* [1993]; W. Grudem, *Systematic Theology: An Introduction to Christian Doctrine* [1994], ch. 47; J. W. Thompson, *Pastoral Ministry according to Paul* [2006]; R. E. Schweitzer in *ABD*, 4:835–42.) R. A. BODEY

Minni min′i (מִנִּי H4973, meaning unknown). A kingdom that, along with ARARAT (Urartians) and ASHKENAZ (prob. SCYTHIANS), was summoned by God to attack BABYLON (Jer. 51:27). Its people, identified as the Manneans (Mannaeans, Assyrian *Mannai*), occupied the area to the S of Lake Urmia in western Iran from the 9th to the 7th centuries B.C. They are mentioned as a warlike people in the Assyrian inscriptions of SHALMANESER III, Shamshi-Adad V, SARGON, SENNACHERIB, ESARHADDON, and ASHURBANIPAL, and in the Urartian inscriptions of Menua, Argishti, Sardur III, and Rusa II. According to the Babylonian Chronicle they sided with the Assyrians when the Babylonians attacked in 616 B.C. Four years later, when NINEVEH fell to the Babylonians, Medes, and possibly the Scythians, their territory became part of the Median dominion (see MEDIA), and they disappear from the record. Something of the material life of the Manneans can probably be seen from the excavations at Hasanlu S of Lake Urmia, where in Levels IV and III B a fortified citadel and metal work of some merit were found. (See R. H. Dyson in *JNES* 24 [1965]: 193–217; E. Porada, *Ancient Iran* [1965], 108–22; E. Yamauchi, *Foes from the Northern Frontier: Invading Hordes from the Russian Steppes* [1982], ch. 2.) T. C. MITCHELL

Minnith min′ith (מִנִּית H4976, meaning unknown). Apparently one of the "twenty towns" of the Ammonites which JEPHTHAH conquered (Jdg. 11:33). See AMMON. According to the description of Jephthah's campaign, which took him from AROER "to the vicinity of [*lit.*, till you come to] Minnith," this city must have been the easternmost limit of his victories. In his *Onomastica* (132.1–2), EUSEBIUS identified it with a place called *Maanith*, 4 mi. from HESHBON on the road to Philadelphia (i.e., Amman or RABBAH of the Ammonites). Its location is unknown, but proposed identifications include Umm el-Hanafish (Umm el-Basatin, halfway between Heshbon and el-Yadudeh) and Khirbet-Hamzeh (4 mi. NE of Heshbon). Ezekiel mentions the "wheat from Minnith," suggesting its exceptional quality (Ezek. 27:17; cf. 2 Chr. 27:5). Some scholars, however, emend the text (cf. RSV, "olives"). P. A. VERHOEF

minstrel. See MUSIC V.B.

mint. An aromatic herb (*Mentha longifolia*, of the *Libiatae* family). The plant has notched leaves and grows taller than the usual mint grown in Europe and the USA — often, in fact, 3 ft. high (see further *FFB*, 143–44). Dried, powdered mint leaves apparently were assiduously tithed by the Pharisees (Matt. 23:23 = Lk. 11:42; Gk. *hēdyosmon G2455*). The synagogues in our Lord's days had sprigs of mint sprinkled on the floor, so that the fragrance arose when they were walked on (cf. H. Shaw, *Plants in the Missouri Botanical Garden* [1884]). See also FLORA (under *Libiatae*). W. E. SHEWELL-COOPER

minuscule. A cursive writing style. The term is also applied to medieval MSS that use this type of writing. See TEXT AND MANUSCRIPTS (NT), II.B.

Miphkad mif′kad. See MUSTER GATE.

miracle. A term commonly applied to extraordinary events that manifest God's intervention in nature and in human affairs (but see qualifications below). There are at least three reasons for studying the subject of miracles. First, one may wish to judge the claims of religious groups or individuals to continue the apostolic power to perform miracles. Second, the so-called scientific view of the world declares that miracles are and always have been impossible; to meet this objection the believer must work out a theory of natural law, a philosophy of science, or in some way relate miracles to ordinary events without impairing the unity of his or her worldview. Third, a Christian thinker has a divinely imposed obligation to know what the Bible teaches (cf. 2 Tim. 3:16), and since miracles are a part of Scripture, they too must be understood.

   I. Biblical data
   II. Theology and science

III. Science and theology
IV. Modern miracles

I. Biblical data. The first miracle is the CREATION of the heavens and the earth. Or was creation really a miracle? No doubt the formation of EVE out of one of ADAM's ribs is a miracle, but is the initial creation properly so classified? What then is a miracle? How is it defined? Without a knowledge of this definition, how could one tell, for example, whether or not to include the birth of SAMUEL (1 Sam. 1)? Was DAVID's escape from SAUL's spear a miracle (18:10–11)? Unless one has the definition first, no list of miracles can be constructed. On the other hand, if there is no inclusive list, if the various miracles cannot be identified, how can one discover their common characteristics or otherwise study them? There is no escape from this dilemma without a survey of the biblical accounts and a tentative identification of the events that might possibly be miraculous.

Here only a selection, nothing like a complete list, can be made. After the creation, and after the expulsion of Adam and Eve from the garden, we come to the account of the flood. This deluge was spectacular enough, and if this is the test of the miraculous, the flood was certainly a miracle (see FLOOD, GENESIS). Rain, however, is not a miracle; hurricanes and typhoons are not miracles; the earthquakes and the breaking up of the fountains of the great deep which accompanied the rain may not be miracles. How much rain, then, and upheaval are needed to make a storm a miracle? The confusion of tongues at BABEL seems to qualify. Was the destruction of SODOM a miracle, or a natural disaster?

God commanded MOSES to throw his staff on the ground, whereupon it became a snake (Exod. 4:2–4). When Moses picked it up again by the tail, it changed back into his staff. Again, God told Moses to put his hand into his bosom, and when he took it out, it was leprous as snow. Repeating the action, his hand was restored (4:6–7). Consider the ten plagues: AARON smote the NILE with his rod and the water turned to blood; next he brought frogs to cover the land of Egypt. Then the magicians with their enchantments also turned the water into blood, and also brought frogs upon the land. Can heathen magicians perform miracles as well as Moses and Aaron?

For the third plague Aaron produced gnats (Exod. 8:16), but this time the magicians failed to duplicate the phenomenon and said to Pharaoh, "This is the finger of God" (v. 19). What is there about gnats, as distinguished from frogs, that would indicate the third plague to be the finger of God? Finally, the firstborn in every Egyptian family died in one night. Death is a natural event, and if two people die at once, it is not a miracle. But when the firstborn of every family, and not younger children, die, all during the same night, it clearly is more than a coincidence. But if this is a miracle, may a miracle be nothing more than many ordinary events happening at the same time? See PLAGUES OF EGYPT.

Consider the exodus itself. The Israelites had begun their march out of Egypt; now they faced the RED SEA and Pharaoh was in pursuit. Here the Scripture reads, "Then Moses stretched out his hand over the sea, and all that night the LORD drove the sea back with a strong east wind and turned it into dry land. The waters were divided, and the Israelites went through the sea on dry ground, with a wall of water on their right and on their left" (Exod. 14:21–22). See EXODUS, THE.

Miracle is sometimes defined as an immediate act of God, that is, an act in which God uses no means. If there were such an act, it undoubtedly would be a violation of natural law, for all natural processes involve means. But most of the events commonly called miracles were accomplished with the use of means. In the present instance, the crossing of the Red Sea, it is expressly stated that God used a strong eastern wind. Possibly one might insist that no means were used in the VIRGIN BIRTH (except Mary herself) and in the RESURRECTION OF CHRIST. In that case these would be the only miracles in the Bible. However, Mary is a means in the INCARNATION, and if no one is sure how the resurrection was effected, there remain only two divine acts that by their nature completely exclude all means. These two are the creation of the world from nothing and the continuous upholding of the existence of the universe in its entirety. Yet neither of these is ordinarily considered a miracle.

To return to the exodus, note once more that the wind was not only a means, but also a natural phenomenon. Strong winds have blown back water at other times and in other places. At these other times no persecuted slaves escaped from a pursuing army. May one then call the escape of the Israelites a miracle? Or a coincidence? Literally, the safe crossing of the Red Sea was a coincidence. Two events took place at the same time. There is a good reason why Christians do not like to use the word *coincidence*, for its connotation suggests an unforeseen, unplanned, accidental event. On the other hand God had planned this coincidence from all eternity. Not only did he control wind and wave at the crucial moment, but he also prepared Moses, hardened Pharaoh's heart, and instilled courage into the Israelites to accept Moses' leadership.

For a final instance in the life of Moses, there was the PILLAR OF FIRE AND CLOUD. By these means God directed the Israelites when to march and when to make camp. These pillars seem to be neither natural nor a coincidence (except in the trivial sense in which everything is a coincidence). They also were noteworthy because, in the absence of any indication as to how they were produced, they could be thought of as immediate acts of God. On the other hand, if God rested from his work of creation, as stated in Genesis, one cannot suppose that now he created something from nothing.

Numerous other miracles follow in the OT accounts, such as BALAAM's talking donkey (Num. 22:28–30); the fall of the walls of JERICHO (Josh. 6:1–21); the fall of DAGON's image (1 Sam. 5:1–5); ELIJAH and the widow's oil (1 Ki. 17:8–16); her son raised from the dead (17:17–24); the fire from heaven on the soaked sacrifice at Mount Carmel (18:20–40); and the chariot of fire with the fiery horses, when a whirlwind took Elijah to heaven (2 Ki. 2:1–12). Two other persons were raised from the dead (2 Ki. 4:32–37 and 13:20–21). The Assyrian army was destroyed in one night (19:20–37). Then there were the three young men who were not burned by NEBUCHADNEZZAR's superheated furnace (Dan. 3:1–30); the handwriting on the wall (5:1–30); and DANIEL in the lion's den (6:1–28); and finally there was JONAH and the great fish (Jon. 1–2).

The NT miracles may be divided into two groups. The first are those in which no human agent was involved. Such are the virgin birth of Christ, the star of Bethlehem, the earthquake that rent the veil of the temple and opened the graves for some saints to rise, and the resurrection of Christ himself. The second set, in which human agents are prominent, may be subdivided into two subsets: the miracles of Jesus and those of the apostles.

The miracles of Jesus are also of two varieties (see JESUS CHRIST VII). First, the HEALING miracles include the three cases in which Jesus raised the dead, as well as his expulsion of demons. The other and more ordinary miracles of healing are not only those of named individuals, but also of large crowds (cf. Matt. 8:16 and 12:15). Second, there are certain "nature miracles," few in number; and while it is obvious that the Gospels do not record all the healing miracles, it seems likely that the nature miracles are totally enumerated. They are the water turned into wine (Jn. 2:1–11); Peter's draught of fishes (Lk. 5:1–11 [miracle, coincidence, or exercise of omniscience?]); the stilling of the storm (Matt. 8:23–27; Mk. 4:35:41; Lk. 8:22–25); the multiplication of the loaves and fishes (Matt. 14:15–21; Mk. 6:30–44; Lk. 9:10–17; Jn. 6:1–14); walking on the water (Matt. 14:22–44; Mk. 6:45–51; Jn. 6:15–21); the second miraculous feeding (Matt. 15:32–39; Mk. 8:1–10); the coin in the fish's mouth (Matt. 17:24–27 [miracle or omniscience?]); and the withering of the fig tree (Matt. 21:28–20; Mk. 11:27–33; Lk. 20:1–8). The accounts of these nature miracles have a bearing on the claim that

Water flowing from red granite rock at Rephidim. Somewhere in this region God told Moses to strike a rock and produce water for the Israelites.

miracles, if they can be defined, have occurred in medieval and modern times.

The miracles of the apostles and some of their converts include the deaths of ANANIAS and SAPPHIRA (Acts 5:1–11); PETER's deliverance from prison (12:1–19); certain undescribed miracles by STEPHEN (6:8); PHILIP transported from Gaza to Azotus (8:39); the light on the Damascus road (9:3); PAUL's blindness and his recovery (9:8, 18); several healing miracles, some by means of Paul's handkerchiefs and aprons (19:12); EUTYCHUS raised from the dead (20:9–12); and, if it was indeed a miracle, Paul's not being hurt by the viper (28:3–6). To these one may add the widespread and spectacular instances of speaking in tongues (10:45–46; 19:6). The list, of course, is not exhaustive.

The biblical accounts may be completed by an addition to one point already mentioned. During the life of Moses the magicians were able to duplicate some of his miracles. Deuteronomy 13:1–2 warns against the miracles of false prophets, even when their prophecies prove true. The NT as well teaches the possibility and the actuality of miracles by evil powers: "For false Christs and false prophets will appear and perform great signs and miracles to deceive even the elect—if that were possible" (Matt. 24:24). According to Acts 8:9, "a man named Simon had practiced sorcery in the city and amazed all the people of Samaria." Whether this magic or sorcery was miraculous or whether it was merely clever tricks is uncertain.

The RSV ascribes to SATAN "pretended signs and wonders," suggesting that the events referred to are not real miracles (2 Thess. 2:9). This, however, is a poor translation, or at best an unnecessary interpretation. The actual phrase is "wonders of falsehood," and can mean either miracles produced by a false and evil power, or wonders intended to produce falsehood in human minds. The Greek does not suggest that the wonders are merely magic tricks. Note also that in Deuteronomy the evil miracles were not merely apparent or pretended; nor in Matthew; nor are they such in Rev. 13:13, which ascribes great signs, even making fire come down from heaven, to the beast that spoke like a dragon (cf. 16:14; 19:20).

The occurrence of miracles wrought by evil powers complicates the theological problem of defining a miracle and rules out the popular definition of a miracle as an event wrought by the immediate power of God. As some divine miracles are not immediately wrought, so too Satan, and not God only, works miracles.

To avoid some of the theological and scientific tangles hinted at, one may point out that Scripture does not really speak of miracles at all; that is to say, the Hebrew and Greek words do not carry the precise connotations of the modern English word. It may be, for example, that the terms translated "wonder" (cf. Heb. *pele'* H7099 and Gk. *teras* G5469) indicate that such events are wonderful and amazing; similarly, "power" (Gk. *dynamis* G1539) shows the need of a more than human endowment; and "sign" (Heb. *'ôt* H253 and Gk. *sēmeion* G4956) refers to the purpose of these events. But a knowledge of Hebrew, Greek, or English words as such will not take us beyond their ordinary meanings, much less avoid any real problems, and still less solve them.

As a transition to these problems one should note that, contrary to some recent views, REGENERATION and ordinary answers to PRAYER are not considered miracles. In Gen. 19:21–22 the answer to LOT's prayer, namely, that a certain small city not be destroyed along with Sodom, does not look like a miracle. After ELIEZER prayed, standing by the well, none of REBEKAH's words and actions, which answered his prayer, was in any way miraculous (Gen. 24:10–27). Nor was Ezra's safe journey, prayed for in Ezra 8:21–23 and answered in 8:31, a miracle. Neither is regeneration a miracle, for the events to which Scripture applies the designation are public, visible, spectacular events.

They must be visible events, for this is essential to their purpose. One of the words by which Scripture designates these events is SIGN. They are signs, not so much to the agent as to the general public; hence they must be easily observable. In various places Scripture states the purpose of miracles. In Exod. 4:5 God told Moses to perform miracles "so that they may believe that the LORD, the God of their fathers … has appeared to you." Thus the miracles attested Moses' divine mission. In the NT miracles attested Christ's claims. The man born blind reproached the Pharisees: "Now that is remarkable! You don't know where he comes from,

A view of the Bitter Lakes region in Egypt. The miraculous dividing of the water at the time of the exodus probably took place near this location.

yet he opened my eyes" (Jn. 9:30; cf. 3:2 and Matt. 9:6; 14:33).

The miracle does not always so directly attest the divine messenger; sometimes in a more general way it impresses the beholder with the nature and attributes of God. The series of miracles mentioned in Exod. 15:13 express God's mercy; the miraculous punishment of DATHAN and ABIRAM declared them to have been enemies of the Lord, and so served as a warning to others (Num. 16:30), and God's mighty acts demonstrate his greatness and power (Deut. 3:24). There is also the miracle of the virgin birth. Thus, miracles by their purpose must be events in the external world, and not inward workings of providence and grace.

II. Theology and science. This survey of the biblical data has touched on two closely intertwined problems. The first may perhaps be viewed as theological because theologians would like to have a definition of *miracle*. Yet the desire to frame such a definition is not motivated merely by a desire to find the common element in all these events, but rather to relate these events to the ordinary course of nature. In particular, since secular science often has denied the possibility of miracles, a Christian must know what they are before he can relate them to scientific law.

This problem early attracted the attention of AUGUSTINE. Holding the view that God created nature and that therefore any event in the visible world was natural, he concluded that miracles violate not nature itself, but what we know about nature. In one place he gives the impression that a miracle consists of accelerating natural processes, for when Christ turned the water into wine, he took only a moment to do what rain does by being absorbed by the vine and then fermenting into wine. Christ's healing miracles also can easily be thought of as an acceleration of natural recuperation. But surely the virgin birth, walking on the water, and the resurrection from the dead do not so easily fit Augustine's theory.

The scheme of Thomas Aquinas is more intricate than that of Augustine. He asserts, for example, that "God can do something outside this [natural] order created by him, when he chooses — for instance, by producing the effects of secondary causes without them" (*Summa theol.* I, Q. 105, A. 6). Apparently this means that natural events are tied together in a series of causes and effects. The law of nature then is the law of causality. On this showing, a miracle is an event that has no cause — no natural, secondary cause, but the primary cause only, that is, God. The secondary causes are presumably the efficient causes rather than the material causes, for in the case of Christ's turning the water into wine, it is obvious that Christ used water as the matter on which he imposed the form of wine. This miracle seems to be a proper example of the definitive phrase. Yet the example Aquinas actually gives is that of a man who lifts a heavy body: this, he says, is against nature, for it is against the nature of a heavy body to move upward. To our modern scientific mind there is nothing "against" natural law in picking up a rock; and to our Protestant Christian minds picking up a rock is a poor example of a miracle.

Strangely enough, Aquinas immediately proceeds to argue that "Where God does anything against that order of nature which we know and are accustomed to observe, we call it a miracle." This may be merely a repetition of Augustine; nevertheless there is some difficulty in the explanation of this proposition. What is the relation between a miracle and our knowledge? Is it our knowledge (or rather our ignorance) that makes an event a miracle? Aquinas allows that an eclipse does not seem miraculous to an astronomer, who knows its cause; though to a rustic who does not know its cause the eclipse seems miraculous. Is then the same event a miracle to a rustic and a natural occurrence to an astronomer? Of course Aquinas does not settle for any such simple unsatisfactory account of miracles. An eclipse is not a miracle, even if the rustic thinks so; for a miracle is not an event whose cause is hidden merely from uneducated people. The cause of a miracle is hidden from all people, and this cause is God.

Some difficulty still remains. There are undoubtedly orders of nature still undiscovered and unknown by learned scientists. Nuclear fission was universally unknown less than a century ago; and if this is what takes place in the sun and in novae, were these processes miraculous prior to their discovery? Similarly there must be other discoveries yet to be made. We do not know the cause of various diseases, but does this make them miracles? Then when their secondary cause is discovered, will they no longer be miracles?

If, now, these suggestions are unacceptable, the explanations must be amended. Aquinas wrote, "Therefore those things which God does outside the cause which we know are called miracles." He ought to have written that those things are miracles whose causes will never be known. Even this amendment faces difficulties, however. First, no one can tell what new laws may be discovered; therefore no one could possibly know that an event was a miracle. This first objection depends on the indefinite extension of the knowledge of how nature works. There is also a second and more modern difficulty, a supposition that would not have occurred to Aquinas. It is the supposition that science never has discovered, and never will discover, any laws of nature. In this case every event would be a miracle because of our total ignorance of how nature works. Absurd as this would have sounded to Aquinas, it is no idle speculation today. Operationalism, a modern philosophy of science discussed below, is such a theory; and combined with the last quotation from Aquinas, it would imply that every event is a miracle. Even aside from operationalism, Sir Isaac Newton freely admitted that he did not know the cause of gravitation, but surely this does not make the fall of a pebble a miracle.

Another difficulty in Aquinas's view is that God must be the immediate and sole cause of a miraculous event. The "effect" must occur without the aid of secondary causes. There are, in fact, two difficulties in this conception. First, although a mysterious disease might thus be quickly ruled out of the category of miracles on a superficial view, yet more profoundly it seems necessary to know what the cause of the disease is in order to know that God is not its cause. As long as we remain ignorant of the cause, the possibility remains open that God is the cause and every case of this disease is a miracle.

The second difficulty is this: if God must be the cause of a miracle then demons cannot work miracles, as the Bible says they can. Naturally, Thomas is well aware that the Bible attributes signs and wonders to demons and false prophets. He tells us that "Pharaoh's magicians made real frogs and real serpents; but they will not be real miracles, because they will be done by the power of natural causes, as stated in the First Part, Q. 114, A. 4" (*Summa theol.* II ii, Q. 178 Art. 1, Reply Obj. 1). The reference in the First Part says, "If we take a miracle in the strict sense, the demons cannot work miracles, nor can any creature, but God alone; for in the strict sense, a miracle is something done outside the order of the entire created nature.... But sometimes miracle may be taken, in a wide sense, for whatever exceeds human power and experience. And thus demons can work miracles."

This explanation seems to be an evasion and subterfuge. There are indeed certain biblical miracles where no created being was the agent; for example, the virgin birth, in which Mary was the patient, not the agent. But if the term *miracle* is to be restricted to such as this, the miracles of Moses are ignored. If, on the contrary, one wishes to explain the mighty works of Moses, Elijah, and the miracles of Paul, one cannot rule out demons. Both Paul and the demons are created beings. To ignore their miracles by an arbitrary choice of "a strict sense," is to neglect the greater part of the material.

Therefore Aquinas must and did say something about miracles "in a wide sense." Aquinas explains how the magicians produced frogs: "All the transformations of corporeal things which can be produced by certain natural powers, to which we must assign the seminal principles [that exist in the elements, and by which nature transmutes matter from one form to another], can be produced by the operation of the demons, by the employment of these principles; such as the transformation of certain things [a staff, or the water of the Nile] into serpents or frogs, which can be produced by putrefaction."

One should not judge Aquinas too severely for his reliance upon the science of his medieval society; but it still seems within the realm of scholarly propriety to question whether, apart from the science, the paragraph adds to our understanding of demonic miracles. Even if frogs are not produced by putrefaction, the account pictures the demons as advanced scientists, able to utilize the laws of nature in a manner not yet discovered in the 13th cent. And were the apostles advanced scientists also?

The *Catholic Encyclopedia* of 1911 (10:338) bases its theory of miracles on the Thomistic position. It insists, as Aquinas had done, that miracles must be evident to the senses. This is essential because of their purpose. They are to excite admiration, accredit a prophet, or in some way impress God's glory on the beholder. When, however, miracles are said to be evident, the intention must be, not only to rule out invisible spiritual experiences, but chiefly to maintain that the visible event is identifiable as a miracle. Identification, however, requires a criterion. By what criterion can a miracle be distinguished from any other unusual event?

To be identifiable as a miracle, says this encyclopedia, the event must be either "above" nature (i.e., something nature cannot do, like the resurrection of Lazarus) or "outside" nature (like the multiplication of the loaves, which nature can do, but not in the manner actually used) or "contrary" to nature (no example is given). "In a miracle God's action relative to its bearing on natural forces is analogous to the action of a human personality [who uses nature but does not violate natural law]. Thus, e.g., it is against the nature of iron to float, but the action of Eliseus in raising the axe-head to the surface of the water ... is no more a violation, or a transgression, or an infraction, of natural laws than if he raised it with his hand."

Now, it is surprising that a Catholic theologian would reduce Elisha's miracle to the level of picking up the iron with his hand. Confusion follows surprise because in the next paragraph the argument seems to assume that miracles violate natural laws. The question is, how can a miracle be identified? The encyclopedia explains that this depends on knowledge of natural forces: if certain events are natural, others that do not qualify are miracles. To quote: "In enlarging our knowledge of natural forces, the progress of science has curtailed their sphere." Since the advance of science has extended rather than curtailed the sphere of law, the author of this article probably means that the advance of science has curtailed *the sphere of miracles*, and he actually concludes: "Hence as soon as we have reason to suspect that any event, however uncommon or rare it appears, may arise from natural causes ... we immediately lose the conviction of its being a miracle." This view, however, seems to abolish all miracles. For if knowledge of natural law enables one to identify a miracle (on the supposition that by this knowledge one can know what is not natural), no event could be so identified as long as science can advance and eventually bring the event in question under a law not now known.

Protestant theologians also have fallen into similar confusion. One of them summarily disposed of objections to miracles on the ground that if we can violate the law of gravitation by picking up a weight, there is no reason to suppose that God cannot. Unfortunately, on the basis of Newtonian science, picking up a weight neither violates the law nor interrupts its action. To avoid such confusion theologians should consider the status of natural law.

III. Science and theology. Thus the discussion of miracles requires a philosophy of science. At this point the modern attack on the possibility of miracles begins. David Hume (1711–76), the most famous opponent of miracles, defined a miracle as a transgression of a law of nature. He then argued that since the laws of nature have been established by a firm and unalterable experience, there must be a uniform experience against every miraculous event.

This argument, though simply stated, contains several complexities. First, it is not consistent with Hume's main position. In arguing against miracles Hume appeals to certain laws of nature, firmly established by uniform experience. But Hume's empiricism does not permit the assertion of any uniform or universal law of any kind. This was one of Kant's main points against Hume (see KNOWLEDGE).

If, in the second place, one wishes to retain the attack on miracles, and avoid inconsistency by dropping Hume's empiricism, several other difficulties come into view. From the standpoint of strict logic the argument is invalid. To say that an unalterable experience has established these laws and that therefore violations cannot have occurred is to beg the question. The argument says no more than that miracles cannot have happened because no one ever saw a miracle. Such an argument offers as proof the very proposition it claims to prove. Though the circularity of the argument is obvious, naturalistic scientists support it with massive buttresses. Experimentation, so they claim, has repeatedly confirmed certain mathematical equations, and these equations accurately describe the phenomenon in question; therefore these equations, so repeatedly confirmed, must describe phenomena outside the laboratories, both in the distant past and in the distant future.

Of course, neither the distant past nor, much less, any of the future has ever been observed. This was precisely Hume's point in his argument against universal truths, and it is difficult for an experimenter to escape the strictures of Hume's skeptical empiricism. The claim that all nature must conform to a minuscule section is a statement of faith based on something other than a firm and unalterable experience. It is not based on experience at all. To produce a philosophy that would justify this claim is difficult to do. With the help of a somewhat intricate argument, the thesis may be shown to be both impossible and even implausible.

The argument must proceed in two stages: first, the Newtonian science, regnant from 1685 to 1900, under which Hume's argument and the scientific materialism of the 19th cent. were formulated, must be analyzed and evaluated; second, the scientific revolution of the 20th cent. also must be taken into account. Newtonian science was essentially the philosophy of mechanism. Mathematical equations, formulated on the basis of experimentation, were supposed to be accurate descriptions of how natural processes took place. These equations enabled scientists both to predict and to understand. As Laplace put it: Given the positions and velocities of every particle in the universe, one can calculate their positions at any future time. Lord Kelvin claimed to understand if, and only if, he could construct a mechanical model of a natural phenomenon. When these laws and others not yet discovered are universalized, that is, when every motion and process

God's extraordinary creation of the world stands behind the Christian belief in miracles.

throughout the universe is said to be describable by differential equations, miracles are ruled out. Life and mind are ruled out too, unless these words are used behavioristically to designate certain sets of physical motions.

This mechanistic philosophy was asserted with great confidence. Ludwig Büchner's *Kraft und Stuff*, which passed through at least seventeen German and twenty-two foreign editions, claims absolute certainty on several pages and states, "It follows with absolute certainty that motion is as eternal and uncreatable … as force and matter"; and, "With the most absolute truth and with the greatest scientific certainty can we say this day: There is nothing miraculous in the world" (*Force and Matter: Empirico-Philosophical Studies, Intelligibly Rendered* [1891], 58–66 and 74–81).

Similarly Karl Pearson wrote, "The goal of science is … the complete interpretation of the universe. … It claims that the whole range of phenomena, mental as well as physical—the entire universe—is its field" (*Grammar of Science* [1911], 14, 24). And he further asserted that science can pronounce "absolute judgments." Ernest Nagel's presidential address in 1954 before the American Philosophical Association depended substantially on Hume's type of argument when he said, "The occurrence of events … and the characteristic behaviors of various individuals are contingent on the organization of spatio-temporally located bodies, whose internal structures and external relations determine and limit the appearance and disappearance of everything that happens. That this is so, is one of the best-tested conclusions of experience. … There is no place for … an immaterial spirit directing the course of events." Hans Reichenbach expresses similar confidence: the results of science are "established with a superpersonal validity and universally accepted" (*Modern Philosophy of Science* [1959], 136, 149).

This confidence is misplaced, and it is strange that Reichenbach repeats a sentiment of 1900 sixty years later. So wide-sweeping are the changes science has undergone during the past century that the Newtonian laws are no longer universally accepted; and so rapid and so profound have these changes been, promising still wider changes to come, that no one can any longer believe that science has the absolute and final truth. If anything is universally recognized, it is that the results of science are tentative. But to convince a stubborn mechanist who may still think that the new laws, however different from Newton's, and some further equations will describe nature and rule out miracles, an analysis of laboratory procedures can show that such equations do not describe natural processes.

To justify these criticisms, the law of the pendulum will serve as an adequate example. This law states that the period of the swing is proportional to the square root of the length. If, however, the weight of the bob is unevenly displaced around its center, the law will not hold. The law assumes that the bob is homogeneous, that the weight is symmetrically distributed along all axes, or more technically, that the mass is concentrated at a point. No such bob exists, and hence the law is not an accurate description of any tangible pendulum. Second, the law assumes that the pendulum swings by a tensionless string. There is no such string, so that the scientific law does not describe any real pendulum. And third, the law could be true only if the pendulum swung on an axis without friction. There is no such axis. It follows, therefore, that no visible pendulum accords with the mathematical formula and that the formula is not a description of any existing pendulum.

Further analysis supports the same conclusion. All experimentation depends on measuring a line, perhaps the length of mercury in a thermometer, perhaps the distance on a balance between the zero mark and another mark on the scale, or perhaps some other line. Whatever the line may be, the scientist measures it many times, and his readings all differ. The temperature is never the same and the weight always changes. Now, when the scientist adds up his readings and computes their mean, one may ask why the arithmetic mean describes the natural object more accurately than one of the actual measurements. One also may ask why, if an average must be used, the arithmetic mean is a more accurate description of nature than the mode, or perhaps the median.

These two considerations, the example of the pendulum and the measurement of a line, suffice by themselves to show that the laws of science are not descriptions of nature's workings. But a third and more technical point is utterly conclusive. After the scientist calculates his mean, he calculates the variable error. That is, he subtracts each reading from the mean and takes the average of these differences. This gives him some such figure as 19.31±.0025. The plus-or-minus quantity designates a length and not a point. The significance of this lies in the fact that when the scientist draws his curve (equation) on a graph, he is not restricted to points, but may draw his curve anywhere through certain areas. This means that the experimental observations, already modified mathematically, never limit the scientist to any one law, but allow him to choose from among an infinite number of equations. Since in this situation there is zero probability of selecting the law that actually describes nature, it would be a miracle if he did so. What is worse, even if the miracle should occur, the scientist could never know it.

Therefore Newtonian science (quite apart from the amazing advances of more recent times) could never rule out miracles because its methods do not result in a knowledge of how nature works. Contemporary science is no more successful in this regard, although it is incredibly more successful in other ways. Newtonian physics was overthrown for several reasons. Its first law of motion is scientifically unverifiable; its need for simultaneous measurements cannot be met; the quantum theory replaced the untenable wave theory of light, and produced a confusion that scientists can utilize but cannot explain; a new equation for the addition of velocities was needed; and the law of gravitation proved inconsistent with the distribution of galaxies in distant space.

What is important in this for miracles is not any of the scientific details, but the new philosophy of science that these advances stimulated. Traditionally science had been regarded as an attempt to understand and describe nature. This is still the popular view, but it no longer commands universal assent among scientists. Many physicists consciously accept a new theory called operationalism, and presumably all physicists have at least some operational ideas embedded in their thinking.

Operationalism is the theory that the concepts of science, instead of referring to or describing natural objects, are defined by and express the operations of laboratory procedure. Length, for example, is not a characteristic of a pendulum, it is a set of operations. Since the operations of measuring a pendulum are quite different from those by which the diameter of a molecule is measured, and these are vastly different from the operations of measuring distances in stellar space, there is not one concept of length or distance, there are three. In ordinary English one word may be used, but it has three vastly different meanings; it refers to three different things; it refers to three sets of operations.

The aim of science therefore is not to understand or describe the actual processes of nature. The aim of science is to utilize nature for human purposes. One can easily make clear that utilization may occur without an understanding of natural processes; and it is worthwhile to make it clear because invention and its accompanying prediction often are used to defend the truth of scientific laws.

The argument claims that if a scientist can predict an eclipse or produce television, the result confirms the laws he used and proves them true. This argument is a logical fallacy that goes by the name of "asserting the consequent." It may be true that a given equation implies the occurrence of an eclipse at a certain moment, or that other equations imply the success of television; but the occurrence of the eclipse does not imply or justify the law. One might as well argue: if it is raining, I carry an umbrella; look, I am carrying an umbrella, therefore it is raining. The flaw in the fallacy of asserting the consequent lies in the fact that although Kepler's laws actually imply an eclipse, many other sets of possible laws also imply the same eclipse. Therefore the occurrence of the eclipse does not confirm one set rather than another. Successful prediction and invention, accordingly, is no proof of the truth of any law of science.

If one were now to brush aside considerations of logic and were to make the optimistic claim that, whatever flaws Newtonian science may have suffered with, the second half of the 20th cent. discovered the absolute and final truth—so final that no more changes will ever occur—it would remain undeniably obvious that the invention of the steam engine, telegraph, incandescent bulb, and airplane was accomplished through the application of laws we now know to be false. Why then cannot the present laws be false without preventing still more amazing inventions?

The argument therefore is this: since science can make no pronouncement on how nature operates in its ordinary course, it has no basis on which to conclude that miracles cannot happen. Such a defense of the possibility of miracles has been rather minimal or negative; it has put the matter in the worst possible light. No doubt this is proper strategy against enemy attack, but the full force of the case for miracles requires something more positive.

It has been shown that the attack on miracles was not based solely on laboratory observation; nor even on the subsequent mathematical manipulation. Rather there was a nonobservational, a priori assumption that mechanism was universal and that either there is no God at all, or at most some impersonal principle unable to operate in the world otherwise than through mechanism.

The Christian position on miracles is not set in such a materialistic or pantheistic background, nor even in a more neutral or noncommittal background. Under any such conditions miracles would be suspicious, freakish, or out of place. When, however, one adopts a view of the world as God's creation, and when God is regarded as a living, acting, personal Being, the appropriateness of miracles depends on God's purposes. In such a theistic worldview, where God desires to have some converse with mankind, the occurrence of miracles is no longer an anomaly.

Also to be noted is the fact that apart from the purpose of God no connotative definition of miracles can be derived from the biblical events usually so regarded. A denotative list is all that can be had and is all that is necessary. The Christian is not obliged to defend a "transgression of a law of nature" or any other definition: he needs only defend the occurrence of the events described in the Bible. Furthermore, the biblical view takes account of human SIN, another anomaly in pantheism or scientism; and if God has plans of redemption, miracles may be confidently expected.

When the biblical miracles are taken out of their proper setting, the argument against them can seem plausible. Hume tried to compare the resurrection of Christ with a hypothetical resurrection of Queen Elizabeth. Since few people would believe that Queen Elizabeth had risen from the dead, even if twelve or five hundred witnesses said so, Hume wishes to conclude that we should not believe that Christ rose.

In spite of a superficial plausibility, Hume's argument contains several defects. First, even he admits that he could not account for the apparent death of Elizabeth, although this apparent death is necessary if witnesses to a resurrection are to be mistaken. Second, Queen Elizabeth may have been the virgin queen, but she was not virgin born, nor did she work miracles, nor was her reign prophesied hundreds of years beforehand. Hume is trying to place a resurrection in a life where it does not fit. Christ's life was quite otherwise. Then, finally, and most profoundly, Hume's argument acquires its superficial plausibility by refusing to face the question of divine providence and revelation. He shows that a resurrection is alien to *his* concept of world history. But this is irrelevant, for the miracles of Christianity take place in a different sort of world.

If God lives, miracles are not only possible, they are appropriate; and whether or not one has occurred is not a question for secular science, but is a matter of testimony by divinely appointed witnesses.

IV. Modern miracles. At the beginning of this article one of the reasons given for studying the subject was the evaluation of certain postbiblical claims. The Roman church claims to have performed miracles throughout the Middle Ages and down to date. Currently there are popular evangelists who claim to heal. A magazine has advertised a prayer cloth that when placed on the forehead will relieve a headache. Then there is the phenomenon of speaking in tongues, earlier restricted to the Pentecostals, but now having spread into other denominations.

The scientific argument just completed does not permit a common argument often used against faith healing. Instead of denying the cures claimed by Roman Catholics and Pentecostals, some people admit the events occur but assert that they can be explained by natural, perhaps psychological, laws, and therefore are not miraculous. The analysis of scientific procedure shows that no one has ever discovered a natural law, and therefore these cases of healing cannot be so classified.

Nor did the earlier examination of scriptural data discover any common characteristic of all miracles, on the basis of which one could decide whether a contemporary cure exhibits the necessary traits. The only characteristic discoverable in Scripture is the fact that miracles are unusual and amazing; otherwise, to all appearances, they were performed in a variety of ways. But amazement comes in many degrees, for which reason the question under consideration is difficult.

Many alleged miracles are patently fraudulent. B. B. Warfield in his *Counterfeit Miracles* (1918) gives some medieval examples, such as the starving Christina Mirabilis nourishing herself with her own virgin milk. But no matter how many fraudulent miracles there may be, it does not prove that all are. Similar is Warfield's comparison of the cures at Lourdes with sudden and remarkable cures in hospitals by the command of a physician, without any medical treatment, all in a situation where no suggestion of divine intervention is present. This may be sufficient to cause us to lose confidence in Lourdes; but it provides no valid implication with respect to other alleged miracles. One must admit the same thing concerning speaking in tongues. The phenomenon was fraudulent and contrived in the Irvingite movement; presumably it is usually the result of extraordinary emotional strain, and in no way amazing; but the possibility still remains that some cases are a gift of the Holy Ghost. See TONGUES, GIFT OF.

It does not seem possible therefore by any direct and conclusive argument to demonstrate that miracles do not occur today. Even if they were not very numerous, an advocate of modern miracles could point out that biblical miracles were not equally numerous in every century. Sometimes two, three, or even four centuries went by without a recorded miracle.

Yet this fact of the sporadic occurrence of biblical miracles lends itself to a somewhat indirect argument, not technically valid, but which nonetheless decreases one's confidence in modern claims. The miracles of the Bible occurred at times of great crises and, as has been shown, were intended to attest a divine messenger—Moses, Elijah, or Christ—and thus to initiate a new stage of religious history. The present world crisis is more political than religious, and resembles the fall of Roman civilization more than a religious upheaval such as Christ and the apostles accomplished. The charismatic movements have not brought a new revelation on a par with the Bible; thus their tongues and faith healing must be viewed with suspicion.

This indirect and not quite conclusive argument against modern miracles is well stated by Warfield in the book already mentioned: miracles ceased to occur in the 1st cent.; writers during the 2nd cent. do not mention any as having happened in their day; the beginning of medieval superstitions is in the late 3rd or 4th cent.; and since true miracles were intended to support the authority of the apostles, none have occurred since. The crux of this argument lies in connecting miracles exclusively with special REVELATION. And indeed this is consistent with the biblical statements about the purpose of miracles. Support for this conclusion also may be found in 1 Cor. 13:8, "But where there are prophecies, they will cease; where there are tongues, they will be stilled." Others question the validity of these arguments (e.g., J. Deere, *Surprised by the Power of the Spirit: A Former Dallas Professor Discovers That God Still Speaks and Heals Today* [1993]; W. Grudem, *Systematic Theology: An Introduction to Christian Doctrine* [1994], ch. 17).

But if the exegesis is doubtful and the tie between miracles and revelation a little loose, a firm conclusion may nonetheless be drawn that there is no conclusive proof that miracles actually have taken place since apostolic times. The burden of proof lies heavily on those who assert modern miracles. Their claims would become more plausible if one of them were to walk on the Sea of Galilee, feed 5,000 people with five rolls and two fishes, or raise the dead. This would be amazing; it would indeed be miraculous.

(See further A. B. Bruce, *The Miraculous Element in the Gospels* [1886]; F. R. Tennant, *Miracle and its Philosophical Presuppositions* [1928]; C. S. Lewis, *Miracles: A Preliminary Study* [1947]; G. H. Clark, *The Philosophy of Science and Belief in God* [1964]; D. Bridge, *Signs and Wonders Today* [1985]; C. Brown, *That You May Believe: Miracles and Faith—Then and Now* [1985]; E. N. Gross,

Miracles, Demons, and Spiritual Warfare: An Urgent Call for Discernment [1990]; G. H. Tweflftree, *Jesus the Miracle Worker: A Historical and Theological Study* [1999]; C. J. Collins, *The God of Miracles: An Exegetical Examination of God's Action in the World* [2000]; C. Hitchcock, ed., *Contemporary Debates in Philosophy of Science* [2004]; A. Rosenberg, *Philosophy of Science: A Contemporary Introduction*, 2nd ed. [2005]; D. Corner, *The Philosophy of Miracles* [2007].)   G. H. CLARK

Miriam mihr′ee-uhm (מִרְיָם *H5319*, derivation disputed, with proposals including Egyp. *mryt* ["beloved"], Akk. *rym* ["gift"], Heb. מָרָה *H5286* ["to be obstinate"], and others; see also MARY). **(1)** Daughter of AMRAM and JOCHEBED, and sister of MOSES and AARON (Num. 26:59; 1 Chr. 6:3). Miriam is first mentioned by name on the occasion of her leading the women in the chorus of the Song of Moses at the time of the crossing of the RED SEA by the Israelites on dry land when they left Egypt (Exod. 15:20–21). At an earlier time she had watched the ark that her mother had prepared for the baby Moses (2:3–8). The little ark was put into the river and floated until PHARAOH's daughter took the child from the ark. Miriam, seeing all of this, alertly offered to the princess the services of Moses' real mother to care for the child.

In the book of Numbers she is mentioned frequently. With her brother Aaron, she opposed Moses at Hazeroth because of his wife who was a CUSHITE WOMAN (Num. 12:1). The opposition was more deep-seated than this, however, for it is clear that a jealousy over his leadership was involved (v. 2). God completely vindicated Moses at this time and rebuked Miriam and Aaron for their challenge to his leadership (vv. 4–8). Miriam was probably the instigator, for the brunt of the punishment for this insurrection fell upon her and she became leprous (v. 10). Aaron interceded before Moses for her and Moses pleaded to God that she be healed (vv. 11–12), and she was healed; however, she was compelled to remain outside the camp of Israel for seven days after the cleansing.

The death of Miriam is recorded. She died in the wilderness of ZIN at KADESH BARNEA and was buried there. The punishment of Miriam continued to be a warning in Israel that they should not rebel against the Lord's chosen ones. Moses recalled the punishment of Miriam to the people in his address to Israel just before his own death (Deut. 24:9). She is long afterward still recognized as one of the great leaders of Israel in the wilderness (Mic. 6:4). She is called a prophetess and undoubtedly was highly regarded in Israel long after her death. (Jewish tradition identifies Miriam further as an ancestor of BEZALEL; cf. Jos. *Ant.* 3.6.1 §105.)

(2) Son of MERED (apparently by his wife BITHIAH, Pharaoh's daughter) and descendant of JUDAH through CALEB (1 Chr. 4:17; note that NRSV, to clarify the sense, includes here part of v. 18). Some leave open the possibility that this Miriam too was a woman.   J. B. SCOTT

Mirma mihr′muh. KJV form of MIRMAH.

Mirmah mihr′muh (מִרְמָה *H5328*, possibly "deceit"). KJV Mirma. Son of SHAHARAIM and descendant of BENJAMIN; a family head (1 Chr. 8:10). Mirmah was one of seven children that were born to Shaharaim in MOAB by his wife HODESH after he had divorced Hushim and Baara (vv. 8–9).

mirror. In biblical times a mirror was a polished metal surface held in the hand to see the reflection of objects, especially of the face. (The KJV rendering "[looking] glass" is an anachronism, since glass mirrors were not introduced until some time in the 1st cent. after Christ.) Women donated bronze mirrors to make the LAVER for the TABERNACLE (Exod. 38:8; Heb. *mar'â H5262*). Many ancient bronze mirrors have been found in Egypt, usually with a round or oval surface and a handle, which often is decorated. Excavations in Palestine have unearthed bronze mirrors imported from Egypt or influenced by Egyptian models. The bright yellow summer sky on a hot day before a wind storm is compared to a molten mirror (i.e., one made of cast bronze, Job 37:18; Heb. *rĕ'i H8023*). The only other possible reference to mirrors in the OT is a difficult text (Isa. 3:23; the Heb. term here is *gillāyôn H1663*, which the NRSV renders "garments of gauze").

The common Greek term for "mirror" is *esoptron G2269*. There are two references in the APOCRYPHA: the need of constantly watching to avoid harm from an enemy is compared to the chore of pol-

Collection of copper mirrors from Egypt.

ishing a metal mirror to keep away corrosion (Sir. 12:11); and wisdom is said to be a spotless mirror of the activity of God (Wisd. 7:26). In the NT, Paul compares our present knowledge of divine things to seeing indirectly and imperfectly in a mirror (1 Cor. 13:12), while James compares the person "who listens to the word but does not do what it says" to someone "who looks at his face in a mirror" but "immediately forgets what he looks like" (Jas. 1:23). When Paul says that believers "with unveiled faces all reflect the Lord's glory" (2 Cor. 3:18), he may imply that Christians should be mirrors of Christ; however, the verb *katoptrizō* G3002 possibly means "to contemplate as in a mirror," in which case Paul is suggesting that believers *see* the Lord's glory "as though reflected in a mirror" (NRSV). (See N. Hugedé, *La metaphore du miroir dans les épitres de St. Paul aux Corinthiens* [1957]; D. H. Gill, "Through a Glass Darkly," *CBQ* 25 [1963]: 427–29; W. C. van Unnik, "With Unveiled Face," *NovT* 6 [1963]: 153–69.)   J. Alexander Thompson

Misael mis′ay-uhl. KJV Apoc. form of Mishael (1 Esd. 9:44).

mischief. This English term occurs about fifty times in the KJV as a rendering of several Hebrew words (Gen. 42:4 et al.; in the NT only once, Acts 13:10). It occurs much less frequently in the NRSV, and not at all in the NIV. Modern versions prefer such renderings as "harm, evil, injury, trouble," and others.

Misgab mis′gab. The KJV transliteration of Hebrew *miśgāb* H5369, treating it as the name of a place in Moab (Jer. 48:1). It is more likely to be taken as a common noun meaning "stronghold" or "fortress."

Mishael mish′ay-uhl (מִישָׁאֵל H4792, "who is like God?" or "who belongs to God?"). **(1)** Son of Uzziel and descendant of Levi through Kohath (Exod. 6:22). One of Uzziel's brothers was Amram (father of Moses), so Mishael was Moses' first cousin. Mishael and his brother Elzaphan were called by Moses to carry out the bodies of Nadab and Abihu after their sin and death (Lev. 10:4–5).

(2) One of the prominent men (not identified as priests) who stood near Ezra when the law was read at the great assembly (Neh. 8:4; 1 Esd. 9:44 [KJV, "Misael"]).

(3) The Jewish name of Meshach, one of Daniel's three companions in Babylon (Dan. 1:6–7 et al.). See Shadrach, Meshach, Abednego.

Mishal mi′shuhl (מִשְׁאָל H5398, possibly "[place of] request, inquiry"). A town within the tribal territory of Asher (Josh. 19:26 KJV, "Misheal"); it was one of the four towns allotted to the Levites descended from Gershon (Josh. 21:30–31). The town is called Mashal in the parallel passage (1 Chr. 6:74), and it is attested in Egyptian texts (in the form *mšir*; see Y. Aharoni, *The Land of the Bible: A Historical Geography*, rev. ed. [1979], 144, 160). The site has not been positively identified, but one possibility is modern Tell Kisan, about 5 mi. SE of Acco.

Misham mi′shuhm (מִשְׁעָם H5471, derivation unknown). Son of Elpaal and descendant of Benjamin (1 Chr. 8:12).

Misheal mish′ee-uhl. KJV form of Mishal.

Mishma mish′muh (מִשְׁמָע H5462, possibly "hearing," i.e., "obedient"). **(1)** Son of Ishmael and grandson of Abraham (Gen. 25:14; 1 Chr. 1:30). E. A. Knauf (*ABD*, 4:871) has proposed a connection with the Isammeʾ, apparently an Arabian tribe described in Assyrian sources as "a confederation of (the worshipers of) the god Atarsamain" (*ANET*, 299a). See also Mibsam.

(2) Son of Shaul or, more likely, of Mibsam; included in the genealogy of Simeon (1 Chr. 4:25).   E. B. Smick

Mishmannah mish-man′uh (מִשְׁמַנָּה H5459, possibly "fat" or "noble" [cf. *HALOT*, 2:649]). A Gadite who joined DAVID's forces at ZIKLAG (1 Chr. 12:10). The Gadites are described as "brave warriors, ready for battle and able to handle the shield and spear. Their faces were the faces of lions, and they were as swift as gazelles in the mountains" (v. 8). See GAD, TRIBE OF.

Mishnah mish′nuh (postbiblical Heb. מִשְׁנָה, "repetition, teaching [by recitation], oral law" [from שָׁנָה H9101, "to repeat"]). Also Mishna. The collection of halakic traditions (legal rulings and discussions—see HALAKAH) transmitted orally by rabbis for a number of generations, but finally codified and written down about A.D. 200 by Rabbi Yehudah ha-Nasi, that is, Judah the Prince. (The term, however, is sometimes used of Jewish religious instruction in general during that period, or of collections of teachings by individual rabbis. Moreover, a *mishnah* refers to a specific proposition within the Mishnah.) Because it thus embodies the *oral law* (i.e., "the tradition of the elders," Matt. 15:2–6; Mk. 7:3–13; cf. Gal. 1:14), the Mishnah is distinguished from, but viewed as correlative to, the Mikra (*miqrāʾ* H5246, "reading," later "biblical reading or teaching"), that is, the Scriptures or the *written law*.

According to one tradition, the Mishnah goes back to Mount SINAI, where God supposedly gave to MOSES oral instruction in addition to the tablets of the law, and that instruction was passed on by word of mouth through the generations (cf. *m. ʾAbot* 1:1). It is possible that the historical origins of the halakic teachings contained in the Mishnah go back to the time of EZRA or soon after, but some scholars dispute even that. Certainly most of the material developed from the 1st cent. B.C. to the 2nd cent. A.D. The rabbis who taught during this period are referred to as the *Tannaim* (from Aram. *tĕnê*, "to repeat, teach," cognate of Heb. *šānāʾ*). Some of them—such as Rabbi AKIBA, who lived during the first decades of the 2nd cent.—probably made their own collections of halakic traditions, which in turn were used by Rabbi Judah.

The Mishnah is divided into six sections or *orders:* Zeraim (seeds, i.e., agriculture), Moed (feasts), Nashim (women), Neziqin (damages), Kodashim (holy things), and Toharot (purities). Each of these in turn contains from seven to twelve tractates. Much of the material, written in very terse Hebrew, consists of debates among the rabbis concerning legal regulations, but the work is characterized by complex interconnections and presents a fairly comprehensive worldview. The Mishnah would later become the basic part of the TALMUD.

(See further H. Danby, *The Mishnah: Translated from the Hebrew with Introduction and Brief Explanatory Notes* [1933]; J. Neusner, *The Mishnah: A New Translation* [1987]; P. Blackman, *Mishnayoth: Pointed Hebrew Text, Introductions, Translation Notes, Supplements*, 7 vols., 2nd ed. [1990]; H. L. Strack and G. Stemberger, *Introduction to the Talmud and Midrash* [1992]; M. S. Jaffee, *Torah in the Mouth: Writing and Oral Tradition in Palestinian Judaism, 200 B.C.E.–400 C.E.* [2001]; A. Samely, *Rabbinic Interpretation of Scripture in the Mishnah* [2002]; J. Hauptman, *Rereading the Mishnah: A New Approach to Ancient Jewish Texts* [2005].)

Mishneh. See SECOND DISTRICT, SECOND QUARTER.

Mishraite mish′ray-it (מִשְׁרָעִי H5490, gentilic form of the unattested name מִשְׁרָע). The Mishraites were a Judahite clan descended from CALEB through HUR and SHOBAL; they made up one of several families associated with KIRIATH JEARIM (1 Chr. 2:53). Their name apparently derives from an otherwise unknown ancestor or place called Mishra.

Mispar mis′pahr (מִסְפָּר H5032, possibly from a word of the same form meaning "number"). An Israelite mentioned among leading individuals who returned from BABYLON with ZERUBBABEL (Ezra 2:2; called "Mispereth" in Neh. 7:7, and "Aspharasus" in 1 Esd. 5:8).

Mispereth mis-pee′rith (מִסְפֶּרֶת H5033). See MISPAR.

Misrephoth Maim mis′ruh-foth-may′im (מִשְׂרְפוֹת מַיִם H5387, "burnings [*i.e.*, limekilns] at the water"; some scholars suggest vocalizing the second element as מִיָּם, "on the west"). Also Misrephothmaim. A place in the vicinity of SIDON, mentioned in Josh. 11:8 in connection with Israel's defeat of the kings of N Canaan, and in Josh. 13:6 as one of the places still in the hands of the Canaanites. These passages suggest that Misrephoth Maim was on or near the S border of Sidon, but its location is uncertain. It is often identified with Khirbet el-Musheirefeh, just S of the promontory known as the LADDER OF TYRE (Ras en-Naqura), though some have preferred a nearby collection of warm springs known as ʿAin Mesherfi. It has also been suggested, however, that Misrephoth Maim is the same as the Litani River, which flows into the Mediterranean about 6 mi. NNE of TYRE (Y. Aharoni, *The Land of the Bible: A Historical Geography*, rev. ed. [1979], 238). P. A. VERHOEF

mission. See APOSTLE.

mist. Water particles in the atmosphere near the earth. Mist is caused by water vapor filling the air until it is only partially transparent. Mist or fog is not common in PALESTINE and SYRIA at sea level, but occurs almost daily in the mountain valleys, coming up at night and disappearing with the morning sun (Wisd. 2:4). The rare Hebrew word *ʾēd H116*, which apparently means "stream" (Gen. 2:6), perhaps can also be rendered "mist" (Job 36:27 NRSV, NIV mg.). The usual word for "cloud," *ʿānān H6727*, may in some contexts refer to the morning mist or fog (Hos. 13:3 et al.). In Acts 13:11, the Greek word for "mist," *achlys G944*, describes incipient blindness, and has been so used since Homer. Human life is compared to a mist or vapor "that appears for a little while and then vanishes" (Jas. 4:14; Gk. *atmis G874*), while false prophets are compared to mists or clouds driven by the storm because of the confusion they bring to unwary believers (2 Pet. 2:17; Gk. *homichlē G3920*). E. RUSSELL

Mitanni mi-tan´ee. An important kingdom in N MESOPOTAMIA that flourished during the period c. 1500–1340 B.C. The ruling class of this kingdom seems to have been Indo-Iranian; its capital, the ruins of which have not yet been identified, bore the name Washshukanni (some think it may have been located in what is now Tell el-Fakhariyeh near Gozan). Their names are linguistically Indo-Iranian, containing recognizable names of Indic deities such as Indra, Mitra, Varuna, etc. The Indo-Iranian term for such warlords seems to have been *maryannu*. They are thought to have introduced into the ANE at this time techniques for the training of chariot horses. A manual for the training of chariot horses has been found at the ancient HITTITE capital. Its author, a certain Kikkuli, employs technical terms for the craft which are clearly Indo-Iranian.

The rank and file of Mitanni's citizenry, on the other hand, were not Indo-Iranians, but HURRIANS, and it is the Hurrian and Akkadian languages that the Mitannian kings employed for official correspondence. At the height of Mitanni's power it controlled Mesopotamia, SE ASIA MINOR (Kizzuwatna), all of N SYRIA, and most of S Syria. Mitannian princesses entered the harems of the pharaohs of Egypt and became quite influential in the Egyptian court. An end was put to the Mitannian kingdom as an independent state by the Hittite emperor Suppiluliuma I (c. 1345 B.C.), who recognized as a vassal ruler of the conquered state a certain Kurtiwaza (formerly read Mattiwaza).

The name Mitanni does not occur in the OT, but the Hurrians, who made up the majority of Mitanni's citizens, also constituted a significant minority group in pre-Israelite Palestine. It is possible that Hurrian customs underlie many mysterious actions in the patriarchal narratives, and more than one personage in the OT bears a Hurrian name. It is also likely that the ethnic term HORITE owes its existence in one form or the other to the term Hurrian, *Hurri*. (See I. J. Gelb, *Hurrians and Subarians* [1944]; E. A. Speiser in *JAOS* 68 [1948]: 1–13; H. Klengel, *Geschichte Syriens im 2. Jahrtausend v. u. Z.* [1965]; *CAH*, 2/2, 3rd ed. [1975], 1–8 et passim; D. Oates et al., eds., *Excavations at Tell Brak. Vol. 1: The Mitanni and Old Babylonian Periods* [1997]; *ABD*, 4:874–75; *CANE*, 2:1243–54.) H. A. HOFFNER, JR.

mite. This English term, meaning "a small coin," is used by the KJV to render Greek *leptos G3321* (Mk. 12:42; Lk. 12:59 [NIV and other versions, "penny"]; 21:2). The Greek term, as an adjective, means "thin, small, slight"; as a noun, it refers to a copper coin of the smallest value, approximately 1/128 of a DENARIUS.

Mithcah mith′kuh (מִתְקָה H5520, "sweet [place]"). Also Mithkah. A stopping place of the Israelites during their wilderness journeys (Num. 33:28–29). It was between Terah and Hashmonah, but the location of these sites is unknown.

Mithkah mith′kuh. See MITHCAH.

Mithnite mith′nit (מִתְנִי H5512, gentilic form of an unattested name such as מֶתֶן). A descriptive title applied only to a certain Joshaphat, one of DAVID's mighty warriors (1 Chr. 11:43). It is not known whether the form Mithnite derives from an ancestor or a place name.

Mithradates mith′ruh-day′teez. See MITHREDATH.

Mithraism mith′ruh-iz′uhm. The cult of Mithras, a Persian sun-god, which reached Rome in or about A.D. 69, by the agency of the eastern legions who set up VESPASIAN as emperor (Tac. *Hist.* 3.24). It is possible that the cult was known in the capital a century before, but it was the latter half of the 1st cent. of the Christian era which saw its strong dissemination in the West, and indeed its notable challenge to Christianity. Based on the trials, sufferings, and exploits of Mithras, the cult appealed to soldiers; and two Mithraea on HADRIAN's Wall, one excavated in 1948 at Carrawburgh, and another still covered at Housesteads, reveal the popularity of Mithraism with the British legions.

Professor Ian Richmond has established a sequence of destruction and rebuilding at Carrawburgh which he interprets as indicative of the practice of Mithraism or Christianity at local headquarters. The same shrine has a place of ordeal under the altar, for the initiate advanced through various grades by way of physical suffering and endurance. The archaeologists on the same site were able to establish the fact that chickens and geese were eaten at the ritual feasts, and that pinecones provided aromatic altar fuel. December 25 was the chief feast of Mithras, and in fixing on that date for Christmas, the early church sought to overlay both the Mithraic festival and the Saturnalia. Christianity triumphed over Mithraism because of its written records of a historic Christ, and its associated body of doctrine adapted for preaching, evangelism, and the needs of every day. Christianity, too, was universal, excluding neither woman, child, nor slave. It preached salvation by faith and demanded no stern ordeals. (See M. J. Vermaseren, *Mithras: The Secret God* [1963]; C. Manfred, *The Roman Cult of Mithras: The God and His Mysteries* [2000]; E. M. Yamauchi, *Persia and the Bible* [1990], ch. 14; R. Beck, *The Religion of the Mithras Cult in the Roman Empire* [2006]; *ABD*, 4:877–78; *DDD*, 1083–89.) See also MYSTERY RELIGIONS. E. M. BLAIKLOCK

Mithras mith′ruhs. See MITHRAISM.

Mithredath mith′ruh-dath (מִתְרְדָת H5521, from Pers., "gift of Mithras" [see MITHRAISM]; LXX, Μιτραδάτης). (1) The treasurer of King CYRUS (Ezra 1:8; 1 Esd. 2:11 [here spelled *Mitēridatēs*]).

(2) One of three Persian officials who wrote a letter of complaint against the Jews to King ARTAXERXES (Ezra 4:7; 1 Esd. 2:16).

(3) Mithradates was the name of seven PARTHIAN kings of the Arsacid dynasty. The Romans fought a series of three wars against Mithradates VI Eupator, called "the Great," between 88 and 64 B.C. This war prohibited the Romans from taking effective control over Palestine until 63 B.C. Although Persian, the Mithradatid rulers were Hellenistic in outlook and preserved this way of life in Syria-Palestine for a century after the other Hellenistic kingdoms had fallen to Rome. See HELLENISM. W. WHITE, JR.

Mithridates mith′ruh-day′teez. See MITHREDATH.

mitre. See TURBAN.

Mitylene mit′uh-lee′nee (Μιτυλήνη G3639). Also Mytilene. Chief city of Lesbos, the largest of the Greek islands off the ASIA MINOR coast. Mitylene was situated on the SE coast of the island, on a magnificent and capacious harbor that always kept the city on the fruitful crossroads of trade. It is mentioned as a stopping place during PAUL's third journey (Acts 20:14).

Mitylene was populated by Aeolian Greeks, and it was in the Aeolic dialect that both Sappho and Alcaeus wrote, in the early 6th cent. B.C., the songs that were the foundation of Greek lyric poetry. Both poetess and poet lived in Mitylene and took an ardent part in the city's stormy politics. The city had its brief period of local imperialism, during which it clashed with ATHENS. It fell under Persian dominance when the great empire flowed W to the shores of the AEGEAN, and had an ill-starred share in the Ionian cities' revolt. When Persian power receded and Athens became dominant in the E Aegean, Mitylene found it expedient to join the Delian League, but was an uneasy partner, twice seceding (428 and 419 B.C.), each time with the loss of her ships, her fortifications, and considerable territory. In the 4th cent. she was a more steady ally of Athens.

After the death of ALEXANDER THE GREAT, Mitylene—too weak now for the successful maintenance of independence in a world of emerging great powers—fell successively under the rule of the Greek states that strove for power in the disrupted borderlands of the W Asiatic coast. At first on good terms with Rome, Mitylene revolted after the Mithridatic War and was broken by the republic. POMPEY restored the city's freedom in his reorganization of Asia. It has little more history to record. E. M. BLAIKLOCK

mixed multitude. This phrase (also "mixt multitude") is used by the KJV to render the Hebrew word *ʿēreb H6850* in two passages: in Exod. 12:38 (NIV, "other people") it refers to the heterogeneous camp followers who escaped with the Israelites from Egypt but were not descended from JACOB; similarly, in Neh. 13:3 it refers to people "of foreign descent" (NIV, NRSV) who were excluded from Israel after the return from exile. The Hebrew word is also used of foreigners in Jeremiah, where the KJV renders it as "mingled people" (Jer. 25:20, 24; 50:37). In addition, the KJV uses the phrase "mixed multitude" to translate Hebrew *ʾăsapsup H671*, "rabble," with reference to a group (apparently the same non-Israelites who left Egypt) that "began to crave other food" in the wilderness (Num. 11:4). J. REA

Mizar miʹzahr (מִצְעָר *H5204*, "small"). The name of a mountain in the HERMON range (Ps. 46:2); alternatively, the word may be a common adjective, used to contrast the mighty Hermon with a small mountain (Mount ZION?). In either case, the precise site is not known. (See *ABD*, 4:879.)

Mizpah, Mizpeh mizʹpuh, mizʹpeh (מִצְפָּה *H5207*, מִצְפֶּה *H5206* [Josh. 11:8; 15:38; 18:26; Jdg. 11:29 bis; 1 Sam. 22:3; in Josh. 13:26, רָמַת הַמִּצְפֶּה], "watchtower"). The KJV uses the form Mizpeh twenty-three times, whereas the NRSV uses it only when the Hebrew is *mispeh*; for consistency, the NIV uses Mizpah throughout.

(1) One of three names given to the covenant heap of stones erected by JACOB and LABAN (Gen. 31:49; see GALEED). It was so named because Laban called on the Lord to watch between him and Jacob. Some believe that this place is the same as #2 below.

(2) A town in GILEAD where JEPHTHAH the judge lived (Jdg. 10:17; 11:11, 29, 34; cf. Hos. 5:1). Its location is uncertain, but some identify it with modern Khirbet Jalʿad, some 14 mi. S of the JABBOK River. See also RAMATH MIZPEH.

(3) A town in MOAB (1 Sam. 22:3). When DAVID was being pursued by SAUL, he took his parents there and left them with the king of Moab, while he returned to his followers in Judah. Since KIR HARESETH (modern Kerak) was at one time the capital of Moab, some have thought that Mizpeh is another name for Kir. Most scholars regard this place as unidentified.

(4) An area in the extreme N of GALILEE is called "the region [*lit.*, land] of Mizpah" and "the Valley of Mizpah" (Josh. 11:3, 8). The precise identification is uncertain since the descriptive phrases are too vague. The first passage indicates that the HIVITES "below Hermon" lived there, while the second refers to it as the eastward terminus of JOSHUA's pursuit of the Canaanites after his victory over them in the battle at the Waters of MEROM. It is not clear whether in these passages Mizpah might have been a town or only the name of a general area.

(5) A town in the SHEPHELAH of JUDAH (Josh. 15:38). It was in the same district as LACHISH, but its location is unknown.

(6) The most important place bearing the name Mizpah was a town allotted to the tribe of BENJAMIN (Josh. 18:26). Scholars differ in its identification.

Tell en-Naṣbeh, a widely favored identification of biblical Mizpah in the territory of Benjamin.

Some favor Nebi Samwil, about 5 mi. WNW of JERUSALEM, though most scholars today prefer Tell en-Naṣbeh, 7.5 mi. NNW of Jerusalem. The present writer believes the evidence favors Nebi Samwil (but see BEEROTH and GIBEAH #3); this site fits the etymology of Mizpah perfectly, for it is a high mountain peak looking directly down upon the Valley of AIJALON, which is the best route between the Mediterranean coast and the Jordan Valley. Joshua used this route for his conquest of Palestine. Tell en-Naṣbeh, on the other hand, lacked any defensive military features. Indeed, the city had some of the heaviest walls of any Palestinian fortress because it was so vulnerable to attack.

The most helpful historic passage on Mizpah is 1 Sam. 7:1–14. SAMUEL called the leaders of Israel to Mizpah to a great confessional religious service before God, following the return of the ARK OF THE COVENANT to Israel. Earlier there had been a great PHILISTINE victory in which the ark was captured, but later it was returned by the Philistines because of a tragic plague that was depleting their population, and which the Philistines had attributed to the vengeance of the God of Israel (1 Sam. 4:1-7:3). In view of the return of the ark, Samuel called a national conference—not to gloat over its return, but to confess Israel's sin for treating the ark as a pagan fetish in their war against the Philistines.

This religious assembly, however, was instantly interpreted by the Philistines as an Israelite military move against them. The Philistines started up the Valley of Aijalon to crush the rebellion at once.

This episode was an exact duplication of the earlier Joshua story in this same Aijalon Valley. Israel was occupying the heights of Mizpah above the valley, and the Philistines were advancing through this valley from their Mediterranean cities. Samuel asked the Lord for help, and, as in Joshua's case, a great thunderstorm and cloudburst completely demoralized the attacking army, and the Israelites then pursued them down the valley to BETH CAR. As a result "the Philistines were subdued and did not invade Israelite territory again" (1 Sam. 7:13). The lesson was not lost on Israel. Never again did the nation use God's ark as a fetish. The nation learned that prayer is the way to secure God's help. The identification of Tell en-Naṣbeh as Mizpah completely misses the parallel between the Joshua and the Samuel episodes. Later Samuel called a new national conference at Mizpah; it was here that Israel chose Saul as their king (1 Sam. 10:17–27).

Two other references favor Nebi Samwil as the identification for Mizpah. In the GEDALIAH story (Jer. 40:6—41:16) Nebi Samwil is closer to Jerusalem than Tell en-Naṣbeh; and the passage refers to

GIBEON, which is in the Valley of Aijalon directly below Nebi Samwil (41:16). After destroying Jerusalem, the king of Babylon appointed Gedaliah as military governor over the conquered Jerusalem area, with a new capital at nearby Mizpah. After the murder of Gedaliah, Mizpah is not mentioned until NEHEMIAH rebuilt the walls of Jerusalem.

There is a close juxtaposition of Mizpah and Gibeon in Nehemiah's list of the towns building the sections of the city wall next to the OLD GATE (Neh. 3:6–7). Citizens of Mizpah repaired the FOUNTAIN GATE (3:15) and a section of the wall that extended "from a point facing the ascent to the armory as far as the angle" (v. 19). Mizpah must have been an influential town in the postexilic period.

In the episode of the Levite's concubine (Jdg. 19:1—21:25), Mizpah was the rallying point for the Israelite tribes, and Gibeon was the only town between Mizpah (Nebi Samwil) and Gibeah. BAASHA of Israel invaded the southern kingdom and began the fortification of RAMAH in Judah's territory (1 Ki. 15:16–22; 2 Chr. 16:1–6). BEN-HADAD of DAMASCUS compelled him to retreat; ASA of Judah took the materials used in fortifying Ramah, and built Geba and Mizpah. Tell en-Naṣbeh is farther N than Nebi Samwil and in Ephraimite territory. It is easy, therefore, to favor the former site for Mizpah. On the other hand, the geographic terrain around Nebi Samwil is much stronger for military defense. The evidence in this episode is evenly divided. (See further F.-M. Abel, *Géographie de la Palestine* [1933]; W. F. Albright in *Excavations and Results at Tell el-Fûl (Gibeah of Saul)*, AASOR 4 [1924], 90–112; C. C. McCown, *Tell en-Nasbeh* [1947]; *NEAEHL*, 3:1098–1102.)

J. L. KELSO

Mizpar miz´pahr. KJV form of MISPAR.

Mizraim miz-ray´im (מִצְרַיִם *H5213*, possibly "[two] boundaries"). This English transliteration is used by the KJV and the NIV only with reference to one of the sons of HAM (Gen. 10:6, 13; 1 Chr. 1:8, 11; NJPS uses it also in 1 Ki. 10:28–29 and 2 Ki. 7:6, but the form does not occur at all in NRSV or TNIV). In the Hebrew Bible, however, *miṣrayim* occurs very frequently as the name for EGYPT and its people. Thus the man Mizraim is regarded as the eponymous ancestor of the Egyptians. The descendants of Mizraim, moreover, included several other important people groups, such as the PHILISTINES (Gen. 10:14; 1 Chr. 1:12). See also NATIONS II.A.3.

Mizzah miz´uh (מִזָּה *H4645*, derivation uncertain). Son of Reuel and grandson of ESAU by BASEMATH; an Edomite clan chief (Gen. 36:13, 17; 1 Chr. 1:37).

Mnason nay´suhn (Μνάσων *G3643*). A friend of PAUL mentioned only in Acts 21:16. Three facts about him are known. First, he was from CYPRUS, like BARNABAS, and probably a Jew, though bearing a common Greek name (some think it may have been regarded by Hellenistic Jews as corresponding with the Hebrew name MANASSEH). Second, he was "one of the early disciples," converted perhaps at PENTECOST or soon afterward, though it has been suggested that he may have been a disciple of Jesus. In its context this description may imply exemplary fidelity. Third, he was hospitable, welcoming Paul and his Hellenistic companions, including LUKE, to his house at Jerusalem. The "Western" text locates the house at a village between CAESAREA and JERUSALEM, but this detail may be simply an attempt to account for the unusual construction of v. 16, so that it is possible to translate either "bringing with them Mnason" or "bringing us to Mnason." It also is possible that he was one of Luke's authorities for the course of events in the early days of the church at Caesarea and Jerusalem. (See C. K. Barrett, *A Critical and Exegetical Commentary on the Acts of the Apostles*, ICC, 2 vols. [1994–98], 2:1003–04.)

W. J. CAMERON

Moab moh´ab (מוֹאָב *H4565* [Gen. 19:37; 36:35] and *H4566*, derivation uncertain; gentilic מוֹאָבִי *H4567*, "Moabite"). A Transjordanian state with its inhabitants, lying E of the DEAD SEA and occupying the plateau between the Wadis ARNON and ZERED. At certain periods the N boundary reached beyond the Arnon, and while the S extremities of Moab were never recorded, they probably were marked by Wadi el-Ḥesa (the usual identification of the Zered).

I. Name and origin
II. Topography
III. Sources
   A. Biblical
   B. Nonbiblical
   C. Cuneiform texts
IV. History
   A. Prebiblical
   B. Biblical
V. Language
VI. Religion

I. Name and origin. The ancestor of the Moabites was Moab, the son of LOT by incestuous union with his eldest daughter (Gen. 19:30–38). The son was born in the hills above ZOAR, presumably in S Moab; no further mention of him occurs in the Bible. Both the descendants of this man and the land were known as Moab, the predominant use of this term in the OT being of the people themselves, and only sporadically of the country. The inhabitants were also known as Moabites, a usage found in the Assyrian royal inscriptions and elsewhere. The MT gives no etymology, but the SEPTUAGINT, after the phrase "she named him Moab" (19:37), adds the gloss, *legousa ek tou patros mou*, "saying, [he is] from my father," which may indicate that the Hebrew text used by the Greek translators explained the name as derived from *mēʾābî* ("from my father"). Etymologies proposed in modern times include "desirable" (from *yāʾab* H3277) and "[land of] the sunset" (cf. Arab. *maʾab*; see *ABD*, 4:882).

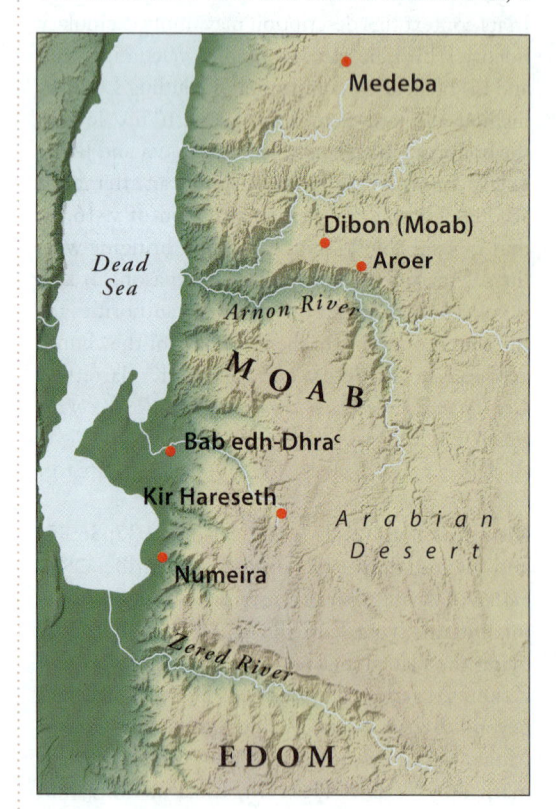

Moab.

II. Topography. The principal inhabited area of Moab was the plateau situated immediately E of the Dead Sea and about 4,300 ft. above the level of that body of water. The core of Moab was located between the Wadi Arnon and the Wadi Zered, although during periods of national strength the extreme N to S extent of the country was a little over 6 mi. in length. When the Moabites were weak, however, this distance was cut down to about one-half. The E to W extent of the terrain was some 25 mi., though not all of this area could be cultivated, due to the presence of deep transverse gorges and portions of arid land to the E bordering on the desert.

The coastal regions of Moab contained several fertile lowland areas, particularly in the SW corner of the country and to the N of the Wadi Arnon. To the E of the coastal area were the Moabite highlands, which contained numerous fertile valleys and tablelands lying both N and S of the Wadi Arnon. Conditions in these areas were excellent for viticulture, agriculture, and the grazing of herds and flocks. During times when Moab was densely occupied, every available part of the land was cultivated, including some of the steep hillsides of the wadis. The raising of sheep was a major occupation in antiquity, with the flocks moving E to the Syrian desert during the lush spring season and returning W in the long hot summer.

The inhabited regions of Moab were well watered by rainfall, particularly in the W region of the highlands, but to the E the rainfall average declined rapidly, making for a marked transition from cultivated terrain to desert land. All the wadis were in flood during the rainy winter season but became dry during the hot summer, when the people depended upon a few perennial springs and reservoirs or cisterns of water. Permanent springs were formed when the rain fell on the highland areas, filtered through the limestone to the solid layers of hard underlying rock, and flowed W along underground channels to the western slopes, or erupted in the valleys of the highlands. Despite these important natural reserves, the land of Moab was by no means amply supplied with water.

The most important river to the S, the Wadi el-Ḥesa, probably formed the boundary between Moab and Edom, taking its rise from the latter. This wadi has frequently been identified with the Zered, which divided the desert from the cultivated land. There is some doubt about this, however, since the Israelites camped at Iye Abarim in the desert E of Moab, and went from there to the valley of Zered. Since this was the last site prior to the crossing of the Wadi Arnon, it presents certain difficulties for the identification of Zered with the Wadi el-Ḥesa. For much of its length the wadi flows through a deep gorge, which became much shallower at its E end.

The ideal N border of Moab, which actually was seldom realized, stretched E from the Wadi Heshban and Khirbet er-Rufaiseh, about 5 mi. N of the Dead Sea. At times the N boundary of Moab extended as far as the Wadi Nimrin, the N limit of a rich and well-watered area known as the Plains of Moab, which extended S for about 80 mi. to the Dead Sea. This territory was apparently occupied by the Moabites early in their political history, since it had already acquired its designation when the Amorite raider Sihon occupied Moabite territory S to the Wadi Arnon. However, at most periods of Moabite history this latter chasm frequently formed the N boundary for practical purposes.

III. Sources

A. Biblical. The main sources relating to Moab are unfortunately not Moabite in origin, but comprised records from neighboring peoples with whom the Moabites were often at war. However, such information is sufficiently objective in character to be used with confidence in the reconstruction of Moabite history and life. The primary source for such a task is the OT, and although the historiographic concerns of the various authors were different in character from those of writers in other times and cultures, their descriptions of events in Moabite history give every indication of being

A sample of the topography of Moab.

objective and therefore reliable. The Israelite feeling of disdain toward the Moabites seems reflected in the narrative describing their incestuous origin (Gen. 19:30–38), since the offspring rather than the unnamed daughters of Lot were the object of discussion.

The itinerary in Num. 21 included a battle against Sihon before the Hebrews reached the plains of Moab. Another account of the Israelite approach to Moab (Deut. 2:8–29) commented upon the relations between the Israelites and Moabites, as well as to some pre-Moabite inhabitants. According to the tradition preserved by this section, the Israelites passed the land of Edom to the E and went due N without entering Moabite territory. When Israel requested permission to travel along the king's highway that crossed the plateau, the Moabites refused (Jdg. 11:17), although they may have had some trading contacts with Israel (Deut. 2:28–29). Moses was prohibited from attacking the Moabites (2:9) despite their unfriendly behavior, even though from then on they were to be excluded from Israel (23:3–6; cf. Neh. 13:1). Concern on the part of Balak, king of Moab, at the success of the Israelites prompted him to enlist a gifted Mesopotamian seer named BALAAM to curse the enemy, who at that time were settled across the Wadi Arnon (Num. 22; Josh. 24:9). Just before they crossed the Jordan the Israelites encamped in the Plains of Moab (Num. 22:1; Josh. 3:1) and were seduced by pagan Moabite and Midianite women so that they participated in idolatrous behavior.

The book of Judges records that EGLON, king of Moab, invaded Canaan as far as JERICHO and subjugated the Israelites for eighteen years before being assassinated by EHUD the Benjamite (Jdg. 3:12–30). The narrative of the book of Ruth, which is admirably consonant with "the days when the judges ruled," records that ELIMELECH of BETHLEHEM had migrated to Moab and had begotten sons, who subsequently married two Moabite women named ORPAH and RUTH. Under adverse circumstances the latter returned as a widow to Israelite territory and subsequently married BOAZ, thereby becoming the ancestress of DAVID (Ruth 4:18–22).

The records of the early monarchy did not give particular prominence to the conflicts with Moab, with the result that the wars of SAUL and David with this nation were mentioned only in summarized form. No information was furnished regarding either the cause or the course of the war against the Moabites, but only the fact that they were defeated by Saul (1 Sam. 14:47). David brought his parents to the king of Moab for protection when he was being pursued by Saul, and was accorded a courteous reception (22:3–4). The account of a Moabite defeat at the hands of David (2 Sam. 8:2, 11–12) described the punitive measures of decimation adopted by the Israelite ruler, as well as mentioning the tribute that the Moabites had to pay.

Information concerning Moab in the books of Kings is also sparse, making it necessary on occasion for inferences to be drawn from the context. SOLOMON married a Moabite woman as one of his many wives (1 Ki. 11:1, 7), and it would seem probable from 1 Ki. 11:7 and 2 Ki. 23:15 that he allowed her to build a high place where CHEMOSH, the Moabite deity, could be worshiped. After the death of Solomon the Moabites broke free from Israelite control, but were subdued in the time of OMRI of Israel (885/4–874/3 B.C.).

Toward the end of the reign of AHAB of Israel (874/3–853) the Moabites once again began to break free. In an attempt to regain control of the situation JEHORAM, the son of Ahab, enlisted the help of JEHOSHAPHAT, king of Judah and ruler of Edom, but the campaign proved abortive (2 Ki. 1:1; 3:4–27). At a later time Judah itself was invaded by a coalition of Moabites, Ammonites, and Edomites, but dissension broke out among these allies and Judah was delivered (2 Chr. 20:1–30). This particular record constituted one of those campaigns in the life of Jehosphaphat not mentioned in Kings, and most probably occurred after the events of 2 Ki. 3:4–27.

A brief narrative (2 Ki. 10:32–33) records that HAZAEL, king of ARAM, seized from JEHU of Israel the territory normally regarded as Moabite which lay to the N of the Wadi Arnon, and which still belonged to Moab at the time of Jehoram. In the year that ELISHA died, some Moabite companies carried out sporadic raids on Israelite territory (13:20), while in the time of JEROBOAM II (782/81–753) the expansion of Israelite holdings to the E of the Jordan must have involved the conquest of at least a part of Moabite territory (14:25). This campaign fulfilled the prophecy of Amos 2:1–3, which spoke of coming retribution for a particularly abhorrent crime.

During the latter part of the 8th cent., the Moabites were compelled to become tributaries to ASSYRIA (Isa. 15–16), but when the Assyrian empire collapsed the Moabites were free from domination once again. In the days of JEHOIAKIM of Judah (609–597) the Moabites made scattered incursions into Judah (2 Ki. 24:2), and when Jerusalem fell to the Babylonians in 586 some of its inhabitants fled to Moabite territory for safety, later returning to Judah when GEDALIAH became governor (Jer. 40:11; the Moabites are briefly mentioned in the postexilic period, Ezra 9:1; Neh. 13:1, 23). Several of the prophets refer to Moab as the recipient of divine judgment (e.g., Isa. 25:10–12; Jer. 9:26; 25:31; 27:3; Ezek. 25:8–11; Amos 2:1–3; Zeph. 2:8–11).

B. Nonbiblical. Purely Moabite sources have come to light through archaeological investigations, though nothing of importance has been uncovered that in any way compares with the finding of the stela of King MESHA at Dhiban (DIBON) in 1868. This black basalt inscription, the celebrated MOABITE STONE, measuring almost 4 ft. high and 2 ft. wide, was made to commemorate the revolt of Mesha against Israel, and his subsequent rebuilding of many important towns (2 Ki. 3:4–5). It was discovered by a missionary on his travels through the territory once occupied by the tribe of Reuben E of the Dead Sea. Shortly afterwards, C. Clermont-Ganneau of the French Consulate in Jerusalem obtained a rough impression of the material contents by means of a "squeeze."

The interest of the archaeologists in the stela prompted the local Arabs to break the stone up into fragments to be used as charms for the blessing of crops, but Clermont-Ganneau was able to recover several of the small pieces and ultimately reconstructed the stela, now in the Louvre. Out of an estimated 1,100 letters in the original inscription, approximately 669 were recovered, but this loss was offset to a large extent by the original "squeeze," which preserved the greater portion of the narrative. Because this stela is the only source in the Moabite tongue, it is of great value both for the study of Moabite history and the language (see LANGUAGES OF THE ANE II.F). The inscription is generally dated about the middle of the 9th cent. B.C.

Other fragmentary inscriptions coming from the same period have been recovered. One of them, discovered in Dhiban and published in 1952, was first thought to have been part of the Mesha stela, but further study showed that it probably came from a larger and different inscription; its brief text cannot be reconstructed. More important is a fragment found in KERAK around 1958, which apparently gives the name of Mesha's father as *kmšyt*, that is, Chemoshyat or Chemoshyatti (the first consonant is missing; in the Mesha stela only the first three consonants of the name are preserved). These fragments are too small to throw any light on Moabite history, but their very existence shows that the Mesha stela was no isolated phenomenon in 9th-cent. B.C. Moab.

A monument discovered in 1930 about 15 mi. N of KIR HARESETH and known as the Baluʿah stela has also survived from ancient Moab, though in badly weathered form. The first photographs of this stela were published in 1932, showing on the upper part an almost completely indecipherable inscription of four lines in extent. Underneath this material were three figures depicted in relief. The inscription has been assigned tentatively to the Early Bronze Age by Albright, though this date was reduced by over a millennium by Drioton, who placed it in the 12th cent. B.C. However, the indecipherable nature of the inscription makes any attempt at dating unreliable. From a supposed correspondence with the Linear B script, Alt thought that the stela had been erected originally by the Emites migrating from W Palestine, who were subsequently conquered by early Moabite settlers and absorbed into the native population. This suggestion, however, is purely speculative in nature.

C. Cuneiform texts. Some of the Assyrian kings came into contact with the Moabites during their forays in the land of *Amurru*, and these encounters were recorded in the Assyrian royal inscriptions. Of interest is the fact that, while the latter were sparse when compared with OT references to the Moabites, they contained more names of Moabite rulers than the OT narratives, and this during a period when the OT took little notice of Moabite history. One such source was recovered during the excavations at Nimrud (biblical CALAH), comprising letters dealing with affairs in Syria and Palestine. Of these, a diplomatic communication written during the last third of the 8th cent. B.C. had reference to an attack upon Moab by a marauding tribe, probably BEDOUIN in nature. Another document from the same period spoke of Palestinian emissaries journeying to Nimrud with tribute. Other Moabite relations with Assyria were mentioned in the annals of ASHURBANIPAL, SENNACHERIB, and ESARHADDON.

Egyptian sources for Moabite history are almost negligible, since there was no sedentary occupation of Moab when Egyptian influence in Palestine was at its height. However, the name Dibon possibly occurs (as *tpn*) on the city list of THUTMOSE III in the temple of Amon at Karnak (this identification is questioned by some). From the list itself the place was located in the area of Upper Retenu, and can thus be identified with Tell Dibbin. The name Moab has been thought to be present on the list of RAMSES II in the temple of Luxor, and other Moabite designations have been recognized on ostraca, graffiti, and papyrus fragments recovered from Saqqara in 1926.

Moab was mentioned occasionally in noncanonical Jewish literary sources such as the Hebrew text of Sir. 36:10, which reads, "crush the heads of Moab's princes," and preserves the general sentiments of the OT writers toward Moab. The country is mentioned five times in the book of JUDITH, but the references are of no historical value. JOSEPHUS preserved a number of facts relating to the Moabites, one of which, concerning the destruction of Ammon and Moab by NEBUCHADNEZZAR (*Ant.* 10.9.7), is not included in the OT record. Though the event cannot be verified readily from other sources, there is no reason to dismiss it as necessarily untrustworthy.

IV. History

A. Prebiblical. The most obvious prebiblical remains in Moab are the *menhirs* (large erect stones sometimes found in rows or circles) and the *dolmens* (stone chambers made from massive slabs of rock and frequently buried under a mound of earth or stones). Such monuments occur throughout TRANSJORDAN, and the Moabite examples come from the Neolithic period (6000–4500 B.C.).

During the Early Bronze IV to Middle Bronze I era (c. 2200–1900 B.C.), there was a high level of sedentary occupation throughout Transjordan, and Moab itself was intensively settled. The inhabitants protected themselves by building fortified cities along the caravan routes which crossed Transjordan from N to S. Indications of firmly established agricultural settlements point to an advanced level of civilization. While the cultivation of crops often was carried on outside fortified sites, some fields of ten acres in area were walled in for purposes of defense. Cultivated lands generally were located near a spring or stream so as to insure a reasonably continuous water supply, and this careful use of land was in evidence throughout the sedentary periods in Moab. The pottery of the early settlers was a rough, handmade variety, of a character with its counterparts in contemporary W Palestine.

In the period under study there was a well-established trading route through Moab, and when the army of KEDORLAOMER traveled down this road as far as EL PARAN in Edom (Gen. 14:5–7), it was able to reduce the fortified sites en route one by one. Ancient Moabite strongholds may originally have been built as the result of internal political disunity, and this factor doubtless contributed to defeat at the hands of the marauding Mesopotamians. Quite possibly also the invasion hastened the disappearance of the EMITES, a group of the REPHAITES said to have inhabited Moab prior to the Moabites (Deut. 2:10–11). At the end of the 19th cent. B.C. the established culture gradually dwindled, and between 1900 and 1300 there was apparently a break in sedentary occupation of the territory S from the river JABBOK. Political and economic factors seem to have been principally responsible, with the AMORITE movement of Mesopotamia exerting a great influence in this direction. After 2200 B.C., AMORITE nomads traversed the FERTILE CRESCENT and went as far S as Egypt, and when sedentary occupation declined in Moab, the Amorites had free access to the territory. This was an important consideration, since they depended upon pasturage for their herds and flocks. Studies in surface archaeology thus far seem to indicate that the general picture of nomadic occupation described above existed in Moab until the 13th cent. B.C.

B. Biblical. The end of the Late Bronze Age witnessed a settling-down of the nomadic populace, along with the rise of the historic kingdoms of Edom, Ammon, and Moab, and the "Amorite" regimes of Sihon and Og. Moab is mentioned in the topographical lists of Ramses II at Luxor, while in the OT Moab is placed in parallel form to the "sons of Sheth," the latter perhaps being an archaic tribal name and the Hebrew form of the Egyptian Shutu (*šwtw*), the Amarna Age designation of an area of Palestine perhaps roughly equivalent to later Ammon and Moab.

The descent and settlement of the Moabites has not been preserved in any detail, for OT references simply described the final establishing of the Transjordanian peoples as an event already accomplished by the time of their first contact with the Israelites. Nothing can be deduced from the etymology of the name Moab regarding their descent, though the fact that they were connected genealogically with

On the plateau of Moab, a shepherd walks amid his sheep and goats.

the Ammonites (Gen. 19:37–38) and mentioned with them (Deut. 23:3) would imply a common ancestor. It has been suggested that the earliest Moabites came from a group of nomadic tribes that lived in the Syrian-Arabian desert, occupying the territory of Moab in some strength during the 14th cent. B.C., though this is far from certain.

At all events, it is probable that the new settlers occupied land unused by the Emites, and as they grew in numbers they subjugated the latter in the manner reflected in the Baluʿah stela. If, as the lack of direct archaeological evidence seems to imply, the original Emite settlement failed to achieve significant depth, it would be a comparatively simple matter for a vigorous nomadic people to dispossess the sedentary inhabitants, or at the least to absorb them into their own cultural patterns without difficulty. Since the Moabites do not appear to have met such firm opposition in settling down as did the Israelites, the period of formal occupation of Moabite terrain would be correspondingly shorter and could well have begun early in the 14th cent., if not earlier.

The absence of Moab from the names mentioned in Gen. 10 can be taken as implying that it was one of the junior NATIONS of the ANE, although it would appear that Moab became sedentary prior to the descendants of ABRAHAM (ch. 19). That the social development of the Moabites was more advanced than that of Israel is apparent from the fact that when the Hebrews encountered them during the exodus period they already were governed by a king. The surface archaeological surveys conducted by N. Glueck in Transjordan indicated that by the last quarter of the 13th cent. the kingdoms of Ammon, Edom, and Moab were firmly established, a situation aided in part by the ending of the Egyptian domination of Palestine at the close of that century.

The Iron Age inhabitants of Moab defended their country by means of a strong chain of border forts. At the point where the plateau descended to Wadi el-Ḥesa there were a number of fortified sites that protected the entrance of the king's highway into S Moab. The pass, some 17 mi. E of the place where the wadi emptied into the Dead Sea, was important for purposes of trade and general communication, as well as being close to the fertile area watered by the springs of Aineh. One of the principal fortresses, el-Medeiyineh, was located on an almost impregnable hill, and was rectangular in form. It commanded a strategic position on the king's highway, since the latter had to skirt the fortress as it wound to the top of the plateau. Before gaining the high land, the highway was protected by a second fort, el-Akuzeh, built on a rocky outcrop overlooking the ancient caravan route. The strong walled fortress of Dhubab was located in the SW corner of the country, somewhat below the edge of the plateau.

The fort known as Medinet er-Ras was located separately on a hill farther N and on the plateau proper, and had an outer defensive wall some 6.5 ft. thick. This complex formed an important bastion in the defense of SW Moab, and was linked with those which guarded the descent to the Dead Sea on the W border of Moab. Because of the way in which the E border merged with the desert, it was particularly important for strong defensive fortifications to be established there. The S extremity of the border was protected by the fortress of Mahaiy, a rectangular structure over 500 yards long, and between 100 and 250 yards wide. It was erected on the top of a steep hill that commanded a clear view of the desert areas to the N and NE, and controlled access to the slope leading to Wadi el-Ḥesa. So strategic was the position of this fort that no large marauding band could enter Moab from the SE without coming into contact with it.

To the N of Mahaiy, and frequently within sight of one another, were constructed numerous defensive positions reaching N along the entire E border of Moab. Some of these strong points were of major proportions, while others were in the nature of blockhouses designed to supplement the larger structures. A great many hills in the area still carry the remains of fortresses or watchtowers, most of which were built in the Iron Age. In the region of the Arnon the Moabites constructed several powerful fortresses in rather inaccessible and inhospitable terrain, and these doubtless needed to be provisioned from outside sources.

The border defenses of N Moab are less pronounced in character because of the rather fluid nature of the border itself. In any event, most of the major centers in the interior were strongly fortified, so that an invader from the N would be faced with the prospect of having to reduce them one by one in order to gain access to central Moab. The Iron Age population was dense, and all available land was tilled by the inhabitants. Whereas Early Bronze Age settlers had been forced to rely for their water upon the few springs or perennial streams in the country, the Iron Age inhabitants had mastered the technique of making water-tight cisterns by using a plaster compound of slaked lime. They were thus much more independent of natural sources of water, and were able to locate their settlements in strategic positions such as on hilltops. The cisterns they built were often hewn out of the natural rock and could be situated either on the hillside near the settlement or located close to the buildings themselves. A great number of these reservoirs have survived to the present and have been cataloged by archaeologists.

Early Iron Age pottery in Transjordan exhibited sufficient peculiarities to mark it out from contemporaneous W Palestinian forms. This situation has been attributed in part to Syrian influences, with the Moabite pottery showing high artistic and technical skill in manufacture. From the available evidence it would appear that contemporary Moabite culture was well advanced, and by no means inferior to that of W Palestine.

By assimilating with the Emites and other indigenous elements, the Moabites had developed into a powerful nation by the 13th cent. B.C. The Israelites seem to have encountered them at the first stage of the Iron Age kingdom, shortly after the Amorite king Sihon had defeated a Moabite ruler (Num. 21:26) and occupied the N segment of the country as far as the Arnon. After this victory Sihon ruled over an area of Moabite territory which probably reached N to the Plains of Moab. The taunt song (21:27–30) apparently alluded to the Amorite campaign against the Moabites, and although the Amorites claimed the destruction of "Ar of Moab," they never actually controlled the territory to the S of the Arnon. Boundary lines at that period seldom were clearly defined, and it is quite probable that there were some Moabite settlements within the limits of Amorite occupation.

The Israelite itinerary through Transjordan is far from easy to establish, but it would seem that the Hebrews had detoured round Edom and camped at OBOTH (Num. 21:10). After this they moved to IYE ABARIM, and subsequently to the valley of the Zered. After crossing the Arnon they camped in several locations (21:10–20; 33:41–49) before reaching a valley overlooked by a craggy ridge W of the desert (21:20; see PISGAH). The Israelite circuit of Edom may have led the Moabites to think themselves superior to the Hebrews, and according to the address of JEPHTHAH (Jdg. 11:17) they forbade the Israelites to approach their territory.

For their part the Hebrews were warned not to fight Moab, since they would not be given any part of the Moabite territory (Deut. 2:9). However, the Moabites of AR had some trading relations with them a little later (2:28–29), quite possibly convinced that Israelite nonaggression could be taken as establishing a tacit political agreement (Num. 21:13; Jdg. 11:18). The victory over Sihon, after which the Israelites sang the Amorite taunt song, and the conquest of Og, not merely gave the Hebrews access to Canaan but also showed that they were quite capable of defeating the Moabites alone if necessary. This threat to his land prompted Balak, king of the Moabites, to enlist the services of the Mesopotamian seer Balaam, with unfortunate prospects for Moab (Num. 22–24). Greater success was encountered in enticing Israel into idolatrous practices (25:3) at a pagan festival. The resultant punishment kindled Israelite anger against Moab and perpetuated a prohibition (Deut. 23:3–4). The grazing facilities of Moab attracted the attention of the Reubenites and Gadites, and on being allotted this territory they later rebuilt many former Moabite towns (Num. 32:34–38). Just before the entrance into Canaan, Moses died and was buried in a Moabite valley opposite BETH PEOR.

During the judges period Moabite power increased, and Eglon invaded Canaan as far N as Jericho, subjugating the local populace for eighteen years. This action was reinforced when Eglon made an alliance with Amalekite and Ammonite groups, and deliverance for Israel only came with the work of Ehud (Jdg. 3:12–30). The Moabites were expelled from W Jordanian territory and a period of peace ensued. The book of Ruth, which purports to describe events "in the days when the judges ruled" (Ruth 1:1), gives no information as to precisely where the family of Elimelech settled in Moab, though it seems clear that easy movement between Israel and Moab pointed to a time of friendly relations between the two people. Not merely were the Israelites periodically subjected to Moabite power in the period of the judges, but they were also in bondage to their gods, as well as to those of neighboring people (Jdg. 10:6). See JUDGES, PERIOD OF.

In the early monarchy the Moabites sought to exploit the temporary weakening of the Hebrew forces resulting from the defeat of NAHASH the Ammonite by Saul at JABESH GILEAD, a site little more than 30 mi. N of Moab. Accordingly the Moabites gained control of territory N of the Arnon, which resulted in Israel's waging a defensive campaign against Moab, Ammon, Edom, and the king of Zobah in the NE (1 Sam. 14:47). The Moabites were driven S beyond the Arnon, but were not made tributaries by Saul.

Prior to becoming king of Israel, David had friendly contacts with Moab (1 Sam. 22:3–5) and attracted some support for his cause (1 Chr. 11:46). During the civil war between David and Ish-Bosheth (2 Sam. 2–4), the Moabites apparently reasserted themselves and were later subjugated by David (2 Sam. 8:2; 1 Chr. 18:2). This dominance was maintained during the reign of Solomon, and it is probable that part of N Moab fell within one of the twelve administrative districts (1 Ki. 4:13–14). The provision of a high place for Chemosh, "the abomination of Moab" (11:7 NRSV), might imply that Solomon was sympathetic to, or at least tolerant toward, the pagan worship of Moab.

An important period of Moabite history began shortly after the division of the united monarchy. Early in the 9th cent. B.C. Moab seems to have tried to regain its holdings N of the Arnon. Only when OMRI came to the throne (885/4–874/3) was Israel able to reassert control of the disputed territory, and that, according to the Moabite Stone, because Chemosh "was angry with his land." The "forty years" of Moabite subjection mentioned in the inscription are meant to indicate a generation, namely from the middle of the reign of Omri (c. 879) to the middle of that of his son Ahab (874/3–853). If this was the case it does not seem necessary to interpret the "son" of the Moabite inscription as "grandson" (the reference thus being to Jehoram [852–841], the second eldest son of Ahab, rather than to Ahab himself). Omri did not in fact conquer all the land as far S as the Arnon, since Dibon and Aroer were Moabite holdings prior to the time of Mesha.

At the battle of Qarqar (853 B.C.) a coalition of peoples including Israel, Aram, and Ammon confronted SHALMANESER III of Assyria, and the absence of Moab from this list shows that it was not then an independent state. Shortly afterward the Moabites, along with the Ammonites and some MEUNITES, invaded Judah from the S (2 Chr. 20:1-3), perhaps prompted by BEN-HADAD II of Aram. The allies penetrated Judah as far as EN GEDI on the W shore of the Dead Sea, but some dissension broke out and they began to fight one another (20:1-30). Just before the death of Ahab, Mesha of Moab rebelled against Israel (2 Ki. 3:5-8), and about the year 850 Jehoram and Jehoshaphat allied and marched on Moab, inflicting a series of defeats on Mesha, but ultimately withdrawing (3:27).

Subsequent to this event, Mesha regained the land of MEDEBA and took the territory of ATAROTH from the tribe of Gad. NEBO also was recaptured with heavy Israelite losses, and this victory marked the virtual recovery of Moabite independence. According to the stela, Mesha fortified various cities and began a program of public works to insure the prosperity of his land. After the death of Hazael, c. 796 B.C., Adadnirari III marched W and subdued Syria and Palestine, though apparently not Moab, which made periodic raids on Israelite territory (2 Ki. 13:20). Despite Mesha's success, Moab began to decline from the beginning of the 8th cent., even though circumstances favored a revival of Moabite and Ammonite power when in 743 TIGLATH-PILESER III made MENAHEM of Israel tributary.

The limitations imposed on Moab after AMAZIAH of Judah campaigned successfully against Edom (2 Ki. 14:7) and gained control of the S Arabian commercial trade were implemented when UZZIAH rebuilt the port of ELATH (14:22), made Ammon tributary, and most probably subjugated Moab also. A further danger to the Moabites lay in the resurgence of Assyrian power from 745 onward with the threat of invasion from the NE, and in 734 Moab became one of a number of Palestinian states to be subjugated by Tiglath-Pileser III. Moab seems to have been a member of a coalition that was defeated in 711 by SARGON, but the country is not mentioned by name in the Assyrian annals. In a Palestinian campaign a decade later, SENNACHERIB suppressed certain rebellious states and Moab was again involved. In a letter to ESARHADDON (681-669), Moab was listed as paying only a small amount of tribute, along with building materials for the palace at NINEVEH.

During a period of civil war in Assyria under ASHURBANIPAL (669-627), Arab tribes invaded E Syria and Palestine, and while they were mostly repulsed from Moabite territory, they seriously weakened the autonomy of Moab (cf. Isa. 15; 16; Jer. 48). While Ammon was strong in the time of JOSIAH, Moab was declining in influence, and when the Assyrian kingdom fell to the Babylonians, Moab, with Palestine proper, was assigned to NABOPOLASSAR (626-605), though it was not until after the Battle of CARCHEMISH in 605 that Moab paid formal tribute to Babylon. When Jehoiakim revolted against Nebuchadnezzar, groups of Chaldeans, Syrians, Moabites, and Ammonites raided Judah in reprisal (2 Ki. 24:2).

Shortly after 598 the Moabites found it politically desirable to ally with Egypt against the Babylonians, and this, combined with the revolt of ZEDEKIAH against Nebuchadnezzar, made it necessary for the latter to march into Palestine. In 586 Jerusalem was laid waste, and some Jews actually fled to Moab for refuge, only to return under Gedaliah (Jer. 40:11-12). According to JOSEPHUS (*Ant.* 10.9.7), Nebuchadnezzar ultimately conquered Moab, after which bedouin tribes had free access to the land from the E. Their inroads compelled many Moabites who had remained in the hill country after the Judean exile to migrate to the depopulated land of Judah, where they would be safe from bedouin attack.

During the Persian period a considerable number of Moabites were to be found in Judah, and in the time of EZRA and NEHEMIAH a hostile attitude was adopted toward them (Ezra 9:1, 12; Neh. 13:1-2), in conformity with the provisions of the Torah (Deut. 23:3). The name "Moabite" became equivalent to "sinner" and "impious," reflecting the attitudes of earlier Judean prophets (Amos 2:1-3; Jer. 9:26; 25:21; et al.), and the land itself was regarded by APOCALYPTIC writers as the seat of iniquity.

Several centuries intervened during which ancient Moab had no sedentary occupation, but from the 2nd cent. B.C., if not earlier, the land once again was occupied by another dense population, that of the NABATEANS. Unmentioned by name in the OT, these people were of Arab stock and originated in NW ARABIA. Before entering Moabite and Edomite territory, the Nabateans were typically Arab in character, traveling on camels, living in tents, and feeding on dates and animal flesh. On becoming sedentary they inherited the trade routes of the Edomites, and their camel caravans traversed the whole of Palestine and even went as far NW as ASIA MINOR. Archaeological evidence shows that they began to settle in Transjordan in the 4th cent. B.C. in ancient Edom and Moab, and by the 1st cent. B.C. they had even infiltrated into the S NEGEV. They reconstructed the fortress system of the earlier inhabitants and extended it to the S and E. At first they were nominally subject to the Persian regime, but became independent prior to the Greek period. The Nabateans were notable for their agricultural zeal, a situation made necessary by the fact that, at its height, their population was twice as dense as that of the Moabites. They utilized every possible source of water, tilled previously uncultivated land, established settlements in thinly populated areas of the Negev, worked the Edomite copper and iron mines, and established trading relations with neighboring peoples. They flourished as a separate nation until A.D. 106, when almost all of the Nabatean territory was made into a Roman province by order of TRAJAN.

Archaeological remains have left no doubt as to the advanced nature of ancient Moabite culture. Typical Moabite pottery found S of the Wadi Arnon and elsewhere is comparable in quality and design with the best contemporary Palestinian ceramic ware. While Egyptian influence was present in the early stages of Moabite history, the land had its own skilled artisans who developed native styles. The writing on the stelae resembles the old Hebrew script and was executed with considerable dexterity, testifying to the artistic abilities of the Moabite craftsmen. Although there are obvious traces of Syro-Phoenician influence upon Moabite culture, there is a sufficient degree of independence evident to warrant the conclusion that for centuries it pursued a vigorous individual pattern of development.

V. Language. The only major inscription in Moabite, a language closely related to biblical Hebrew, is the stela of King Mesha. The forms of the letters are important to the epigraphist in illustrating the development of Canaanite scripts during the second half of the 9th cent. B.C. Grammatically, Moabite had elements in common with Ugaritic, Phoenician, Aramaic, and Arabic, while it shared with Hebrew such important features as the *waw consecutive*, the use of the relative particle, the accusative particle *ʾet*, and other familiar Hebrew forms. Words were divided by means of points, following the pattern of the SILOAM inscription and a few others from 8th-cent. B.C. Aramaic sources. The use of *matres lectionis* (consonants functioning as vowels) is the exception rather than the rule in the Mesha stela, as opposed to the orthography of some later Hebrew documents (such as 1QIsa^a). Regarding the Hebrew "diphthongs" *ay* and *aw*, the Moabite language contracted them to *e* and *o* respectively. Whereas in Hebrew the final consonant of masculine plural and dual forms was *m*, in Moabite it was replaced by an *n*. Again it is difficult to tell from the Moabite Stone whether a feminine noun with a pronominal suffix is singular or plural in number, a distinction which is made clear in biblical Hebrew. See also ARAMAIC LANGUAGE; HEBREW LANGUAGE; LANGUAGES OF THE ANE II.

VI. Religion. As with their history and language, the religion of the Moabites reflected their relationship with the other inhabitants of ancient Palestine. Again, unfortunately, just as Moabite history has had to be reconstructed largely from non-native sources, so their religious beliefs and practices have to be inferred from statements in the writings of other peoples, since there are hardly any sources dealing with Moabite religion proper. Quite obviously, therefore, the nature of their views on theological concepts such as sin, grace, immortality, and the like cannot be ascertained from what is known of Moabite religion.

Much of the present information concerning their beliefs comes from an early period in the history of Moab, and largely on the strength of this evidence scholars have seen marked similarities between Moabite and Canaanite religious forms. Sacrificial procedures were mentioned in the Balaam narratives (Num. 22:40), apparently in honor of a local deity. The seduction of the Israelites near SHITTIM and their participation in the sacrificial rites of BAAL PEOR (23:1–4, 14; 25:1–5) has important elements in common with Canaanite cultic worship, but nothing specific can be deduced about its nature from the etymology of the name Baal Peor.

Pottery figurines of male deities sometimes depicted them as mounted on horseback, while female statuettes generally represented the mother goddess Astarte (ASHTORETH), and as such were similar to those from other areas of Palestine. From the Iron Age artifacts found at Khirbet ʿAyin Musa, Kerak, and elsewhere, the female deity, named Ashtar-Chemosh in the Mesha inscription, often was depicted as clutching some sacred object in front of her upper torso, possibly a symbol of fertility. Pottery fragments of animal figurines found by Glueck could perhaps have formed the pedestals for images of gods and goddesses.

The mother goddess was worshiped in Moab in conjunction with Chemosh, and the Baluʿah stela relief may indicate that these two deities were being worshiped when Moabite tribes first entered the land. Chemosh was mentioned in the Amorite mocking song (Num. 21:27–30), one of the most ancient sources relating to the Moabites, and gives ground for the contention that he was the preeminent deity in Moab. Although revered as the god of warfare who subdued all his enemies (cf. Jdg. 11:24), he also was recognized as the one who provided for all aspects of daily life. Unlike the later Hebrews, the Moabites did not hesitate to address their deity by his personal name. He was worshiped at altars of unhewn stone erected on hilltops. Presumably temples were built in his honor in Moab, yet it remains true that though a Bronze Age temple has been found, no comparable structure from the Iron Age has been excavated to date.

There are no indications of a priestly hierarchy in the cult of Chemosh, which evidently was headed by the reigning king, as illustrated by the position of Balak in seeking the help of Balaam. This situation had not changed in the time of King Mesha, who, according to the Moabite Stone, acted under the direct instructions of Chemosh, and took the lead in the rite involving the sacrifice of his eldest son. Canaanite kings generally possessed priestly authority, and the Moabite rulers were no exception to this rule. In early Moabite sacrifice, bulls and rams were offered (Num. 23:1, 14, 29), and these animals have been represented in figurines from Khirbet el-Medeiyineh and Saliyeh. As with the Hebrew tradition, only the best quality sacrificial animals were acceptable to Chemosh, though more specific prescriptions relating to Moabite sacrifice are unknown. Whether incense was burned during cultic rites is also uncertain, since no altars of incense similar to those occurring in Canaan have been recovered from Moab.

As with other ANE peoples, the Moabites practiced the institution known as the BAN (*ḥerem* H3051, "that which is devoted to destruction or cultic use"), in which the spoils of war were devoted to the god of the victors. Brutality and ruthlessness in destruction were common features of Amarna age life in the ANE, and even later it was the normal practice for captured warriors to be killed, and the inhabitants of entire cities to be put to the sword. Generally speaking, such slaughter was deemed necessary for conciliating an angry god, and in this regard the Moabites were no exception. Nor did their religion survive the collapse of other pagan faiths in the ancient world.

(See further N. Glueck in AASOR 14 [1934] and 18–19 [1939]; F.-M. Abel, *Géographie de la Palestine* [1933], 1:278–81; F. V. Winnett in *BASOR* 125 [Feb. 1952]: 7–20; A. D. Tushingham in *BASOR* 133 [Feb. 1954]: 6–26; W. F. Albright, *The Archaeology of Palestine* [1956]; A. H. Van Zyl, *The Moabites* [1960]; N. Glueck, *The Other Side of the Jordan*, rev. ed. [1970]; J. Kautz in *BA* 44 [1981]: 27–35; A. Hadidi, ed., *Studies in the History and Archaeology of Jordan*, 3 vols. [1982–87]; J. F. A. Sawyer and D. J. A. Clines, eds., *Midian, Moab and Edom: The History and Archaeology of Late Bronze and Iron Age Jordan and Northeast Arabia* [1983]; P. Bienkowski, ed., *Early Edom and Moab: The Beginning of the Iron Age in Southern Jordan* [1992]; G. L. Mattingly in *Peoples of the Old Testament World*, ed. A. J. Hoerth et al. [1994], 317–33; B. MacDonald et al., eds., *The Archaeology of Jordan* [2001]; B. E. Routledge, *Moab in the Iron Age* [2004].)   R. K. HARRISON

The famous Moabite Stone mentions conflict between Mesha of Moab and Omri of Israel.

Moabite Stone. A votive inscription of MESHA, king of MOAB, referring to his victory over Israel and building activities. Also known as the Mesha Stela.

In 1868 a German missionary, F. A. Klein, was shown an inscribed basalt slab (3'10" high x 2' wide x 2.5" thick) with rounded top and thirty-nine lines of writing in an early cursive Hebrew type script. When both the German and French consuls aided by local Turkish officials evinced a competitive interest in the object, the Arabs broke the monument into several pieces to disperse it. Fortunately C. Clermont-Ganneau had obtained a "squeeze" of the major part of the unique text and thus was able to recover some 669 of an estimated 1100 letters, or almost two-thirds, when the larger pieces were bought and rejoined in the Louvre Museum in 1873.

The monument recounts how Mesha, king of Moab, the Dibonite son of Chemosh (to be restored as Chemoshyat[ti] on the basis of a different inscription found in KERAK), who had earlier ruled for thirty years, dedicated a high place to the god CHEMOSH in Qrhh (Qarhoh?) in gratitude for having delivered him "from all the kings and letting me see my desire over all my enemies." It was presumably at this sanctuary that the stela originally had been erected. The text then goes on to outline the occasion for its dedication. "Omri, king of Israel, had oppressed Moab for many days for Chemosh was angry with his land. His son succeeded him and he too said, 'I will oppress Moab.' In my time he said [this] but I triumphed over him and over his house, while Israel has perished for ever! Omri had taken possession of the land of Medeba and [Israelites] had settled there in his time and half the time of his son, that is forty years; but Chemosh dwelt in it again in my time."

The text would seem to supplement 1 Ki. 16 in regarding OMRI as the conqueror of northern Moab. The forty-year domination by Israel, if not intended as a generalization to cover a full generation, must comprise the reign of Omri (885–874 B.C.), his son AHAB (874–853), AHAZIAH (853–852), and half of the rule of JEHORAM (852–841). If this is so, the son here referred to must be Omri's "grandson" Jehoram, in whose reign there was an attempt to crush the Moabite rebels (2 Ki. 3:4–27). There is no reason to interpret the stone as implying that Mesha broke from Israel before the death of Ahab. This would be contrary to 2 Ki. 1:1. The overthrow of the Omrids by Jehu was doubtless interpreted by the Moabites as vengeance upon them wrought by the national god Chemosh.

The text continues: "I built Baal-Meon and made a pit [cf. Jer. 18:20] in it and I built Qaryaten [KIRIATHAIM, 48:1]. Now the men of Gad had built Ataroth for themselves, but I fought against the town and took it, slaying all the people of the town as a satiation for Chemosh and Moab. I brought back from there Oriel its chief [or read 'the altar-hearth of David'] and dragged him before Chemosh in Qerioth [KERIOTH, Amos 2:2]. There I settled men of Sharon and Maharith. Chemosh said to me, 'Go, seize Nebo from Israel!' So I went up by night, fought against it from daybreak to noon and took it, slaying everyone; seven thousand men, boys, women, girls and maidservants, for I had consecrated it to Ashtar-Chemosh. And I took from there the vessels of Yahweh, hauling them before Chemosh. The king of Israel had built Jahaz and stayed there while he was fighting against me, but Chemosh drove him out before me. So I took two hundred Moabites, all experienced fighting men, and sent them against Jahaz which, after capture, I annexed to Dibon [Jer. 48:21; 48:18, 22]."

The text shows clearly that the Moabites, like Israel, practiced the total destruction of towns and the annihilation of the inhabitants as an offering to their national deity to whom they ascribed victory. At the same time it describes Israelite penetration and building in Moab not expressed in the OT. The citing of the name of the God of Israel is of special interest.

Mesha continues with a claim to have built Qarhoh, both the wall around the park and citadel, its gates, towers, and royal residence, and reservoirs within the town. "Since there was no cistern within the town at Qarhoh I said to all the people, 'Let each of you make a cistern in your own house.' With Israelite captives I had irrigation ditches dug for Qarhoh." Mesha also had built AROER (cf. Jer. 48:19, modern ʿAroʿir S of DIBON) and a highway in the valley of the ARNON. He rebuilt ruined Beth Bamoth (cf. BAMOTH, Num. 21:19–20) and BEZER using men from Dibon. Other reconstruction work was carried out at MEDEBA, BETH DIBLATHAIM (Jer. 48:22), and BETH BAAL MEON as centers for sheepbreeders. Altogether he added more than a hundred towns and villages to his territory. The broken inscription ends with the call of the god Chemosh to Mesha to go and fight the Hauranites.

This major inscription in Moabite, a Semitic dialect akin to biblical Hebrew, is in a 9th-cent. hand and is probably to be dated soon after the year 841. The style is free narrative reminiscent of the OT. It is of much importance for the historical, linguistic, religious, and economic insights it affords.

(See further G. A. Cook, *A Text-Book of North Semitic Inscriptions* [1903], 1–14; S. R. Driver, *Notes on the Hebrew Text of the Books of Samuel* [1913], lxxivff.; W. F. Albright in *ANET*, 320–21; E. Ullendorf in *Documents from Old Testament Times*, ed. D. Winton Thomas [1958], 195–98; J. C. L. Gibson, *Textbook of Syrian Semitic Inscriptions* [1971], 1:71–83; J. A. Dearman, ed., *Studies in the Mesha Inscription and Moab* [1989]; *ABD*, 2:561–68 and 4:708–9, s.vv. "Epigraphy, Transjordanian" and "Mesha Stele.")   D. J. WISEMAN

Moadiah moh´uh-di´uh (מֹעַדְיָה H5050 [Neh. 12:5], "ornament of Yahweh"; the alternate form מוֹעַדְיָה H4598 [12:17], if genuine, perhaps means "assembly of Yahweh"; cf. MAADAI). One of the priestly leaders who returned from the EXILE with ZERUBBABEL (Neh. 12:5 NIV; the KJV and other versions have "Maadiah"). Both his family and that of MINIAMIN were headed by Piltai (Neh. 12:17). Some believe that Maadiah and Moadiah are two different individuals. Scholars who believe that the two names refer to the same person explain the spelling variation in different ways (see the discussion in *ABD*, 4:430–31, s.v. "Maadiah").

Mochmur mok´muhr (Μοχμούρ). A WADI or brook apparently SE of DOTHAN (Jdt. 7:18). If the name is not fictitious, it may be the same as Wadi Makhfuriyeh (which runs S of SHECHEM, modern Nablus) or Wadi Qana (see KANAH).

mocking. This English term and its cognates are used to render a variety of Hebrew and Greek words. Mocking may be harmless teasing, as the boy ISHMAEL with baby ISAAC (Gen. 21:9; the Heb. verb here is *ṣāḥaq* H7464, a play on Issac's name). Or it may be a lover's complaint, as of DELILAH with SAMSON (Jdg. 16:10, 13 KJV, rendering Heb. *tālal* H9438; NIV, "you have made a fool of me"). SANBALLAT and others "mocked [*lāʿag* H4352] and ridiculed [*bāzâ* H1022]" the Jews rebuilding Jerusalem (Neh. 4:1; cf. Ps. 80:6). Mocking may be biting sarcasm, as of ELIJAH against the prophets of the fertility god (1 Ki. 18:27 KJV, Heb. *hātal* H2252; NIV, "taunt"). JEREMIAH felt scorn directed at him (Jer. 20:7; cf. Ps. 119:51).

Israel's record of mocking God's messengers and prophets brought his wrath in the Babylonian captivity (2 Chr. 36:16; Heb. *lāʿab* H4351). The mockery of the OT is not confined to human reactions! God made sport of the Egyptians (Exod. 10:2; 1 Sam. 6:6 RSV). The psalmist says he holds all nations in derision (Ps. 59:8), especially when they rebel against him (Ps. 2:4). God "mocks proud mockers" (Prov. 3:34; using the verb *lîṣ H4329* and the noun *lēṣ H4370*).

In the NT, mocking may be public laughter at a failure, as in the parable of the unfinished tower (Lk. 14:29; Gk. *empaizō G1850*, a verb used also of the MAGI in the sense that they had "tricked" or "outwitted" HEROD the Great, Matt. 2:16). When the apostolic band spoke in tongues at PENTECOST, unbelievers mocked saying the disciples were drunk (Acts 2:13; Gk. *diachleuazō G1430*, NIV, "made fun of"). The members of the AREOPAGUS likewise mocked by gesture and word the message of the resurrection that PAUL brought (17:32; Gk. *chleuazō G5949*). Dedicated Christians will constantly meet scoffers (Jude 18), especially when they speak of the second coming (2 Pet. 3:3). Mockery may even advance to derisive torture (Heb. 11:36). Sinners, thinking they can "get away" with their sins, turn up their noses at God and his laws, but they cannot outwit him (Gal. 6:7; Gk. *myktērizō G3682*).

Jesus foretold his own mockery by the Romans (Matt. 20:19), and it came to pass (27:29). Jesus also was mocked in the Jewish trial (Lk. 22:63), and it was repeated with the men of Herod Antipas (23:11) and by the soldiers at the cross (23:36).

W. G. BROWN

Modad moh´dad. See ELDAD AND MEDAD (MODAD), BOOK OF.

Modein moh´deen (Μοδεΐν). A town where MATTATHIAS and his sons initiated the Maccabean Revolt (1 Macc. 2:15 et al.). It is identified with modern Midyah (more specifically, el-Arbaʿin), about 17 mi. NW of JERUSALEM. See MACCABEE.

modernism. An approach that accommodates the Bible and theology to contemporary thought, devaluing traditional views of biblical authority and supernaturalism. See BIBLICAL CRITICISM.

Moeth moh´eth. Apoc. form of NOADIAH (1 Esd. 8:63).

Moladah moh´luh-duh (מוֹלָדָה *H4579*, from יָלַד *H3528*, "to give birth"). One of "the southernmost towns of the tribe of Judah in the Negev toward the boundary of Edom" (Josh. 15:26); also listed in the allotment to the Simeonites (Josh. 19:2; 1 Chr. 4:28). In the postexilic period Moladah was one of the villages where "the people of Judah" settled (Neh. 11:26). This region was afterward occupied by the Edomites, and some think that it should be identified with a fortress in IDUMEA called *Malatha* (Jos. *Ant.* 18.6.2 §147). The idea that Moladah was a shrine where women came to pray for children cannot be deduced from the name as such.

Moladah was evidently close to BEERSHEBA, but the precise location is uncertain. EUSEBIUS and JEROME describe it as being 20 Roman mi. to the S of HEBRON on the road to Aila (Elath). If Moladah is the same as Josephus's Malatha, the town should be identified with Tell el-Milḥ, 14 mi. SE of Beersheba (cf. *NEAEHL*, 3:934–37, s.v. "Malḥata, Tel"). Most recent scholars, however, prefer Khereibet el-Waṭen, some 5.5 mi. E of Beersheba. Since one of the descendants of JERAHMEEL bore the name MOLID (1 Chr. 2:29), some have speculated that Moladah was a part of the Jerahmeelite settlement, which is known to have been in the S of Judah (1 Sam. 27:10).

P. A. VERHOEF

molding. This English term is used to render Hebrew *zēr H2425*, which occurs with reference to a shaped rim around the ARK OF THE COVENANT (Exod. 25:11, 24–25; 37:2), a similar rim around the altar of incense (30:3–4; 37:26–27; see INCENSE, ALTAR OF), and still another one around the table for the SHOWBREAD (37:11–12). In all three cases the molding was of pure gold and was ornamental, giving a finished appearance to the objects.

E. RUSSELL

mole. This term is used by the KJV and other versions to render the conjectured Hebrew word *ḥăparpārâ H2923*, which occurs only once: "On that day people will throw away to the moles [MT, *laḥpōr pērôt*] and to the bats their idols of silver and their idols of gold, which they made for themselves to worship" (Isa. 2:20 NRSV; NIV, "rodents"; NJPS, "flying foxes"). This translation is doubtful. No true mole (*Insectivora*) is found in this area, but the small heaps of soil pushed up by the Syrian mole rats (*Spalax ehrenbergi*) are an obvious and frequent sight in all areas with a rainfall of over four inches.

Moles are rodents of a specialized family. They spend most of their life underground and their eyes have disappeared; the feet, but mostly the enormous protruding incisor teeth, are used for burrowing. Mole rats are entirely vegetarian and feed on roots, bulbs, etc. The smallest is about 4 in. long, others reach 8 in. In the winter rainy season they build breeding mounds, like those of pocket gophers, that may be 5 ft. long and 3 ft. tall. (See *FFB*, 54–55.) Some scholars argue that the passage refers to the shrew (*Crocidura religiosa*), which apparently was worshiped in Egypt (see *HALOT*, 1:341). (The KJV uses "mole" also to render Heb. *tinšemet* H9491 in Lev. 11:30, but this term more likely refers to the CHAMELEON. The NJPS has "mole" for *ḥōled* H2700 in v. 29; see WEASEL.)   G. C. CANSDALE

Molech moh′lek (מֹלֶךְ H4891, prob. מֶלֶךְ H4889, "king," with the vowels of בֹּשֶׁת H1425, "shame"; Μολόχ G3661). Also Moloch (Amos 5:26 KJV; Acts 7:43 KJV, NRSV); TNIV Molek.

I. Meaning. Most scholars accept one of two meanings for "Molech." Some contend that it is a generic noun denoting a particular type of sacrifice, "a votive offering." This view is based primarily on the use of *mlk* in a number of Punic and Neo-Punic inscriptions dated roughly from the 4th to the 1st cent. B.C. from N Africa and engraved upon stelae that commemorated a sacrifice. The word *mlk* occurs alone or compounded with expressions, the most remarkable of which are *mlkʾmr* and *mlkʾdm*. Several stelae, dated from the end of the 2nd cent. or beginning of the 3rd cent. A.D., bear an analogous Latin inscription vocalized *molchomor*, which is evidently a transcription of the Punic *mlkʾmr*. Thus one can reckon *molk* as the vocalization of the first element.

O. Eissfeldt then showed that the word had a ritual sense denoting a sacrifice made to confirm or acquit a vow (*Molk als Opferbegriff im Punischen und Hebräischen und das Ende des Gottes Moloch* [1935]). Probably *mlkʾmr* and *mlkʾdm* mean respectively "offering of lamb" and "offering of man," and refer to the sacrifice of an infant or of a lamb substitute. Furthermore, although these inscriptions and texts are of late date, R. Dussaud read *mlkʾmr* on a stela from Malta of the 7th or 6th cent. B.C.

Moreover, Sanchuniathon (as quoted by Porphyry according to PHILO JUDAEUS [*De abstinentia* 2.56], a text also taken up by EUSEBIUS [*Praep. ev.* 4.16.6]), said that the Phoenicians sacrificed children at a much earlier date, and Quintus Curtius (*HAM* 4.3.23, translated by H. Bardon in the Budé Collection) said explicitly that this rite was transmitted from Phoenicia to Carthage. Although *mlk* never appears with a sacrificial meaning in the Phoenician inscriptions, this silence is explicable because Quintus Curtius also said the practice had been in abeyance for centuries before the founding of Carthage.

The Ras Shamra texts (see UGARIT), roughly contemporaneous with the period in which Philo places Sanchuniathon, may use *mlk* for a type of sacrifice but the texts are not decisive (cf. C. H. Gordon, *Ugaritic Textbook* [1965], glossary #1483). More compelling is the mention of *mlkm* at the end of a list of divinities among the first alphabetic tablets discovered in 1929. A tablet from excavations in 1956 contained the same list in syllabic Akkadian in which *mlkm* is represented by "the Maliks" (pl. form), and these *mlkm* come among a group of cult objects or actions which are divinized. It is possible, then, that the *mlkm* gods are divinized *molk* sacrifices.

The major objection to this view is the statement in Lev. 20:5, which condemns those who prostitute themselves by following Molech. Here Molech must be a divinity and not a sacrifice. On the contrary the references to Molech in all the biblical texts can be understood as a divine name.

The term traditionally has been explained, and recently has been defended, as a deliberate misvocalization of the title "King"—referring to the god of the Ammonites—by inserting the vowels of *bōšet* H1425, "shame" (cf. ASHTORETH; ISH-BOSHETH). This title is a divine epithet which enters into the composition of many Phoenician and Hebrew names, where it changes places with proper names of divinities. The epithet is found also under the forms *muluk* and *malik* in the name lists of MARI at the beginning of the 2nd millennium B.C. Accordingly, it may be construed as an alternate form of MILCOM. J. Gray argued that the proper name of the god was Athtar, an astral deity (*I and II Kings: A Commentary*, 2nd ed. [1970], 275ff.).

II. The cult. It usually is assumed that the cult of Molech involved sacrificing the children by throwing them into a raging fire. The expression "passed through [the fire] to Molech" (Lev. 18:21; 2 Ki. 23:10; Jer. 32:35) normally is so interpreted for the following reasons: (1) it is assumed that the same rite is mentioned in 2 Ki. 16:3; 21:6; 23:6; Isa. 30:33; Jer. 7:31; 19:5; Deut. 12:31; (2) this rite is abundantly verified among the Canaanites in both literary texts and artifactual evidence; and (3) there is a significant connection between 2 Ki. 23:10, which informs us that Josiah "desecrated Topheth [incinerator], which was in the Valley of Ben Hinnom, so no one could use it to sacrifice his son or daughter in [*lit.*, to pass his son or daughter through] fire to Molech," and Jer. 7:31, which says, "They have built the high places of Topheth in the Valley of Ben Hinnom to burn their sons and daughters in the fire." The verbal connections between these two passages are so close that "to burn" seems to be equivalent "to pass through the fire."

N. H. Snaith, however, contended that the disputed expression means the children were given up by the parents to grow up and be trained as temple prostitutes (see *VT* 16 [1966], 123–24). His best evidence is that in Lev. 18 the writer throughout the whole chapter is concerned with illegal sexual intercourse, and especially so in vv. 19–23. Moreover, the phrase was so interpreted in the Talmud. The apparently foreign insertion in Lev. 18:21 is difficult to explain (cf. R. de Vaux, *Studies in Old Testament Sacrifice* [1964], 87 n. 137). On the other hand, the rabbis also luridly describe a statue of Moloch according to the first view. The origins and specific character of the Molech cult remain open questions in scholarly research.

(See further G. F. Moore in *JBL* 16 [1897]: 161–65; J. Carcopino in *Révue de l'histoire des religions* 106 [1932-B], 592–99; W. Kornfeld in *Wiener Zeitschrift für die Kunde des Morgenlandes* 61 [1948–52]: 287–313; W. F. Albright, *Archaeology and the Religion of Israel* [1953], 162–64; K. Dronkert, *De Molochdienst in het Oude Testament* [1953]; E. Dhorme in *Anatolian Studies* 6 [1956]: 57; J. Hoftijzer in *VT* 3 [1958]: 288–92; M. Weinfeld in *UF* 4 [1972]: 133–54; G. C. Heider, *The Cult of Molek: A Reassessment* [1985]; *DDD*, 581–85.)
B. K. Waltke

Molek moh′lek. TNIV form of Molech.

Moli moh′li. KJV Apoc. form of Mahli (1 Esd. 8:47).

Molid moh′lid (מוֹלִיד H4582, "descendant" or "begetter"). Son of Abishur and descendant of Judah through Perez and Jerahmeel; his mother's name was Abihail (1 Chr. 2:29).

Moloch moh′lok. See Molech.

molten image. This phrase is used by the KJV and other versions to render the Hebrew word *massēkâ* H5011 (from *nāsak* H5818, "to pour"); it is usually rendered "cast idol" by the NIV. The word refers first of all to an image of a god cut from stone, shaped from clay, or carved from wood, but it also includes images cast from metal (Lev. 19:4; Deut. 27:15). Such an image was made by pouring molten metal, gold, silver, iron, or bronze, over a prepared form or into a mold (Isa. 40:18–20). The term is used of the golden calf made by Aaron (Exod. 32:4) and of the two calves set up at Bethel and Dan (place) by Jeroboam (1 Ki. 14:9). See calf, golden.

By divine commandment the Israelites were explicitly forbidden to make graven images (Exod. 20:4; Deut. 5:8). This commandment also pertained to the making of molten images, the words "graven" and "molten" referring to the manner in which the forbidden image was constructed. The making of such idols, in keeping with the Decalogue, was strictly forbidden by the entire Mosaic law (Exod. 34:17; Lev. 19:4). The prophets also unreservedly condemned it (Isa. 30:22; Hos. 13:2; Hab. 2:18; cf. also Ps. 106:19). The command not to make graven or molten images does not forbid practicing the arts of sculpture, painting, and the like. The prohibition refers only to the practice of making images for the purpose of bringing the deity within human reach. See idolatry.
S. Woudstra

molten sea. See sea, molten.

money. During OT times, the Hebrews did not use coinage to exchange goods and services. Bartering, including precious metals, was used instead.

Silver, for example, would be weighed according to accepted units, such as the SHEKEL. The NT, however, does mention several Greek and Roman COINS. The Roman DENARIUS (equivalent to the Gk. DRACHMA) was the basic unit, being generally regarded as a day's wage for a laborer. One hundred denarii made up one MINA, and sixty minas made up a TALENT. The denarius was divided into sixteen assaria (Matt. 10:29; Lk. 12:6); each assarion into four quadrans (Matt. 5:26; Mk. 12:42; Lk. 12:59); and each quadrans into two lepta (Mk. 12:42; Lk. 12:59; 21:2). See also DIDRACHMA; MITE; MINA; PENNY.

money changer. This term renders Greek *kollybistēs* G3142 (from *kollybos*, "small [copper] coin," the regular term for the fee received by the money changer for his services), which occurs in the story of Jesus' cleansing of the temple when he "overturned the tables of the money changers" (Matt. 21:12; Mk. 11:15; Jn. 2:15; the latter passage, in v. 14, also uses the synonym *kermatistēs* G3048, from *kerma* G3047, "small change").

The function of these money changers was to convert the currency of a worshiper at the Jerusalem TEMPLE into a type of money acceptable for purposes of a sacrificial offering. Since there was no Jewish currency in silver (there apparently had never been any such minted even back in HASMONEAN times), ecclesiastical approval had for some reason been granted to the Tyrian half-shekel or DIDRACHMA, and the Tyrian SHEKEL or tetradrachma (even though they bore the effigy of Baal Melkart, the patron god of TYRE) as acceptable for the temple poll tax, which amounted to a yearly levy of one half shekel per male citizen. (Cf. the episode in Matt. 17:27, where PETER is told to use the shekel he had found in the mouth of the fish he had caught, in order to pay the temple tax for himself and for Jesus.) It may have been necessary for smaller offerings to be converted into acceptable bronze coinage, such as the lepta or MITES minted by the Jewish rulers of the Hasmonean dynasty.

At any rate, granted the legitimacy of this taboo against pagan currency as a medium for sacrifice (in place of clean animals sacrificed on the altar), the money changer seems to have performed a useful function. It could not have been because of anything inherently reproachful in their activity that they aroused Christ's ire in the temple. Undoubtedly they served the convenience of the public, especially where birds, animals, or cake-offerings had to be purchased by city dwellers not possessing livestock of their own. In these transactions it must have been necessary to make small change available if the buyer was not to be cheated, and of course the banker who provided this service was entitled to some sort of a fee, in order to make a living.

There seem to be only two possible grounds on which they incurred our Lord's indignation: either their charges for money changing were excessive and tended to gouge the poor and pious, or else they had their tables set up so close to the section of the temple set apart for worship and sacrifice as to interfere with these sacred functions. On either count, or on both counts, Christ could have leveled the charge of turning the house of God into "a den of robbers." It is likely that Jesus took exception to the corruption which money changers and merchants brought into the temple itself, especially during the highly lucrative PASSOVER season. No doubt priests were often in on the profit, since they approved the exchange.

Money changers evidently sat at tables or benches, stacked high with various types of coins used in the Mediterranean world at the time. It is quite conceivable that the loud and passionate haggling that undoubtedly accompanied this activity of changing money in an oriental setting was completely disturbing to genuine devotion; and when this commotion was augmented by the lowing of

Replica of stone carving on a funerary stela (Hungary, late 2nd cent. A.D.), depicting a money changer and his servant counting daily income.

cattle, the bleating of sheep and goats, and the cooing of pigeons and doves, the resulting hubbub must have made devotional exercises most difficult for the sincere worshiper. At any rate, Jesus found it necessary to clear them all out, and thus relegate them to a suitable distance from the place of sacrifice and prayer. G. L. ARCHER

monkey. See BABOON.

monotheism. The belief that there is only one God. It stands in opposition to polytheism, which acknowledges many gods. With the application of the principle of evolution to the study of history, particularly religious history, the effort has been made to classify all religions on a scale moving from the simple to the sophisticated, and to equate this spectrum with the historical development of the race. On such a scheme, monotheism is the final stage in the evolution of the human religious consciousness. Its "discovery" is said to have been the achievement of the great ethical PROPHETS of Israel, much as the Greek mathematicians discovered the fundamental laws of numbers. The latter displayed a genius for rational abstract thought, the former for religion and ethics.

For anyone who accepts the witness of Scripture, however—and there is nothing in the evidence outside of Scripture that contradicts this witness—the knowledge of the one true God can hardly be the mere product of the interplay of factors in the environment on the social organism of Israel. Israel's doctrine of God is based on historical events that are capable of only one interpretation. By his mighty power God had delivered Israel from Egyptian slavery and made them his elect people. "What other nation is so great as to have their gods near them the way the LORD our God is near us whenever we pray to him?" (Deut. 4:7). For Israel, from the beginning, there could be only this one God. This is why the religious faith of Israel was able to survive even the crisis of the EXILE. It was the God of Israel, not the false gods of ASSYRIA AND BABYLONIA, who was in charge of all these events. The Assyrian was only "the rod of [his] anger" (Isa. 10:5); NEBUCHADNEZZAR, his "servant" (Jer. 25:9); and CYRUS, his "anointed" (Isa. 45:1).

The doctrine of the TRINITY, which is rejected by the great monotheistic religions of Judaism and Islam as a denial of the truth that God is one, really rests on the same foundation as the monotheism of the OT. The concept of the Trinity is not the product of Greek speculation, but rather the result of believing reflection on the great events of the INCARNATION and PENTECOST, which are at the heart of the Christian faith. Because these events are the fulfillment of the promises made to the fathers, the apostles saw no incongruity in identifying themselves as strict monotheists, while at the same time proclaiming that God is the Father, the Son, and the Holy Spirit (cf. 1 Cor. 8:6). It is true that the elaboration of this belief, in terms of the dogma of the Trinity, involves the use of categories of Greek thought. But to say that God is three persons, though one in his essential being, however it may transcend human comprehension, in no way denies, but rather strongly affirms, the unity and oneness of God as a fundamental affirmation of the Christian faith.

If God is the one only true and living God, and if this knowledge rests on his self-disclosure in the events of the incarnation and Pentecost, what of all the peoples of the earth to whom he has not revealed himself as the Redeemer? With respect to this question, the Scriptures teach that God was known to human beings from the beginning (cf. the opening chapters of Genesis), and that even though they have fallen into sin, they are not wholly without a knowledge of the true God. Paul wrote that "since the creation of the world God's invisible qualities—his eternal power and divine nature—have been clearly seen, being understood from what has been made, so that men are without excuse" (Rom. 1:20).

The belief, therefore, in many gods, and the idolatrous practices connected with such beliefs, are the result of the sinner's alienation from the true God, and no matter how widespread and ingrained such beliefs may be, they really constitute no evidence that there are more gods than one. As a matter of fact, even in cultures where there is a belief in many gods, there is sometimes the belief that one of these is above the others; the gods themselves have a god. Researchers in the field of the history of religions have noted the belief in a supreme high god even among primitive peoples.

Joel 2:31]). In a prophecy, Rev. 6:12 sates that "the whole moon turned blood red." The woman of Rev. 12:1 (whether Christ, the Church, or Israel) is pictured as having the moon under her feet, etc. In the eternal state, the new Jerusalem will not need the moon to shine (Rev. 21:23). (See further *DDD*, 585–93.) — W. H. Mare

Moossias moh´uh-si´uhs. KJV Moosias. One of the descendants of Addi who had married foreign women (1 Esd. 9:31; cf. Maaseiah in Ezra 10:30).

Morasthite moh´ruhs-th*it* (מוֹרַשְׁתִּי *H4629*, gentilic of מוֹרֶשֶׁת). A descriptive title applied to Micah the prophet, according to the KJV and some other versions (Jer. 26:18; Mic. 1:1; the NIV and NRSV render "of Moresheth"). See Moresheth Gath.

Mordecai mor´duh-k*i* (מָרְדֳּכַי *H5283*, apparently based on the Babylonian name Marduk). **(1)** An Israelite mentioned among leading individuals who returned from Babylon with Zerubbabel (Ezra 2:2; Neh. 7:7; 1 Esd. 5:8 [KJV, "Mardocheus"]).

(2) Son of Jair and descendant of Benjamin who lived in Susa during the rule of the Persians (Esth. 2:5); his great-grandfather Kish was among those who had been deported from Jerusalem to Babylon by Nebuchadnezzar (v. 6). Mordecai was the protector of Esther, who was the daughter of his uncle Abihail (vv. 7, 15). Esther was chosen as queen by Ahasuerus (Xerxes I), who ruled Persia from 486 to 465 B.C. At the time of the choosing of the queen, Mordecai warned her not to reveal that she was Jewish (v. 10). He kept in constant contact with his cousin and became a prominent man himself, sitting in the gate of the king (v. 19); Esther in turn continued to obey Mordecai as a child would obey her father (v. 20).

Soon after Esther became queen, Mordecai overheard a plot against the king by two of the king's eunuchs, Bigtha(na) and Teresh (Esth. 2:21). He reported this plot to Esther, and the king successfully thwarted their plan (v. 22). At that time, providentially, no further recognition or reward was given Mordecai, but his deed was recorded in the official records of Persia.

When the king promoted Haman among his nobles, Mordecai would not bow to him (Esth. 3:1–4). The reason for his refusal is not given. Perhaps the most likely explanation is that Haman may have been considered a descendant of Israel's ancient enemies, the Amalekites, as his gentilic Agagite suggests; or maybe this title simply is a way of indicating that Haman was full of hatred for the Jewish people (see K. H. Jobes, *Esther*, NIVAC [1999], 119–21). In any case, Haman became angered and sought to destroy all Jews (3:5–6). When Mordecai learned of this evil plot he went into mourning. This attracted Esther's attention and, on inquiry, she learned of the plight of the Jews (4:4–7). Bravely, Mordecai ordered Esther to go to the king for the sake of her people. He did this in spite of the great risk to her should she earn the king's displeasure (4:14).

The hate between Mordecai and Haman increased. Finally, at the suggestion of his wife Zeresh, Haman planned to have Mordecai hanged on a gallows he would make (Esth. 5:14). Providentially again, God stirred the mind of the king to have the book of the chronicles of the kings of Persia read to him on a sleepless night (6:1). He hoped the dull reading of the chronicles would put him to sleep. Instead, it startled him as the chronicler read aloud the record of Mordecai's uncovering the plot against his life some years before. Ironically, Haman was ordered by the king to honor Mordecai before all the people (6:4–11). Then at Esther's banquet it was revealed that Haman plotted to destroy her people. The king was so enraged by this news that he had Haman hanged on his own gallows (7:10).

The authority and glory that once had belonged to Haman now was given to Mordecai (Esth. 8:2). By this new power he was able to annul the former decree against the Jews by a counter decree (8:11). Copies of the decree went to all the provinces of Persia (8:13). Mordecai, now wearing the royal robes of blue and white, led the Jews in celebration of this great deliverance. The Feast of Purim was established on this day. The name Purim came from the term *pûr H7052*, which means "a lot" (9:24). Since lots were to be cast against the Jews, this great deliverance day became known as Purim (9:26). In 2 Macc. 15:36 it is called "Mordecai's day." Mordecai became a man to reckon with in the kingdom of Ahasuerus. He was not only great among the Jews, but found favor also with the king. He always sought the good of his own people (10:3).

The hill of Moreh. (View to the N from Mt. Tabor.)

In secular history there is no mention of the name Mordecai in the annals of King Xerxes. A possible reference to a Marduk, a finance officer in the Persian court of Xerxes' day, is suggested from a CUNEIFORM document, but no solid secular evidence is yet available. (See C. Pfeiffer, *Exile and Return* [1962], 119–23; *ABD*, 4:902–4.)   J. B. SCOTT

Moreh mor´eh (מוֹרֶה *H4622*, "teacher"). **(1)** A place near SHECHEM. When Abram (ABRAHAM) first entered Canaan, he "traveled through the land as far as the site of the great tree of Moreh at Shechem" (Gen. 12:6; NRSV, "the oak of Moreh"; KJV incorrectly, "the plain of Moreh"). There God revealed himself to Abraham with the promise to give Canaan to his descendants, whereupon Abraham responded by building his first altar to the Lord in Canaan. The phrase "the great tree [*ʾēlôn H471*] of Moreh" may also be translated "the teacher's [or diviner's] tree." (However, it is unlikely that this is the same place as the DIVINERS' OAK, or "soothsayers' tree," of Jdg. 9:37; cf. J. Simons, *The Geographical and Topographical Texts of the Old Testament* [1959], 212 n. 194.) It must have been a "holy" tree, and the place an old Canaanite sanctuary. Although it is difficult to understand Abraham's motives for visiting this place, there is no reason to suggest that he recognized the sacred character of the place and willfully adapted himself to it. The reference merely serves to indicate the place where Abraham camped and built his own altar. Elsewhere, the expression "the great trees of Moreh" serves to indicate the general location of Mounts EBAL and GERIZIM (Deut. 11:30). Some have thought that there is a connection with "the oak at Shechem" (Gen. 35:4; cf. Jdg. 9:6).

(2) The "hill of Moreh" was a place near which the Midianites were camping when they were attacked by GIDEON (Jdg. 7:1). This hill was at the E end of the Valley of JEZREEL (6:33) and is generally identified with Jebel Nabi Dahi (sometimes wrongly called the Little Hermon), about 8 mi. NNW of Mount GILBOA, and just S of NAIN.
    P. A. VERHOEF

Moresheth mor´uh-sheth. See MORESHETH GATH.

Moresheth Gath mor´uh-sheth-gath´ (מוֹרֶשֶׁת גַּת *H4628*, "possession of Gath"; LXX, κληρονομίας Γεθ; Vulg., *hereditatem Geth*). Also Moresheth-gath. One of several towns in the SHEPHELAH of JUDAH that were going to be conquered (Mic. 1:14). The passage is full of wordplays, and some believe that this name alludes to the term *mĕʾōreśet* (from *ʾāraś H829* piel, "betroth, become engaged to"; cf. the

This mound (Tell el-Judeideh) may be the site of Moresheth Gath, home of the prophet Micah. (View to the NW.)

pual ptc. in Deut. 22:23). If so, the figure is that of Judah having to part with one of its towns and giving a dowry besides (cf. J. M. P. Smith, *A Critical and Exegetical Commentary on Micah*, ICC [1911, bound with several other Minor Prophets], 48).

It is generally thought that the prophet Micah's gentilic, "the Morasthite" (KJV in Mic. 1:1 and Jer. 26:28, where the NIV and other versions say "of Moresheth"), refers to Moresheth Gath. The addition "Gath" is to define more precisely Moresheth's situation as in the vicinity of, or as belonging to, GATH. According to EUSEBIUS, it was located just E of Eleutheropolis. Some scholars have thought that it is the same as the better known city of MARESHAH (Mic. 1:15; Josh. 15:44; et al.), but most think it was a distinct village and tentatively identify it with the modern Tell el-Judeideh, about 7 mi. SE of Gath and 6 mi. NE of LACHISH (Z. Kallai, *Historical Geography of the Bible* [1986], 381 and 386, prefers Tell ʿEtun, while identifying Tell el-Judeideh with LIBNAH). The MEDEBA map shows a vignette NE of Eleutheropolis with the note: "Morasthi, from which the prophet Micah came." (See further J. Jeremias in *PJ* 29 [1933]: 42–53; K. Elliger in *ZDPV* 57 [1934]: 119ff.)

P. A. VERHOEF

Moriah muh-ri′uh מֹרִיָּה *H5317*, derivation uncertain; by popular etymology, "the place where Yahweh provides [*or* appears]," Gen. 22:14). **(1)** The region to which God instructed ABRAHAM to go so that he might offer up ISAAC on one of its mountains (Gen. 22:2; LXX, *tēn gēn tēn hypsēlēn*, "the high land"; Vulg., *terram Visionis*, "the land of apparition"). The district may have received its name from the incident in which Yahweh *provided* a sacrifice and *appeared* to Abraham (22:8, 14). The SAMARITANS connected Moriah with MOREH (in the vicinity of SHECHEM) so as to identify it with GERIZIM (for a refutation, see James A. Montgomery, *The Samaritans* [1907], 234ff.). The precise location of the mountain is not given in Genesis beyond the statement that it was a three days' journey from BEERSHEBA (22:4).

(2) The rocky hilltop of JERUSALEM N of the City of David (see ZION) where Yahweh appeared (Heb. *nirʾâ*) to DAVID when he presented offerings on the threshing floor of ARAUNAH the Jebusite (2 Chr. 3:1). Some argue that the author of Chronicles is indirectly identifying this hill with the place where Abraham offered Isaac. Such an identification was widely accepted in ancient times (Jos. *Ant.* 1.13.2 §226; 7.13.4 §333; *Jubilees* 18.13; Jerome, *Hebrew Questions on Genesis* [on Gen. 22:2]; and rabbinic literature generally). The Muslim mosque known as the Dome of the Rock presently sits on the site. Many modern scholars, however, regard this identification as unlikely or even impossible, and explain the connection between the two passages in other ways (see *ABD*, 4:905).

B. K. WALTKE

morning sacrifice. See SACRIFICE AND OFFERINGS.

morning star. This term is applied to Venus (occasionally to other bright planets) because it is often visible in the eastern sky before sunrise, heralding the appearance of the sun (see ASTRONOMY II.D). The expression is used by the NIV to render Hebrew *hêlēl H2122* ("shining one"), which occurs only once, in an oracle against the king of BABYLON (Isa. 14:12; NRSV, "Day Star"); see LUCIFER.

In the NT the phrase once renders Greek *phōsphoros G5892* (lit., "light-bringer," but a common term for Venus in Greek literature), which Peter uses as a symbol of Christ's SECOND COMING (2 Pet. 1:19; KJV, "day star"). It also appears twice in Revelation as a literal rendering of the phrase *ho astēr ho prōinos*. In one of these passages (Rev. 22:16), the reference to Jesus is explicit. The other occurrence, in a promise to the church of THYATIRA, is somewhat obscure: "To him who overcomes and does my will to the end, I will give authority over the nations. ... I will also give him the morning star" (2:26–28). Various interpretations have been proposed (cf. G. R. Osborne, *Revelation*, BECNT [2002], 168), but there is likely a connection with 22:16; if so, Christ is promising that those who persevere will share in his coming messianic glory. All three NT passages seem to allude to the prophecy of BALAAM, "A star will come out of Jacob" (Num. 24:17).

morsel. This term is used a number of times in the KJV in the OT, especially in the expression "a morsel of bread" (e.g., Gen. 18:5, where the NIV has "something to eat"), and once in the NT (Heb. 12:16, where the Greek really means "one meal," not "one piece of food"). The NIV uses the word only twice in the expression "choice morsels," which renders a participial form of the rare verb *lāham H4269* (Prov. 18:8; 26:22; NRSV, "delicious morsels," but KJV wrongly, "wounds," as though it were from *hālam H2150*, an old conjectural emendation followed also by Luther).

mortal. As an adjective ("subject to death"), this English term is used by the KJV once in the OT (Job 4:17, where "mortal man" renders the common Heb. noun *ʾĕnôš H632*) and five times in the NT to render the Greek adjective *thnētos G2570* (Rom. 6:12; 8:11; used substantivally in 1 Cor. 15:53, 54; 2 Cor. 4:11; another substantival use, 2 Cor. 5:4, is rendered "mortality" by the KJV). See DEATH; IMMORTALITY. As a noun meaning "human being," the term *mortal* does not occur in the KJV, but is so used a number of times in the NIV, especially in Job (Job 4:17; 9:2; 10:4–5), and very frequently in other modern versions.

mortal sin. This precise expression is not found in the Bible, though it is clear that SIN in itself, and therefore every manifestation of a depraved nature, issues unto DEATH (Rom. 6:23 et al.). In Roman Catholic theology, however, mortal sin is contrasted with "venial" sin, which is seen as less aggravated and therefore much less damaging to the soul than mortal sin. This distinction is not explicitly asserted in Scripture.

In 1 Jn. 5:16–17, the apostle distinguishes between "sin unto death" and "sin not unto death" (the NIV renders, "sin that leads to death"; the NRSV, "mortal sin," which may be misleading). Inasmuch as he directs that no prayer should be offered for the former, this passage has been quite naturally related to Matt. 12:31–32 (and parallels); Heb. 6:4–6; 10:26–31 (sometimes also 2 Pet. 2:20–22). It is not certain that all of these passages refer to the same kind of transgression; but if this be so, the sin in view would appear to be the hardening of the heart against the offer of the divine light in its most unmistakable form. This interpretation commends itself to the evangelical scholar at many points.   R. NICOLE

mortar. This English term has two distinct meanings, both of which occur in the Bible. In the sense of "a utensil for pounding material," especially for the purpose of crushing grain, it renders Hebrew *mĕdōkâ H4521* (Num. 11:8, with reference to the beating of MANNA so that it could be cooked) and *maktēš H4847* (Prov. 27:22, used figuratively with reference to the fool, whose folly cannot be removed even by grinding him in a mortar). With regard to "the Mortar" (Zeph. 1:11 NRSV), see MAKTESH.

The second sense is "a substance used for uniting brick or stone in construction." In this meaning, *mortar* is the proper rendering of Hebrew *ḥōmer* H2817, which also means CLAY (e.g., Job 4:19). According to Gen. 11:3, the builders of the Tower of BABEL used "tar" (*ḥēmār* H2819; NRSV, "bitumen") in place of "mortar." The use of BITUMEN (or asphalt) for mortar is attested in Babylonia by archaeological evidence; and its occurrence in the Valley of SIDDIM (Gen. 14:10 NRSV) beside the JORDAN, near the DEAD SEA, renders its use in Palestine possible. Biblical references and archaeological evidence show that some kind of clay commonly was used for mortar in Egypt and Palestine.

Modern mortar differs from ancient in that it is made of one part by volume of slaked lime and three parts of sand, mixed with enough water to form a paste. When applied to brick or stone it sets, becoming stiff as the water evaporates; then it hardens, as the slaked lime absorbs carbon dioxide from the atmosphere and is converted into calcium carbonate. Mortar in biblical times was sometimes bitumen or asphalt, where this was found in nature, as in Babylonia and in Palestine, though its use for mortar in Palestine is less surely attested. Bitumen is a sticky, pitchy substance occurring as liquid in wells, or exposed in pools where it is more or less hardened. It was used in Egypt for waterproofing PAPYRUS boats and for preserving mummies. In Egypt and Palestine the usual mortar was moistened natural clay, which hardened by exposure to the air. The term *clay* is loosely used in the Bible, referring sometimes to true potter's clay, sometimes to mud or mire of many types. Bitumen was too sticky to be trodden out, but clay, mixed with water, was trodden by barefooted men, until it was the proper consistency for use (cf. Nah. 3:14). E. RUSSELL

mortgage. This English term occurs just once in the Bible, in the context of a time of drought and want: "Others were saying, 'We are mortgaging our fields, our vineyards and our homes to get grain during the famine'" (Neh. 5:3). The verb is *ʿārab* H6842, which is used of pledging or pawning personal property in all other passages (see PLEDGE), but here of real estate, which is put up as collateral for a loan. The root basically refers to exchanging or trading merchandise (the verb is so used in Ezek. 27:9, 27), but it also can be used of becoming surety or guarantor of a loan made to some borrower. Although a specific reference to mortgaging real property occurs only in Neh. 5:3, there can be no question that this was a much-practiced mode of securing loans from the time of the Hebrew conquest and onward. According to the PENTATEUCH, one of the duties of the kinsman-redeemer (see GOEL) was to purchase the mortgaged property of his indigent relative. This was one of the services performed by BOAZ for NAOMI, his dead kinsman's widow (in addition to his LEVIRATE marriage of RUTH). See also BORROW, LEND. G. L. ARCHER

mosaic. This English term refers to a surface ornamentation of designs or pictures, and sometimes inscriptions, made by inlaying in patterns small pieces of colored stone, glass, shell, or other material. (The word derives from Medieval Latin *mūsāicum*, "of the Muses"; it is therefore to be distinguished from *Mosaic* as an adjective derived from the name MOSES.)

Although no Hebrew term in the OT specifically means "mosaic," in Esth. 1:6 a pavement in the palace at SUSA is described as made of porphyry, marble, mother-of-pearl, and precious stones (the NIV and other versions regard this as a "mosaic pavement"). Mosaics were very ancient in MESOPOTAMIA. In the latter half of the 4th millennium B.C. cone-mosaics appear. These were made of terra-cotta, usually 7–8 cm. long, and were thrust into the soft plaster on the walls or other features. The ends were dipped in paint before insertion, and sometimes the heads were inset with colored stones, or sheathed in bronze. An outstanding example is the Pillared Hall at Warka (biblical ERECH). This form of decoration persisted through the Ubaid period. The temple of Nin-khursag at Tell al-ʿUbaid had columns (of palm trunks) with a mosaic sheathing of black, red, and white triangles of mother-of-pearl, red sandstone, and asphalt. The triangular tesserae recall the texture of the tree trunk. A masterpiece of mosaic is the "Standard" from the Royal Cemetery of UR. It is a double-sided panel, with small figures in shell or mother-of-pearl, which are inlaid in bitumen against a mosaic of lapis lazuli. One side shows a battle with chariots and infantry, the other, a victory feast.

Mosaic from the synagogue in Hamat Tiberias, with a dedication to its founder.

Roman mosaics, both pavement and wall, had widespread use as a decoration both stable and impervious to moisture. Only stone tesserae were used for pavements, but glass and gold leaf on stones were used for walls. Mosaics reached their highest point of development in early churches and synagogues, and especially in the Byzantine period. Prime examples are to be seen at ANTIOCH OF SYRIA, Tabgha (near TIBERIAS), GERASA, MEDEBA, and the Beth Alpha synagogue near JEZREEL. The mosaicist's art involved geometric designs and figured compositions, assembled from the basic shapes of the square, star, triangle, lozenge, circle, pelta, and hexagon. Mosaics are (1) decorative, (2) descriptive (telling a story), and (3) identifying (advertising shops, etc.).

(See further M. Avi-Yonah, *The Madeba Mosaic Map* [1954], 18–20; S. Lloyd, *The Art of the Ancient Near East* [1961], passim; A. Graber, *Byzantium* [1966], 102–66; R. Meiggs, *Roman Ostia* [1960], 446–53; M. Ben-Dov and Y. Rappel, *Mosaics of the Holy Land* [1987]; K. M. D. Dunbabin, *Mosaics of the Greek and Roman World* [1999]; R. Talgam and Z. Weiss, *The Mosaics of the House of Dionysos at Sepphoris* [2004]; L. Becker and C. Kondoleon, *The Arts of Antioch: Art Historical and Scientific Approaches to Roman Mosaics* [2005].) M. H. HEICKSEN

Moserah, Moseroth moh-see'ruh, -ruhth (מוֹסֵרָה *H4594*, "bond," also in the pl. form מֹסְרוֹת *H5035*). A place where the Israelites encamped on their journey from Egypt to Canaan (Num. 33:30–31), and where AARON was said to have died (Deut. 10:6). The site is unknown, but it must have been near Mount HOR, by the border of EDOM. Some scholars regard the latter passage as a variant tradition, because elsewhere Aaron is said to have died at Mount Hor itself (Num. 33:38; cf. 20:22). According to KD (*Pentateuch*, 3:245), the problem could be solved by relating the two passages to different journeys: in Deut. 10:6–7 the reference is to the fortieth year, when the Israelites went from KADESH to Mount Hor, encamping in the ARABAH first at the wells of the Jaakanites (see BEEROTH BENE-JAAKAN) and then at Moserah, with Aaron dying on Mount Hor, which was nearby. This would have been the second visit to these places (cf. W. H. Gispen, *He boek Numeri* [1959–64], 2:268). Some, deriving the name Moserah from *yāsar H3579*, suggest that it means "chastisement" because Aaron's death was regarded as a punishment for the trespass at MERIBAH (Num. 20:24; Deut. 32:51); most scholars, however, derive the name from *ʾāsar H673*, "to bind."

P. A. VERHOEF

Moses moh'zis (מֹשֶׁה *H5407*, derivation uncertain, but by popular etymology, "drawn out [of the water]"; Μωϋσῆς *G3707*). According to Exod. 2:10, Moses received his name from PHARAOH's daughter, who said, "I drew him out of the water" (some have argued that the subject of the verbs "she called [his name]" and "she said" is in fact Moses' mother). The Hebrew verb for "draw out" here is *māšâ H5406* (its only other occurrence is in 2 Sam. 22:17 = Ps. 18:16, where the hiphil conjugation is used).

It is often thought, however, that the name is Egyptian, derived from the root *mśy*, "to bear," a common component in theophoric names (e.g., THUTMOSE or Thutmosis, "[the god] Thoth is born"; alternatively, *Moses* could be identified with the noun *mesu* [*mśw*], meaning "child"). Many have speculated that the child was given a compound Egyptian name, such as Ramose(s), and that he dropped the divine component when he later identified with the Hebrews. If so, the meaning given in Exod. 2:10 is a wordplay suggested by the similarity in sound between the Hebrew and Egyptian words (on the linguistic problems, see J. G. Griffiths in *JNES* 12 [1953]: 225–31, summarized by J. K. Hoffmeier in *ISBE*, rev. ed., 3:417).

Alternatively, if Moses was originally a Hebrew name, perhaps it was Pharaoh's daughter who assimilated it to the Egyptian form (cf. K. A.

Kitchen in *NBD*, 783–84; Y. Muchiki, *Egyptian Proper Names and Loanwords in North-West Semitic* [1999], 217). In any case, while the name occurs more than 750 times in the OT, no further explanation is given; and like the names of some other prominent OT characters, it is given to only one person, the great leader and lawgiver of Israel.

    I. Background
   II. The first forty years
      A. Birth
      B. Infancy
      C. Life in Egypt
      D. The flight
  III. The second forty years
      A. Moses in Midian
      B. Moses and Jethro
      C. Moses at the bush
      D. Moses returns to Egypt
  IV. The third forty years
      A. Moses and Pharaoh
      B. Moses and Israel
   V. The fortieth year
      A. Failure at Kadesh Barnea
      B. Defeat of Arad and the Amorites
      C. Arrival at Jordan
      D. Moses' valedictory: Deuteronomy

I. Background. With the word "Now" (Exod. 1:1 KJV; Heb. *wĕ-*), the historian passes from the death of Joseph, who saved the PATRIARCHS from starvation in Canaan by bringing them down into Egypt, to the time of Moses, who led their descendants forth from bondage. He first lists the tribes who were in Egypt and stresses their amazing fruitfulness (v. 7), the rise of a king who knew not Joseph, the fears aroused in the heart of the reigning pharaoh by their increase, the steps he took to control it, the refusal of the midwives to obey his command to destroy the male infants, and finally the command to his own people to drown the Hebrew boys (v. 22).

Thus the stage is set for the birth of Moses, which occurred nearly 300 years after the death of Joseph. This background is sketched very briefly. Nothing is said about Egypt except what directly concerns Israel. The names of the two Hebrew midwives and of the two cities that the Israelites built are given, but not the name of the pharaoh who knew not Joseph nor of the pharaoh who oppressed Israel, nor of the princess who became the foster mother of Moses. The writer omits them as immaterial to his story.

II. The first forty years

A. Birth. Moses is introduced to the reader in a striking way. Sometimes the ancestry of a person is given in some detail; here it is stated in the broadest of terms: "Now a man of the house of Levi married a Levite woman" (Exod. 2:1). From the words that follow, "and she became pregnant and gave birth to a son," one might infer that Moses was their first child. This inference is promptly corrected by the mention of a sister whose name is not mentioned until much later (15:20), but who was old enough to watch over the babe in the little ark and shrewd enough to seize upon the remark of the royal princess concerning the parentage of the babe and produce the mother of the foundling to serve as its nurse. There is a touch of irony in the result that the Hebrew mother was paid by Pharaoh's daughter to nurse her own child. Moreover, Pharaoh aimed to destroy every male child born in Israel, with the result that his own daughter took under her protection the Hebrew baby who was to become the future deliverer of his people, and she even adopted him as her son. (For a detailed study that traces interpretive developments in postbiblical Judaism, see J. Cohen, *The Origins and Evolution of the Moses Nativity Story* [1993].)

B. Infancy. The statement that "the child grew older" is indefinite. The mother probably kept the child for two or three years (cf. 1 Sam. 1:19–24). Perhaps she kept him longer, bringing him frequently to the princess, who must not be allowed to forget him, while at the same time cultivating in his young heart a love and loyalty to the race from which he sprang. Regarding these formative years, however, nothing is related. Moses had an older brother, AARON, who would later be proposed to Moses as his spokesman (Exod. 4:14) and sent to meet him at the mount of God (v. 27). Aaron was three years Moses' senior (7:7), a statement of special interest because it implies that the command that all male children be drowned (1:22) was

Basket coffin (Egypt, 1st–3rd dynasties). Moses' mother may have placed her son in a basket coffin like this one.

not given until after Aaron was born. The names of Moses' father and mother are mentioned later (6:20). All these facts that are gradually introduced serve to show how much is omitted in the brief statement with which ch. 2 begins.

C. Life in Egypt. Nearly forty years lie between the "grew" of Exod. 2:10 and the "grown up" of v. 11. With reference to this period, STEPHEN stated that "Moses was educated in all the wisdom of the Egyptians and was powerful in speech and action" (Acts 7:22), which implies that Moses received an education befitting an Egyptian prince. The parents "were not afraid of the king's edict" (Heb. 11:23), which may indicate that they were willing to risk the danger of detection before the baby was hidden in the bulrushes, or else that after his adoption by the princess, they used every opportunity to instill in the heart of their child a love for his people and his God. The biblical account devotes only fifteen verses to this formative period of Moses' life.

Five verses now suffice to describe its dramatic and unhappy conclusion, yet they are significant because of the light they throw on the development of Moses' character. The comment, "One day, after Moses had grown up" (Exod. 2:11), introduces two closely related incidents that marked the close of the first forty years of Moses' life (Acts 7:23). Moses "went out where his own people were and watched them at their hard labor. He saw an Egyptian beating a Hebrew, one of his own people." This is the first expression of what became a master motive in Moses' life: his love for his Israelite brethren (Heb. 11:23–24). His love may have been aroused suddenly by the act of injustice which he imprudently punished too severely, but it seems more probable that it was only the sudden unleashing of a passionate desire which he had long cherished and which came to sudden expression.

Probably this was not a sudden act on Moses' part. He may often have watched the Hebrews toiling at their burdens, and the word *people* suggests how powerfully kinship and parental teaching may have influenced this adopted son of an Egyptian princess. It reveals Moses as a man of powerful emotions, impulsive in action, yet he was now a mature man of forty, to whom such a scene must have been quite familiar. He then assumed the role of deliverer. His response was not one of uncontrollable anger, for he first glanced "this way and that" to make sure no one could see him. He then "killed" the Egyptian who had been "beating" his countryman (Exod. 2:12). The same Hebrew verb is used for both actions (*nākâ H5782*, hiphil, "to smite"), but Moses' blow was deadly, so he endeavored to cover up his violent act by burying his victim in the sand.

D. The flight. "The next day he went out" (Exod. 2:13). Was it to determine whether his act had been discovered? If so, he soon found out the facts. For an attempt to play the role of "peacemaker" between two of his fellow Hebrews brought upon him the accusation of murder: "Are you thinking of killing me as you killed the Egyptian?" (v. 14). The tragedy in this charge is brought out by the words of Stephen: "Moses thought that his own people would realize that God was using him to rescue them, but they did not" (Acts 7:25). So Moses fled for his life. It may seem a little strange that Moses made no effort to excuse or justify his conduct. He was a man of princely rank among the Egyptians, and his victim apparently was not a man of any prominence, possibly at most only an Egyptian "taskmaster." It would certainly seem that he might have been able to "brazen it out" before Pharaoh. Apparently Moses did not think so; and he already may have shown his sympathy with his oppressed people too plainly for his own safety. At any rate his fear was fully justified—Pharaoh sought to slay him. So Moses "fled from Pharaoh" (Exod. 2:15).

The travels of Moses.

III. The second forty years

A. Moses in Midian. Forty years had passed swiftly (Acts 7:23). This adopted son of an Egyptian princess now sat by a well in the land of MIDIAN, an exile from the court of Pharaoh and with a price on his head. Again the situation serves to reveal the man. While he was resting, seven maidens came to the well and he watched them draw water for their flock. Then he saw a group of shepherds come and drive the girls away from the troughs. Moses might well have said to himself, "This is no concern of mine. I am sitting here a wanderer and fugitive as a result of meddling with other people's affairs. These girls and their sheep are nothing to me." Instead Moses stood up and rescued them from the roughness of the shepherds (Exod. 2:17). Moses' act was not merely an expression of kindness and sympathy but also an evidence of high courage. It also indicates that there was something in his appearance and bold intervention that overawed the shepherds, who apparently quailed before a single unknown stranger who had the valor to oppose them.

The daughters may have thanked him, but they left him. They called him "an Egyptian" (Exod. 2:19) and probably were wary of foreigners, so their father had to make amends for their lack of oriental hospitality. In this incident there is not the slightest suggestion of any prior connection or contact of Moses with JETHRO or the Midianites. It was as a total stranger that this Egyptian came to this locality, and he was treated as such.

B. Moses and Jethro. In a compressed narrative (Exod. 2:21–22) we are told that Moses accepted Jethro's offer and agreed to stay in his home, that he married one of Jethro's daughters, ZIPPORAH, and that she gave birth to a son. The name given his first child, GERSHOM—which Moses explained with the words, "I have become an alien [*gēr H1731*] in a foreign land"—may suggest that Moses was far from happy in his new environment. This second period of forty years (Acts 7:30) concludes with a reference to the homeland from which Moses had been forced to flee: "During that long period [*lit.*, in those many days], the king of Egypt died"

(Exod. 2:23). The date is not given, but it was probably toward the end of the forty years (cf. NRSV, "After a long time"), since it was Pharaoh's death that prepared the way for Moses' return to Egypt.

C. Moses at the bush. The first two forty-year periods of Moses' life, both of which end in a startling and climactic event, have been largely covered by a single chapter of Exodus. The event with which the second period ends, however, introduces and determines the whole of the third period of forty years that is to follow. It begins by describing what may have been Moses' chief occupation for forty years: "Now Moses was tending the flock of Jethro his father-in-law," and by slow stages he led the sheep "to Horeb, the mountain of God" (Exod. 3:1; it is uncertain whether the name "mountain of God" is used proleptically, anticipating what later would happen).

Perhaps he had led the flock here many times before, but now something wonderful happened. The call of Moses is perhaps the most revealing—as it was the most momentous—event in his entire life. The angel of the Lord appeared to Moses "in flames of fire within a bush" (Exod. 3:2). Moses no doubt had noticed often that a thorn bush burns rapidly and with a great crackling (Eccl. 7:6), so he marveled that the bush kept on burning. "I will go over and and see this strange sight—why the bush does not burn up" (Exod. 3:3). When he approached, God called to him and warned him that he was on sacred ground. Moses not only put off his shoes as commanded, but also hid his face "because he was afraid to look at God" (v. 6)—an act of reverence and awe.

Then God revealed himself as the God of Moses' forebears, of Abraham, Isaac, and Jacob, and told Moses that he had heard the cry of their descendants and had come to deliver them. He then made a truly amazing proposal to Moses: "I am sending you to Pharaoh to bring my people the Israelites out of Egypt" (Exod. 3:10). Forty years had gone by since Moses, an important figure at Pharaoh's court, had slain one Egyptian for mistreating one Hebrew and had tried to make peace between two of his fellow Israelites. Now suddenly he was challenged to undertake on a vast scale what he had so signally failed to achieve in a small way.

Little wonder that Moses replied, "Who am I, that I should go to Pharaoh and bring the Israelites out of Egypt?" (v. 11). If Moses' reply was exactly what one should expect from someone in his position, the answer of the Lord was quite startling: "I will be with you. And this will be the sign to you that it is I who have sent you: When you have brought the people out of Egypt, you will worship God on this mountain" (v. 12).

The sign was a double challenge to Moses: to his faith in the God of his fathers and to his love of his people, a people who on his first attempt to serve them had met him with hostility and rejection. Moses at first apparently parried the challenge by asking what name he should give to the God whom he was to represent to the people as their deliverer. He asked the question as if he meant to imply that he knew the name of the God of his fathers, but was not sure just how he should speak of him to the people when they ask the name of this God who will deliver them. Perhaps he was asking the question as much for himself as for them. The answer was, "I AM WHO I AM" (Exod. 3:14); the Hebrew can also be rendered, "I will be what I will be."

This language suggests the immutable God, who is unchangeable in his being, the same yesterday, today, and forever—the same as when he called ABRAHAM to go forth from Ur of the Chaldees to the land of promise. Or it may stress rather the activity and energy of this God of the fathers, who will act sovereignly and effectively in behalf of his people in the future as he has done of old. Then the Lord at once used the well-known name, "The LORD [*yhwh* H3378], the God of your fathers" (Exod. 3:15), and added: "This is my name for ever, the name by which I am to be remembered from generation to generation." Hence the Tetragrammaton (four-consonant word) is properly viewed as the memorial or COVENANT name of the God of Israel. See GOD, NAMES OF; I AM.

The command then was repeated that Moses go to the Israelites and announce to them God's promise of deliverance and of entrance into the good land promised to their fathers. Moses was given the assurance that they would obey and that he would go with them to Pharaoh to request permission for a three days' journey into the wilderness to worship the God of their fathers who had appeared to them through Moses. The request they were to propose was modest, designed to show the unreasonableness of Pharaoh's refusal; and they were to make it as a request, not as a demand (Exod. 3:18; the Heb. particle *nā᾽* H5528 is sometimes translated with "please," as in 4:13). But they were to be told that Pharaoh would not let them go "unless a mighty hand compels him." Then God's purpose to use force to affect the deliverance is plainly stated, and the result would be that Pharaoh would let the people go (3:20).

Moses raised the natural objection that the people would not believe that God had sent him to deliver them from Pharaoh. The Lord gave him three signs: his rod becomes a serpent, his hand becomes leprous, and the water turns into blood. There is a striking difference between the sign given Moses for himself (Exod. 3:12) and these signs for the people and for Pharaoh. The latter signs appeal to the physical senses; they are ocular proof of the power of God; they are intended to *compel* belief, to certify Moses as the servant of a higher power, the God of their fathers. Moses' sign was a challenge to faith in God and to love of neighbor.

Furthermore, these signs also represented a definite challenge to Moses. The venomous serpent terrified Moses and he "fled" from it. Yet he obeyed, apparently without demur, the command to take it by the tail; and the wriggling, hissing snake became again his familiar shepherd's rod. Leprosy is a terrible disease. The sight of his leprous hand must have filled Moses with loathing and fear. Yet he put it again into his bosom, and it became clean. Water turned to blood was a disgusting thing, undrinkable as it was later to prove (Exod. 7:20–21). Fear, courage, and obedience all were involved in these simple tests, and Moses stood the test. One need not present a detailed argument for the reality of these signs. They are represented as supernatural and form an integral part of that series of mighty acts by which the God of Israel delivered his people from seemingly hopeless bondage (Deut. 34:11).

Moses raised still another objection: he was not qualified for the task to which God was calling him. He never had been "eloquent" (Exod. 4:10; lit., "a man of words"), and God's call to extraordinary service had not changed this limitation in any way.

God's answer was that human speech is God-given, as are all human faculties. Despite this indisputable fact, which was supported by the promise that God would teach him what to say, Moses still resisted with the words, "O Lord, please send someone else to do it" (v. 13), meaning, "anyone but me." So God in anger and also in compassion gave him as a spokesman his brother Aaron, who would be to him a "mouth" while Moses would be to Aaron as God (v. 16). Finally, Moses was to take the staff, the serpent rod, with him in order to perform these signs, and others far greater than he had yet performed (v. 17).

D. Moses returns to Egypt. Moses returned to Jethro, told him nothing of the divine commission that he had received, offered a plausible and adequate excuse (cf. 1 Sam. 16:2–3) for a visit to Egypt, and received Jethro's consent, as well as God's assurance that it was safe for him to return (Exod. 4:18–19). We read that he put his wife and sons on a donkey and set out for Egypt with the staff of God in his hand (v. 20; the reference to a single donkey suggests that both children were quite young, possibly indicating that he did not receive Zipporah as his wife until toward the end of the forty years, or else that she, like RACHEL, had to wait a long time until the crown of motherhood was given her). Although Moses was forewarned that his attempt to secure Pharaoh's consent to his mission would fail, yet he also was told what would be God's final word to Pharaoh—the slaying of the first-born (vv. 21–23).

As Moses was returning to Egypt, a strange thing happened that throws a little more light on his life in Midian and supports the view that Moses' children were very young at that time (Exod. 4:24–26). The incident at the inn is best understood as indicating that Moses had failed to circumcise the baby before leaving home. This may have been due partly to haste and preoccupation with the mission that had been given him. But it was more probably due to Zipporah's objection to the performance of the rite. Whether she had objected in the case of Gershom, we do not know. Here at the inn, when she realized that Moses' life was in danger and apparently felt that she was responsible, she performed the rite herself, but evidently with great reluctance (as is shown by her words, twice repeated, "you are a bridegroom of blood to me"). Whatever the reason, Moses had sinned in failing to perform the covenant rite of CIRCUMCISION, which was required of every Israelite under penalty of death (Gen. 17:13–14).

Before Moses arrived in Egypt, the Lord sent Aaron (first mentioned in Exod. 4:14) to meet him (v. 27). It is perhaps significant that they met at the mountain of God. This apparently involved a considerable detour. It may mean that Moses wanted to visit again the spot where God had called and commissioned him and thus to gain fresh confidence and strength in preparation for the conflict that lay ahead of him. There at the mount Aaron met Moses "and kissed him," an act of affection not often mentioned in the OT, and which showed the strong feeling of kinship that united these brothers who had been parted for forty years. Moses had much to tell Aaron—"everything the Lord had sent him to say, and also about all the miraculous signs he had commanded him to perform" (v. 28).

IV. The third forty years. If Moses' slaying of the Egyptian and his flight from Egypt marked the close of the first period of Moses' life, the call he received at the mount of God may be regarded as marking the ending of the second period. If so, the third begins with Moses' entering upon the God-assigned task of delivering Israel from Egyptian bondage. This period then consists of two parts that somewhat overlap. The first is the conflict with Pharaoh, which ends with the triumph song of Exod. 15. The second phase is the contest with Israel, which aptly is described and summarized by Moses' own words, "You have been rebellious against the Lord ever since I have known you" (Deut. 9:24). This struggle fully occupied Moses' mind and heart from the day of his call to the day of his death.

A. Moses and Pharaoh

1. The first request. After Moses and Aaron had accredited themselves to the elders and people of Israel (Exod. 4:29–31), and Aaron had performed his proper role, acting and speaking for Moses, they at once presented themselves before Pharaoh with the Lord's demand: "This is what the Lord, the God of Israel, says: 'Let my people go [*lit.*, Send my people away], so that they may hold a festival to me in the desert'" (5:1; the idea is not expressed as courteously here as in 3:18). The demand was at first a moderate one, but it was met with disdain and flatly denied: "Who is the Lord, that I should obey him and let Israel go? I do not know the Lord and I will not let Israel go" (5:2). So the notion of "letting go" (i.e., sending away) becomes the issue, the *mot de combat* between the God of Israel and Pharaoh, king of Egypt. Pharaoh's first step was to charge the Hebrews with idleness and to make their task more arduous; now they were not to be supplied with straw, yet they were to make just as many bricks as before. When the Israelite "foremen" (i.e., scribes or tally-keepers, Heb. *šāṭar* H8853) were thus ill-treated (v. 14), they complained to Moses and Aaron (vv. 20–21). Moses carried the complaint to the Lord and bitterly objected that instead of the Lord helping Israel as promised they are worse off than ever. Moses had lost the preliminary skirmish!

2. The contest with Pharaoh. "Then the Lord said to Moses, 'Now you will see what I will do to Pharaoh: Because of my mighty hand he will let them go; because of my mighty hand he will drive them out of his country'" (Exod. 6:1). That the conflict is now to begin in earnest is indicated by the fact that, as if in answer to Pharaoh's contemptuous words, his opponents are now carefully identified.

Painting from the tomb of a nobleman (Rekhmine) who died during the Egyptian New Kingdom period (c. 1500 B.C.). It shows workers making bricks from mud and straw.

First is the God of Israel, who identifies himself with the words, "I am the Lord [YHWH]: I appeared to Abraham, to Isaac and to Jacob as God Almighty [El Shaddai], but by my name the Lord I did not make myself known to them" (Exod. 6:3). This statement seems clearly to imply that the God of the fathers is now to manifest his redemptive power by deeds of covenant faithfulness mightier than any which the patriarchs had known or experienced. The meaning of these words has been much debated. R. D. Wilson (in *PTR* 22 [1924]: 119), after a thorough study of this passage in the original Hebrew and in the versions, proposed the following rendering: "And God spake unto Moses and said unto him: I am Jehovah and I appeared unto Abraham, unto Isaac, and unto Jacob in the character of the God of Might (or, mighty God), and in the character of my name Jehovah I did not make myself known unto them" (alternatively, the last part may be rendered as a question). Wilson added, "Consequently, it is unfair and illogical to use a forced translation of Exodus 6:3 in support of a theory that would destroy the unity of authorship and the Mosaic origin of the Pentateuch."

In view of the failure of their first meeting with Pharaoh, the Lord reaffirmed his promises to the people, assuring them of his entire awareness of their distressing situation and his purpose to rescue them. When Moses gave this reassurance to the people, they were too dispirited to listen to him. When Moses was again told to demand the release of Israel, he complained that it was useless to do so. For if the people would not listen to him, how could he expect Pharaoh to do so? Yet the Lord simply repeated his purpose of deliverance.

Second, the Lord's champions are identified by means of a brief genealogy, showing the descent of Moses and Aaron from the "heads of their families" (Exod. 6:14–27; note the repetition in the last two verses, "It was this same Aaron and Moses. ... It was the same Moses and Aaron"). The narrative continues with a repetition of the Lord's instruction to Moses to speak to Pharaoh, but again Moses pleads his incompetence: "Behold, I am of uncircumcised lips; how then shall Pharaoh listen to me?" (v. 30 RSV; NIV, "I speak with faltering lips"). "Uncircumcised" recalls the giving of the covenant sign to Abraham (Gen. 17) and perhaps indicates also that Moses remembers the near tragic episode at the inn (Exod. 4:24–26). The use of the word here in a figurative sense is noteworthy. Then follows the amazing statement: "See, I have made you like God to Pharaoh, and your brother Aaron will be your prophet" (7:1)—what God says, the prophet says.

The controversial issue of God's hardening the heart of Pharaoh was first referred to in Exod. 4:21, and now was to be repeated more than a dozen times. Sometimes it was used of the state of Pharaoh's heart (7:14, 22; 8:19; 9:7). Sometimes it is stated that Pharaoh hardened his heart (8:15, 32; 9:34); more often, that God hardened or would harden it (4:21; 7:3; 9:12; 10:1, 20, 27; 11:10; 14:4, 8). The best commentary on this subject is the biblical one given in Rom. 9–11, ending with the wonderful doxology that celebrates the "wisdom and knowledge of God" (Rom. 11:33).

The ten plagues then were sent upon Egypt to show the omnipotence of the God of Israel, his sovereign control over nature, and to convince Pharaoh and the Egyptians of the folly of resisting the divine will. See PLAGUES OF EGYPT. It is pointed out again and again that the aim of these divine judgments was that Pharaoh and his people might "know" (i.e., come to understand) the power of the God of Israel (Exod. 7:5, 17; 8:10, 22; 9:14, 29; 11:7; 14:18) and that Israel might know it also (6:7; 10:2; 11:7; 14:31; cf. 29:46; 31:13). Pharaoh's first reply to the demand that he free the Israelites had been, "Who is the Lord that I should obey him and let Israel go? I do not know the Lord and I will not let Israel go" (5:2). The plagues were sent to enlighten his ignorance and to break down his stubborn will. Furthermore it was no mere chance that brought about this confrontation of Pharaoh with the God of Israel. To this very God whom he defied Pharaoh owed his throne and power (9:16; cf. Rom. 9:17).

The last plague was the most terrible of all. It is introduced by the words, "I will bring one more plague on Pharaoh and on Egypt." It would accomplish what all the others had failed to do. Not merely would Pharaoh let Israel go: "he will drive you out completely" (Exod. 11:1). That matters had come to a head is indicated by what had just taken place; Pharaoh had dismissed Moses and threatened him with death if he came before him again.

In the case of all the plagues that preceded, Moses and Aaron played an important but a rather impersonal role; here appear two personal touches. One is the statement that "Moses himself was highly regarded in Egypt by Pharaoh's officials and by the people" (Exod. 11:3). The other is that Moses left Pharaoh "hot with anger" (11:8). Moses had been greatly tried by Pharaoh's vacillation, by his persistent refusals to yield to the demands made of him in the name of Moses' God. Finally Moses' wrath found vigorous expression. If Pharaoh would not yield, his own people would implore Moses to leave. Pharaoh would not yield. The Lord hardened Pharaoh's heart in order that he might not yield until the sovereign power of the God of Israel was fully manifested in the last and most terrible plague (11:9–10), the death of the FIRSTBORN.

The death of all the firstborn children evoked such a reaction from the Egyptians that Pharaoh was compelled to release the Israelites. Under Moses' leadership they celebrated the PASSOVER and marched out of Egypt, taking with them their children, cattle, household goods, and the bones of Joseph. See EXODUS, THE. The statement, "Moses took the bones of Joseph with him" (Exod. 13:19), suggests that this was an act of piety Moses performed without receiving special instruction from God. Amid all the confusion and the many demands upon his time and leadership, Moses thought of the oath that Joseph, looking forward confidently to this event, had imposed on his brethren; now after a lapse of centuries Moses fulfilled this sacred obligation. This mention of what Moses did, apparently on his own initiative, is especially interesting and significant as affording a glimpse into his sense of personal responsibility.

3. The pillar of cloud and of fire. In Exod. 13:21 this supernatural guide is first mentioned which was to lead the children of Israel on their journeyings to the land of promise. The pillar represented the manifested presence of God; and three times the angel of the Lord is referred to as being in it (14:19; 23:20; 32:34). Apparently the pillar varied greatly in size. In 14:19 it is said to have separated the Israelites from the army of Pharaoh; in 33:9 it stood at the door of the TABERNACLE and the Lord talked with Moses from it. In Num. 12:5 it is called a "pillar of cloud" through which the Lord spoke to Moses, Aaron, and Miriam. More frequently it is referred to as "the cloud"; and in 9:15–23 occurs the fullest account of it (cf. 10:11–12, 33–36; Deut. 1:33).

The chief purpose of the cloud was guidance, or rather the manifested presence of God. The mention of the ARK OF THE COVENANT in that connection (Num. 10:33) indicates that the cloud then hung suspended above the ark. There are frequent allusions to the GLORY of the Lord as manifesting itself to Israel in the cloud (Exod. 16:10). Numbers 10:33–36 describes impressively how Moses at the beginning and ending of each journey sought the guidance of the Lord during the years of wandering. This manifestation in the cloud and pillar was continuous (Exod. 13:22), preparing for and following the tremendous theophany at Sinai.

The guiding cloud led the Israelite host into a situation in which they were trapped between the sea and the pursuing chariotry of Pharaoh; and when the latter drew near, the Israelites were terrified and bewailed their perilous state (Exod. 14:11–12; cf. 5:21; 6:9). Moses was not dismayed; he encouraged them with words of the utmost confidence: "Do not be afraid. Stand firm and you will see the deliverance of the LORD" (14:13). Israel's extremity was God's opportunity! Israel was to go forward to the sea and Moses was to open up a path through the sea, a tremendous challenge to Moses' faith! Israel would pass through it on dry ground. The Egyptians would follow after them to their own destruction. Israel passed through the sea safely; Pharaoh's army was drowned in the returning waters. Israel saw "the great power" of the Lord and believed in him and in his servant Moses (14:31). Then Moses and the people sang a paean of triumphant praise to the God who had so wonderfully delivered them.

B. Moses and Israel. Pharaoh and the Egyptians were finally beaten; the chariotry of Egypt was overwhelmed in the returning waters, never to trouble Israel again (Exod. 14:13). Then began Moses' struggle with Israel, signs of which had already plainly appeared (5:21; 14:11). This far longer struggle proved a greater testing of Moses' patience and faith, and of his love of God and for his people, than the one which preceded it.

1. The murmuring in the wilderness. Having seen the great work of deliverance and recognizing the hand of God in it under the leadership of Moses (Exod. 14:31), three days later the people murmured against Moses saying, "What are we to drink?" (15:24). This time they were supplied from the waters of MARAH. The trial of their obedience came again in the wilderness of Sin when they bemoaned their departure from Egypt (16:12); there they were provided with quail and manna; and they saw the glory of the Lord for the first time (vv. 7, 10). The QUAIL are mentioned only briefly as a single occurrence (v. 13), while the MANNA that was their food for nearly forty years is fully described (vv. 14–36). Again they murmured because of thirst (17:1) and they were supplied with water from the rock at Horeb (v. 6). There they also were given a military victory over AMALEK under circumstances that should have greatly increased their confidence in Moses as the servant of their God.

2. Jethro's visit. At this point Jethro came to see Moses, bringing Moses' wife and sons with him, having heard of the Lord's deliverance of Israel from Egypt (Exod. 18:1–4). Jethro rejoiced and declared, "Now I know that the LORD is greater than all other gods, for he did this to those who had treated Israel arrogantly" (v. 11). Jethro's joy in the Lord's victory and his sharing in the communal meal with the elders of Israel does not imply, as some claim, that Jethro was a worshiper of Yahweh and that he at this time inducted Moses and the elders into the worship of his god. The advice he gave Moses (vv. 13–23) had to do entirely with secular affairs; and in following it Moses merely freed himself from the deciding of matters of minor importance. Then Jethro left Moses and returned to his home. He did not accompany Israel to Sinai. He had no part in the ratification of the covenant there.

3. The theophany at Sinai. The tremendous and terrifying scene that accompanied the giving of the law at SINAI provides further insight into the character of Moses. The awesomeness of the spectacle is described (Exod. 19:18). When the Lord called Moses to come up to the top of Sinai, he obeyed; God then told Moses to go down and warn the people not to draw near to it (v. 20). When the Lord uttered the TEN COMMANDMENTS his voice so terrified the people that they asked that God speak to them only through Moses, "or we will die" (20:18–19). The NT states that so terrifying was the sight that even Moses said, "I am trembling with fear" (Heb. 12:21). Of this fear in Moses' heart nothing is said in the exodus account. It simply states that Moses calmed the people and that while they stood afar off, "Moses approached the thick darkness where God was" (Exod. 20:21).

4. Aaron and the seventy elders. The difference between Moses and the rest of the people, including the seventy elders and Aaron and his sons, is emphasized by the fact that while these representatives of the people were to come up and worship afar off, Moses alone was to come near to the Lord. This ceremony followed the solemn ratification of the covenant, which involved the reading of the book, the solemn acceptance by the people, and the sprinkling of "the blood of the covenant" (Exod. 24:8). Then these representatives of the people went up into the mount. There "they saw the God of Israel" (v. 10), but apparently all they saw was what looked like a sapphire footstool, "a pavement" under the feet of Deity; and they "ate and drank" (v. 11).

Moses then spent forty days in God's presence, and during this time he neither ate nor drank. Like his Lord, Moses had meat to eat that the people knew not of (Jn. 4:32). The mention of JOSHUA in Exod. 24:13–14 and in 32:17 indicates that he was near Moses during the first forty days, while in the case of the second forty-day period it is stated expressly that no one was to be with him or even on the mountain (34:3), during which time Joshua was left in charge of the tent (33:11).

5. Moses and the tabernacle. After the tremendous scene that attended the proclaiming of the Decalogue and the sight of the glory of their God which was given to Aaron and the seventy elders, the glory abode upon Mount Sinai for seven days. Then Moses was summoned to come up to the mount. He left Aaron and Hur in charge (Exod. 24:14), and they apparently returned with the elders to the camp. "Then Moses entered the cloud as he went on up the mountain," where he stayed "forty days and forty nights" (v. 18). The purpose of his long stay there was that he might receive God's instructions for the construction of the TABERNACLE: "Make this tabernacle and all its furnishings exactly like the pattern I will show you" (25:9, 40: cf. Heb. 8:5). Finally God gave Moses the tablets of stone on which the testimony was "inscribed by the finger of God" (Exod. 31:18).

6. The first apostasy. Later, while Moses was in the mount receiving instructions as to the conditions under which their God would dwell in their midst, the people apostatized from this God, whom they had promised to obey. "Come, make us gods who will go before us" (Exod. 32:1). They had lived in such an environment of IDOLATRY for centuries that it had left its mark on them. And Aaron, Moses' brother, whose glorious apparel and sacred duties had been described to Moses on the mount (chs. 28–30), tamely acquiesced (32:2) and made a molten calf. When the people said, "These are your gods, O Israel, who brought you up out of Egypt," Aaron announced, "Tomorrow there will be a festival to the LORD" (vv. 4–5). See CALF, GOLDEN.

In this terrible situation, it was no wonder that the Lord at once revealed to Moses what had taken place and threatened to destroy Israel. Moses at once interceded with God for the deliverance of his people. When he descended the mountain, he was filled with great anger upon seeing what had taken place, and he destroyed the tablets of the Decalogue, ground the golden image to powder, scattered it on the water and forced the people to drink it (Exod. 32:19–20). Then he turned upon Aaron himself, demanding an explanation for this "great sin" (v. 21). After hearing Aaron's lame and fainthearted explanation, Moses called for volunteers to execute the Lord's judgment on the idolaters, an impartial judgment that would fall upon all who had been guilty, whether Levites or laypeople. The men of Levi responded and they slew about 3,000 men, an act of loyalty to Yahweh for which they were later praised and rewarded (Deut. 33:9). That Aaron himself was spared from death was due to Moses' special intercession for him (9:20).

7. Moses' intercession. Then Moses returned to the Lord, confessed Israel's "great sin" (Exod. 32:31), and requested that if it could not be forgiven he might be blotted out along with the rest of his people (v. 32). Obtaining God's pardon for chastened Israel, he received the command to lead the people to Canaan (v. 34). In this incident there is a deeper insight into the character of Moses. Moses did not try to minimize or excuse the sin of calf worship either for Aaron or for the people. It was a "great sin." In reply to the Lord's amazing offer (v. 10) to substitute him for Israel and make of him a great nation in place of unworthy Israel (a proposal which doubtless was intended to be a test of Moses' love for his people), he proceeded to appeal to God's love for the nation, as shown in his earlier deliverance of Israel from Egypt in fulfillment of the promises made to the patriarchs. Next he deplored the damage that would accrue to God's own reputation if he should destroy Israel in the desert (v. 12). As for himself, he asked only that if Israel must be blotted out, he might perish with them.

We read that when Moses entered the "tent of meeting," the Lord would speak to him there "face to face, as a man speaks with his friend" (Exod. 33:11). Moses secured God's promise that his "presence" would go with Israel. Then he made a plea for himself, namely, that the Lord would show him his glory; and when this privilege was promised to him, he hewed out two new tablets of stone

Aerial view of the Wilderness of Sinai. It was in desert terrain like this that the Israelites murmured against God and Moses.

to replace the ones he had broken, and ascended the mountain once more. There the Lord descended in a cloud and passed by before Moses and proclaimed his own name, Yahweh: "The LORD, the LORD, the compassionate and gracious God, slow to anger, abounding in love and faithfulness" (34:6). During this second stay of forty days on the mount with God, Moses pleaded that the Lord would continue to accompany Israel on their journey. He received and repeated further instructions for the people, notably a renewed warning against idolatry, because "the LORD, whose name is Jealous, is a jealous God" (34:14). It is in his conduct with regard to this terrible apostasy of the people (as well as the one narrated in Num. 14) that the true greatness of Moses—his humility, his love of his people, his love of God and zeal for his honor and glory—were most severely tested and most clearly revealed.

8. The veil on Moses' face. After the second stay of Moses on the mount, as he came down "his face was radiant" and the Israelites "were afraid to come near him" (Exod. 34:29–30; because the verb *qāran* H7966, "to shine," is related to the noun *qeren* H7967, "horn, protrusion, ray," the VULGATE mistranslates, saying that Moses' face had *cornuta*, "horns," which is the reason Michelangelo's famous statue of Moses includes protrusions on the head). We then read that when Moses finished speaking to the people, "he put a veil over his face" (v. 33; the KJV rendering is misleading). The meaning is not that Moses covered his face because the people were afraid to look at him. The apostle PAUL gives us the true explanation of the use of the veil. It served to prevent the people from seeing the heavenly light gradually fade away from Moses' face (2 Cor. 3:13), since it was only when in the presence of God that the radiance of the divine presence was reflected in it (cf. Matt. 17:2; Acts 9:3; Rev. 1:14).

9. The tabernacle and its ritual. In regard to the construction of the tabernacle and all of the ritual vessels and vestments, it is important to recognize the emphasis that is placed on the heavenly origin of the pattern (Exod. 25:9, 40; 26:30; 27:8; 39:32, 43; cf. Heb. 8:5). Whether Moses learned much or little in Egypt about the plan and construction of Egyptian temples and their rituals of worship was immaterial: he was to follow the pattern shown him in the mount, during the twice-forty days spent there in communion with God. In Exod. 39–40, which describe the construction and dedication of the tabernacle, the words "as the LORD commanded Moses" become a kind of refrain, occurring about a dozen times. And the cloud and the glory which filled the tent (40:34) are the divine certification of the fidelity with which Moses "finished the work" (v. 33).

10. The investiture of Aaron and his sons. As the proclamation of the Decalogue (Exod. 20) is followed by the law of the altar, so the dedication of the tabernacle with which Exodus concludes is followed at once in Leviticus by instructions regarding the ritual of sacrifice. Two chapters (Lev. 8–9) are devoted to the ordination and investiture of Aaron and his sons, which was performed by Moses. In view of the provision that is made in chs. 1–7 for the physical needs of the priests, it is noteworthy that there is only one reference anywhere to Moses' portion (8:29). Then the solemn installation of the priests who are to officiate there is described. Detailed specifications for the vestments of the priests and particularly of the high priest and of their sanctification already had been given (Exod. 28; 29; 39:1–31, 41).

The solemn ordination and installation was all performed by Moses (Lev. 8–9). The priesthood is a *Mosaic* institution. It is significant that nothing is said here or elsewhere about Moses' apparel. Moses' staff and his shining face were described, but unlike Aaron nothing is said about Moses' vesture. The reason for this is that Aaron's position was symbolical, ritualistic, and hereditary (6:22; 16:32). Before he died Aaron was stripped of his holy garments and they were placed on ELEAZAR his son (Num. 20:22–28). Moses had no successor. He was the lawgiver; and the law that was given through him was not to change with the changing generations of people (Josh. 1:7; Mal. 4:4).

11. Nadab and Abihu. After this solemn rite, there occurred one of the most amazing events in Israel's history, the sacrifice offered by NADAB and ABIHU. Aaron had four sons: he and they were all anointed, and they only, to the office of priest. Nadab and Abihu, however, "offered unauthorized [Heb. *zār*

H2424, 'strange, forbidden'] fire before the LORD, contrary to his command" (Lev. 10:1). It might seem as if the willfulness and disobedience of the nation found typical expression in this act, which was so severely punished. Moses' comment was: "This is what the LORD spoke of when he said: / 'Among those who approach me / I will show myself holy; / in the sight of all the people / I will be honored'" (v. 3). Moses was so deeply impressed with the sinfulness of the act which had been committed, that he expressed no personal sorrow at the fate of his nephews. But he gave instruction that "your relatives, all the house of Israel, may mourn for those the LORD has destroyed by fire" (v. 6).

12. The departure from Sinai. The book of Numbers begins with the numbering of the tribes, and it then gives their "stations" in the camp with reference to the tabernacle. Following certain laws dealing with impurity and jealousy, Moses was given the words of the beautiful "Blessing" that the priests were to pronounce upon the people and, in so doing, "put [God's] name on the Israelites" (Num. 6:23–27).

The fullest statement regarding the manner in which Moses was accustomed to receive his instructions from the Lord is significantly placed after the record of the dedication of the altar (Num. 7). It was when standing in the tabernacle before the veil that he was to hear the voice of God speaking to him, as if the voice came from one seated upon the ark, his throne between the two cherubim (7:89).

Numbers 9 deals with the Passover celebrated a year after the exodus, and in connection with it instructions are given regarding a second Passover to be held a month after the regular one for those providentially hindered from observing it at the proper time. When this problem first arose, Moses told those concerned to wait until he could inquire of the Lord about the matter. This detail shows clearly that Moses was given instructions when and as they were needed and that he constantly was seeking divine guidance (cf. Num. 15:32–35).

It may seem somewhat strange that in connection with the departure from Sinai (Num. 10:29–30) Moses invited HOBAB to accompany Israel, urging him with the words: "Please do not leave us. You know where we should camp in the desert, and you can be our eyes" (v. 31). This request might seem to indicate lack of confidence on Moses' part in the sufficiency of the divine guidance. It probably means simply that Moses, fully conscious of the difficulties and perils of the journey that lay ahead for Israel, was eager to secure any assistance which Hobab, who presumably knew these regions well, might be able to supply. It shows Moses as a sensible believer in divine guidance. He was ready to use human skill where and when it might prove helpful or necessary.

13. The murmuring over manna. Scarcely had the journeying resumed when the murmuring began again (Num. 11:1). The reason for it was such as to arouse the anger of the Lord and cause him to send a fire to punish them, a burning ("Taberah," v. 3) in the outskirts of the camp. The complaint was not because of lack of food; but rather, they were tired of eating manna, the bread from heaven (cf. Exod. 16), and demanded meat (Ps. 78:18–31). This situation so distressed and distracted Moses that he offered an anguished plea (Num. 11:11–15) that he might die rather than continue to suffer at the hands of a mutinous people. He evidently was brokenhearted and at his wit's end. How could he furnish "meat" to feed 600,000 footmen (v. 21)! The answer of the Lord was twofold. Moses was to be given the help of the seventy elders in judging the people; and the nation was to be given quail for a whole month and in such abundance that they would gorge themselves with it and be punished by illness and death for their greed.

14. Miriam and Aaron. An incident occurred that Moses must have felt most keenly, a personal attack by his own sister and brother. It is significant that Miriam is mentioned first. This, and the fact that it was she who was punished, indicates that she was the prime mover; and the occasion was another woman. Who the woman was is unknown. That she was a CUSHITE WOMAN (Ethiopian) indicates that she could not have been Zipporah. It was not long since Jethro had brought Zipporah back to Moses (Exod. 18:5); and it may be assumed that she and her sons remained with him. When or why Moses married this woman, whose name is not even mentioned, is not stated. It may be that Miriam resented it as an affront to Zipporah.

The matter assumed great importance for Moses personally and especially for his influence as leader. "Now Moses was a very humble man, more humble that anyone else on the face of the earth" (Num. 12:3). This parenthetical statement often has been challenged by critics as unsuitable on the lips of Moses and probably a later insertion. It is to be noted, however, that the word rendered by "humble" (Heb. ʿānāw H6705) may also by a slight modification (the letter *yod* instead of *waw*) represent the word for "afflicted" (ʿāni H6714). To say that Moses was "greatly afflicted" would be perfectly true, in view of all his trials and sufferings, and especially of the situation described in the preceding context (11:15).

Moses made no reply to his brother and sister. He did not need to. The Lord suddenly intervened and emphasized to these next of kin the unique position which their brother enjoyed. He then inflicted leprosy on Miriam and removed it only when Moses interceded in response to Aaron's agonized supplication. The fact that the Lord dealt so suddenly and severely and that Miriam was made such a public example made this incident a significant occurrence in the eyes of the people, and turned it into a notable confirmation of the unique authority of Moses.

15. Rebellion and rejection. The sending of the spies into Canaan is represented as taking place by command of God (Num. 13:1–2) and at the request of the people, a request that Moses approved (Deut. 1:22–23). Both statements were true, for Moses acted at the command of the Lord, but also in response to the demand of the people. The search that followed was both representative and thorough. A leader of each tribe was appointed, and the search party devoted forty days to its task. The majority report began favorably enough (Num. 13:27), but soon became adverse: the land was full of enemies, the sight of whom was terrifying. CALEB's appeal for obedience and faith was rejected. Moses and Aaron were blamed for inept leadership, and the further appeal of JOSHUA and Caleb was met with the threat to stone them. This rebellious reaction of the congregation provoked a threat from Yahweh to exterminate them all (cf. Exod. 32:10).

Once again Moses' love for his people was put to the test. On the previous occasion Moses pleaded for the people who had so ungratefully rejected him, but because he was concerned only for God, he urged that the Lord's honor would be impugned if Israel were to be wiped out. He concluded with the words, "forgive our wickedness and our sin, and take us as your inheritance" (Exod. 34:9). Now the Lord's response was to declare that "ten times" the people have tested him by their willfulness (Num. 14:22), and he swore by himself ("as surely as I live," 14:21, 28; cf. Heb. 6:13–20) that all the earth would be filled with his glory, and that none of those who had seen his glory and his miracles and had provoked him would see the good land promised to their fathers, a land they themselves had refused to enter. This remarkable oath is mentioned in the Pentateuch only in Deut. 32:40.

V. The fortieth year

A. Failure at Kadesh Barnea. Numbers 20 reverts back to KADESH BARNEA, where Miriam died. Again the people quarreled with Moses (cf. Exod. 17:2), because the region was barren and there was no water. Then occurred one of the most tragic events in the entire life of Moses. He was commanded to take the staff, gather the people, and "speak to" the rock that it might give forth water (Num. 20:7). Moses and Aaron therefore gathered the congregation together before the rock, and "he said to them" (v. 10 NRSV; it may be that it is Aaron who *speaks*, since Moses is the one who *strikes* the rock with the rod), apparently speaking for both of them: "Listen, you rebels, must we bring you water out of this rock?" So Aaron and Moses were both involved, and God's sentence upon them is, "Because you did not trust in me enough to honor me as holy in the sight of the Israelites, you will not bring this community into the land I give them" (v. 12).

What a tragedy! For forty years Moses and Aaron had led the people and put up with their conduct (Acts 13:18), and now these leaders were forbidden to enter into the fruit of their labors. Centuries later the psalmist wrote regarding Moses' sin that the people "made his spirit bitter, and he spoke words that were rash" (Ps. 106:33 NRSV). It might seem that the punishment did not fit the crime. It is to be remembered that Moses and Aaron occupied a

The Israelite spies traveled N into the Promised Land through this general area in the Arad region. (View to the N toward the Judean hill country.)

preeminent place in the life of Israel and that they had been signally favored and honored by the Lord. Their sin apparently was a sin of presumption and disobedience for which the punishment under the law was death. Shortly afterward Aaron died on Mount Hor (Num. 20:23–29). Moses, in spite of his personal grief, which is mentioned elsewhere, at once resumed the march toward Canaan. He sent a courteously worded message to the king of EDOM, who nevertheless refused Israel passage through his land (21:4). So Israel journeyed to Mount Hor, where Aaron died after his high priestly vestments had been transferred to his son Eleazar (v. 28).

B. Defeat of Arad and the Amorites. The king of ARAD attacked Israel without provocation and suffered total destruction (Num. 21:1–3). Soon after this victory Israel once again complained against God and against Moses (vv. 4–5), who was commanded to make a bronze snake (v. 8), because the people were bitten by "fiery" serpents (v. 6 KJV). This incident was given special significance by Jesus' reference to it in Jn. 3:14 as a type of his coming crucifixion. Then the great victories over the two AMORITE kings, SIHON and OG, are described briefly. They seem to be described in this way to show how quickly God might bring about the conquest of Canaan if only Israel would trust and obey him.

C. Arrival at Jordan. Finally Israel arrived in the plains of Moab opposite Jericho in full view of the land of promise, poised for conquest (Num. 22:1). The BALAAM story (chs. 22–24) does not mention Moses and does not directly concern him. But it is of great interest because of its great prophecies and promises regarding Israel. It is followed (ch. 25) by the account of yet another of Israel's long list of transgressions, the whoredom with the Midianites. This seduction was brought about by the counsel of Balaam, who was to perish later in the vengeance visited on Midian (31:8). His sin and its punishment are referred to elsewhere as a terrible example and warning (Josh. 13:22; 2 Pet. 2:15; Jude 11; Rev. 2:14). This story is in a sense a prophecy of Israel's history in the land of promise. For the first time since leaving Egypt God's people encountered the seductions and allurements of that licentious idolatry which they were to meet in the land of Canaan, and because of which its inhabitants were to be dispossessed by Israel. They yielded to this seduction to such a degree that their leaders were severely

Mount Nebo as seen from the south.

punished, and 24,000 of the people perished in a plague, while the zeal of Phinehas for the Lord is commended and rewarded (Num. 25:10).

The plague was followed by the second census (Num. 26), which is recorded in a different manner from the first and which gives somewhat different figures for each of the tribes, yet a total for all of them which is only slightly less (601,730) than that for the first census, while that of the Levites shows a slight increase (23,000). The phenomenal increase of Israel in Egypt came to an end when the generation that came out of Egypt refused to go forward to possess the land of promise. These years were years of stagnation; and the covenant sign, circumcision, was not observed (Josh. 5:2–9).

The case of the daughters of Zelophehad, relating to inheritance, was raised (Num. 27:1–11), and a preliminary decision was rendered. Then Moses received instructions as to Joshua's succession (27:12–23). Instructions followed regarding feasts and offerings, notably those of the seventh month (ch. 29), and vows (ch. 30).

The vengeance on the Midianites is described with minute detail concerning the disposition of the spoil, both of humans and of livestock, all of which is based on the census figures given in Num. 26:51. The apostasy of Baal Peor was the last of the transgressions recorded of Israel during the wilderness period. Like the apostasy at Sinai, it involved licentious idolatry and it gave an ominous foreview of the situation in Canaan, when Israel would forsake Yahweh and go whoring after Baal. That such tragedy took place at the end of the journey while Moses their great leader was still with them, and in sight of the land of promise, is a final evidence of that incorrigible waywardness with which Moses contended for forty years. Specially noteworthy are the words of the Lord to Moses: "Take vengeance on the Midianites for the Israelites. After that, you will be gathered to your people" (31:2). This act of retributive justice was required by the Holy God of Israel. It was in a sense the last act of Moses.

The request of the two and a half tribes that they might possess the lands E of the Jordan (Num. 32) was granted by Moses, but only after solemn warning by him, and equally solemn pledges by them, to do their full part in the task of conquering the land of Canaan to the W.

D. Moses' valedictory: Deuteronomy. If the abrupt and almost trivial ending of the book of Numbers is intended to indicate that the great story of Israel's beginnings as a nation is not ended, the book of Deuteronomy no less clearly forms the conclusion of this great history of deliverance. In it Moses is not merely, as in the three preceding books, the chief actor; here he is also the only speaker, and in the discourses that constitute the main part of the book we find both his summary and his application of that history for Israel. That it is Moses, the leader and lawgiver who speaks to Israel, and through her to all the Israel of God in the generations to come, is made clear by express statements to that effect, and also by the fact that the utterances themselves are so markedly and characteristically Mosaic.

Moses accepted mutely the sentence that he would not lead the people into Canaan (Num. 27:12–17). Three times in his first address (Deut. 1:37; 3:23–27; 4:21–24), he expressed his poignant grief that he was deprived of this fulfillment of his heart's desire. In all three passages he lays the blame for this disappointment on the people: the Lord was angry for their sakes; and he twice drew from this tragic disappointment a lesson on obedience for Israel. Similarly, he pointed out that it was because of his intercession that Aaron was not slain for the sin of making the golden calf (9:20).

The first eleven chapters are largely retrospective and climax in the account of the giving of the law at Mount Sinai, the first tablet of which is epitomized in the Shema, "Hear, O Israel: The Lord our God, the Lord is one. Love the Lord your God with all your heart and with all your soul, and with all your strength" (Deut. 6:4–5; cf. Matt. 22:37–38). Although Christ's summary of the second tablet, "Love your neighbor as yourself," is actually quoted from Lev. 19:18, yet it finds its full expression in the repeated exhortations in Deuteronomy to care for the poor, the stranger, the widow, the fatherless, and the Levite (e.g., Deut. 15:7–8; 16:11; 24:10–22). In fact, nowhere is the essence of the second tablet of the Decalogue more emphasized than here in Deuteronomy.

In Deut. 12 Moses begins to deal more particularly with the conquest of the land and its possession, and especially with that place in the land in which the Lord will choose to place his name (v. 5). This place, which like the tabernacle of the wilderness journey is to be the center of worship for all Israel, is referred to nineteen times, most frequently in ch. 12. In no one of these passages is its location specified or its name given. The same is true of other great features in Israel's life in the land, kingship (17:14–20) and prophecy (18:15–22). They lie in the future. Moses has much to say about that future and gives laws that are to govern Israel in the land they were about to possess. But his great concern for Israel after his forty years' experience in leading is that they take possession of the land of promise and worthily administer it. In his mind their continuance in the land was even more serious a matter than its conquest; and success in both cases was dependent on faithful obedience to him who promised it to the fathers, to Abraham, to Isaac, and to Jacob.

Moses then expresses all his hopes and fears for Israel in a song, followed by a final discourse (Deut. 32–33). These passages have a distinctive poetic form, and they show how readily the eloquence of impassioned oratory that appears so often elsewhere in the Mosaic books can pass into poetry. What may be regarded as Moses' last words (Deut. 33:26–29; cf. 2 Sam. 23:1–7) find their echo in the prayer recorded in Ps. 90. Moses, the prophet without peer in the OT, foresees with the anguish of a great love all the misery and suffering which their sins of disobedience will bring on his people. Solemnly he warns: "This day I call heaven and earth as witnesses against you that I have set before you life and death, blessings and curses. Now choose life, so that you and your children may live" (Deut. 30:19). With such words of counsel and admonition, this great lover of God and of the people of God passed to his reward.

The finest and truest tribute to Moses' memory is given in the words of his epitaph: "Since then, no prophet has risen in Israel like Moses, whom the Lord knew face to face, who did all those miraculous signs and wonders the Lord sent him to do in Egypt—to Pharaoh and to all his officials and to his whole land. For no one has ever shown the mighty power or performed the awesome deeds that Moses did in the sight of all Israel" (Deut. 34:10–12). Multitudes of believers both of OT times and in the days of the New Covenant have accepted them as their own tribute to "Moses the servant of the Lord."

(See further F. E. Hoskins, *From the Nile to Nebo* [1912]; M. G. Kyle, *Moses and the Monuments* [1920]; O. T. Allis, *The Five Books of Moses* [1943];

G. T. Manley, *The Book of the Law* [1957]; M. Kline, *Treaty of the Great King: The Covenant Structure of Deuteronomy* [1963]; H. M. Buck, *People of the Lord* [1966], 125–49; K. A. Kitchen, *Ancient Orient and the Old Testament* [1966]; W. A. Meeks, *The Prophet-King: Moses Traditions and the Johannine Christology* [1967]; E. Auerbach, *Moses* [1975]; G. W. Coats, *The Moses Tradition* [1993]; J. Van Seters, *The Life of Moses: The Yahwist as Historian in Exodus–Numbers* [1994]; J. K. Hoffmeier, *Israel in Egypt: The Evidence for the Authenticity of the Exodus Tradition* [1997]; J. L. T. Kok, *The Sin of Moses and the Staff of God: A Narrative Approach* [1997]; G. Phillips, *The Moses Legacy: In Search of the Origins of God* [2002]; B. M. Britt, *Rewriting Moses: The Narrative Eclipse of the Text* [2004]; J. Lierman, *The New Testament Moses: Christian Perceptions of Moses and Israel in the Setting of Jewish Religion* [2004]; A. Graupner and M. Wolter, eds., *Moses in Biblical and Extra-Biblical Traditions* [2007].) O. T. ALLIS

Moses, Apocalypse of. See ADAM AND EVE, LIFE OF.

Moses, Assumption of. Also *Testament of Moses*. A composite Jewish work, dating probably to the 1st cent. A.D., and containing a speech of MOSES to JOSHUA. Believing that the original document included an account of Moses' death and translation to heaven, scholars have traditionally referred to it as the *Assumption of Moses*, but since the extant text does not include such an account, recent writers prefer to call it the *Testament of Moses* (both titles are mentioned in patristic writings).

I. Text. Only one MS of *As. Mos.* has survived. This is a palimpsest written in Latin, the style and orthography of which belong to the 5th cent. It was discovered in the Ambrosian library in Milan by A. M. Ceriani and published by him in 1861 (*Monumenta sacra et profana*, 1/1 [1861], 55–64). Much of the text is corrupt and some passages are almost undecipherable.

II. Contents. The work contains twelve chapters, the contents of which are briefly as follows: Moses appoints Joshua to succeed him, and Joshua is to bring the people into the land of promise after which time they will fall into idolatry (*As. Mos.* 1–2). A king from the E is to destroy Jerusalem and to bring the people into captivity for seventy-seven years, after which a few will return (chs. 3–4). Then a succession of wicked priests and kings will appear, culminating in the reign of a particular tyrant for thirty-four years (chs. 5–6). In the first six chapters of the work, the history of Israel from Moses to Herod is constantly alluded to. The final six chapters look forward to times of increasing turmoil, wickedness, and persecution, in which a certain individual named Taxo chooses unresisting death, rather than to break the law. In the end, the Most High intervenes with punishment for the Gentiles and blessing for Israel.

III. Unity. In the various lists of apocryphal books in the ancient church, there is usually mention of a *Testament of Moses*, followed immediately by an *Assumption of Moses*. In the existing MS, however, there is little indication that Moses' death was so unusual as to merit the designation "assumption." The 5th-cent. writer Gelasius of Cyzicum, for example, assigns a passage found in this document (*As. Mos.* 1.4) to the same source as a quotation concerning a dispute between MICHAEL and SATAN, namely, to what he calls "the book of the Assumption of Moses." Other Greek patristic writings are to the same effect and, in fact, the epistle of Jude is believed by many to draw from some such book (Jude 9; cf. also v. 16 with *As. Mos.* 5.5; 7.7, 9). There is probably sufficient reason for concluding, as R. H. Charles does (*APOT*, 2:407–9), that there were originally two independent works which were subsequently edited together. The *Testament of Moses* would therefore be represented by the Latin MS, whereas the *Assumption of Moses* proper is known only from the various patristic quotations. Some scholars, however, still use the latter title to designate the composite whole. Others believe that the two titles refer to two distinct and unrelated documents.

There appears to be sufficient evidence to indicate that the Latin MS was derived from an earlier Greek work and that the Greek was, in turn, derived from an earlier Semitic source. The Greek fathers give no indication that they are quoting from other than Greek sources, and there are instances in the Latin MS where, for sense, one must translate, not from the Latin, but from the Greek presupposed by it. Also, certain words in the Latin text are best explained as transliterations of underlying Greek words (e.g., Lat. *heremus* in 3.11 for Gk. *erēmos*; *acrobistia* in 8.3 for *akrobystia*). The suggestion that the Greek is in turn based on a Hebrew (or Aramaic) original seems to be a necessary conclusion (cf. D. H. Wallace in *TZ* 11 [1955]: 321–28). Certain Semitic idioms seem to have survived in the Latin MS, and there appear to be vestiges of a *waw-conversive* (e.g., in 8.2). Added to that is the fact that, in a work claiming to have been written by Joshua at the dictation of Moses, the probabilities would lie in favor of a Hebrew original.

IV. Authorship. The author of the book is aptly characterized by Charles as a "Pharisaic Quietist" (*APOT*, 2:411). He could not have been a SADDUCEE, for he speaks strongly against that party and he looks forward to a theocratic kingdom on earth. He could not have been a ZEALOT, for, although he shows a good acquaintance with the Maccabean movement, he is silent concerning their uprising. Further, his ideal hero, Taxo, is not pictured as trusting in an arm of flesh, but as one who, with resignation, commits his cause to God. The author cannot have been an ESSENE, for he took a keen interest in the fortunes of the temple and in the character of its sacrifices. Thus, says Charles, "he was a Pharisee of a fast-disappearing type, recalling in all respects the Chasid of the early Maccabean times, and upholding the old traditions of quietude and resignation" (ibid.). See PHARISEE.

V. Date. The *As. Mos.* gives sufficient information to narrow the limits for its dates of composition quite considerably. Since the book frequently mentions the profanations of the priesthood and of the temple, and yet fails to mention the destruction of the latter, the latest date for the composition of the book must be A.D. 70. In addition, however, ch. 6 clearly refers to the reign of HEROD, and the comment that his children would reign for shorter periods after him (both Philip and Antipas in fact reigned for longer periods than their father) implies that the writing took place before A.D. 30. Indeed, Archelaus was the only son who reigned less than the period of his father, and he was deposed in A.D. 6. As to the earliest date, Charles argued that, judging by 6.6, Herod must have already died; he thus concluded that the probable period for the composition of the book was A.D. 7–30. This approach has been widely accepted, although some scholars have argued that the original document dates back to the Maccabean period and that chs. 6–7 are a later interpolation (cf. J. Licht in *JJS* 12 [1961]: 95–103). The view that the work was composed around the time of the BAR KOKHBA revolt (A.D. 132–135) has attracted little support.

VI. Theology. The author shows little affinity with rabbinic thought, but is thoroughly steeped in the spirit of the OT. While moral responsibility is insisted upon, God's COVENANT with his people is still seen as based upon his grace and not upon human merit. No MESSIAH is mentioned in the book, possibly because of the growing Pharisaic idea that the Messiah was to be a man of war. The kingdom would be brought in by a day of repentance and God himself would intervene. Moses is seen as having a unique relation to Judaism, for he had been appointed from the foundation of the world to be the mediator of God's covenant. He served as Israel's intercessor during his lifetime and he was to continue that function even in the spiritual world after death.

VII. Influence on the NT. The alliance between the teachings of the *As. Mos.* and those of Jesus is notable in that the conception of religion as unaligned with any particular school of politics is common to both. The parallels with the epistle of Jude have already been noted. One may also compare 2 Pet. 2:13 with *As. Mos.* 7.5, 8, and Acts 7:36 with *As. Mos.* 3.11. (For the Latin text, with emendations and notes, see R. H. Charles, *The Assumption of Moses* [1897]; for a recent English trans., J. Priest in *OTP*, 1:919–34.) H. G. ANDERSEN

Moses, Testament of. See MOSES, ASSUMPTION OF.

Moses' seat. See SEAT, MOSES'.

Mosollam, Mosollamon moh-sol′uhm, moh-sol′uh-muhn. KJV Apoc. forms of MESHULLAM (1 Esd. 8:44; 9:14).

Most High. See EL ELYON; GOD, NAMES OF.

most holy. This expression renders the Hebrew phrase *qōdeš qādāšim* (lit., "holy of holy things") and is applied to various accoutrements of the TABERNACLE, such as the altar (Exod. 29:37), and to the various offerings (Lev. 6:17, 25; 7:1; et al.). Once it is used with reference to the coming MESSIAH (Dan. 9:24). The variant phrase *qōdeš haqqādāšim* ("holy of the holy things") is applied specifically to the Most Holy Place. See also HOLINESS I.D; TEMPLE.

Mot. The god of death in the Canaanite pantheon (cf. Heb. *māwet H4638*, construct form *môt*). He is regarded as the son (or the beloved) of EL and as the adversary of BAAL. Some biblical passages personify DEATH (e.g., Job 18:13; Hab. 2:5), but it is not certain whether these refer, directly or indirectly, to the Canaanite deity. (See *ABD*, 4:922–24; *DDD*, 598–603.)

mote. This English term, meaning "small particle," is used by the KJV to render Greek *karphos G2847* ("chip [of wood], piece [of straw], bit [of wool]," etc.), which occurs only in two passages in the metaphorical sense of a minor fault (Matt. 7:3–5; Lk. 6:41–42; modern versions typically use the term "speck").

moth. Both the Hebrew term *ʿāš H6931* (Job 4:19 et al.) and the Greek *sēs G4962* (Matt. 6:19–20; Lk. 12:33; cf. *sētobrōtos G4963*, "moth-eaten," Jas. 5:2) refer to the clothes moth or *Tineola pellionella*. Small moths of the family *Tineidae* are now largely confined to human surroundings and have been serious destroyers of clothes, fur, and feather since early times. Soon after emerging from the pupae, the female moths lay eggs among clothes, and damage has already started before they are seen flying. The larvae are up to half an inch long, and they make a silk-lined case, covered with debris, out of which only the head protrudes. They feed on a range of fibers, but clothes seldom are damaged if they are thoroughly clean and dry. Some think that the WORM in Isa. 51:8 (Heb. *sās H6182*) is the larva of the moth (see *FFB*, 55–56). Many species of butterflies and moths are found in Palestine, including such conspicuous forms as the swallowtail butterfly and the large hawk-moths, but none seems to have mention in the Scriptures.

G. S. CANSDALE

mother, mother-in-law. See FAMILY.

Mount, Sermon on the. See SERMON ON THE MOUNT.

mountain goat. See IBEX; WILD GOAT.

mountain sheep. This term is used by the NIV and other versions to render Hebrew *zemer H2378*, which occurs only once in a list of animals that the Israelites were allowed to eat (Deut. 14:5; the KJV, "chamois," is not possible, for that term refers to a type of antelope that probably was never found in Palestine). The context shows only that this animal is a wild ruminant, and the rendering "mountain sheep" is indefinite, for it is applied to several distinct species. Various identifications have been proposed, including the WILD GOAT (cf. *FFB*, 36), the GAZELLE (so *HALOT*, 1:274), the mouflon (*Ovis orientalis* and *O. musimon*), and the aoudad or "barbary sheep" (*Ammotragus lervia*, a wild bovine, not closely related to true SHEEP, which seems never to have lived outside the mountains of N Africa, including Egypt). The mouflon in particular is found in S Europe and SW Asia, mostly in Asia Minor; earlier perhaps, in the hills of Palestine. This is a true sheep, dark reddish brown in color, with white and yellow flank patches developing in winter. It is thought to be, in small part, an ancestor of domestic sheep. This species is the more likely identification, but not at all certain.

G. S. CANSDALE

Mount Ephraim. See EPHRAIM, MOUNT. Similarly for other mountains that have proper names (e.g., HERMON, MOUNT; NEBO, MOUNT; TABOR, MOUNT; etc.).

mount of assembly. See CONGREGATION, MOUNT OF THE.

Mount of Beatitudes. A slope on the NW shore of the Sea of Galilee where Jesus delivered the

The Mount of Olives (ridge with the 3 towers) rises above the Kidron Valley. (View to the E, with the temple mount visible in the middle far right.)

Sermon on the Mount, part of which consisted of the Beatitudes (Matt. 5:3–12; Lk. 6:20–23). Apart from Matthew's statements that Jesus was on a mountain (Matt. 5:1; 8:1) and Luke's account that the sermon was on a level place (Lk. 6:17), the only other help in locating the site is the record that Jesus went from there directly to Capernaum. The older suggested location was the Horns of Hattin (Qarn Ḥaṭṭin), 7 mi. W of Tiberias. Now the more popular site is the slope up from the Sea of Galilee SW of Capernaum. There is a Catholic church in this place. R. L. Alden

Mount of Olives. A N-to-S ridge about two miles long, across from the Kidron Valley E of Jerusalem, known for its abundance of olive trees. There is reason to believe that in ancient times the Mount of Olives had many more olive groves on it than it does today, which accounts for the derivation of its name (Heb. *har hazzētim*, Zech. 14:4; Gk., *to oros tōn elaiōn*, Matt. 21:1 et al.; its modern Arabic name is Jebel Zaitun, which has the same meaning).

I. Geography. The mount is really a ridge running parallel to the Kidron Valley E of Jerusalem. There are undulations along it separating several high points. Although the northernmost of these has been connected with Nob (Isa. 10:32) and Mount Scopus (Jos. *War* 2.11.4, 7; 5.4.1), that is probably incorrect. The northernmost peak is not on the usual route to Jerusalem from the N. Today this is called Ras el-Mesharif. On the S part of that elevated area today are the original Hadassah Hospital and the Augusta Victoria German Lutheran Hospital. The road from Jerusalem goes due E from the N part of the old city and up the mountain where there is a shallow depression.

To the right or S is the beginning of the village of eṭ-Ṭur (*the mount* or *tower*), which is strung southward along the hill. This middle height is sometimes named after the Greek Orthodox monastery of Viri Galilaei. It is directly opposite the Ḥaram es-Sharif of Old Jerusalem. The Mount of Olives drops off to the S where the modern road to Jericho runs. The third and southernmost summit, which some do not even consider a part of the same ridge, is the Mount of Offense, so named because of Solomon's placing pagan worship shrines for his many foreign wives on the location (1 Ki. 11:7; 2 Ki. 23:13; see below). On its slopes is the Jerusalem suburb of Silwan.

The center part of the Mount of Olives or Olivet rises c. 100 ft. higher than Jerusalem or c. 2,700 ft. above sea level. To the E is a magnificent view of the JORDAN Valley and the DEAD SEA, c. 15 mi. distant in a straight line. Beyond are the mountains of MOAB. To the S and SE one can see the expansive wilderness of JUDEA. To the W the finest, most unforgettable, panoramic view of the old city of Jerusalem is available.

The hill is made of cretaceous limestone with a chalk-like top layer. The olive tree, which is one of the hardiest trees, thrives here, but there are many pines as well. The wind blows hard from the NW and gives many of the trees a decided bent to the SE. In fact, the southernmost peak is called by the Arabs Jebel Baṭn el-Hawa (the Mount of the Belly of the Wind) because it blows so hard through that valley separating it from the central summit.

II. In the OT. Considering the proximity of the Mount of Olives to Jerusalem, there are surprisingly few mentions of it. It first occurs in 2 Sam. 15:30 where one reads that DAVID "continued up the Mount of Olives" (lit., "went up the ascent [maʿăleh H5090] of the olives"). ABSALOM had been wooing the men of Israel and it had become unsafe for David to remain in Jerusalem. We then read that "David arrived at the summit, where people used to worship God" (v. 32 NIV). Up to this point no mention had been made of a sanctuary here, but knowing the propensity of ancient peoples to worship on mountains, it would not be a surprise to find a shrine there. David met HUSHAI there, dispatched him back to Jerusalem, and continued on his way toward the wilderness.

The next chapter opens with David passing over the summit where he met ZIBA, the servant of MEPHIBOSHETH. Then he went to the village of BAHURIM (2 Sam. 16:5) and eventually down to the Jordan River (v. 14). Bahurim has been identified tentatively with Ras et-Temim on the E slope of the hill and N of the old Jericho road, which went straight over the hill rather than around its S slope as the modern one does. Because of the word "ascent" in 15:30, some have figured his route as the almost staircase-like trail that bears left up the hill past the Roman Catholic Garden of GETHSEMANE and reaches the top near the Greek Orthodox monastery.

It is easy to connect a religious sanctuary on the Mount of Olives with the references to Nob, the city of priests, and AHIMELECH the priest (1 Sam. 21:1; 22:9, 11, 19). There is also the possibility of a connection between the biblical ANATHOTH, a city where priests lived, and the modern Anata just N of the Mount of Olives range (Jer. 1:1). The "hill east of Jerusalem" where SOLOMON built altars to foreign gods (1 Ki. 11:7) was located "on the south of the Hill of Corruption" (2 Ki. 23:13; see CORRUPTION, HILL OF). There may be a play on words in the latter passage: the Hebrew word meaning "corruption" (mašḥit H5422) is similar to the word for "anointing" (mišḥâ H5418), which would allude to the Mount of Olives, where anointing oil was produced.

The other occurrence of the name Mount of Olives is in a powerful eschatological passage: "On that day [i.e., the day of the Lord's coming] his feet will stand on the Mount of Olives, east of Jerusalem, and the Mount of Olives will be split in two from east to west, forming a great valley, with half of the mountain moving north and half moving south" (Zech. 14:4).

III. In the NT. The Mount Olivet is most important in the closing week of Jesus' life on earth. Undoubtedly he crossed over it many times in his going to and from festivals in Jerusalem. Since the custom was not to pass through SAMARIA, Galileans probably detoured across the Jordan in the N and then recrossed to the W bank near Jericho. This would account for Jesus' appearances in Jericho, the geography of his parable of the Good Samaritan, and his presence in BETHANY and BETHPHAGE.

One passing reference to the mount is in the textually uncertain account of the woman taken in adultery (Jn. 8:1). All other references have to do with events during and after PASSION week. Both Mark and Luke mention Bethany, Bethphage, and the Mount of Olives together in their record of the triumphal entry (Mk. 11:1; Lk. 19:29). The descriptions and location of biblical Bethany fit well with the Arab village of el-ʿAziriyeh SE of the mount astride the modern Jericho Road. Bethphage is adjacent to Bethany, but nearer the top of the Mount of Olives; it is identified with the village of eṭ-Ṭur on the very top.

As Jesus came over the crest of the hill and caught sight of the Holy City, he wept (Lk. 19:41). When he returned from the city that night he went to Bethany, apparently again to the home of Mary, Martha, and Lazarus or the home of Simon the leper (Mk. 11:11; 14:3). The next day he went into the city again, and on his way cursed a fig tree (Matt. 21:19; Mk. 11:13). It was probably to the Mount of Olives that the Savior referred when he said, "if you have faith and do not doubt … you can say to this mountain, 'Go, throw yourself into the sea,' and it will be done" (Matt. 21:21).

The following day, after having spent the previous night in Bethany and having returned from the temple, Jesus was sitting on the Mount of Olives with his disciples as he discoursed about the destruction of Jerusalem and the end of the world (Matt. 24:3; Mk. 13:3). In a summary statement Luke says that every night after teaching in the temple Jesus went out to the Mount called Olivet (Lk. 21:37). For a Galilean, the seclusion from the hustle of the city that the groves on the hillside offered undoubtedly was welcome. Furthermore, there was probably no room in the inns of Jerusalem at Passover time.

It was in the Garden of Gethsemane on the W slopes of the Mount of Olives that Jesus agonized with the Father (Matt. 26:30, 36; Mk. 14:26, 32; Lk. 22:39; Jn. 18:1), and there JUDAS ISCARIOT betrayed his Lord. Lastly, it was from the Mount called Olivet that the disciples returned after witnessing the ASCENSION OF CHRIST (Acts 1:9–12; cf. Lk. 24:50).

IV. The shrines on the mount. Apart from the city of Jerusalem, there is probably no greater concentration of shrines than on the Mount of Olives. To trace the history, significance, and denominational connection of each would be an impossible task. About the only things that are certain are the location of the hill itself and the location of Bethany to the SE. There are three "Palm Sunday" trails over the hill, three Gardens of Gethsemane, two or three sites for the ascension, two Jericho roads, and so forth. Faithful devotees of Jesus and the land on which he walked have marked with the church of Dominus Flevit the exact spot where he wept over Jerusalem, and have recovered the stone on which he stepped as he mounted the donkey on Palm Sunday in Bethphage. A Muslim shrine called Inbomon, built within the ruins of an octagonal church originally constructed in 375, later destroyed but restored by the crusaders, contains a footprint in the rock floor reputed to be the last footprint of Christ on earth. The credit for the most extravagant enterprise must go, however, to the Arab selling rides on a white donkey which he claimed was a direct descendant of the one Jesus rode!

The first sanctuary on the mount was begun in A.D. 325 by Helena, the mother of Constantine, on the S end of the central hill. Called the Eleona (*Olives*), the structure sheltered a grotto in which Jesus was to have taught the disciples. The Persians destroyed it in the 7th cent., but over it in 1869 was built the Church of the Pater Noster on the assumption that the LORD'S PRAYER (the "Our Father") was given there (Lk. 11:1–4). That church has the Lord's Prayer written on panels on the walls of the sanctuary and cloister in forty different languages.

In addition to the Inbomon, with its footprint, is the Russian Orthodox Monastery of the Ascension with its tall and most distinctive bell tower. Another monastery, a Greek Orthodox one called Viri Galilaei, may be named from the words in Acts 1:11, "Men of Galilee, why do you stand looking into heaven?"

On the W slope of the hill near the bottom are the Gardens of Gethsemane. Three churches with three gardens are there for the pilgrim's choice. Nearer the center of the hillside is the Russian church of Mary Magdalene with its typical Byzantine architecture. Below it is the famous Roman Catholic Church of All Nations sheltering the "Rock of Agony." This site has a long tradition behind it. In the garden to the N are 1,000-year-old olive trees. Farther N is a church built c. A.D. 455 over the supposed tomb of Mary. It is maintained by the Greeks and the Coptics.

On the N end of the ridge of the Mount of Olives is the magnificent Augusta Victoria Hospital built by Kaiser Wilhelm II. It is not intended to mark a biblical site, however, although in the digging of the foundations in 1907 remains of a very ancient settlement were discovered. A modern luxury hotel now dominates the S end of the central ridge overlooking the many tombstones of the centuries-old Jewish cemeteries. (See further G. Dalman, *Sacred Sites and Ways* [1935], 261–70;

K. Kraeling, *Bible Atlas* [1956], 396–98; C. G. Rasmussen, *Zondervan NIV Atlas of the Bible* [1989], 188–200.)

R. L. ALDEN

mount of the congregation. See CONGREGATION, MOUNT OF THE.

mourning. The act of expressing sorrow and grief, especially upon the death of a loved one. Many Hebrew and Greek words in the Bible are used to indicate various aspects and signs of mourning. The most common are Hebrew ʾēbel H65 (Gen. 27:41 et al.) and Greek *penthos* G4292 (Jas. 4:9), with their cognates.

I. Occasions for mourning

A. Death. The most common occasion for mourning in the Bible is the DEATH of a closely related person. Great detail is given regarding the mourning of ABRAHAM for SARAH (Gen. 23:2); of JACOB for JOSEPH (Gen. 37:34–35); of the Israelites for AARON (Num. 20:29), for MOSES (Deut. 34:8), and for SAMUEL (1 Sam. 25:1); and of DAVID for SAUL and JONATHAN (2 Sam. 1:12), as well as for ABNER (2 Sam. 3:31–32). In the NT there is a more subdued but nevertheless heartfelt sadness when MARY and MARTHA mourn for LAZARUS (Jn. 11), and when devout believers mourn for STEPHEN (Acts 8:2).

B. National calamity. Mourning also comes to expression in a variety of situations other than death. Calamities that have overwhelmed the individual often are presented as occasions calling forth the most abject sorrow and grief (Job 1:20–21; 2:8). In the later phases of OT history there are also numerous examples of mourning due to national disasters. The prophets give vivid expression to the mourning that resulted from the collapse of Judah and the subsequent exile of the people (Jer. 9:1; Joel 1:13; see also Exod. 33:4 and Num. 14:39). In Jer. 14:2 national mourning is called for because of a drought. National mourning is extensively and graphically depicted in the poetic language of the book of LAMENTATIONS.

C. Before a calamity. Trouble and calamity that are threatening and impending also are occasions for mourning (Neh. 1:4; Esth. 4:3). Generally such threats are due to a dissatisfied deity and call for an attitude of penitential mourning in the hope that God's favor might be restored. Mourning in the actual presence of death is spontaneous emotional feeling whose expression custom rigidly prescribed, while the mourning associated with the prophetic prediction of national disaster is an activity motivated by the hope of altering the path of impending doom. The thought seems to be that to mourn before a disaster is better than mourning afterward, particularly if it is efficacious in averting the calamity. In an era when it was firmly and widely believed that God is present and that he controls human affairs, it can be seen that penitential mourning would be urged upon a nation by the prophets. As in the case of PRAYER, it was sincerely felt that mourning changes things.

It would be one-sided, however, to think of these national expressions of mourning in the OT as hypocritical activities designed solely to change God's mind. On the contrary, national mourning was intended also to be an expression of a heartfelt contrition at having ignored or violated the word of the Lord. To avoid the divine displeasure, return to compliance with God's will was expressed by the ceremonies of mourning marking the death of that which had produced the divine disfavor. The prophet Joel shows the repentant attitude in mourning clearly when he calls for a mourning that is a rending of the heart, rather than a rending of the garment in order to persuade God to turn and repent (Joel 2:12–17).

A good instance of mourning offsetting an impending disaster is in Jon. 3:5–10, following the prophet's reluctant preaching. JEREMIAH, unsuccessfully, attempted to call the nation to mourning for its sin in order to gain God's favor (Jer. 9:17–19; 14:12; 36:9). More successful was HEZEKIAH's donning of SACKCLOTH (2 Ki. 19:1–14) to secure God's aid in overruling the Assyrian threat. The same hope of protection was again realized following a period of fasting and mourning (Ezra 8:21; cf. also 1 Ki. 8:33; Esth. 4:16; Mal. 3:14).

David's breach of custom in behaving in a mournful fashion before the death of BATHSHEBA's child, instead of after his death, was probably the definitive example that gave sincere mourning the purposeful character of influencing God rather than remaining simply a spontaneous manifestation of grief (2 Sam. 12:15–23).

II. Mourning customs

A. Personal behavior. Weeping is a universal expression of mourning; in the Hebrew language the verb for weeping or wailing (*bākâ H1134*) is a common term for mourning. The capacity of the Hebrew for tears is immense, though the psalmist is using hyperbole when he speaks of "flooding" his bed during the night with tears (Ps. 6:6). Loud cries frequently are associated with weeping as a sign of grief (Gen. 50:10; Ruth 1:9; 2 Sam. 13:36). Accompanying these cries is the characteristic action of beating the breast, which is suggested (but not always so translated) in the word *sāpad H6199*. This practice is urged as a token of sincere repentance for an apathetic attitude toward sin (Isa. 32:12).

A similar sign of repentance is the lifting up of hands (Ezra 9:5; Ps. 141:2). Other behavioral traits associated with mourning in the OT are lying or sitting in silence (Jdg. 20:26; 2 Sam. 12:16) and bowing the head (Lam. 2:10). FASTING for varying lengths of time was also common (2 Sam. 3:35). The sprinkling of ashes, dust, or dirt upon oneself seems to be associated more with mourning arising out of personal tragedy (2 Sam. 1:2; 13:19), national calamity (Josh. 7:6; 2 Sam. 15:32; Esth. 4:1–3; Rev. 18:19), or threatening calamity (Jer. 6:26; Mic. 1:10).

Prohibited from being a part of the Jewish mourning rites were certain practices found among pagan neighbors, such as gashing the flesh or shaving the head or beard (Lev. 19:28; Deut. 14:1; Jer. 16:6; cf. the priests of BAAL on Mount Carmel, 1 Ki. 18:28). These pagan customs of propitiating and honoring the spirits of the dead by blood letting or offering hair to them were clearly too much like the Canaanite agricultural festivals which the Mosaic code castigated. It has been suggested that the practices of covering the head (2 Sam. 15:30; Esth. 6:12; Jer. 14:3) and the beard were introduced to replace the forbidden rituals (*A Standard Bible Dictionary*, ed. M. W. Jacobus [1909], 562), but little evidence can be found in the Bible for making the one a substitution instead of the other.

B. Clothing. The clothing that is worn is another stylized form that confirms the dismal internal feeling. The common mourning garment was a black (Rev. 6:12), coarse article, similar to a grain sack, usually made of goat's hair, which was called a SACKCLOTH (Gen. 37:34; 2 Sam. 3:31; 21:10; Jer. 6:26; Joel 1:8). Adornments were also removed (Exod. 33:4) and the mourner went about barefoot (2 Sam. 15:30; Ezek. 24:17).

"Rending of the garments," or tearing a slit in the bottom of an item of apparel, was a universal sign among the Hebrews signifying grief and distress (Gen. 37:29; 44:13; 2 Sam. 3:31; 2 Chr. 34:27; Joel 2:13). It was also a pious method of showing holy indignation and zeal (Ezra 9:3; Acts 14:14). The high priest pretended to have such feelings when he tore his robe at Jesus' trial (Matt. 26:65). Gaster feels that rending is either "a later form of the more primitive practice of gashing the flesh," or an ancient "method of disguising oneself so that hovering demons may be foiled" (T. H. Gaster, *Customs and Folkways of Jewish Life* [1955], 162). A more biblical interpretation of this rite suggested by R. de Vaux is that it expresses natural sorrow as well as religious piety and duty, but without any thought of forming a cult of the dead (*Ancient Israel* [1961], 61).

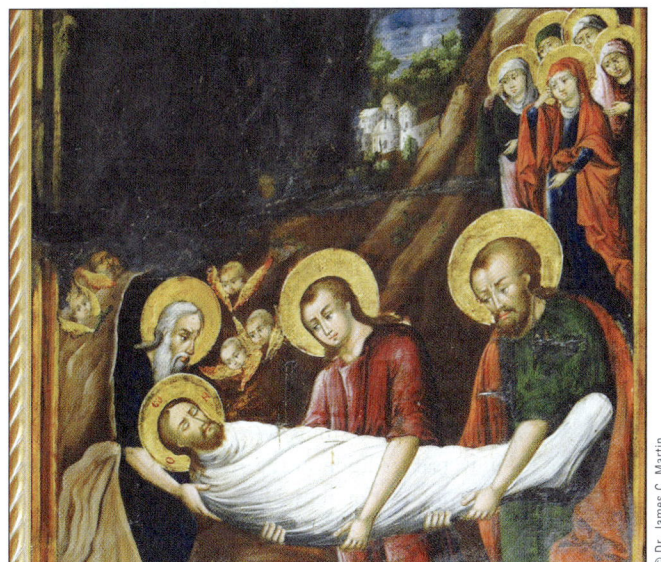

Painting from the Church of the Holy Sepulchre in Jerusalem depicting those mourning the death of Jesus as they take him to the tomb.

C. Formal lamentations. In the later part of the OT paid professional mourners, generally female, take an important place in the mourning rituals. Known as "wailing women" or "skillful women" (used in parallel in Jer. 9:17) or as "singing women" (2 Chr. 35:25), these individuals embellished the funeral rites with skillfully contrived dirges and eulogies (Amos 5:16). Sometimes they were accompanied by flutes (Matt. 9:23). Their office was passed on from mother to daughter (Jer. 9:20). In due time these mournfully sung elegies became a stylized treatment of a limited number of themes which could readily be applied to almost any individual.

David probably popularized and stylized the practice of formal lamentation with his lengthy elegy sung at the funeral of Saul and Jonathan (2 Sam. 1:17–27) and a shorter one at Abner's burial (3:33–34). Some of the features of formal lamentation included sections introduced by "how" or "what," frequent use of "ah" or "alas," extravagant praise, references to the tragic circumstances of the death, vivid imagery contrasting past splendor with present misery, and the consolation that the person's name will be remembered. An interesting reversal of many of these features is found in a satirical lament (Isa. 14:4–21) for the king of Babylon. The book of Lamentations uses these elegiac forms extensively. The form of a funeral elegy is used to express communal despair over national misfortunes and penitential sorrow for personal sins (Jer. 22:18; Ezek. 19:1–14; 26:17–18; 27:2–9, 25–36; Amos 5:16; 1 Macc. 9:21).

III. The meaning of mourning. Various explanations are given of mourning. Some scholars speak of the mourning rituals as a token of submission to the dead who are thought to have power to help or hurt the living; others argue that men are disguising themselves from a god or spirits of the dead who may otherwise choose them next after having struck so close (*SHERK*, 8:31–32). Undoubtedly the Hebrew customs were closely related to the universal tradition of the ANE peoples, but there is no foundation in the Scriptures for holding that these outward practices represented any form of a cult for the dead.

In the OT the outward signs of mourning were called for in situations of repentance and supplication as well as sorrow. This would indicate that the rituals were more than natural expressions of sorrow. Paul's words to the Thessalonians, "we do not want you ... to grieve like the rest of men, who have no hope" (1 Thess. 4:13), show grief as a natural expression that is transformed by religious belief. Likewise, for the Hebrew aware of the presence of a loving God, mourning rites could be neither mere expressions of sorrow nor forms of cultic veneration.

In the NT tender sympathy is expressed toward those mourning the loss of a loved one (Jn. 11:35; Rom. 12:15; 1 Thess. 4:13), but mourning in its religious aspects is seen also as helpfully uncovering some of the unique facets of the gospel. Thus, Jesus' personal advent brought suffering and lamentation (Matt. 2:16–18) as did his death (Lk. 23:27). Moreover, it is declared that his followers will also weep and lament (Jn. 16:20), and it is even demanded of them that they suffer with him (Rom. 8:17). In a manner more glorious than in the OT, penitential and supplicational mourning turn into glory and rejoicing with Christ as he is found to be the messenger of joy (Jn. 16:20, 22; Rom. 8:17). The NT exalts in an eschatological and existential hope: "Blessed are those who mourn, for they will be comforted" (Matt. 5:4). (See further X. H. Y. Pham, *Mourning in the Ancient Near East and the Hebrew Bible* [1999]; S. M. Olyan, *Biblical Mourning: Ritual and Social Dimensions* [2004].)   T. M. GREGORY

mouse. The Hebrew term ʿ*akbār H6572*, which may be accurately rendered "mouse" or "rat," was probably applied to a wide range of small rodents. In parts of Africa today, one term includes all uniformly colored rats and mice up to the size of a brown rat. Thus when the Hebrew term is found in a list of unclean animals (Lev. 11:29; see UNCLEANNESS), it likely refers to the whole group, even though in many parts of the world it is usual, and safe, to eat many small rodents. The real object of the ban was probably to exclude black rats, carriers of dangerous diseases. Isaiah speaks of those who deliberately defile themselves by eating mice and other forbidden meat (Isa. 66:17 RSV; NIV, "rats"; NRSV, "rodents").

The word appears in only one other passage, in connection with the plague that afflicted the

A sand rat, common in the Middle East and North Africa.

PHILISTINES when they captured the ARK OF THE COVENANT (1 Sam. 6:4–5, 11, 18). This incident took on new significance in modern times when the relationship between rats, PLAGUE, and humans was discovered. Although rats are not specifically blamed for the epidemic that affected both Philistines and Israelites, the causal relationship between the tumors and the rats was clearly recognized by the priests of DAGON when they sent gifts of golden rats and TUMORS with the ark back to Israel. Bubonic plague began in the E and for many centuries has caused numerous deaths in many countries; the Plague of London was one such outbreak, with 70,000 deaths in London alone. Plague is, in fact, primarily a disease of rats, transmitted by several species of flea, which seek other hosts, including humans, when the rat dies. One of the classic symptoms is the tumor or bubo that forms in the groin and elsewhere. Black rats have now spread all over the world and are the main ship rat. (See A. R. Short, *The Bible and Modern Medicine* [1953].) In addition Palestine has many species of small rodents, some of which become serious pests in the intensive agriculture now practiced. Some believe that the rodent referred to in this passage is the Levant vole (*Microtus guentheri*; see *FFB*, 57); other identify it as the jerboa (*Jaculus jaculus*, a jumping rodent of the family *Dipodidae*; see W. L. Holladay, *A Concise Hebrew and Aramaic Lexicon of the Old Testament* [1971], 272). G. S. CANSDALE

mouth. The cavity at the beginning of the alimentary tract, located between the jaws and leading into the pharynx (throat). It contains the teeth, gums, and tongue. Into it are poured the secretions of the salivary glands, namely, the parotid glands, the submaxillary glands, and the sublingual glands. These secretions contain enzymes for digestion of food. The mouth contains the organs of taste. It also serves in mastication and impregnation of food with saliva, and in respiration, speech articulation, expectoration and sucking. One of the most astounding statements of fact presented to the writer as a medical student was that the mouth without exception is the dirtiest part of the human body (the nutrients that go into the human mouth are good culture media for growing bacteria that cause diseases, and the saliva in the mouth tends to discourage the growth of all other bacteria except those that are disease-producing in human beings).

Both Hebrew *peh* H7023 and Greek *stoma* G5125 are used literally (1 Sam. 1:12; Acts 23:2; et al.) as well as figuratively. Among the latter uses, the word "mouth" can refer to an entrance, such as of a cave (Josh. 10:27), the grave (Ps. 141:7), a sack (Gen. 42:27), and a well (29:10). It is used metaphorically to refer to the absolute sovereignty of God in the fiat of his words in judgment, as in the phrases "rod of his mouth" (Isa. 11:4) and "out of his mouth comes a sharp sword" (Rev. 19:15). Jesus taught that "the things that come out of the mouth come from the heart, and these make a man 'unclean'" (Matt. 15:18 and parallels; cf. also Rom. 3:14). P. E. ADOLPH

mow. To cut down the standing grass or other herbage. The Hebrew noun *gēz* H1600 (which twice refers to wool or fleece, Deut. 31:20; Job 31:20), is used of mown grass or a mown field in two passages (Ps. 72:6; Amos 7:1). In the latter, the phrase "the king's mowings" (NIV, "share") refers to the first cut of spring herbage, which was to be given as tribute to the kings of Israel to feed their horses; after that the owner of the field could have his portion. The word occurs in the NT once as the rendering of Greek *amaō* G286 (Jas. 5:4).

Moza moh'zuh (מוֹצָא H4605, "[act or place of] going out"). Some scholars believe that this is a place name, rather than a personal name, and that it possibly should be related to MOZAH. **(1)** Son of CALEB by Ephah his concubine, included in the genealogy of JUDAH (1 Chr. 2:46).

(2) Son of Zimri and descendant of SAUL through JONATHAN (1 Chr. 8:36–37; 9:42–43). Several of the names in this section of the genealogy correspond to towns within the tribal territory of BENJAMIN.　　　　　　　　　E. B. SMICK

Mozah moh′zuh (מֹצָה *H5173*, perhaps "[water] source" or "[oil] press"). A town within the tribal territory of BENJAMIN (Josh. 18:26). Because the name is stamped on the handles of vessels excavated at JERICHO and Tell en-Naṣbeh (MIZPAH), it is thought that Mozah was a center for the manufacture of pottery. The town was evidently near such W Benjamite cities as Mizpah and KEPHIRAH, but its precise location is uncertain. Many scholars believe that the site is at or near the Arab village of Qaloniyeh (Qalunyah), about 5 mi. WNW of JERUSALEM on the road to Tel Aviv. The ancient name may survive in nearby Khirbet Beit Mizzah and has been adopted by the Jewish colony of Moṣah W of Qaloniyeh, which some think may also be the EMMAUS of the NT. (See J. Simons, *Geographical and Topographical Texts of the Old Testament* [1959], 176–77; *ABD*, 4:925.)　　　　　P. A. VERHOEF

muffler. This English term, referring to a scarf worn around the neck, is used by the KJV to render Hebrew *rĕʿālâ H8304*, "veil," which occurs only once (Isa. 3:19).

Mugharah, Wadi el- (Arab. "valley of caves"). A valley S of Mount Carmel where Stone Age remains have been found (see CARMEL, MOUNT). Between 1929 and 1934 an archaeological expedition under the leadership of Dorothy Garrod and Theodore McCown of the British School of Archaeology excavated four caves in the Wadi el-Mugharah. About two miles in from the Mediterranean Sea on the S side of the valley, three of these caves produced extensive artifacts and skeletal remains of several Stone Age cultures. The oldest items were from the Early Paleolithic Period and the most recent from the Mesolithic. A subdivision of the latter known as the Natufian Period (so named from the nearby Wadi en-Natuf, which Garrod also discovered) was also well represented. The subdivision has been redivided on the basis of the artifacts found at the Mugharah caves.

The Natufian people did not make pottery or domesticate animals but raised crops and hunted; most of their artifacts were flint arrowheads, spearheads, knives, and scrapers. In common with other previous cultures, they left their dead unburied in a contracted position, as evidenced from the skeletons in the es-Skhul and el-Wad caves. These skeletons resembled those of the Homo sapiens of the Upper Paleolithic Period more than the Neanderthal.

The cave of el-Wad represents in its several strata a transition period between the Mousterian and the Upper Paleolithic. These judgments are based on the shape of the flint tools and bone objects found there. In the cave called el-Tabun, some of the earliest artifacts of all appeared in the form of crude scrapers and untoothed knives. Neither Wadi el-Mugharah nor any of its caves are mentioned in the Bible. (See D. A. E. Garrod et al., *The Stone Age of Mount Carmel*, 2 vols. [1937–39]; E. Anati, *Palestine Before the Hebrews* [1963], parts 2 and 3.)　　　R. L. ALDEN

mulberry tree. The Greek term *moron*, referring to the black mulberry (*Morus nigra*, grown for its edible fruit), is used once in the APOCRYPHA (1 Macc. 6:34); its juice was somehow effective in provoking elephants to fight (see J. A. Goldstein, *I Maccabees*, AB 41 [1976], 320). Another term, *sykaminos G5189*, occurs once in the NT (Lk. 17:6). See also BALSAM TREE; FLORA (under *Moraceae*); SYCAMINE; SYCAMORE.

mule. The mule is a hybrid, the offspring of a male donkey (see ASS, DONKEY) and a female HORSE (the reverse cross, by stallion and a donkey mare, is called a *hinny*, which is much less useful and rarely bred). Mules are sterile; the few records of fertile mules, mostly old, are not generally accepted. The mule combines some of the size and strength of the horse with the patience, surefootedness, and endurance of the donkey, and can work efficiently in country too hard for horses. The Israelites were specifically forbidden to breed such hybrids (Lev. 19:19), and mules were regularly imported from countries that specialized in this work (cf. 1 Ki. 10:25; Heb. *pered H7234*). They were highly regarded, and their use in the OT is largely confined to the nobility; for example, they first appear in 2 Sam. 13:29, ridden by DAVID's sons (cf. also 1 Ki. 1:33, 38, 44, where the alternate form *pirdâ H7235* is used). The one possible exception is Ezra 2:66, repeated in Neh. 7:68, where 245 mules were part of the transport bringing back the exiles to Judah. (The KJV rendering "mule" is probably incorrect in Gen. 36:24; Esth. 8:10, 14.) The mule's stubbornness is proverbial today, but this characteristic is referred to only once in the Bible (Ps. 32:9, where the mule is classed with the horse as lacking understanding).

G. S. Cansdale

Muppim muh′pim (מֻפִּים *H5137*, derivation unknown). Son of Benjamin and grandson of Jacob (Gen. 46:21). This name does not occur in the other genealogies of Benjamin, although many scholars identify Muppim with Shephupham (Num. 26:39 MT; KJV and NIV, "Shupham"), Shuppim (1 Chr. 7:12, 15; NIV, "Shuppites"), and Shephuphan (1 Chr. 8:5). See discussion under Shephupham; see also Huppim.

Muratorian Canon myoor′uh-tor′ee-uhn. Also known as the Muratorian Fragment, this 7th/8th-cent. Latin document provides a very early list of accepted NT books. It was discovered by L. A. Muratori (1672–1750) in the Ambrosian Library of Milan and published by him in 1740. Although some recent scholars have argued that the original Greek work from which it was translated may have been produced in Syria or Palestine as late as the 4th cent., it is widely believed that the Muratorian Canon is the earliest existing list of its kind, composed originally c. A.D. 180–190 in or near Rome. For a discussion of its significance, see canon (NT) V.

S. Barabas

murder. See bloodguilt; crimes and punishments I.B.

murrain. This English term, meaning pestilence or plague, is used once by the KJV to render the common Hebrew word *deber H1822* (Exod. 9:3). See also plagues of Egypt.

Mushi myoo′shi (מוּשִׁי *H4633*, derivation uncertain; the same form [מוּשִׁי *H4634*] is used as a gentilic, "Mushite"). Son of Merari and grandson of Levi (Exod. 6:19; Num. 3:20; 1 Chr. 6:19, 47; 23:21, 23; 24:26, 30); eponymous ancestor of the Mushite clan of Levites (Num. 3:33; 26:58). It has been argued that the name is derived from *mōšeh H5407* (Moses), and some speculate that the Mushites constituted an early priesthood competing with that of Aaron.

Mushite myoo′shit. See Mushi.

music, musical instruments

I. Introduction
II. Music in the OT
   A. Community life
   B. Temple and synagogue
   C. Musical style
III. Music in the NT
   A. Actual instances of music making
   B. Instructions having to do with music making
   C. Supernatural and eschatological mentions of music
   D. Temple and synagogue worship in early Christianity
   E. The importance of the NT perspective
IV. Musical instruments
   A. Idiophones
   B. Membranophones
   C. Aerophones
   D. Chordophones
V. Terms relating to performance
   A. Vocal
   B. Instrumental
VI. Musical terms in Psalm superscriptions
   A. Types of songs
   B. Names of melodies
   C. Other musical terms introduced by ʿal
   D. Remaining musical terms in the superscriptions

I. Introduction. Words about music are secondary to music itself. This is the dilemma of historians, whose obligation it is to bring enlightenment and perspective to music making. They are successful only if their work finally draws the reader to music itself, and if they avoid the temptation of allowing word impressions to replace the musical ones.

Music is the most abstract of the arts. Its components—pitch, duration, texture, rhythm, color, and ultimately form—speak their own language.

The composing experience, which brings these together in a satisfying wholeness, is to be matched in the listening experience, which then must comprehend this wholeness. Hence, the final meaningfulness of music lies in the aural experience. Other experiences are merely adjuncts or glosses on the acoustical event.

All of this is true whether one is dealing with music for its own sake, a comparatively recent phenomenon in Western culture, or music that is inseparable from function, as in the case of music in the Bible. In either instance, the primary problem is the hearing and understanding of inherent musical sound as it occurs in its cultural contexts. Furthermore, music is gone as soon as it is made. It is a time art: its sounds do not coexist as the parts of a painting do; they succeed each other chronorhythmically. Their recapture or repetition does not guarantee entire faithfulness to the original. We cannot return to a performance of a concerto or a folk song the way we can to a painting or an artifact. The advent of electronic media only partially solved this problem, since a very important element, the performer, is still missing, and absolute fidelity to the original sound is unattainable even with the most sophisticated equipment.

The historian's problem is further complicated when the primary data (instances of the music itself) are partly or completely missing, and when the secondary data (the historical contexts) are removed by vast cultural and linguistic distances. The success with which these barriers are overcome determines how accurately deductions can be made as to what the music of another culture in another time might have been, what its instrumentations were, as well as what its formulae and functions entailed.

Many recent archaeological discoveries, coupled with heightened musicological skills and insights, have clarified much of what had been previously obscure or highly romanticized. Still the primary task in the field of biblical music is to be assumed by the biblical scholar, whose insights into ancient history are coupled with a mastery of the languages of biblical contexts. The role of the musicologist comes into play only when judgments are to be made in the presence of musical data that surface one way or another. The danger in such work is apparent. Musicians must avoid betraying their amateurism when speaking biblically or theologically. Biblical scholars must be careful when attempting to speak musically. Incisive scholarship is often pivotal. It is not necessarily to be equated with a single perspective, but conscientiously used to serve whatever perspective is consistently and honestly searched out. While the first two sections of the present article depend to a great extent on the outstanding researches of such scholars as Eric Werner (in *IDB*, 3:457–76), Abraham Z. Idelsohn (*Jewish Music in Its Historical Development* [1967]), and Egon Wellesz (*A History of Byzantine Music and Hymnography* [1949]), it assumes a different theological and biblical perspective from theirs.

II. Music in the OT

A. Community life. The book of Genesis mentions JUBAL (a name possibly related to *yôbēl* H3413, "ram's horn") as the protomusician (Gen. 4:21). The distance, both stylistic and chronological, between him and the later music making of the Jewish community can only be a matter of speculation. The real importance of Jubal is in the attention given to music making this far back in sacred history, and further, that such attention is focused on its natural appearance along with other human and cultural activities. Jubal's brother, JABAL, was a cattle breeder; his half-brother TUBAL-CAIN, the first smith. This is important, for music is first described in a functionally neutral sense. Jubal is the "father of all who play the harp and flute." His music making is not religiously caused or primarily associated with WORSHIP, nor is it necessarily an activity which, by contrast, bears only the association of any number of so-called secular activities. Even though Yahweh was to be worshiped in his sanctuary, the earth with all its fullness was also his; and as man's habitat, and with the command given him to be its steward, the world was to be an arena for praise. Accordingly, the use of music is as much an integral part of the gathering of harvest as the worship in the sanctuary. The uniqueness is that while harvest songs are sung, they are sung to the Lord of the harvest; that while battle songs are sung, Yahweh is to win the battle.

Thus if there is one consistent strand concerning music in the OT, it is that it is inseparable from all of life. Although in its earliest stages, or as related to certain activities, it may have been little more than noise making, music accompanied work, worship, merrymaking, and military activities (Gen. 31:27; Exod. 32:17–18; Num. 27:17; Jdg. 11:34, 35; Isa. 16:10; Jer. 48:33). There are instances of music making connected with specific acts of God: the collapse of the walls of JERICHO (Josh. 6:4–20), the enthronement of kings (1 Ki. 1:39–40; 2 Ki. 11:14; 2 Chr. 13:14; 20:28), music for the court (2 Sam. 19:35; Eccl. 2:8), and for feasting (Isa. 5:12; 24:8–9), as well as for the restoration of prophetic gifts (2 Ki. 3:15) and the soothing of personality disturbances (1 Sam. 16:14–23).

These latter two instances superficially seem to belong to the psychological realm or to the blatantly magical. Along with the narrative in Josh. 6:4–20, in which the combination of trumpet sounds with people shouting precede the felling of Jericho's walls, an immediate relation is seen by some biblical scholars between music and MAGIC. It cannot be denied that this relationship is assumed in the myths and legends of the religious systems surrounding Judaism. Nor can it be denied that music and magic are linked in religious systems of primitive cultures everywhere. Furthermore, the more sophisticated doctrine of ethos which developed within the Greek philosophical system still has overtones in much of today's thinking regarding musical values. In one way or another, the Christian church has to some extent adopted this philosophy. Current uses of music in psychotherapy further seem to suggest that music has somewhat intrinsic powers to change behavior.

Although this is not the place to discuss this problem at great length, it is necessary to mention a few distinctions that speak to both the biblical and the contemporary issues. First, music already has been seen to have accompanied all of Jewish life. Therefore it may be assumed that there is a difference between that which accompanies an event and that which causes it. Second, the parallel practices in other religious systems are only relevant if the basic perspectives of these systems are parallel to the system under discussion. This is patently not the case. Third, the uniqueness of the Jewish religion is seen in the fact that Yahweh is the one who calls all things into being and controls all events. Furthermore, he

Ceramic figures of flute players (Middle Elamite, late 2nd millennium B.C.).

calls and controls purposefully in terms of which people, places, and things are instruments of his purpose. Therefore, God brings walls down while people and their activities participate in the event. Fourth, the fact that music, among other created and cultural things, is purported by primitives and sophisticates alike to have power is more a matter of the dislocation of priorities than anything else.

It is possible to sense in the earliest parts of Scripture that the created order is to be subject to human dominion and that it is good. Human beings are to be sovereign over it and not the reverse; the goodness of creation is a reflection of God's handiwork, but it is a goodness not in the sense of inherently causing good, otherwise it would be sovereign over man and the cultural mandate would be irrelevant. In addition, even though CREATION has been ravished by SATAN, this does not mean that it has become intrinsically bad in the moral sense. Ultimately the Judeo-Christian perspective maintains that human beings are interiorly wrong and that until they are right they will place the blame for their condition outside themselves. Hence, they will assume that created things or activities, as is often the case with music, have power over them and their activities. Consequently the parallels that are drawn in comparative religious studies between Judaism and its contemporary systems are in fundamental error because fundamental perspectives are overlooked.

B. Temple and synagogue. The idea of special creative skills in cultic worship occurs long before the advent of professional musicians. In the building of the TABERNACLE, people were chosen to "make artistic designs" and were given the HOLY SPIRIT to do so (Exod. 31:3–11; 35:30—36:2). The ability to devise these works is interestingly related to intelligence, knowledge, and finally craftsmanship. The mention of music, however, is minimal in the matter of WORSHIP in the tabernacle (Exod. 28:34–35 describes gold bells that were attached to the lower hem of AARON's robe so that their sound could be heard when he entered the Holy Place).

The trained musicians that eventually appear around the time of DAVID and SOLOMON mark a distinctive change in the history of Jewish music. Before this time much of the music was made by women. MIRIAM led a group of her own sex in singing and dancing (Exod. 15:20–21) after MOSES and the Israelites had sung to the Lord in celebration of the overthrow of the Egyptians (vv. 1–18). JEPHTHAH's daughter met her father with timbrels and dance upon his return from battle (Jdg. 11:34). Women sang, danced, and played for the conquering David (1 Sam. 18:6–7).

With the professionalization of music in the royal courts and more especially in TEMPLE worship, music making was restricted to men. This is not to say that in the nonprofessional realm women ceased making music; this continued as before. In the accounts in Chronicles that give the statistics of the temple ministries, 4,000 of the 38,000 Levites chosen by David for temple service were musicians (1 Chr. 15:16; 23:5). These were the singers who were "to sing joyful songs, accompanied by musical instruments: lyres, harps and cymbals." In 1 Chr. 25:6–7, the number of musicians is listed at 288, divided into 24 orders of 12 each.

The descriptions of the musical activities that occur thereafter give the impression of an awesome spectacle: "The priests then withdrew from the Holy Place. All the priests who were there had consecrated themselves, regardless of their divisions. All the Levites who were musicians—ASAPH, HEMAN, JEDUTHUN, with their sons and relatives—stood on the E side of the altar, dressed in fine linen and playing cymbals, harps and lyres. They were accompanied by 120 priests sounding trumpets. The trumpeters and singers joined in unison, as with one voice, to give praise and thanks to the LORD. Accompanied by trumpets, cymbals, and other instruments, they raised their voices in praise to the LORD and sang: 'He is good; his love endures forever.' Then the temple of the LORD was filled with a cloud, and the priests could not perform their service because of the cloud, for the glory of the LORD filled the temple of God" (2 Chr. 5:11–14).

The parallel between this rich array and the existence of professional guilds of musicians in the neighboring kingdoms of Egypt and Assyria is obvious. In the transition from an unsettled nomadic life to one of a centralized monarchy, there was the opportunity for training and the regulation of a musical system that would serve the needs of the royal court and the worship in the temple. No efforts, it seems, were spared in the full realization of this goal. The importation of musical instruments and musical systems was no doubt carried out. The normal cultural intercourse during Israel's sojourn was formalized in the monarchy. The MIDRASH alludes to a tradition in which King Solomon's Egyptian wife included 1,000 musical instruments in her dowry. More concrete archaeological evidence makes it clear that the instruments of the ancient world were similar from culture to culture. This would imply a similarity of musical systems, although it would not rule out the possibility of indigenous change.

There have been many highly romanticized and exaggerated speculations about a never-to-be-repeated musical situation in the temple. These have distorted a true contextual sense of what might have happened, and since there is no precise knowledge of the full musical style, one must remain content with the central concept of a solemn yet exuberant mode of worship. Moreover, it is important to remember that though these musical activities were quantitatively and qualitatively professional, the matter of functionality mentioned earlier still prevailed. The central importance in temple ritual was sacrificial. All else served this centrality. The system of daily sacrifices, morning and evening, was minutely regulated. The liturgical activities were complex and cumulative. The MISHNAH (which possibly preserves reliable information from the Second Temple period) gives the number of instruments in the temple as follows: "never less than two harps or more than six ... never less than two flutes or more than twelve ... never less than two trumpets, and their number could be increased without end … never less than nine lyres, and their number could be increased without end; but of cymbals there was but one" (*m. ʿArak*. 1:3, 5).

The choir consisted of a minimum of twelve adult male singers, the maximum limitless. The singers served between the age of thirty and fifty with a five-year training period preceding this. The lack of mention of a large percussion group as well as the absence of a corps of dancers might indicate an attempt to evade a similarity to pagan forms of worship, although this can only be conjecture. It certainly has to be balanced with those occasions in which dance is mentioned as a legitimate way of praise elsewhere in the OT (2 Sam. 6:14; Pss. 149:3; 150:4).

Although a good part of the musical performance must have been left to the trained singers and players, the congregation was also musically involved. There is record in the 1st cent. of three forms of public singing of the Scriptures including the Psalms, each based on the response principle. *First Form:* the leader intoned the first half verse, repeated by the congregation; the leader then sang each succeeding half line, but the congregation responded with the same first half-line, which became a refrain throughout the entire song. *Second Form:* the leader sang a half-line at a time and the congregation immediately repeated what had just been sung. *Third Form:* the leader would sing the whole first line and the congregation would answer with the second line of the verse; this type was true responsive singing.

Not long after the destruction of the temple instrumental music fell into disuse and for some reason or other was never revived. Vocal tradition and practice however continued, and as such became the central musical feature of SYNAGOGUE worship. In contrast to the temple with its system of sacrifice, the synagogue was primarily for public worship and instruction as well as secular assemblage. It was and is, in Werner's terms, a "layman's institution" in which the Torah, its study and interpretation, readings from the Scriptures, and devotional prayers took the place of the sacrificial ceremonies of the temple. There was only one temple but numberless synagogues. The TALMUD claims that there were 394 synagogues alone in Jerusalem at the time of the destruction of the temple (*b. Ketub*. 105a).

The quantity of synagogues as contrasted to the unique singularity of the temple is explained not only "theologically," in that there was but one place for sacrifice and many places for instruction. It was also logistical. The DIASPORA, a dispersion over a vast geographical spread, deprived the Jew of temple worship. The synagogue helped fill this need for corporate solidarity and for communion with God. It is within the framework of synagogue worship, however, that the vocal elements of temple worship were most likely perpetuated. The intonations of the Psalms and the Pentateuch and perhaps the recitation of prayers were all a part of this perpetuity. Furthermore, these intonations or cantillations, mentioned as far back as the 1st cent., were cast into a system of modes or formulae, one for each of the books of the Bible intended to be publicly read. These are: the Pentateuch, the Prophets, Esther, Lamentations, Ruth, Ecclesiastes, Song of Songs, Psalms, and in some communities, Job. As to when the transition from declamatory to musical reading was first evidenced there is little knowledge except that it is known that the PSALMS were sung in the temple worship. Idelsohn and Werner are both convinced that the chanting of Scripture, in one form or another, went back perhaps as far as EZRA, 5th cent. B.C., and that its eventual complexity and organization was the result of hundreds of years of crystallization.

C. Musical style. For a full and informative treatment of this particular subject, the reader is referred especially to Idelsohn and Werner, to whom much of the following is in debt. The crucial task in determining matters of style is one of identifying relationships that are found in available music and that can be shown to have also been present in music which is not available. Through a combination of linguistics, history of culture, and comparative musicology, discoveries have been made that make this possible to quite some extent. Excavations have produced ancient instruments from Ur, Kara-Tepe, Mesopotamia, and Egypt, as well as from Israel. Liturgies, whole or in part, from Sumer, Akkad, Egypt, and Ugarit have been reconstructed. Finally, comparative musicology has endeavored to examine the oldest melodic elements of the ANE and to set forth criteria for their age and locale.

As a result of all these efforts certain distinguishing characteristics of Semitic music are identified by Idelsohn. (1) *Modality.* This is not to be confused with the later Western use of the term. A mode comprises a number of motives within a certain scale, each of which has different functions. The resulting composition is an arrangement and combination of these motives.

(2) *Ornamentation.* The modes and their motivic partials are, within the arrangements of (1), subject to ornamentation and decoration, often very florid and extended. To a large extent this depends upon the skill and training of the singer, whose object it is to keep within the perimeters of the mode itself while at the same time enhancing its basic profile with ornaments. The contour of such ornamentation is basically step-wise; skips of more than a third are rare. Thus the style is eminently vocal.

(3) *Rhythm.* Idelsohn incorrectly uses the term *unrhythmical* to describe Jewish chant. All music is rhythmic in the sense that its sequence of tones is subject to virtually infinite temporal variations. Metrical music is that which is subject to regularly recurring, equally divided measures. Within each of these, rhythmic development takes place. The characteristic of Semitic music is its lack of regularly recurring meters. Nonetheless it is freely and richly rhythmic; its rhythmic structure is as complex as its ornamentation. In fact, it may be said that rhythm is to meter what ornamentation is to scale.

(4) *Scale.* The general nature of melody is diatonic, although this is mixed with a certain feeling for quarter tones, a distinctive foreign to most Occidental music.

(5) *Monophony.* Jewish music is unharmonized and depends for its beauty on elaborate ornamentation of the melody alone. Occasionally in group singing intervals of fourths or fifths appear, more out of limitation in vocal range than an inherent harmonic vocabulary. However, it probably is true that the natural acoustical compatibility of these intervals allows for departure from the unison and, by virtue of this, gives room for speculation as to the relation of this kind of primitive harmony to the development of harmonic procedures. When vocal music was instrumentally accompanied, heterophony (a way of embellishing the basic melodic line; a concurrent decoration) was often employed.

(6) *Improvisation.* The performer and composer were the same person. The modal formulae were elaborated upon as seen in (1) and (2). A combination of long training and inherent ability were necessary to accomplish this.

For several centuries musicians sensed an essential identity between archetypes of Christian chant and Hebrew counterparts, but it has not been possible to substantiate this connection until recently. The French musicologist Amédée Gastoué established the first concrete evidence and support of this claim. Then Idelsohn was able to establish the essential identity of certain melodic archetypes in the Yemenite tradition with the earliest Gregorian chant. The significance of this is that the Yemenites had left Palestine during the beginnings of Christianity and had remained isolated from contact with the church ever since. In addition to the work of Gastoué, Idelsohn, and Werner, the names of Peter Wagner and Egon Wellesz are important in the furtherance of such studies.

III. Music in the NT

A. Actual instances of music making. Superficially the NT appears almost to disregard music. Outside of the book of Revelation, in which music is part of a rich eschatological drama, there are not more than a dozen passages in the entire canon that shed light on music making. Of these, five mention music metaphorically (Matt. 6:2; 11:17; Lk. 7:32; 1 Cor. 13:1; 14:7–8). The remaining cast important light, especially when seen in broader context—that of the rich heritage of temple and synagogue worship known and practiced by the early Christians.

There are four relevant passages in the Gospels, two of which are parallel: Matt. 26:30 and Mk. 14:26 mention the use of a hymn by Christ and his disciples at the conclusion of the Last Supper (see LORD'S SUPPER). Although there is debate as to the exact nature of the Last Supper with regard to its full content and relation to Jewish traditions and practices, as well as the attendant possibilities of adaptation and change by Jesus himself, it probably is true that the words and music that were used were traditional. This is the only specific mention in the NT of Jesus himself singing, although it is probable another) in psalms, hymns, and spiritual songs. If there are omissions concerning instrumental music or the dance, they need not necessarily be construed, as some would, as a sign that since these were used in the orgiastic Greek mystery rites (see MYSTERY RELIGIONS), or for that matter, in the worship of the now hostile Jewish cult, they were wrong. For one thing, the primitive church was transient, temporarily quartered in homes, ships, beaches, and public squares. It often was hidden away from those who tried to stamp it out. It had no time for anything but the most simple musical devices and activities in its own worship.

More important, certain types of music might have been avoided, not because of an intrinsic wrongness, but by the strong associations in the minds of some who were brought from pre-Christian experiences, either Jewish or pagan. However, the radically Christian principle which ruled was that certain things were to be avoided because they could offend a weak conscience, not because they were intrinsically empowered to change behavior. The distinction therefore between the pagan concept of the empowerment of things and the Christian concept of discernment among things, none of which are impure *in themselves* (Rom. 14:14) and are not empowered, overrides any claim that the early church set a standard in music that was rigid, unchangeable, and limited. The range of musical practice is rather to be construed as broadly as possible because it is based on a principle that speaks to a total way of life, including music.

IV. Musical instruments.
The problem is one of correlating the terms apparently denoting musical instruments with the archaeological data in the form of actual artifacts or artistic representations of them on coins, seals, monuments, manuscripts, etc. Particular caution must be exercised so as not to read modern forms of instruments into the biblical terms. Attention throughout is given to the terminology used by C. Sachs (*The History of Musical Instruments* [1940]; *The Rise of Music in the Ancient World* [1943]).

A. Idiophones (made of naturally sonorous materials).
(1) *Pairs of similar instruments struck together.* The usual word for cymbals is *mĕṣiltayim* H5199 (found almost a dozen times in 1–2 Chronicles; also Ezra 3:10; Neh. 12:27; cf. Ug. *mṣltm*); this Hebrew term is always translated *kymbalon* G3247 in the SEPTUAGINT. It probably denotes the small cymbals portrayed in Assyrian art. Another word from the same root, *ṣelṣelîm* H7529, is usually taken as a synonym, as it is by the LXX in Ps. 150:5. This verse speaks of cymbals of "sound" (*šemaʿ* H9049; NIV, "clash of cymbals") and cymbals of "shout" (*tĕrûʿâ* H9558; NIV, "resounding cymbals"); if two different instruments are meant, one possible distinction is between small cymbals that perhaps were held vertically, and large ones held horizontally (W. L. Holladay, *A Concise Hebrew and Aramaic Lexicon of the Old Testament* [1971], 307). The term *ṣelṣelîm*, however, is used in only one other passage, 2 Sam. 6:5, where the LXX renderings of the various words are confusing (they may reflect textual variants), while another cognate term, *mĕṣillâ* H5197, certainly does not mean "cymbal" (it occurs only in Zech. 14:20 and apparently refers to bells). Paul's depreciation of the cymbal in 1 Cor. 13:1 may refer specifically to the use of the instrument in pagan cults (cf. *TDNT*, 1:28).

(2) *Instruments that were shaken.* The Hebrew word *mĕnaʿanʿîm* H4983 (from the root *nûaʿ* H5675, "to quiver, waver, shake") occurs only in 2 Sam. 6:5 and apparently denotes a shaken idiophone. The reference could be either to a rattle (e.g., beads in a hollow gourd; cf. NRSV, "castanets") or to a sistrum (so Vulg.; cf. NIV). The latter, consisting of a small frame with metal pieces loosely attached, was more common, especially in Egypt.

(3) *Instruments that were struck.* Bells are mentioned in a few passages (Exod. 28:33–34; 39:25–26; Zech. 14:20), but apparently not in a strictly musical sense.

B. Membranophones (drums).
The main instrument in this class is the *tōp* H9512 (for which the LXX usually has *tympanon*, "kettledrum"). The fact that women used it in dance (Exod. 15:20; 1 Sam. 18:6; et al.) suggests that it was usually a small (hand-beaten) drum, that is, a timbrel or tambourine. It has been suggested that the Aramaic word *sûmpōnĕyâ* H10507 (Dan. 3:5, 10, 15) reflects Greek *tympanon* and thus designates a drum (cf. NRSV), but the word must rather represent *symphōnia*

G5246, which can simply mean "music" (Lk. 15:25) or "in unison" or "musical band," though here it may refer to a kind of bagpipe (cf. NIV) or to the double-flute (for the latter, see P. Grelot in *VT* 29 [1979]: 23–38, esp. 36–38; for further discussion of Nebuchadnezzar's orchestra, see T. C. Mitchell and R. Joyce in *Notes on Some Problems in the Book of Daniel* [1965], 19–27).

C. Aerophones (blown). (1) *Instruments played with lips vibrating.* The Hebrew term *šôpār H8795*, usually translated "trumpet," refers specifically to a "ram's horn" used as a sound instrument for communicating signals and announcing important events (e.g., 1 Ki. 1:34). The characteristic of this animal horn is its curved shape and relatively wide, conical bore. The same instrument can be referred to with the word *yôbēl H3413* ("ram" or "ram's horn"), used either by itself (Exod. 19:13) or in combination with *šôpār* or *qeren H7967* (Josh. 6:4–8, 13). On the other hand, the common term *ḥăṣōṣĕrâ H2956* (Num. 10:2 et al.), also translated "trumpet," designates a tube of straight, narrow bore. The main difference between the two types of instrument was one of tone quality, but it is likely that a secondary difference was the often metallic construction of the *ḥăṣōṣĕrâ*. For either instrument only a limited number of pitches (two or three) could be produced, so that they are far removed from the modern trumpet.

(2) *Pipes.* All other blown instruments can be called pipes and fall into two groups. Reed pipes have either one or two reeds (as in the present-day clarinet and oboe, respectively) into which air is blown, while with flutes the air is blown against one edge of the mouth-hole. Flutes can be end-blown (vertical), cross-blown (hole in side, held transversely like the modern flute), or whistle flutes. Certain Hebrew terms designate instruments belonging to the general class of pipes, but it is difficult to be more specific. The *ḥālîl H2720*, translated *aulos G888* in the LXX and "flute" in modern English versions ("pipe" in KJV), was probably a reed pipe, an interpretation that fits the context of lament in Jer. 48:36. Since in antiquity two reed pipes often were played simultaneously by the same person, this might also have been true of the *ḥālîl* (some believe that the word refers specifically to the double-pipe). The *nĕḥîlôt H5704* (mentioned only in the title of Ps. 5) may have been another form of this instrument.

The Aramaic term *mašrôqi H10446* (cf. Heb. *šāraq H9239*, "to whistle, hiss") probably signifies some type of flute, preferably vertical or whistle (Dan. 3:5 et al.). Of the four occurrences of Hebrew *ʿûgāb H6385*, two passages indicate only that it is a musical instrument (Gen. 4:21; Ps. 150:4), and the other two imply that it is normally used to express rejoicing (Job 21:12 [a verse that also mentions a membranophone and a chordophone]; 30:31). The TARGUM interpreted it as a pipe, but the LXX translated it variously (*kithara*, a stringed instrument; *organon*, a general term for musical instrument; and *psalmos*, music made with a stringed instrument). There is no reason to think that it was a set of pipes or an organ.

D. Chordophones (strings). The Hebrew term *mēn H4944*, "string," occurs in the plural as a general word for stringed instruments (Pss. 45:8; 150:4). Although modern types can be bowed, plucked, or struck, there was apparently no bowing in use in antiquity.

(1) *Lutes* have strings stretched along a neck attached to a resonating body as in guitar-like and violin-like instruments. Although lutes are represented in Egyptian, Mesopotamian, and Hittite art, it is uncertain whether they are mentioned in the Bible. The English term is used by the NIV twice to render two different Hebrew words (1 Sam. 18:6; 2 Chr. 20:28), while the NRSV also uses it twice, but other Hebrew words occur (Pss. 92:3; 150:3; cf. also 1 Macc. 4:54). The simplicity of the lute (possibly originating from the hunting bow being plucked) should caution one against assuming that it did not exist in Israel. In Greece the lute was usually

Jewish man blowing the shofar or ram's horn trumpet.

A silver lyre from c. 2600 B.C.

called *pandoura* (possibly reflecting ultimately the Sumerian *PAN. TUR*).

(2–3) *Harps and lyres.* Harps have the neck at an angle to the body, either arched (of the same piece as the body) or angular (neck fastened to body at near right angle), whereas lyres have a body with two arms joined by a crossbar, the strings going from body to crossbar. It is difficult to determine which Hebrew words refer to which of these stringed instruments. The NIV usually has "harp" for *kinnôr H4036* and "lyre" for *nēbel H5575*, terms that are often found in the same context (e.g., 2 Sam. 6:5; 1 Ki. 10:12; et al.). Other translations, however, reverse these two words (e.g., TNIV, NRSV, NJPS). In the historical books, the LXX renders them by means of unhelpful loanwords (*kinyra* and *nabla*), but in the poetic and prophetic literature it uses respectively *kithara* (a triangular lyre or lute with seven strings) and *psaltērion* (psaltery or a type of harp; cf. Aram. *pĕsantērîn H10590* in Dan. 3:5 et al.). The reference to a ten-string lyre or harp (Pss. 33:2; 144:9) probably indicates that normally a different number of strings was employed. According to Bo Lawergren (in *BASOR* 309 [Feb. 1998]: 41–68), *kinnôr* refers to a "thin" lyre, consisting of no more than eight strings, whereas *nēbel* refers to a "thick" lyre, which can have as many as thirteen.

(4) *Other instruments.* Zithers have many strings stretched across a body, either struck (dulcimer) or plucked (psaltery). It is problematic whether such instruments are mentioned in the Bible, although both NIV and NJPS use "zither" to render Aramaic *qîtrōs H10630* (from Gk. *kithara*, Dan. 3:5 et al.). Another Aramaic term in the same passage, *śabběkāʾ H10676*, is rendered "lyre" by the NIV, but "trigon" by the NRSV and NJPS (the KJV's "sackbut," referring to a medieval trombone, is wrongly based on the similarity of sound between the Aram. and Eng. words). Hebrew *šālîš H8956* (from the word for "third"), which may refer to a three-stringed or three-sided instrument, occurs only once and is translated variously (1 Sam. 18:6; NIV, "lutes"; NJPS, "sistrums"; NRSV, "musical instruments"). Another Hebrew word, *něgînâ H5593*, which appears in the title of several psalms (e.g., Ps. 4) and elsewhere, may be a general term for "stringed instrument." (For a fine survey of musical instruments in the Bible, including valuable illustrations, see P. J. King and L. E. Stager, *Life in Biblical Israel* [2001], 290–98.)

V. Terms relating to performance

A. Vocal. Several Hebrew terms refer to vocal music. The very common verb *šîr H8876* (Exod. 15:1 et al.) means "to sing," and the cognate noun *šîr H8876* (Jdg. 5:12 et al.; less frequently *šîrâ H8878*, e.g., Num. 21:17) is translated "song," although it may perhaps lose its connection with music and mean simply "poem" (Cant. 1:1). The singing may be to the accompaniment of instruments, typical ones being cymbals, harps, and lyres (Neh. 12:27; 1 Chr. 15:16; 25:6).

The verb *ʿānâ H6702*, which occurs about a dozen times, usually means "to sing"; although it has a different derivation from the very common verb *ʿānâ H6699*, "to answer," the two may have been linked by popular etymology (the former perhaps could suggest "sing in response"; cf. Syr. *ʿny*). One is impressed by the brevity of the texts introduced by this verb (Exod. 15:21; Num. 21:17; 1 Sam. 18:7; 21:11; 29:5; Ezra 3:11), and some have speculated that the piece was sung repeatedly, one person or group answering another rather than singing alternate lines. Another verb, *rānan H8264*, properly means "shout [for joy]," but in various contexts it seems to have a quasi-musical sense and can be translated "sing [for joy]" (e.g., 1 Chr. 16:33; Ps. 5:1). See also the next section (instrumental terms).

Greek terms for vocal music include the verbs *adō G106* and *psallō G6010*, as well as the nouns *hymnos G5631*, *psalmos G6011*, and *ōdē G6046* (all five words occur in Eph. 5:19, and four of them in the parallel, Col. 3:16).

B. Instrumental. The verb *nāgan H5594* (usually piel) refers to instrumental music, since it can be done with the hand (1 Sam. 16:23). In Ps. 68:25 it stands in contrast to singing and playing the hand-drum, and whenever the instrument is mentioned, it is a lyre or harp, *kinnôr* (1 Sam. 16:23; Isa. 23:16). The participle *měnaggēn* (2 Ki. 3:15; qal ptc. *nōgěnim* in Ps. 68:26) may mean "string player, harpist," or more generally "minstrel, musician." The verb *zāmar H2376* (always piel; cf. also the cognate noun *zimrâ H2379*) has a wide semantic range and thus is somewhat ambiguous: in a few passages it seems to have the general meaning of "to make music, play [an instrument]" (e.g., Ps. 33:2), but more often it means "to sing [praise]" (2 Sam. 22:50 et al.), and is always directed to God (see also the next section, VI.A).

VI. Musical terms in Psalm superscriptions.

Because many of these (semitechnical) terms are of uncertain meaning, the following classification should be regarded as only tentative.

A. Types of songs. The common term *mizmôr H4660* (it occurs in the title of 57 psalms, beginning with Ps. 3) is traditionally rendered "psalm" (following LXX, *psalmos*). Like its cognate verb *zāmar*, it probably has a general meaning, such as "song with musical accompaniment," or perhaps "song with string accompaniment." The meaning of *šiggāyôn H8710* (only in the title of Ps. 7 and the plural in Hab. 3:1) is obscure, and Bible versions simply transliterate it. It probably derives from the verb *šāgâ H8706* ("to go astray, stagger"), so some have suggested the meaning "dithyramb" (i.e., a song with rapidly changing mood or with sporadic rhythm); others appeal to Akkadian *šegû* and translate "dirge, lament," characterized by a wandering style.

Another uncertain term that Bible versions usually transliterate is *maśkîl H5380* (in the title of 14 psalms, beginning with Ps. 32). It derives from the common verb *śākal H8505* (hiphil, "to understand," but also "act devoutly"), so suggested meanings include "meditation" and "skillful poem." Two other terms are the common noun *těhillâ H9335*, which clearly means "praise, song of praise" (e.g., Ps. 40:3), and *miktām H4846* (in the title of Ps. 16 and 56–60), which perhaps means simply "inscription" (see discussion under MIKTAM).

B. Names of melodies. Some phrases, usually introduced by the preposition ʿ*al H6584*, "upon," seem to designate the melody to be sung by referring to words commonly associated with the melody, a practice attested in Babylonian music. If so, these phrases possibly do not give any information regarding the psalm itself. Alternatively, these terms have been interpreted as referring to content, mood, or occasion. For example, the phrase ʿ*almût labbēn* in the title of Ps. 9 may mean, "concerning the death of the son," and ʾ*el-šōšannîm ʿēdût* in Ps. 80 (notice the use of a different preposition) can be rendered, "concerning the lilies of testimony" (KJV, "Shoshannim-eduth"; cf. also Pss. 45; 60; 69; for other interpretations, see *HALOT*, 4:1455). In the case of ʾ*al-tašḥēt* (Pss. 57–59 and 75), the first element is not a preposition but a negative particle; this phrase means, "do not destroy." The difficulty of interpreting the phrases according to the context of the psalm, witnessed to by the multiplicity of renderings by the ancient versions, enforces the impression that they are names of melodies.

C. Other musical terms introduced by ʿal. The similarity of these to the preceding class raises the possibility of their also being explained as melodies. However, other explanations are possible. For example, the phrase ʿ*al-haggittît* (Ps. 8; 81; 84) could refer to some musical instrument associated with the city of GATH or it may indicate "vintage time" (see

GITTITH). In 1 Chr. 15:20–21 we read that certain musicians "were to play the lyres according to *alamoth*," while others "were to play the harps, directing according to *sheminith*." The first of those technical terms (also found in the title of Ps. 46) is apparently the plural form of ʿ*almâ H6625*, "maiden," and some have speculated that the song was set to a higher (woman's) range. The second term (also in Ps. 6; 12) appears to be the feminine form of *šĕmînî H9029*, "eighth," which suggests either an "eight-stringed instrument" or "the eighth tone, octave" (it is doubtful whether the Israelites had an eight-tone scale, although on the basis of a four-tone scale it could mean "double octave"). Others have thought that the word derives from the verb *šāmēn H9042* ("to grow fat"; the hiphil can mean "to make dull") and that it indicates "the dull, heavy range." Both *nĕḥîlôt H5704* (Ps. 5) and *māḥălat H4714* (Pss. 53; 88) may refer to pipes or flutes, although the second term is particularly obscure (other suggestions for it include "with dancing," "sorrowfully," and "for sickness").

D. Remaining musical terms in the superscriptions.

A frequently occurring phrase, *lamnaṣṣēaḥ* (found in fifty-five superscriptions and in Hab. 3:19), is to be interpreted by 1 Chr. 15:21, where the verb *nāṣaḥ H5904* is applied to certain men playing stringed instruments. It does not designate the general directing of the music since that is the function of the three cymbalists (v. 19). Rather, it would describe those who provided the musical introduction and accompaniment and thus "led" the singing. If this passage is relied on, the term in the Psalms could mean "to be begun by an accompanist." In this connection, it should be noted that all of the superscriptions containing an indication of the accompaniment (musical instrument or tune; about thirty) have this term, nearly always as the first element. Usually, however, *lamnaṣṣēaḥ* is taken to mean "to the leader" (NRSV) or "for the director of music" (NIV) in the sense of the person leading the music in the Israelite nation or in a local worshiping community. One wonders, however, why psalms would have to be thus designated, since this would be a matter of course and would be an appropriate designation for many that are not given this term. Others understand the phrase to mean "from the director's collection," but it is not clear why such information would be pertinent. None of these interpretations is supported by the ancient versions, which give meanings like "to the end," "to the conqueror, conquering."

The phrase *šîr hammaʿălôt* or *šîr lammaʿălôt* is found in the titles of Pss. 120–134. It is usually translated literally, "a song of ascents" (from *maʿălâ H5092*, "a going up, a step"; KJV, "a Song of degrees"), and has been taken to refer to the characteristics of the psalm (a shift in theme or key word, but this view cannot account for the definite article), or to origins (going up from Babylon, but the preposition argues against this), or to location (the Levites' going up the temple steps as they sang), or to use (sung when going up to Jerusalem for a feast). Most modern interpretations tend to this last view. If so, these are psalms designated as suitable for those traveling up to the various pilgrimage feasts (the verb ʿ*ālâ H6590* is used frequently of going to Jerusalem).

The term *lĕʿannôt H4361* (used with *māḥălat* in the title of Ps. 88) is obscure; it appears to be the infinitive of ʿ*ānâ H6699*, and if so it may refer to antiphonal performance, either of singing or dancing. Two other technical terms occur in the body of various psalms. One of them, *higgāyôn H2053*, elsewhere means "talk, murmuring, meditation," but it can also mean "sounding, melody" (Ps. 92:3), and the technical use in Ps. 9:16 has been taken as "loud, resounding music" or "music of strings." Finally, the word *selâ H6138* occurs seventy-one times in Psalms and three times in Hab. 3. Some scholars, deriving it from *sālal H6148*, suggest that it refers to the "lifting up" of the voice (or raising the pitch) in singing a benediction. Others think that it indicates a pause or instrumental interlude (cf. the LXX rendering *diapsalma*), or that it means "forever," or that it is an acronym, each consonant standing for the first letter of a word (the resulting phrase might be an instruction to go back to the beginning and repeat, or it might indicate a change of voices).

(In addition to the works mentioned in the body of this article, see P. Gradenwitz, *The Music of Israel* [1949]; C. C. J. Polin, *Music of the Ancient Near East* [1954]; C. C. Keet, *A Study of the Psalms of Ascents: A Critical and Exegetical Commentary upon Psalms CXX to CXXXIV* [1969]; J. Rimmer, *Ancient Musical Instruments of Western Asia in the British*

Museum [1969]; A. Sendrey, *Music in Ancient Israel* [1969]; E. Werner, *The Sacred Bridge* [1970]; W. Madge, *Bible Music and Its Development* [1977]; J. Braun, *Music in Ancient Israel/Palestine: Archaeological, Written, and Comparative Sources* [2002]; T. W. Burgh, *Listening to the Artifacts: Music Culture in Ancient Palestine* [2006]; *ABD*, 4:930–39; *CANE*, 4:2601–13.)
H. M. BEST; D. HUTTAR

mustard. The Greek term for "mustard," *sinapi G4983*, occurs in two NT contexts: in the kingdom parable of the mustard seed (Matt 13:31 = Mk. 4:31 = Lk. 13:19) and in Jesus' comment about having "faith as small as a mustard seed" (Matt. 17:20 = Lk. 17:6). The tree known in Palestine as the mustard tree (*Nicotiana glauca*) has minute seeds and yellow flowers; it is grown widely in the Mediterranean and is a member of the *Solanaceae* family. Most Bible students, however, agree that the plant mentioned in the NT is the black mustard, *Brassica nigra*. This is the plant grown for the production of the normal mustard, though in our Lord's day it was grown possibly for its oil content.

A field of mustard plants in Israel.

Its seed "has a section of 1 mm and weighs 1 mg" (*FFB*, 145). The plants are usually not large, but when isolated they may grow to a height of 15 ft. and have a thick main stem, with branches strong enough to bear the weight of a bird. Jesus described it as "the largest of garden plants" (Matt. 13:32 = Mk. 4:32), and the black mustard certainly fits this description.

Because of its Greek name, some believe that the plant must be *Sinapis alba*, the white mustard, but this grows only 2 ft. high. The Royal Horticultural Society prefers the evergreen *Salvadora persica*, the kilnel oil plant (sometimes called the mustard tree). This tree grows on the sides of the Dead Sea, and the Arabs give it the name of *khardal*, which could be translated "mustard tree." It does not, however, have tiny seeds, but small "stones," smaller than those of the damson. Such "stones" would not have been broadcast by a farmer as described in the NT.
W. E. SHEWELL-COOPER

Muster Gate. A gate in Jerusalem, not far from the TEMPLE. The Hebrew name *ša‘ar hammipqād*, which occurs only once in connection with NEHEMIAH's rebuilding of the wall of JERUSALEM (Neh. 3:31), is rendered "the gate Miphkad" by the KJV, "the Muster Gate" by the NRSV, and "the Inspection Gate" by the NIV. The Hebrew word *mipqād H5152* can mean both "regulation, appointment" (cf. 2 Chr. 31:13) and "counting" (as when mustering troops, 2 Sam. 24:9 = 1 Chr. 21:5). The exact location of the Muster Gate is uncertain, but it was apparently opposite the temple on the NE part of the city, between the EAST GATE and the SHEEP GATE (Neh. 3:29, 32), and some identify it with the BENJAMIN GATE. According to Ezek. 43:21, the bull for the sin offering was to be burned *bĕmipqād habbayit*, a phrase usually rendered "in the designated [appointed] place of the temple." Some, however, understand it as "the place of review [inspection] in the temple," suggesting a connection with the Muster Gate. See also JERUSALEM II.D.2. and III.A.

Muth-labben myooth-lab´uhn. The Hebrew musical term ‘*almût labbēn* (in the superscription of Ps. 9) is rendered by the KJV and other versions as "upon [NRSV, according to] Muth-labben" (the NJPS has "almuth labben"). The meaning is obscure. Interpreting the phrase as a reference to a particular melody, the NIV renders, "To the tune of 'The Death of the Son.'" See MUSIC VI.B.

mutilation. See CRIMES AND PUNISHMENTS III.B.

muzzle. The Israelites were commanded not to muzzle (Heb. *ḥāsam H2888*) the ox when it was treading out the grain, that is, THRESHING (Deut. 25:4). The muzzle was a guard placed on the mouth of the oxen to prevent them from biting or eating. The threshing ox was to have ample opportunity of feeding, thus making the labor more agreeable. The injunction is in harmony with the spirit of the Deuteronomic exposition of the Mosaic law throughout. PAUL quotes this injunction to illustrate, with an appropriate light touch of humor, his view that it is proper to pay the minister for his work in the gospel (1 Cor. 9:8–11 [Gk. *kēmoō G3055*]; 1 Tim. 5:17–18 [*phimoō G5821*]; on the question of whether Paul's use of Scripture here is allegorical and invalid, see D. E. Garland, *1 Corinthians*, BECNT [2003], 409–11).   E. RUSSELL

Myndos min′dohs (Μύνδος). KJV Myndus. A city on the coast of CARIA in ASIA MINOR at the far end of the peninsula, noted for silver mines; identified as modern Gumushli. It is one of the places to which the Roman senate, in 139 B.C., sent a letter in behalf of the Jews (1 Macc. 15:23), and it was therefore probably independent of the Carian confederacy.   S. BARABAS

Myndus min′duhs. KJV Apoc. form of MINDOS.

Myra mi′ruh (Μύρα *G3688*, meaning uncertain). A city of LYCIA, in SW ASIA MINOR. The apostle PAUL visited the town on his journey to ROME, and the fact that he changed ships there indicates its importance as a port (Acts 27:5). The origins of Myra are lost in antiquity; it was known as an ancient town, achieved some importance as the chief city of the Lycian district, and actually was called a metropolis. It is described by ancient writers as the "best and most sparkling" city of Lycia. Its public buildings were distinguished, and included a GYMNASIUM with an arcade furnished with recesses and seats, a theater, a bath, a stoa or roofed colonnade, a temple of Peace, and during the Christian era several churches.

Myra had a large territory, extending 2.5 mi. S to the sea, where the port city Andriaca lay. It spread widely to the N and W as well. Some notion of the influence of the place may be gathered from the fact that many citizens of Myra also held citizenship in other cities. This was a common form of recognition in the Hellenistic world. It is strange that for such an influential city only one product, rue (from which oil was pressed, and a flavoring for wine extracted), is mentioned, and two occupations: something having to do with flax or fishing-nets, and tavern-keeping. Perhaps these are things for which Myra was particularly known and do not represent the sole business activity of the city.

In spite of its importance, little is known of the actual history of Myra. In 88 B.C. PTOLEMY IX of Egypt, fleeing from his mutinous army, took refuge there. In 42 B.C., during the troubled period following the death of CAESAR, the city was attacked and capitulated to Brutus. It suffered extensively from a severe earthquake in A.D. 141 and was rebuilt largely by the contributions of one of its prominent citizens. Little is known of its subsequent history. (See W. Ruge in Pauly-Wissowa, *Realencyclopädie der classischen Altertumswissenschaft* 16/1 [1933], 1083–89; J. Borchhardt, *Myra: Eine lykische Metropole in antiker und byzantinischer Zeit* [1975]; *ABD*, 4:939–40.)   R. C. STONE

myrrh. There are twelve instances of the Hebrew noun *mōr H5255*, generally dealing with perfuming, as in Ps. 45:8, "All your robes are fragrant with myrrh"; or in Prov. 7:17: "I have perfumed my bed

Myrrh, a fragrant gum harvested from trees in Arabia.

with myrrh." S〇L〇M〇N mentions it again and again in his Song (e.g., "My lover is to me a sachet of myrrh," Cant. 1:13). Oil of myrrh was also used as part of beauty treatment (Esth. 2:12). Another Hebrew term, *lōṭ H4320* (only in Gen. 37:25; 43:11), is rendered "myrrh" by some (cf. KJV, RSV, NIV), but others think it is the resin or mastic of the *Pistacia mutica* (cf. NRSV) or else ladanum (the gum of the rockrose *Cistus salvifolius*; cf. NJPS). Myrrh is mentioned also in the NT (Gk. *smyrna G5043*, but *myron G3693* in Rev. 18:13 [KJV, "ointments"; cf. Jn. 11:2]): the MAGI brought some (Matt. 2:11), and our Lord was embalmed with it (Jn. 19:39).

This myrrh is a fragrant gum that exudes from trees in ARABIA, and particularly from the *Balsamodendron myrrha*. It is said to have been part of the composition of the "anointing oil" (Exod. 30:23–25). There are pictures of these trees on the Egyptian temple of Deir el-Bahari. The inscriptions speak of Punt in Africa as the home of these trees and a source of myrrh.

It is generally agreed, however, that myrrh came from *Commiphora myrrha*, which grows in Somaliland, Ethiopia, and Arabia. The trunk and branches exude a gum that produces the delicious fragrance (according to *HALOT*, 2:630, *C. abessinica*). This *C. myrrha* is related to *C. kataf*. Both are small trees, often called thorny shrubs, and both bear small plum-like fruits. Though the gum exudes naturally from the branches, any artificial incision will, of course, produce an immediate supply. The sap as it first oozes out is oily, but as it drops onto wooden squares or stones on which it is collected, it solidifies. The gum obtained from the *Commiphora kataf* is not the true myrrh, though it often is mixed with it. (See G. van Beek in *JAOS* 78 [1958]: 143; *FFB*, 147–49.) See also FLORA (under *Burseraceae* and *Cistaceae*); SPICES.   W. E. SHEWELL-COOPER

myrtle. The Hebrew term *hădas H2072* occurs six times, sometimes referring to myrtle branches (Neh. 8:15), often as myrtle trees (Zech. 1:8, 10–11). ISAIAH uses it in eschatological contexts (Isa. 41:19; 55:13). Because they are evergreen, the boughs were used at the Feast of Tabernacles. NEHEMIAH ordered that myrtle branches should be cut to make booths for this festival (Neh. 8:15); they are still gathered in Palestine for a similar purpose. "Myrtle" is the meaning of Queen ESTHER's Hebrew name, HADASSAH.

The myrtle is undoubtedly *Myrtus communis*, a dense evergreen shrub that grows abundantly in Palestine and particularly around the Lake of Galilee and near Samaria and Jerusalem. With age it becomes a small tree, up to 15 ft. tall with equal spread; the leaves are small, shiny, slightly-scented, and leathery. The white or pinkish flowers are scented, and are followed by blue-black berries, which can produce a perfume. The fascinating fragrance of Russian and Turkish leather comes from the fact that the roots and bark of myrtle are used during tanning. The queens of England carry sprigs of myrtle in their wedding bouquets as a symbol of peace. (See *FFB*, 149–50.) See also FLORA (under *Myrtaceae*).   W. E. SHEWELL-COOPER

Mysia mis´ee-uh (Μυσία *G3695*). A region in NW ASIA MINOR bounded by the AEGEAN, the Hellespont, the Propontis, BITHYNIA, PHRYGIA, and LYDIA; it includes the historic TROAS and the areas of Aeolian Greek settlement on the Aegean coast. In Greek times it shared the fortunes of the W stub of the peninsula, fell to the Romans in 133 B.C. as part of the royal legacy of Attalus III, and in Roman days was part of the province of ASIA. This is why Mysia, never itself an independent political

Mysia.

entity, lacks precise boundaries (cf. Strabo, *Geogr.* 12.4.4–6; 12.8.1–3). It was a mountainous and, in early times, well-forested region, traversed by some of the main trade routes. The Troas area was part of Mysia, and PERGAMUM itself lay within its somewhat vague boundaries. The early inhabitants of Mysia were probably of Thracian origin. Like the Trojans, who held their strategic foothold in Mysia near the entrance to the Hellespont, and the HITTITES, whose great empire at times held dominance this far, they probably were an Indo-European stock, an early wave of the great invasions of the peoples who, with their kindred dialects, were to settle all Europe. Mysia was traversed by PAUL in the course of his second journey (Acts 16:7–8), but no pause was made there save at Troas. There is evidence, however, of church foundations of a very early date. E. M. BLAIKLOCK

mystery. In the NT, the Greek word *mystērion G3696* refers to the counsel of God, unknown to human beings except by REVELATION, especially concerning his saving works and ultimate purposes in history. The word occurs in the SEPTUAGINT as a translation of Aramaic *rāz H10661* (Dan. 2:18–19, 27–30, 47; 4:9 [MT 4:6, LXX 4:18]; it also occurs a number of times in the APOCRYPHA, but usually with the meaning "secret"; however, see Wisd. 2:22). This term occurs almost thirty times in the NT, and in none of the passages is its use casual. On the contrary, it is a carefully chosen term of significance for biblical theology. It is relevant to such major topics as REVELATION, ESCHATOLOGY, ecclesiology (see CHURCH), and CHRISTOLOGY. Moreover, it is a significant term in pagan and Jewish religion; but if its interpretation in biblical contexts is to be informed by its nonbiblical usage, it is extremely important that such data be precise and judiciously applied.

I. Background

A. Issues. The general study of comparative religions and the quest for historical and semantic precedents as an aid to biblical interpretation have resulted in considerable discussion over the meaning of the term. The obvious fact that Christianity was contemporaneous with, and challenged by, the so-called MYSTERY RELIGIONS, has naturally caused scholars to probe the pagan concept of mystery as a background to NT usage. For some time, however, the limitations of this pursuit have been recognized, and attention has turned to Semitic parallels. A combination of sound methodology and adequate data is required. Further, the interpretation of the biblical term must be derived primarily from exegesis of the passages involved. The basic meaning of these passages is clear enough from the respective contexts to prevent overdependence on nonbiblical frames of reference.

B. Secular and pagan. Relevant secular occurrences are rare. The very nature of the word attracts it mainly to discussions on the issues of life, which are basically religious and philosophical (for source references, see G. Bornkamm in *TDNT*, 4:802–28). Conversely, in the apocryphal books of JUDITH and TOBIT the term is used in a secular sense (Jdt. 2:2; Tob. 12:7, 11), referring to the secret counsel of the king. While direct connection is unlikely, there is an interesting similarity between the "king's mystery" in Tobit and the "mystery of the kingdom" in Matthew.

The mystery religions offered the initiates a religious awareness and experience not enjoyed by others. This was imparted at the initiation and possibly in later stages. It has been a natural supposition that the contemporary idea of a mystery or secret revealed only to initiates should find its way into Christian thought. This supposition was apparently supported by other alleged parallels between Christianity and these cults. The supposed parallels may be challenged, however. Further, while the term *mystery* is common in the NT, related terms are never used (e.g., *mystēs, mystikos, mystagōgos*; see A. D. Nock in *JBL* 72 [1933]: 131–39). The stress in the NT is not on a mystery *hidden* from all except a select few initiates, but rather on the *revelation* of the *formerly* hidden knowledge. The term also lent itself to philosophical and gnostic usage and could not be considered the distinctive property of any one system or belief. It occurs throughout contemplative literature, from Plato (e.g., *Symposium* 249e) to the HERMETIC WRITINGS (*Poimandres* 16).

Later writers have further maintained that the ample usage of the term in Jewish literature causes alleged pagan parallels to lose their significance. R. E. Brown (*The Semitic Background of the Term*

"Mystery" in the New Testament [1968]) has concluded from his extensive research in the Semitic materials that Greek parallels need not be seriously considered. Nevertheless, while pagan concepts and cultic meanings have not penetrated NT thought, the widespread occurrence of the term indicates its significance as an expression of the quest for the meaning and purpose of life. The problems of evil and suffering, and the frustrations of man's finitude, cause people in all cultures to seek illumination.

C. Jewish. If the hypothesis of influence from the mystery cults is wanting, what can be concluded from the usage in the literature of JUDAISM? The passages in Daniel referred to above stress the contrast between Daniel and the pagan seers. Only the true God knows and reveals the future, and he reveals such to his chosen prophet. It is noteworthy that the word *rāz* used here is found again in the vocabulary of Qumran (see below). The Greek term occurs twelve times in the Apocrypha and frequently in the PSEUDEPIGRAPHA, showing that there is adequate Jewish precedent for its use in the NT. Some of these passages may show an awareness of the mystery cults (cf. Wisd. 6:22). Other contexts are clearly far removed from such concerns and deal instead with the creative and providential decrees of God (e.g., *1 En.* 41.3). Still others, some perhaps contemporary with Christianity, deal with what is known as the problem of evil, and with God's chosen way of future judgment and vindication (e.g., *1 En.* 68.5; 103.2; *2 Bar.* 81.4; *2 Esd.* 14:5). The SON OF MAN will be revealed and will express the hidden counsel of God in the day of judgment (*1 En.* 48.7; 51.3; 62.1–2).

This concern with future vindication was also developed in the literature of QUMRAN (see DEAD SEA SCROLLS). Among the documents discovered, the commentary on Habakkuk (1QpHab) provides a prime example of the sect's attitude to revelation. Taking the word *rāz*, the commentary purports to provide an interpretation (PESHER) of the mysteries and of all the prophetic symbols, which supposedly found their fulfillment in that sect. An example is found in the commentary on the familiar words "so he may run who reads" (Hab. 2:2), which are said to refer to the sect's "Teacher of Righteousness to whom God has revealed all the secrets of the words of his servants the prophets" (1QpHab VII, 1–5).

The universe and the affairs of both men and angels are under the sovereign providence of God, whose ways, known only by revelation, are wonderful (1QS XI, 3–8; 1QH XII, 13–14). At Qumran there existed also a strong dualistic persuasion that pitted the counsel of God against that of the spirit of evil. The mysteries seem in some cases to be related to the devices and fate of the evil beings who reject the mysteries and counsel of God (1QS IV, 18). There is a mystery pertaining to evil ("iniquitous mysteries," 1QH V, 36), which concept may be relevant to the exegesis of 2 Thess. 2:7.

R. E. Brown has also observed the occurrence of the word *sôd* H6051, "plan, counsel, council." It is his particular theory that this word is related to the concept of the mystery, and that in the OT it refers to a heavenly "council" wherein the conduct of the world is discussed. The prophets are, as it were, given access to the decisions of the council. In the DSS, however, it is the evil counsel of BELIAL that is mentioned (1QS IV, 1). One need not decide completely on Brown's conclusions to recognize that the prophets were indeed granted knowledge of God's counsel in advance of his acts (Amos 3:7). To associate the word *mystery* with the decrees of God is a thoroughly biblical concept and basic to NT usage. Further, the conflict in the DSS between calculated evil and God's benign will constitutes another expression of the problem of evil, which is relevant to the NT use of the term.

To what extent the NT authors were aware of any of the literature or beliefs surveyed thus far is difficult to say. However, where the uses of the term in Jewish and in pagan literature differ significantly in meaning, the Jewish usage should take precedence as being more closely related to (and more consistent with) that of the NT. Inasmuch, however, as the very meaning of the word in the Scriptures signifies divine revelation, the only certain canon of interpretation is to derive the basic sense of the word from its biblical context.

II. Interpretation of significant passages

A. The Gospels. The context in Matt. 13:11; Mk. 4:11; Lk. 8:10 is twofold: the inability of unbelievers to understand the mystery in its parabolic form, and the issue of the reign of God. These constitute two basic aspects of mystery: (1) human sin and ignorance, and (2) the revelation of God's sovereign decrees. The first problem was expressed in Isa. 6:9–10. It may be noteworthy that in this prophetic context, there is also an expression of the counsel of God ("Whom shall I send? And who will go for us?" v. 8), a participation of the prophet in this dialogue, and the question, "For how long, O Lord?" (v. 11; the element of waiting is important in the mystery passages). It should be observed also that the mystery of God is not capriciously hidden, but is withheld from those who are disposed to reject it anyway. Further, the revelation itself is a sovereign act of grace; as Jesus expressed it, "The knowledge of the secrets of the kingdom of heaven has been given to you, but not to them." So also God made his ways known to MOSES, but spoke to others in enigmas (Num. 12:8 [LXX, *ainigma*]; cf. 1QS III, 20–23; *2 Bar.* 81.4).

The meaning of the mystery of the KINGDOM OF GOD is open to some diversity of interpretation. It is useful to bear in mind that one aspect of Jewish thought on the kingdom is the subjugation of all evil. Conversely, one aspect of the mystery is the persistence of evil in God's world. Therefore, one of the teachings of the kingdom parables seems to be that, unlike Jewish speculation, the kingdom, in its present form, coexists with evil.

B. Romans. The problem of evil is apparent also in the context of Rom. 11. The present state of Israel is, however, temporary. God will work in human affairs to bring about his gracious will for Israel (vv. 17–26). This interim period of Israel's hardening is a mystery (v. 25). Indeed, part of God's mystery, long hidden but now revealed, concerns how he will bring about obedience to the faith, to his own glory, through Christ (16:25–27).

C. First Corinthians. No human rhetoric or sophistry is capable of declaring God's mystery, according to 1 Cor. 1:18—2:16. The mystery, however, is not hidden, but revealed. What no eye has seen God *has* revealed. Once again the mystery concerns human history and the power of evil. It was decreed before the ages began, and the rulers of this age could not discern it. There is a significant connection here between God's mystery, his decrees, and his wisdom. This WISDOM is imparted to the *teleioi* (*teleios* G5455, "perfect, mature"), a word which referred in the mystery religions to the initiates. Here, however, the background is more likely the familiar *tāmim* H9459, used in the OT and Jewish literature to describe "complete"—i.e., devout, mature—believers (cf. 1QS IV, 22; Lk. 1:6).

In 1 Cor. 15:51, Paul further stresses the transcendence of divine wisdom and power over fleshly limitations. The mystery here relates to the newness of the spiritual body, a matter, like other mysteries, known only by revelation and received by faith. The familiar problem of evil, as it relates to death, and the element of apparent delay also find expression. The expected moment comes suddenly, at the end times, which are the focal point of mysteries.

The remaining uses of the term in this epistle are in 1 Cor. 13:2 and 14:2, where it apparently refers in general to inspired utterances of divinely revealed truths. The whole context of chs. 12–14 is concerned with the SPIRITUAL GIFTS that transcend human limitations, and the proclamation of mysteries properly belongs in this category.

D. Ephesians, Colossians, 1 Timothy. The entire letter to the EPHESIANS is an exposition of the counsel of God and his mystery. The first chapter is interspersed with expressions conveying the idea of divine purpose ("chose," "destined," "will," "purpose," "counsel," etc.). Thus "the mystery of his will" (Eph. 1:9) is an appropriate expression. In the fullness of time (note again the element of delay and expectation), all things will be brought into an orderly and meaningful relation to Christ. The present chaotic disorder will be ended, but during this time of waiting it is only by the Spirit of wisdom and revelation that one may understand this "hope" (1:17–18). Meanwhile, God is working out his mystery: by grace (2:8–10), divinely revealed (3:2–3), through Christ (3:4), in the church (3:9–10), which is composed of Jews and Gentiles in one body, a mystery not previously so revealed (3:5–6).

The word *mystērion* appears in all these passages, and is associated in Eph. 3:9–10 with the wisdom of God (cf. 1 Cor. 1–2) and with *oikonomia* G3873, that is, God's administrative plan. The concept of an orderly divine sequence of saving acts and of a meaningful consummation of history is thus introduced. Since *oikonomia* also is used to describe Paul's stewardship within God's administration, it is not difficult to see why Paul considers his preaching of the gospel to be linked with the mystery itself (Eph. 6:19; 1 Cor. 4:1; Col. 4:3).

Not only does Paul preach the mystery, but he also bends every effort by God's grace to present believers mature in Christ (Col. 1:28–29). The reason is that the mystery centers in Christ, and it is in Christ that the future final glorious revelation of the mystery will be realized. The unseen presence of Christ in the church is the hope of this glory (1:26–27). Indeed, the mystery is not only of God but also of Christ (2:2).

Since mystery is related to the perception by faith of God's saving work in history, and since Christ is the agent and center of God's mystery, the creedal statement (1 Tim. 3:16) is called "the mystery of godliness" (NRSV, "of our religion"; cf. "the mystery of the faith" in 3:9). The verbs represent the language of mystery: "appeared," "vindicated," "seen," "preached," "believed," "taken up in glory."

It is generally held that *mystery* in Eph. 5:32 is used to signify an allegorical meaning of Genesis that is here explained (see ALLEGORY). This usage of the term is found later in patristic literature. Likewise the mystery is said to designate the symbols used in Rev. 1:12–20. While this may be true, one must not ignore the fact that in both contexts Christ and the church are the subjects, consistent with the mystery passages in Ephesians and Colossians. The term may, therefore, still refer to the content of the revelation and not to the allegorical element.

E. Second Thessalonians, Revelation.

A contrasting negative use is found in 2 Thess. 2:7 and Rev. 17:5, 7. The former passage deals with the mystery of iniquity and the man of lawlessness (2 Thess. 2:3; see ANTICHRIST), while the passage in Revelation discusses the symbolic "mother of prostitutes," BABYLON. While the term *mystery* in Revelation may indeed also relate to the matter of allegory and revelation, the two passages are related by the common concept of a mystery of evil. This may reflect earlier Jewish speculation (e.g., 1QH V, 36). The questions raised are typically those of the mystery: How long must the consummation of God's kingdom wait? How long must the saints wait before they are vindicated and evil judged? Why is evil permitted to continue and how does it flourish? Both passages respond firmly by putting a time limit on the progress of evil and by stressing the judgment of God.

Another verse, Rev. 10:7, makes the definitive statement, "the mystery of God will be accomplished." The passage concerns the SOVEREIGNTY OF GOD over creation, his activity in final judgment, the end of delay (v. 6; KJV, "time"), and the previous revelation to the prophets. These are all familiar elements of mystery, and we may conclude that the book of Revelation presents the consummation of that very mystery that has occupied the thoughts of generations of believers and that is progressively revealed in Scripture.

III. Mystery as a theological term.

Mystery in the NT does not deal with the unknowable, but with what is imparted by revelation. God has shared his plan, especially regarding the future judgment of unbelievers and the vindication of believers. Since the problem of evil is involved, and the ways of God are vindicated, mystery may also be considered a term of THEODICY. The concept of mystery in the NT owes nothing to the mystery cults. (In postapostolic times, however, the term was employed with conscious reference to cultic usage to describe the SACRAMENTS.)

From the human side, the existence of evil in God's world (even after the coming of Christ and his proclamation of the kingdom) and the seemingly interminable waiting for justice and vindication constitute a mystery. From the biblical perspective, the mystery concerns God's wise counsel and the certain progress toward fulfillment of his decrees and saving work. The revelation of the mysteries to the biblical authors is itself an act of grace, as is the saving work of Christ therein described. Though thus revealed, the content of the mystery is received only by faith: the INCARNATION (1 Tim. 3:16), the presence of the kingdom (Matt. 13:11–17), the presence of Christ in his church (Col. 1:27), the meaning and purpose of the church (Eph. 3:8–12), future resurrection (1 Cor. 15:51), and final judgment (Rev. 14:7).

Mystery thus is related to biblical inspiration and revelation, the providence and decrees of God, the problem of evil, the kingdom, the person and work of Christ, the place of Israel and the Gentiles, the

MYSTERY RELIGIONS

church, and eschatology. (In addition to the works mentioned in the body of the article, see E. Hatch, *Essays in Biblical Greek* [1889], 57–62; id., *The Influence of Greek Ideas and Usages upon the Christian Church*, 2nd ed. [1891], 283–309; K. Prümm in *Sacramentum verbi: An Encyclopedia of Biblical Theology*, ed. J. B. Bauer [1970], 2:598–611; J. Marcus, *The Mystery of the Kingdom of God* [1986]; M. N. A. Bockmuehl, *Revelation and Mystery in Ancient Judaism and Pauline Christianity* [1990].)

W. L. LIEFELD

mystery religions. Secret cults that flourished in the Hellenistic world several centuries before and after the time of Christ.

I. Significance. The mysteries appealed to a deep and growing sense of need, in the Hellenistic period, for a personal religious experience and future salvation. Perpetuating ancient agrarian rites and FERTILITY CULTS, most of these mysteries (sometimes called "oriental") took shape in the eastern part of the Roman empire. MYTHS were developed around locally recognized deities, and such myths were reflected in initiation rites and other celebrations. These latter were repugnant to the Roman mind, and their full acceptance at Rome took centuries. The cults, especially MITHRAISM, offered a challenge to the early Christians. Some of them employed rituals, myths, and terminology that have points of resemblance to Christianity. It has been maintained that the oriental religions had a significant influence on Christian doctrine and worship. The alleged relationship between these mysteries and Christianity will be discussed, following a survey of the cults themselves.

II. Description

A. The Eleusinian mysteries. These were well known and honored in classical times, and are mentioned in literature from the time of the Homeric *Hymn to Demeter*. Native to GREECE, their center was ELEUSIS, near ATHENS. Evidently growing out of an agrarian festival, the rites celebrated the annual production of crops. Demeter, goddess of the harvest (and naturally of fertility also) and her daughter, Persephone (Kore), were the main figures

In this grave stone of a Roman legionnaire named Aurelius Surus (1st cent.), the deceased is described as having "served the subterranean gods for 18 years."

of the Eleusinian myth. Persephone was abducted by Pluto, god of death. Demeter's mournful quest for her through the underworld and her subsequent withdrawal, followed by the reappearance of Persephone, are reflected in the rites, which connect the myth with the changing seasons. To understand this, or any, mystery cult, the importance of the seasons in daily life must be remembered (including the fact that summer was a time of withering, not growth).

The rites that supported this myth were complex and were performed in several stages. After the initiation (*myēsis*) and dedication (*teletē*), there was a final revelation (*epopteia*). This ritual involved not the inculcation of doctrine or the performance of sacred acts, but the witnessing of a drama, probably the reenactment of the Demeter-Persephone myth. The use of the word *descent* in an ancient description suggests that the initiates went down into a dark area, symbolizing the underworld to which Persephone was taken. From there they ascended into bright light, where with great emotion and a sense of identification they were shown certain sacred objects, probably symbolizing fertility. Participants in this drama received the blessedness of a better life after death.

B. Dionysus. Another ancient festival was that of DIONYSUS, the god of wine. Traditionally Tracian in origin, the religion of Dionysus was widespread. His name has been found even among ancient inscriptions in CRETE. The celebration of rites varied from place to place, but they were generally known to be emotionally excessive. (The terms *bacchic* and *bacchanalian* are derived from the other name of Dionysus, Bacchus.)

The ancient cult of Orphism employed a myth about Dionysus. In it, an ancient COSMOGONY is described in which Dionysus, son of ZEUS, was destroyed by the Titans, who ate his flesh. A new Dionysus emerged from his heart, which had been preserved. From this myth the cult justified a belief in a kind of metempsychosis (the passing of the soul to another body) and ultimate release of the soul. In spite of the crude mythology and rites of Orphism, it did, unlike most other mystery cults, promulgate specific doctrines, urge a consistency of life (even if the practices seem strange to us), and preach retribution for evil.

Sabazios was a hybrid god, symbolized by a snake, who was identified with Dionysus. Various characteristics of other cults were absorbed into his own, which apparently even drew on Judaism. His worship was connected with that of Cybele.

C. The Magna Mater. The remaining cults, unlike the foregoing, are clearly eastern in origin. In the area of Anatolia (see ASIA MINOR), the people of PHRYGIA worshiped Cybele, who came to be known as the Magna Mater, or Great Mother. The goddess of fecundity, she received the sacrifice of the virility of her lover, Attis. He recovered from this, coming, in a sense, back to life. Self-castration became a practice of those who would be his priests. Naturally this was highly objectionable to the Romans, to whose doors all the eastern religions (including Christianity) eventually came. Although Cybele was accorded a place in Roman worship in 205 B.C. (because of an oracle prescribing her acceptance as the only means of victory in the Hannibalic War), severe restrictions were placed on the cult. After the rise of Christianity, the rite of the Taurobolium came to be practiced. A bull was slaughtered on a platform above an adherent. The blood dripped between the boards over the face of the person, even into his mouth. This was alleged to bring rebirth.

D. The Dea Syria. The fertility goddess worshiped in SYRIA was ATARGATIS. She became known as the Dea Syria, the Syrian Goddess, but the merging of deities common in the ancient world meant that in spite of historical and geographical distinctions, Atargatis is but one form of the almost universal figure. The name of Astarte (see ASHTORETH) also is associated with Syrian worship. ADONIS, who may be compared with the ancient TAMMUZ, bears much in common with Attis. Sexual excesses characterized this cult complex also.

E. Isis and Osiris. The Egyptian Isis stands in some contrast to the preceding goddesses. Her rites and processions were attractive, she was considered a model of wifely devotion, and great saving power was attributed to her. In the myth, her husband OSIRIS was killed, and after the body had been recovered by Isis, it was dismembered by the evil god Set. Isis faithfully searched for the members of his body, which had been widely scattered, and brought him back to life. Identification with Osiris thus was seen as a way of surviving death. Isis was elevated as a representative deity, identified with many other goddesses, in the syncretistic spirit of the day. Adherents of other cults could thus appropriate her also. Osiris likewise was a symbol of syncretism. His very name became hyphenated with that of the bull-god, Apis. Under the resultant hybrid name, SERAPIS, he was widely worshiped.

F. Mithraism. The cult of Mithra was observed across the Empire, especially on the strategic frontiers where Roman troops, its strongest adherents, were stationed. As noted above, it was competitive with early Christianity. The rites were performed in a shrine called a Mithraeum. Those discovered are small, indicating that the local groups were not large, though the movement was widespread.

As with the other cults, details of origin and doctrine are not completely clear. The cult of Mithra is certainly eastern in origin, and was given structure in Persia, but it predated ZOROASTRIANISM and was not fully compatible with it. The myth featured Mithra's slaying of the bull. The rite celebrating this included the representation of sexual power. Mithra was exalted also as the victorious sun-god, and it is clear from the iconography depicting his conquests that the beliefs of the cult included IMMORTALITY and the ultimate triumph of good over evil. This reflects the dualistic nature of the theology, but even more, it portrays the vigor and attractiveness of the cult. Initiates proceeded through a ritual that still is not fully known. They evidently progressed through seven stages in a hierarchical structure, following an ascension theme. This, with the accompanying discipline, had great appeal to the military personnel. See MITHRAISM.

III. Meaning and relationship to Christianity.

The available data permit several general observations about the mystery religions. While they are diverse in myth and in ritual, they are similar in having an agrarian origin. This gives them a seasonal character, which is seen in the cyclical nature of the motif of dying and rising. This theme does not issue from the death and resurrection of a historical figure, one event at a particular time and place, but from the observed course of nature, celebrated in the experiences of a mythical deity. Closely connected with the agrarian or nature characteristic of the cults is the symbol of fertility in the female deity. Womb and soil are related. While some aspects of the initiations and other celebrations were no doubt beautiful, there is no question about the sexual meaning in much of the symbolism.

Except where there is evidence of conscious modification, the cults had little moral or ethical content. Where this was present, it marked perhaps something of an advance over the "classical" Greek and Roman religions, which were on the whole detached from the moral and personal needs of men and women. The mysteries spread to fill the void left by the other religious forms, a void that was felt increasingly in the Hellenistic period. They were both sexual and sensual in their appeal. Initiation was more a matter of seeing and participating than of believing and accomplishing. They also appealed to the anxiety and hope of man regarding life after death.

A comparison of these characteristics with those of Christianity has led to the hypothesis that the early Christians, Paul in particular, borrowed much from the mysteries. This theory was stated most forcibly during the decades when *Religionsgeschichte*, or history of comparative religion, was not only establishing patterns but also hypothesizing cause-and-effect relationships. The rite of lustration, ceremonial washing, was seen as a precursor to BAPTISM, that of a sacral meal to the LORD's SUPPER, and the dying and rising of a god to the Christian doctrine of RESURRECTION.

Such assumptions, given plausible form by such scholars as Bousset, Reitzenstein, and Loisy among others, have been negated by competent scholars. The word of A. D. Nock has been especially penetrating. For example, his article on the word *mystērion* (*Harvard Studies in Classical Philology* 80 [1951]: 201–4) is devastating to the aforementioned assumptions, showing that even where similar vocabulary might suggest a relationship, such is not factually supported. Rahner, Bouyer, and Metzger are among more recent scholars who have addressed this issue. The present state of the evidence may be summarized as follows: The NT lacks (and possibly avoids) such key mystery terms as *mystēs* and *katharsis*, while those apparently similar terms that are found (*mystērion* and *teleiōsis*) are different in meaning and usage.

The rites themselves were secret. This means they were not open to scrutiny. Further, the information that has survived is scanty enough as to require caution before sweeping comparisons are made. There are obvious differences between the rites of communal eating and of lustrations. Even where an analogy may appear striking, the probability is that the practice, or at least the evidence for it, is post-Christian. The taurobolium, for example, with its alleged life-giving properties, followed the time of Christ by a hundred years or so.

The foundations of the mysteries were mythical and natural, not historical and revelatory. The "death" of the mythical gods was usually involuntary and meaningless, in contrast to the loving, voluntary sacrifice of Christ. "Dying and rising" was cyclical, not historical and unrepeatable. The "resurrection" of these gods was not in the sphere of history, and the stories are weird and complex. While there were promises of salvific benefits, the nature of the redemption promised was different from that of the NT.

It is alleged that some of the mystery cult ideas and practices did indeed penetrate later Christian religion. This is dealt with especially by the Catholic theologian H. Rahner (*Greek Myths and Christian Mystery* [1963]). The issues are somewhat different from those pertaining to the canonical Scriptures. The NT itself is free from any such formative influence.

(See further F. Cumont, *The Mysteries of Mithra* [1910]; id., *Oriental Religions in Roman Paganism* [1911]; H. A. A. Kennedy, *St. Paul and the Mystery Religions* [1913]; F. Legge, *Forerunners and Rivals of Christianity*, 2 vols. [1915]; J. G. Machen, *The Origin of Paul's Religion* [1921]; S. Angus, *The Mystery Religions and Christianity* [1925]; E. Rhode, *Psyche, the Cult of Souls and Belief in Immortality among the Greeks* [1925]; R. Reitzenstein, *Die hellenistischen Mysterienreligionen*, 3rd ed. [1927, Eng. trans., *Hellenistic Mystery-Religions*, 1978]; R. Willoughby, *Pagan Regeneration* [1927]; S. Angus, *The Environment of Early Christianity* [1929]; S. J. Case, *Experience with the Supernatural in Early Christian Times* [1929], 106–45, 221–63; V. D. Macchioro, *From Orpheus to Paul* [1930]; A. D. Nock, *Conversion* [1933]; M. P. Nilsson, *Greek Popular Religion* [1940]; W. W. Hyde, *Paganism to Christianity in the Roman Empire* [1946]; M. P. Nilsson, *Greek Piety* [1948]; W. K. C. Guthrie, *Orpheus and Greek Religion* [1935, 1952]; B. M. Metzger in *HTR* 48 I [1955]: 1–20; F. C. Grant, ed., *Hellenistic Religions* [1953], 105–49; M. P. Nilsson, *Geschichte der griechischen Religion*, 2 vols., 3rd ed. [1955–74]; E. O. James, *The Cult of the Mother Goddess* [1959]; id., *Comparative Religion* [1961]; G. E. Mylonas, *Eleusis and the Eleusinian Mysteries* [1961]; A. D. Nock, *Early Gentile Christianity and its Hellenistic Background* [1964], 109–45; M. J. Vermaseren, *The Legend of Attis in Greek and Roman Art* [1966]; A. L. Campbell, *Mithraic Iconography and Ideology* [1968]; R. Duthoy, *The Taurobolium: Its Evolution and Terminology* [1969]; M. J. Vermaseren, *Cybele and Attis* [1977]; W. Burkert, *Ancient Mystery Cults* [1987]; M. Giebel, *Das Geheimnis der Mysterien: Antike Kulte in Griechenland, Rom und Ägypten* [1990]; M. B. Cosmopoulos, ed., *Greek Mysteries: The Archaeology and Ritual of Ancient Greek Secret Cults* [2003]; S. I. Johnston, ed., *Religions of the Ancient World: A Guide* [2004]; C. Bonnet et al., eds., *Religions orientalles: nouvelles perspectives* [2006]. For an extensive classified bibliography, see B. M. Metzger in *ANRW* 2/17/3 [1984]: 1259–1423.) W. L. LIEFELD

myth, mythology. The term *myth* (from Gk. *mythos* G3680, "story, fable") is usually applied to traditional stories about gods, narrated in a communal setting and regarded as occurrences of permanent significance; typically, they presuppose and give expression to a particular view of the world (but see "Problems of Definition" below). The term *mythology* frequently denotes any body of myths, although more strictly it refers primarily to the study of myths.

   I. Problems of definition
      A. The modern discussion
      B. Greek literature
  II. ANE mythology and the OT
      A. Questions about specific OT passages
      B. Problems of a more general kind
 III. Myth and the NT: the debate about demythologization
      A. Bultmann's contentions about myth in the NT
      B. Difficulties about Bultmann's contentions
      C. The subsequent course of the debate
      D. The five allusions to "myth" in the NT

I. Problems of definition. Definitions of myth are notoriously controversial, and they remain acutely relevant to questions about the relationship between myth and the Bible.

A. The modern discussion

1. Recognizable characteristics of myth. Some features of myth are less controversial than others, and most writers agree on the following points:

a. *Content and narrative form.* Myths may be distinguished from legends in that they depict gods, rather than people, as their central figures, although some writers admittedly blur this distinction (e.g., M. Dibelius). There is total agreement, however, that myths use only narrative form. They express ideas or events as tales which embody imaginative features; they are never abstract generalizations or analyses.

b. *Communal setting.* Myths emerge from within the life of a community. They answer to some significant feature of its common belief and culture.

c. *Supposed truth-status.* In their own community setting, myths possess, or at least once possessed, the status of believed truth. The popular notion of myth as fabricated fiction is strictly secondary, stemming from the fact that all but their earliest narrators regarded, say, the myths of ancient Greece as notorious falsehood. (Cf. esp. M. Eliade, *Myths, Dreams and Mysteries* [1960], 23ff.)

2. Disputed characteristics. a. *Relation to polytheism.* Otto Eissfeldt contends that "a real myth presupposes at least two gods" (*The Old Testament: An Introduction* [1965], 35). But to Emil Brunner (*The Mediator* [1934], 377–96), John Knox (*Myth and Truth*, 2nd ed. [1966]), and other writers, "myth" remains compatible with biblical monotheism. The issues at stake, however, are chiefly (1) whether polytheism constitutes an essential, or merely a usual, feature of myth; and (2) whether, given either definition, writers use it consistently and unambiguously.

b. *Relation to cultus and to primitive attitudes.* Myth presupposes a particular understanding of the world. But is this worldview exclusively the expression of prescientific notions? Positive answers were given in the 18th cent. by Lowth, and in the 19th cent. by Heyne; and G. Hartlich and W. Sachs have shown how deeply their answers influenced 19th-cent. work on the OT from Eichhorn onward (*Der Ursprung des Mythosbegriffes in der Modernen Bibelwissenschaft* [1952], 6–19, 148–64). In the 20th cent., apart from the questions raised by Rudolf Bultmann, the philosopher Ernst Cassirer has elaborated a view of myth as a distinctively prephilosophical tool of knowledge and communication. On the other hand, Mircea Eliade (*Myths*, 23–56, 232–46) follows Jaspers and Jung in insisting that myth remains fundamentally relevant to moderns (cf. also K. Jaspers in H. W. Bartsch, ed., *Kerygma and Myth*, 2 [1962], 144). To Eliade, it is certainly not the notion of a three-story universe that constitutes the essence of myth. Rather, it is the mythical concept of time, whereby the great archetypal events of the past can be "repeated" to give fresh shape or meaning to the present (cf. M. Eliade, *The Myth of the Eternal Return* [1954]).

Myth, in practice, is an extraordinarily complex phenomenon (cf. Eliade's definition in *Aspects du mythe* [1963], 14–15). B. S. Childs is almost certainly correct in his general analysis of mythical attitudes to space and to the cultus, as well as to time (*Myth and Reality in the Old Testament*, 2nd ed. [1962], 17–21, 73–94). Normally it is specifically in the drama of the cult that primeval events are supposedly actualized in the present (ibid., 19). Contentions about myth and cult in biblical thought justly encounter controversy. Few Christians would deny that God's saving acts of the past become "contemporary" in the sense of shaping, and giving meaning to, the present; but when Eliade speaks of "reactualizing" the PASSION of Christ specifically in liturgy (*Myths*, 27–31), this is a different matter altogether.

c. *What kind of truth is claimed?* While most writers agree that myth has been narrated as truth, some view this as factual truth, and others as existential truth. The difference is significant. For example, if creation-myths are given "factual" status, most of them would logically exclude the truth-claims of the others. But, if they are merely concrete expressions of man's finitude, one COSMOGONY may be said positively to complement another. Some writers illustrate this difference by comparing the "truth" of a map with the "truth" of a painting. Admittedly a concept emerged in developed Greco-Roman thought of things which "never happened but are eternally true" (e.g. Sallustius and Julian on Attis mythology). Many writers doubt whether earlier cultures were also conscious of this distinction. Knox insists that "it is precisely this distinction which in mythology is obscured or drops from sight" (*Myth and Truth*, 23). On the other hand, if this is so, it is not an outlook which characterizes the OT, with its emphasis on historical event (cf. G. E. Wright, *God Who Acts* [1952], 116–28).

B. Greek literature

1. Varying uses of the term. The ambiguity of the term *myth* is not modern. Originally *mythos* could mean "thought," "account," or "account of the facts" (e.g., Homer, *Odyssey* 3.94; 11.492). Quickly, however, the term came to mean "story" or "tale," without implying any particular judgment of its truth. It then functioned increasingly as an antonym of *logos* G3364 to mean either "myth" in a fully technical sense, or "fiction," "fable," "allegory," or "fairytale." Two specialized uses significantly developed. First, it came to denote the plot of a drama. The importance of this is that just as a plot dictates its dramatic action and the drama enacts its plot, so myth dictates a ritual, while ritual supposedly actualizes its myth. Second, the term could also denote pictorial or imaged thinking. Thus Suidas in his *Lexicon* defined *mythos* as *logos pseudēs, eikonizōn tēn alētheian* ("a false word, giving the semblance of the truth").

2. Varying attitudes to mythology. Greek literature reflects a phenomenon roughly parallel to more modern notions of demythologization. Many thinkers—including Plutarch, Euripedes, and Aristophanes—criticized the ancient myths as insults to intelligence and ethics. Others believed that the myths reflected certain insights, and could be of educative value in communicating them in concrete images. The Stoics viewed myths as early philosophy in historical dress, and subjected them to reappraisal by allegorical interpretation. Plato carried the process further, although he himself and especially Aristotle express simultaneous criticism of the traditional myths (cf. G. Stählin in *TDNT*, 4:762–95; Sallustius, "On the Gods and the World," in G. Murray, *Five Stages of Greek Religion* [1935], 200–225; and J. A. Stewart, *The Myths of Plato* [1905]).

II. ANE mythology and the OT

A. Questions about specific OT passages

1. The creation accounts in Genesis. In addition to other foreign creation-myths, two particular epics of the ANE have invited intense comparison with the description of CREATION in Gen. 1:1—2:7. The Babylonian *Creation Epic*, commonly known by its opening words as ENUMA ELISH, was discovered during the 19th cent. and published in 1875 (cf. *ANET*, 60–72; and A. Heidel, *The Babylonian Genesis*, 2nd ed. [1951]). Its main concern is to depict relationships between deities of the Babylonian pantheon. It includes a COSMOGONY in which MARDUK utilizes the body of TIAMAT for creating the world. There is not yet unanimity about its dating, and W. G. Lambert (in *JTS* ns 16 [1965]: 287–300, esp. 291) concluded that it is not a genuine norm of Babylonian or Sumerian cosmology. In spite of these and other difficulties, it has been argued repeatedly that the biblical book of Genesis reflects borrowings from this source. The other writing is the Babylonian *Epic of Atrahasis*. Only about a fifth of it was known before 1965 (cf. *ANET*, 104–6), but up to four-fifths of it can now be recovered (cf. A. R. Millard, *TynBul* 18 [1967]: 3–18). It recounts mythical acts of gods that include both a creation and a cosmic flood. It cannot be dated later than 1630 B.C. For examples of other creation-myths, cf. *ANET*, 3–155. Questions about the relationship between Genesis and these foreign myths turn mainly on the following points.

a. A questionable argument from etymology. In Gen. 1:2, the Hebrew word *tĕhôm* H9333 ("the deep") suggests an etymological connection with Tiamat, the Babylonian goddess or personified sea monster.

This terra-cotta plaque (800–500 B.C.) depicts the Babylonian god Marduk in the form of a dragon.

Many have cited this point to support the view that Genesis draws on foreign myth (cf. Childs, *Myth and Reality*, 37–39). But how direct is the connection, and what significance is to be attached to it? It has been pointed out (1) that in OT poetry, this term is roughly equivalent to *yām H3542*, "sea"; and (2) that both terms probably constitute independent derivations from *tiāmtu*, "ocean" (cf. Lambert in *JTS* ns 16 [1965]: 293; Heidel, *Babylonian Genesis*, 98–101; D. F. Payne, *Genesis One Reconsidered* [1964], 10). No firm inference can be drawn from this etymological argument. See SEA.

b. *Contentions about a primeval chaos.* As part of the Tiamat nexus of ideas, Babylonian myth contains the notion of a primeval chaos existing alongside the creator and prior to creation. Other mythologies reflect similar ideas. But can the same be said of Gen. 1:2? Three issues must be considered. (1) The words traditionally rendered "without form and void" (*tōhû wābōhû*) could admittedly denote confusion and waste, or a trackless wilderness, but there is no evidence that they ever signified something personal and active (cf. BDB, 96, 1062; G. von Rad, *Genesis* [1961], 47–48). (2) In terms of syntax, it is possible to translate Gen. 1:1–2 as "When God began to create ..., the earth was without form and void," thus implying that "the void" was prior to creation; but such a rendering is unnecessary and raises difficulties (see E. J. Young in *WTJ* 21 [1958–59]: 133–46 and 23 [1960–61]: 151–78; for further bibliography, Childs, *Myth and Reality*, 31–43). (3) In addition to its allusion to "the deep," Gen. 1:2 also explicitly mentions "water(s)"; the prominence of "primeval water" in Babylonian mythology has been overestimated (see Lambert in *JTS* ns 16 [1965]: 293).

Two conclusions deserve respect. B. S. Childs argues that Genesis transforms myth into "broken" myth. The purpose of this is to contrast creation with active chaos, not with "nothingness." On the other hand, Young argues that in Gen. 1:2 it would be wiser to abandon the word "chaos" altogether, since the terms in question simply mean that the earth was not yet ready for man (but cf. D. Kidner, *Genesis* [1967], 45).

c. *Theories about primeval conflict.* If Genesis had genuinely borrowed from the myth of Tiamat, why does it not seem to reflect a conflict theme? In 1895, H. Gunkel suggested an answer, and modifications of his theory have been widely held. The OT reflects the conflict, he suggested, primarily in its poetic books. Allusions to RAHAB (MONSTER), LEVIATHAN, and DRAGON (*tannîn H9490*) all look back to the primeval battle. The passages are cited below (section 4), but here it is perhaps sufficient to point out that none of the passages sets the conflict before creation.

d. *The order of creation.* Although the parallels are not exact, the order of creation is roughly the same in Genesis as in Babylonian myth. Opinions vary as to whether this correspondence necessarily indicates some kind of relationship. For example, no inference can be drawn from the creation of dry land before the appearance of vegetation, which could not otherwise exist. More has been made of the mention of light before the existence of luminary bodies. On the other hand, in many religions "light" is hardly contingent on sources within the world.

e. *Acts of "dividing."* In the Babylonian *Creation Epic* (4.136–38) Marduk "divides" the body of Tiamat. In Genesis God "divides" light from darkness (Gen. 1:4) and heaven from earth (Gen. 1:6–8). But the giving of form to creation inevitably involves differentiation. Hence, similar "dividings" also appear in Egyptian, Hittite, and other mythology.

f. *The creation of man.* In *The Epic of Atrahasis* man is created by Nintu's mixing clay with the blood of a god, and by the gods' then spitting on the clay. God forms man of dust and breathes life into him (Gen. 2:7). But the parallel does not arise from a common mythological setting. Rather, it expresses the basic recognition that man stands in solidarity with creation, and yet also transcends it.

g. *The Sabbath.* In many Akkadian or Babylonian myths the creation of man brings rest to some of the gods (e.g., *Creation Epic* 7.27–30). God rests from his work on the seventh day (Gen. 2:2–3). But the context of ideas is radically different. In Babylonian myth the gods are relieved of routine chores such as providing food for the pantheon. In Genesis God "rests" only from the work of creation (but see SABBATH).

h. *Further note on the Enuma Elish epic.* Valid assessments of the relationship between Genesis and foreign myths cannot be made by comparing

The centaur was a half-man and half-horse figure that originated in Greek mythology.

conditions reappear at the end-time (cf. Childs, *Myth and Reality*, 75–84). In Genesis, however, Eden remains "part of a traveled road that cannot be traversed again" (von Rad, *Genesis*, 73). Biblical ESCHATOLOGY uses the imagery of a renewed nature (Isa. 11:6–9) and sometimes may depict redemption as a reversal of the FALL. As Childs rightly argues (*Myth and Reality*, 90), the new creation contains an additional content above and beyond the original *Urzeit*. In this sense, Eden cannot be regarded as myth.

The serpent has been connected with various myths (Gen. 3:1–5). H. Gressmann associated it with a mythical god of the underworld, on the basis of its "eating dust," and its connection with death. Others have viewed it as part of the general dragon mythology of the E, associating it with Tiamat, Leviathan, or the Ugaritic *Tannin* (see below). One difficulty about all these conjectures is that the serpent in Gen. 3 enters the scene as a created animal; but chiefly the emphasis of the whole narrative is on Adam and Eve rather than on the serpent.

preselected parallels only. By contrast, the following will indicate the main outline of the Babylonian *Creation Epic*: The epic depicts domestic tensions between the pantheon, with extreme anthropomorphism. The older gods are given sleepless nights by the noise of the younger (1.22–50). Gods use deceit and spells (1.60ff., 152ff.; 2.42), and have petulant moods (2.75, 117). The high point of the epic is where Marduk slays Tiamat with the support of winds, a bow and arrow, and a net (4.35–103). Tiamat's corpse provides materials for creation (4.137ff.). And the creation account takes very little space, chiefly introducing the ascription of honorific titles to Marduk (6.45 to the end).

2. Paradise and the fall. Myths of paradise occur here and there all over the world, and often reflect such features as harmony with heaven and absence of death (M. Eliade, *Myths*, 57–71). Hence discussions about EDEN (Gen. 2:8–17) focus less on specific myths than on general mythological patterns. Mythology often embodies the *Urzeit-Endzeit* pattern, according to which primeval

3. The flood. Allusions to a great flood appear not only in mythology, but also in the ancient Sumerian king list (*ANET*, 265). Probably the *Epic of Gilgamesh* constitutes the best-known parallel to the flood account (Gen. 6–8). It was published in 1872 and is dated by Speiser and Heidel at about 2000 B.C. (cf. *ANET*, 72–99; A. Heidel, *The Gilgamesh Epic and Old Testament Parallels*, 2nd ed. [1949]; N. K. Sandars, *The Epic of Gilgamesh* [1960]). Much of it tells of ordinary human life and might better be called legend than myth; but the famous tablet 11 tells of a cosmic flood in the setting of polytheistic myth. It includes the following similarities to Genesis: (1) a divine decree is revealed (11.187; Gen. 6:13); (2) a boat is built according to careful measurements, and sealed with bitumen (11.24, 50–69; Gen. 6:14–16); (3) the family and many animals enter (11.84–5; Gen. 6:18–20); (4) the flood rises (11.96ff.; Gen. 7:11ff.); (5) birds are sent out three times and these include a dove and a raven (11.147–154; Gen. 8:6–11); and (6) a sacrifice is made at the conclusion (11.155; Gen. 8:20). Finally, recently recovered material in the *Epic of Atrahasis* adds a further parallel which is lacking in the *Epic of Gilgamesh* (cf. Millard in *TynBul* 18

[1967]: 11–14). Atrahasis, the Babylonian Noah, is saved for his distinctive piety.

Estimates of the significance of these parallels vary. Here we have space to make only a general comment. In terms of history, the similarities are more striking than the differences; while in terms of myth, the differences are more striking than the similarities. For example, the sequel to the flood in Genesis is a solemn covenant (Gen. 8:20—9:17). The mythical sequel in Gilgamesh is that ENLIL is rebuked for having jeopardized the gods' food supply, while the other gods crowd "like flies about the sacrificer" (11.161ff.). On the other hand, the many similarities of narrative detail, together with the inclusion of a cosmic flood in the Sumerian king list may suggest the possible survival of reports and memories of the biblical flood (but cf. Kidner, *Genesis*, 95–97). See FLOOD, GENESIS.

4. Other OT passages. Lack of space prevents more than a bare mention of other passages that have been said to reflect foreign myth. Perhaps the most difficult is Gen. 6:1–4. Childs (*Myth and Reality*, 50–59) argues that it embodies what was originally a Canaanite etiological myth explaining the origin of "giants." Biblical writers, he believes, subsequently transformed it into no more than an example of increasing sin. The enigmatic character of such terms as NEPHILIM (KJV, "giants") and SONS OF GOD tends to obscure all but the final significance Childs suggests, and various explanations of the terms have been put forward (see respective articles).

The chief problem in the poetic books is to distinguish between myth and metaphor (see below). A number of passages depict cosmic or historical combat in terms of conflict with "Leviathan" (Job 41:1; Pss. 74:14; 104:26; Isa. 27:1), "Rahab" (Job 9:13; Ps. 89:10; Isa. 51:9), and "dragon/monster" (Ps. 74:13; Isa. 27:1; 51:9). As mentioned earlier, Gunkel's theory that all this imagery reflects the conflict theme of Tiamat mythology has met with difficulties, and the Ugaritic texts suggest a different source for the nexus of ideas. However, the origins of the terms are less significant than their actual functions in the biblical writings. There is abundant evidence that the terms can be used metaphorically (e.g., in Ezek. 32:2, of Pharaoh), and it is doubtful whether the term *myth* would

describe this, other than misleadingly. (On the original mythological context, cf. T. H. Gaster in *IDB*, 3:481–84; on the metaphorical use cf. K. Kitchen, *Theological Students Fellowship Bulletin* 44 [1966]: 3–5; Childs, *Myth and Reality*, 65–72; E. Dhorme, *Job* [1967], 134; and especially W. F. Albright, *New Horizons in Biblical Research* [1966], 32–35; on messianic imagery, cf. also E. J. Young, *The Study of Old Testament Theology Today* [1958], 44–59.) See also JOB, BOOK OF, VII.

B. Problems of a more general kind

1. Divergent results in modern research. Modern writings suggest a bewildering variety of conclusions on the present subject. However, their divergences often are due to differences in method and approach, some of which may be distinguished as follows:

a. Early comparative investigations. Toward the end of the 19th cent., three archaeological events gave a new impetus to OT studies. (On earlier work, cf. Hartlich and Sachs, *Der Ursprung des Mythosbegriffes*.) The publications of the *Gilgamesh Epic* in 1872 and of the *Creation Epic* in 1875 were followed in 1887 by the discovery of the TELL EL-AMARNA tablets, which suggested close cultural interchanges between ANE peoples. These discoveries seemed almost to recast the OT as one of many perhaps similar contemporary writings. In the enthusiasm of such inquiry, overstatements often were made. H. Winckler and A. Jeremias tried to explain too much in terms of Babylonian ideas. Robertson Smith and J. G. Frazer investigated a wide range of primitive cultures, but they were hampered both by the anthropology of the time and by inadequate archaeological knowledge, and Frazer sometimes sacrificed accuracy and relevance for sheer quantity of comparative material. Little from this early period is of unqualified value today, although many see a turning point in the more cautious work of H. Gunkel.

b. Myth and ritual: Mowinckel, Hooke, and Bentzen. In the 1920s myth figured notably in S. Mowinckel's studies in the Psalms. Noting that certain psalms implied liturgical settings, he claimed that they also involved a ritual which, in turn, looked back to ancient myth. This applied

3. "Demythologization" in Paul and John. Bultmann stresses that the NT invites demythologization, first by contradictions, and second by its own conscious example. Contradictions are symptoms of myth. For instance, the death of Christ, Bultmann claims, cannot be simultaneously both a sacrifice and a cosmic event, unless it is in the realm of mythical thought. Similar telltale "contradictions" exist between "Messiah" and "Second Adam," or between freedom and predestination. However, at least in eschatology, he argues, Paul and especially John began to become alert to the situation. Paul endeavored to translate the myth of apocalyptic into the existential language of Christ-union. John transposed eschatology entirely into the present. As a concrete example, Bultmann suggests that John reinterpreted the mythological ANTICHRIST into a historical series of "false teachers" (*JCM*, 32–34).

4. Modern demythologization. a. *Premises about the function of myth in the NT.* Bultmann claims to the very end that his proposals follow only what the NT genuinely suggests. But he admits, in effect, that his claim rests on premises about the purpose and function of myth. The purpose of myth, he assumes, is not to portray the external world, but "to express man's understanding of himself in the world in which he lives" (*KM*, 1:10). It constitutes a means of arriving at, or expressing, *self*-understanding. But second, Bultmann suggests, myth functions with an undesirable effect. It obscures and impedes the very purpose which it exists to serve (*KM*, 1:11). In addition to involving "contradictions" such as we noted above, it does appear, after all, to describe external, extrinsic, or "objective" realities. This is perhaps the deepest reason Bultmann cannot leave "myth" as it is. In his view, it positively demands existential interpretation.

b. *Mythology and existential interpretation.* Existentialism serves as an ambiguous label for a number of individual philosophies. Bultmann draws his existentialist categories almost entirely from Martin Heidegger's *Being and Time*. But he insists, "I learned from him not *what* theology has to say, but *how* it has to say it" (*TRB*, 276, Bultmann's italics; cf. 273–78; *KM*, 1:22–33; and J. Macquarrie, *An Existentialist Theology* [1955]). There is certainly a common emphasis both in Heidegger and in the NT on individual challenge and decision, and on human finitude with its consequent pressures. Heidegger, Bultmann argues, speaks also with the voice of modern secularism and thereby provides categories of expression that must be exploited. Thus the NT "myth" of the imminent end can supposedly be translated by taking up Heidegger's language about the pressures of earthly cares and the engulfing onrush of time (cf. *JCM*, 24–29). The "myth" of the new creation can be cashed as letting go the false securities of the "old" and known, to yield oneself to whatever new future God may give (cf. *JCM*, 31; *TRB*, 268–71).

c. *Contrasts between Bultmann and earlier liberalism.* Bultmann notes that the earlier liberals used different methods from his own of dealing with myth. Most of them hoped to extract "timeless truths" from the historical or mythical husks which they freely discarded. Bultmann strongly insists that his own approach differs from theirs in two decisive ways. First, he does not propose to jettison mythology without trying to replace it with something better. He aims to interpret myth rather than to eliminate it. Second, he does not regard the gospel as a system of timeless truths; it remains, he stresses, the proclamation of a unique *event*. He consistently defends these two points, whatever his critics may have said (*KM*, 1:12–16; *TRB*, 258, 271).

B. Difficulties about Bultmann's contentions

1. Assumptions about the biblical worldview. Although Bultmann treats this issue as virtually self-evident, writers have drawn attention to the following difficulties:

a. *Myth and metaphor.* We earlier noted W. F. Albright's timely warning against underestimating the logical capacity of the Hebrew mind (see above, II.B.2). P. S. Minear similarly insists that even the apostle John did not believe naively in a three-storied universe (W. Klassen and G. Snyder, *Current Issues in New Testament Interpretation* [1962], 34). Examining Bultmann's assumptions, G. R. Beasley-Murray (in *ThTo* 14 [1957]: 61–79, esp. 66) asks whether the "horses" of Rev. 19:14, 18 had really been groomed in heavenly stables, and how the wife of the Lamb could be a city whose height was 12,000 furlongs, but whose wall, in any case, was a mere 144 cubits (21:16–17). G. B. Caird (in *ExpTim* 74 [1962–63]: 103–5) concludes that while Revelation utilizes mythical imagery, it does so with the insight of a political cartoonist. Facts such as these cast serious doubts on Bultmann's assessment of the NT worldview.

b. *Myth and miracle.* Many have questioned whether a belief in miracles has anything at all to do with an obsolete worldview. J. Macquarrie, whose criticisms of Bultmann are normally moderate, argues that his notion of miracle comes from an outdated pseudoscientific view of the universe as a closed system (*An Existentialist Theology*, 168). The criticism is developed by D. Cairns, who consistently reserves the term *prodigy* to designate Bultmann's *miracle*, because he believes that it has little in common with the concept in the NT and in current thought (*A Gospel Without Myth?* [1960], 112–35; for a strong attack from the conservative viewpoint cf. P. E. Hughes in *EvQ* 20 [1948]: 184–95; id., *Scripture and Myth* [1956], 19–20).

c. *The NT and Gnosticism.* According to Bultmann, the NT borrowed much of its myth from Gnostic sources. But quite apart from serious problems of dating, a comparison with GNOSTICISM serves all the more to bring into relief the studied restraint of the NT in avoiding cosmological naiveties.

2. Ambiguities in Bultmann's concept of myth. The linguistic philosopher R. W. Hepburn goes to the heart of the matter when he points out that Bultmann defines myth in two very different ways ("Demythologizing and the Problem of Validity," in A. Flew and A. MacIntyre, eds., *New Essays in Philosophical Theology* [1955], 227–42, esp. 229–30). One of Bultmann's definitions is purely formal: "the use of imagery to express the other worldly in terms of this world" (*KM*, 1:10n). The other is in terms of content: "supernatural forces intervene … miracles are by no means rare" (ibid., 1). The *formal* definition, Hepburn reminds us, makes demythologizing "a logically impossible task." For, clearly, it must include symbol and analogy in general, but on Bultmann's own inevitable admission, language about God remains "certainly analogical" (*KM*, 1:197). Hepburn concludes that the two definitions are incompatible, urging Bultmann to "greater logical rigor."

Each type of definition has also invited its own criticisms. Clearly on the basis of the formal definition, H. Thielicke protests that we can no more abandon myth than we can cease to think in space-time categories (*KM*, 1:141); while H. Gollwitzer asserts that Bultmann vitiates his own discussion by a clumsy confusion between myth and analogy (*The Existence of God as Confessed by Faith* [1965], 43–44). J. Macquarrie examines this question with greater sympathy, but he also concludes that Bultmann's position is unsatisfactory (*The Scope of Demythologizing* [1960], 202–6). A defense, however, comes from S. M. Ogden (*TRB*, 108–16). "Myth" in Bultmann, he claims, is not merely analogy, but a mode of thinking which conceptualizes the divine as though it were an object of scientific observation. Ogden's clarification shows the doubtful relevance of certain criticisms, but it also pinpoints a difficulty about the "narrower" definition of myth. Why does Bultmann refuse to take at face value language which "objectifies" spiritual realities? For as H. P. Owen points out (*TRB*, 47), it is impossible to believe "in" unless one first believes "that"; and to have "objective" concepts *about* someone does not at all imply that one is viewing that person as an "object" rather than as a person. Yet Bultmann explicitly declares, as Owen shows, that any cosmic process which is said to happen objectively "outside" us would be "nothing other than a myth" (*TRB*, 45; see also below).

3. History, factuality, and language. a. *Criticisms and replies.* From 1942 onward it has been urged repeatedly that Bultmann's conclusions fail to do justice to the historical factuality of the gospel. H. Thielicke declared that Bultmann had reduced the gospel to the status of a philosophy (*KM*, 1:141ff.), a censure repeated by others, such as W. Künneth (*The Theology of the Resurrection* [1965], 40–107). Finally, "demythologizing" was officially condemned by the United Evangelical Lutheran Church of Germany (cf. E. Kinder, ed., *Kerygma and History* [1962]; and *KM*, 2:1–82). Bultmann replied that his critics had misread the issue, and F. Gogarten published a defense of his attitude to history in the well-known book, *Demythologizing* *and History* (1955; cf. also *TRB*, 258, 260). Nowadays it is widely recognized that Bultmann did not intend completely to evaporate the gospel's factuality. Indeed this is the point at issue between him and his "left-wing" critics. However, there are many who remain unconvinced that he has logically succeeded in his stated aim (see below, 3.c).

b. *Falsification and criteria of meaning.* We have space only to refer to literature on this subject. A trenchant exposé comes from R. W. Hepburn, who characterizes Bultmann's position as a flight from the evidential ("Demythologizing," 230ff.; cf. also his *Christianity and Paradox* [1958]). In *The Scope of Demythologizing*, J. Macquarrie is sympathetic, but nevertheless critical (see pp. 81–101; 186–221; cf. *TRB*, 141). Heinrich Ott's contentions about the problem of meaning and history are relevant to the concept of "eschatological verification" (*TRB*, 51–64).

c. *Event and interpretation.* Bultmann is rightly concerned that nothing should obscure the existential thrust of the Bible. His account of the function of myth (see above, A.4) tends too easily to suggest that it can be translated into existential terms with almost no factual remainder. An example will serve to throw the problem into relief. How are we to interpret the "myth" of the doctrine of creation? Admittedly, biblical writers intend that it should be cashed in existential terms (e.g., as thanksgiving for life, or stewardship of resources). But does this exhaust its significance? If both God and creation are said to be realities, does this not also imply a relationship between them that is independent of the believer's self-understanding? The biblical doctrine gives certainly *more* than mere information; but it hardly gives *less* than this. One writer complains about the exclusiveness of Bultmann's alternatives, when he speaks of *either* cosmology *or* anthropology, as if a mixture of both could never be found (Minear in *TRB*, 77). In fact, the existential depends on the historical, as effect on cause. Macquarrie pertinently asks how does it make sense to talk of dying and being raised with Christ, unless we first have some assurance that Christ actually died and was raised (*TRB*, 141).

The problem is rooted in the larger question of the relationship between event and interpretation. Ian Henderson (*Myth in the New Testament* [1952], 31) draws an illuminating distinction between two types of interpretation. Some interpretations, like the decoding of a message, will allow the subsequent disposal of their original source; others, like a commentary on a masterpiece, can never substitute for their original. It is arguable that "demythologization" mistakes the second for the first, for there remains an inseparable relationship between the original events of Scripture and the original interpretations that came with them (cf. K. Kantzer's excellent essay in C. F. H. Henry, ed., *Jesus of Nazareth: Saviour and Lord* [1966], 241–64).

4. Basic theological problems. a. *Theology transposed into a doctrine of man.* Many have argued that if Bultmann's notions of myth were right, the gospel could give man news only about himself. It becomes virtually impossible to maintain the traditional distinction between knowledge of God and knowledge of man in theology (cf. H. P. Owen in *TRB*, 49). G. Bornkamm, however, emphatically defends Bultmann against this criticism, on the ground that he preserves at all costs the "offense" of the gospel (*TRB*, 15). Since both sides often appeal to the subsequent course of the debate, conclusions are perhaps best arrived at in that context.

b. *Christology transposed into soteriology.* Bultmann and his critics agree on the issue at stake: according to the NT perspective, does Jesus help the believer because he is "Son of God," or is he "Son of God" because he helps the believer? If "Son of God" Christology is myth, it allows only the latter alternative. But many believe that the NT asserts the former (e.g., Karl Barth in *KM*, 2:96ff.; L. Malevez, *The Christian Message and Myth* [1958]).

C. The subsequent course of the debate. If Thielicke and Kinder argued that Bultmann had gone too far, others maintained that he had not gone far enough. Fritz Buri expounded this view in 1952 (cf. *KM*, 2:85–101), and S. M. Ogden developed it in *Christ Without Myth* (1961). Yet, in spite of their arriving at opposite conclusions, both sides, Ogden points out, share the common belief that Bultmann's view is "an uneasy synthesis of two ... incompatible standpoints" (ibid., 115). If myth is to be interpreted in terms of human self-understanding, on what logical basis can faith be retained in the uniqueness of an event proclaimed in the NT kerygma? Jaspers describes Bultmann's special pleading as "altogether orthodox and illiteral" (*KM*, 2:174). Buri demands not merely "demythologizing," but also "dekerygmatizing" as its logical conclusion. Similarly Ogden comments in a recent critique of Bultmann, "As I read the NT it knows of no basis for man's authentic existence except the primordial love of God" (*TRB*, 121). Finally, Herbert Braun goes even further than Buri and Ogden. If the language of the NT is no more than a vehicle of self-understanding, cannot the same be said about its postulate "God"? (For a critique of Braun, cf. Gollwitzer, *The Existence of God*, 35–39.)

The claims of Bultmann's "left-wing" critics tend perhaps to vindicate some of the criticisms of his more conservative ones. There have certainly been vigorous reactions against underestimating the biblical concern about history, and these can be seen not only in New Quest School and in emphases on salvation-history, but also in the concerns of such writers as W. Pannenberg. Indeed, it is worthy of note that since the aftermath of the Bultmannian debate in the 1960s, biblical scholarship has shown relatively little interest in mythological issues surrounding the NT.

D. The five allusions to "myth" in the NT.

Four occur in the Pastoral Epistles and one in 2 Peter (1 Tim. 1:4; 4:7; 2 Tim. 4:4; Tit. 1:14; 2 Pet. 1:16). In every case myths are repudiated as profitless, but each passage adds particular characterizations or contrasts. In 2 Pet. 1:16 "cleverly devised myths" (NRSV, Gk. *sesophismenois mythois*) seems to denote the spurious embroidery of speculative prophecies in contrast to the faithful proclamation of historical truth by "eyewitnesses." First Timothy associates them with speculations about "genealogies" (1 Tim. 1:4) and describes them explicitly as "godless" and "silly" (*graōdēs* **G1212**, "old-womanish," 4:7). They stand in general contrast with "the truth" (2 Tim. 4:4), while in Tit. 1:14 they are specified as "Jewish" and contrasted with health or soundness in the faith (cf. v. 13).

Discussions about these allusions generally turn on (1) whether all have some connection with Judaism, or only the reference in Titus; (2) whether they can be directly associated with Gnostic speculations; (3) whether they might indicate a sincere but misguided attempt by Christians (or Jews) to allegorize pagan myths for homiletical purposes (see above, I.B.). G. Stählin (in *TDNT*, 4:783) considers it "highly probable" that the Pastorals refer to an early form of Gnosticism that flourished on the soil of Hellenistic Jewish Christianity, in some ways comparable with what is reflected in Colossians; while C. K. Barrett (in *ExpTim* 68 [1956–57]: 348) views the third alternative as a strong possibility. There is insufficient data, however, to allow firm conclusions (cf. also D. Guthrie, *The Pastoral Epistles* [1957], 57–58). In the SEPTUAGINT, "myth" occurs only in the APOCRYPHA, and only twice (Wisd. 17:4; Sir. 20:19).

(In addition to the works referred to in the body of the article, see H. Riesenfeld in *The Background to the New Testament and its Eschatology*, ed. W. D. Davies and D. Daube [1956], 81–95; G. R. Driver, *Canaanite Myths and Legends* [1956]; G. V. Jones, *Christology and Myth in the New Testament* [1956]; B. H. Throckmorton, *The New Testament and Mythology* [1960]; H. Ridderbos, *Bultmann* [1960]; E. O. James, *The Ancient Gods* [1960]; G. Miegge, *Gospel and Myth in the Thought of Rudolf Bultmann* [1960]; S. G. F. Brandon, *Creation Legends of the Ancient Near East* [1963]; R. H. Fuller, *The New Testament in Current Study* [1963], 9–32; A. N. Wilder, *Early Christian Rhetoric* (=*The Language of the Gospel*) [1964], 126–36; J. Macquarrie, *God-Talk* [1967], 168–91; W. Schmithals, *An Introduction to the Theology of Rudolf Bultmann* [1968], 249–72; J. W. Rogerson, *Myth in Old Testament Interpretation* [1974]; A. C. Thiselton, *The Two Horizons: New Testament Hermeneutics and Philosophical Description* [1980]; A. Dundes, ed., *Sacred Narrative: Readings in the Theory of Myth* [1984]; J. N. Bremmer, *Interpretations of Greek Mythology* [1987]; R. A. Johnson, *Rudolf Bultmann: Interpreting Faith for the Modern Era* [1987]; B. F. Batto, *Slaying the Dragon: Mythmaking in the Biblical Tradition* [1992]; N. Wyatt, *Myths of Power: A Study of Royal Myth and Ideology in Ugaritic and Biblical Tradition* [1996]. W. G. Doty, *Myth: A Handbook* [2004]; R. A. Segal, *Myth: A Very Short Introduction* [2004].)

A. C. THISELTON

Mytilene. See MITYLENE.

The Nile River at sunset.

N

Naam nay´uhm (נַעַם H5839, possibly short form of אֶלְנַעַם H534, "God is pleasantness"; see ELNAAM). Son of CALEB and descendant of JUDAH (1 Chr. 4:15).

Naamah (person) nay´uh-muh (נַעֲמָה H5841, possibly "pleasantness"). **(1)** Daughter of LAMECH and ZILLAH, sister of TUBAL-CAIN, and descendant of CAIN (Gen. 4:22). She is the only daughter named in the lineage of either Cain or ABEL (Gen. 4:17—5:32).

(2) Ammonite wife of SOLOMON and mother of REHOBOAM (1 Ki. 14:21, 31; 2 Chr. 12:13). See AMMON. An addition to the Greek text of 1 Ki. 12:24 identifies Naamah (*Naanan*) as the daughter of HANUN (*Ana*), son of NAHASH (*Naas*), the Ammonite king (cf. 2 Sam. 10:1–2), but there is no way to confirm this tradition, which would indicate that Solomon's marriage was politically motivated. It is often assumed that Naamah was one of the many foreign women that Solomon married when his heart was turned away from God (cf. 1 Ki. 11:1–8); Rehoboam's age, however, suggests that this marriage had taken place when Solomon was relatively young, and some have speculated that it was a diplomatic arrangement on the part of DAVID. In any case, it is possible that Naamah played a role in Judah's disaffection from Yahweh and Rehoboam's introduction of "high places, sacred stones and Asherah poles," and "even male shrine prostitutes" (14:23–24). B. K. WALTKE

Naamah (place) nay´uh-muh (נַעֲמָה H5842, possibly "pleasantness"). A city in the SHEPHELAH allotted to the tribe of JUDAH (Josh. 15:41). It was apparently near MAKKEDAH, but its precise location is unknown. Proposals have included modern Naʿneh (6 mi. S of LOD) and ʿAraq Naʿaman (more properly, Khirbet Fared, near TIMNAH), but the biblical text suggests a site much farther S. See also NAAMATHITE. B. K. WALTKE

Naaman nay´uh-muhn (נַעֲמָן H5845, "pleasantness"; gentilic נַעֲמִי H5844, "Naamite" or "Naamanite"; the name is attested both as a proper name in the administrative texts from Ras Shamra [see UGARIT] and as an epithet of royal personages). **(1)** Listed among the "sons" of BENJAMIN in Gen. 46:21, but elsewhere identified more specifically as a son of BELA and therefore as Benjamin's grandson (Num. 26:40; 1 Chr. 8:4, 7 [the Heb. syntax in vv. 6–7 is ambiguous]). He became the eponymous ancestor of the Naamites (Num. 26:40; NJPS, "Naamanites").

(2) The Aramean commander who was cured of a skin disease by ELISHA (2 Ki. 5). Prior to this incident, the king of ARAM, probably BEN-HADAD II (Jos. *Ant.* 18.15.5), had credited Naaman's victories to his military genius (v. 1). The phrase "highly regarded" (NIV) reads literally "he was lifted up of face," referring to the gesture of the king stretching forth his scepter and touching the face of the suppliant bowed to the ground before him, and raising the face up (cf. Esth. 8:3–4). When the king referred to him as "my servant" (2 Ki. 5:6), he meant that he was a high officer, possibly, though not necessarily, bound to him in feudal service. In any case, Naaman was a "valiant soldier" who suffered from "leprosy" (see below). In spite of the young girl's assertion that the prophet in SAMARIA could cure the leprosy (v. 4), the king took no regard of the prophet, but in accord with the ancient conception of the king as the channel of divine blessing, he made the request directly to the king of Israel, who also ignored the prophet.

379

Elisha directed Naaman to wash in the Jordan River in order to be healed from his leprosy.

Unaware that Yahweh was using him (cf. v. 1), Naaman was a proud man: (1) he came to ELISHA's house with all the pomp of his status (v. 9); (2) "to me" (v. 11) is in an emphatic position, suggesting, "to a person like me"; (3) the expression "he would surely come out" (v. 11, rendering the Heb. infinitive absolute construction) also emphasizes the fact that Naaman considered it the duty of Elisha, whom he regarded as his social inferior, to come out to him; (4) he refused to carry out a plan not according to his own formulation (vv. 11–12).

Yahweh used several agents to bring about Naaman's conversion from a proud, self-sufficient man to a believing (v. 15), humble (v. 18, "your servant"), and reverent man (v. 18), the qualities Yahweh desires of all, including those he employs to discipline his people. First, Yahweh afflicted him with a skin disease. Leprosy here is not the same as the modern "Hansen's disease" (see DISEASE). In any case, it was not of that kind which debarred him from society. J. A. Gray (*I and II Kings*, 2nd ed. [1970], 452–58) concluded, "the disease of Naaman must have been what Herodotus calls *leukē* as distinct from *leprē*." Only God could cure this disease (v. 7). Second, Yahweh used believing servants of a much inferior social position (the captured Israelite girl, v. 2, and Naaman's own servant, v. 13). Finally, he used the man of God who recognized his authoritative position under God (v. 10), the need for child-like faith in the Word of God (vv. 11–14), and the truth that God's salvation is a free gift (vv. 15–16). Naaman's cure was alluded to by the Lord Jesus as an example of God's gracious concern for the non-Israelite (Lk. 4:27). B. K. WALTKE

Naamathite nay´uh-muh-th*i*t (נַעֲמָתִי *H5847*, "of Naamah"). Descriptive title of ZOPHAR, one of JOB's three friends (Job 2:11; 11:1; 20:1; 42:9). It evidently refers to his place of origin. The Judahite town of NAAMAH (Josh. 15:41) is almost certainly not in view. Since the other two friends (ELIPHAZ and BILDAD) apparently came from the Arabian desert, the term Naamathite may point to a place such as Jebel el-Na‘ameh, in NW ARABIA, or to a Sabean clan (*n‘mt*) in S Arabia (for the latter, see *ABD*, 4:968).

Naamite nay´uh-m*i*t. See NAAMAN #1.

Naarah (person) nay´uh-ruh (נַעֲרָה *H5856*, "young woman"). One of the two wives of ASHHUR, a descendant of JUDAH; she bore him four sons (1 Chr. 4:5–6).

Naarah, Naaran (place) nay´uh-ruh, -ruhn (נַעֲרָה *H5857*, "watermill"; also נַעֲרָן *H5860*). A city listed as marking part of the SE border of the tribe of EPHRAIM (Josh. 16:7 [KJV, "Naarath"]; called Naaran in 1 Chr. 7:28). It is mentioned between

ATAROTH and JERICHO. A note from JOSEPHUS (*Ant.* 17.13.1) says that Archelaus (see HEROD IV), after rebuilding JERICHO, "diverted half the water with which the village of Neara used to be watered," thus locating Neara (Naarah) near Jericho and associating it with a good water supply. EUSEBIUS (*Onom.* 136.24) reports that the town of *Noorath* was 5 Roman miles (c. 4.5 mi.) from Jericho. Accordingly, N. Glueck (*Explorations in Eastern Palestine*, 4 vols. [1934–51], 4:412–13) identified Naarah with Khirbet el-ʿAyash. Most scholars, however, favor Tell el-Jisr, just below the springs ʿAin Duq and ʿAin Nuʿeimeh at the foot of the Judean hills, less than 2 mi. NW of Jericho. These springs qualify as "the waters of Jericho" lying E of the border (Josh. 16:1). Other nearby sites have been proposed (cf. Z. Kallai, *Historical Geography of the Bible* [1986], 163–66; see also *NEAEHL*, 3:1075–76).   L. J. WOOD

Naarai nay´uh-ri (נַעֲרַי *H5858*, possibly short form of נְעַרְיָה, "young man [*or* attendant] of Yahweh"). Son of Ezbai, listed among DAVID's mighty warriors (1 Chr. 11:37); in the parallel passage he is called "Paarai the Arbite" (2 Sam. 23:35). See discussion under EZBAI.

Naaran nay´uh-ruhn. See NAARAH, NAARAN (PLACE).

Naarath nay´uh-ruhth. KJV form of NAARAH.

Naashon nay´uh-shon. KJV alternate form of NAHSHON (only Exod. 6:23).

Naasson nay´uh-son. KJV NT form of NAHSHON (Matt. 1:4; Lk. 3:32).

Naathus nay´uh-thuhs (Ναάθος). One of the descendants of Addi who agreed to put away their foreign wives in the time of EZRA (1 Esd. 9:31). The name does not occur in the parallel, though some think it may correspond to Adna (Ezra 10:30).

Nabal nay´buhl (נָבָל *H5573*, "foolish," possibly by popular etymology; the name originally may have derived from a root meaning "noble"). A wealthy descendant of CALEB who lived in MAON, some 8 mi. SE of HEBRON (1 Sam. 25:2–3). He owned 3,000 sheep and 1,000 goats which he pastured in the vicinity of CARMEL (present Kirmil just N of Maon). He is described as "surly and mean" (v. 3). DAVID, a fugitive from SAUL, had been in the neighborhood for a period when sheepshearing time, normally festive, came for Nabal. David had been giving protection to Nabal's flocks from marauding BEDOUINS (vv. 15–16) and so sent ten of his men now to extend good wishes to Nabal, remind him of his service to him, and request a gift in return.

Nabal showed his ungrateful character in not only refusing the reasonable request but also returning insulting remarks, regarding David as a vagrant, escaped from his master like many others of the era. Immediately David prepared with 400 men to bring retaliation. However, Nabal's wife ABIGAIL, described as "intelligent and beautiful" (v. 3), came quickly to David to make amends. She brought a bountiful gift of food, needed by David and his men, and made humble apology for her husband's conduct, asking David not to inflict his intended reprisal. David agreed. When Abigail later told her husband of his narrow escape, "his heart failed him" (v. 37), and ten days later he died. David then made Abigail one of his wives. (See J. D. Levenson in *CBQ* 40 [1978]: 11–28.)   L. J. WOOD

Nabariah nab´uh-ri´uh (Ναβαριας). One of the prominent men who stood near EZRA when the law was read at the great assembly (1 Esd. 9:44 [KJV, "Nabarias"]; the name does not appear in the parallel, Neh. 8:4).

Nabarias nab´uh-ri´uhs. KJV Apoc. form of NABARIAH.

Nabateans nab´uh-tee´uhnz (Ναβαταῖοι). Also Nabataeans. Although this name does not occur in the OT or NT, the Nabateans were an influential, Aramaic-speaking people who were active in the NW part of ARABIA and TRANSJORDAN from about the 4th cent. B.C. to the beginning of the 2nd cent. A.D. Some earlier scholars sought to link the Nabateans (root *nbṭ*) with the name of ISHMAEL's firstborn, NEBAIOTH (*nĕbāyôt H5568*, Gen. 25:13 et al.), and with the Nabayat mentioned in the Assyrian chronicles, but Jean Starcky showed

Aerial view near Ein Avdat along the Nabatean trade route from Petra to Gaza. In the foreground are stone walls located in the valley floor to slow the flow of water over the agricultural fields.

that the identification is not valid (*BA* 18 [1955]: 85–86). However, nonbiblical sources and archaeological evidence indicate that after the close of the OT period, and especially in the 1st cent. of the Christian era, the Nabateans were a significant political power in the ANE.

The Nabateans usually are associated with the magnificent ruins of PETRA, SSE of the DEAD SEA, but their political domain extended at times W to the NEGEV and N as far as DAMASCUS. Their origin is obscure: many scholars have sought it among the Arab tribes inhabiting S ARABIA, while others favor a NW Semitic (Aramaic) context (for the latter, cf. J. T. Milik in *Studies in the History and Archaeology of Jordan*, ed. A. Hadidi, 3 vols. [1982–87], 1:261–65). Although their native language was probably an early form of Arabic, they adopted ARAMAIC, the lingua franca of the Persian Empire, as their primary means of communication. Located in the territory of ancient EDOM, the Nabateans controlled some of the rich trade routes linking the major areas of the FERTILE CRESCENT. The first historical reference to them is in connection with their refusal to recognize the authority of Antigonus, the successor of ALEXANDER THE GREAT in this area (Diodorus Siculus, *Bibl. Hist.* 19.94–96). Attempts to subjugate the Nabateans were unsuccessful.

The classical period or Golden Age of the Nabateans was the 1st cent. B.C. and the 1st cent. of this era. In this period they settled extensively in the lands once occupied by the Edomites and Moabites and intensively cultivated the soil. In addition, they incorporated the Negev and Sinai into their kingdom. In this period they developed a brilliant civilization with a dynamic creativity and speed scarcely paralleled in history. The sudden end came with the Roman conquest in the beginning of the 2nd cent.

JOSEPHUS and a few inscriptions provide some information about certain Nabatean kings. The first king mentioned in the sources is ARETAS I (cf. 2 Macc. 5:8), ruler in the 2nd cent. B.C. at the time of the Maccabean Revolt. About 100 B.C. Aretas II ruled the Nabateans and expanded the territory of his kingdom at the expense of the waning SELEUCID power in Palestine. Aretas II was succeeded by his son, Obadas I, who recovered much of MOAB and GILEAD from the HASMONEAN ruler of Palestine, Alexander Jannaeus, whom he defeated in battle about 90 B.C. Under Aretas III, the Nabateans became a powerful and independent nation in Transjordan and withstood Roman domination for the next century and a half, in spite of attempts by the Romans and the Herodians to subjugate them.

About this time they also gained control of the trade of MYRRH and FRANKINCENSE from S Arabia to the Mediterranean (some scholars have speculated that the MAGI were in fact Nabateans or that they shopped in Petra on their way to Judea).

In this period their greatest king was Aretas IV Philodemus, who ruled from 9 B.C. to A.D. 40. Although assisting the Romans in subduing the Jews upon the death of HEROD the Great, Aretas initially had good relations with Herod Antipas, son of Herod the Great and tetrarch of PEREA and GALILEE (see HEROD V), who married Aretas's daughter. About A.D. 27 Herod Antipas divorced her in favor of his brother's wife HERODIAS. This led to two troublesome conflicts in Herod's life. The first was with JOHN THE BAPTIST, who roundly denounced him for his marital activity (Matt. 14:3–5; Mk. 6:17–20; Lk. 3:19–20). The other conflict was with Aretas IV, the father of his first wife. In A.D. 36 Aretas defeated Herod in battle and regained much territory, possibly as far N as Damascus. An attempt by the Romans to avenge Herod by an attack on Aretas foundered upon the death of Emperor TIBERIUS.

At the time of PAUL's escape from DAMASCUS following his conversion (Acts 9:23–25), an ETHNARCH of Aretas was guarding the city (2 Cor. 11:32–33). The exact nature of the Nabatean presence in Damascus is not known, but the text does indicate some type of military or police control of the city. Successors of Aretas IV included Malichus II (A.D. 40–70) and Rabbel II, the last king of the Nabateans, who died in A.D. 106. During the reign of TRAJAN, the legate of SYRIA, A. Cornelius Palma, in a campaign in A.D. 105 to 106 annexed Nabatea to the Roman empire. Bostra became the capital of the new province called Arabia (see BOZRA #3). This was the beginning of the Era of Bostra, frequently used in the datelines of inscriptions in this area in subsequent centuries.

The most extensive ruins of the Nabateans are found at Petra, S of the Dead Sea. In this valley surrounded by virtually impassable mountains are the ruins which illustrate the unique type of architecture developed by the Nabateans. The structures were carved into the living rock and reveal a remarkable engineering skill. The typical Nabatean façade consists of a row of pillars (carved *in situ*) with niches containing sculptures between the pillars, which support a crossbeam decorated with a frieze. Above this is a split gable with a domed structure in the middle similar to an inverted urn. The pendantive type of dome may have been developed by the Nabateans (Safwan K. Tell, *Annual of the Department of Antiquities of Jordan* 14 [1969], 35–37 [in Arabic]). They had a unique method of dressing stones—lines cut diagonally across the face of the stone or rock face. Most of the rock-hewn structures in Petra appear to be mausoleums in connection with a cult of the dead, rather than temples. Another major Nabatean site is located on Jebel et-Tannur (excavated by Nelson Glueck in 1937), SE of the Dead Sea, where a series of successive sanctuaries with numerous carved figures and designs were uncovered—perhaps the most significant being the statues of ZEUS (HADAD) and the goddess ATARGATIS.

The Nabateans have made a unique contribution to Palestinian ceramic ware. "Nabatean ware" is very thin and smooth—almost like porcelain. The shapes were beautifully symmetrical, often with delicate decorations in dark brown or black paint on the red ware. The material is so characteristic that the presence of a small sherd on a site strongly suggests Nabatean occupation. (See J. Patrich, *The Formation of Nabatean Art: Prohibition of a Graven Image among the Nabateans* [1990].)

Prior to the discovery of the DEAD SEA SCROLLS, which include some papyri in Nabatean, the only literary remains in Nabatean were inscriptions and graffiti in Sinai and Transjordan, especially in Petra. Nabatean was a form of Aramaic with a strong Arabic influence. The Nabatean papyri, dated in the 1st cent. of the Christian era, provide new data for the study of the dialect. The script developed by the Nabateans is similar to the Hebrew and Aramaic scripts of the time, but the letters are strangely elongated vertically—a practice that allows for close packing of the letters. This script is thought to have a been a precursor of the Arabic alphabet.

The principal Nabatean deity was a god named Dushara (hellenized form, Dushares), symbolized by a block of stone or obelisk. At Tannur the chief god was Hadad, the Syrian storm-god, equivalent of the Greek Zeus. Atargatis, equivalent of the Greek ARTEMIS, appears to have been a type of fertility goddess (see FERTILITY CULTS). Evidence of the religious practices of the Nabateans can be seen in the "high places" (open-air sanctuaries of the gods), such as the Conway High Place and the Great High Place of Robinson at Petra, with processional ways, altars, and pools or lavers. Places for the ritual sacrifice of animals are also found, for example, above ed-Deir in Petra. As archaeological research continues, especially in the Negev and Transjordan, more information can be expected about the Nabateans, who in many respects were one of the most remarkable and vigorous people in the eastern Mediterranean world during the Roman period.

(The fundamental work is J. Cantineau, *Le nabatéen*, 2 vols. [1930–32]. See further N. Glueck, *The Other Side of the Jordan*, rev. ed. [1970], ch. 6; P. C. Hammond, *The Nabataeans: Their History, Culture and Archaeology* [1973]; G. W. Bowersock, *Roman Arabia* [1983]; A. Negev, *Nabatean Archaeology Today* [1986]; A. Kasher, *Jews, Idumaeans, and Ancient Arabs* [1988]; J. F. Healey, *The Religion of the Nabataeans: A Conspectus* [2001]; J. Taylor, *Petra and the Lost Kingdom of the Nabataeans* [2002]; G. A. Crawford, *Petra and the Nabataeans: A Bibliography* [2003]; G. Markoe, ed., *Petra Rediscovered: Lost City of the Nabataeans* [2003]; S. M. Rababeh, *How Petra Was Built* [2005]; *NEAEHL*, 4:1181–92.)

B. VAN ELDEREN

Nabonidus nabʹuh-niʹduhs (Lat. form of Gk. Ναβόννηδος [cf. Jos. *Ag. Ap.* 1.149–53; in Herodotus *Hist.* 1.74, Λαβύνητος]; from Akk. *Nabū-naʾid*, "[the god Nabu] is to be revered"). The last king of Chaldean Babylonia, 556–539 B.C. See ASSYRIA AND BABYLONIA; CHALDEA.

I. Sources. An eighty-four line tablet known as the Nabonidus Chronicle (British Museum 35382), three stelae from Haran, and a libelous "Verse Account" of his reign by CYRUS are among the direct historical sources (cf. *ANET*, 305–7, 308–16, 560–63). These may be supplemented by numerous contemporary business and economic documents and by the later accounts of Greek historians, namely, HERODOTUS and Berossus (the latter preserved in Jos. *Apion* 1.20–21 and Euseb. *Prep. Evang.* 9.41). The fall of BABYLON is described in Dan. 5 (on which Jos. *Ant.* 10.11.2 relied). This has been compared with the account of the madness of NEBUCHADNEZZAR (Dan. 4:23–33). Since Herodotus calls both Nebuchadnezzar and Nabonidus by the same name (Labynetus), it has been argued that the prayer in Dan. 4:23–33 may refer to Nabonidus himself (see NABONIDUS, PRAYER OF).

II. Family. Nabonidus was the only son of Nabū-balāssu-iqbi, a "wise prince and governor" at Haran, otherwise unknown. His mother, Adda-guppiʾ, was an influential votary of the gods Sin, Ningal, Nusgu, and Sardarunna, who died in 547 B.C., aged 104, and was given a state funeral and public mourning. Both were probably of royal blood, and Nabonidus possibly was related to Nebuchadnezzar through marriage so that his son and coregent Bēl-šar-uṣur (BELSHAZZAR) could claim to be a descendant of that illustrious monarch (so Dan. 5:11, 18). He made a daughter, Bēl-šalti-nannar, high-priestess of the moon-god Sin at Ur.

III. Reign. If identical with the person of the same name in a contract of the eighth year of Nebuchadnezzar, he was then a chief official of a Babylonian city and could thus have been the Labynetus who acted as the Babylonian intermediary, with Syennesis of CILICIA, between Alyattes of LYDIA and Astyages of MEDIA in 585 B.C. Nebuchadnezzar was succeeded by a period of family strife during which the rulers were his son EVIL-MERODACH (for two years), his son-in-law Neriglissar (for four years), and another son, Labashi-Marduk, who was recognized as king only for two months, May-June 556 B.C., in part of Babylonia. Nabonidus, who was supported by other cities, was accepted as sole ruler by the end of June.

Two years later Nabonidus entrusted the rule of Babylon to his son Belshazzar, whom he had made coregent (cf. *ANET*, 313b). He himself moved to Haran, where restoration work on the temple of the moon-god Sin, Ehulhul, was begun after its ruin by the Medes, as indicated to him in a dream. See HARAN (PLACE). From there he moved S to attack Adummu (EDOM) and the sheikh of Teimaʾ (TEMA) in NW ARABIA, who was killed. Here Nabonidus settled with his Babylonian and Syro-Palestinian troops and gained control of an area S to Dedan and Yathrib (Medina).

Various theories have been put forward to explain the ten years Nabonidus spent in this area. It has been considered an act of madness (Dan. 4) or an astute economic move to control the valuable spice routes from S Arabia to the N, to Babylonia, and to Egypt. Commercial tablets show that the king kept in touch with his capital, Babylon, and it is clear that no such sojourn could have been possible without the peaceful relations with the Arabs he claimed. It is possible that the move was connected with the dire famine that was rife in Babylonia and attributed by Nabonidus to the impiety of the people. Prices there increased by fifty percent during the decade between 560 and 550, while in Teimaʾ the rains never failed. It is unlikely that the voluntary exile was due to any desire to avoid close contact with the increasing power, since Astyages was not captured by Cyrus till 549 B.C.

According to the Haran stela, there was a change in the attitude of the kings of Egypt (Amasis II) and of the Medes (at this time Cyrus). The Arabs and other rulers were said to have also resumed good relations. On the seventeenth day of Teshrit in 545, Nabonidus therefore returned to Babylon, where he carried out work on various shrines, including that of the sun-god Shamash at Sippar. The weakness of the state was evident in both its economy and defense. The Medes overran the zone E of the Tigris River; the Elamites, parts of southern Babylonia. In 547 he brought the gods of the principal cities into Babylon in an attempt to save them from the advancing enemies, now aided by the defector Gobryas of Gutium.

The Persians moved on Babylon in 539. The city was entered by a stratagem and without a battle on October 12. On that night Belshazzar was put to death (Dan. 5:30). Nabonidus, who had fled to Borsippa, reentered the city and was taken prisoner. According to one tradition, he died in exile in Carmania (Jos. *Apion* 1.20). Seventeen days later Cyrus himself entered the city and took over the throne. The political power at Babylon now passed from Semitic into Persian hands.

IV. Religion. It has been customary to see in Nabonidus a reformer who aimed to replace MARDUK and make the worship of the moon-god Sin paramount in Babylonia. On this view he was thwarted by a priestly party in the country that forced him into exile in Arabia, where he was able to indulge in such worship unhindered. Against this, his inscriptions show that while interested in Sin shrines for family reasons he showed the customary piety in restoring the temples of other deities, including that of Marduk at Babylon and Shamash at Sippar. Due regard is paid also to other deities in his building inscriptions. His activity in the work of restoration has led him to be designated a "royal archaeologist," but his interest in the past, exemplified by the copies of earlier texts found in the course of restoration work, especially at Ur, only follows ancient Babylonian tradition.

The account of Cyrus certainly aims to vilify Nabonidus, accusing him of injustice, lack of regard for property, and the failure to observe the correct rites of the New Year Festival. This may well be a later attempt to justify the Persian conqueror in the eyes of the vanquished, though some of the historical information included is no doubt accurate. Evaluation of the two points of view must await the discovery of further texts.

(See further S. Smith, *Babylonian Historical Texts Relating to the Capture and Downfall of Babylon* [1924], 27–123; R. P. Dougherty, *Nabonidus and Belshazzar* [1929]; J. Lewy in *HUCA* 19 [1946]: 405–89; J. T. Milik in *RB* 62 [1956]: 407ff.; C. J. Gadd in *Anatolian Studies* 8 [1958]: 35–92; P.-A. Beaulieu, *The Reign of Nabonidus, King of Babylon, 556–539 B.C.* [1989; cf. also his summary in *CANE*, 2:969–79]; R. H. Sack in *ABD*, 4:973–76; D. J. Wiseman in *CAH* 3/2, 2nd ed. [1991], 243–51; P.-A. Beaulieu, *Legal and Administrative Texts from the Reign of Nabonidus* [2002].)

D. J. WISEMAN

Nabonidus, Prayer of. A fragmentary ARAMAIC MS discovered in Qumran Cave IV (4QPrNab = 4Q242) and dated to the 1st cent. B.C., though the original composition may be one or two centuries older. The reconstruction of this brief text is problematic in some of its details, but it evidently relates a prayer of King Nabonidus (*nbny*) when he had been smitten by a severe skin disease for seven years while in Teiman (Teimaʾ; see TEMA). After the king has confessed his sin, a Jewish exile tells him to worship the God Most High. Scholars have been intrigued by the similarities of this document with the account of the madness of NEBUCHADNEZZAR (Dan. 4:23–33), and some argue that the latter derives from the former or that both reflect a common tradition. (See F. M. Cross in *IEJ* 34 [1984]: 260–64; F. García Martínez, *Qumran and Apocalyptic: Studies on the Aramaic Texts from Qumran* [1992], 116–36; É. Puech in *Targumic and Cognate Studies: Essays in Honour of Martin McNamara*, ed. K. J. Cathcart and M. Maher [1996], 208–27.)

Nabopolassar nab´uh-puh-las´uhr (Akk. *Nabū-apla-uṣur*, "may [the god] Nabu protect the son!"). First king (626–605 B.C.) of the Neo-Babylonian ("Chaldean") Dynasty, and the father of NEBUCHADNEZZAR II. See ASSYRIA AND BABYLONIA; CHALDEA. Nabopolassar was originally a petty chieftain in S Babylonia, but at the death of King ASHURBANIPAL of Assyria in 626 B.C., he became king of BABYLON and quickly thereafter seized NIPPUR and Uruk (ERECH) from Sin-šar-iškun of Assyria. In a few years he had control of all Babylonia and made a significant alliance with Cyaxares, king of the Medes (see MEDIA).

In 615 B.C. he failed to seize ASSHUR, but when it fell in 614 to the Medes he shared the spoils. To bind a treaty made between Nabopolassar and Cyaxares, king of the Medes, the latter gave his daughter Amytis in marriage to Nabopolassar's son, Nebuchadnezzar. After this treaty with Cyaxares, there was no fear of the mountain tribes, and Nabopolassar was able to compel the former vassals of Assyria, as far as Palestine and Cilicia, to pay tribute to him. His army was well-trained in Assyrian methods of fighting, and eventually in 612 he and his ally took NINEVEH. This conquest meant that the Assyrian empire was divided, with the southern part falling to Nabopolassar. In 609 Haran, the last Assyrian stronghold, fell to the Babylonians. See HARAN (PLACE).

In 606 Nabopolassar took up the EUPHRATES front, where the Egyptian hold on CARCHEMISH posed a threat to the entire western part of his newly won empire. Pharaoh NECO II of Egypt had invaded Palestine and Syria in order to get his share of the fallen Assyrian empire, and it was Nebuchadnezzar, the crown prince, acting for his ailing father, who achieved the conquest of Carchemish and drove the Egyptian army back home in 605. King Nabopolassar had returned to Babylon in the spring of the same year, and died there on 15 August.

Nabopolassar represented himself as a pious man who rose from humble origin to kingship, but he referred with great pride to his victory over Assyria. He started various constructions at Babylon and elsewhere that were completed by his son Nebuchadnezzar. These included improvement of the irrigation around Babylon, as well as beautifying the city itself.

Although Nabopolassar is not mentioned in the Bible, JOSIAH of Judah may have been friendly with him (as HEZEKIAH had been an ally of the Babylonians), for Josiah lost his life at MEGIDDO in a futile attempt to stop Pharaoh Neco II from going to the aid of the Assyrians. (See further D. J. Wiseman, *Chronicles of the Chaldean Kings* [1956], 5–21; G. Roux, *Ancient Iraq*, 2nd ed. [1980]; S. Zawadzki, *The Fall of Assyria and Median-Babylonian Relations in the Light of the Nabopolassar Chronicle* [1988]; P-A. Beaulieu, *The Reign of Nabonidus, King of Babylon 556–539 B.C.* [1989]; J. Oates in *CAH* 3/2, 2nd ed. [1991], 162–93.) L. L. WALKER

Naboth nay´both (נָבוֹת H5559, "growth, sprout," possibly short form of a theophoric name, such as "scion of Yahweh" [cf. LXX Ναβουθαι]). The owner of a vineyard desired by King AHAB because it lay near his alternate royal palace in JEZREEL (1 Ki. 21:1–29), probably on the E side of the city (2 Ki. 9:25–26). Ahab offered Naboth either money or the exchange of a better vineyard. Naboth refused on the valid ground that it was part of his paternal INHERITANCE. Patrimonies belonged to families, not individuals, and Naboth would have wronged his descendants by selling it, as well as having broken God's law (Lev. 25:23–28; Num. 36:7–9).

Ahab himself did not force the issue, but his wife JEZEBEL did. She showed her cruel, ruthless character by arranging a "legal" method by which to take Naboth's life, and apparently also the lives of his sons (2 Ki. 9:26). She ordered Jezreelite officials to suborn false witnesses and so bring about the death-deserving conviction because Naboth had blasphemed both God and king. Her orders were carried out, revealing the strength of her control in the land. This gave Ahab access to the vineyard,

Arial view of the remains of Jezreel from the SE. Adjacent to this town was Naboth's vineyard.

but when he came to possess it, ELIJAH met him and pronounced God's judgment upon him and the entire royal house. When Ahab repented, temporary respite was given (1 Ki. 21:27–29) until his death at RAMOTH GILEAD. Dogs then licked his blood at the pool of SAMARIA when it was flushed off his chariot (22:38). Complete fulfillment came through JEHU when he slew Ahab's second son, JEHORAM (2 Ki. 9:24), caused the death of Jezebel in Jezreel (9:33), and then the execution of Ahab's remaining sons in Samaria (10:1–11). (See C. F. Keil, *The Books of the Kings* [1872], 269–73; F. I. Andersen in *JBL* 85 [1966]: 46–57; Y. Zakovitch, addendum in M. Weiss, *The Bible from Within* [1984], 379–405; P. T. Cronauer, *The Stories about Naboth the Jezreelite* [2005].)   L. J. WOOD

Nabu. See NEBO (DEITY).

Nabuchodonosor nab´uh-kuh-don´uh-sor. KJV Apoc. form of NEBUCHADNEZZAR (Jdt. 1:1 et al.).

Nachon nay´kon. KJV form of NACON.

Nachor nay´kor. KJV alternate form of NAHOR (only Josh. 24:2; Lk. 3:34).

Nacon nay´kon (נָכוֹן H5789, possibly "established"). KJV Nachon; TNIV Nakon. The owner of a threshing floor next to which UZZAH died because he touched the ARK OF THE COVENANT while it was being transported toward JERUSALEM (2 Sam. 6:6; 4QSam^a has *nwdn*, and the parallel passage in 1 Chr. 13:9 reads *kidōn*). Some have speculated that the form here is not a proper name and that the phrase should be rendered "a certain threshing floor" or "the threshing floor of striking" (i.e., destruction). See discussion under KIDON.

Nadab nay´dab (נָדָב H5606, possibly short form of נְדַבְיָה H5608, "Yahweh is willing"). **(1)** Eldest son of AARON and ELISHEBA (Exod. 6:23; Num. 3:2; 26:60; 1 Chr. 6:3; 24:1). He and his next younger brother, ABIHU, were permitted to accompany Aaron and seventy Israelite elders while ascending Mount Sinai to see a representation of God and to eat and drink in God's presence (Exod. 24:1, 9–11). This official group represented Israel in intimate fellowship with God in keeping with the new covenantal relationship just ratified earlier the same day (24:3–8).

Nadab and his brothers, Abihu, ELEAZAR, and ITHAMAR, were admitted to priestly office with their father, Aaron (Exod. 28:1; Lev. 8:1–36). After several days of consecration, on the eighth day when official service began, Nadab and Abihu sinned in offering "unholy" (NIV, "unauthorized") fire before the Lord. They were immediately consumed in death by fire from the Lord (Lev. 10:1–2; Num. 3:4). To emphasize the seriousness of the sin, MOSES forbade Aaron and the two living sons to observe customary mourning ceremonies for them (Lev. 10:6). Both men died without offspring (Num. 3:4; 1 Chr. 24:2).

The exact nature of the sin is not clear. Moses' words (Num. 3:3) imply that the sin issued from hearts that were not in tune with God's HOLINESS and GLORY. Apparently their hearts were proud. The term *zār* H2424 ("strange, unlawful"), designating that which they offered, suggests error in the nature of the fire used. Some passages (Lev. 16:12; Num. 16:46) imply that fire from the brazen altar was to be used in offering incense. Nadab and Abihu may have taken live coals from elsewhere. Their act is described as putting fire in censers and laying INCENSE on it while yet in the censers. This was to be the procedure on the Day of Atonement (Lev. 16:12–13), but otherwise incense was to be offered on the golden altar (Exod. 30:7–8; see INCENSE, ALTAR OF). Further, they seem to have offered at a wrong time. Incense was to be offered morning and evening (Exod. 30:7–8), but the time implied was some other period during the day, between the sacrificial activity of Lev. 9 and the ceremonial eating of Lev. 10:12–20. Further still, the injunction of Lev. 10:9–10 perhaps suggests that the brothers were under the influence of strong drink at the time.

(2) Son of Shammai and descendant of JUDAH through JERAHMEEL (1 Chr. 2:28, 30).

(3) Son of JEIEL and descendant of BENJAMIN; apparently a great-uncle of King SAUL (1 Chr. 8:30–33; 9:35–39).

(4) Son of JEROBOAM I and king of Israel about 910–909 B.C. (1 Ki. 15:25–31). His two years of rule (v. 25) were really only parts of two years (cf. vv. 25, 28, 33). It is said that he laid siege to GIBBETHON (v. 27), a city belonging to the tribe of Dan (Josh. 19:40–46) and assigned as a Levitical city (Josh. 21:23). At this time it was held by PHILISTINES (1 Ki. 15:27; 16:15). Though comparatively small, Gibbethon must have been considered important, for twenty-six years later OMRI, then general under King ELAH, laid siege to it again (16:15–17). SARGON too besieged it, even picturing the city on a panel in his Khorsabad palace, calling it Gab-bu-tu-nu. Nadab was killed by his successor, BAASHA, during his siege of Gibbethon. Baasha exterminated the whole house of Jeroboam, thus fulfilling AHIJAH's prophecy (14:10–11).

(5) Nephew of Ahikar who attended the wedding of TOBIT's son, Tobias (Tob. 11:18). Later Nadab, having plotted to kill Ahikar, received God's condemnation (14:10). He is called Nadan in the Mesopotamian legend known as *The Words of Ahikar* (see AHIKAR). L. J. WOOD

Nadabath nad′uh-bath (Ναδαβαθ). A place mentioned once in the APOCRYPHA (1 Macc. 9:37). Jonathan and Simon MACCABEE, avenging the execution of their brother John by the "children of Jambri," a NABATEAN tribe, ambushed a wedding procession. The bride was brought from Nadabath to MEDEBA. This Transjordanian city is perhaps the ancient Moabite town of NEBO, referred to as Nabatha in JOSEPHUS (*Ant.* 13.1.4). Others identify it with the modern Khirbet et-Teim, just S of Medeba. (For a different approach, see J. Goldstein, *I Maccabees*, AB 41 [1977], 384–85.)

P. A. VERHOEF

Naggai nag′i (Ναγγαι G3710). KJV Nagge. Son of Maath, included in Luke's GENEALOGY OF JESUS CHRIST (Lk. 3:25).

Nagge nag′ee. KJV form of NAGGAI.

Nag Hammadi Library nahg′huh-mah′dee. In 1945, a dozen Coptic MSS (plus part of a thirteenth) were accidentally discovered near the modern Egyptian town of Nag Hammadi. These leather codices apparently were found by the village of Faw Qibli (near al-Qaṣr, ancient Chenoboskion); they had been hidden in a jar behind a large rock at the base of a cliff called Jebel al-Ṭarif. Over time they were acquired by the Coptic Museum in Old Cairo. The significance of these MSS soon became clear when they were shown to date to the 4th cent. A.D. and to contain more than fifty tractates that give expression to what may be called Gnostic Christianity. It appears that these writings had originally been composed in Greek a century or two earlier.

Prior to this discovery, our knowledge of Gnostic ideas in early Christianity had been largely limited to partial (and hostile) descriptions in the patristic literature. Now, however, it became possible to read firsthand, and in context, the writings associated with that movement. The various tractates are quite diverse in character: some have a strong tie to Jewish traditions, others reproduce non-Christian philosophical treatises, still others consist of HERMETIC texts. Many of the documents contain obscure myths, made even more difficult by their fragmentary nature and by the fact that in the course of transmission numerous copying and translation errors were introduced. Still, these writings have opened up a new world to students of early heterodox Christianity, shedding considerable light on religious developments after the apostolic period. In addition, some scholars have argued that a few of the texts provide a direct and independent link to the teachings of Jesus (see LOGIA; THOMAS, GOSPEL OF).

Following is a complete list of the tractates in each MS (NHC = Nag Hammadi Codex); note that copies of several of the tractates are preserved in more than one codex. See separate articles for a brief summary of individual tractates. (An authoritative and convenient English translation of all the tractates may be found in *NHL*. For a more complete edition, which includes the Coptic texts and commentaries, see J. M. Robinson, ed., *The Coptic Gnostic Library* [2000]. See also K. Rudolph, *Gnosis: The Nature and History of Gnosticism* [1984], esp. 34–52; S. Giversen et al., eds., *The Nag Hammadi Texts in the History of Religion* [2002]; *ABD*, 4:982–93.) For a discussion of the Gnostic worldview and further bibliography, see GNOSTICISM.

I, 1: Prayer of the Apostle Paul
I, 2: Apocryphon of James
I, 3: Gospel of Truth (cf. XII, 2)
I, 4: Treatise on the Resurrection
I, 5: Tripartite Tractate
II, 1: Apocryphon of John (cf. III, 1 and IV, 1)
II, 2: Gospel of Thomas
II, 3: Gospel of Philip
II, 4: Hypostasis of the Archons
II, 5: On the Origin of the World (cf. XIII, 2)
II, 6: Exegesis on the Soul
II, 7: Book of Thomas the Contender
III, 1: Apocryphon of John (cf. II, 1 and IV, 1)
III, 2: Gospel of the Egyptians (cf. IV, 2)
III, 3: Eugnostos the Blessed (cf. V, 1)
III, 4: Sophia of Jesus Christ
III, 5: Dialogue of the Savior
IV, 1: Apocryphon of John (cf. II, 1 and III, 1)
IV, 2: Gospel of the Egyptians (cf. III, 2)
V, 1: Eugnostos the Blessed (cf. III, 3)
V, 2: Apocalypse of Paul
V, 3: First Apocalypse of James
V, 4: Second Apocalypse of James
V, 5: Apocalypse of Adam
VI, 1: Acts of Peter and the Twelve Apostles
VI, 2: The Thunder, Perfect Mind
VI, 3: Authoritative Teaching
VI, 4: Concept of Our Great Power
VI, 5: Plato's Republic (only 588B–589B)
VI, 6: Discourse on the Eighth and Ninth
VI, 7: Prayer of Thanksgiving
VI, 8: Asclepius (only 21–29)
VII, 1: Paraphrase of Shem
VII, 2: Second Treatise of the Great Seth
VII, 3: Apocalypse of Peter
VII, 4: Teachings of Silvanus
VII, 5: Three Steles of Seth
VIII, 1: Zostrianos
VIII, 2: Letter of Peter to Philip
IX, 1: Melchizedek
IX, 2: Thought of Norea
IX, 3: Testimony of Truth
X, 1: Marsanes
XI, 1: Interpretation of Knowledge
XI, 2: A Valentinian Exposition
XI, 2a: On the Anointing
XI, 2b: On Baptism A
XI, 2c: On Baptism B
XI, 2d: On the Eucharist A
XI, 2e: On the Eucharist B
XI, 3: Allogenes
XI, 4: Hypsiphrone
XII, 1: Sentences of Sextus
XII, 2: Gospel of Truth (cf. I, 3)
XII, 3: Fragments
XIII, 1: Trimorphic Protennoia
XIII, 2: On the Origin of the World (cf. II, 5)

It should also be noted that a Coptic papyrus codex in Berlin (BG 8502) contains the *Apocryphon of John* (NHC II, 1, et al.) and *Sophia of Jesus Christ*

Nahalal nay′huh-lal (Heb. נַהֲלָל H5634, also נַהֲלֹל H5636 [Jdg. 1:30], "water place"). A city allotted to the tribe of ZEBULUN (Josh. 19:15; KJV, "Nahallal"), later given to the Levites descended from MERARI (21:35). Zebulun was unable to expel the Canaanite inhabitants who dwelt among them, but the latter became subject to forced labor (Jdg. 1:30; here the name occurs in the form "Nahalol"). Nahalal was evidently close to SHIMRON, but the precise location is uncertain. There is a modern town named Nahalal about 6 mi. N of MEGIDDO, and some sites near it have been identified with the biblical town (cf. J. Simons, *The Geographical and Topographical Texts of the Old Testament* [1959], 182). W. F. Albright had earlier favored Tell en-Naḥl, which is much further W (c. 6 mi. E of the Mediterranean, N of the KISHON River near the S end of the Plain of Acco; see AASOR 2–3 [1923]: 26), but this identification requires that the tribal territory of Zebulun had expanded to include part of ASHER. There is not sufficient evidence to confirm the various suggestions.   P. A. VERHOEF

Nahaliel nuh-hay′lee-uhl (נַחֲלִיאֵל H5712, "river [or palm-grove] of God"). A stopping place of the Israelites in TRANSJORDAN toward the end of their wanderings (Num. 21:19). Nahaliel was evidently between MATTANAH and BAMOTH, but the precise location of these sites is unknown. If the name alludes to a wadi, it might be one of the northern tributaries of the ARNON.

Nahallal nuh-hal′uhl. KJV alternate form of NAHALAL (only Josh. 19:15).

Nahalol nay′huh-lol. Alternate form of NAHALAL.

Naham nay′ham (נַחַם H5715, "comfort"). Brother of HODIAH's wife, included in the genealogy of JUDAH (1 Chr. 4:19).

Nahamani nay′huh-may′ni (נַחֲמָנִי H5720, "comfort," possibly short form of נְחֶמְיָה H5718, "Yahweh has comforted," with double ending -ān and -i [Noth, *IPN*, 39, 175]; see NEHEMIAH). An Israelite mentioned among leading individuals who returned from Babylon with ZERUBBABEL (Neh. 7:7; apparently called "Eneneus" in 1 Esd. 5:8 [KJV, "Enenius"; RSV conjectures "Bigvai"]; the name is omitted in the parallel in Ezra 2:2).

Naharai nay′huh-ri (נַחְרַי H5726, perhaps "diligent" or "gaunt"). A man from BEEROTH who served as armor-bearer for JOAB and who was included among DAVID's mighty warriors (2 Sam. 23:37 [some eds. of KJV, "Nahari"]; 1 Chr. 11:39).

Nahari nay′huh-ri. KJV alternate form of NAHARAI.

Nahash nay′hash (נָחָשׁ H5731, "serpent"; but cf. also Akk. *Naḫšu*, from *naḫāšu*, "to be luxuriant"). **(1)** King of AMMON in the late 11th cent. B.C. Soon after SAUL became king of Israel, Nahash besieged JABESH GILEAD and agreed to make a treaty with its inhabitants "only on the condition that I gouge out the right eye of every one of you and so bring disgrace on all Israel" (1 Sam. 11:1–2). This incident caused Saul to prove himself as king in the way he rallied Israel against Nahash and defeated him (1 Sam. 11:4–11; cf. 12:12).

One of the DEAD SEA SCROLLS (4QSam^a) precedes this story with a paragraph that many scholars consider original. It is included in the NRSV as follows: "Now Nahash, king of the Ammonites, had been grievously oppressing the Gadites and the Reubenites. He would gouge out the right eye of each of them and would not grant Israel a deliverer. No one was left of the Israelites across the Jordan whose right eye Nahash, king of the Ammonites, had not gouged out. But there were seven thousand men who had escaped from the Ammonites and had entered Jabesh-gilead. About a month later…" (here the scroll picks up the text at 1 Sam. 11:1; cf. Jos. *Ant* 6.5.1 §§68–70). If this material is indeed authentic (but see, e.g., T. L. Eves in *WTJ* 44 [1982]: 308–26), it indicates that the siege of Jabesh Gilead was only one (the last) in a series of repressive acts by Nahash against the Transjordanian tribes of Gad and Reuben.

According to 2 Sam. 10:1–2 (= 1 Chr. 19:1–2), after "the king of the Ammonites died," DAVID said to himself, "I will show kindness to Hanun son of

Nahash, just as his father showed kindness to me." Many scholars assume that Nahash must have aided David when the latter was fleeing from Saul, their mutual enemy. One scholar has speculated that the specific kindness mentioned here refers to a much later time when David, during ABSALOM's rebellion, received provisions from Nahash's son SHOBI (2 Sam. 17:27; see P. K. McCarter, Jr., *II Samuel*, AB 9 [1984], 273–74). The chronology is problematic, however; in addition, some have thought that the Nahash in the latter passage is a different individual altogether (cf. KD, *Samuel*, 434). It has also been suggested that the Nahash referred to in 10:2 was a descendant of the one mentioned in 11:1, though the biblical text gives no indication that two different people are meant. See also #2 below.

(2) Father of ABIGAIL, the sister of ZERUIAH (2 Sam. 17:25). Both women are called sisters of David (1 Chr. 2:16), even though David's father was named JESSE, not Nahash. Perhaps the best explanation is that Nahash was the first husband of David's mother; if so, these two women were half-sisters of David and stepdaughters of Jesse. Some have argued that this Nahash is the same as #1 above, in which case David would have had a connection with the Ammonite royal family even before the conflicts between Saul and Nahash (note that the Ammonite crown was placed on David's head after he captured RABBAH, 2 Sam. 12:30; see *ABD*, 4:496).

(3) Possibly the name of a town in Judah. See IR NAHASH. P. A. VERHOEF

Nahath na′hath (נַחַת *H5740*, possibly "rest" or "pure"). (1) Son of Reuel and grandson of ESAU by BASEMATH; an Edomite clan chief (Gen. 36:13, 17; 1 Chr. 1:37).

(2) Son of Zophai, descendant of LEVI through KOHATH, and ancestor of SAMUEL (1 Chr. 6:26; possibly the same as TOAH in v. 34 and TOHU in 1 Sam. 1:1, both of whom are identified as being a son of ZUPH).

(3) A Levite who, in the time of King HEZEKIAH, was a supervisor of the temple offerings (2 Chr. 31:13). S. BARABAS

Nahbi nah′bi (נַחְבִּי *H5696*, possibly "timid"). Son of Vophsi, from the tribe of NAPHTALI, and one of the twelve spies sent out by MOSES to reconnoiter the Promised Land (Num. 13:14).

Nahor nay′hor (נָחוֹר *H5701*, meaning uncertain; Ναχώρ *G3732*). KJV also Nachor (only Josh. 24:2; Lk. 3:34). (1) Son of Serug, descendant of SHEM, father of TERAH, and grandfather of ABRAHAM (Gen. 11:22–25; 1 Chr. 1:26); included in Luke's GENEALOGY OF JESUS CHRIST (Lk. 3:34). After the birth of Terah in his twenty-ninth year, Nahor "lived 119 years and had other sons and daughters" (Gen. 11:25).

(2) Second son of Terah, and brother of Abraham and HARAN (Gen. 11:26–29; Josh. 24:2). A list is given of the twelve children of Nahor (Gen. 22:20–24), eight by his wife MILCAH, who was the daughter of his brother Haran (Gen. 11:29; 24:15, 24, 47), and four by his concubine REUMAH. The contention that these "children" of Nahor must have represented the names of twelve Aramean tribes or places does not necessarily follow from the text. LABAN is once called the "son" of Nahor (29:5 NRSV) but the Hebrew word *bēn H1201* can refer to a descendant, thus a grandson (cf. NIV). In concluding the covenant at MIZPAH, Laban called upon "the God of Abraham and the God of Nahor, the God of their father" (31:53). The indication is that Laban distinguishes between the deities of JACOB and himself (cf. vv. 29 and 42; this distinction, however, does not apply to the God of the patriarchs, as was proposed by A. Alt, *Der Gott der Väter* [1929]).

(3) A city mentioned in Gen. 24:10. The reference may be either to a city called Nahor, or else it may be understood as the personal name, referring to #2 above; in the latter case, the passage may be rendered, "the city where Nahor lived," that is, Haran. See HARAN (PLACE). The Akkadian name *Naḫur*, however, occurs frequently in the MARI texts, referring to a location in northern Mesopotamia. It must have been near to Haran (Gen. 27:43; 28:10; 29:4–5; cf. J. Simons, *Geographical and Topographical Texts of the Old Testament* [1959], 219). P. A. VERHOEF

Nahshon nah′shon (נַחְשׁוֹן *H5732*, "little snake"; Ναασσών *G3709*). KJV also Naashon (Exod. 6:23) and Naasson (Matt. 1:4; Lk. 3:32). Son of Amminadab, descendant of JUDAH, grandfather (or ancestor) of BOAZ, and ancestor of DAVID; included in the GENEALOGY OF JESUS CHRIST (Ruth 4:20; 1 Chr. 2:10–11; Matt. 1:4; Lk. 3:32). Nahshon was the leader of the tribe of Judah as they camped in the wilderness (Num. 2:3). As such, he assisted MOSES in taking a census of the Israelites (1:7) and brought offerings to the Lord on the first day of the dedication of the TABERNACLE (7:12–17). Since this tribe led the way when the whole nation moved, Nahshon was an important man (10:14). His sister ELISHEBA married AARON (Exod. 6:23). R. L. ALDEN

Nahum nay´huhm (נַחוּם *H5699*, possibly "[God] comforts" or "comforter"; Ναούμ *G3725*). **(1)** An ELKOSHITE, author of a prophetic book (Nah. 1:1). See NAHUM, BOOK OF.

(2) Son of Esli, included in Luke's GENEALOGY OF JESUS CHRIST (Lk. 3:25; KJV, "Naum").

Nahum, Book of. The seventh book among the Minor Prophets. It belongs to that class of prophecies known as the *prophetiae contra gentes* (prophecies against the nations); it foretells the fall and destruction of NINEVEH, the haughty capital of the mighty Assyrian empire (see ASSYRIA AND BABYLONIA).

I. Unity. The consensus of critical scholarship regards only Nah. 2:3—3:19 as original. It is argued that 1:2–10 is a secondary addition mainly because this passage is construed partly as an alphabetic (ACROSTIC) psalm, and because it is supposedly not related to the central theme of the book. These arguments, however, are not decisive. First, it is evident that the acrostic is incomplete and that the opening letters of vv. 2–10 have a disturbed order: 1, 10, 3, 5, 12, 9, 6, 13 and 11. "Only by the most radical emendations and reshuffling of verses can the acrostic theory be made out" (G. L. Archer, Jr., *A Survey of Old Testament Introduction*, rev. ed. [1994], 392). The theory that this type of acrostic poetry did not become popular until the 4th cent. B.C. presupposes a late dating of Lam. 1–4 and of Pss. 34; 37; 111; 112; 119; 145. There is no reason why someone with such a distinguished poetical ability as Nahum could not have written this passage. Second, the charge of the absence of a reference to Nineveh is, of course, contradicted by the fact that Nineveh is mentioned in the title and alluded to especially in v. 8. This section is, indeed, an appropriate introduction to Nahum's prophecy, emphasizing both RETRIBUTION toward God's enemies and consolation toward those who take refuge in him.

Division of opinion exists in regard to the intervening passage (Nah. 1:11—2:2). According to some, this section is partially redactional and partly an original section of Nahum's prophecy. The main objection against its originality is the "artificially balanced" representation of judgment upon the enemy and of promise toward God's people. These two aspects of the prophecy, however, belong together in the sense of cause and effect.

II. Authorship. The second part of the title (Nah. 1:1) assigns "the book" to Nahum of Elkosh (see ELKOSHITE). According to some scholars (Smit, Goslinga), this part of the title was added to preserve the name of the prophet and to characterize the oracle as "book." There is however no reason to doubt the validity of the title in connection with Nahum's authorship of the prophecy. The name Nahum (*naḥûm H5699*, signifying "comfort, consolation") occurs nowhere else in the OT, but is found in Lk. 3:25 and on OSTRACA. Nothing is known of this prophet outside the book that bears his name.

III. Date. Two major events define the approximate date of this prophecy: the fall of THEBES (Walter Maier, *The Book of Nahum: A Commentary* [1959], 34) in 668/7 B.C., and the fall of NINEVEH in 612. The first event is referred to in Nah. 3:8–10 as a fact of history, and the fall of Nineveh is predicted as a future occurrence. Within these limits a wide range of conflicting dates has been advocated. Most critical scholars prefer a date shortly before the fall of Nineveh. According to Pfeiffer "the poem was undoubtedly written between 625 and 612, and probably between 614 and 612" (*Introduction to the Old Testament* [1941], 596). The main reason for this viewpoint is the supposition that the fall of Nineveh is thought of as imminent. According to J. M. P. Smith, "the invasion of Assyria has already begun" (*A Critical and Exegetical Commentary on Nahum*, ICC [1911], 275).

This imminence, however, is read into the text. The internal evidence of the book itself points to

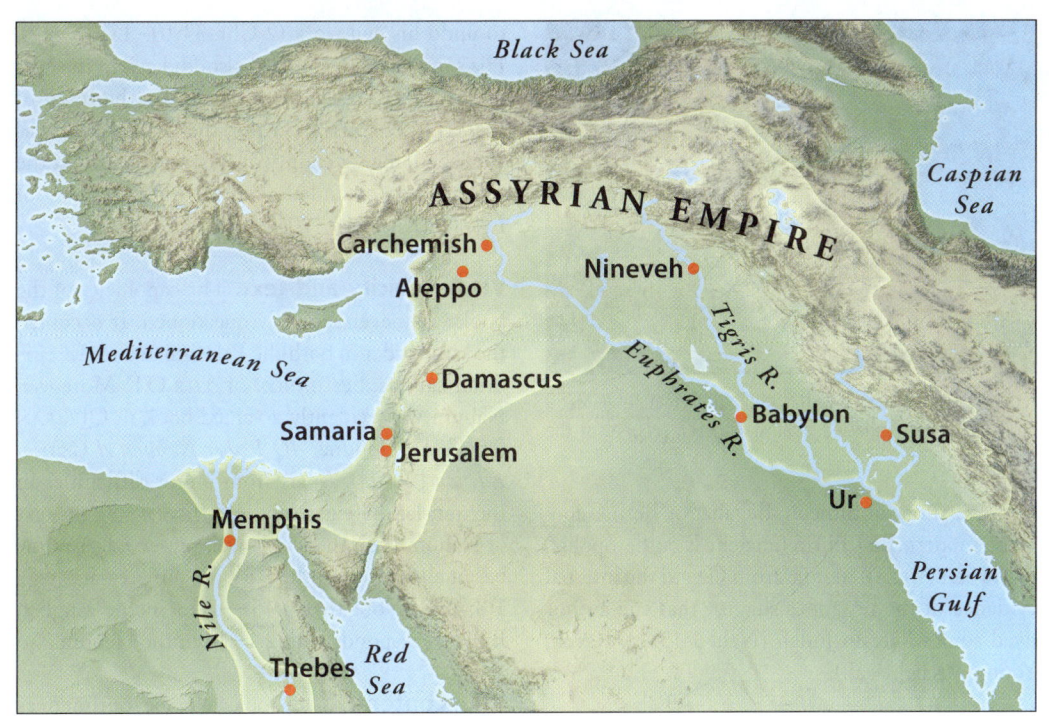

The book of Nahum foretells the collapse of the Assyrian Kingdom and the fall of Nineveh.

a much earlier date. The description of Nineveh presupposes a city bathing in grandeur and might, and this could hardly have been applied to Nineveh shortly after the death of ASHURBANIPAL in about 626. It is known that Assyria had lost its authority over the territories in the W during the reign of JOSIAH, king of Judah (639–609). When Nahum wrote his prophecy Judah was still subjected to the Assyrian tyranny (Nah. 1:13) and plundering (2:2, cf. 1:15). During the reign of Josiah, however, there was no occasion for the prophet to represent the deliverance and rejoicing of Judah as a result of the fall of Nineveh, for at that time Judah was no longer experiencing the rule of Assyria (cf. 2 Ki. 23).

Two other dates have been advocated, one shortly before 626, in connection with a supposed attack on Nineveh led by Cyaxares, the Median king, and one shortly before 652–648, with reference to the Babylonian rebellion led by Shamash-shum-ukin. These theories are hypothetical, based upon the assumption that the prophecy of Nahum must have had a basis in specific historical events. The present writer prefers a date shortly after the fall of Thebes. The reference to this event as an argument against Assyria gains in effectiveness under the assumption that the prophecy was uttered shortly after Thebes was captured and destroyed by Ashurbanipal. Perhaps it would be safe to date the prophecy before 654, because at that time Thebes began to rise from its ruins (cf. Maier, *Nahum*, 36). Extreme positions have been taken by scholars who date Nahum *post eventum* (Sellin, Humbert), or even in the Maccabean age (O. Happel).

IV. Place of origin. Contrary to the rendering of the TARGUM, according to which Nahum was from the "house of Koshi," scholars are agreed that "Elkoshite" is a designation of his native town (cf. Mic. 1:1). There are, however, four different theories in regard to the identification of this place: (1) an unlikely Islamic tradition from the 16th cent. refers to the supposed grave of Nahum in el-Qush near Mosul; (2) Jerome identified it as Elcesi (apparently modern el-Kauze) in GALILEE; (3) according to others CAPERNAUM really signifies "the village of Nahum"; (4) the theory that is favored by many identifies Elkosh with Elkesei, which according to Pseudo-Epiphanius was in the vicinity of "Begabar"

NAHUM, BOOK OF

A pedestal from Nineveh with mythological creatures (c. 2250 B.C.). Nahum prophesied against Nineveh, capital of the Assyrian empire.

in the territory of Simeon. Begabar or Beth Gabre is the modern Beit Jibrin (ancient Eleutheropolis), in the SHEPHELAH, not far from GATH; the internal evidence of the text does suggest that the author lived somewhere in Judah (Nah. 1:15; cf. Raven, Young, Archer et al.).

V. Background. During the first half of the 7th cent. B.C. the international scene was dominated by Assyria. ASHURBANIPAL (669–626), the son of ESARHADDON (680–669), played a high hand in international affairs. He conquered Egypt the first year of his kingship (669), and repeated his victory in 663 (or 661). Some scholars apply the reference in Nah. 3:8–10 to this occasion. Little is known of the last part of Ashurbanipal's reign. His country was surrounded by mighty enemies: the SCYTHIANS in the N, the Medes in the E (see MEDIA), and the Chaldeans in the S (see CHALDEA). Egypt had previously regained its independence (645). The hour of Assyria's fall was drawing near. In the year 612, Nineveh was conquered and destroyed by the Medes and Chaldeans, and in 609 the mighty Assyrian empire vanished from the map.

Judah's internal situation was determined by the long reign of MANASSEH (c. 696–641). Being a vassal of Assyria (cf. the relevant inscriptions in *ANET*, 291, 294, 295), he introduced into Judah the official cult of the Assyrians (cf. 2 Ki. 21:1–18; 23:8–9; 2 Chr. 33:3), along with a whole host of heathen practices. Later he was taken captive (2 Chr. 33:11), and afterward was brought back to Jerusalem, where he repented of his sins and tried to undo his evil work (2 Chr. 33:10–13, 15–17). His son AMON (641–639) also "did evil in the eyes of the LORD" (2 Ki. 21:20). During the reign of JOSIAH (639–609), however, the heathen cult was abolished, the suzerainty of Assyria ended, and the reformation extended even into the territory of Israel (2 Ki. 23:15–20; 2 Chr. 34:6–7).

VI. Canonicity and text. The canonicity of the book was never seriously questioned. It occupied the same order in both the Palestinian and Alexandrian canons. See CANON OF THE OT. Moreover, Nahum was evidently a valued book in QUMRAN (cf. G. L. Doudna, *4Q Pesher Nahum: A Critical Edition* [2001]). Apart from minor difficulties in the translation (e.g., Nah. 1:10, 12; 2:7–8), the text of Nahum is on the whole well preserved. A number of alterations in the RSV are unnecessary (e.g., 1:8; 2:3). Note that 1:15—2:13 in the English Bible corresponds with 2:1–14 in the Hebrew.

VII. Content. The book may be outlined as follows:

A. The title (Nah. 1:1) characterizes the prophecy as a burden or oracle (*maśśāʾ* H5363) concerning Nineveh.

B. In an introductory statement (1:2–8) Nahum describes the power and patience of God, his wrath toward his enemies, and his goodness for those who seek refuge in him. The divine resolve to destroy Nineveh (v. 8) is implied.

C. The prediction of Nineveh's doom on account of her sins is meant as a consolation for Judah (1:9–15).

D. The next section (2:1–13; Heb. 2:2–14) depicts in a vivid manner the conquering of Nineveh. The precautions to defend the city against the instrument of doom (2:1–5) will be in vain. The city will be flooded (2:6), her people taken captive (2:7–8), and her treasures plundered (2:9). Terrifying fear will prevail (2:10), and Nineveh, that self-assured lion's den (2:11–13), will be destroyed.

E. In ch. 3 the fall of Nineveh is again announced, and described in highly poetical language. The murderous city (3:1) will be captured by the instrument of God's judgment (3:2, 3). Since this city acted like a harlot, she will be treated in like manner (3:4–7). She will fare no better than the mighty and well-fortified Thebes in Egypt, which went down in bloody defeat (3:8–10). Nineveh's defense will be in vain (3:11–14). Her multitudes of merchants and military leaders will desert the doomed city (3:16–17). Its inhabitants will be scattered, never to be gathered again (3:18). Amid universal applause Nineveh will disappear forever (3:19).

VIII. Theology. Some scholars unjustly degrade the religious significance of Nahum's prophecy on the ground that the prophet was "filled with a detestation of foreign oppressors." The allusion to Nahum's supposed chauvinistic attitude and concern with the sins of foreign nations only is extremely subjective. His prophecy was concerned primarily with the "consolation" for the people of God, who at that time were in subjection to the Assyrians. The affliction of Judah (Nah. 1:12) presupposes her sins, and the deliverance out of the bondage of Assyria (1:13) must be seen as an act of God's mercy (2:2).

The main point, however, is that this prophecy has its roots in the preceding history of the divine revelation (cf. Nah. 1:2–3a with Exod. 20:5; 34:7; Num. 14:18; Nah. 1:4 with Pss. 18:16; 104:7; Nah. 2:1 with Isa. 52:7; and Nah. 3:7 with Isa. 51:19). In the prophecy of Nahum the history of God's judgments in connection with Assyria (cf. Isa. 10:5–19; 14:24–27; 17:12–14; 18:4–6; 29:5–8; 30:27–33; 31:5–9; 33; 37:6–7, 21–35) reaches its climax. At the same time the prophecy of Nahum links up with the subsequent history of revelation, inasmuch as the antithesis between Assyria and Judah is deepened to represent the world power as enemy of God and his kingdom. This is especially evident in the description of Nineveh as harlot, which figure is again reflected in the visions of Rev. 17:1, 2, 15, 18; 18:23. In the announcement of judgment upon this enemy the people of God are "consoled."

(Important commentaries include O. Happel, *Das Buch des Propheten Nahum* [1902]; J. M. P. Smith et al., *A Critical and Exegetical Commentary on Micah, Zephaniah, Nahum, Habakkuk, Obadiah and Joel*, ICC [1911]; W. A. Maier, *The Book of Nahum: A Commentary* [1959]; R. L. Smith, *Micah-Malachi*, WBC 32 [1984]; O. P. Robertson, *The Books of Nahum, Habakkuk, and Zephaniah*, NICOT [1990]; R. D. Patterson, *Nahum, Habakkuk, Zephaniah* [1991]; J. J. M. Roberts, *Nahum, Habakkuk, and Zephaniah*, OTL [1991]; T. Longman III in *The Minor Prophets: An Exegetical and Expository Commentary*, ed. T. McComiskey [1992–98], 2:765–89; K. Spronk, *Nahum* [1997]; K. L. Barker and W. Bailey, *Micah, Nahum, Habakkuk, Zephaniah*, NAC 20 [1998]; J. K. Bruckner, *Jonah, Nahum, Habakkuk, Zephaniah*, NIVAC [2004]; H.-J. Fabry, *Nahum übersetzt und ausgelegt*, HTKAT [2006]. See also P. Haupt in *JBL* 26 [1907]: 1–53; C. Goslinga, *Nahum's Godsspraak tegen Ninevé* [1923]; P. Humbert in *Revue d'histoire et de philosophie religieuses* 12 [1932]: 1ff.; A. Haldar, *Studies in the Book of Nahum* [1947]; K. K. Cathcart, *Nahum in the Light of Northwest Semitic* [1973]; and the bibliography compiled by W. E. Mills, *Nahum-Malachi* [2002].) P. A. VERHOEF

Naidus nīʹduhs (Ναιδος). One of the descendants of Addi who agreed to put away their foreign wives in the time of EZRA (1 Esd. 9:31); the parallel list (Ezra 10:30) differs considerably, but it is often thought that Naidus may correspond to BENAIAH.

nail. This English noun is used to render several Hebrew terms, such as *masmēr H5021* (1 Chr. 22:3 et al.). The nails of the carpenter and cabinet maker were widely used from ancient times and differed little in size and shape from those used today. Made usually of bronze or iron, they were hand-forged and tapered more gradually than the machined nails of today. Nails with gold or silver heads have been found that were used for decorative purposes. Six different words are used in the Bible for nails.

In the sense of the heath that protects the human finger, Hebrew has the term *ṣippōren H7632*. In the ANE, women in time of MOURNING let their persons go uncared for, sometimes as long as a year. The end of mourning was marked by dressing the hair and cutting the nails. The captive woman was given a month to mourn her separation from her people (Deut. 21:12). Then to indicate the end of her mourning, and perhaps the putting off of her heathenism, she cut her nails, groomed herself, and joined the community of Israel.

In the NT, "nail" renders Greek *hēlos G2464*, which occurs in only one passage with reference to the iron spikes used in the CRUCIFIXION of Jesus

(Jn. 20:25; but cf. the verb *proseloō G4669* in Col. 2:14). Such large nails have been found dating to Roman times. P. C. Johnson

Nain nayn (Ναΐν *G3723*). During his great Galilean ministry, following the healing of the Roman CENTURION's slave in CAPERNAUM, Jesus journeyed about 25 mi. S to a city called Nain (Lk. 7:11–17). As he approached the city, he met the funeral procession of a widow's son, apparently a well-known person, since the procession consisted of a large crowd from the city. Touched by the desolate state of the widow, Jesus miraculously restored the young man to life to the astonishment and gratitude of the whole city and neighboring territory. Luke is the only evangelist to report this episode.

About 6.5 mi. SE of NAZARETH, near Kefar Yeladim, is the modern village of Nein, identified with the NT city. The present village is a Muslim settlement. It lies at the foot of the lower N slope of the hill Mount MOREH (at the northern edge of the Plain of ESDRAELON). It is intriguing that on the S side of the same hill lies the OT town of SHUNEM, where ELISHA also restored a child to life (2 Ki. 4:8–37). At Nein, a small chapel erected by the Franciscans in 1880, supposedly upon the foundations of an ancient sanctuary, marks the site of one of the most touching scenes in the life of Jesus — the raising of the widow's son.

JOSEPHUS (*War* 4.9.4–5) mentions a village called Nain, which a revolutionary named Simon fortified in an attempt to usurp the command of the Jews shortly after the death of Galba in A.D. 69. This, however, is located in IDUMEA, S of MASADA, and obviously is not the village referred to in Lk. 7:11. B. Van Elderen

Naioth nay′yoth (נָיוֹת *H5766*; the *Ketib*, however, is נויִת, prob. to be pointed נְוָיִת, and in 1 Sam. 20:1 many MSS, including Leningradensis, have the common noun נָוֹת, which is the form preferred by *HALOT*, 2:679, with the meaning "grazing place, township"). A place in RAMAH to which DAVID fled from SAUL (1 Sam. 19:18—20:1). When Saul went to this location, "the Spirit of God came even upon him, and he walked along prophesying until he came to Naioth. He stripped off his robes and also prophesied in Samuel's presence" (19:23–24a).

The site is unknown, however, and many believe that the word is not a proper name, but rather a common noun to be rendered "camps" or the like (cf. P. K. McCarter, Jr., *I Samuel*, AB 8 [1980], 328). Since SAMUEL lived in Ramah (modern er-Ram, c. 5 mi. N of Jerusalem), some think that "the camps/dwellings at Ramah" described the domicile of Samuel and his school of prophets (v. 20).
R. L. Alden

nakedness. The first use of the word *naked* (Heb. *ʿārôm H6873*) in the Bible gives insight into the meaning in many other contexts: "The man and his wife were both naked, and they felt no shame" (Gen. 2:25). In the unfallen state the exposure of the body would not provoke TEMPTATION. The sense of SHAME at nakedness is illustrated graphically in the account of NOAH's drunkenness and the reaction of his sons to his consequent exposure (Gen. 9:20–23). The expression "to uncover nakedness" (*lĕgallôt ʿerwâ*) is used to describe forbidden degrees of cohabitation (Lev. 18:6 et al.).

The terms *naked* and *nakedness* are used figuratively in many ways. "To be naked" may mean to be without full covering (Jn. 21:7; Gk. *gymnos G1218*), or destitute (Job 22:6), or impoverished (Gen. 42:9). JOB used the word to indicate the transience of earthly possessions (Job 1:21). The expression "nakedness of the land" (Gen. 42:9 NRSV) indicates exposure and helplessness. The spiritual state of the church in LAODICEA was "wretched, pitiful, poor, blind and naked" (Rev. 3:17) — a vivid characterization of its utter bankruptcy.
D. L. Blaiklock

Nakon nay′kon. TNIV form of NACON.

name. The first and most important experience that a newborn Hebrew underwent was the receiving of a name. Just as God in his CREATION named "day" and "night," "seas," and so on (Gen. 1:3–10), and even each star (Isa. 40:26), so he likewise gave to ADAM, the creature made in his image, this high privilege of naming each of the animals (Gen. 2:20) and each of his children (Gen. 4:1, 2, 26).

  I. Terminology
    A. Hebrew
    B. Greek

II. Biblical onomatology
  A. Names of persons
  B. Names of places
III. Name in the OT
  A. The giving of a name
  B. The change of a name
  C. The significance of a name
IV. Name in the NT
  A. Name and personality
  B. Name and authority
  C. Name and reputation
  D. The name of Christ

I. Terminology. In the OT, "name" is usually the rendering of Hebrew *šēm H9005* and Aramaic *šum H10721*, which occur over 770 times. The Greek *onoma G3950* (used in the LXX to render *šēm*) appears almost 200 times in the NT. There are a few related words that will be discussed below, but the statistical data for this concept is indeed impressive and thereby indicates its importance in the Bible.

A. Hebrew. In 1872 Redslob (in *ZDMG*, 751–56) argued that *šēm* was derived from the root *šmw*, "to be high," and that therefore its basic meaning was one of height and then (1) a monument (Gen. 11:4; 2 Sam. 8:13; Isa. 55:13) or mausoleum (Isa. 56:5), and (2) excellence or majesty (Ps. 54:1). However, P. Lagarde (*Uebersicht über die im Aramäischen, Arabischen und Hebräischen übliche Bildung der Nomina* [1889], 160) and W. R. Smith (*Kinship and Marriage in Early Arabia*, new ed. [1903], 248–49) argued for the Arabic root *wšm*, "to mark or brand," indicating that *šēm* originally meant a "sign" or "token." Which was the original meaning of our root is uncertain, but the development of the word includes both sets of ideas in its range of meanings.

The prepositional combinations with *šēm* are instructive. The idiom "to call the name (of someone) over" (preposition ʿ*al*) is found eighteen times. Isaiah describes a future day in a depopulated Jerusalem when seven women shall ask one man, "only let us be called by your name," that is, the husband's protection and ownership as signalized by his name (Isa. 4:1). In 2 Sam. 12:28, DAVID speaks of calling his name over a conquered city. In Amos 9:12 God's name is called over the heathen just as it extends over Israel (Isa. 63:19). Other prepositions used with the noun include *lĕ*-, "to, for" (over 50 times, usually with reference to the name of Yahweh), *bĕ*-, "in" (some 130 times), *min* partitive and comparative (3 times), *lĕmaʿan*, "for the sake of" (16 times), *kĕ*-, "as" (7 times), and once *baʿăbûr*, "for the sake of" (cf. H. Bietenhard in *TDNT*, 5:252–53).

A less frequent noun is *zēker H2352*, "memory, remembrance," which sometimes is used in parallel with *šēm* (cf. Exod. 3:15; Job 18:17; Prov. 10:7; Isa. 26:8), and in some cases is properly rendered "name" (e.g., Pss. 30:4; 97:12). The verb *zākar H2349*, "to remember," appears in the hiphil stem as a set formula with the noun *šēm* as a direct object six times (Exod. 20:24; 24:21; 2 Sam. 18:18; Ps. 45:17; Isa. 26:13; 49:1), and in four other cases it appears with the preposition *bĕ*- and the noun *šēm*. These uses have led scholars like B. Jacob, J. Begrich, and B. S. Childs to interpret the hiphil of this verb as a denominative of *zēker*, thus "to name the name," an act of utterance rather than an act of remembering, as in the qal stem.

Roman marble cinerary chest in the form of an ancient tomb with names inscribed (1st cent. A.D.). The names of those who have died are often preserved on tombs and monuments as memorials.

(The etymology of the root *zkr* still remains unsolved even though a great deal of effort has been expended on solving the problem. Gesenius's first edition of his *Thesaurus* represented the major consensus up to that time when he connected it with the noun *zākār* **H2351**, "male," since the male was thought to be the sex by which the memory of parents and ancestors was preserved. Gesenius changed that opinion in later editions of his lexicon and argued that the root idea was one of pricking or piercing, and from that came the noun used with reference to the *membrum virile*. Memory was, on this theory, a penetrating or fixing in the mind. This theory and others have all failed due to a lack of positive evidence.)

B. Greek. The SEPTUAGINT consistently translates Hebrew *šēm* and Aramaic *šum* by the Greek *onoma*, "name." This Greek term also was used to render other Hebrew words (e.g., Gen. 21:23; Num. 14:15; Josh. 6:27), including *zēker* (Deut. 25:19). Then the LXX sometimes adds *onoma* before mentioning a name of a person or place for stylistic reasons (e.g. Gen. 21:31; 1 Chr. 2:1). For the Hebrew term *zēker*, it usually prefers Greek terms meaning "memory, remembrance" (*mneia* **G3644**, *mnēmē* **G3647**, *mnēmosynon* **G3649**).

The NT writers used *onoma* much as the Hebrews used their words for "name." Thus a name is a "reputation" (Mk. 6:14; Phil. 2:9; Rev. 3:1); the "authority" and "power" by which one acts (Matt. 7:22; Mk. 9:39; Acts 4:7); the "character" of its possessor (Matt. 6:9; Jn. 12:38); the "whole system of divine doctrine," the "content of revelation," or "divine truth" (Jn. 17:16, 26; Heb. 2:12 quoting Ps. 22:22); the "rank" or "category" (as of a prophet, Matt. 10:41); and in the plural, "persons, people" (Acts 1:15; Rev. 3:14; 11:13; Acts 18:15).

The prepositional combinations will be treated in more detail below, but these also show the same Semitic influence rather than the typical classical meanings. The dative form of *onoma* is found with *en* (40 times) and *epi* (at least 14 times). These forms are used almost as a formula for "by the authority of" or "in the power of" God or Jesus Christ. The genitive (3 times) and the accusative (4 times) is found with the preposition *dia*; the former designating the means and agency for the results described, while the latter has the name as the grounds and basis upon which the action rests. It would appear that *eis* with the accusative often functions like *lĕšēm*, "with regard to, in thinking of, for the sake of, to the benefit or account of." Some of the other prepositions are *heneka* (Matt. 19:29; Lk. 21:12); *peri* with the genitive (Acts 8:12); *pros* with the accusative (Acts 26:9); and *hyper* with the genitive (Acts 5:41; Rom. 1:5).

II. Biblical onomatology. Neither the unscientific etymologies of Plato and Aristotle nor the more systematic but nevertheless speculative wordplays of PHILO JUDAEUS provide a solid base for the study of biblical names (they were effective, however, in setting the tone for some fifteen centuries). The STOICS, led by Zeno and Chrysippus, developed a whole doctrine of speech, but still included etymologizing as the means of unfolding the moral, religious and metaphysical truth in words.

With the advent of scientific lexicography and grammar and comparative Semitics, major contributions to the subject began to appear (e.g., M. Hiller, *Onomasticum sacrum* [1706]); J. Simonis, *Onomasticum Veteris Testamenti* [1741] and *Onomasticum Novi Testamenti* [1762]; E. Nestle, *Die israelitischen Eigennamen* [1876]; G. B. Gray, *Studies in Hebrew Proper Names* [1898]; and several others, esp. M. Noth, *Die israelitischen Personennamen im Rahmen der gemeinsemitischen Namengebung* [1928]). Through the 20th cent., such studies were significantly complemented by detailed comparisons between Hebrew and other Semitic languages (e.g., J. J. Stamm, *Die akkadische Namengebung* [1939]; I. J. Gelb et al., *Nuzi Personal Names* [1943]; H. B. Huffmon, *Amorite Personal Names in the Mari Texts* [1965]; F. Gröndahl, *Die Personennamen der Texte aus Ugarit* [1967]; and many others). Added to these materials are Jewish names recorded in the 5th-cent. B.C. Aramaic papyri from ELEPHANTINE, the LACHISH letters, and the Samaritan OSTRACA. Nevertheless, some questions remain, and not all of the meanings attributed to the names listed below are accepted by all specialists.

A. Names of persons. The Hebrews were a mononymous people; that is, each child received only one name at birth without a family name or middle name. If a distinction was necessary, the individual could be identified easily by adding the name of his father and any other ancestor's name in ascending order as these occasions required. Most scholars classify Hebrew names according to their formation: simple and compound.

1. Simple names. These are the most difficult, since there is only one element and it is generally some being, object, description, or circumstance known in this cryptic form by the contemporaries but not as easily known to us. Single-element names are often *hypocoristic*, that is, they are shortened forms of names that originally consisted of more than one element (see *ABD*, 4:1017–18; however, as noted by J. D. Fowler, *Theophoric Personal Names in Ancient Hebrew* [1988], 149, this label is not the most appropriate one, since it technically refers to diminutives or pet names). A simple name may be an adjective, or an abbreviation of a compound name (with the divine element omitted in some instances or the noun of kinship in other cases), or a verb in the third person singular (e.g., Nathan, "he has given"). Sometimes one element simply is replaced by an ending on the remaining element, and these abbreviated and apocopated forms then become simple names.

a. *Nature names.* There are three groups of nature names: (1) animal, (2) plant, and (3) meteorological. The first group is represented by twenty-two preexilic southern names of which some of the better known are: Deborah (bee), Rachel (ewe), Caleb (dog), Huldah (weasel), Acbor (mouse), Shaphan (rock badger), Jonah (dove), and Tola (worm). In addition to these examples of Hebrew animal names, there are eleven foreign names in the OT of this type, including Zeeb (wolf), Eglah (calf), Oreb (raven), Hamor (ass), Jael (mountain goat), Nahash (serpent), Epher (young gazelle), and Zipporah (lady bird). Plant names, however, are rarer. Illustrations of this class are Tamar (date palm tree), Hadassah (myrtle), Elon (oak), Zethan (olive), Rimmon (pomegranate); in the Apocrypha and NT, Susanna (lily).

While one cannot dogmatically affirm just what the intention was in every case, it is possible to parallel these names with a plethora of animal and plant names from other lists of names of high antiquity in the ANE. It must be said that a theory that is equally as justifiable as the totem theory for which there is some support is the idea of endearment and tenderness as the reason for using these names; this might be especially true where small animals, albeit unclean ones, are used for names!

People in the Bible are sometimes named after animals. For example, the name Rachel means "ewe."

Some meteorological names are Barak (lightning), Samson (little sun), and Nogah (sunrise). This class may be wholly derived from pagan theophorics or slight modifications thereof.

b. *Physical characteristics.* These few names seem to divide easily into four categories: (1) color, (2) size, (3) defects, and (4) sex. Some examples are: Laban and Libni (white), Zohar (reddish white), Haruz (yellow), Edom (red), Phinehas (bronze-colored Nubian), Hakkatan (small one), Korah and Kareah (baldy), Heresh (dumb), Ikkesh (crooked), Gareb (scabby), Gideon (maimed?), Paseah (halting), and Geber (male).

c. *Circumstances at birth.* Often the name indicates something about (1) time of birth, (2) place of birth, (3) order of birth, and (4) events at birth. Some examples are: Haggai and Haggith (festal, i.e., born at feast time), Shabbethai (sabbatical, i.e., born on the Sabbath), Judith and Jehudi (Jewess or Jew, perhaps originally, of Judah), Cushi (Ethiopian), Beker (firstborn), Yathom and Yathomah (fatherless, orphan), Azubah (forsaken, perhaps by mother at birth?), and Thomas (twin).

d. *Miscellaneous.* There are a few additional simple names that refer either to the qualities of the person, such as Nabal (fool) and Naomi (perhaps pleasant), or to various objects like Peninnah (corals), Rebecca (cord for tying sheep), Rizpah (pavement), Bakbuk (pitcher), and Acsah (anklet). Other names in this category are active or passive participles, such as Saul (asked), Baruch (blessed), Menahem (comforting); names with the diminutive (affectionate) endings -*on*, -*an*, -*om*, or -*am*, such as Nahshon (small serpent), Samson (small sun); names ending in -*ai* or -*i* for possession or gentilics, or for abbreviation, such as Mordecai (votary of Marduk), Omri; and those ending in -*a*, such as Gera (guest).

2. Compound names. This class of names by far exceeds the former class. Especially numerous are the theophorous names, that is, names that explicitly mention Deity. Compound names in the OT consist of two or more independent words. The relationship between these words may be: (1) two substantives functioning as nominative and genitive, the so-called construct state; and (2) a complete sentence. In the construct bond, often the first element ends in -*i*. This usually is regarded as a survival of the old case ending system, but occasionally it does indicate the presence of the first person singular suffix, "my." Infrequently, a preposition may appear before this noun in the construct, for example, Bezalel (in the shadow of God). Sentence names are common in the Semitic languages, and Hebrew has its share of them. Some that quickly come to mind are the names of Isaiah's children, Shear-Jashub (the remnant shall return) and Maher-Shalal-Hash-Baz (plunder has hastened, spoil has sped), as well as Hosea's children, Lo-Ruhamah (she has found no mercy) and Lo-Ammi (he is not my people). The name Hephzibah (my delight is in her, 2 Ki. 21:1; Isa. 62:4) also illustrates this usage.

a. *Theophorous names.* Generally these names are sentence names formed with the divine names EL or Yahweh (see I AM). The sentence may appear with a nominal predicate indicating assurance or confidence, such as Joel (Yahweh is God); or with a verbal predicate, for example, in the perfect tense expressing thanksgiving, such as Jonathan (Yahweh has given). Since the subject may come at the beginning or the end (contrast Nathanael and Elnathan), often it is difficult to decide which is the subject and predicate; this is especially true when the MT vocalization may be in question on a particular name. Some verbs are in the imperfect tense or the jussive, and thereby can express a wish or desire, such as Jehoiachim (may Yahweh establish). Some authorities even claim to find an imperative form of the verb in these names (e.g., Hoshea, save!) but this is by no means clear.

The greatest number of these compounds contain the element for Yahweh either at the beginning or end of the name. It appears as *yĕhô* or *yô* (Eng. Jeho-, Jo-) in the first position, and *yāhû* or *yā* (Eng. -iah, -jah) in the second position. Gray (*Studies in Hebrew Proper Names*, 149) has counted 156 different names of over 500 persons in the OT with this divine name. The Elephantine papyri give evidence of this same high frequency, with as many as 170 Jews bearing a Yahweh compound name. Ranking second in the number of occurrences is the El compound name. The OT has, according to Gray (p. 163–65), 135 names compounded with a form of El, of which 113 are Hebrew personal (or tribal) names.

The meanings found in these theophorous names cover almost the complete range of God's being, person, gifts, and works for human beings. T. Nöldeke, in his monumental article on "Names" in *Encyclopedia Biblica* (1902), arranges these meanings according to the following groupings: God's sovereignty—he is just, rules, judges, is possessor, is the Lord; God's gifts—he gives, increases, opens the womb, gives freely; God's graciousness—he blesses, has mercy, loves, helps, saves, is good, confers benefits, is with man; God's creating ability—he makes, builds, sets up, establishes, accomplishes; God's knowledge—he remembers, knows, weighs, sees; God's salvation—he delivers, comforts, heals, redeems, preserves, keeps in safety, conceals; God's power—he holds fast, is strong, is a refuge, strengthens; God's immanence—he hears, answers, speaks, swears, promises; and God's being and attributes—he is great, perfect, high, glorious, lives, is incomparable, dwells, comes, passes by, meets, contents, shoots, thunders, rises, is glad, is light, is fire. This is just a sample of the many roots and ideas. (For a thorough and more recent investigation, see J. D. Fowler, *Theophoric Personal Names in Ancient Hebrew* [1988]; cf. also *ABD*, 4:1018–19.)

Rizpah (2 Sam. 21:7–8); and (5) Ahaziah (1 Ki. 22:40; 2 Ki. 8:16–18, 26).

2. To a place. Many of the place names in Canaan are older than the Israelite contacts or occupation of that land. The chief evidence for this statement comes from the EXECRATION TEXTS, the TELL EL-AMARNA letters written by the city-state kings of Canaan to Egypt, the Karnak inscription of THUTMOSE III, Amenhotep II's two military expeditions, and the lists of Seti I, RAMSES II, and MERNEPTAH. In the Thutmose III list alone, which is the most detailed information extant on the land of Canaan, there is evidence for some fifty place names found in the OT in a list extending to 119 names in two copies and 350 in a third.

The OT traces the names of some of these places back to the eponymous hero who settled in that region or who captured the site (Gen. 4:17 [cf. 10:2–7 et al.]; Num. 32:42; Deut. 3:14; Josh. 19:47). When JOAB was about to defeat the Ammonite capital, RABBAH, he warned DAVID to capture the city lest he should do so and the city then be called after his name (2 Sam. 12:28). Thus the proclaiming of one's name over a place signified one's ownership of that town.

B. The change of a name. There are about a dozen examples of a change of a name in the OT. These each signalized the introduction of a new relationship, a new quality of character, a new phase of life, and perhaps a new vocation. Just as ANE monarchs assumed a new name expressive of a new era or policy at its inauguration, so God renamed his men and women when they inaugurated new aspects of the promise of God. This was so for Abram, whose name became Abraham (Gen. 17:5), and Sarai, who was renamed Sarah (Gen. 17:15). Other examples are: God renamed Jacob as Israel (Gen. 32:28; 35:10); Pharaoh renamed Joseph as Zaphenath-Paneah (Gen. 41:45); Moses changed Hoshea into Joshua (Num. 13:16); Pharaoh Neco turned the name Eliakim into Jehoiakim (2 Ki. 23:34); Nebuchadnezzar changed Mattaniah into Zedekiah (2 Ki. 24:17); and the Babylonian prince of the eunuchs renamed Daniel, Hananiah, Mishael, and Azariah as Belteshazzar, Shadrach, Meshach, and Abednego respectively (Dan. 1:7). In every case, there is a change of position expressed; either an exaltation to a new dignity or a reduction to dependency. These examples remind one also of "the new name" to be given to Jerusalem at its future restoration (Isa. 62:2) and of the fact that God will give his servants "another name" (Isa. 65:15; LXX, "new name"), announcing a corresponding change of dignity. (See further *ABD*, 4:1011–17, s.v. "Names, Double.")

C. The significance of a name. As it already has been indicated in some of the above discussion, the name is more than the distinguishing title of God or a person. The people of Israel were aware of the significance that could be attached to a name, and therefore their usage of the concept demonstrates this broad range of meanings.

1. The name and personality. It would appear that the Hebrew term that comes closest to our modern Western concept of "personality" (i.e., the total picture of a person's organized behavior) is *šēm*, "name." Thus the sum total of a person's internal and external pattern of behavior was gathered up into his or her name. In this way, one could give honor to the person of God (Pss. 5:11; 7:17). Knowing someone's name was equivalent to knowing that person's essence: "Those who know your name will trust in you" (Pss. 9:10; 91:14).

To change the name was to imply a change in the character and mission, thus the dozen or more examples referred to above. Not only does the changing of the name indicate the close ties that the name has with the person and his personality, but the person was so intimately connected with his name that "to cut off the name" was tantamount to destroying the person or the place (1 Sam. 24:21; 2 Ki. 14:27; Ps. 83:4; Isa. 14:22; Zeph. 1:4). One's existence in his earthly form was bound in with his name. When the name had been destroyed, the person had for all intents and purposes also been dealt a death blow. What else does a person actually own, in the last analysis, beside his personality?

This connection is best seen in the plural forms of the Hebrew and Greek words for "name" that could actually be rendered as "persons" (Num. 1:2, 18, 20; 3:40, 43; 26:53; Acts 1:15; 18:15; Rev. 3:4; 11:13). Perhaps this was part of David's problem in taking the census of 2 Sam. 24. To list the names of the persons was in effect to muster the men into the servitude of military missions not explicitly commanded by God.

The name, since it was the person, also could act and speak. Often Israel, as representatives of the name of God, fought and acted magnificently with his strength. God's name was more than mere approbation of the mission; it was the power, strength, courage, and presence of God himself. Thus Israel was successful because the name acted and won (Ps. 44:5; Mic. 4:5; 5:3). The name of God can support, defend, hide, and give comfort to the righteous, and all who will run to it (Ps. 20:1; Prov. 18:10). So also was the matter of speaking in his name. Frequently this expression meant that one was God's representative, but it also meant in reality that if one would dare speak in the name of the Lord, this would be the same as if the person whose name was being used had actually spoken himself (Deut. 18:19; Jer. 26:20; 44:16).

Even the names of cities had a personality inherent in their names. For example, Jerusalem is called "the City of Righteousness" (Isa. 1:26), "the City of the Lord" (60:14), "My Delight Is in Her" (62:4 NRSV), and "Sought After, the City No Longer Deserted" (62:12)—new names for an old city, giving a new character and pattern of behavior.

2. Name and authority. When one gives a name to another, he thereby establishes a relation of dominion or possession to him. Already in Eden, Adam demonstrated that part of the *imago Dei* which promised to him the subjugation and rulership over all things upon the earth by naming the animals (Gen. 2:19–20; see IMAGE OF GOD). This right is held on loan from God, who already has not only made the world, but named it as well (Gen. 1:5, 8, 10). Man in turn names his wife "woman" (Gen. 2:23). The psalmist (Ps. 8) cannot contain himself as he reflects on the magnificence of humanity in this capacity as sovereign over the works of God's hands. The excellence of God's name (Ps. 8:1) is witnessed in all the earth, yet he has set all these things under human authority!

Whatever a man owns, he names, whether it be a conquered city (2 Sam. 12:28), his land (Ps. 49:11), or his wives (Isa. 4:1). Even children are important to one's name, for they preserve the memory of that name (Ps. 72:17). The whole institution of LEVIRATE marriage was just for this reason: to keep the family name and the family alive in Israel (Deut. 25:5–10; Ruth 4:5).

Likewise Yahweh not only gives to the stars their names (Ps. 147:4; Isa. 43:1), but he also has his name called over the ARK OF THE COVENANT (2 Sam. 6:2), the temple (Jer. 7:10), Jerusalem (Jer. 25:29; Dan. 9:18), and Israel (2 Chr. 7:14; Isa. 63:19). God also promises to "put his Name" in a place he will "choose as a dwelling for his Name" (Deut. 12:5, 11). This promise was made to the Israelites before they entered Canaan and is just a continuation of the older promise that wherever God should cause his name to be honored, he would come and bless his people (Exod. 20:24). Contrary to G. von Rad's suggestion (and all of modern criticism) that the Deut. 12 passage represents the key issue of the centralization of the Jerusalem temple, this passage in an indefinite and anticipatory way (with regard to the actual place, whether in Jerusalem or elsewhere) betokens only the equation of the name of Yahweh and "the place." The authority to worship at this place which will be declared is to be found in the presence of the Name. Linked with the concept of authority is the idea of protection. What God or people own, they must thereby protect (e.g., 1 Ki. 8:43; 2 Chr. 7:14; Jer. 7:10, 11, 14, 30; 14:9; 34:15; Dan. 9:18, 19; Amos 9:12).

3. Name and reputation. Names can grow, be great, be bad, and collect honor and praise. This is simply an extension of the equation of the person and his name. The name comes to have a reputation, fame, renown, and glory all its own. In Gen. 6:4 the aristocracy ("the sons of God") took wives, and these "heroes" (or "mighty tyrants," from *gibbôr H1475*) had children who also became "men of renown" (lit., "men of the name"). Again, the builders of the tower had as their motivation the acquisition of a name (Gen. 11:4). Moses was later to be confronted by 250 princes of Israel who were "well-known" (lit., "men of a name," Num. 16:2). The guests and witnesses at the marriage of Ruth and Boaz wished this couple God's blessing when they prayed that their family would do courageous things and "be famous" (lit., "a name be called") in Bethlehem (Ruth 4:11). Certain "brave warriors" are described as "famous men" ("men of names," 1 Chr. 5:24). By the same token, "nameless" people were "disreputable" (NRSV) men who were infamous by virtue of their lack of a (good) name (Job 30:8). Indeed, "A good name is more desirable than great riches" (Prov. 22:1), and "A good name is better than fine perfume" (Eccl. 7:1; cf. Cant. 1:3). Even the way one speaks and acts toward a name affects the reputation and character of that name and thereby some have given "a bad name" to others (Deut. 22:14, 19).

4. The name of Yahweh. A great theological theme is to be found in the name of Yahweh. It appears most frequently with the Hebrew inseparable prepositions "to" and "in." One may "call upon," "speak in," "prophesy in," "bless," "serve," "walk in" the name of the Lord. See GOD, NAMES OF; I AM.

a. *The revelation of the name.* Few passages in the Bible have been made so pivotal for our modern understanding of the OT as Exod. 6:2–3. The passage was indeed a crucial one for Moses and Israel as they received a further development to the promise theology of the patriarchs: God now would redeem his people from the bondage of Egypt. The modern question is, simply put, had God previously withheld his name Yahweh from the patriarchs in favor of using as his self-designation the name EL SHADDAI? Does he here declare that only now will he make himself known as Yahweh?

The proper answer to this question lies in denying to the patriarchs the knowledge of the *significance* of the name Yahweh, not in denying to them the knowledge of the name itself. The two verbs "to appear" and "to make known" are both in the niphal stem, which here conveys a reflexive sense, that is, "I showed myself" and "I did not make myself known." The Hebrew preposition *b* before El Shaddai and the absence of any Hebrew preposition before Yahweh is most crucial. An English translation will demand some preposition in the second case as well, and we believe those renderings to be best which view both prepositions as having the same force. Although the Hebrew preposition most frequently means "in," its use in contexts such as this one is often designated *beth essentiae*, to be translated "as." The meaning is, "I showed myself to Abraham, to Isaac, and to Jacob *in the character of* [with the attributes of] El Shaddai, but *in the character of* my name Yahweh, I did not make myself known to them." The name plays an important function here: it reveals the character, qualities, attributes, and essence of the name.

The correctness of this interpretation can be checked by noting the question asked earlier by Moses when God promised that he would be with him. He queried: "Suppose I go to the Israelites and say to them, 'The God of your fathers has sent me to you,' and they ask me, 'What is his name?' Then what shall I tell them?" (Exod. 3:13). As Martin Buber and others have noted, the interrogative *mâ H4537* ("what?") is to be distinguished from *mî H4769* ("who?"). The latter asks only for the title or designation of an individual, while the former, especially since it is associated with the word "name," asks the question of the character, qualities, power, and abilities resident in the name. The thrust of their anticipated question was, "What does the 'God of our fathers' have to offer in a situation as complex and difficult as ours?" This is precisely the question God answers by declaring his name to be Yahweh, that is, the God who will be present there in that situation for them.

b. *The being of God.* Often the expression "the Name [of Yahweh]" and the name Yahweh itself are used interchangeably (Deut. 28:58; Job 1:21; Pss. 18:49; 68:4; 74:18; 86:12; 92:1; Isa. 25:1; 26:8; 48:9; 56:6; Ezek. 20:44; Amos 2:7; Mal. 3:16). At times "the Name" functions almost like an appearance of Yahweh. The surest passage leading to this conclusion is Exod. 23:20–21, where God says of the

God's covenant name YHWH (Heb. יהוה) is written with early Hebrew characters in some Jewish MSS (see first line, second word from the right).

ANGEL whom he sends before Israel, "my Name is in him." Israel is to beware of the angel and to obey him, because "he will not forgive your rebellion." In Isa. 30:27, what is normally credited to Yahweh is attributed to his name. The Name of Yahweh comes from afar and burns with his anger, while his lips are full of indignation and his tongue is as a devouring fire! The Name then, like the angel of God (of the Lord) or the GLORY of the Lord, is the one who will be present for them and who is to be feared and obeyed just like Yahweh himself, if indeed he is not Yahweh himself.

c. *The doctrine of God.* At times the name of God is used to indicate the whole system of divine truth and doctrine revealed in the Scriptures. The psalmist seems to have intended this when he wrote, "I will declare your name to my brothers" (Ps. 22:22; quoted in Heb. 2:12). The messianic psalm refers to the life and doctrine of the promised One who was to come. When he came, he said, "I have manifested you [*lit.*, your name] to those whom you gave me," and "I made you [your name] known to them" (Jn. 17:6, 26). Obviously the proclamation of the name was the declaration of the doctrine of God. Thus it was possible for the people to live according to the teaching appointed and approved by God: "All the nations may walk / in the name of their gods; / we will walk in the name of the LORD / our God for ever and ever" (Mic. 4:5).

d. *The theological development.* G. von Rad (*Studies in Deuteronomy* [1953], 37–44) views the appearance of a "name-theology" as the distinctive contribution of the Deuteronomic movement that replaces the older "Glory-of-the-Lord Theology" associated with the ark and the phenomena of the cloud and fire. Yet he too (p. 38) is aware of passages like Exod. 20:24, which appear earlier. Rather than saying with von Rad that the ideas move from a crude concept of Yahweh's material presence to a more sophisticated tendency toward hypostasis, we believe the concepts of the ark, the angel, the face, the glory of God, and the name of God are intended as a representation and pledge (earnest) of Yahweh's presence. This removes the developmental idea away from an identity concept to a representation concept. Thus the name comes to represent the presence of God himself, for example, in the temple; but while he is there present, he is not contained within that temple (Th. C. Vriezen, *An Outline of Old Testament Theology* [1958], 248).

(The APOCRYPHA has about a hundred verses illustrating the uses of *onoma* that are almost identical to those seen in Hebrew *šēm*. Neither does the PSEUDEPIGRAPHA illustrate any new features when compared to the OT. Its most frequent reference is to the name of God; otherwise it does not exhibit any noteworthy features for the purposes of this article. See *TDNT*, 5:261–64, 266–67.)

IV. Name in the NT. Often when the NT gives instances of "name," it actually is quoting the OT and therefore the above discussion would hold true for this section of the Scriptures as well (Matt. 6:9; 12:31; 23:39; Jn. 17:6; Acts 2:21; Rom. 15:9; Heb. 2:12). A few distinctive examples can be given now.

A. Name and personality. "Name" again appears in the plural meaning "persons" (Acts 1:15; Rev. 3:4; 11:13). It also denotes the character or work that someone does or will do, such as the name of JOHN THE BAPTIST (Lk. 1:13, 59–63) and that of JESUS (meaning "Yahweh is salvation"), because "he will save his people from their sins" (Matt. 1:21). Jesus has "the name that is above every name" and "at the name of Jesus every knee should bow" (Phil. 2:9–10). A change of name meant a corresponding change of character, vocation, or status. For example, Simon is changed to PETER (Matt. 16:17–18); James and John are renamed BOANERGES, that is, "sons of thunder," men characterized by a bombastic temperament (Mk. 3:17).

B. Name and authority. The name of Jesus is his authority given to his disciples so that they might work miracles, preach, or pray to the Father. When the question arises "by what name have you done this?" the answer is always in terms of the authority and power of Jesus (Matt. 7:22; Mk. 9:39; Lk. 24:47; Acts 4:7; 16:18; 19:17). That name was authoritative and powerful enough to justify sinners (Acts 10:43; 1 Cor. 6:11) and to forgive them their sins (1 Jn. 2:12).

C. Name and reputation. This usage is rare in the NT. The only references are Mk. 6:14; Lk. 6:22; Rev. 3:1; and perhaps Phil. 2:9.